C.P.E. Bach and the Rebirth of the Strophic Song

C.P.E. Bach and the Rebirth of the Strophic Song

William H. Youngren

The Scarecrow Press, Inc.
Lanham, Maryland, and Oxford
2003

SCARECROW PRESS, INC.

Published in the United States of America
by Scarecrow Press, Inc.
A wholly owned subsidiary of The Rowman & Littlefield Publishing Group, Inc.
4501 Forbes Boulevard, Suite 200, Lanham, Maryland 20706
www.scarecrowpress.com

PO Box 317
Oxford
OX2 9RU, UK

Copyright © 2003 by William H. Youngren

Cover image courtesy of Paul Corneilson, Ph.D.
Author photograph by Virginia R. Youngren

This book is based on the doctoral dissertation "The Songs of C.P.E. Bach"
Brandeis University, Waltham, Massachusetts, 1999

All rights reserved. No part of this publication may be reproduced, stored in a retrieval system, or transmitted in any form or by any means, electronic, mechanical, photocopying, recording, or otherwise, without the prior permission of the publisher.

British Library Cataloguing in Publication Information Available

Library of Congress Cataloging-in-Publication Data
Youngren, William H.
    C.P.E. Bach and the rebirth of the strophic song / William H. Youngren.
       p. cm.
    Includes bibliographical references and index
    ISBN 0-8108-4840-6 (cloth : alk. paper)
    1. Bach, Carl Philipp Emanuel, 1714–1788 Songs.   2. Songs–History and criticism.   I. Title.
    ML410.B16Y68 2003
    782.42168'092–dc22   2003059587

∞ The paper used in this publication meets the minimum requirements of American National Standard for Information Sciences–Permanence of Paper for Printed Library Materials, ANSI/NISO Z39.48-1992.

Designed and typeset by JCGraphics, Brattleboro, Vermont.

Manufactured in the United States of America.

For Virginia

Σύν μοι πῖνε, συνήβα, συνέρα, συστεφανηφόρει...

Contents

Preface ix

Acknowledgments xi

The Background

Chapter One – C.P.E. Bach: Forgotten Master of a Neglected Genre 1

Chapter Two – The Songless Time 35

Chapter Three – The *Aufschwung* 57

Chapter Four – Rationalist Aesthetics: Rules 89

Chapter Five – Rationalist Aesthetics: Taste 107

Chapter Six – *Ars poetica* 123

Chapter Seven – "Das *Unum* des Horaz" 139

The Songs

Chapter Eight – Bach's Earliest Songs 165

Chapter Nine – The Gellert Songs 203

Chapter Ten – From Gellert to Cramer 241

Chapter Eleven – The Cramer Psalms 271

Chapter Twelve – Folksongs for Voss 311

Chapter Thirteen – A Cantata for Gerstenberg 341

Chapter Fourteen – The Sturm Songs 379

Chapter Fifteen – The Last Songs 411

Appendix One 455

Appendix Two 457

Notes 465

Bibliography 487

Index 497

About the Author 519

Preface

First, I must apologize for having written such a long book; I had not intended to do so. But when I discovered how little is generally known about the songs of C. P. E. Bach (and how good many of them are), I felt impelled to give a full and detailed view of his output, which numbers almost 300 songs. And since so few of those songs are in print, it seemed necessary to supply copious musical examples.

Whenever possible, I took my examples directly from the original 18th-century prints. Some of these are either faint or mildewed, and for that, too, I apologize. But often there was only one library that had the songs I needed, and I had to take what I could get. The reason I decided to use the 18th-century prints is that the few existing modern editions often contain wrong notes and mistakes in phrasing and almost always fill out the keyboard accompaniment. Bach almost never used figured-bass notation in his songs, and so the keyboard player does not have the liberty of voicing the chords just as he wishes. Indeed, Bach's keyboard accompaniments often seem so carefully planned that any added notes would spoil them, while at other times it appears that some added notes are required. Therefore it is best to leave the songs as he wrote and published them, with his intentions ambiguous, and to add notes only when it seems absolutely necessary.

Using the 18th-century prints does create one small problem for the modern singer and accompanist. Bach's songs are printed on two staves: the upper staff gives the vocal line and the keyboardist's right-hand part, while the lower staff gives his left-hand part. But while the lower staff is written in our familiar bass clef, the upper, in all but a few of Bach's last songs, is written not in our treble clef but rather in the antiquated soprano or descant clef, with middle C on the bottom line. Thus the modern musician accustomed to treble clef must "transpose" everything in the upper staff down a third—rather as one does for A clarinets in an orchestral score: what looks like E is really C, what looks like B is really G, and so on. This may at first seem a formidable obstacle, but a few hours' practice will accustom even an amateur to making the shift.

The two halves of my title are intimately related to each other: one cannot understand the significance and the progress of C. P. E. Bach's career as a composer of songs without understanding how and why the strophic song went out of fashion in Germany in the 1680s and then, after half a century, was reborn in the 1730s. I have therefore drawn heavily, particularly in the earlier chapters, on the writings of contemporary critics and aestheticians. In the dissertation upon which this book is based, "The Songs of C. P. E. Bach" (Brandeis University, 1999), all the passages cited from German writers appeared in the original, without accompanying translations. (So too did those from English writers, while those from French writers appeared in contemporary English translations.) In this book, however, which is intended for the musically informed general reader, I have translated the German passages and omitted their originals—the inclusion of which would have vastly increased the size of a book already too long. Anyone who wishes to check the originals of the cited German passages will find them in my dissertation—except for those passages which occur in my book's first chapter.

I have not, however, translated the poems set by Bach and the other composers I have discussed, but have left them in German. This may seem an inconsistency on my part, but I did not feel competent to get into the business of translating poetry. Most people to whom this book will be of interest, I figured, will have at least some knowledge of German. Besides, I have tried, in my analyses of the poems, to make clear their general content.

When I first began to work on Bach's songs, it did not occur to me that I would wind up analyzing a large number of poems in a language not my own. But songs are, after all, musical settings of poems or some other sort of verbal document. If you want to understand a song—why it is as it is, whether it is any good or not, how it might well have been quite different—you must have a thorough knowledge of the text it sets. In fact, one thing wrong with almost all the books on songs I read in preparation for writing this book was that their authors, in analyzing a particular song, usually had little or nothing to say about the relation between music and text—or, as they said in C.P.E. Bach's day, *Ton und Wort*. As we shall see, the successful forging of this relation was almost an obsession with German poets and musicians of the 18th century. Therefore, despite my keen awareness of my linguistic shortcomings, I had no choice but to analyze as closely as possible the poems that Bach and his contemporaries chose to set—an adventure that I thoroughly enjoyed.

Music historians have not devoted much attention to the 18th-century German song—indeed, reading some of them, one might conclude that the modern German lied began with Schubert. But, as we shall see, the song composers of north and central Germany were immensely productive during the last two thirds of the 18th century, and the importance that the strophic lied held for them was intimately related to other important developments in German music and letters. C.P.E. Bach was virtually the unanimous choice of contemporary critics as the best of these composers, even though (or perhaps because) his aims and methods were rather different from theirs.

C.P.E. Bach is perhaps a more popular composer just now than at any time since his death, in 1788. But for reasons that I trace in Chapter One, he is still, as in the 19th century, thought of by most listeners as an instrumental, rather than a vocal, composer. There are many recordings of his symphonies, chamber music, and solo keyboard pieces, and a complete recording of the keyboard concertos and sonatinas—perhaps his most interesting and least known instrumental music—is now in progress. Yet in recent years there have also been good recordings of all Bach's major choral works, and now, at last, the songs are beginning to find their way onto disc. More of them will soon do so, and as they do, I hope this book will serve as an increasingly helpful guide.

Acknowledgments

I am most grateful to the many people who had a hand in the making of my dissertation and, now, of this book. The late Bill Kiraly, a violist with the Cleveland Orchestra who developed a passionate interest in Baroque music and went back to school in middle life to get a higher degree in musicology, gave me the idea of doing the same thing. When I approached Lewis Lockwood and Christoph Wolff of Harvard, and Allan Keiler of Brandeis, they did not think I was crazy to start on a second Ph.D. in my early fifties. In fact, they very kindly encouraged me. The choice between the two universities, a difficult one, was made for me by a rule—which no one seems to know about and no one can explain—that you cannot become a regular student in the Harvard Graduate School of Arts and Sciences if you already have a Ph.D.

My years of taking seminars at Brandeis were some of the happiest of my life. Eric Chafe, Robert Marshall, and Allan Keiler were demanding and stimulating teachers who have now become close friends. When I decided to write about C. P. E. Bach's songs, Professor Chafe agreed to direct me, and Professor Marshall to be my second reader. To them, and also to Professor Wolff, who served as my outside reader, I am indebted for their enthusiastic reception of my work and for their many helpful suggestions.

Along the way I also had help from Steve Clark, who introduced me to the world of C.P.E. Bach scholars and scholarship; Professor E. Eugene Helm, the dean of C.P.E. Bach studies, who generously volunteered to read (and comment on) my 975-page dissertation; the late Harry Zohn of Brandeis and Professor Ute Brandes of Amherst College, who saved me from many "howlers" in my struggles with the German poems; D'Anna Fortunato, Nancy Armstrong, and Mark Kroll, who were interested enough in Bach's songs to give a superb private concert of them at Boston's St. Botolph Club; Joel Flegler, editor of *Fanfare*, who kept (and keeps) me well supplied with C.P.E. Bach discs to review, Jessee Carter, Stephen Owades, and Kira Razee, who elegantly computerized my primitive typescript; Alice Klein, for a superb index; and, finally, my family. The path to completion was smoothed by the love and support of my wife, Virginia, and my children—especially my younger daughter Valerie, who proved an unfailing source of encouragement and good cheer.

The Background

Chapter One

C. P. E. Bach: Forgotten Master of a Neglected Genre

The music of Johann Sebastian Bach's second son, Carl Philipp Emanuel (1714–1788), has been growing steadily in popularity over the last couple of decades. Though not often performed in the concert hall, it is heard frequently on FM "concert-music" stations, and a great deal of it has now been recorded. Yet the C.P.E. Bach with whom this book deals, C.P.E. Bach the composer of songs, is almost completely unknown—even to music-lovers familiar with his keyboard sonatas, symphonies, and chamber music. But over his long career Bach wrote about 300 songs, depending on what we choose to count as a song. For while the vast majority of his short vocal compositions are ordinary strophic songs, some are chorales, rather in the style of his father, which he contributed to Lutheran songbooks, while others are extended into something like cantatas. Bach did not publish (or perhaps even compose) any songs until 1741, when he was 27 years old, but his last ones were composed in 1788, the year of his death.

Though today Bach is thought of almost entirely as a composer of instrumental music, his songs and large choral works were equally esteemed by his contemporaries. This is clear from the publication figures in E. Eugene Helm's *Thematic Catalogue of the Works of Carl Philipp Emanuel Bach* (New Haven and London: Yale University Press, 1989). Of Bach's almost 300 songs, only six remain in manuscript, the others having all been published—all but a few of them during his lifetime. Of the 335 solo keyboard pieces to which Helm assigns the numbers H. 1-337, 213 had been published by 1792. That these two genres should have been so popular makes perfect historical sense. Like the verbal literacy that produced the enormous increase in the number of novels published in all European countries, musical literacy too grew and spread rapidly in the mid-18th century. Thus was born a new class of musical amateurs, hungry for new music that could be performed in the home. The two genres best suited to their needs were of course the solo song and the solo keyboard piece.

The percentage of Bach's works accorded early publication falls off sharply as we move into the other instrumental genres. Of his 18 symphonies, only five were published during the 18th century. Of the more than 70 concertos and "sonatinas" (miniature concertos) for keyboard and orchestra, a mere 15 appeared in print during Bach's lifetime. But for the genre that Helm calls "Chamber Music With a Leading Keyboard Part," like the songs and the solo keyboard pieces a species of *Hausmusik*, the figure is higher: 13 out of 40. The other sorts of chamber music fare far less well: four of the 25 trio sonatas, just one of the solo wind and string sonatas, three of the pieces for miscellaneous combinations—these make up the meager totals of works that were published during Bach's lifetime, and that therefore could have been known to contemporaries who were not members of his immediate circle. Interestingly enough, all of Bach's few large choral works were published either during his lifetime or not too long after his death—if we stretch that period to include the 1829 Simrock edition of the 1749 *Magnificat*. Since these were obviously not works suited to domestic performance, their early publication would seem to offer further evidence, quite independent of the widespread desire for *Hausmusik*, of Bach's high reputation as a vocal composer.

How then did it happen that C. P. E. Bach the composer of songs is now, as my title has it, the forgotten master of a neglected genre? The answer is quite complex, and has several parts to it. Let us begin by looking at some of the critical writing about Bach that appeared shortly before and after his death.

I

General histories of music, and even more specialized histories of song, often give the impression that the German lied began with Schubert—or perhaps with his immediate forerunners, late in the 18th century. Quite understandably, Schubert's overwhelming greatness has led us to think of the lied as a Romantic genre. Yet the simple strophic song was actually a most important genre of German music during the last two-thirds of the 18th century. This fact has been lost sight of because the vast majority of the songs of that period were composed and published in north and central Germany. Most music historians, writing about the 18th century, concentrate their attention on Vienna or south Germany from about 1750 on, because it was there that the Classical style was forming and the first Classical masterpieces would soon be produced. In Catholic Austria, as opposed to Lutheran north and central Germany, the vocal literature was traditionally in Latin rather than the vernacular. Though Haydn, Mozart, and Beethoven all wrote songs, a few of which are still heard, they did not write many, and their songs are a very minor part of their respective *oeuvres*, dwarfed in importance by their instrumental music and, in Mozart's case, operas.

In fact, it was during the second half of the 18th century that the humble song attained a higher level of dignity in intellectual circles than it had ever known before. A number of French linguistic theorists, arguing against the Cartesian rationalists, maintained that human language originated in instinctive, animal-like cries, uttered in response to the environment. Étienne Bonnot de Condillac (1715-1780), in his *Essai sur l'origine des connaissances humaines* (1746), saw these cries as prompted, at least in part, by social need. Jean-Jacques Rousseau (1712-1778), in the *Discours sur . . . l'inégalité* (1755) and *Essai sur l'origine des langues* (c. 1760), saw them as growing solely out of private, passionate need and therefore as logically prior to society. Either way, language—in its most basic, most primitive form—comes out as very close to song; conversely, song becomes enthroned as the essential form of human expression and communication. These and similar ideas were transmitted to Germans chiefly by Johann Gottfried von Herder (1744-1803), in his *Abhandlung über den Ursprung der Sprache* (1772).[1]

One of the most important and representative writers on music in late 18th-century Germany was Christian Friedrich Daniel Schubart (1739-1791), who was also a poet and composer. In Schubart's *Ideen zu einer Ästhetik der Tonkunst*,[2] a work written in 1784-1785 but not published until 1806, we immediately feel the influence of Herder's ideas. "The art of music is as old as the world," Schubart begins the sketch of music history that opens his book. "One could just as well define man as a singing creature as, with Aristotle, a speaking creature" (p. 3). From the assumed temporal priority of song in human development Schubart concludes that it is also logically prior to other forms of music and even to language itself:

> That song appeared long before instrumental music is thus undeniable. For the investigation of physical objects that produce tones is too difficult for the childhood of the human race. Song, on the other hand, is so natural, and flows forth so freely and artlessly from our hearts, that every feeling of happiness or of sweet melancholy, or every passionate impulse, is sufficient to open our lips in song.

[P. 5]

In Schubart's book we also find warm praise for the music, and in particular the vocal music, of C.P.E. Bach. Schubart speaks of Bach as "the German Orpheus" (p. 37), and in a longer passage later in the book, he writes: "What Raphael is to painting, and Klopstock to poetry, so, essentially, is Bach to harmony and musical composition" (pp. 178-179). In that same passage Schubart rhapsodizes about Bach's many accomplishments: as master of all the keyboard instruments, as unmatched accompanist, as keyboard composer, as theorist. Significantly, however, Schubart saves for last Bach's work as a composer of songs:

> He has also demonstrated brilliance as a song composer. His cantatas, his chorales, for which he chose Gellert's, Cramer's, and Klopstock's texts, are full of pathos, full of novelty in the course of their melodies, unique in their modulations—in short, true music of the spheres. His diligence is as great as his creative spirit. No genius has ever written as much as he has, and everything—even the most trifling little song or minuet—bears his original stamp.
>
> [P. 180]

It is perhaps natural that Schubart should have valued Bach's song output so highly, for he himself was both a composer of songs and a poet, four of whose poems, the most famous of which is "Die Forelle," would later be set by Schubert.

For Schubart, then, an enthusiasm for Herder's ideas could coexist comfortably with an appreciation of Bach's songs. But this situation was changing even as Schubart was writing his book. Ironically, it was in large part the view of songs contained in the writings of Herder and his French predecessors that helped to bring about the decline in Bach's reputation as a composer of songs—even as it dramatically raised the prestige of songs generally. From the view of the relation between language and song expressed in *Abhandlung über den Ursprung der Sprache* it was but a short step to the elevation, above all other kinds of song, of the simple, natural, artless songs of ancient and primitive peoples. It was, apparently, Herder who coined the German word *Volkslied,* and he included in his 1773 manifesto *Von deutscher Art und Kunst* a brief essay called *Auszug aus einem Briefwechsel über Ossian und die Lieder alter Völker.* Herder, like Goethe and many other prominent men of letters in both Germany and England, accepted James Macpherson's volumes of "translations" from the fictitious Ossian as authentic ancient poetry of the Celts. Goethe in fact studied Gaelic in order to grasp more securely the spirit of the supposed ancient bard.

In 1778 and 1779 Herder produced two volumes entitled *Volkslieder,* the word *Lied* being used, as had by then become customary, to mean not only a song but also a poem without musical setting that was, however, well adapted to being set. Their effect on composers was instantaneous. The best-loved song collections of the next decade were the three volumes of *Lieder im Volkston* (1782, 1785, 1790) by Johann Abraham Peter Schulz. It was Schulz who, in the preface to the second (1785) edition of the first volume of *Lieder im Volkston,* created the slogan of the folksong movement by coining the phrase "der Schein des Bekannten"—the appearance or illusion of what is known and familiar—to characterize the effect he was striving for in his songs. Other young poets and composers attracted to the *Volkslied* or *Volkston* movement included G. A. Bürger, L. C. H. Hölty, Matthias Claudius, C. G. Neefe (later the teacher of Beethoven), and J. F. Reichardt.

Johann Friedrich Reichardt (1752-1814) was also a critic and a prominent commentator on the musical scene; it is in his writings that we see most clearly the decline in Bach's reputation as a composer of songs. Every book on C.P.E. Bach will tell you that Reichardt, in *Über die Deutsche comische Oper* (1774),[3] praises Bach in terms very much like those that would be used by Schubart: "We have only one Bach and his manner is wholly original and belongs to him alone" (p. 15). And you will also learn that Bach receives similar praise in both parts of Reichardt's *Briefe eines aufmerksamen*

Reisenden die Musik betreffend (1774, 1775).[4] Hearing a passion of Bach's in Hamburg, Reichardt feels that he has encountered a new side of the composer, and he is filled with new respect for him:

> At St. Peter's they performed a passion of his that was characterized by originality, appropriately strong and novel expression, stunning power, and passionate fire. One recognizes Bach's original genius in all his works, even in the smallest pieces; all bear the stamp of originality; and all are distinguishable among a hundred other pieces, though each possesses invention and novelty.
>
> [I, 111]

When he actually meets the great man, Reichardt is suitably enraptured:

> Whenever I visit Herr Bach, he plays me three, four, or even more sonatas from different times of his life. One recognizes in each his individual spirit—the greatest proof that his originality is not affectation—but also, at the same time, his manysidedness and his inexhaustible richness. Each sonata has something special that clearly distinguishes it from all the others.
>
> [II, 10]

What one is usually not told is that Reichardt later turned against Bach. In *Briefe eines aufmerksamen Reisenden* he enthusiastically recounts how Bach played through for him the whole of his oratorio *Die Israeliten in der Wüste*. In words that recall his earlier experience with the passion, Reichardt remarks that he has learnt "once again to know a completely new side of the great man":

> This is the sort of masterpiece by Herr Capellmeister Bach that completely strikes down any remaining objections from those who, out of malice or ignorance, envy him. For it is pervaded by flowing, pleasing, natural song of the sort found earlier only in [Reinhard] Keiser and [C. H.] Graun.
>
> I myself was astonished at how this great man had so completely forsaken his accustomed height—as natural to him as it is to the eagle to fly near the sun—and had been able to sing a song so easy, so readily comprehensible to us poor sons of earth.
>
> [II, 14]

In other words, Reichardt is surprised that Bach, whose greatness lies in elevation and sublimity, can write such pleasant, natural song. Taken out of context, the passage looks like unalloyed praise for a master's versatility. In context, however, what stands out is not so much Bach's achievement as Reichardt's astonishment.

In the very first letter of Part I Reichardt singles out Nature as being what Pope in *An Essay on Criticism*, a poem Reichardt would surely have known, had called "At once the *Source*, and *End*, and *Test* of Art":

> And should not the musician study Nature, and his Ramler and Batteux, just as closely as do the poet and the painter? In Nature he has the noblest thing of all, man, to study; but unfortunately we have as yet no Ramler or Batteux in our art. All this calculating, all this fussing over harmony—excellent! I understand perfectly well that we can never sufficiently thank a Bach, a Marpurg, a Kirnberger for their exceedingly edifying works.
>
> [I, 12]

The irony seems clear enough, but it gets still clearer as we read on. Reichardt proceeds to compare the operas of Hasse with those of C. H. Graun. While Hasse receives high praise for his fire and strength of passion—qualities similar to those Reichardt values in Bach—it is Graun who carries the day: "But Graun is in such songs so simple, and at the same time so moving, that every listener who is moved—and who would not be moved to tears?—believes it is he himself who sings" (I, 17). It was, we recall, Graun whose naturalness Reichardt was so astonished to find Bach matching in *Die Israeliten in der Wüste.*

Charles Batteux (1713-1780) was the author of *Les Beaux-Arts réduits à un même principe* (1746) and also of *Cours de belles lettres* (1747-1748), in which the theory of the earlier book is applied to various works of art. The one principle to which Batteux traced the nature and efficacy of all the arts was imitation, but imitation of a somewhat idealized nature rather than a literal copying of ordinary reality. He was one of the most influential aestheticians of the 18th century, and the German poet and critic Carl Wilhelm Ramler (1725-1798), who translated the *Cours de belles lettres* as *Einleitung in die schönen Künste* (1756-1758), was one of Batteux's first and most prominent German followers.[5] Both men thus stood for the special kind of "naturalness" that Reichardt was praising in Graun, a quality that Bach's learned, and therefore somewhat artificial, "fussing over harmony" usually prevented him from attaining. We shall encounter both Batteux and Ramler again.

What emerges is that Reichardt is deeply ambivalent about such seeming virtues as originality and genius and sublimity: is there not a danger that genius may become so dazzlingly original, and may provide us with works so sublimely above common human nature, that we (like the great artist himself) may, in our bedazzlement, lose sight of the all-important fact that the "principal goal" ("Hauptendzweck") of music, as of all the arts, is (in Reichardt's words) to portray "those passions and feelings of men" that "have always been and will eternally remain the same" (I, 12, 15)? In the years following Bach's death, Reichardt's ambivalence hardened into a distaste for Bach's vocal music. In the *Musikalischer Almanach* for 1796, Reichardt maintains that in all his vocal works but the brief choral work *Heilig,* Bach "appears more as a great instrumental composer, to whom the study of language and poetry, fine and deep feeling, and that taste for nobly simple beauty that issues from the whole being of the inner man are simply lacking."[6]

I have lingered so long over Reichardt not only because his shift of opinion concerning Bach's vocal music was characteristic of the time but also because it shows how easily (and, in Reichardt's case, uneasily!) the conviction that the task of art is to portray those feelings and passions that are always and everywhere the same, which we ordinarily consider a "neoclassical" idea, could coexist with the "Romantic" (or anyway "pre-Romantic") tendency to exalt original genius. The reason that Reichardt eventually had trouble reconciling these two notions is not that he came late in the 18th century, on the threshold (as it were) of the Romantic movement. One of the main, continuing tasks of European critical thought, from Boileau and Dryden through Pope and Addison in England, and Gottsched in Germany, right up to Dr. Johnson and even beyond, to Coleridge, was to find ways of forging such a reconciliation. That is why the critics of this period reserve their highest praise for works of art that manage to reconcile such seemingly opposed qualities.

Johnson, scarcely a "pre-Romantic," praised Pope's *The Rape of the Lock* because it exhibited, "in a very high degree, the two most engaging powers of an author. New things are made familiar, and familiar things are made new."[7] Just so, Coleridge, surely the principal "theorist" of Romanticism in English, defined the characteristic power of a poet as revealing itself "in the balance or reconciliation of opposite or discordant qualities: of sameness, with difference; of the general, with the concrete; the idea, with the image; the individual, with the representative; the sense of novelty and freshness, with old and familiar objects."[8] Indeed, it is this constant struggle to reconcile opposing qualities that answer to opposing needs in us, the consumers of art, that makes the aesthetics of the late 17th and 18th centuries—usually, as we shall see later, dismissed as simplemindedly "rationalist"—so extraordinarily interesting and valuable.

Yet Reichardt's shift of opinion was indeed characteristic of his time. Moreover, as the masterpieces of Schubert and Schumann, along with the finest songs of such lesser masters as Franz and Loewe, accumulated, the memory of Bach's songs, and of those by most of his north German contemporaries, was eclipsed. Indeed, though there were a few specialized histories of the German song, and, later in the 19th century, even of the 18th-century German song, the message most of them conveyed was that the German lied was essentially a Romantic genre that had begun, more or less, with Schubert, and that the short strophic song had not been a genre of any cultural importance or musical distinction in 18th-century Germany.

The history of the German lied began formally to be written shortly after the midpoint of the 19th century. The point of view of one of the earliest histories, A. H. Hoffmann von Fallersleben's *Unsere volksthümlichen Lieder* (1859), is fairly suggested by its title. Though Bach's idiom as a composer of songs was, as we should expect from his instrumental music, not usually that of folklike simplicity—and of course this fact figured largely in the decline of his reputation—the three of his songs that receive attention from Hoffmann are praised, rather halfheartedly, for their similarity to folksongs. Bach is accorded cursory, patronizing treatment in K. E. Schneider's *Das musikalische Lied in geschichtlicher Entwickelung* (1863–1867) and August Reissmann's *Geschichte des deutschen Liedes* (1874). Even E. O. Lindner's 1871 *Geschichte des deutschen Liedes im XVIII. Jahrhundert*,[9] the first book of consequence to be devoted entirely to the 18th-century German lied, gives Bach only three pages—and the first of those three pages is padded out with quotations from the 18th-century English music historian Dr. Charles Burney. Lindner then briefly discusses the songs in Bach's 1762 collection, *Oden mit Melodien*:

> What one would prefer to praise about them is their generally clear and comprehensible declamation. For they lack immediate warmth, an intrinsic "conception" [*"Empfängniss"*] that would bring the conjunction [*Anschluss*] with the word into the melodic flow. Thus the melody becomes angular and remains unattractive.
>
> [P. 59]

Lindner concludes with this comment on Bach's last collection, the 1789 *Neue Lieder-Melodien*: "Despite occasional bold harmonic changes of direction [*Wendungen*] reminiscent of C.P.E. Bach's keyboard fantasies, these compositions too are dry and unattractive" (p. 60).

This is pretty much how things stood at the end of the 19th century. The 18th-century German lied had not amounted to much, and anyway Bach was too learned, too sophisticated, too full of "calculating" and "fussing over harmony" (as Reichardt put it) to achieve the necessary folksong-like simplicity and naturalness. A neglected genre, indeed! But during most of the 19th century the attention of most music historians was not primarily directed toward vocal music. The great flowering of instrumental music during the Classical era had raised a host of new and troubling questions for music historians; it was in trying to answer these questions that they gave C.P.E. Bach a new and rather glamorous position in the history of music. In doing so, however, they still further discouraged any close and critical examination of his songs.

II

The characteristic method of the music history written during the 18th century was biographical and anecdotal. But toward the end of the century, as early as E. N. Forkel's *Allgemeine Geschichte der Musik* (1788, 1801), we can already see the shaping influence of the great Enlightenment idea of Progress. The earliest 19th-century progressivist histories of music adhered to a rather simple, usually three-stage, scheme to chart music's advance through the ages. But the development of evolutionary biology and social theory, even before the publication of Darwin's *The Origin of Species* in 1859, gave progressivist historians a more detailed and suggestive model on which to base their work.

The 18th century posed special problems for music historians committed to a progressivist model. Darwin was fond of citing the old proverb *Natura non facit saltum* (Nature does not make jumps). But even before Darwin, progressively minded historians had always wanted to tell a smoothly continuous story, a story without significant jumps or gaps. Early in the 19th century, however, they had already begun to see the preceding century as divided into two quite different ages, which we call the Baroque and Classical eras but they were likely to speak of as the age of Bach and Handel and the age of Haydn and Mozart. The former was generally held to run until about 1750, the year of J. S. Bach's death, while the latter was viewed as beginning in about 1775, with the first Classical masterpieces: Mozart's Symphonies, K. 200 and 201 (Nos. 28 and 29), and E-flat Piano Concerto, K. 271; Haydn's post-*Sturm und Drang* Symphonies and his Op. 20 and Op. 33 String Quartets. But what was to be done with the gap of a full quarter century between 1750 and 1775?

The two periods that flank this musical no-man's-land are dominated by five men who indisputably rank among the very greatest Western composers: Bach and Handel on one side of the divide; Haydn, Mozart, and (early) Beethoven on the other. Their work, taken as a body, constitutes the standard by which, consciously or unconsciously, we judge all later Western music—and, indeed, it set the standard most later composers strove to match. On the other hand, the only two important composers who flowered during the 25-year interregnum, while certainly worthy and serious, are not really great and, more important, are both somewhat enigmatic.

Even C. P. E. Bach's earliest surviving music, written during the 1730s and 1740s, does not really sound like Baroque music. On the other hand, the later symphonies, solo keyboard pieces, keyboard concertos, and chamber works by which he is mainly known are conspicuously marked by abrupt discontinuities, seemingly wanton changes of tempo and texture, that set them apart from the Classical style, with its grandly satisfying formal symmetries. Haydn, all through his long life, declared his indebtedness to Bach—but just what, and how much, he learned from the older composer has been a matter of dispute for almost 200 years.[10] Mozart's less well-known remark about Bach, "He is the father, we are the sons," is still more puzzling. For Bach's music, though it often has a quirky humor all its own, lacks the pervasive wit and irony of the mature Classical style. In his brief autobiography, Bach expressed regret at the extent to which the humorous element ("das Komische") was taking over modern music. He thought it was far more important to move the heart than to tickle the fancy, and he was probably speaking specifically of comic opera—but as D. F. Tovey once remarked, "Mozart's whole musical language is, and remains throughout, the language of comic opera."[11] The same could be said of the mature Haydn, whose own comic operas, though not in a league with Mozart's, are far finer than is usually believed,[12] and also of more of Beethoven, and not just early Beethoven, than most people realize.

The other composer who dominates this troublesome quarter century is Christoph Willibald Gluck (1714–1787), who is Bach's almost exact contemporary, having been born in the same year and having died a year earlier. Gluck's fame rests, of course, on his famous "reform" of opera, which consisted in making dramatic action, rather than theatrical spectacle, paramount. His concern with drama might seem to link him to the Classical style, which is nothing if not dramatic, but his great and characteristic works are very serious, with nobly tragic classical subjects and music that is rigorously austere. They have nothing in common with the operatic comedies that played so important a role in the formation of the Classical style during the 1770s and 1780s. Friedrich Nicolai, a Berlin journalist visiting Vienna in 1781, noted that while Gluck was "the most famous musician in Vienna," and was "highly praised there, as elsewhere," he nonetheless had, "to my knowledge, not exerted any very marked influence on the city's musical taste."[13] In November 1787, Goethe, who had recently tried his hand at writing a libretto to an opera influenced by Gluck, lamented: "All our endeavor . . . to confine ourselves to what is simple and limited was lost when Mozart appeared. *The Abduction from the Seraglio* conquered all, and our own carefully written piece has never been so much as mentioned in theater circles."[14] The restrained and austere classicism or neoclassicism cultivated by Goethe and his circle was powerfully influenced by J. J. Winckelmann's *History of the Art of Antiquity,* and its ideal of "noble simplicity and calm grandeur." It had as little in common with the wit and emotional breadth of the Classical style as did the music of Gluck.

Thus music historians, attempting in the 19th century to tell the story of the preceding century's music as one of more or less steady and orderly progression from the world of Bach and Handel to that of the three great Classical composers and beyond, into the Romantic era, were forced to fill the gap represented by the century's third quarter by invoking either C. P. E. Bach or Gluck or both. Neither composer, viewed from the comfortable distance of more than 200 years, seems a very promising candidate for the job.

One of the earliest three-stage progressivist histories is the 1827 *Darstellungen aus der Geschichte der Musik* by the Göttingen philosopher Christian Friedrich Krause (1781-1832).[15] Krause's three stages of music's development are marked, respectively, by the predominance of melody (ancient music), polyphony (Christian music), and harmony (modern music).

It soon becomes clear that Krause is far more interested in vocal than in instrumental music. He sees Handel, "fully accomplished in harmony and rhythm, original and thoughtful in his melodies" (p. 95), as having forged the synthesis of elements that make up modern music. But J. S. Bach possesses, in addition to all of Handel's good qualities, a special depth and seriousness, an intellectual and spiritual distinction: "He never wrote for the crowd; he had always in view his high artistic ideal" (p. 104).

The relation of Hasse to Gluck is quite similar. Hasse's works, like those of Handel, are "equally accomplished in melody, harmony, and rhythm" (p. 110). But it is Gluck who has deepened and perfected this fusion of elements. Krause's answer to the question of how the transition from the Baroque to the Classical era came about is therefore that it "was made by the Ritter von Gluck, one of the most original, innovative figures in the field of dramatic music, which he has brought to the high point of its development, and has thereby begun a whole new epoch of this art" (p. 111). There is only one passing reference to C. P. E. Bach in Krause's book: merely as one of J. S. Bach's composer sons, and not at all as a transitional figure between the two eras.

The next important general history of music, on a grander scale than Krause's and the most significant survey to appear since Forkel's, is *Geschichte der europäisch-abendländischen oder unserer heutigen Musik,* by Raphael Georg Kiesewetter (1772-1850), a Viennese nobleman who held state offices but whose first love clearly was music. Published in 1834, it was followed by a second edition in 1846 and an English translation in 1848.[16]

As his firmly insistent title implies, Kiesewetter, unlike Krause, sees "our" European or Western music not as issuing from other sorts of world music in a grand developmental progression but as something quite special, set apart, unique. The only other sort of music he even deigns to mention is Greek music, toward which his attitude is unmitigatedly hostile. For our European music—and here one senses the influence of Herder—is basically natural and instinctual, "a very simple, artless song of nature, free from the trammel of rules" (p. 3). Greek music, on the other hand, was nothing but rules, a theoretical system "strictly confined by the authority of the philosophers" (p. 2).

This view of Western music as originating in spontaneous song leads Kiesewetter virtually to discount instrumental music until his final chapters, and to see opera, and specifically Neapolitan opera, as the grand culmination of Western music's natural development. "There can be no doubt," he concludes, "but that the style of the Neapolitan school was universally adopted by composers in Italy and other countries, and that the music of the present day"—and here we must recall that Kiesewetter is writing in the early 1830s!—"is still essentially that of Naples" (p. 222).

Gluck does not stand alone, as he so often does in later histories of music, but rather completes and perfects the line of development that began with Carissimi, or perhaps even with Monteverdi.

Kiesewetter's conviction that Western music is basically vocal music, and that opera is therefore its final flowering, is, if anything, even stronger than Krause's. It is thus no surprise that he ends his chapter on Gluck by reaffirming: "Thus may be said to have been prepared by Gluck the epoch of Haydn and Mozart" (p. 239), a conclusion similar to Krause's.

Yet Kiesewetter finds himself impelled immediately to add that "it would scarcely be proper to conclude the present chapter without mentioning the meritorious son of the great Johan. Sebastian Bach, Carl Philipp Immanuel, who, without forsaking the school of his father, was able nevertheless to unite its seriousness and solidity with the gracefulness of modern compositions" (p. 239). At this point Kiesewetter recalls his earlier insistence that the vocal line is the important one, and adds that C.P.E. Bach's "works in the department of Church music, the grand sacred cantata, and oratorio, are quite as valuable as his numerous instrumental productions" (p. 239). Only then can he permit himself to write of Bach: "He was in some measure the precursor of our celebrated Haydn" (p. 239). This, as we shall see, was the view of Bach's place in history that was soon to become a commonplace. But while later historians were to see Bach's influence on Haydn as being entirely through the former's instrumental music, Kiesewetter, true to form, leaves the impression that Bach's vocal music was at least equally responsible.

In 1835, a year after Kiesewetter's book, Gustav Schilling (1803-1881), director of the Stoepel Music School at Stuttgart, began publication of his seven-volume *Encyclopädie der gesammten musikalischen Wissenschaften, oder Universal-Lexicon der Tonkunst.*[17] The only German music encyclopedia published during the first half of the 19th century, it was an impressive job of research and years ahead of its time. Schilling had the assistance of many of the finest contemporary musical scholars, the most prominent perhaps being Adolf Bernhard Marx (1795-1866), an important theorist and minor composer who had already (1824-1830) served as editor of the *Berliner allgemeine musikalische Zeitung* and was director of music at the University of Berlin. As it happens, Marx was the author of the entries in Schilling's *Encyclopädie* that are of most concern to us. To move from Krause and Kiesewetter to the subtle and intricate, eloquently flowery, carefully cadenced prose of Marx is to enter a new world. His articles on Gluck, C.P.E. Bach, Haydn, and Mozart are minor masterpieces of psychological portraiture.

The very first sentence of Marx's entry on Gluck introduces him as "this most profoundly thoughtful of composers, the perfector of French grand opera" (III, 254)—thus suggesting a career marked by both artistic greatness and worldly success. And indeed Gluck, as it turns out, achieved both. Yet throughout Marx's little sketch the repeated German word *einsam* (lonely or solitary) tolls like a death knell.

Though Gluck gained a certain amount of success with his first operas, the main thing he learned from the experience, Marx tells us, was that "he himself could not be satisfied" (III, 254). More success followed, culminating in the mixed reception accorded *Alceste*—initial ridicule followed by gradually deepening appreciation—in the late 1760s. In the dedication to the score of his next opera, *Paride ed Elena* (1770), Gluck wrote: "Only in the hope of finding imitators did I decide to publish the music of *Alceste,* flattering myself that others would be eager to follow the path I had taken, and to destroy the abuses that have crept into Italian opera and have disgraced it. But my hope was in vain" (quoted III, 256). At last, frustrated and exhausted by quarrels and intrigues, Gluck died at Vienna in 1787. Marx gives him a stark, one-sentence obituary: "Er starb reich und einsam" ("He died rich and alone") (III, 257).

But this is far from the end of Marx's account. Indeed it is just here that the word *einsam* begins to be heard again and again, as a sort of refrain, reinforcing the strange, paradoxical, deeply moving picture that Marx is giving us of Gluck's life and work. After eloquently evoking the peculiar mixture of chaste coldness and passionate truth embodied in Gluck's operas, Marx asks: "Is it possible that this man could continue to stand alone [*einsam*] with his achievement, without mechanically imitative followers, abandoned in his fatherland? It could not be otherwise" (III, 259). For Gluck's works belong to an imaginative world remote from us; his heroic figures find in our fragmented and enervating lives their complete antithesis. "And so Gluck's creations could find no permanent place in Germany" (III, 259). One is particularly struck by the fine irony behind Marx's bland assumption—an assumption that he implies might have been shared by the unhappy composer—that any imitator or imitation of Gluck would of course necessarily be merely mechanical: in hoping for imitators Gluck was putting himself in yet another no-win situation by making a wish that, even if granted, could have brought him no satisfaction.

The entry closes with detailed evocations of some of these heroic figures. Of the abandoned sorceress Armida, heroine of the only one of Gluck's late operas to end tragically, Marx writes: "Then, veiled, she will go off alone [einsam] into the night, and beneath her flying feet her paradise will crumble to ashes" (III, 260). And of *Iphigénie en Tauride*: "Then, after 15 miserable years, we meet Iphigenia again, in Tauris. Once again are heard those happy melodies with which the happy bride was greeted at the camp. But dark veils obscure the charming sounds, which grow darker and darker in the chorus of lonely [einsamen] virgins as minor strain succeeds minor strain" (III, 260). While Armida may be literally alone at the end of Gluck's opera, she is nonetheless armed and seeking vengeance, and thus not exactly *einsam*; nor are the priestesses at the beginning of *Iphigénie en Tauride*.

In his repeated use of the word, Marx is stretching a point to make the lonely, inimitable Gluck seem like one of his own tragic figures: grand but solitary, undone by the very qualities that make him great. Marx concludes: "For two centuries and longer, man had dreamt of reviving the tragedy of the Greeks, and had striven to do so in Italy and France. Images both successful and distorted, Italian opera and the *drame lyrique,* had arisen out of these dreams. To a German, Gluck, their fulfillment was granted. With his passing the succession of these forms came to an end" (III, 260).

Marx's view of C. P. E. Bach is utterly different—and far less complex. "In everything he did there was a completely thought out plan, a precisely defined, industriously sought, and capably achieved goal" (I, 381). Or again: "No lack of any sort of preparation stood in the way of his completing his creations; he was a born genius and a fully formed artist, master, and advancer of his art" (I, 382). Marx singles out for praise Bach's sonatas and fantasias, in which this overarching sense of purpose is combined with "the charm of a heightened variety of ever-changing feeling. This touch of humor, this happily varied play of feeling in the midst of the surest, most powerful cohesion of the whole, was surely what mainly so deeply attracted the spirited and humorous Joseph Haydn" (I, 382). Far from standing alone in solitary tragic eminence, Bach is the direct inspirer of the first of the great Classical composers. Yet despite—or perhaps because of—the warmth and generosity of Marx's praise, the happy, successful, perfectly organized and competent Bach seems a trifle dull beside the unforgettable figure of Gluck.

Franz Brendel (1811-1868) was educated at the Freiburg Gymnasium; the University of Leipzig, where he met Schumann; and the University of Berlin. In 1845 he succeeded Schumann as editor of the *Neue Zeitschrift für Musik,* and he soon became an avid (though often troublesome) disciple of Wagner. From 1846 Brendel also taught music history and aesthetics at the Leipzig Conservatory. When he published Wagner's *Judaism in Music* in the September 1850 issue of the *Neue Zeitschrift für Musik,* his Conservatory colleagues, who included the great violinist Joseph Joachim and the composer and pianist Ignaz Moscheles, unanimously demanded his removal. But he retained his Conservatory position, and until his death he continued to edit the *Neue Zeitschrift für Musik,* in whose pages he promoted German unification as well as the music of Wagner and Liszt. Brendel's two most important books are the 1852 *Geschichte der Musik in Italien, Deutschland und Frankreich,* a compilation of his Leipzig lectures, and the 1854 *Die Musik der Gegenwart und die Gesammtkunst der Zukunft,* a survey of the contemporary musical scene that is, as its title suggests, heavily influenced by Wagner's writings.[18]

In the lecture in *Geschichte der Musik* that deals with Bach and Handel, we can see at once the influence (and perhaps one of the causes) of Brendel's preoccupation with Wagner's music of the future. Though Brendel is of course most respectful toward Bach, Handel obviously interests him more, for it is Handel who has devoted "the long series of years" between his early sacred works and his later oratorios "almost exclusively to his activities in the field of opera" (p. 238). Moreover, his oratorios are, in Brendel's view, "definitely to be considered a first step toward the later opera" (p. 240)—one can almost feel the presence of Wagner, waiting impatiently in the wings.

One of Handel's great achievements, in his role as harbinger of modern opera, is that he made Gluck possible. Far from being Marx's solitary, tragic figure, at odds with his age even as he gives it just the sort of tragic drama it requires, Brendel's Gluck is the product, the logical result of Handel's work in the theater. With Gluck, Brendel grandly proclaims, "begins the reign of secular music" (pp. 260-261). For Brendel, Gluck is not so much the reviver of Greek tragic drama as he is the ideal composer for the age of Kant.

Far from dying rich and alone, Brendel's Gluck moved from success to success, and died crowned with fame and blessed with admiring followers. Indeed, how could it have been otherwise, seeing that Gluck is the next stepping-stone on the path to Wagner? Just as Handel made Gluck possible, so Gluck made Mozart possible: "Mozart was the greatest result that Gluck produced" (pp. 287-288).

One way Gluck had accomplished this feat was by destroying the rigid forms of earlier opera in order better to serve dramatic truth. It is interesting that for Brendel, at least when it comes to opera, *form* is something of a dirty word. Gluck, he tells us, "recognized the need to make everything flow [*Alles in Fluss zu bringen*], to shift around arias, recitatives, choruses as the moment demanded, without first working through each piece in purely musical terms and bringing it to a definite conclusion" (p. 284). In a sense this is true. Yet Gluck's operas, like Mozart's after them, are still "number operas." Brendel's metaphor of making everything flow—or of turning everything into a river, which is another sense of *Fluss*—strongly recalls (and prefigures) Wagner, with his endless melody.

When Brendel leaves opera and begins to talk about the 18th century's development of an autonomous instrumental music, a topic that seems of somewhat less interest to him, he of course has to speak of form in a more positive way. Yet while he notes the importance of sonata form, he does not describe either its workings or its evolution in any detail. "Instrumental music," he tells us, "completely corresponds to the modern spirit" (p. 300), and it is C. P. E. Bach, "as the first representative of the new age in this area, to whom the rise of modern instrumental music is most closely linked" (p. 301). His strong individuality and imaginative freedom have in fact made Bach "the founder of the modern direction in composition, in a further sense of the word the founder of the Romantic direction, the direct forerunner of Joseph Haydn" (p. 305).

Thus while for Krause and Kiesewetter, and in a way for Marx as well, the line of vocal music was more important than that of instrumental music not only for the troublesome period 1750-1775 but for the whole of the 18th century, for Brendel the two seem about equally important—though he is clearly more interested in vocal music, particularly in opera. For the historians that follow, the emphasis definitely shifts to instrumental music, and particularly to the forms of instrumental music as they were developing in the years just preceding the production of the first Classical masterpieces by Haydn and Mozart.

August Reissmann (1825-1903), the author of many books on music and also a minor composer, taught at the Stern Conservatory in Berlin and was awarded an honorary doctorate by the University of Leipzig. Despite also having been, for a time, a student of Liszt's, Reissmann campaigned against the "new music" of Liszt and Wagner as passionately as Brendel campaigned for it.

Like Brendel, Reissmann sees Gluck not as a loner or sport but rather as the result of previous developments in operatic composition—though for him Gluck's most important forerunner is Rameau, not, as for Brendel, Handel. Thus in the third and last volume of his *Allgemeine Geschichte der Musik* (1863-1864),[19] Reissmann is not dismissive, as Brendel had been, of the French opera composers. Also in contrast to Brendel, Reissmann talks a good deal about form—a concept that for him has a positive value. For Reissmann, the mark of progress in music, whether we are speaking of opera or of instrumental music, is that its forms grow more *bestimmt*, more fixed and definite, that they attain greater *Bestimmtheit*, greater clarity and definition.

This sort of formal clarity or definition is especially important in instrumental music. "Before Bach," Reissmann tells us, "composers felt and conceived purely in vocal terms; the instrumental side of music lagged behind and was adapted to the requirements of the vocal" (p. 158). It was Bach and his contemporaries who "first began to make instrumental music independent, but still mostly within the stricter forms of vocal music" (p. 158). Why does Reissmann think of the forms of vocal music as "stricter"—than the forms of independent instrumental music, presumably? At least partly, I think, because not only the forms but also the character of vocal music are largely controlled by the text being set.

We are accustomed to purely instrumental music having an arsenal of fairly strict forms. But during the 18th century, as we shall have ample occasion to see later, there was considerable concern about how, and to what degree, textless music should or could be organized. The fact that instrumental music, by its very nature, lacks a form or shape that is preordained by a verbal text led many aestheticians and critics to declare that instrumental music was therefore less determinate, less *bestimmt*, in its emotional or cognitive content than vocal music, in which the emotions or ideas to be communicated to the listener are named, or otherwise indicated, in its text. The two terms that dominated this discussion were *bestimmt* and *allgemein*—in the sense of general or universal, with overtones of vagueness. Instrumental music, it was often said, is inferior to vocal music in that it can only express emotions or ideas that are *allgemein*, not *bestimmt*.

Once instrumental music, or much of it at any rate, abandoned the determinacy provided (or supposedly provided) by a verbal text, there was therefore a need for it to gain that determinacy in some other way. The way, of course, was through the development of purely instrumental forms, particularly sonata form. Reissmann gives a brief history of sonata form, as found in the keyboard works of Domenico Scarlatti, Mattheson, and, finally, C.P.E. Bach, whom he, like Brendel, singles out as Haydn's main forerunner, "the most important representative of this transitional period, whose direct pupil Haydn declared himself to be" (p. 159). Of Haydn, Reissmann writes:

> He was, indeed, in the incomparably favorable position of being able to take possession immediately of the newly won territory that his predecessors had obtained.... Because instrumental music lacks the definiteness [*Bestimmtheit*] of expression found in vocal music, it requires a greater stock of means by which it can reveal itself as self-sufficient. It must seek to compensate for [its lack of] precise definiteness [*Bestimmtheit*] through greater fineness of detail [*Ausführlichkeit*].
>
> [P. 162]

Reissmann then draws a parallel between vocal and instrumental music. "If the continuity of inner organic development is acknowledged to be the primary basis of vocal music, then for instrumental music the introduction of certain self-sufficient sections, which above all stand in no connection of inner necessity [*Nothwendigkeit*] to the main content is necessary [*nothwendig*]" in order to "set this [main content] in a new light and make it throughout more comprehensible" (p. 163). There is much here that is confusing.

Why should "inner organic development" be a natural property of vocal music but (by implication) not of instrumental music? To us it is just as natural to speak of organic development in a movement from a Beethoven symphony as in a Schubert song or Monteverdi madrigal. Again we must recall that the ascendancy of untexted instrumental music was, in Reissmann's time, still a relatively recent event. Moreover, theory lagged badly behind practice. As has often been pointed out, no detailed analytical descriptions of sonata form appeared until well into the 19th century: in the final volume of Anton Reicha's *Traité de haute composition musicale* (1826), the third volume of Marx's *Die Lehre von der musikalischen Komposition* (1845), and Carl Czerny's *School of Practical Composition* (1848).[20] Reissmann is, after all, the first of the music historians we have examined to treat the question of form in instrumental music in any detail.

It would probably have been natural to Reissmann and his contemporaries to think of a verbal text as already containing the continuity provided by its own "inner organic development," which could (and presumably would) be translated by the composer into musical terms. A purely instrumental piece, on the other hand, lacking a text, might well seem at least potentially chaotic. Whereas the sections of a (suitably composed, appropriate) vocal work would indeed have a "connection of inner necessity" to the content of its text, it was logically necessary—or at least unavoidable, in the nature of things—that the sections of an instrumental work should have no such necessary connection to the work's emotional or cognitive content. For men of Reissmann's generation, I think this was still a very real problem. Certainly the tortured quality of his prose—the paradoxical play on *nothwendig*—suggests that he is struggling with it. We must realize that these ideas, so familiar to us, are new to Reissmann; that sonata form, and the wonders it can work in the hands of a Haydn or Mozart or Beethoven, still seems something of a miracle, demanding yet resisting rational explanation.

Reissmann is thus the first of our historians for whom the line of instrumental music that runs from Bach and Handel through C.P.E. Bach to Haydn is clearly of more importance than the operatic line that runs from the French composers and Handel through Gluck to Mozart and beyond. He is therefore also the first one to take a positive interest in form and the problems of form in instrumental music, and the first to introduce analysis into music history.

Arrey von Dommer (1828–1905) was born in Danzig. He attended the University of Leipzig, and taught briefly there before moving on, in 1863, to Hamburg, where he served for seven years as music critic for the *Hamburgische Correspondent*. Though he published a few compositions, he is best known for his *Handbuch der Musikgeschichte,* which appeared first in 1868 and then, in an enlarged edition, in 1878.[21] The book was popular enough to be given yet another edition, in 1914, thoroughly revised by Arnold Schering.

Like Reissmann, Dommer is far more interested in the instrumental line than in the vocal or operatic one. Even his respect for Gluck has something grudging about it. If Gluck has succeeded in increasing the importance of drama in opera, that is at least partly because "His gift was indisputably more for the dramatic than for the specifically musical; his artistic inspiration was primarily poetic, only secondarily musical. He was protected from the extravagances of the Italians not only by his strong character and the clear purity of his artistic vision but also by the narrow bounds of his musical imagination" (p. 542).

Shortly after entering Dommer's chapter entitled "The Epoch of Haydn, Mozart, and Beethoven," we find ourselves awash in a sea of contorted, quasi-philosophical prose even rougher than that stirred up by Reissmann. But the source of the difficulty is the same: Dommer too is trying to describe exactly how, and in what respects, the instrumental music of the Classical period is rendered *bestimmt* by its forms. Moreover, Dommer is also trying to show the difference between that music and the instrumental music of J. S. Bach's time. Though it is very difficult to follow Dommer's thought here, the effort must be made: just as with Reissmann, the lapse of an ordinarily clear writer into such tortured prose clearly indicates that he is struggling with ideas that are of the greatest importance to him—and, I would add, to his age.[22]

Though Dommer obviously loves Bach's instrumental music, his feelings about it are ambivalent—and in a most interesting way. "The highest fulfillment of the older instrumental music came about through Sebastian Bach" (p. 571), and yet "The essential content of the older instrumental music, with Sebastian Bach at its summit, is purely musical [*rein musikalisch-kunstmässiger*], its poetry that which resides in musical sound and its artistically correct [*kunstgerechten*] combinations" (p. 572). The phrase "purely musical" and the whole notion of art (*Kunst*) seem double-edged: does Dommer mean that the instrumental music of Bach and his contemporaries was artistically perfect and correct but cold, impersonal, lacking in humanity? Not exactly. "Such musical creations," he pointedly reassures us, "can only be the product of a rich and profoundly inspired life of the soul, because otherwise they would merely elicit from us admiration of their artistic technique, and in other respects would leave us cold" (p. 572). What then is missing?

Only after elaborately protesting that we admire this music not only for its "artistic technique" but also for "the unity and harmony, perfected by art, in which all operative elements are combined with one another, the ideal interconnection of all greater and lesser parts, the organic state of self-realization from within outward," and various other commendable virtues, does Dommer feel free to write:

> But the mood content is nonetheless merely general [*allgemeiner*], the style merely artistic [*kunstmässiger*], a purely objective expression of the universal [*allgemeinen*] life of feeling, as it passes, still without essential modification, through the individual subjectivity of the artist into the work of art.
>
> [P. 572]

The two opposed terms that dominated the 18th-century discussion of whether or not purely instrumental music could attain the definiteness and clarity of vocal music were, we recall, *bestimmt* and *allgemein*. Even though the instrumental music of Bach's time possesses all the virtues laboriously enumerated by Dommer, and has besides "definite [*bestimmte*] and uniform coloring and demeanor" (p. 572), the music's content is irremediably *allgemein*: general, universal, objective rather than subjective, true of or applicable to all of us rather than just the artist alone, and therefore finally deficient.

This older instrumental music does indeed present us not merely with a demonstration of technical expertise but also with a vividly realized "life of the soul" or "life of feeling." But this life, though vividly realized and presented, is recognizably the life of common humanity rather than that of a particular (and therefore special) human being. What is missing therefore is intimate imaginative contact or communion with a person who reveals himself as markedly different from ourselves. Dommer is, in other words, a Romantic who is having difficulty explaining his love for Bach's quite un-Romantic but nonetheless deeply compelling music—a love that he himself seems somewhat surprised by.

The instrumental forms employed by Bach and his contemporaries were mostly too rigid and confining: "through the universality [*Allgemeinheit*] of the basic feeling, the artist's fantasy, imagination, and emotion remained held within certain boundaries" (p. 573). In certain exceptional types of piece, however—fantasias, toccatas, preludes, and the like—"the stream of fantasy . . . flowed more freely, and the more subjective moods spoke a freer language, resulting in a quicker and more lively alteration of expression, sharper contrasts, and generally a more vigorous life in the whole piece" (p. 573). Dommer thus describes the transition to the instrumental music of the Classical era in rather surprising (and very Romantic) terms: "As the stricter forms now fell under such boundless power of the fantasy, they did not resist the demand, now stirring in the new instrumental music, for the embodiment of more subjective feelings and more individual utterance, which made for a freer handling of the artistic medium" (p. 573).

Yet Dommer is at pains immediately to point out that this increase in subjectivity, in freedom and fantasy, did not lead to any blurring or indefiniteness of either form or content:

> The more far-reaching and ramified became the content that the instrumental forms were to receive into themselves, the more definite [*bestimmter*] and clear it appeared, with all its modifications and contrasts; and the more the universal [*allgemeine*] human subjectivity showed itself in the individual subjectivity of the artist, the

more must they [i.e., the forms] extend their borders yet at the same time divide and group themselves, in their inner configuration, all the more definitely [*bestimmter*] and clearly in order now to remain clear and distinct.

[Pp. 573-574]

This remarkable passage embodies a double-sided paradox that is, in a sense, the key to Dommer's whole view of the relation between Baroque and Classical instrumental music.

The first side of the paradox is that as the content of instrumental music became "more far-reaching and ramified" owing to the letting loose of fantasy and imagination, the intrusion into the music of what Dommer calls individual (as opposed to universal) subjectivity, that content did not become vague, blurred, indefinite in all the ways that we sometimes associate with Romanticism. Quite the opposite: it became clearer, more definite.

The second side of the paradox is perhaps the more surprising and important. For all his talk of fantasy and individual subjectivity, that is not all that Dommer wants from (and finds in) the new instrumental music of the Classical era. So far he has spoken of the change from Baroque to Classical instrumental music in terms of an increase in the individual subjectivity of the artist. But what about that universal subjectivity that was present in the older instrumental music? Will it disappear? Or will it simply remain, but with the artist's individual subjectivity added to it? Dommer's language makes it clear, I think, that he is saying that even as the amount of individual subjectivity increases, so will that of universal subjectivity.

It is, however, on the particular rather than on the general or universal that Dommer lays his final stress. In the closing paragraphs of this extremely difficult passage, he tells us that as music moved from Haydn to Beethoven, the demand for greater directness of expression and greater variety of form led to a desire for music that would "bring to view, by means of analogy, through the movement of tones, a poetic idea that validates itself in a definite [*bestimmten*] process of feeling" (p. 574). That is, the substance and movement of the music will not be determined by abstract formal and musical considerations, or at least not to the degree that was true in the older instrumental music, but will embody or dramatize, so as to re-create in the listener's mind, by analogy as Dommer puts it, a particular movement of thought or feeling in an individual human sensibility, an emotional or psychological process.

Dommer then concludes: "Thus in this case there lies, at the base of the musical work, an inner experience with psychological consequences, an experience that the listener will be induced also to live through; instrumental music will then be . . . the means for representing concrete feelings and experiences of the soul" (p. 574). Far from instrumental music, owing to its lack of words, being vaguer and less definite than texted vocal music, the suggestion here is that the very absence of words will, through the mediation of the new and freer forms, allow for a greater directness and immediacy of communication than is possible with words: the "concrete feelings and experiences" will pass directly from the soul of the composer through the music and into the soul of the listener, without loss of concreteness or of anything else.

Once he has got himself (and us) through this intricate, paradoxical, almost mystical celebration of the miraculous fusion of general and particular, and of form and content, made possible by the development of sonata form, Dommer's prose returns to normal. He traces the antecedents, in Sammartini and the Mannheim composers, of sonata form, gives a brief analysis of the form itself, and at last pronounces C.P.E. Bach to be Haydn's most important predecessor in the form's development. The particular details of Dommer's history and analysis of sonata form are not relevant; the point is how pressing the whole question of sonata form and its development had come to be and how naturally C.P.E. Bach now fell into place as the middle term between the Baroque and the Classical composers, the historical slot that he would occupy for at least the next half century.

In the decades that followed, the historians' accounts of just how the binary forms of the Baroque evolved into ternary Classical sonata form would become increasingly detailed, both historically and analytically. After the publication, in 1859, of Darwin's *The Origin of Species,* music historians began trying to chart the step-by-step development or evolution of particular instrumental forms, and especially of sonata form, just as Darwin and other biologists, with the aid of the fossil record, were charting the evolution of various species of plants and animals. Since, as we know, *Natura non facit saltum,* there had to be middle terms or missing links discoverable between stages. As the focus of the historians changed from vocal to instrumental music, C.P.E. Bach became the crucial link in the development of sonata form—for no better reason than that he was the most important instrumental composer active during the crucial years 1750–1775.

In 1868, however, a dissenting voice was heard when C. H. Bitter's two-volume *Carl Philipp Emanuel und Wilhelm Friedemann Bach und deren Brüder,* the first extensive examination of C.P.E. Bach as a composer, appeared.[23] Carl Hermann Bitter (1813–1885) was not a professional musicologist. After study at the Universities of Berlin and Bonn, he followed his father into the Prussian civil service, and from 1879 to 1882 he served as Bismarck's minister of finance. He wrote several books on music, which occasionally drew the fire of such professionals as Philipp Spitta and Friedrich Chrysander. The most interesting thing about his book on the Bach sons is how utterly out of step it is with the historical writing we have been examining.

It is clear from the outset that Bitter thinks of C.P.E. Bach primarily as a vocal, not an instrumental, composer. He speaks of Bach's "melodic tuneful style" (I, 2), and further on he sees Bach's development as a composer mainly in vocal terms:

> In the course of his development the most important factor was his talent for simple song. He saw it as his special mission to write instrumental music that was singable because he wanted it to be moving and affecting, for the cultivation of melody was well suited to his special gifts. Therefore he was at pains to strip away everything Baroque, harsh, and unyielding that had come down from the contrapuntal school.
>
> [I, 138]

One can find ample support for this view of Bach's nature and aims as a composer in the chapter on performance that ends Part I of his treatise *Versuch über die wahre Art das Clavier zu spielen.*[24]

Bach begins the chapter by insisting that mere technique, while all very well in its way, is not enough for a keyboardist. For "the continuity and flow of the melody suffer" at the hands of technicians who "do nothing more than play the notes" (p. 147). When Bach describes the sort of playing he values, he almost invariably mentions song. The performer's goal is to attain "the ability through singing or playing to make the ear conscious of the true content and affect of a composition," the "rounded, pure, flowing manner of playing which makes for clarity and expressiveness" (p. 148). Bach's final advice to keyboardists is to "lose no opportunity to hear artistic singing," and in fact "to sing instrumental melodies in order to reach an understanding of their correct performance": "This way of learning is of far greater value than the reading of voluminous tomes or listening to learned discourses" (pp. 151–152).

Because Bach thinks of instrumental music as a kind of offshoot or subsidiary of vocal music, he does not share the doubts that were soon to set in, about whether or not untexted instrumental music could acquire the definiteness and precision of content that a verbal text gives to vocal music. If the performer thinks of the instrumental piece as though it were vocal music, and comes to understand it through singing it, that will do the job. (As we shall see later, in the fall of 1773 Bach had a very interesting correspondence, with the poet Heinrich Wilhelm von Gerstenberg, about just this question.)

Nor does Bitter share these doubts. Therefore he has no interest in the questions that so concern Reissmann and other late-19th-century music historians, as to just how sonata form and the other instrumental forms manage to give definiteness and precision of content to untexted instrumental music. He is far more concerned with describing the stylistic qualities of Bach's keyboard sonatas than he is with analyzing their formal structure: "Noble melody, unity of thought, elegance, and harmonic mastery are here, as in all Bach's keyboard pieces, in rich profusion" (I, 71). When he discusses Bach's 1780 "orchestral symphonies"—that is, symphonies scored for winds in addition to the string choir—Bitter does several times mention sonata form, and at one point he refers to "the three-part sonata form so often employed by Bach" (I, 237). But it soon becomes clear that when he speaks of "three-part sonata form," he is not speaking of the internal structure of the first or any other movement, but rather of the whole sonata-form work: the three parts are the three movements (fast-slow-fast, without minuet).

Therefore Bitter does not see Bach's historical importance as residing in his having been Haydn's main forerunner in the development of sonata form. In fact he goes out of his way to stress how different Bach's symphonies are from Haydn's:

> They had not yet taken on the symphonic character passed down from Haydn to the present day. Basically, they were simple in nature, without the splendor of blended orchestral effects, constructed only on the more or less profound content and skilled development of their ideas.
>
> [I, 237-238]

For Bitter, Bach's historical importance lies mainly in his vocal works, in his being "the founder and creator of the German song in its modern form" (I, 142-143). And Bitter insists, quite rightly, that Bach's "great service to the German song, to which he was doubtless the first to give color and life, has until now not been justly valued" (I, 153).

Bitter, then, is the odd man out in this game of deciding where to place C. P. E. Bach historically. From his general awkwardness of language and his out-and-out mistakes we can recognize his amateurishness. Spitta and Chrysander were probably fully justified in their objections to his work. Yet his book should not be either missed or dismissed. Blessedly free of knowledge about Darwin and evolution, Bitter looked at the music before him, and he saw a great deal—though he often had trouble describing what he saw. Moreover, he is right where the tradition of music history accumulating around him is wrong: C. P. E. Bach should not be so easily assigned the role of principal forerunner of Haydn, sonata form, the Classical style, and the whole glorious golden age that culminates in Beethoven. He was genuinely different from the Viennese masters—as also were his north German contemporaries—and one symptom of that difference is that songs were so much larger a part of his *oeuvre* than they were of Haydn's, Mozart's, or Beethoven's.

The next important (or at least well-known) music history written in Germany was Emil Naumann's *Illustrierte Musikgeschichte: Die Entwickelung der Tonkunst aus frühesten Anfängen bis auf die Gegenwart,* which appeared in two volumes in 1880-1885, and which almost immediately, in 1886, received an English translation.[25] Naumann (1827-1888) was the grandson of the composer and Dresden Capellmeister Johann Gottlieb Naumann (1741-1801), whom we shall meet later in connection with a collection of songs to which both he and C. P. E. Bach contributed. A composition student of Mendelssohn's while still in his teens, the younger Naumann earned a doctorate from Berlin University and, like his grandfather, settled in Dresden, where he was professor of music history. His book, however, is astonishingly superficial. Its historical importance lies in the fact that it was one of the first illustrated histories of music, which helps to account for its popularity. One is not surprised to learn that a Nazified edition was prepared by Eugen Schmitz and published at Stuttgart in 1934.

Naumann's book is of interest here merely because it shows that the idea that C. P. E. Bach's main distinction was to have been Haydn's most important forerunner had, by the 1880s, hardened into a cliché. Indeed, the book is nothing but a tissue of clichés, a shapeless bundle of received opinions. As is generally true in such books, the bits of wisdom that the author has sedulously culled from earlier writers often collide with one another, producing nonsense. In Naumann's hilariously muddled history of sonata form, C.P.E. Bach's music is marked by a "stiff conventionality" (p. 857), yet he is "the writer who surpasses all others in breaking with the cast-iron monothematic tradition" (p. 875). Thus Bach emerges as both old fogy and forward-looking rebel!

Perhaps the most ambitious and far-reaching single-author history of music in the late 19th century was that planned by August Wilhelm Ambros (1816-1876), a nephew of Kiesewetter. But Ambros's death prevented his magnum opus from advancing beyond the early 17th century. His three completed volumes were published in 1862, 1864, and 1868, with a fourth volume, edited from his notes by Gustav Nottebohm, appearing posthumously in 1878.

Soon after Ambros's death, his publisher asked Wilhelm Langhans to complete the work. Langhans (1832-1892) was trained as a violinist and composer at the Leipzig Conservatory, and later played in the Leipzig Gewandhaus and Düsseldorf Orchestras. The two volumes of his completion of Ambros's history, *Die Geschichte der Musik des 17. 18. und 19. Jahrhunderts,* appeared in 1881 and 1887.[26]

Langhans is distinctly more chauvinistic in temper than the other historians we have examined. After recounting Gluck's career, he describes the composer's Paris triumph with *Iphigénie en Tauride*: "Thus the German musical genius—unfortunately we cannot say 'German art'—with this opera scored the first decisive victory over the Italian" (p. 60). Why can we not call this a triumph of German art? Though Gluck restored "the lost unity of poetry and music," he was forced "to leave his fatherland and disown his native tongue in order to develop his principles," and thus "the unfavorable conditions of the time prevented him from attaining the complete balance between the languages of word and tone through which, we may assume, ancient tragedy made its powerful effect on the emotions" (p. 66). Now, however, the achievement of Wagner enables us to see both "what he [i.e., Gluck] accomplished and what it was denied him to accomplish" (p. 66).

As for C.P.E. Bach, Langhans refers to Dommer's description of him as "an authentic child of his age, a *galant* salon musician . . . who felt at home with the excessive prettiness, endlessly trifling charm, and ornamented superfluity of the rococo." But Langhans goes on to insist, more strongly than Dommer had done, that there is more to Bach than this: "if one approaches him more closely, one soon recognizes, under the conventional exterior, the true essence, the superbly schooled musician filled with pure enthusiasm for his art, who understood how to breathe life into the forms that he inherited" (p. 121).

Up to the 1880s, almost all of the serious work in music history had been done by Germans. There had, to be sure, been some important contributions in French, notably the many books by the Belgian polymath François-Joseph Fétis (1784-1871), which span the half century between the early 1820s and the late 1860s. But the English had done almost nothing, depending mostly on German books, many of which, as we have seen, were translated into English. That began to change in the late 1870s. In 1878 were held the first of the meetings that would eventually lead to the opening of the Royal College of Music five years later, with the newly knighted Sir George Grove as its director. The following year, the first volume of the first edition of *Grove's Dictionary of Music and Musicians* appeared.[27]

Some of the longest and most impressive entries in the first edition of Grove's *Dictionary*—particularly those on Form, Harmony, Melody, Modulation, Sonata, Symphony, and Variations—were written by the young composer and scholar Hubert Parry (1848-1918), a member of Grove's handpicked staff at the RCM. In 1893 Parry's book, *The Art of Music,* perhaps the most important English contribution to music history since the 18th century, would appear.[28] The book, much of which still reads very well, was a great success. Because its title was felt to be misleading, and also because Parry was even more indebted to Darwin than the Germans who preceded him, in 1896 the book was retitled *The Evolution of the Art of Music*. In 1930 a new edition, brought up to date by new chapters by H. C. Colles but otherwise unchanged, was issued.

In Parry's chapters on the 17th, 18th, and early 19th centuries, he is mainly concerned with tracing in detail the development of what he calls "harmonic design":

> The essence of design in harmonic music of the modern kind is that groups of chords and whole passages shall have a well-defined connection with certain tonal centres; and that the centres round which the successive passages are grouped shall have definite and intelligible relations of contrast or affinity with one another. The simplest dance tune or street song is now constructed upon such principles no less than the greatest masterpieces. But the early experimenters had no experience of such effects, and jumbled up their chords together inconsequently.
>
> [P. 141]

Plainly, this is a point of departure quite different from that adopted by the other historians we have examined. Whereas they began their historical accounts by talking about forms and genres, Parry is taking a deeper cut (so to speak), starting with an examination of the changes that took place in the interrelations among keys and chords, the basic harmonic building blocks of music.

Through several chapters, and with the help of copious musical examples, Parry charts his course through the increasing sensitivity to harmonic relations on the part of composers and the increasing complexity of harmonic design that it produced in their music. What Parry terms "real artistic development," free of any dependence upon a verbal text, could not be achieved "till men changed their point of view and developed their feeling for tonality and for the classification of harmony" (p. 165). This happened only with Corelli, who has left us "the earliest examples of pure instrumental music which have maintained any hold upon lovers of the art" and which "therefore mark the point where imperfect attempts are at last replaced by achievement" (pp. 165-166).

Parry closes this chapter with a statement that illuminatingly sums up his own general "point of view" and is therefore worth citing at some length:

> The progress of this somewhat immature period shows the inevitable tendency of all things from homogeneity towards diversity and definiteness. In its widest aspects art is seen to branch out into a variety of different forms. The difference in style and matter between choral movements and instrumental works begins to be more definite and decisive. The types of opera, oratorio, cantata, and of the various kinds of church music become more distinct, and are even subdivided into different subordinate types, as was the case with Italian and French opera. Instrumental music, from being mainly either imitations of choral music, or vague toccatas and fantasias, or short dance tunes, established a complete independent existence, and began to branch out into the various forms which have since become representative as sonatas and symphonies.
>
> [Pp. 169-170]

Like his German predecessors, Parry wants independent instrumental music to become definite, and finds that it did so during the period we are considering. For him as for them, definiteness is the mark of success. But it is important to note that he is also saying that modern instrumental music, like "all things," has also moved "from homogeneity towards diversity"—as well as "definiteness." This claim is new, and it shows that Parry is more closely linked to Darwin than were his German predecessors.

In the introduction to *The Origin of Species*,[29] Darwin notes that a naturalist, reflecting upon such matters as the distribution and mutual affinities of species, might well come to the same conclusion that he himself has come to, namely, "that each species had not been independently created," as the

Bible teaches, "but had descended, like varieties, from other species" (p. 4). But then Darwin adds a most important qualification: "Nevertheless, such a conclusion, even if well founded, would be unsatisfactory, until it could be shown how the innumerable species inhabiting this world have been modified, so as to acquire that perfection of structure and coadaptation which most justly excites our admiration" (p. 4). Darwin, though coming at it from the other side, is making the same double assertion as Parry.

Darwin's main point of course is that species were not all individually and simultaneously created, each to remain forever the same, by divine fiat, but that they have modified and diversified themselves over time. But he also wants to insist that the modifications and the diversification have been steadily producing improvements that will lead at last to perfection. "As natural selection works solely by and for the good of each being," he writes in his concluding chapter, "all corporeal and mental endowments will tend to progress towards perfection" (p. 395). Parry's main point, on the other hand, is that during the 17th and 18th centuries, music was steadily improving as composers developed the feeling for harmonic design that would at last make possible an independent instrumental music possessing the requisite definiteness. But he also wants to insist that this process has not simply been one of improvement on the part of individual genres—keyboard sonatas getting better, orchestral suites getting better, and so on—but that it has involved constant and increasing diversification: forms splitting off from one another and producing new forms. Just as Darwin's goal is "perfection of structure," so Parry's is "harmonic design"; and the path that leads to each of these goals is one marked by constant diversification. The reason that Darwin does not use the word *design* in these contexts but prefers such near synonyms as *structure, pattern, framework, system, scheme,* and *contrivance,* is probably that he does not want to evoke associations with the theological "argument from design," long employed to prove the existence of God.

We need not investigate in detail the rest of the process by which Parry sees instrumental music arriving at its more or less predestined culmination, the greatest works of Beethoven. The most interesting thing about his treatment, in contrast to those of his German predecessors, is that Parry is completely free of the desire to speculate philosophically, let alone to become somewhat mystical, about the ways in which definiteness and clarity were achieved without the aid of verbal texts. One of the many advantages he has gained from his more literal and thoroughgoing adoption of Darwin's theory is a cool, critical, quasi-scientific approach to his subject. Like Darwin, Parry produces a wealth of examples, and he stresses the need for composers, just like biologists, to engage in extensive taxonomy: harmonies must be classified, sorted, ranked according to their "relations of contrast or affinity with one another." It is no surprise that Parry's close examination of the history and development of sonata form, when it finally arrives, is far more elaborate and detailed than that of any of the preceding historians.

Where does all this leave C. P. E. Bach? Parry's few references to him show a genuine, if qualified, respect, and a stronger interest in his relations to his father and to the Italians than to Haydn and Mozart. In the midst of lamenting the general low quality of music in our troublesome period, the third quarter of the 18th century, Parry writes of Bach: "even he, the sincerest composer of the following generation [i.e., after J. S. Bach], was infected by the complacent, polite superficiality of his time; and was forced, through accepting the harmonic principle of working, to take with it some of the empty formulas and conventional tricks of speech which seem to belie the genuineness of his utterances, and put him out of touch with his wholehearted father" (p. 211). Yet after scornfully listing the German composers who "adopted Italian manners to suit the tastes of the fashionable classes," Parry notes that "there were a few here and there who did not bow the knee to Baal; and noteworthiest of these was Philip Emmanuel Bach" (p. 224). If he did not actually invent the harpsichord sonata, "he was for some time its most prominent representative" (p. 224). As for Bach's symphonies, Parry finds them "harmonic in style, but not so decisively so as his sonatas"; though they are "remarkably vigorous, animated and original in conception, they have not led to any further developments in the same line" (p. 229).

It is clear then that Parry does not see C.P.E. Bach's main historical importance as residing in his role as Haydn's forerunner in the development of sonata form. Here too I think Parry has been helped by Darwin—as well as by the flood of 18th-century music that had recently begun to be published, giving historians a clearer picture of the century's latter half. For Darwin's constant stress on diversification and ramification, along with his habit of relentlessly citing chapter and verse to enforce his every point, evidently made it clear to Parry that his subject was far too complex for the old search for Haydn's one and only forerunner to be anything but a rather foolish, trivial game. It is interesting that Parry, unlike his recent predecessors, shows an appreciation of C.P.E. Bach's oratorios. Because his Darwinian habits of mind and his broad knowledge of the development of sonata form left Parry free to avoid sticking Bach in the Haydn's-chief-forerunner pigeonhole, he was free also to listen to Bach's vocal music with an open mind.

After Grove's *Dictionary,* the fourth and last volume of which appeared in 1889 and which received its second edition in 1904–1910, the next great milestone in English musicology was the *Oxford History of Music,* the first edition of which appeared, in six volumes, in 1901–1905. The volume of concern to us, Volume V, *The Viennese Period,* was written by W. H. Hadow (1859–1937), lecturer in music at Oxford and general editor of the *Oxford History*, and was published in 1904.[30]

Hadow, like Parry, is an evolutionist, but a far more superficial one. Describing the development of sonata form out of the Baroque forms, he writes: "the history of this Binary form shows a continuous development, until at last it breaks its own bounds and passes into a higher stage of evolution" (p. 191). While his treatment of this process is nearly as detailed as Parry's, to which it owes a good deal, Hadow is a less cool and detached writer than Parry, more melodramatic in the old-fashioned "great-man" style. Describing the state of things at J. S. Bach's death, Hadow writes:

> Italian music was apparently going from bad to worse, and its popularity throughout Europe was proportionally increasing. The case appeared little short of desperate....
> It is not too much to say that for a few years the fate of European music depended on Emanuel Bach.
>
> [P. 66]

Or, placing Bach in his familiar role as precursor to Haydn, Hadow can write: "to C.P.E. Bach fell the opportunity of seeing in the fulness of time that the threefold form was possible, and that no other could any longer satisfy the requirements of the sonata" (p. 195).

This breathlessly dramatic view of Bach's position and accomplishment is, like most such views, achieved at the cost of distorting its subject's career. "We are here less concerned with a criticism of Bach's ability," Hadow writes, "than with a statement of his place in the history of musical forms." That place, he admits, Bach owes, "almost wholly," to his very early "Prussian" and "Württemberg" sonatas, which were published in 1742 or 1743 and in 1744, respectively. "In the eyes of Burney he was the kindly old virtuoso, in whose writings the instrumental music of the eighteenth century attained its consummation: in ours he is the inspired pioneer who cleared the path for the feet of his Viennese successors" (p. 200). It is indeed a fact that Bach's earliest sonatas make the best case for his direct influence on Classical form; his later keyboard works developed in ways that drew them ever further from the work that Haydn and Mozart were doing in Vienna. Hadow writes as though C.P.E. Bach, to whom the dazzling possibilities of "the threefold form" had been revealed in his youth, had then tried to become Haydn or even Beethoven, to realize completely the dimly glimpsed future—but (the implication is clear) had failed to do so. Actually, however, Bach, a highly intelligent and self-aware man, was trying to become a rather different sort of composer, and was succeeding quite well at it. Teleology is a dangerous master.

Much of Hadow's actual criticism of Bach's music is, however, quite acute. After citing a passage from one of the keyboard works, he points out that "the curious, abrupt changes are determined not by the requirements of the drawing, but by the wish to set points of colour into strong contrast and relief," and he finds "the nearest analogue" to such writing in the fantasias of Haydn and Mozart, and (still more insightfully) in Schumann (p. 73). Moreover, while Hadow naturally wants to insist that Bach's "main historical interest lies" (p. 183) in the role he played in the development of sonata form, that achievement by no means exhausts his own interest in Bach's music. For Hadow is the first of our historians who has read Bitter's book on the Bach sons, and so he has taken the trouble to investigate Bach's vocal music, and has found that it is by no means "weak"—as earlier historians had assumed, almost as a matter of course. In his chapter on oratorios and church music, Hadow praises Bach's "fine manly setting of the *Magnificat*," and he judges *Die Israeliten in der Wüste,* the *Passions-Cantate,* and the *Auferstehung und Himmelfahrt Jesu* to be "three important works" in which "we find a definite revolt against the old traditions, and, on some sides, a definite anticipation of later methods" (pp. 144–145).

More surprisingly, Hadow is interested in Bach's songs. Rather than adopting the common 19th-century view that the German lied was almost solely a product of the Romantic movement, Hadow writes that Schubert "was born at a time when German song, matured through half a century of noble achievement, offered itself in full measure for his acceptance" (p. 324). And he approvingly cites Bitter's praise of Bach's Gellert songs: "With these beautiful and noble works, Emanuel Bach became the founder and creator of the German lied in its present-day meaning" (quoted p. 328). Still, however, we find traces of the evolutionist: Hadow also cites Reissmann's praise of Bach as "the father of the through-composed song" (quoted p. 328). As we shall see, Bach was no such thing, and to celebrate him for having fathered the through-composed song—of which he actually wrote very few—is as misguided, as out of line with his nature as a composer and with the development of his career, as finding his main historical significance to lie in his shaping influence on Classical sonata form.

But that way of seeing Bach's position in music history was soon to change—had in fact already begun to change shortly before Hadow's *Oxford History* volume appeared. For it was in the last decades of the 19th century that the great multivolume editions of early music from various parts of the German-speaking world were launched: *Denkmäler der Tonkunst in Österreich* in 1888, *Denkmäler deutscher Tonkunst* in 1889, and *Denkmäler der Tonkunst in Bayern* in 1900. The impact of these volumes on the writing of music history was immediate and lasting. Suddenly a wealth of music that contradicted the favored clichés of music historians was made easily available for inspection. Since the whole problem of the nature and development of sonata form had, as we have seen, become something close to an obsession with music historians as the 19th century drew to a close, it was one of the problems on which the editors of the *Denkmäler* volumes were most eager to shed light.

The change in C.P.E.Bach's historical position can perhaps be most easily seen in the writings of Hugo Riemann. Riemann (1849-1919) was so powerful and versatile a figure that he is hard to sum up in a few sentences. He first studied law, Germanic philology, and history at the University of Berlin. Then, while serving in the Franco-Prussian War, he studied philosophy at Tübingen and wrote poetry. But once decided upon a career in music, he moved with great speed. In 1871 he entered the Leipzig Conservatory and the University of Leipzig, by 1872 he was publishing articles on music theory in the *Neue Zeitschrift für Musik,* and in 1873 he received his doctorate from the University of Göttingen. He spent the rest of his life teaching at the University of Leipzig and the Hamburg Conservatory, and writing on virtually every conceivable musical subject. The Festschrift published in 1909 to celebrate his 60th birthday lists 58 books, 209 articles and editions of musical works, and many original compositions.

During the years 1888-1894 Riemann published a number of what he called "catechisms," elementary books on musical subjects that were cast in a question-and-answer form. In Riemann's *Katechismus der Musikgeschichte,* which was published in 1888 and appeared four years later in an

English translation,[31] a question about the development of instrumental music after the time of J. S. Bach is answered thus: "the next step forwards in the direction indicated, was made by J. S. Bach's second son, Karl Philipp Emanuel, who is very properly regarded as the father of modern instrumental music.... It is certainly wonderful that precisely the son of the last master of the old school became the founder of the new school" (p. 123).

But less than a decade later, Riemann had apparently had second thoughts. In 1897 he published a brief essay entitled "Die Söhne Bachs" in *Blätter für Haus- und Kirchenmusik,* an essay that was reprinted in 1901 in the third and final volume of his *Präludien und Studien.*[32] Riemann tells us that he has seen early editions of two of the symphonies Bach composed in 1773 (Wq. 182/1 and 4; H. 657 and 660), and that he hopes to publish editions of his own—as he in fact did, later in 1897. However, he is certain that these so-called symphonies are really string quartets because of the "genuine quartet style, sprightly invention, and finely imagined development, especially of the G-major quartet [Wq. 182/1; H. 657]" (p. 178). All of which leads Riemann to a most surprising conclusion: "In view of this quartet, it must certainly be conceded, without any reservation: Haydn is the spiritual father [*Geistesvater*] of Philipp Emanuel Bach" (p. 178). The well-known fact that Haydn acknowledged C. P. E. Bach as an early influence should not be allowed to rule out the possibility—considerably more than a possibility in Riemann's view—that the influence may later have flowed in the other direction, and that at least so far as the composition of string quartets is concerned, Haydn was the forerunner of Bach, rather than the other way around.

While chronology would certainly have permitted this to have been the case, it does not, on the face of it, seem likely. Bach's 1773 symphonies do not sound particularly like Haydn: to us, knowing far more of Bach's music than was available to Riemann, they sound like characteristic mature Bach works, full of the abruptness and surprise that Haydn may well have learnt from Bach but lacking the concentration on large-scale symmetry and balance that makes up the other half of the Classical synthesis forged by Haydn and Mozart. In any case, Ernst Fritz Schmid tells us in his book *C. P. E. Bach und seine Kammermusik*[33] that he discovered autograph manuscripts of four of these symphonies, and that they contained "a special figured-bass part for the continuo player": "there can therefore be no talk of 'string quartets': these are normal orchestral symphonies for strings and harpsichord, perhaps with concertante soloists" (p. 117n.).

The point, however, is that Riemann has, for whatever reason, felt impelled to reverse the conventional wisdom and to see Haydn as the forerunner of Bach. The unlikelihood of this being true, in addition to the somewhat random quality of Riemann's remarks concerning Bach, makes one feel that he has sensed that the conventional wisdom will no longer do and is groping for some other answer to the "forerunner" question. A few years later he found it.

In 1902 Riemann edited the first of three volumes of the newly launched *Denkmäler der Tonkunst in Bayern,* entitled *Sinfonien der Pfalzbayerischen Schule,*[34] that contained symphonies by Johann Stamitz (1717-1757) and other composers connected with the court of Elector Palatine Carl Theodor at Mannheim, in southwest Germany. Mannheim had long been known for the excellence of its orchestra, to which both Mozart and Burney offered eloquent contemporary testimony, and as the birthplace of certain "modern" orchestral effects, such as the gradual crescendo and diminuendo. But Riemann, in his preface to the first of these *DTB* volumes, argued forcefully that 18th-century Mannheim had also been "the seat of an established school of composition" whose main representatives had "inaugurated a new stylistic trend" that constituted "one of the most important early steps in the development of the symphony" (pp. x-xi). The influence of these composers, Riemann contended, had spread to France, England, and the Netherlands. That their works were now almost completely forgotten he blamed not only on "the splendor of the great Viennese triumvirate Haydn-Mozart-Beethoven" (p. xi) but also on the "jealousy" (p. xxi) of the north Germans, specifically of the 18th-century Berlin and Leipzig critics and the 19th-century biographers of Haydn and Mozart, who had claimed that C. P. E. Bach was the link between the Baroque and Classical eras.

Riemann concluded his review of the evidence by triumphantly proclaiming, in boldface type, that Johann Stamitz was "the so long sought-for forerunner of Haydn" (p. xxiv).

Riemann's attempt to install Stamitz in the position so long occupied by C.P.E. Bach did not go unchallenged for long. In 1908 Guido Adler (1855-1941), founder of the Musicological Institute at the University of Vienna and founding editor of *Denkmäler der Tonkunst in Österreich,* contributed a preface to a *DTÖ* volume, *Wiener Instrumentalmusik vor und um 1750,*[35] that contained symphonies by a number of mid-18th-century Viennese composers, notably Matthias Georg Monn (1717-1750) and Georg Christoph Wagenseil (1715-1777). In his preface Adler spoke, somewhat mystically, of the "organic life" of the Viennese Classical School, reminded his readers that Austria was "the ripening place [*Fruchtkammer*] of Joseph Haydn's boyhood and early youth" (p. ix), pointed out the Austrian origin of Riemann's Mannheim composers, and insisted that "the Viennese School was in full bloom [*Entfaltung*] when certain Austrians were called to Mannheim" (p. x). "The basic qualities that formed the Viennese School and grew to greatness," Adler concluded, "took root in home soil" (p. xii).

Riemann, a combative man and a colorful writer, did not take this lying down. In his 1913 *Handbuch der Musikgeschichte*[36] he asserted the significance of the Mannheimers even more emphatically than before, and he poked fun at the "better organization" and "greater harmonic correctness" of C.P.E. Bach and the other north German "well-schooled wig-wearers," which he contrasted with the "brightly colored and various" style of the "south German hotheads [*Brauseköpfen*]" (p. 130). As for the Viennese, Riemann judged Monn to be "a perfectly respectable composer" but found Wagenseil's symphonies "primitive and poor" (p. 149). Riemann also tried to show, by comparative musical examples, that C.P.E. Bach was directly influenced by Stamitz (pp. 143-145), and repeated his curious idea that Bach's 1773 symphonies were really string quartets influenced by those of Haydn (pp. 167-168).

Adler had the last word in this entertaining regional competition only because he outlived Riemann, who died in 1919. In 1924 Adler too produced a *Handbuch der Musikgeschichte,*[37] though he acted only as contributing editor and not as sole author. In his chapter on "The Viennese Classical School," he rhapsodized at great length, not only about the greatest works of Haydn, Mozart, and Beethoven, but also about the "School" itself, as a mystical entity that—"in its emergence, its unfolding, its formation, its power, its noble artlessness and eloquent greatness, . . . its congruence of form and content, its truth and depth of expression, . . . its permeation in beauty and perfection, . . . its incomparable blending of deep seriousness with gaiety and high spirits, its complete combining of tragic and comic," and so on—summed up all that was best and brightest in the human spirit (p. 768). Though Riemann is not mentioned by name, Mannheim comes in for some hard knocks: "The Mannheim School remained one of the outposts of the Viennese Classical School, fell into superficial mannerisms . . . because it abandoned its native soil [*Mutterboden*], and lost its natural motive power" (p. 776). As late as 1932, nine years before his death, Adler was still singing the same old song: "The fundamental note of true Viennese classical music is a metaphysical blend of the serious and the gay. . . . Its real starting-point, its native soil as it were, is Austrian folk-song, or, in its purest form, the music of the Viennese people, a mixture of the original German stock with foreign neighbors."[38]

There was of course no way of settling the Riemann-Adler quarrel. As Parry perhaps realized, the whole search for the one missing link between Baroque and Classical music or styles or forms was doomed to failure because it was radically misconceived. But it took music historians a long time to see this, and that is why the quarrel has such significance. In 1969 the English musicologist Gerald Abraham in fact began an essay entitled "18th-Century Music and the Problems of its History"[39] by declaring: "It is arguable that the first important step in the direction of a comprehensive history of the music of the 18th century was taken . . . when in 1902 Hugo Riemann published a volume of Mannheim symphonies in the second (Bavarian) series of *Denkmäler deutscher Tonkunst*" (p. 49). No longer was it possible to think of the 18th century as neatly divided between the age of Bach and Handel and the age of Haydn and Mozart, with C.P.E. Bach and/or Gluck somehow managing smoothly to bridge the enormous gap between the two ages. No longer was it possible to see the formation of the Classical style as (in Hadow's apt phrase) "the growth of the sonata," the gradual, orderly, unitary evolution, out of the so-called "architectural" forms of the Baroque era, of the far more "dramatic" sonata form, with its first themes, second themes, and bridge passages, and its three-part structure of exposition, development, and recapitulation.

The history of music's development in the 18th century could no longer be seen as a straight line that tidily connects the dots—that is, the comparatively few composers and works from the period with which we are well acquainted. Too much hitherto unknown 18th-century music, beginning with Riemann's Mannheimers and Adler's Viennese, was becoming available and known for the old schemes and the old ways of thinking to remain viable. Writers like Parry were beginning to approach both Baroque and Classical works more "scientifically": not measuring them against the fixed, stereotyped ideas of the various forms derived from 19th-century composition textbooks but analyzing the works freshly and seeing how they were actually put together.

The first and most important writer to begin looking at the 18th century in a new way was D. F. Tovey (1875–1940), composer, pianist, and Reid Professor of Music at the University of Edinburgh. Tovey had been a pupil of Parry, and in all his writings he loyally paid homage to the man he often referred to as "my beloved master" and to the mode of analysis he had learnt from Parry. Just what this method of analysis entailed, Tovey makes a point of telling us right at the beginning of his best-known work, the six-volume *Essays in Musical Analysis*:[40]

> Parry's method of analysis taught me that no piece of music can be understood from *a priori* generalizations as to form, but that all music must be followed phrase by phrase as a process in time. It is very unlikely that this principle has been essentially violated in these volumes.
>
> [I, 2]

A little later in the same volume he adds: "A true analysis takes the standpoint of a listener who knows nothing beforehand, but hears and remembers everything" (I, 68).

The one essential point on which Tovey disagreed with Parry was in not believing in progressivist or evolutionary views of the arts. In *The Integrity of Music*,[41] a series of lectures he delivered at the University of Glasgow in 1936, Tovey pointed out that Parry, like other men of his generation, "suffered from an inveterate and deliberately developed tendency to regard all works of art as leading to something beyond. Mozart and Haydn at their best were for Parry necessary processes leading to Beethoven and destined to be superseded by him" (p. 64). Tovey, on the other hand, liked to describe himself as not believing in Art with a capital A but only in individual works of art. Having grown up in the 1890s, Tovey was very much a believer in "Art for Art's Sake": it was the piece of music that counted, not—or not usually, at any rate—the conditions under which it came into being or the biography of the man who composed it.

In the general essay on music that he wrote, shortly before 1910, for the 11th edition of the *Encyclopaedia Britannica*[42] Tovey barely mentions C.P.E. Bach. Of the transition period between Baroque and Classical, he observes that "its boldest rhetorical experiments, such as the fantasias of Philipp Emanuel Bach, show a security of harmony which, together with the very vividness of their realization of modern ideas, must appear to a modern listener more like the hollow rhetoric of a decadent than the prophetic inspiration of a pioneer" (XIX, 79). It is hard to know what to make of this. Continuing, Tovey, who was always a lover of rather donnish paradoxes, points out that during a transition period "the work that is most valuable artistically tends to be that which is of less importance historically": "Thus, far more interesting artistically than the epoch-making earlier pianoforte works of Philipp Emanuel Bach are his historically less fruitful oratorios, and his symphonies" (XIX, 79).

Again we are left in the dark because Tovey explains neither the historical importance of one group of works nor the artistic value of the other.

In the version of this entry as it was rewritten for the 1929 edition of the *Encyclopaedia* and may be conveniently found in Tovey's *Musical Articles from the "Encyclopaedia Britannica,"*[43] these sentences do not appear; of Bach, Tovey merely remarks: "we regard Philipp Emanuel Bach as bridging the gulf between his father's and the new art; but Philipp Emanuel was writing quite mature sonatas in the year of his father's B minor Mass and his last set of sonatas was produced in the year of Mozart's *Don Giovanni*" (p. 126). Here is something to catch hold of: though Tovey is no friend to history, at least when it comes between us and a work of art, he is devoted to the facts of chronology, which he was one of the first musicologists to use imaginatively to combat the stale clichés of music history.

In the analysis he wrote of the one C. P. E. Bach symphony (Wq. 183/1; H. 663) included in *Essays in Musical Analysis,* he has fleshed out the remark in his 1929 encyclopedia article; the passage is worth citing at length:

> Philipp Emanuel Bach is, as all the world knows, the link between the polyphonic style and forms of his father and those of Haydn and Mozart. . . . The trouble begins when we find that Philipp Emanuel Bach was writing in a well-developed style of his own at the time when his father produced the B minor Mass, and that his last set of sonatas was produced in the year of Mozart's *Don Giovanni*. The present symphony was, as far as I can make out, composed in 1780, and is thus a year later than Mozart's epoch-making Paris Symphony. In style and form it has not the remotest resemblance either to his father's work or to the styles of Mozart and Haydn. Unlike the pianoforte works, it is not really on sonata lines at all, except in certain superficial matters. In relation to contemporary music, it is in line with Gluck's opera overtures, and it shares with them a doubtful collateral ancestry with the early concerto grosso.
>
> [VI, 9-10]

Tovey then declares that Bach's symphony "has the right of a mature work of art to exist on its own merits," and apologizes for his little excursus into music history: "Its historical origins have needed this amount of explanation, because without them the listener is sure to approach the work under preoccupations equally historical in appearance, but entirely misleading as to its character" (VI, 10).

In two essays collected in his volume *Essays and Lectures on Music,*[44] Tovey goes still further. In a 1929 essay on Haydn's chamber music, on the basis of his "study of some eighty sonatas, besides many rondos and fantasias," of Bach's, he concludes that "C.P.E. Bach never shows an inkling of the special idea of 'development' in sonata style" (pp. 27-28). Later, having posed the question of what Haydn's "real debt" to Bach is, Tovey replies:

> It is a pity that the word "rhetoric" has been degraded to a term of abuse, for it means an art the perfection of which is as noble as the noblest cause in which it can be used. Rhetoric is what Haydn learnt from C.P.E. Bach: a singularly beautiful and pure rhetoric, tender, romantic, anything but severe, yet never inflated.
>
> [P. 28]

While he admits that "the example of Bach's chaotically wild rondos and fantasias may have been necessary in order to stimulate Haydn's far more realistic sense of adventure" (pp. 28-29), Tovey firmly insists that Haydn did not learn from Bach the guiding principles of sonata form. In a 1934 essay on Gluck, also contained in *Essays and Lectures on Music,* Tovey sums up as follows:

Not only the splashy theatrical texture, but also the larger aspects of Gluck's musical form owe much to Sammartini. The sonata style of Haydn and Mozart is inveterately dramatic, to an extent of which its reputed pioneer Philipp Emanuel Bach had no conception. But it is not through the sonata forms that Gluck arrived at his dramatic style.... Strange to say, the classical symphony itself was an offshoot from operatic overtures in this style and did not immediately coalesce into the genuine sonata forms. Philipp Emanuel Bach was a lyric rhetorician whose style grew steadily more aloof from dramatic action.

[P. 76]

Tovey's point about Bach's "rhetoric" is well taken. But I do think he goes too far—perhaps understandably, given the power and influence of the position he is endeavoring to refute—in saying that Bach "never shows an inkling of the special idea of 'development' in sonata style." There are, in fact, many places, in both the early keyboard sonatas and the later symphonies and keyboard concertos, where we do feel a sense of "development" at work. Finally, however, Tovey wants to shift the credit for helping to create the Classical style from Bach to Gluck. In his 1929 *Encyclopaedia Britannica* entry under Music, he writes, in a style noticeably more blunt and decisive than usual:

It is inadequate to call Gluck a "reformer" of opera. Music itself was not dramatic before Gluck made it so. Hence it is a mistake to separate Gluck's "reform" from the whole process of the development of the sonata style.

[P. 124]

This Gluck, we note, is the absolute antithesis of Marx's lonely tragic figure. While there are certainly links to be made between what was happening in opera and the formation of the Classical style, here too Tovey seems to have allowed his polemical zeal to carry him a bit too far.

In the years since *Essays in Musical Analysis* appeared, a great deal of hitherto unknown 18th-century music has become available, and a great deal has been written about it. Manuscripts have been discovered in monasteries; differences among regional styles of music have been minutely examined; the relations between developments in opera and in instrumental music have been more closely analyzed than ever before. By 1973, in the *Age of Enlightenment: 1745-1790* volume of the *New Oxford History of Music*,[45] Egon Wellesz and F. W. Sternfeld could write: "Research suggests that well over 7,000 symphonies (or overtures used in concerts) dating from the period 1740-1800 are still extant and there is evidence of many more that have disappeared" (p. 366).

With such a flood of new music confronting them, it is no wonder that some musicologists concerned with the 18th century have grown quite depressed about their prospects of ever really understanding their period. During a 1969 conference, H. C. Robbins Landon, co-editor of the Union Catalogue of 18th-century symphonies, more than doubled that preposterous figure of 7,000. In response to the hopeful suggestion that it should now be possible "to put the [Classical] period into some perspective" in a comprehensive book, Robbins Landon replied:

The trouble with that book is that even if it is just a survey, it is going to be hopelessly large. And unless it is in three volumes of, let's say, 600 or 700 pages each, it is going to be so superficial as to be useless. It will have to cover some 15,000 symphonies written between 1740 and 1800, to say nothing of other forms. And even *such* a book would tend to be too much of a survey.[46]

This, surely, is the counsel of despair.

Despite Robbins Landon's rather dire pronouncement, there have in fact been at least two writers in the last 30 years who have done an excellent job of putting the Classical period in perspective. Both have also commented, in detail and with deep firsthand understanding, on C. P. E. Bach, his music, and his relation to his century.

The first of these writers is Charles Rosen, who was known first as a brilliant concert pianist but has now also earned a high place among music historians. The two books of Rosen's that are relevant here are *The Classical Style: Haydn, Mozart, Beethoven* (1971) and *Sonata Forms* (1980).[47] Both books clearly show the influence of Tovey, and in fact the latter one owes him its title. When asked to write an article for the 11th edition of the *Encyclopaedia Britannica* on sonata form, Tovey protested that the title must be "Sonata Forms" if the article were to be historically accurate. When asked to contribute a similar entry to the 1980 *New Grove*, Rosen made the same stipulation but was turned down: hence the book.

While Rosen, in *The Classical Style,* by no means singles out Bach as Haydn's main forerunner, he makes him a more important influence than Tovey did. In Bach's keyboard works "all kinds of 'sonata' patterns exist, with and without complete development sections, with partial and complete recapitulations, etc." (p. 32). But for Rosen Bach is primarily the composer of music that is "violent, expressive, brilliant, continuously surprising, and often incoherent" (p. 44). Of our troublesome third quarter of the 18th century, Rosen writes: "It is the lack of any integrated style . . . between 1755 and 1775 that makes it tempting to call this period 'mannerist'" (p. 47). As examples he cites "The neo-classicism of Gluck, with its wilful refusal of so much traditional technique, the arbitrarily impassioned modulations and the syncopated rhythms of Carl Philipp Emanuel Bach, the violence of many of the Haydn symphonies of the 1760s" (p. 47).

The difference between Bach and Haydn is that in Bach's music the extreme mannerisms "exist in and for themselves, with little relation to any conception of the whole work" (p. 48), while for Haydn the "violence" and general rhythmic disorganization of the early symphonies soon disappear: "C. P. E. Bach's horizon is wider harmonically, but his practice is incoherent: he is more interested in local effects—he delights in harmonic shock, as did Haydn; but Haydn knew how to weld his effects together, and his most disparate harmonies are not only reconciled but even explained by what follows as well as implied by what precedes" (p. 79). In "the synthesis that Haydn gradually developed, in the late 1760s and the early 70s, out of dramatic irregularity and large-scale symmetry," even his "most dramatic effects were essential to the form—that is, justified the form and were justified (prepared and resolved) by it" (p. 112).

Sonata Forms is a shorter but more technically detailed book. Rosen's account of Bach and his relation to the development of sonata form is very similar to that given in *The Classical Style,* but his emphasis is a little more on Bach's positive contributions, a little less on his eccentricity and his concentration on effects of the moment without regard to form and continuity. There is thus less talk of violence and incoherence than in the earlier book: "Haydn was the first composer to relate the dissonances in the opening thematic material coherently to the large structure; Philipp Emanuel Bach, from whom he learned so much, was even more sensitive to the expressive properties of dissonance, but less consistent in his structural use of it" (p. 232). Rosen also seems to be arguing against Tovey's contention that Bach "never shows an inkling of the special idea of 'development' in sonata form":

> . . . the themes of C. P. E. Bach are capable of transformation, of "development," and remain sufficiently memorable for their identity to be clear through the transformations. Both the strikingly individual motif and development by transformation and fragmentation exist in Baroque style, but it was C. P. E. Bach above all who made them available for sonata style and showed how they could be used in the creation of forms.

[Pp. 137-138]

The other writer is Giorgio Pestelli, whose book *L'età di Mozart e di Beethoven* was published in Italy in 1979, and appeared in English translation, as *The Age of Mozart and Beethoven*,[48] in 1984. Pestelli has an interesting interpretation of the Riemann-Adler controversy: "This controversy, which, since it caused a considerable amount of music to be unearthed and studied, was very useful, was nevertheless based on a misunderstanding, the belated consequence of the romantic conception of the genius who would spontaneously invent for himself the forms that he needed" (p. 17). Actually, of course, "the growing evidence uncovered in recent decades has shown that sonata form grew up simultaneously in all the nerve-centres of a Europe united in taste and cultural exchanges as at few other times in its history" (p. 18).

Pestelli sees C.P.E. Bach as less important in the development of sonata form and the Classical style than does Rosen:

> In spite of the discussions about form that have suggested it, Emanuel did not have a vocation for and possibly not even a deep interest in formal structure, or at least in sonata form; the forms that suited him most were the fantasia and the rondo, with its cyclical structure. Perception of the complete arch of sonata form was, for him, secondary to the possibilities offered in the way of independent details and meaningful interjections.
>
> [P. 24]

Indeed, Pestelli, like Parry, seems more interested in Bach's ties to the musical past than in his influence on music's future. He finds that Bach's symphonic output "was remarkable for its quantity, instrumental richness and fully discursive style, but it had something backward and old-fashioned, especially on account of the themes he used, which were in his father's mould and in the style of Corelli and Vivaldi, going back to the 'intricate' flights of fancy of the baroque concerto" (p. 37). For Pestelli, the two most important forerunners of the modern symphony are Sammartini and Stamitz—though he also cites Adler's Viennese and a number of Parisian composers. Finally, Pestelli is at one with Rosen (and opposed to Tovey) in seeing Gluck's work in opera as, at most, very tenuously connected to the growth of sonata form. "Sonata form was foreign to Gluck," he writes: "In Gluck's music, with its basic impermeability to sonata form, the orchestra's expressive function, cut off from the principles of harmonic operation that motivate its progress on the symphonic level, acquired total and absolute prominence" (p. 76).

As the memory of the 18th-century German lied faded from historians' minds, and they became preoccupied with the problems raised by the autonomous instrumental music born during the Classical era, C.P.E. Bach, as we have seen, found his historical place as the crucial link in the developmental chain leading to the instrumental works of Haydn, Mozart, and Beethoven. Though the simplemindedness of this judgment was revealed as more of the music of the 18th century became available and historians became more sophisticated in their views and methods, C.P.E. Bach has remained, right down through the excellent books of Rosen and Pestelli, an instrumental composer as far as the great majority of music historians have been concerned. Earlier we traced Bach's sinking reputation as a composer of songs, from just before his death to almost 1900. Let us now conclude by seeing what happened to that reputation in the 20th century, as he began to lose his position as Haydn's main forerunner in the development of sonata form.

III

Shortly after 1900 two works appeared that helped to reawaken interest in Bach's songs. The first of these was Max Friedlaender's massive compendium, *Das deutsche Lied im 18. Jahrhundert*, which was published in 1902.[49] Friedlaender (1852–1934) was not only a musicologist but also a professional singer and a friend of Brahms. Most of his professional life was devoted to collecting, publishing, and commenting upon songs. *Das deutsche Lied im 18. Jahrhundert* was the first attempt at a systematic, year-by-year catalogue, with critical commentary, of all the song collections published in Germany during the 18th century. In the second section of the first of his two volumes, Friedlaender also reprinted many of the songs discussed. His second volume was devoted to the poets involved. Friedlaender had a great liking for C. P. E. Bach's music, and in his introduction he made clear, for the first time since Bitter's book more than 30 years earlier, just how important a figure Bach had been in the development of the 18th-century lied.

Of three early songs that Bach contributed to J. F. Gräfe's four-volume *Sammlung verschiedener und auserlesener Oden* (1737–1743), Friedlaender writes: "Among the five composers in Gräfe's collection who are of interest, Philipp Emanuel Bach, despite the small number of his contributions, stands out because of his more profound melodic progressions [*Züge*], superior sense of form, and richer harmonies" (I/i, 91). When he comes to the first collection that bore Bach's name on its title page, the 1758 settings of Christian Fürchtegott Gellert's *Geistliche Oden und Lieder,* Friedlaender goes on to discuss ten of Bach's other collections, right up through the posthumous *Neue Lieder-Melodien* of 1789. Of the Gellert songs, the ones in which Bach really found his voice as a song composer, Friedlaender notes:

> In some of these compositions Bach offers distinguished works of art that are of great interest as regards their use of counterpoint. That the technical work is masterly does not need saying when one is dealing with a composer of Bach's standing.
>
> [I/i, 138]

The other of the two important turn-of-the-century works I mentioned earlier is *Thematisches Verzeichnis der Werke Carl Philipp Emanuel Bach,* compiled by the Belgian bibliographer and librarian Alfred Wotquenne (1867–1939) and published in 1905. This at last gave a reasonably complete and coherent picture of Bach's compositional output and made it possible to regard his work as all of a piece.

We can see the influence of both Friedlaender and Wotquenne in the brief yet respectful treatment accorded Bach in W. K. von Jolizza's 1910 *Das Lied und seine Geschichte*:[50] of Friedlaender in the fact that Jolizza selects as musical examples two of the songs reprinted by Friedlaender; of Wotquenne in the detailed statistical account of Bach's *oeuvre* with which Jolizza prefaces his discussion of the songs. His final judgment of Bach as a song composer, which we may contrast sharply with that of Lindner some 40 years earlier, runs thus:

> Philipp Emanuel Bach's songs certainly do not attain the high level of his keyboard pieces, yet we owe to his cultivated sensitivity to the concurrence [*Übereinstimmung*] of poetry and melody the first attempts to make of the strophic song one that is through-composed—that is, to give each strophe of the song a melody that corresponds to the content of the text. His songs are technically accomplished and well formed throughout yet not vocally conceived; rich in syncopation and ornamentation, they betray at every turn the keyboard virtuoso of his time.
>
> [Pp. 263–264]

Still more enthusiastic was the verdict of Hermann Kretzschmar, in his 1911 *Geschichte des neuen deutschen Liedes.*[51] Unlike earlier writers, Kretzschmar not only pays lip service to Bach's well-known "originality"; he also makes a concerted effort to show how Bach's 1758 settings of Gellert's *Geistliche Oden und Lieder* are different from those by his north German contemporaries:

Without precedent in the history of the religious song, Bach's Gellert songs are alien to the songs of the Berlin school, both in their technical range and in their spirit. They are similar to the Berlin songs only in their compactness of form. One seldom encounters, among the Berliners, Bach's art of establishing the mood in the first bar in a way that gives to the rest of the song, despite a sparkling variety of ideas, a sense of concentration and unity. One never encounters the distinctly musical organic development [*Zug*] found in his songs, their richness and freedom of modulation, their virtuosity of contrast and detail.

[P. 241]

Fond of far-flung comparisons, Kretzschmar writes of these same Gellert songs: "As in his instrumental works, so also in these songs is Philipp Emanuel Bach the inspired, resourceful improvisor. They are the unmediated effusions of lofty hours, and are thus stylistically related to the monologues and recitative scenas of Monteverdi and his school, as also to the last quartets of Beethoven" (p. 240). In the keyboard accompaniments to Bach's 1774 settings of Johann Andreas Cramer's poetic versions of the Psalms, Kretzschmar even hears foreshadowings of Liszt (p. 241).

This sort of enthusiasm was to reach still greater heights a decade later in the still more highly colored prose of Otto Vrieslander, in the chapter devoted to the songs in his book *Carl Philipp Emanuel Bach*.[52] Vrieslander is at one with Kretzschmar (and at odds with most earlier writers) in seeing a continuity (rather than an opposition) between Bach's instrumental works and his songs. In fact he takes earlier historians to task for praising the instrumental works yet being unable to see the value of the songs: "It is not a little surprising that history, which unconditionally bestows upon him the honor of having been a pioneer in the realm of keyboard compositions, does not acknowledge the same honor in his songs" (pp. 103-104). To Vrieslander, the Bach of the Gellert songs is Schubert's "acknowledged forerunner in the area of psychological detail," a composer who "successfully endeavors to extend, elevate, and enrich the song as an artform" (p. 116). One particular Gellert song, "Wider den Übermut," Vrieslander finds to be "already thoroughly in the spirit of Schubert" (p. 116).

In 1928, five years after Vrieslander's book, came what apparently was the first German doctoral dissertation on Bach's songs, Hertha Wien-Claudi's *Zum Liedschaffen Carl Philipp Emanuel Bachs*.[53] For a German dissertation, it is almost scandalously short: a mere 84 pages! Though written in a lively and entertaining style, Wien-Claudi's little book is an almost total disappointment. The first third rehearses the familiar facts of Bach's life and career; the remainder is an arbitrary, off-the-cuff collection of remarks about songs that happened to appeal to Wien-Claudi.

There seems not to have been another German dissertation on Bach's songs for almost 30 years. Gudrun Busch's *C. Ph. E. Bach und seine Lieder*[54] is the standard work on the subject, and is, indeed, indispensable to anyone doing work on Bach's songs. It is divided into two parts. The first, and more important, of these is a detailed description of the various collections and periodicals in which Bach's songs were published, generously larded with quotations from the letters that passed between him and the many composers, poets, editors, and critics whom he knew in Berlin and Hamburg, and with whom he collaborated. It was Busch who first painstakingly established a reliable chronology for Bach's songs—a chronology, I might add, that was adopted almost wholesale by E. Eugene Helm in his 1989 *Thematic Catalogue of the Works of Carl Philipp Emanuel Bach*.

The second part of Busch's dissertation is of somewhat less interest. It consists of a tightly compartmentalized analysis of the "Einzelelemente" that make up Bach's songs: "Die Melodie," "Der Satz," "Die Form," "Der Ausdruck"—each of which is in turn broken down into subcategories. There are many valuable insights along the way, but the mode of analysis is too atomistic, too rigidly taxonomic, to demonstrate the actual feel or construction of any whole song or to give much sense of how Bach's style as a composer of songs might have changed over the years. Also, Busch tends to view the songs in isolation from the poems that they set. Though she may fairly be said to have settled for good virtually all questions of chronology and provenance, there is thus a good deal of analytical work left to be done on Bach's songs.

Since Busch's dissertation, there has been no substantial work devoted to Bach's songs. As we have seen, the publication of Friedlaender's compendium and Wotquenne's catalogue helped to bring about a slight reawakening of interest in Bach as a song composer. Yet aside from those writers who sought to compensate for earlier neglect by praising Bach's songs excessively and absurdly overestimating their historical importance, most of the praise given to them, and in fact to the German 18th-century lied as a genre, has been accompanied by an assurance that the only real reason for studying the 18th-century lied is to see how it led to Schubert, and also often by an expression of regret that Bach and his contemporaries did not have the wit to write through-composed songs instead of strophic ones. Many of Schubert's, and even of Brahms's, finest songs are strophic; yet the assumption among music historians, at least since the mid-19th century, has been that through-composed songs are more "advanced," more sophisticated formally, and therefore necessarily more effective, than strophic songs.

In his 1965 *Music in the Classic Period*,[55] Reinhard G. Pauly notes that north German song composers of the 18th century "favored simple, light songs" (p. 28), and cites as an example an extremely simple (and wholly uncharacteristic) folksong-like effort by Bach (p. 30). Later Pauly writes: "while the Lied was not central to the work of Classic-period composers," study of their songs will nonetheless "show that Schubert's Lieder have ties to the past and to the work of composers around him" (p. 178).

Rosemary Hughes, in the 1973 *Age of Enlightenment* volume of the *New Oxford History of Music*, does somewhat better by Bach, citing a powerful setting of one of Christoph Christian Sturm's poems and rightly pointing out that Bach's contemporary fame as a song composer "rested on his settings of Gellert's religious poetry" (pp. 347–348). Yet even for Hughes the main advantage to be gained from a study of the 18th-century song is a sense of the "gathering movement away from Italianate operatic elaboration toward unstudied simplicity," and of various other features of "the incipient Romantic movement" (p. 349).

Still more to the point, Philip Radcliffe, writing in the 1960 collection *A History of Song*,[56] pronounces Bach "by far the most interesting and individual" (p. 232) of the German songwriters of his period, but generalizes thus about his songs: "One or two, such as *Selma* or *Doris,* are on a large scale, with contrasted sections, but for the most part they are highly compressed" (p. 231). Bach composed two settings of Albrecht von Haller's poem "Doris," one strophic and one through-composed; and he wrote two vocal pieces called "Selma" to two different poems of that title by J. H. Voss, one of which was a through-composed cantata and the other a simple strophic song. Radcliffe's phrase "with contrasted sections" makes clear that it is the through-composed works he is singling out for praise; "on a large scale" means through-composed while "highly compressed" means strophic.

From these two implicit equations we can see that Radcliffe was thinking not of songs as they are experienced in performance, but rather of songs as they appear on the page. A through-composed song looks more large-scale on the page because it takes up more space than a strophic song; a strophic song looks highly compressed because it takes up less. But a strophic song is not just the one bit of music that appears on the page: it is that music repeated, with suitably varied expression, for all the stanzas of the poem that it sets. The composer of a strophic song must compose a brief piece of music that will, somehow, be malleable enough to suit all the different stanzas of the poem. The strophic song is thus not necessarily a compromise form, a necessary second-best to the through-composed song that musically follows every twist and turn of the poetic content. If managed properly, the strophic song is, rather, a synthesis of change and stability, the dramatic change that takes place over the course of a lyric poem and the unity of feeling or imaginative color that makes the poem (and the song) a cohesive work of art.

It will be one of the main contentions of this book that the strophic song is a very special sort of work of art that has distinct advantages of its own. The strophic song is of course a far older form than the through-composed song, with its roots deep in those primitive cultures that so fascinated Herder and men of his generation. But this does not mean that all strophic songs are necessarily primitive, or less "advanced" artistically than through-composed songs. During the years of what is known as the first Berlin song school, from about 1740 to 1770, the composers of north and central Germany, with Bach leading the way, brought to the strophic song all the musical sophistication they had gathered from their work in other genres. The result was the immense body of work that constitutes the unjustly neglected genre of this chapter's title.

As for the forgotten master, it is hard to think of a worthy composer who has been so often misrepresented in so many different ways as has C.P.E. Bach. As we have amply seen, he has been pegged as Haydn's forerunner, as the composer of feeble and unattractive vocal works, and as the father of the through-composed song—none of which reputations suits him in the least. Moreover, some of the same qualities in his instrumental music that led to his being singled out as the herald of the Classical style—his complete harmonic mastery, his fondness for contrast and surprise—were also responsible for his vocal music's being pronounced dry and unattractive by some historians, innovative and forward-thinking by others.

What was he then, really? A unique, *sui generis* master of almost (yet not quite) the first order who had no real followers and founded no school or movement. At some point in the not-too-distant future, we shall at last be able to develop an accurate and comprehensive view of this fascinating artist. When we do, it will be importantly shaped by the nature and range of his career as a composer of songs.

Chapter Two

The Songless Time

One of the most interesting facts about C. P. E. Bach's career as a composer of songs is how late it began. We think of the solo song as a genre to which composers usually (and quite naturally) turn early: the forms are short, and therefore no great developmental or transformational skills are required; the perennial popularity of keyboard accompaniments makes experience with orchestration unnecessary; the chosen verbal text is there as inspiration and continuing guide to composition. Yet aside from three arias (Wq. 211; H. 669), which exist only in manuscript and of whose composition we know only that they were "written in his early years,"[1] Bach's first song was composed in 1741, by which time he had reached the great age of 27.

By 1741 Bach had already served three years as harpsichordist at the Prussian court. By the end of that year he had composed 27 keyboard sonatas (including all but one of the so-called "Prussian Sonatas"); nine keyboard concertos; two sonatas for violin, nine for flute, and one each for oboe and cello; six trio sonatas; his first symphony; and five lost cantatas—but only the one song: his next one would not come until two years later. Moreover, while he wrote only nine songs during the years 1741-1755, he added to his *oeuvre* 75 more sonatas and other major keyboard pieces, 25 more keyboard concertos, and many other chamber works in all categories. It was only in the late 1750s, when he was in his forties, that he began to compose songs with regularity and in volume.

No doubt this curious disproportion was due partly to the requirements of Bach's position as court harpsichordist and composer for various chamber combinations. But it was also due to the fact that his early adulthood overlapped with the later years of what German music historians call "die liederlose Zeit," the songless time.[2] Throughout most of the 17th century, song collections were published in Germany in great profusion. But in the 1680s. publication quite suddenly shrank to almost nothing. The exhaustive bibliography in Max Friedlaender's *Das deutsche Lied im 18. Jahrhundert* has only nine entries for the years 1689-1734. It was only in 1733 and 1737, with the appearance of the first two volumes of Johann Valentin Rathgeber's *Ohren-vergnügendes und Gemüth-ergötzendes Tafel-Confect,* and in 1736, with the appearance of the first volume of *Sperontes Singende Muse an der Pleisse,* that publication of song collections began in earnest once again. By the late 1750s, Friedlaender's bibliography has eight or nine entries for each year! The first important collections to mark this renewal (or "Aufschwung," as the German writers often call it) were the four entitled *Sammlung verschiedener und auserlesener Oden* that J. F. Gräfe brought out in 1737, 1739, 1741, and 1743, and the two volumes of *Oden mit Melodien* edited by C. W. Ramler and C. G. Krause, published in 1753 and 1755. Bach contributed songs to Gräfe's third and fourth collections and to both Ramler-Krause volumes. So he was, as it were, present at the creation of the 18th-century German lied. If we are to understand the particular problems that confronted him and his songwriting contemporaries, we must understand what caused the *liederlose Zeit* and what finally brought it to an end, once again making the strophic song the viable art form that it had long been in Germany.

I

From the beginning, historians of the lied had a hard time dealing with the *liederlose Zeit*. Indeed, most of what they wrote about it tells us less about it than about them, and about their assumptions, conscious and unconscious, as to how history should be written.

The first serious history of the German lied was August Reissmann's *Das deutsche Lied in seiner historischen Entwicklung*, which appeared in 1861. Though it is a slim volume, it traces the development of the lied from the Minnesingers right up to the mid-19th century. Reissmann seems scarcely to recognize the existence of a *liederlose Zeit*. Like many historians after him, he cites a passage from Reinhard Keiser's preface to his 1698 cantata *Gemüths-Ergötzung*, in which Keiser declares that cantatas "have . . . in Germany been granted freedom of the city, and the old citizens, that is the German songs of yesterday, have been completely driven out."[3] But Reissmann's emphasis is far more upbeat than this quotation would suggest. The growing popularity of opera, oratorio, and cantata, far from having driven the lied out of circulation, in fact fulfilled the conditions necessary for the lied's further development: "Through their influence the still unwieldy techniques of vocal music became more pliant, more supple, and thereby more capable of aiding subjective expression. Thus when the lyric poem began once again to be cultivated, German composers returned to it with enthusiasm, though of course gradually at first" (p. 78). These new genres also spawned a whole mass of new forms for the lied—all of which, however (Reissmann is careful to add), "go back to that simple, basic strophic form based on the tonic and dominant" (p. 77).

The next history of the lied, E. K. Schneider's three-volume *Das Musikalische Lied in geschichtlicher Entwickelung*, is very different from Reissmann's although it appeared very soon after it, in 1863-1865. In his preface, Schneider, after noting the newness of the field he has chosen, takes to task Reissmann and another writer who had ventured into the history of the lied for lacking "systematic mastery and organization of the source material."[4] These assets, and others, Schneider then promises to provide. As we move from Reissmann's vaguely optimistic account of the lied and its history to Schneider's highly detailed, painstakingly laid-out story of its step-by-step development, we enter the age of explicitly progressivist music history.

Schneider's view of the history of the lied is in fact progressivist to a degree that almost shocks a modern reader. Like some of the progressivist historians we examined in the preceding chapter, he divides his field of inquiry into three periods: the ages of the chanted song, the contrapuntal or polyphonic song, and the strophic song. At the beginning of his third volume, which covers his third period, the 17th and 18th centuries, he breathes a sigh of relief at having finally arrived at real music: "The two earlier periods fell in the dark ages; their history is an unknown land, even to friends of music: even our lieder-singers have either seldom or never heard of the old composers" (p. iii). Of his second (or polyphonic) period he tells us: "Music, which during this centuries' long period was occupied with forming itself, was not yet able to express any content, whether of religious or poetic texts" (p. 1). His view of his first period is still more dire: "In general the musical passages of this first stage are without relation to the text, and therefore lack both content and character" (p. 1). What then is the difference between the two periods? "The chanted song was sung out of naive instinct, without either intention or art," whereas "The second, contrapuntal period took the naive, monophonic song to the School of Artistic Treatment" (p. 1). In other words, there is no expression, no inner relation between music and text in either period, and the polyphonic period is distinguished from its predecessor only by its cultivation of abstract harmonic and contrapuntal form, mere technical manipulation without human significance.

Of his third period, by contrast, Schneider writes: "The 17th-century song, having rediscovered homophony and persisting in its practice," saw its task as "to reproduce the text with both metrical and psychological fidelity" (p. 157). But this praiseworthy search for greater expressivity led the melody to become "something merely rational, mechanically soulless" (p. 157). A terrible dilemma thus confronted not only composers of lieder but the lied itself, which Schneider personifies as "das kleine Lied" (the little song): "it possessed no power to battle against stagnation; in the confining strophic form there was no spark of life, no means of either enlarging or raising itself; on the contrary, this little form would actually cease to exist as soon as it was enlarged: enlargement would mean the dissolution, the annihilation of the lied" (p. 157). What is to be done? How is the lied to be saved? Faced by the stark alternatives of death by stagnation and death by annihilation, the sympathetic reader feels rather like the viewer of a 19th-century melodrama. Indeed, one great advantage of the air of "science" that the adoption of evolutionary modes of explanation bestowed upon 19th-century historians was that it allowed them to feel free to indulge in this sort of melodramatic writing.

Fortunately, however, the solution to the lied's dilemma is close at hand. "The enlargement of the form," it now turns out, "was from the beginning inseparable from the concept of development"—with, however, a qualification that reminds us of Reissmann: "But this enlargement may only extend to the point where the original strophic scheme is essentially preserved and is still recognizable in the enlarged dimensions" (p. 158). In spite of Schneider's earlier assertion that "enlargement would mean the dissolution, the annihilation of the lied," this condition of expanding the lied's form while still (somehow) remaining true to its original strophic form can, after all, be met. How? Through the influence of the operatic aria!

Of course this happy result could not be achieved all at once: hence the *liederlose Zeit*. And once again melodrama steps in to fill up the void left by an absence of thought: "We stand here before a barren plain, before a desolate, sterile prospect without any songs or song composers or song collections" (p. 159)—and much more of the same. What made the operatic aria so helpful to the lied's further development was of course the former's dramatic intensity. Though this dramatic intensity is indeed foreign to the lied's lyrical essence, it is for that very reason necessary to the lied's full self-realization: "For the lied required this powerful musical expression since it is an essentially lyrical form, an outpouring of feeling; but feeling, if it is to express itself, requires at least that it unite itself with verbal [*sprechendem*] expression" (p. 161). This paradox is extended a few pages later when Schneider, after enumerating the "ornaments such as trills, mordents, turns, etc.," that the previously chaste and simple German lied has picked up from the Italian aria, tells us: "All these characteristics of southern melody now pass over into the German lied and—though not without some contradiction of its original simplicity—help it attain a more active, more pleasing expressiveness" (p. 167). A few pages later, even that apparently insignificant "contradiction" has vanished.

As if all this were not enough, Schneider also wants to insist that the lied's imitation of the aria "led to the desired goal, namely that the rejuvenated art song regained that unity of text and music, of poetic feeling and effective presentation in song, that its character demands" (p. 164). "*Regained*"? Yes, because (surprisingly enough) it turns out that the lied had the desired "unity" once before: "In the folksong alone, and then only in a naive state, did song still possess this close connection between text and melody, the characteristic trait of simple, genuine song" (pp. 163–164). This remark is easy to miss in the thick fog of Schneider's exposition, but it is most important. For later Schneider makes it abundantly clear that what supplanted the "arid wasteland" of the *liederlose Zeit* was "a thickly leaved garden of lieder-flowers, nourished by the mild sun of the southern song, the aria. Under its influence the German lied, in the hands of gifted musicians, was able to release itself from rigidity into freedom and beauty once more, and at last to become, once again, purely German, simple, and of the people" (pp. 173–174). That earlier remark about the "Volkslied" was thus preparing us for the astonishing (and strained) assertion that all those Italian "ornaments" borrowed from the operatic aria have not only enabled the lied to attain the dramatic expressiveness that was, all along, its destined goal, but have also brought the lied back home to the *echt deutsch* simplicity that was its true starting point and remains its essence. All seeming contradictions are reconciled among the stars, end and beginning meet in a paradoxical synthesis, and we sense the influence not only of Darwin but of Hegel as well.

The next history of German song was the first one ever to deal just with the 18th century, Ernst Otto Lindner's *Geschichte des deutschen Liedes im XVIII. Jahrhundert*, posthumously published in 1871. (Lindner had died in 1867.) Because of the restricted scope of his book, Lindner naturally does not go into the 17th-century background of the *liederlose Zeit* as Schneider had done. But Lindner's book marks an important advance over those of his predecessors because he is the first historian of the lied to look closely at any of the criticism that was being written during the years just before the *Aufschwung*, roughly 1720-1740. In fact the point of his very first paragraph is to establish a linkage or interplay between song composition and criticism in the early 18th century.

"At the end of the 17th century," Lindner tells us at the outset, "the secular German art song had found a champion in Reinhard Keiser."[5] Until his death in 1739 Keiser reigned as the arbiter of musical taste in Hamburg, the success of his operas complemented by the fact that "Johann Mattheson simultaneously published his first influential musical writings, the views of which were essentially based on Keiser's musical practice" (p. 1). While Keiser "brought the combination of lyricism and drama to fruition" in the areas of opera, cantata, and oratorio, "Mattheson provided the theory"—specifically, "a theory of the aria, which everywhere was pushing the lied to one side" (p. 1). As illustrations of this theory, Lindner then cites a number of passages from Mattheson's critical works.

The most interesting of these passages are two from *Critica musica*, the first German musical periodical, which appeared between 1722 and 1725. The first is taken from the journal's fourth number, published in August 1722. In the preface to the first of three sections of the Abbé François Raguenet's *Paralèle des italiens et des françois, en ce qui regarde la musique et les opéra* (1702), which Mattheson printed in parallel columns of French original and German translation, he writes:

> Many wish to maintain that songs [*Oden*] are musical; but they should know that in all of music nothing can be more despicable, more tasteless, than to hear the same melody, often repeated over and over, to different words, which also occasionally contain quite contrary *incisiones*.[6]

Strong words indeed! Yet Mattheson is at least refreshingly concrete and particular—especially after Schneider's elaborate dialectical posturing. What Mattheson seems to be saying is that the strophic lied, by its very nature, is incapable of affording that subjective expression, that perfect inner correspondence of *Ton* and *Wort*, of which Reissmann and Schneider spoke at such length. For while the material dealt with in the poetic text, and hence the emotional affect appropriate to it, will usually change from stanza to stanza, the music, repeated stanza after stanza, will necessarily remain the same. While the melody remains "the same," the words will be "different" from stanza to stanza of the poem, sometimes even containing "quite contrary *incisiones*"—clauses or sentences that are mutually contradictory.

This very interesting line of thought is taken up again, but is not elaborated or clarified, in the second passage cited by Lindner from *Critica musica*. This one is taken from the journal's twenty-first number, presumably published in 1725, and comes in the midst of a discussion of the melodic theories of Heinrich Bokemeyer, cantor to the ducal court of Wolfenbüttel:

> To me, songs [*Oden*] are not at all musical. . . . My reasons are that those poems [*Oden*] that one wants to turn into songs will never match well with the music and a good melody because of the different stanzas, except in the melismatic style, since all will be shorn with the same comb.
>
> [*Critica musica*, II, 309; cited Lindner, p. 2]

As before, I give the passage in its entirety, as cited by Lindner: the ellipsis is his. *Oden*, like *Lieder*, was widely used at this time to mean both songs and the sort of poems that were written to be set to music or at least lent themselves to being set to music. The word probably has both meanings here. Once again the problem with *Oden* seems to occur because of the variety of the poetic stanzas that must all be set to just one melody. The resulting music will always be unsatisfactory: "all shorn with the same comb" in Mattheson's homely metaphor or, as we should perhaps say, all of its parts stamped out by the same dye or cookie-cutter. In the chapters that follow, I shall often refer to this particular difficulty with strophic songs as "the strophic problem."

But why does Mattheson add the words "except in the melismatic style"? And what, exactly, does he mean by the melismatic style? Ordinarily, the word *melismatic* is used in connection with chant and early polyphonic music: pieces in syllabic style have one note for each syllable of text whereas ones in melismatic style include melismas or large groups of notes sung to the same sustained syllable of text. But that meaning obviously has no relevance here. For its quite different meaning in the 17th and 18th centuries, we must consult Johann Gottfried Walther's 1732 *Musikalisches Lexicon,* in which we find *Stilo Melismatico* defined as "a natural style in which all the world can sing, almost without art. It is suitable for ariettas, street songs, etc."[7] What Mattheson probably means is that in such a simple style—homophonic, with short and balanced phrases—the relation of music to text is not important or complex enough for the disadvantages of the strophic song to make much difference.

Finally Lindner moves on to discuss some of the song collections that appeared just around the end of the *liederlose Zeit*: the *Sperontes* and *Tafel-Confect* volumes, and the first two of Gräfe's four collections. His stress, which follows directly from his perusal of Mattheson, is on the generally low quality of the songs, the "tastelessness" of it all. But Lindner insists that Gräfe's third (1741) collection, the one that contained Bach's first published song, is quite different from its two predecessors. These differences are due to the influence of the theoretical writing about song composition published in the years intervening between the second and third Gräfe volumes, and since this writing "is directly dependent upon Gottsched's '*kritische Dichtkunst*'" (p. 25), Lindner chooses at this point to discuss Johann Christoph Gottsched (1700-1766) and his followers.

Gottsched's *Versuch einer critischen Dichtkunst vor die Deutschen* was first published in 1730, with revised (and enlarged) editions following in 1737, 1742, and 1751. Appointed lecturer at Leipzig University in 1725, Gottsched rose rapidly to the positions of Professor of Poetry and Professor of Logic and Metaphysics. He had set as his goal the reform (and modernization) of the German language, literature, and theater, and by the late 1730s his impressive series of books had made him the arbiter of German taste in these and other areas. In October 1738 Lorenz Mizler, who had been a student of Gottsched's at Leipzig, devoted part of an issue of his *Neu eröffnete musikalische Bibliothek* to reprinting, with commentary, some of the observations Gottsched had made concerning songs in *Versuch einer critischen Dichtkunst*. Lindner, in turn, comments on what both Gottsched and Mizler had to say.

What apparently interests Lindner is that Gottsched and Mizler seem, to some degree at least, to share a concern similar to Mattheson's: how can a strophic song achieve expressive unity of text and music when one melody must fit all the stanzas of the given poem? Lindner's failure to distinguish between what Gottsched is saying and what Mizler is saying, between what either of them is saying and what Mattheson was saying, and between what any or all of them are saying and what he himself is saying makes it impossible to be quite clear about this, however.

The other contemporary critic cited by Lindner is Johann Adolphe Scheibe, who had also been Gottsched's student at Leipzig and who titled his periodical *Der critische Musikus* in express homage to his master's *Versuch einer critischen Dichtkunst*. Indeed, even before the publication of Gottsched's influential book, the adjective or its cognate noun, in both German and Latin, had become a kind of buzzword to set the reader on notice that he was about to encounter a product of the *Aufklärung*, a contribution to the effort to rethink and reform German letters in order to bring Germany into the 18th century as already defined by writers in France and England. The word, as used in titles, seems to have functioned in somewhat the way that words such as "radical" and "alternative" do in our own time, as a signal that a tough-minded cultural revaluation (or even revolution) is in progress. We can see this from the titles of Mattheson's periodical and Friedrich Wilhelm Marpurg's *Der critische Musikus an der Spree*, *Historisch-Kritische Beyträge*, and *Kritische Briefe über die Tonkunst*, as well as in those of Gottsched's book and Scheibe's periodical; and of course we can also see it in the titles of Kant's three great works.

Scheibe devoted No. 64 of *Der critische Musikus*, dated November 17, 1739, to the problem of the lied. He immediately reveals a far more positive attitude than that of Mattheson, by attacking "certain great and sublime composers, . . . great souls who find even the word *Lied* insulting."[8] Since Scheibe goes on to use the two words *schwülstig* and *verworren* ("bombastic" and "confused"), which he had also used in his famous attack on J. S. Bach two years earlier, to characterize the sort of art preferred by these composers, Lindner's comment that these remarks are "perhaps written not without a glance at J. S. Bach" (p. 29n.) seems overcautious. At any rate, Scheibe plainly believes that the lied is a genre governed by rules that critics may state and composers must heed.

After giving the usual warnings that the composer must match his style to that of the poem and must take careful account of its content and verse form, Scheibe writes: "There are even some [songs][9] that almost throughout require special melodies" (*Critischer Musikus*, p. 587; Lindner, p. 29). Though it is perhaps not quite clear, Scheibe seems here to be recommending *Durchkomponierung*, melodic writing specially contrived to suit the ever-changing content of the poem. This will of course be the exception rather than the rule, but it is nonetheless significant that Scheibe raises the possibility of through-composed songs for it shows that despite his greater respect for the strophic song, he is nonetheless bothered by some of the same worries that bothered Mattheson and Mizler. But because it is the exception, Scheibe continues: since "[almost][10] all song melodies are very short, one must therefore consider well which emotion or feeling most prevails in the whole poem, and which poetic style the poet has really adopted" (*Critischer Musikus*, p. 587; partially cited, Lindner, p. 29). It is by discerning, and musically rendering, this general, overarching *Affect* that the composer will best be able to suit his one, repeated melody to the various stanzas of the poem he is setting, and thus to solve the strophic problem.

Having dealt with the two extreme cases, the quite rare through-composed song and the ubiquitous simple strophic song, Scheibe takes up the intermediate case of what Gottsched called *Wechseloden*, songs in which two different melodies set alternate stanzas of a poem. These Scheibe finds to be "far more welcome to the audience than those songs usually encountered, in which one repeats the melody of the first stanza for all the other stanzas" (*Critischer Musikus*, p. 593; partially cited, Lindner, p. 29). To the description of the *Wechselode* offered by Gottsched, Scheibe adds the stipulation that the melody that goes with the second stanza of the poem (and also with its fourth, sixth, and other even-numbered stanzas) should be composed, if the content of the poem permits it, "as an antithesis to the melody of the first stanza" (*Critischer Musikus*, p. 593; Lindner, p. 29). Lindner comments: "To be sure, this song form goes far beyond the *Wechseloden* recommended by Gottsched and Mizler; but it is essentially just a theoretical chimera since the basic condition of song form, unity of mood, could then be met very seldom and only with difficulty" (p. 29). Still, Lindner generally approves of *Wechseloden*.

At this point Lindner returns from his long digression to consider Gräfe's third (1741) collection—though he never makes clear what it was that the collection owed to the body of critical ideas he has spent so much time belaboring! Yet despite all its confusions, Lindner's treatment of the *liederlose Zeit* is very valuable. For it brings to the fore the questions that contemporary critics—virtually all of whom were, of course, also composers—were asking about songs. Their concern with how traditional strophic form could provide both the unity of mood required of the lied and enough variety to keep a song interesting and appealing was, as we shall see, the central cause of the *liederlose Zeit*; correspondingly, it was finding a solution to the problems raised by that concern that made possible (or at least encouraged) the *Aufschwung*.

Amusingly, Reissmann promptly showed his recognition of the value of Lindner's approach. After *Das deutsche Lied in seiner historischen Entwicklung*, Reissmann published not only *Allgemeine Geschichte der Musik* (1863-1864) but also *Allgemeine Musiklehre* (1864), *Grundriss der Musikgeschichte* (1865) and *Lehrbuch der musikalischen Komposition* (1866-1871), as well as individual books on Schumann (1865), Mendelssohn (1867), and Schubert (1873). Then in 1874, only three years after Lindner's book, appeared *Geschichte des deutschen Liedes*, which, Reissmann immediately assured his readers in his preface, was neither a revision nor an enlargement of his earlier book on the lied, but rather "a completely new arrangement of the same material from a new point of view."[11] Reissmann's new approach shows itself most clearly in the use he makes of contemporary critics, whom he had ignored in his earlier book.

A few examples will make clear Reissmann's specific indebtedness to Lindner. The passage in Reissmann's earlier book, cited above, in which he mentions Keiser's statement that songs had been "completely driven out" by cantatas, has been revised: Keiser is now coupled, in exactly Lindner's manner, with Mattheson. Reissmann also cites many of the same passages from Mattheson, Mizler's discussion of Gottsched, and Scheibe's *Der critische Musikus* as Lindner had done. And in a footnote Reissmann praises Lindner's book for providing "numerous examples" (p. 134n.) from the song collections he discusses. This time Reissmann himself provides many more such examples, and eliminates the rather simpleminded talk about subjective expression that had marked his earlier book.

II

It was more than 35 years before another important history of the lied appeared. In the meantime music history had become a serious subject. For this was the period that saw the publication of the general histories that we examined in the preceding chapter, as well as the first editions of *Grove's Dictionary of Music and Musicians* and the *Oxford History of Music,* and such other important works as Fétis's *Histoire générale de la musique* and Robert Eitner's *Biographisch-bibliographisches Quellen-Lexicon*. In these and other contemporary works we can see the waning of the simple progressivism that we encountered in Reissmann and Schneider. Both musical and extra-musical documents are viewed more seriously and scrupulously—we could see the beginnings of this in Lindner—and music, though often seen as an autonomous, continuously evolving being, is also seen in relation to general culture and other aspects of the *Zeitgeist*. In addition to working deductively, from an assumed story of progress, the historians try to work inductively, rather as they believe all scientists do, from facts gathered from documents.[12] One recalls the two famous statements of Leopold von Ranke from the preface to the first (1824) edition of his *Geschichten der romanischen und germanischen Völker*: that the historian "merely wishes to show how it really was" ("wie es eigentlich gewesen"), and that "strict presentation of the facts, no matter how hypothetical and unlovely it may be, is without doubt the highest law."[13] These statements are often said to embody the creed of 19th-century positivist historiography.

Max Friedlaender's monumental *Das deutsche Lied im 18. Jahrhundert*, published in 1902, is not really a history—and deliberately so. It is, to use the word Friedlaender himself often uses, a "*Verzeichniss*," or catalogue, and thereby an excellent example of Rankean positivism and striving for objectivity. At the outset Friedlaender tells us that he seeks "to describe rather than to pronounce judgments."[14] But of course he realizes that the nature of his subject-matter has not permitted him to maintain at all times a quasi-scientific neutrality, and so he apologizes to his reader in advance: "if a subjective element has nonetheless crept in, it may be excused as, in the nature of the case, unavoidable" (I/i, xi). Anyhow, Friedlaender insists, when one is dealing with the lied, "the dry dates themselves offer . . . very eloquent testimony" (I/i, xiv).

Given Friedlaender's vague pretensions to "science," it is hardly surprising that he thinks badly of his predecessors. Of Reissmann's first book and Schneider's three volumes, he tells us sternly, "they have no scientific value," and as for Lindner's *Geschichte des deutschen Liedes im 18. Jahrhundert*, "this dilettantish work in no sense contains what its title promises" (I/i, xv). It is, however, interesting that Friedlaender has high praise for Ludwig Erk, the friend of Lindner's who prepared his work for posthumous publication. For Erk, unlike Reissmann, Schneider, and Lindner, did not set up as an historian but operated merely as a collector and editor of folksongs—as, that is, the pure neutral scientist that Friedlaender himself would have liked to have been.

But Friedlaender, willy-nilly, must act as an historian, searching out causes and making judgments of value, at least part of the time: namely, in the preface and introduction to his first volume, from which I have been quoting. And as it turns out, his brief account of the history of the German lied is based simply and solidly on mere chauvinistic prejudices, and thus is even less scientific—in any meaningful sense of that word—than the accounts offered by the predecessors for whom he had such scorn. Everything that went wrong with the German lied in the late 17th and early 18th centuries was due to foreign (especially Italian) influence and to the decline of German poetry. So much for the *liederlose Zeit*!

Friedlaender divides the history of the lied into two large periods: from the beginning until the third quarter of the 16th century, when the decline of the polyphonic secular song set in, and from then until the present. The second of these is itself divided into two smaller periods: from about 1550 until the first decades of the 18th century, and from then until now. The decline that began in about 1550 was brought about by the steady growth of Flemish, French, and (especially) Italian influence: "The national hallmark [*Gepräge*] that characterized the German lied until about 1550 was almost entirely absent in the first half of the 17th century" (I/i, xvii). Between 1560 and 1807, Friedlaender tells us bitterly, not a single collection made up entirely of German folk melodies was published, and only about 10 were published in which folklike songs were in the majority. It was only in the early decades of the 19th century that this mysterious "national hallmark" made itself felt once more.

For a man whose theoretical pronouncements evinced such reluctance to make judgments of value, Friedlaender is astonishingly bald in his condemnation of all this foreign influence. There is not even the pretense of intellectual complexity that was embodied in Schneider's dialectic-mongering. Of the process by which opera rose to predominance over the course of the 17th century, Friedlaender says flatly: "This development did not affect the German lied favorably" (I/i, xxix). The only foreign intrusion in which Friedlaender sees any value is that of the French chanson, a process he helps along by printing 12 chansons in the portion of his work devoted to musical examples.

Thus native German composers, apparently helpless against the foreign onslaught, were not primarily responsible for the long decline that culminated in the *liederlose Zeit*. In addition to the seductive charms of Italian opera, they had working against them the inability of German poets to provide them with lyrics fit to be set to music: "This preference for foreign art even in our *Hausmusik* is certainly lamentable—yet one can hardly be surprised by it, since in Germany the number of really singable, easily accessible songs was not great; at that time German lyric poetry had fallen to its nadir" (I/i, xxxiii–xxxiv).

Friedlaender thus has little or nothing of either factual or theoretical interest to tell us about the *liederlose Zeit*. Yet of course the immense amount of research that he did in compiling his massive *Verzeichniss* has been of inestimable value to every subsequent student of the German lied. Indeed, just what is most interesting about him from the standpoint of contemporary positivist historiography is the immensity of the gap that yawns between the simplemindedness of his transparently chauvinistic historical pseudo-explanations and the vast scope and painstaking detail of his compilations.

The next important history of the lied—and, as we saw in the preceding chapter, the first to take advantage of Friedlaender's work—is W. K. von Jolizza's *Das Lied und seine Geschichte*, which appeared in 1910. The sort of theoretical interest that one misses in Friedlaender (and that we saw in a rudimentary form in Lindner's use of contemporary critics) is present right from the opening pages of Jolizza's chapter on the early 17th century. Moreover, throughout that chapter and the following two, on the later 17th and 18th centuries, he gives more musical examples than his predecessors and analyzes them more thoroughly, integrating the analyses into his exposition rather than just leaving them floating on its surface. He is free not only of the simple progressivism we saw in Schneider but also of Friedlaender's equally simple chauvinism.

It is immediately clear that Jolizza does not regard Italy's assumption, in the 16th century, of the musical leadership of Europe as "lamentable" (to borrow Friedlaender's expressive term). Rather, he sees Italy's triumph merely as the natural musical extension of the general Renaissance tendency "to emphasize the element of personal individuality."[15] Nor does Jolizza follow Schneider in denying that any connection between words and music existed in polyphonic vocal music; he simply points out that polyphony had developed to the point where it could no longer serve the newly formed expressive needs of the Renaissance. These needs could better be met by the short forms and homophonic textures of frottolas and villanelles. But all attempts to make music the vehicle of subjective feeling were frustrated by the prestige and predominance of polyphony until the members of the Florentine camerata justified monody as a return to classical models. It is Caccini's *Le Nuove Musiche* of 1602 that Jolizza cites at length and singles out as "*this first work in the new style*" (p. 150).

In time the monodic revolution reached Germany, "the lied's real home and place of cultivation, while the Italians have dedicated themselves wholly to the formation of the dramatic style" (p. 154). In the earliest operas the melodies could not achieve proper development because they were too closely tied to the words. But in the arias of Francesca Caccini's *La liberazione di Ruggiero dall'isola d'Alcina* (1625) "the form of the lied stands out as much more compact and pliable; the melodies are charming and display an effort to characterize each passing mood" (pp. 156-157). These developments reached their culmination in the works of Monteverdi, which had a profound influence on German composers.

Though Schütz was a pupil of Giovanni Gabrieli and, in his 1611 madrigals, an imitator of Monteverdi, it was not Schütz himself but his cousin Heinrich Albert who brought the achievements of Italian monody to bear on the German lied. Of Albert's *Arien und Melodeyn*, which appeared in eight volumes from 1638 to 1650, Jolizza writes: "Here he combines with great skill relatively prosaic declamation and genuinely tuneful song, which often captures the mood of the poem either with tender intimacy or with great gaiety" (p. 176). While earlier historians who spoke about the influence on the lied of developments in opera invariably spoke of arias, Jolizza lays at least equal stress on recitatives. And this makes sense, considering that such qualities as intimacy and naturalness are the ones that he sees both as characteristic of Renaissance musical expression and as especially suited to the lied. For as aria and recitative gradually became distinct areas in early opera, it was not so much the arias as it was the recitatives—the direct descendants of Caccini's monodies—that embodied the close and continuous expression of the poetic text. Jolizza even notes perceptively that it was perhaps through Albert's application of recitative technique to the song that he "laid the first foundation stone of the later through-composed lied" (p. 177).

Unlike Schneider, whose rigidly progressivist schema led him to lump together the 17th-century lied composers, Jolizza is careful to make distinctions among them. And unlike Schneider, Jolizza does not believe that the effort "to reproduce the text with both metrical and psychological fidelity" inevitably led melody to become "something merely rational, mechanically soulless." "Albert's simple monophonic songs," Jolizza tells us, "quickly spread through his circle and found many imitators throughout Germany" (p. 193). The large number of song collections published by mid-century demonstrates "how quickly the monophonic lied came into German *Hausmusik*" (p. 193). Yet while describing the circle of song composers that gathered around Johann Rist in Hamburg, Jolizza freely admits that most of their songs were stiff and mechanical. This is not, however, the inevitable result of the effort to combine *Wort* and *Ton* after the manner of Italian monody but merely a sign that the effort was being made in a pedestrian and literal-minded fashion, worlds away from the "fusion between *Wort* and *Ton*" (p. 176) that Albert achieved and that enabled him to match the intimacy and naturalness of his best Italian models.

In Jolizza's view, it was only in the second half of the 17th century, when German composers began in earnest to compose in the larger Italian forms, that the growth of opera and cantata had a destructive influence on the lied: "Confronted by such rich and complex forms, the little lied was doomed to fade away" (p. 221). Thus although Jolizza has a certain amount of chauvinism, he by no means shares the conviction of the earlier historians that foreign influence on the German lied was in general a disaster. For him the point is not so much the source of the influence as its purely formal implications for the lied:

> The original strophic form of the lied was essentially torn apart, for under the influence of the cantata and opera the striving for precise individualization reached the point where each stanza of the poem had to have its own melody. Thus the lied took on broader and freer forms, and increasingly lost its original character, its simple, folksong-like nature.
>
> [Pp. 221-222]

In these sentences Jolizza has provided a clearer and more emphatic statement of what the critics cited by Lindner were really driving at than either they or Lindner were able to provide.

Like Friedlaender before him, Jolizza also places a good deal of blame for the *liederlose Zeit* on the low quality of contemporary German poetry. But he hastens to point out that even in Albert's time, during the Thirty Years' War, German lyric poetry was hardly inspiring: "on the one hand drily didactic or rough and trivial, on the other full of mawkish, offensive eroticism, for the most part in mythological form, with all the allegorical trappings that were then in vogue" (pp. 245-246). Still, all was well so long as song composers kept to the traditional strophic form. The trouble came when they adopted not only the larger Italian forms but also the elaborate ornamentation of the French chanson: "With the growing influence of French *galanterie,* songs became ever more ornate, more decorated and unnatural, and the connection between word and melody once again appeared to have been completely lost" (p. 248). The result of all this foreign influence was thus, paradoxically, to undo the unity of text and music that had been the original goal of the Italian monodists.

Jolizza dates the end of the *liederlose Zeit* and the onset of the *Aufschwung* rather later than most historians. Both Johann Valentin Rathgeber's *Tafel-Confect* volumes (1733, 1737, 1746) and the many *Sperontes* collections (1736-1745) have sometimes been singled out as hopeful signs that the drought of songs was coming to an end. But Jolizza dismisses the often praised Quodlibets in the *Tafel-Confect* volumes as "virtually worthless and without significance"; and he finds the *Sperontes* collections "radically unsuitable as songs" because in them "text and melody often have no relation to each other" (p. 232). Only with the publication in 1753 of the first Ramler-Krause *Oden mit Melodien* volume was the *liederlose Zeit* definitely at an end.

What then brought about the *Aufschwung*? The criticism of Lessing, the aesthetics of Bodmer and Gottsched with its plea for a "return to Nature" (p. 251), the "enchanting, invitingly pious Nature" (p. 251) depicted in Gellert's poems and the sublimity of Klopstock's odes, Gay's *Beggar's Opera* and the development in Germany of the *Singspiel,* Gluck's reform of opera—all these influences and others combined "to bring poetry and music back to simplicity and naturalness" (p. 279). The immediate result was the 1753 Ramler-Krause volume, the preface of which laid the groundwork for the "volksthümliches Lied"; the ultimate result was the fusion, some decades later, of Goethe's lyrics and Schubert's melodies.

Since Hermann Kretzschmar's *Geschichte des neuen deutschen Liedes* appeared in 1911, Kretzschmar could not take account of Jolizza's book. Kretzschmar does, however, show throughout an awareness of his other predecessors, of whom his clear favorite is Schneider. Although he lacks Schneider's simpleminded progressivist view, and is more detailed and closely analytical even than Jolizza, Kretzschmar has a good deal of Schneider's straightforward chauvinism and general suspicion of foreign influences on German music.

Kretzschmar's book contains only two (very long) chapters, one on the 17th century and one on the 18th. The former begins very much as the first of the chapters from Jolizza's book considered above, with a discussion—far more detailed than Jolizza's, however—of Caccini's *Nuove Musiche*. But even before he embarks on that discussion, Kretzschmar has a surprise announcement: the solo song did not begin in the 17th century, as all his predecessors have unquestioningly assumed, but at least two centuries earlier. Immediately reinforcing the claim in his preface that his book is differentiated form those of his predecessors mainly by his having had at his disposal "richer source material," Kretzschmar writes in his opening sentence: "From numerous old paintings, and also from the reports of writers, it can be established that by the 15th century the lands in which music was cultivated already possessed a solo song accompanied by lute, guitar, or keyboard."[16] But a paragraph later, introducing his discussion of Caccini, Kretzschmar acknowledges that only with the turn into the 17th century was it possible to have an accompanied solo song "that matched the melodic excellence of earlier monody, derived from Gregorian chant and the early Netherlanders, and that incorporated it into the harmonic language developed during the age of counterpoint" (pp. 1-2). This does not literally contradict Schneider's view of the relation of his third period to his first two, but Kretzschmar's emphasis is utterly different: on renewal and enrichment rather than on simple progress.

The title Caccini gave to his collection, Kretzschmar tells us, was fully justified, "for with the introduction of the accompanied solo song a whole new musical age began: opera, oratorio, and cantata are born, instrumental music assumes its position of dominance, music's power—for both good and ill—is doubled: it extends its external area of operation and moves closer to its final destiny, to serve, and be useful, as a universal gift of God" (pp. 2-3). The accompanied solo song played a very special part in this process since "it is the main channel through which high art flows into the *Volk*" (p. 3). Thus, Kretzschmar concludes, it was the 10 arias that conclude *Nuove Musiche*, rather than the 12 madrigals that begin it, that had a crucial influence on the development of the German lied.

This emphasis is both different from and more specialized than Jolizza's in his comments on *Nuove Musiche*, and indeed Kretzschmar's detailed analysis of the three basic song forms exemplified by the work's 10 arias, Nos. 14-23 in the collection, is one of his book's signal contributions. While Nos. 15, 18, 19, 20, and 21 are in simple strophic form, with the same vocal line and bass line for all stanzas of the poem, No. 14 is through-composed, with different music for each stanza, and Nos. 16, 17, 22, and 23 retain more or less the same bass line for all stanzas but vary the vocal line. Kretzschmar then comments on the significance of these three basic forms:

> Of the three song forms that are distributed among the arias of *Nuove Musiche*, that of the repeating strophic lied, found earlier in choral song and in unaccompanied monody, has become the main form of the German accompanied solo song; the strophically varied lied, on the other hand, did not achieve great significance until the end of the 18th century, and the *Koloraturlied* still remains a problem.
>
> [P. 6]

The "*Koloraturlied*," through-composed and elaborately ornamented, was very popular during the Renaissance because it seemed to obey most faithfully the demand for a complete congruence of text and music. But it soon did itself in by making ornamentation an end in itself rather than an expressive means. As for the "strophically varied lied," which Kretzschmar seems to have been the first to single out as a discrete form, it offered composers a way of compromising between the burdensome repetition of the simple strophic song and the potential formlessness of the through-composed song. We shall return to it later.

The beginnings of the accompanied German song, Kretzschmar tells us with some regret, cannot at present be dated very precisely. But unlike Jolizza, who dismissed the possibility of Schütz's having played a role in the development of the lied, Kretzschmar notes that Paul Fleming mentioned Schütz's lieder in one of his poems, and perceptively comments that while no Schütz lieder have survived, such compositions as the "Historie vom Absalon"—by which he presumably means "Fili mi, Absalon," from *Symphoniae Sacrae* I—offer more than sufficient testimony to Schütz's talent for the genre. Moreover, many of the lied composers whose works have survived—Adam Krieger, Albert, Schein, Nauwach, and Hammerschmidt among them—are either known or rumored to have had personal contact with Schütz. The earliest of these to publish his songs was Schein, whose *Musica boscareccia* (1621, 1626, 1628) Kretzschmar discusses at some length. After more discussion and analysis of other early 17th-century song collections, he asks rhetorically whether or not the new songs of Schein and his contemporaries measure up to the old polyphonic songs of Isaac, Senfl, and Hassler. His answer is a resounding "nein"—but for reasons that are disappointingly chauvinistic: "These new compositions were somewhat significant works of art, but both in their overall form and in their inward language they stood at some distance from the lied and under the influence of a foreign, Italian spirit" (p. 17).

It was Albert who enabled the German lied to escape foreign contamination and stand on its own, and whom Kretzschmar therefore views as the German Caccini—and then some: "Albert easily puts Caccini in the shade, since the general cultural and social significance of the German lied is incomparably greater than that of the Italian cantata" (pp. 17-18). Kretzschmar also sees Albert as a mediator and synthesizer: "Out of the mixture of old and new, German and Italian elements there developed a wealth of forms found in Albert's arias, that proved beneficial and that immediately provided the song composition of the future with a variety of new stimuli" (p. 31). Owing to Albert's success, the number of lied collections published increased dramatically: between 1638 and 1650 (coincidentally, the years of Albert's own first and last collections of *Arien*) there were more than 20 collections, involving about 40 German composers. But of course the lied had to do battle, at the end of the 17th century, with the opera and the cantata—a battle for which Kretzschmar expresses his regret that there is not extant documentation as ample as that for the earlier battle between the *prima* and *seconda pratiche*.

But how, exactly, did the *liederlose Zeit* come about? As Kretzschmar toils through the many lied composers who followed Albert, the reader, though constantly intrigued, loses sight of this larger question—because Kretzschmar himself has done so. After about 100 pages dense with analyses, distinctions, and musical examples, one suddenly notices, at the top of Kretzschmar's page, such running heads as "The End of the Religious Song," "The Last Secular Song Publications," and "The Causes of the Decline" (pp. 138, 140, 141). Nothing in Kretzschmar's exhaustive (and exhausting) catalogue of composers, collections, and songs has prepared us for this.

The answer, perhaps not surprisingly, turns out once again to be that there was no poetry worth setting and that Italian opera usurped the prospective audience for the lied. Much earlier, Kretzschmar described how the very popularity of songs, as they were incorporated into 17th-century Venetian and 18th-century Neapolitan operas and also into cantatas, paradoxically helped drive the independent, self-sufficient song out of business in Italy. And he has referred to the German emulation of the foppishly overdecorated Italian *Koloraturlied* as "overcultivation of the lied" (p. 8). But after all this extraordinarily detailed analysis, we expect something much better in the way of explanation. This late in the game it simply will not do to fall back, yet again, on the incompetence of contemporary poets and the vaguely sinister Italian opera. For all the richness of his "source material," Kretzschmar really does no better than his much-admired predecessor Schneider.

In *The Whig Interpretation of History* Sir Herbert Butterfield wrote of the ways in which a particular progressivist paradigm of European history had shaped the work of certain English historians. In the work of Schneider, Kretzschmar, and, to a lesser extent, the other historians of the lied we have reviewed, we can see the shaping effect of a somewhat different paradigm from the one Butterfield had in mind but one that operates in the same ways and with the same results. Butterfield's paradigm was the one seen in the work, most notably, of Macaulay and Trevelyan, according to which the history of Europe in general and England in particular is seen as the gradual rise, out of the Dark Ages and the mysteries of medieval kingship, toward modern, enlightened, Protestant parliamentary democracy. The one we see at work in Schneider, Kretzschmar, and the other historians of the lied is far older.

The path of Western civilization, as it happens, has led roughly northward and westward. In the writings of its newer recipients and beneficiaries about its older ones there has always been a mingled strain of steadfast nativist self-righteousness and gnawing covert envy, the older culture or cultures at hand always being viewed as somewhat decadent (and therefore suspect) yet also as more sophisticated, more accomplished, perhaps even wiser (and therefore enviable). We can find this interesting mix of feelings in Greek writings about the Persians, in Roman writings about the Greeks, in Christian Renaissance writings about both Greeks and Romans, in late 17th-century English writings about the French and Italians, and in American writings about virtually all Europeans. We also find it in the writings of these Germans when they speak of the influence on their *echt deutsch* lied of Italian (and, to a lesser extent, French) musical forms and mannerisms.

But the writing of the Germans has a special edge to it because of the peculiar conditions of the German Enlightenment. As Germans were all too well aware, the Enlightenment came to Germany late. There is no mid-17th-century German figure who ranks with Bacon or Hobbes, Descartes or Montaigne. Moreover, when the Enlightenment did come to Germany, near the end of the century, it was not intimately connected, as it had been in both England and France, with the revolution taking place in science. In fact, as Lewis White Beck points out, the Enlightenment in Germany "arose at a time of religious revival, whereas in England the Methodist revival was to occur later against the Age of Reason and in France the Jansenist movement was already dying."[17] The leading German Enlightenment philosopher was Christian Wolff, whose turgid, system-building philosophical style makes it hard to remember, as Beck remarks, that he was a contemporary of Hume and Montesquieu. Yet it was Wolff who established the modern philosophical vocabulary for German, much as Cicero had done for Latin, and it was Wolff whose thought Gottsched popularized, as part of his program of reform, in *Erste Gründe der gesamten Weltweisheit* (1733-1734). And it was Mattheson who, in 1713, began publishing in Hamburg a moral weekly called *Der Vernünftler*, which was not only explicitly patterned on Addison's and Steele's *Spectator* and *Tatler* but which consisted almost entirely of essays translated from those two papers. These efforts, together with Gottsched's various books and the works of such poets as Günther, Brockes, and Hagedorn, were the result of a realization on the part of educated Germans that they had fallen badly behind the English and French, and needed to catch up.[18]

It is thus no wonder that the German writers whose histories of the lied we have reviewed evince a special sort of touchiness about the Italian and French influences on—or, to put it more aptly, meddling with—the lied, traditionally considered private German property. We can see this curious blend of resentment, pride, and envy in Schneider's mysterious paradoxes about the embellishments of the Italian aria somehow recalling the German lied to its *volkstümlich* origins and essence, and also in the immense gap between the subtlety and detail of Kretzschmar's particular analyses and the flat-footed simplicity of his generalizations about the causes of the *liederlose Zeit*. Butterfield, discussing his "whig" paradigm, pointed out how such a paradigm can continue to exert its hold on the historian's mind even when his detailed research has shown it to be mistaken:

> Further, this whig tendency is so deep-rooted that even when piece-meal research has corrected the story in detail, we are slow in re-valuing the whole and reorganising the broad outlines of the theme in the light of these discoveries; . . . that is, the tendency [is] to patch the new research into the old story even when the research in detail has altered the bearings of the whole subject.[19]

"Exceptions in detail," Butterfield remarks a little later, "do not prevent us from mapping out the large story on the same pattern all the time; . . . There is a magnet for ever pulling at our minds, unless we have found the way to counteract it" (pp. 6-7). This difficulty is precisely what we are up against in reading Schneider, Friedlaender, and Kretzschmar. The immense growth in detailed research does not prevent them from falling back on the old combination of resentment for the Italians' intrusion and admiration for their "more perfect forms" when it comes time to explain what caused the *liederlose Zeit*.

No sooner has Kretzschmar offered his explanation than he suddenly begins denying that the *liederlose Zeit* ever took place at all. Once again calling on his wealth of "Quellenmaterial," he unearths several manuscript collections of songs that he says offer proof that there were, after all, plenty of "friends of the lied" during the years in question and thus can act as "a corrective to the picture given by the number of song publications" (p. 147). Yet apparently most of these collections, including the famous one assembled by the Leipzig student "Clodius" (Christian Klöde), contain not original songs but merely copies or slightly reworked versions of ones already published. As he moves on to list mentions of songs and singing culled from contemporary novels, Kretzschmar feels emboldened to dismiss the *liederlose Zeit* as merely a momentary annoyance: "We know from contemporary novels that at about the time when Clodius was a student, the desire to sing lieder had reached a highpoint—despite the temporary halt in publication of new song collections" (p. 151). But then a few pages later he reverses himself once more: "But none of this changes the essential fact that the new German lied at the end of the 17th century, in its true home and on what had formerly been the most fruitful ground, was near death" (p. 154). This statement, however, refers to north and central Germany. As Kretzschmar presses southward to discuss some manuscripts found in Munich, he turns yet another corner. These manuscripts, he tells us, "show that in the time that we commonly call songless, southern Germany was at work, and was still providing an uninterrupted series of talented lied-composers" (p. 161).

Considering that Kretzschmar is apparently the writer who coined the phrase *liederlose Zeit* in the first place, he does seem to go through an extraordinary number of changes of mind as to how severe it was or even whether it actually occurred. The paradoxes and tensions in his writing surpass even those of his master, Schneider. At any rate, in the second chapter of his book Kretzschmar speedily delivers us from the *liederlose Zeit* and into the arms of the "simple, fresh truth to life" of a newly revived (yet reassuringly traditional) *echt deutsch* poetry and song (p. 186). The *Aufschwung* comes a good deal earlier for Kretzschmar than it did for Jolizza. Unlike Jolizza, Kretzschmar has high praise for the Quodlibets of Rathgeber's *Tafel-Confect* volumes and even for the much scorned Sperontes. In fact Kretzschmar singles out Christian Günther, whose poems were both used and imitated by Sperontes, as the poetic savior who made the great renewal possible. Of Günther he writes:

> To have rendered him at last helpful to the lied is the service of a collection upon whose appearance the *liederlose Zeit* ceased.
> Its full title, which must be made known, reads as follows: . . .
>
> [P. 184]

Kretzschmar then proudly, even reverently, reads into the record the entire title page of the first (1736) *Sperontes* volume!

It is surely very strange to view an historical state or condition as significant, far-reaching, and complex as Kretzschmar at least sometimes takes the *liederlose Zeit* to have been as ceasing so quickly and so totally, vanishing "on an instant" (in Yeats's phrase), with almost magical swiftness and completeness, upon the publication of a single book. And of course it is even stranger if that book is the first *Sperontes* volume, which by fitting new lyrics to preexisting instrumental, often quite unvocal dance pieces, violated everything that the supposed *Wort-und-Ton* revolution brought about by Italian monody had stood for.

What is most to be regretted about Kretzschmar's treatment, however, is that he did not bother to follow up his very interesting remarks about the varieties of song form encountered in *Nuove Musiche*. For it is gradually becoming clear that once we peel away the various versions of chauvinism and the oversimple notions of historical "development" we have encountered, the real historical interest of the *liederlose Zeit* resides in the doubts that the success of opera, cantata, and oratorio raised about the continuing viability of traditional strophic form. This is what worried contemporary critics like Mattheson and Scheibe, and this is what set the problems that song composers of C.P.E. Bach's generation had to solve.

Kretzschmar's book was widely acclaimed, and once again the literature on the lied thins out. Only in the mid-1920s do we encounter two important books that bear—though not very directly or importantly—on our subject. The first of these is Günther Müller's *Geschichte des deutschen Liedes vom Zeitalter des Barock bis zur Gegenwart*, which appeared in 1925. Though it has a 48-page appendix of musical examples prepared by Alfred Einstein, it is really a book of literary history, and hence the word *Lied* in its title means lyric poem. Though Müller does from time to time comment on musical matters, his interest is mainly in themes and verse forms, and is only marginally musical.

Yet *Geschichte des deutschen Liedes* is a very interesting book to anyone who has read the books so far reviewed here. For it is plain that Müller has read them too. At more than one point he gently takes music historians to task for blaming the decline of the lied during the *liederlose Zeit* on poets and poetry. Because he is free of the German music historian's characteristic obsession with the lied as a precious, somewhat fragile native product, to be tenderly cherished and jealously guarded against foreign encroachments, Müller is able to see its temporary downfall at the hands of the operatic and cantata aria in its general artistic context, as a normal (and gradual) Baroque development. "The transformation of the lied into the aria had long been prepared for in the musical world," he writes. "As early as Heinrich Albert the intimacy [of the lied] was occasionally opened outward, and with Adam Krieger, in the 1760s, that was also true of the poetry."[20]

But of course there is a downside to Müller's being a literary (rather than a music) historian: he has no interest in the developing doubts about the viability of the strophic lied as a form in which to embody the content of a dramatic or quasi-dramatic lyric poem. For that we must turn to the other of our two important mid-1920s books, Walther Vetter's *Das frühdeutsche Lied*, published in 1928.

From the outset Vetter makes it clear where his main indebtedness lies: "Kretzschmar belongs among the first and strongest of that epoch of modern musicology that recently has justly become known as 'the age of heroes'."[21] There is something of both regret and anxiety—the "anxiety of influence," as it has recently come to be known[22]—in Vetter's praise of Kretzschmar and his contemporaries: "The younger generation is conscious of being, in many ways, the heirs of a great past, whose most recent representatives, aside from Kretzschmar, were Hugo Riemann and Hermann Abert" (p. xi). This sense that the giants are all under the earth, that the age of heroes is forever past, which surely has something to do with the recent war, curiously inhibits Vetter's sense of how much he (or perhaps anyone else) can accomplish in writing about the German lied. His book, Vetter carefully tells us, cannot be a true history of the German lied but only preliminary studies ("Vorstudien") for such a history: "The time for a musical history of the German lied that is comprehensive and free of omissions, yet at the same time internally and externally concise, has, in my opinion, not yet arrived" (p. xi). After which he feels impelled immediately to add that in saying this he is in no way criticizing Kretzschmar!

The good side of Vetter's elaborate scholarly caution it that he is refreshingly free of the easy categorizations so often found in earlier historians of the lied. Because he is intent on providing as complete as possible a composer-by-composer, item-by-item survey of the 17th-century lied and is not writing teleologically—with his eye on Schubert looming there in the middle distance—Vetter is able to pay more attention than his predecessors to 17th-century survivals of the polyphonic song and to their relation to the solo song. Kretzschmar, we recall, had dubbed Heinrich Albert the German

Caccini. Consequently, when he came to consider Albert's return, late in his career, to writing polyphonic songs, Kretzschmar had to see it as an unfortunate hardship forced upon Albert by the fact that much of his work was occasional, and he denounced the polyphonic songs themselves as mere "rearrangements" of Albert's earlier solo songs. Vetter, on the other hand, suggests that perhaps the polyphonic songs were "realizations of the original idea, and the monophonic songs were 'abridgements' of some sort" (p. 34n.). Vetter also points out that the polyphonic songs of Albert's contemporary Caspar Kittel are his best work, "songs of amazing naturalness," and that when Kittel presented himself "as the advocate of the new Italian artistic ideal" (p. 186), he lost his sureness of touch. Vetter's openness to the more conservative aspects of 17th-century song even enables him, from time to time, appreciatively to note survivals of the old church modes.

The bad side of his scholarly caution is that he has practically nothing to contribute to our view of the *liederlose Zeit*. Very early he makes it clear that he is defining *Lied* so narrowly that the relations to opera and cantata that were so important in bringing about the *liederlose Zeit* will be of no interest to him (pp. 18-20). But Vetter is, by nature and training, very chary of generalizing about anything. Only in his very last pages, when he is describing in greater detail some of the manuscript collections unearthed by Kretzschmar, does Vetter venture to suggest that his work might have any bearing on the glorious future of the German solo song:

> The German propensity for correctness, profundity, and completeness shows itself to advantage even in these south German songs. It lends them an inner orderliness, integrity, stylistic unity, and thereby a wholly individual charm that even the undeniable dependence upon Italy (vocal) and France (instrumental) cannot take away. In this sign shall the German lied conquer a century later, gaining international fame and power.
>
> [P. 338]

It is, one feels, only Vetter's reluctance to generalize, his sense that generalizations don't really belong in the body of a "scientific" work but must—if they are to be present at all—be smuggled in at the very end, that forces him to burden these inconsequential south German manuscript songs with such a weight of assertion.

The next history of the lied was Ernst Bücken's *Das deutsche Lied: Probleme und Gestalten*, published in 1939. Just under 200 pages in length, it traces the development of the lied from 1600 right down to the late 1930s. Bücken begins on an upbeat note that is to be sustained throughout most of the book: "The beginning of the life of the modern German solo song represents a twofold change of direction in the history of the lied. One sees in it the change from the polyphonic to the monophonic lied, but also the change to a lied created and formed by the *Volk*."[23] It is this latter change that interests Bücken, who then launches into a long discussion of how the birth of the German solo song coincided with the breakup of the feudal order, the healing of the rifts that had separated the classes of German society one from another, and the establishment of an almost mystical social unity.

Not that the course of the lied's development always runs smooth, but the *liederlose Zeit* does emerge as surprisingly painless. To be sure, when he comes to Kusser and Keiser, those two mainstays of the Hamburg Opera, Bücken notes: "Already in Kusser's famous aria collection 'Helikonische Musenlust' of 1790 [*recte* 1700] the aria-like lied has been forced into a corner by Frenchified dance songs and Italianate arias." And he compares parallel passages from the 1710 and 1730 versions of an aria from Keiser's *Croesus* to the disadvantage of the latter: "In the second version . . . this German lied-aria has become an arietta with modal effects and coloratura" (p. 30). Yet Keiser is still "the highly gifted Keiser . . . , to whom the German lied is still indebted for some exceptional achievements" (p. 30).

"The point was reached," declares Bücken, "at which the lied lost even its last curious refuge—the aria collections. The aria, as viewed from the standpoint of form, remained the victor over the German [strophic] lied form" (p. 31). But he quickly turns his attention to the work of composers like Wolfgang Franck and Philipp Heinrich Erlebach, who were deeply influenced by opera but whom he sees as having effected a successful compromise or reconciliation "between the foreign-derived arioso style and the [strophic] principle of the German song" (p. 31). He then praises Handel's *Neun deutsche Arien* of 1729, a work not even mentioned by Kretzschmar, as "the high point of the German Baroque song" (p. 33). After citing a passage from the fourth of these arias in which he finds "lyrical intensity" and "completely inward-turning ardor," Bücken sums up his case:

> What does such a creative act tell us when viewed against the rationalists' squabble over the "differences" between cantata, aria and lied! They can be found everywhere that same rationalistic pedantry drew distinctions—which the genius Handel here rendered meaningless when he breathed new life into the sacrosanct da capo aria form and made of it a lyrical demonstration that would not be surpassed by any so-called "song form."
>
> [P. 32]

This seems to me nothing short of astonishing. Earlier in his book Bücken grossly inflated the distinction between aria and lied into a black-and-white value distinction: aria bad, lied good. Here that distinction gets airily dismissed as merely the product of "rationalistic pedantry." Suddenly reason—the faculty that makes and argues for such distinctions—is the enemy: on the pages that follow we find the phrases "music rationalism" and "rational system of rules" used contemptuously against critics like Scheibe, Gottsched, and Gräfe, who attempted to draw such distinctions. In the face of glowing inspiration, genius, the "creative act," reason and argument must, apparently, fall silent. Why should this be?

Looking back over Bücken's language in the early pages of his book, we notice that he, like other writers on the lied, extols a kind of "unity" or "union" that is not only musical and aesthetic but also social and political. But we notice that he also uses terms like "rassisch" (racial), "Stamm" (race, family), and even "Lebensraum" (living space)—terms that figured prominently in the Nazi rhetoric of the time. The song-movement to which other German writers apply the adjective "Berlin" is referred to by Bücken as "Prussian," and a passage in which Vetter innocently (and characteristically) remarks that in the early 17th century polyphonic songs were often more important for the development of the German solo song than was "German monody based slavishly on the principles of the Florentine Hellenists" (*Das frühdeutsche Lied*, p. 136) is transformed by Bücken through the addition of a stirring military metaphor: "Walter [sic] Vetter was right . . . to point out that this victory could not have been won under the banner of the Florentine Hellenists" (p. 18).

Sure enough, by the end of *Das deutsche Lied: Probleme und Gestalten* we find Bücken asserting that in stressful times like the present ones, "the important thing is not the complexity of experience and its embodiment in the lied but rather the necessity and the possibility of capturing great national events in *clear, simple tone symbols*" (p. 192). Among the works that accomplish this task, according to Bücken, are the *Horst-Wessel-Lied* and "the already large cantata cycle of the Hitler Youth Movement" (p. 198). Even worse was to follow two years later, in Bücken's *Musik der Deutschen: eine Kulturgeschichte der deutschen Musik*. By the end of that book, "rationalization" has become the word for the precompositional schemes of decadent Jews like Schoenberg and for the justifications of their music offered by their "Rassegenossen" (co-racialists) in the critical press. It is small wonder that Bücken, with such big political and cultural fish to fry, tells us little of interest about the *liederlose Zeit*.

So far I have discussed only books in German. Though there have been many English-language books written on the German lied, they have almost all begun with Schubert and the early Romantics or, at the earliest, with Haydn and Mozart. It is only recently that English-speaking musicologists have turned their attention to the first and second Berlin song schools. Now, however, there are three books of real though limited relevance to our particular subject. They are: R. Hinton Thomas's *Poetry and Song in the German Baroque* (Oxford: Clarendon Press, 1963); Margaret Mahony Stoljar's *Poetry and Song in Late Eighteenth Century Germany* (London: Croom Helm, 1985); and J. W. Smeed's *German Song and its Poetry, 1740-1900* (London: Croom Helm, 1987). As their titles make clear, none of these books rests squarely in the period that concerns us: Thomas ends a little too early for the *liederlose Zeit*, while Stoljar and Smeed start a little too late. Moreover, the fact that they are non-German writers, writing without the familiar chauvinistic chip on the shoulder, means that the *liederlose Zeit*, which was so intimately connected with foreign influence acting on the German lied, is not of great significance to them. But of course their freedom from the chauvinism that marred so much of the work so far considered is also an advantage.

Thomas's book is by far the best of the three. He begins his Introduction by alluding briefly to the situation in 1750, the year of J. S. Bach's death: "Hagedorn's *Oden und Lieder* had begun to appear ten years before, and, in the songs of Telemann and Görner, at once began to play a crucial part in the transition to the lied in its post-baroque situation. Composers now wanted their songs to be simple, natural, and easy to perform" (p. ix). Later, after tracing in illuminating detail the growth of the solo song and its elaboration under the influence of opera and cantata, Thomas arrives at the crucial years. He tells us that "Mattheson, who was associated with the Hamburg opera, decided by 1722, in the *Critica Musica*, that the strophic lied was intolerably dull" (p. 83)—though he does not tell us what led to Mattheson's decision—and he notes that an "interest in operatic forms" (p. 84) informs Erlebach's *Harmonische Freude Musikalischer Freunde*. "Strophic song, it is true," Thomas concludes, "was soon to return to prominence, but on the basis of a new type of poetry in association with a different conception of music" (p. 89). Thomas singles out Hagedorn's 1740 *Oden und Lieder* as marking "a point of critical change in German poetry," a point that also "marks the stage at which the use of the figured bass begins, with far-reaching implications, to enter its period of decline" (pp. 99-100). The result of these two cooperating tendencies was a "conception of song as an easy tune over a simple bass" (p. 109).

Stoljar's period of coverage does not really begin until about 1770, and so she has the least of the three to tell us about the *liederlose Zeit*. Moreover, since her emphasis is heavily sociological—on "song as social fact, which is to say, song in performance," as "an act of communication between singer and listener" (p. 2)—she naturally does not take a very detailed formal interest in the songs she discusses. But she does talk a little about the beginnings of the first Berlin school, noting that the Ramler-Krause *Oden mit Melodien* of 1753 shows the editors' "awareness of a tendency towards artlessness and sociability in song" (p. 84). This awareness, however, she finds "perhaps surprising" owing to her firm conviction that the German Enlightenment was constrictingly "rationalistic": earlier, discussing the first volume of C.P.E. Bach's *Versuch über die wahre Art das Clavier zu spielen* (1753), she finds it "striking" that "Bach, writing in conservative Berlin at a time when Enlightenment rationalism was certainly the dominant mode of thinking in the circles in which he moved, should have already defined the function of his art in terms that could not be more typical of positions that were to mark the age of sentiment a decade or two later" (p. 65).

Smeed begins rather unpromisingly by implying that he has only reluctantly dwelt on "musical technicalities" since "the ultimate test of a song is what it reveals to the ear, not how much it yields on formal musical analysis" (p. vii)—as though there were no connection between how a piece of music sounds and what an analysis of it might show. But his opening chapter does sketch, in some detail, the reaction that brought about an end to the *liederlose Zeit*. He reproduces some passages from the songs of Albert and "Sperontes," and discusses the views of Gottsched and Mattheson. At one point he draws an interesting causal connection between the *Affektenlehre* and the reinstatement of the strophic form in the early Berlin song collections: "nearly all these early songs are set strophically—a logical consequence of the Affektenlehre, which encouraged the composer to search out the dominating mood of the poem, devise a melody to fit this and stick to it throughout all the stanzas" (p. 12). Later, however, he singles out C.P.E. Bach's through-composed song "Die Küsse" ("Dass ich, bey meiner Lust, durch keinen Zwang"), which was published both in the 1753 Ramler-Krause *Oden mit Melodien* and also in

Bach's own 1762 collection of the same title, as suggesting "how song might progress towards freer forms without sacrificing musical logic and unity" (p. 94). And at another point Smeed notes that Bach's preface to the 1774 *Herrn Doctor Cramers übersetzte Psalmen* shows that the composer "felt that strophic composition imposed a constraint on the composer and blamed his amateur public, who would be incapable of performing more extended and elaborate songs" (p. 70).

Finally, however, the issues that we have seen playing about the fringes of earlier historians' work were met head-on, by Siegfried Kross in his 1989 *Geschichte des deutschen Liedes*. Though well-known as a Brahms scholar, Kross has devoted a good deal of his time for the last 25 years to the study of the German lied. The ongoing series *Dokumentation zur Geschichte des deutschen Liedes*, which he edits and which is published by Georg Olms of Hildesheim, was started in 1973.

In his brief book's opening chapter, "The Beginnings of the Newer German Song in the 17th Century," Kross lucidly and elegantly traces the development of the lied from the time of Schein to the eve of the *liederlose Zeit*. The whole story is told without a hint of chauvinism—there is no envious upbraiding of foreigners, no making of excuses for German composers and poets, as we move inexorably toward century's end: "Such achievements at least make it clear that the ability to compose songs had not been lost, but that the composers' will to form and to express had sought more extensive opportunities for development."[24]

Kross's second chapter, "The 18th-Century Lied," opens with the firm statement: "The time from the end of the 17th to the end of the first third of the 18th century has been called a songless time" (p. 57)—a statement that immediately gets interestingly qualified: "Actually, it is not so much a matter of a songless time as of a genre's loss of aesthetic prestige, which had consequences for its dissemination: whatever did not claim to be a work of art was not published in durable form" (p. 57). There were, after all, Kross reminds us, those manuscript collections of which Kretzschmar and Vetter spoke; it was only the printing of song collections that ceased.

After rehearsing the familiar passages of disapproval from Mattheson, Scheibe, and others, Kross illuminatingly generalizes: "The theoretician's main critical point was that the same melody, repeated for all stanzas, necessarily could not fit the content and character of each individual stanza in the required manner" (pp. 58-59). This, clearly, is what the accumulating evidence of discontent with the limitations of the strophic song has been heading us toward—though none of the historians we have examined has put it so clearly and succinctly.

But once Kross begins to zero in on the problem—to state its causes in more precise formal terms and to show how it got solved—he is less satisfactory. The turning away from counterpoint created a demand for a new type of melody, which was first met by the composers of the Hamburg opera. Kusser's experience with the tradition of French lyric tragedy had taught him "a decidedly simple melodic style, though without closed song forms," and Keiser brought "genuine lieder" into his operas: "The dramatic necessity for the musical characterization of the figures onstage of course justified the entry of the lower style into opera" (p. 60).

But for Kross it was above all Telemann who regained for the lied its stature as a respectable artistic genre. And indeed Telemann's songs do cover a good deal of the *liederlose Zeit*: from the 35 included in J. C. Losius's *Singende Geographie* (1708, but only rediscovered in 1960) to the two in his own *Der getreue Music-Meister* (1728-1729) to the 48 in his *Singe-, Spiel- und Generalbass-Übungen* (1733-1734) to his 1741 collection *24 Vier und zwanzig, theils ernsthafte, theils scherzende, Oden* and beyond, to the songs he contributed to later anthologies. What mainly interests Kross about these songs is that they were written to serve an educational purpose, that they were "functional songs" (p. 62), specimens of what a later century would term *Gebrauchsmusik*. Even the 1741 *Oden*, though not written for a specifically educational work, had an instructive purpose: as Telemann tells us in his dedication, the songs grew out of conversations with Scheibe, who, fresh from his studies with Gottsched, had come to Hamburg in 1736 (in Kross's words) "with the intention of producing for music something comparable to *Versuch der critischen Dichtkunst vor die Deutschen*" (p. 64).

It is thus Kross's sociological preoccupations that divert him from explaining, in sufficiently precise formal terms, just what brought about the end of the *liederlose Zeit,* yet these same preoccupations also provide him with valuable insights. They help him, for example, to explain the exceptional popularity of such seemingly against-the-grain collections as Rathgeber's *Tafel-Confect* and the many *Sperontes* volumes:

> Here it is all too clear that the function of the songs is to be sung at social gatherings, and thus it is permissible that their connection with fashionable dances and poems makes them verge on the frivolous—indeed, songs mocking the educated Enlightenment women crowding the universities were sung to the same melodies. It is these impudent texts, with their suggestive dance tunes that, then as today, provided the charm of the *Singende Muse.* That the collection was a thorn in the eye of the theoreticians, who were endeavoring to give the lied a new foundation as a genre of artistic expression, is understandable. Yet it not only reflects the taste of the urban bourgeoisie; it also contributed decisively to the revival of interest in the lied.
>
> [Pp. 70-71]

Toward the end of his chapter on the 18th-century lied, Kross notes the difficulty of using the predominantly reflective poetry of the time to reanimate "the small vocal form of the lied," especially since the thread of tradition had been broken and the composers were accustomed to writing cantatas: "Thus the generation of Bach and Handel, though it contained the dominating figures of German musical history, was lost to the lied" (p. 72). In sharp contrast to Bücken, Kross asserts of Handel's *Neun deutsche Arien*: "they really have nothing to do with the lied genre" (p. 72). And of Bach he finds only the lovely "Bist du bei mir" (BWV 508) from the *Anna Magdalena Notebook,* which, however, the *New Grove* numbers among Bach's "Doubtful and spurious" works.

The revival of the lied took place, rather, "in the generation born after 1700" (p. 73)—a generation of which Telemann was a sort of honorary older member. Kross's chapter closes with illuminating analyses of several of the post-1740 song composers and critics of the song, for he, more than any of the writers whose work we have reviewed except perhaps for Lindner, believes in the importance of studying songs and critical texts together: "In no other area of music history has there been this sort of broad and intensive analysis of the music; never again have musical practice and theoretical reflection dovetailed so closely as in the generation born around 1700" (p. 74).

Thus we reach the end of our investigation of how the *liederlose Zeit* has been treated by historians of the German song. As I have noted several times along the way, once we strip away the chauvinism and the various historiographical convictions, conscious and unconscious, that have shaped the work of our historians, what remains is the fact that the moment-to-moment, word-by-word depiction or dramatization of poetic texts provided by Italian monody—as found in early opera and solo madrigals, and later in the cantata and oratorio—produced a discontent with the traditional strophic form of the lied. How could the same melody, repeated over and over, possibly follow, with a fidelity comparable to that offered by these other, through-composed forms, the developing content of a stanzaic poem? This discontent, caused by what I have called the strophic problem, was the real cause of the *liederlose Zeit,* and the question that embodied it was certainly a reasonable one.

The odd thing is that our historians had so much trouble accounting for the *liederlose Zeit*—the only one who did so clearly, after all, was Siegfried Kross, writing in 1989. Yet, as we have seen, Mattheson and Scheibe, writing in the midst of the *liederlose Zeit,* knew perfectly well what was causing it. And so did the critics who immediately followed them, and who played a crucial role in the reinstatement of the strophic song. Why then should the matter have presented such a puzzle to 19th-century music historians?

Part of the trouble, as Lindner pointed out, was that most of them had not bothered to read the 18th-century critics. But that was just one result of the general process recounted in the preceding chapter. At about the middle of the 19th century, the attention of music historians shifted from vocal to instrumental music, and they became increasingly preoccupied with questions of form, and how form operated to give order and meaning to music that had no verbal text. Thus they lost sight not only of the songs of C.P.E. Bach and his contemporaries but also of the idea that anyone could be similarly preoccupied with the operation of form in vocal music. This was why they felt impelled to blame the *liederlose Zeit* on foreign meddling or the allegedly low quality of 18th-century German lyric poetry or some other irrelevant (or even nonexistent) state of affairs.

Chapter Three

The *Aufschwung*

Earlier I referred briefly to the fact that the Enlightenment came late to Germany, and to the efforts at modernization and reform made first by the philosopher Christian Wolff, then in a series of popularizing books by Wolff's disciple Johann Christoph Gottsched, and finally in the musical journals founded by Johann Mattheson and by Gottsched's students Lorenz Mizler and Johann Adolph Scheibe. The best of these writers, Gottsched and Scheibe, strove for a prose style that was pointedly transparent, light, and elegant, far from the heavy inflexibility of the German Baroque prose of only a few decades earlier. Some of the poets whose work embodied similar aspirations—and who were to be most important to the composers who helped to reinstate the strophic song—were Johann Christian Günther, who died in 1723 at the age of only 28; Barthold Heinrich Brockes (1680-1747), author of *Irdisches Vergnügen in Gott* (1721-1748) and translator of Pope's *An Essay on Man* (1740) and Thomson's *The Seasons* (1745); and Friedrich von Hagedorn (1708-1754), whose *Oden und Lieder* (1740) decisively marked the beginning of the new poetry.

The musical correlate of the changes taking place in German prose and poetry was a new—or, in some ways, an old, revived—emphasis on simplicity and intelligibility. It is no accident that the famous attack on J. S. Bach was launched in 1737 by Gottsched's former student Scheibe; nor is it any accident that Scheibe's condemnation of Bach's "Schwülstiges und verworrenes Wesen" is so closely matched verbally by Hagedorn's almost exactly contemporaneous condemnation of the Baroque poet Christian Hofmann von Hofmannswaldau (1618-1679):

> Zum Dichter machten dich die Lieb' und die Natur.
> O wärst du dieser stets, wie Opitz, treu gewesen!
> Du würdest noch mit Ruhm gelesen:
> Jetzt kennt man deinen Schwulst und deine Fehler nur.

Martin Opitz (1567-1639), invoked by Hagedorn as the man whose influence might have kept Hofmannswaldau writing about love and nature, thereby saving the latter's good name, was, as we shall see, the 17th-century poet most important to the young poets remaking German poetry in the early 18th century. The *Aufschwung* that brought the strophic song back into prominence as a genre was part of the effort to replace the (alleged) *Schwulst* of Hofmannswaldau and J. S. Bach with something lighter, more elegant, more up-to-date.

As we have seen, the lied as a genre was thrown into disrepute in Germany for upward of 50 years at the end of the 17th and beginning of the 18th centuries. And the reason for this was that the development, over the course of the 17th century, of opera, cantata, and oratorio—genres that permitted a sustained expressive unity of text and music—had thrust into bold relief a seemingly disenabling handicap of the lied's traditional strophic form: that it necessitated the repeated use of the same music for words of at least potentially different emotional weight and significance. It would seem that the reinstatement of the lied as a major musical genre would have required composers to abandon the strophic form either wholly or partially, and to adopt some of the innovations of opera, cantata, and oratorio. Then, perhaps, the strophic lied gradually regained standing over the course of the 18th century. But this was not the case. Right from the beginning of the *Aufschwung* that ended the *liederlose Zeit* in the late 1730s and early 1740s, the overwhelming majority of published songs were in the old (and discredited) simple strophic form.

I

To return to Caccini's *Nuove musiche*. When the collection appeared in 1602, attention was of course drawn immediately to its solo madrigals, in particular to the way in which the freedom of the solo vocal line, liberated both from the distracting movements of other voices and also from the constraints of strophic or other form, could enhance the meaning of individual words and images of the poetic text. Yet as Kretzschmar pointed out, the appeal made by the volume's arias was also of historical significance.[1] Let us look more closely at those arias.

Of the 10 arias that conclude *Le nuove musiche*, Nos. 14–23, five (Nos. 15, 18, 19, 20, and 21) are in simple strophic form; No. 22 (a *Wechselode*) is divided into two sections, which are sung to alternate stanzas: the first to the odd-numbered and the second to the even-numbered ones; in No. 23 the same music is used for stanzas 1–4, but for the concluding stanza 5 the music is expanded and elaborated, though basically unchanged; Nos. 16 and 17 look at first like through-composed songs since the musical setting for each separate stanza is fully written out, but in each case the differences from strophe to strophe, both in vocal line and bass line, are minimal; No. 14, finally, is a genuinely through-composed song: though three of the five strophes are similarly structured internally (roughly, ABBC) and there are motivic relations amongst strophes, each strophe is musically different, both in vocal line and bass line, from all the others.

The arias of *Le nuove musiche* can thus be arranged along a spectrum stretching from simple strophic form to through-composed. The most interesting point on this spectrum, both theoretically and historically, comes between Nos. 16 and 17 (on the one hand) and No. 14 (on the other). At this point all strophes of the music are written out and have the same bass line and underlying harmony (as in Nos. 16 and 17) but the vocal line changes from strophe to strophe (as in No. 14) in order to express more flexibly the changing significance of the text. This form, which has come to be known as strophic variation, enabled composers to have it both ways: a vocal line with something close to the variety and latitude found in the through-composed madrigal could be buttressed by a recurring harmonic pattern, thus fusing expressive freedom and musical unity, simultaneously meeting the needs of *Wort* and *Ton*.

It is no wonder, then, that strophic variation soon became, in Jan Racek's words, "one of the most popular and most interesting forms of the early Italian accompanied monody."[2] It is everywhere in the madrigals and cantatas of the early 17th century, and also in opera. Perhaps the most familiar example is Orfeo's aria "Possente spirto" in Monteverdi's great work.

Yet as John Baron has pointed out, strophic variation "was not suited to the taste or needs of 17th-century Germans."[3] Indeed, Casper Kittel (1603–1639) and Johann Nauwach (c. 1595–c. 1630), both of whom were trained in Italy, are about the only German composers whose names are associated with it. Of Kittel's 1638 collection *Arien und Cantaten,* Baron writes:

> Kittel has been accused by some modern writers of slavishly copying the Italians, and this no doubt stems from his almost unique attempt at German strophic variations

utilizing extensive melismas and other early cantata characteristics. His attempt to experiment with this form failed because it violated basic German song tradition, but it is wrong to assume that he copied the Italians any more slavishly than other Lied composers who experimented with other Italian types of song that happened to be more suitable to and more easily assimilated into German song.

[P. 112]

As a German composer in whom the Italian influence was both strong and direct, Kittel is for Baron something of an exception, for Baron's whole thesis, roughly derived from the work of Hermann Abert,[4] is that the Italian influence, in particular the influence of Italian monody, on the 17th-century German lied was not so strong as earlier historians such as Kretzschmar believed, and that the role played by the native German tradition was considerably stronger than had usually been recognized.

It is widely accepted that the standard for the modern German solo song was set by Heinrich Albert (1604-1651) in his eight volumes of *Arien* (1638-1650).[5] The neatness and symmetry of his mainly syllabic text-setting obviously owe a great deal to the metrical reforms proposed by Opitz in *Buch von der Deutschen Poeterey* (1624), a precursor and early harbinger of the poetic reform that was to take place in Germany in the early 18th century. That over 20 collections of lieder, containing the work of about 40 composers, appeared in Germany between 1638 and 1650, the years during which Albert's *Arien* were being published, is owing in no small part to his success. Of the 190 songs contained in Albert's eight volumes, only 10 are non-strophic and none of those 10 is in strophic variation form.

In the important German song composers who follow Albert, we also find a surprisingly small proportion of non-strophic settings. Of the 68 songs in Andreas Hammerschmidt's three major collections, only seven are non-strophic. All 18 songs in *Erster Theil weltlicher Oden oder Liebesgesänge* (1642) and all 20 in *Ander Theil weltlicher Oden oder Liebesgesänge* (1643) are strophic. The non-strophic pieces all appear in *Dritter Theil geist- und weltlicher Oden und Madrigalien* (1649).[6] Of these, three are through-composed, three are in various sectional forms, and one is in a sort of simplified version of strophic variation.

The only collection that Adam Krieger (1634-1666) published during his brief life was the 1657 *Arien*, which has been lost but partially reconstructed. His posthumous fame rests on the 50 *Neuen Arien* of 1667, reprinted in 1676 with 10 more songs as *Neue Arien in 6 Zehen eingetheilet*.[7] Of these 60 songs, all but three are strophic with instrumental ritornelli. The three exceptions are in sectional form. Most of the reconstructed numbers from the 1657 *Arien* seem also to have been strophic.

One of the last important song composers to publish before the *liederlose Zeit* set in was Johann Wolfgang Franck (1644-c. 1710). Interestingly enough, he was also an opera composer—only one of his operas, however, survives entire. He began his career at Ansbach, moved on to Hamburg in 1679, and left for London in 1687, probably owing to a temporary suspension of operatic activity at Hamburg. During the early 1680s, while he was publishing successful collections of his arias, Franck was also setting the religious verse of the Hamburg clergyman Heinrich Elmenhorst. His 73 settings first appeared, in small groups, in volumes published during the 1680s, and then, all together, in Elmenhorst's *Geist-reiche Lieder* of 1700,[8] which also contained settings by the Lüneburg organist Georg Böhm and the Kiel Kantor Peter Laurentius Wockenfuss. Franck's songs, like all the others in the volume, are strophic. They reveal nothing of the operatic side of his career.

Precisely the opposite is true of Philipp Heinrich Erlebach's two collections entitled *Harmonische Freude Musikalischer Freunde*, published in 1697 and 1710.[9] Erlebach too was an opera composer, based at Rudolstadt in Thuringia, and several of the pieces in his two collections are arias taken from his two otherwise lost operas, *Die Plejades* (1693) and *Die siegende Unschuld* (1702). It is now fashionable to take earlier historians to task for speaking of Erlebach as a representative song composer of his period since what he has given us are not, after all, songs but opera arias. But of course that is precisely the point. That the two most important collections of short vocal pieces published shortly before and after 1700 should be filled with opera (and quasi-operatic) arias is what makes Erlebach the representative composer of the *liederlose Zeit*. Whether we call him a song composer or define the concept *song* so narrowly that we must call him some other kind of composer is really of no consequence.

What Erlebach's collections clearly demonstrate is the tension that was felt during the *liederlose Zeit* between the tradition that decreed songs should be strophic and composers' aspirations to write in the longer and more ambitious dramatic forms that had been imported from Italy and were defining contemporary opera, oratorio, and cantata. For though most of the 75 pieces in his two collections—50 in the 1697 volume and 25 in the 1710 one—do have the appearance of operatic or cantata arias, all but one of them are in fact strophic in form. The one exception is, as we might expect, a *da capo* aria: it was the rise of the *da capo* aria, at just this time, that led to the relatively undramatic strophic aria's being confined to comic and other less serious situations.

Despite their strophic form, a number of Erlebach's pieces are quite complex in their internal structure, and those point up sharply the tension to which I referred a moment ago. For example, No. 41 in the 1697 collection begins *Un poco allegro* with a brief instrumental introduction followed by a florid coloratura vocal passage to the words "Amor, eile und erteile treuen Rat." But then suddenly, in mid-bar, the tempo changes to *Largo* for a passage beginning "sag, was mich betöret hat!":

One can easily imagine the dramatic effectiveness of the character's excitedly summoning love and then, as she asks her question, being suddenly seized by a kind of depression—the vocal line, we notice, droops at this point. But what about the text's other two stanzas? In the second, the *Allegro* passage reads "Ja, ich fliehe und entziehe meine Brust," and the *Largo* passage, "von der Liebe falschen Lust." There is no possible justification in the words for the dramatic turnaround in the music. And the third stanza is almost as bad: "Amor eile und zerteile meine Pein!" is followed by "Ich will ungequälet sein." The one word "ungequälet" would seem to defeat the tempo and shape of the *Largo* passage.

It would not be hard to multiply examples. What this brief and very selective survey of some 17th-century German song composers shows is that in spite of all the influence coming out of Italy, the traditional strophic song form more than held its own in Germany until the 1680s. Moreover, strophic variation form, which offered a most convenient compromise to composers eager to strike out in new expressive directions but unwilling to abandon strophic form completely, made virtually no headway in Germany. Only in the last 15 or so years of the century did the traditional strophic song begin to lose status to the point where compositions like those of Erlebach—neither flesh nor fowl—could step into the void left by the sudden disappearance from the market of ordinary song collections.

II

The passage just cited from Erlebach gives an idea of the sort of *Schwulst* or tumidity—a sort quite different, of course, from that attributed by Scheibe to J. S. Bach—that the influence of the Italian opera aria brought into the German song literature in the early years of the 18th century. Plainly, a counter-response was to be expected. It was most famously embodied in the four volumes entitled *Ohren-vergnügendes und Gemüth-ergötzendes Tafel-Confect*, published at Augsburg in 1733, 1737, and 1746.[10] In vivid contrast to Erlebach's elaborate quasi-operatic productions, the *Tafel-Confect* songs, composed by Valentin Rathgeber (1682-1750), are simplicity itself. The mind-numbing dullness of most of them is fairly represented by the following:

Certainly this blandly generic, one-size-fits-all tune stands at the other end of the spectrum from Erlebach's musico-dramatic complexities. One imagines it would suit equally well each of the 11 stanzas of doggerel printed with it. As we saw, the *Volkslied* quality of some of the contents of the *Tafel-Confect* volumes induced even so acute an historian as Kretzschmar to grant them high marks. But this, surely, is a dead end.

Something else was necessary: something that fed the growing taste for simplicity and naturalness in song yet did not bore the consumers to extinction. It was provided, quite dramatically though in what it soon became clear was a flawed form, by the first installment of *Singende Muse an der Pleisse*, published at Leipzig in 1736—a year earlier, actually, than the second volume of *Tafel-Confect*, which contained the song just cited. The first volume of *Singende Muse an der Pleisse* was a great and instant success, and was reprinted, with various additions and reorderings, in 1740, 1741, and 1747. A new volume appeared in 1742 and was reprinted in 1747; two others followed in 1743 and 1745. All four volumes were combined and reprinted together in 1751.[11]

The most striking thing about *Singende Muse an der Pleisse* was that the poems were set to already existing pieces of music. The second most striking thing was that the identity of the compiler, given under the obvious pseudonym "Sperontes" on the title page of the 1736 volume, was never revealed in any of the subsequent reprintings or supplements, or definitively established by any contemporary critic. Zedler's *Universal Lexicon*, published in 1743, ambiguously stated that Mizler either was or had claimed to be the man. But it remained for J. S. Bach's biographer Philipp Spitta to clear up the matter once and for all in 1885, in a long and brilliant essay published in the *Vierteljahrsschrift für Musikwissenschaft*.[12] Sperontes turns out to have been an otherwise virtually unknown Silesian named Johann Sigismund Scholze (1705–1750). Even Spitta, however, could shed no light on the significance of the pseudonym. One is tempted to connect it to the Latin verb *spero*, to hope, but since *spero* is a first-conjugation verb, the form would presumably have to be "Sperantes"—which Spitta noted had indeed been used by another 18th-century writer (p. 189). Could Sperontes, one wonders, possibly have been a Latinization of Greek σπερόντες, meaning those who will beget or produce, or (a longer shot) σπειροντής, the begetter?

In all, 248 settings of 250 poems appeared in the collection's final form. The settings are mostly short, originally instrumental pieces, either marches or one of the then-current dance forms: polonaises, minuets, or murkies. Spitta traced this "parody" use of preexisting instrumental numbers as vocal settings to France, and in particular to a 1695 collection called *Parodies bachiques, sur les Airs et Symphonies des Opera* that employed pieces by Lully and Charpentier, among others (p. 235).

Once again, the influence of Gottsched can perhaps be traced. Spitta very perceptively noticed that one of the buildings shown in the elaborately engraved view of Leipzig on the 1736 title page was Schellhafers Haus (or Saal), a popular meeting place for the university literary societies or clubs, formed under Gottsched's aegis, that would, among their other activities, sing songs like those gathered in *Singende Muse*. Moreover, the Singende Muse was a contemporary Leipzig bookstore—no doubt another meeting place for the same university coteries (pp. 179-180).

The problem with the songs in *Singende Muse* was that many of them, owing to their instrumental origin, were distinctly unvocal. Thus although the collection was immensely popular—as witnessed by the number of reprints and supplements—its real and lasting value did not lie in its intrinsic artistic worth. It lay, rather, in its influence, in the fruitful catalyzing effect it immediately had upon rival composers and editors. For the necessary gap, often so wide as to be ludicrous, that existed between the preexisting instrumental pieces and the texts with which Scholze provided them only compounded, rather than solved, the formal problems raised by the strophic lied. As we saw, Jolizza dryly remarked of the Sperontes songs that "text and melody often have no relation to each other."

In 1737, only a year after the first Sperontes volume, Johann Friedrich Gräfe (1711-1787) published the first of his four collections entitled *Sammlung verschiedener und auserlesener Oden*—the others followed in 1739, 1741, and 1743. An amateur poet and composer, Gräfe made his living as a postal official and court secretary in his native Brunswick, where he belonged to a poetry circle presided over by Gottsched. In the preface to his 1737 collection he makes it very clear that he is publishing in direct reaction to Sperontes. Poetry and music, Gräfe tells us, come from almost the same source, and share a common aim: the imitation of nature and the pleasing of mankind. It is therefore small wonder that these two arts have been closely connected with each other ever since ancient times. In all ages poems have been sung in order to increase the pleasure of listeners. One needs, however, little proof of the bad taste of our own times in this regard: it will be clear to anyone who will recall how often he has heard such wretched yet well-known songs as "Du strenge Flavia" and "Ihr Sternen hört" praised and performed.

Now "Du strenge Flavia" was a familiar song that combined the old "Folies d'Espagne" melody with a text composed in 1695 by Erdmann Neumeister, best known as the author of cantata texts used by J. S. Bach, Telemann, J. P. Krieger, Erlebach, and others. "Ihr Sternen hört" was a piece that the influential critic Friedrich Wilhelm Marpurg (1718-1795) referred to memorably in a scathing review of the Sperontes volumes:[13]

> Anyone who knows the old beaten-to-death [*ausgestäupte*] murky "Ihr Sternen hört," etc. and other songs of the same nature will have an idea of the compositions in this song collection. That piece, which appears here with a new text, is indeed one of the better offerings. . . . We will not pause longer over this rotten collection, which seems to have come forth from a stable boy rather than from the muse.
>
> [I, 162]

The murky was ordinarily a cheerful dance, but "Ihr Sternen hört" had a rather melancholy text, in which the speaker complains about how badly the world has treated him. The combination of the lugubrious, self-pitying poem and the short, skipping melodic phrases and characteristic broken-octave "murky bass" was, quite simply, grotesque. But Scholze made things still worse by printing the tune with a still more bathetic text, in which a man meditates on his fate, ending by specifying what he wants written on his tombstone. *Ton* and *Wort*, indeed!

After stressing the age-old alliance of poetry and music, and mentioning these two hackneyed old songs in which this alliance is shattered, Gräfe continues his preface by conjecturing that the only reason such pieces are still heard and tolerated is that older musicians keep teaching them to their pupils, leaving them in ignorance of "new arias and so-called *galant* pieces." Remarking that it is precisely to remedy this situation that he has prepared the present collection, Gräfe then plays his trump card: "The music that stands above the poems is completely new, and has been written expressly for the poetry."

Each of Gräfe's four volumes consists of 36 songs. In the 1737 volume, 27 of the musical settings are by Gräfe's friend Conrad Friedrich Hurlebusch, seven are by Gräfe himself, and two are by Carl

Heinrich Graun. Gräfe and Hurlebusch divided the settings in the 1739 volume almost equally between them: 17 for the former and 19 for the latter. In the 1741 volume, however, two new composers were introduced: C.P.E. Bach and a mysterious Italian named de Giovannini, whose history and identity are obscure and whose first name remains unknown. Gräfe provided 12 settings, Hurlebusch 15, Graun three, the mysterious de Giovannini six, and Bach—cautiously testing the waters—just one. (The total is 37 because both Hurlebusch and de Giovannini provided settings for the final poem.) For the 1743 volume the roster of composers was very much the same: Gräfe with 18 settings, Hurlebusch with 12, Graun with three, Bach with two, and de Giovannini with one.

The poems in the four collections mostly come from predictable sources. Gottsched, Günther, and Hagedorn are represented, along with such other important "new poets" as Christian Fürchtegott Gellert (1715-1769) and Johann Adolph Schlegel (1721-1793). Gräfe also wrote a number of poems himself, and others were contributed by Christian Gottfried Krause (1719-1770), a prominent Berlin lawyer whose treatise *Von der musikalischen Poesie* (1752) and subsequent song collections, coedited with poet Karl Wilhelm Ramler (1725-1798), were to play an important part in the resuscitation of the strophic lied. It is no surprise also to find a somewhat older "Horatian" poet such as Friedrich Rudolf Ludwig von Canitz (1654-1699), and of course Opitz is represented. But it is surprising to find five poems by the widely castigated Hofmannswaldau.

Gräfe's collection was, by and large, well received. Of the first volume, which he reviewed in 1737, just after its appearance, Mizler wrote:

> Herr Gräfe, in producing this collection, has done a very good thing. He has given many noble souls the opportunity to amuse themselves and also to spend their time usefully.[14]

Mizler then, characteristically, rather fussily pointed out what he took to be errors, most of which concerned a disparity between word-accent and melodic accent.

In No. 64 of *Der critische Musikus*, discussed in Chapter Two in connection with Lindner's treatment of the early critics, Scheibe alludes in passing to Gräfe's collection. That issue of the journal is dated November 17, 1739, and since Gräfe's preface to the second volume of his collection is dated October 20 of that year, Scheibe could only have seen the first (1737) of Gräfe's four volumes when he wrote his piece. In the course of his argument, Scheibe complains about songs in which the melody contains pauses, accentings or repetitions that may work satisfactorily with the first stanza of the poetic text but do not work with the other stanzas. He then adds: "One sees this mistake very often, and even our best collection of German songs is not completely free of it."[15] That Scheibe had Gräfe's first volume in mind is clear from a long footnote that he appended to that sentence when he prepared the whole of his journal for book publication in 1745. "When I wrote this page," the note begins, "Telemann's song collection had not yet appeared; I must therefore supplement that judgment by adding that the best song collection now available is completely free of that fault" (p. 588n.). Telemann and Scheibe had been friends for some time, and the composer had not only encouraged Scheibe to start his journal but had also apparently planned originally to collaborate with him in running it.[16] But Scheibe does not allow his quite justified enthusiasm for Telemann's *Vier und zwanzig, theils ernsthafte, theils scherzende, Oden*, which had appeared in 1741, entirely to cancel his good opinion of Gräfe's collection:

> In no sense do I wish here to deny the merits of the well-beloved Gräfe collection. On the contrary, I am well aware that several songs contained therein have excellent melodies. But, it must be confessed, there are not very many of those.
>
> [P. 588n.]

Many of the Gräfe songs are not suitable for all voices, or are so artfully contrived that the style, lacking the "completely natural and unforced ease" (p. 588n.) of Telemann's songs, fails to suit the words of the text. "Surely," Scheibe concludes, "Gräfe's collection unarguably contains more bad and mediocre melodies than good ones"; and it is inevitable that this should be the case: "has a Hurlebusch," Scheibe asks rhetorically, "ever been the equal of a Telemann?" (p. 589n.).

Finally, there is Marpurg. His comments on Sperontes that were cited earlier come in the course of a sort of omnibus review of song collections, written in 1759, in which he also comments on Gräfe's four volumes as well as on Telemann's *Oden*. From the comfortable distance of almost 20 years Marpurg writes of Gräfe's collection: "because of the many good pieces—compared with the small number of bad ones—that it contains, it will long remain a collection to be treasured" (*Kritische Briefe*, I, 161). But Marpurg agrees with Scheibe, whom he cites, on the general superiority of Telemann's collection, including in the midst of his praise the oft-quoted remark: "It is also in the nature of Herr Telemann's songs that they can be effective even without accompaniment" (I, 163).

But how do the songs in the Gräfe collection look at this still more comfortable distance of more than two-and-a-half centuries? Gräfe was only 22 when he published the first of his four volumes, and he was, it seems obvious, a novice at musical composition. The seven songs he contributed to that volume are, without exception, amateurish and pedestrian—though Scholze, snatching at straws, paid Gräfe the backhanded compliment of lifting one of those seven songs and reprinting it, with a new text, in the 1742 "Erste Fortsetzung" of *Singende Muse an der Pleisse*. One can discern something of Scholze's methods by noting that the opening line of the Günther poem for which Gräfe wrote his melody, No. 27 in the 1737 volume, is "Stürmt, reisst und rast ihr Unglücks-Winde," while the opening line of the poem with which Scholze coupled it to form No. 32 of his 1742 collection is "Ich bin vergnügt mit meinem Stande"! So much for *Ton und Wort*.

A fair example of Gräfe's work is No. 21 in the 1737 volume, set to a poem by an unnamed author whose initials were, apparently, B. N. It is a conventional enough poem in praise of love, and we need consider only the opening stanza:

> Nichts kan schöner als die Liebe
> Und ihr himmlisch Wesen seyn;
> Denn sie schrenkt ja alle Triebe
> In vergnügte Knechtschaft ein.
> Was wir wünschen, was wir wollen,
> Was die Sehnsucht nur begehrt,
> Wird durch ungeweigert Zollen
> Uns beym Lieben auch gewehrt.

Here is Gräfe's setting:

One is immediately thrown off balance by the unexpected shift of accent to the second beat of the opening bar, which throws the emphasis, disconcertingly, on "kan"—a perfect example of the sort of fault Mizler complained about in his reviews. The silly little decorative turn and the sudden, jerky phrase-ending do not help matters; nor does the fact that the dreadful phrase is immediately repeated. We then get the requisite march to the dominant, the deadness of the bass line and the awkward skips in the melody in mm. 13-15 adding to our sense of incompetence busily at work. After the double-bar we get the equally requisite passage to the subdominant. The bass line is evidently designed to suggest pastoral simplicity, but in the absence of any significant correspondence between melody and text it simply falls flat. We then work our way back through a series of turn-skip phrases that echo those just preceding the double-bar, and this poor tired song shows its one faint sign of life: Gräfe picks up that jerky end to the opening phrase, repeated in m. 28 on the word "Zollen," and fashions a series of descending phrases on it, extending the expected last eight bars to 10 as he repeats the words "uns beym Lieben"—for once showing some awareness of what the text is saying.

The worst thing about this song is that it does not have a singable melodic line. Not that it is particularly difficult; it just goes nowhere. And this is characteristic of Gräfe's contributions to the 1737 volume. But his friend and colleague (and perhaps teacher) Hurlebusch is a different matter. Though surely not an important composer, Conrad Gottfried Hurlebusch (c. 1696-1765) was by 1737 quite an experienced one. He had become closely acquainted with Telemann and Mattheson; had worked in Italy and Sweden as well as in several German cities; and had composed instrumental works and operas, as well as cantatas that had won the praise of Mattheson (in *Critica musica*) and would win that of Gottsched (in the later editions of *Versuch einer critischen Dichtkunst*).[17] His first songs, however, were apparently those that he contributed to Gräfe's collection.[18] Though the 27 contained in the 1737 volume are not all of equal interest, they are all considerably beyond the grasp of an amateur such as Gräfe.

Take for example No. 26, "An Phyllis," which is set to a poem of Günther's that is worth looking at in its entirety:

> Ich verschmachte vor Verlangen
> Meine Phyllis zu umfangen,
> Harter Himmel zürnstu noch!
> Faule Stunden, eilet doch.
> Eilet doch ihr faulen Stunden,
> Und erbarmt euch meiner Noth;
> Wird der Riss nicht bald verbunden,
> Blutet sich mein Herze todt.
>
> Liebste Seele! lass dich finden,
> Ich spaziere durch die Linden,
> Durch die Thäler, durch den Hayn,
> In Begleitung süsser Pein;
> Ich durchkrieche Strauch und Höhlen,
> Euch in Wäldern weit und nah
> Die vertraute meiner Seelen;
> Dennoch ist sie nirgends da.
>
> Ich beschwöre selbst die Hirten
> Bey den Heerden, bey den Myrthen,
> Die vielleicht der Liebe Pflicht
> Um die bunten Stöcke flicht:
> Wisst ihr nicht der Phyllis Spuren?

Habt ihr nicht mein Kind erblickt?
Kommt sie nicht mehr auf die Fluren,
Wo wir manchen Strauss gepflückt?

Die ihr alles hört und saget,
Luft und Forst und Meer durchjaget,
Echo, Sonne, Mond und Wind,
Sagt mir doch, wo steckt mein Kind?
Soll sie schon vergöttert werden?
Beth ich sie vielleicht herab,
Oder ziert sie noch die Erden,
O so reis' ich bis ans Grab.

Sage selbst, entrissne Seele!
Welcher Weinberg, welche Höhle,
Welcher unbekannte Wald
Ist anjetzt dein Aufenthalt?
Sage mir, damit ich folge,
Wär es auch des Nilus Strand,
Wär es auch die kalte Wolge,
Zög ich gern durch Eis und Sand.

Weiss mir nichts Bericht zu geben?
O was ist das vor ein Leben,
Das ich jetzo ohne sie
Als mein Joch zur Bahre zieh.
Himmel, lass dir nicht erst fluchen,
Ich begehre sie von dir,
Bin ich nicht ein Thor im Suchen?
Phyllis lebt ja selbst in mir.

 The poem begins conventionally enough, with the speaker's declaration that he is pining away for the lack of his beloved Phyllis, and that the heart in him will die if the rift resulting from her continued absence is not soon healed. The apostrophe to heaven and the passing hours is grandiose but surely not unusual or unexpected in such a context. "Liebste Seele!" begins the second stanza, and one assumes that the speaker is addressing Phyllis, urging her to let herself be discovered in the sense of presenting herself to him. But he quickly becomes far more absorbed in the search itself than in its ostensible object: what begins as an ordinary walk beneath the lime trees is suddenly a far-flung expedition through valleys and groves, involving (almost grotesquely) creeping or crawling through shrubbery and, surprisingly, caverns. One begins to wonder whether the "Liebste Seele" might also perhaps be taken as his own soul—especially in light of the proximity of "Herze" in the line just preceding—and whether he might be commanding it to find itself because he is (unconsciously perhaps) regarding this search as a journey of self-discovery, a search for his own identity. The pain, we notice, is sweet.

 What indeed is the object of the search? I have printed the penultimate line of the poem's second stanza as it appears beneath Hurlebusch's song in Gräfe's 1737 volume: "vertraute" begins with a small *v*. But in the editions of Günther's poems I have consulted the word is "Vertraute"—as one would expect: Phyllis is the one in whom the speaker's soul has confided, his soul's betrothed. If the word ought indeed to have a lowercase *v*, must it not be taken as a verb? Phyllis then becomes she who confided in or trusted his soul, the reciprocity of the relation thus intensifying its intimacy—the intensification being all the more appropriate if indeed there is a hint that "Liebste Seele" is also to be taken as referring to the speaker's own soul.

In the third stanza, the speaker tells of asking the shepherds if they have seen Phyllis, and his search thus seems again more normal, the pastoral machinery and the notion of a community of shepherd-lovers giving his love a social basis and reference. But in the fourth stanza he is off again, addressing not just his fellow shepherds but the sun, moon, and wind. And while the first question he asks them is predictable enough—"Wo steckt mein Kind?"—his second is a surprise: "Soll sie schon vergöttert werden?" If she has indeed been apotheosized, in some way transformed into a divine being, he will pray to her for intercession ("herab"), as one does to a saint. But then the last two lines are more puzzling still: "Oder ziert sie noch die Erden, / O so reis' ich bis ans Grab." The most natural way for her to still be an ornament of earth would of course for her still to be among the living. But the line that follows, declaring that he will journey to the—apparently to *her*—grave, suggests that she might also be an ornament of the earth by being buried in it—one thinks of Wordsworth's Lucy, "Rolled round in earth's diurnal course, / With rocks, and stones, and trees." But then if that's true, might not the grave he will travel to be his own? The German leaves it, I think, ambiguous, and the ambiguity seems obliquely related to the ambiguity of "Liebste Seele," noted in the second stanza.

This earlier ambiguity is immediately reimpressed upon our minds by the opening line of the next stanza: "Sage selbst, entrissne Seele!" Once again: is the soul that has been snatched away from him Phyllis or his own soul? And, as we read on, is the "Aufenthalt," the stopping place, he seeks to know that of Phyllis or that of his own soul on its journey? Just as before, when he expatiates on the lengths to which he is willing to go—to the Nile or the Volga—the point seems to be at least as much the journey itself as its goal or object. And we also notice, once again, the presence of that odd word "Höhle," which, repeated, gives the journey almost a mythic dimension—all epic heroes, after all, must visit the underworld, and that is surely one of the word's implications here.

Finally we reach the concluding stanza. Have you no report to give me?—the speaker asks distractedly. And he then laments the burdensome life he must lead "ohne sie," a life that he will bear like a yoke, all the way to his bier. But who or what is "sie"? The last feminine noun to which the pronoun could reasonably refer is "Seele," in the first line of the preceding stanza. And that word, as we saw, is itself ambiguous. As we continue on to the end of the poem—as the speaker asks whether or not he is, after all, a fool to embark on this quest—the "sie" seems definitely to fasten itself to Phyllis: "Phyllis lebt ja selbst in mir." But then of course to say that Phyllis lives in him is another way of saying that she and his soul are one and the same. Thus the ambiguities that have hovered all the way through are not resolved at the end but are, rather, clarifyingly reaffirmed. Loved one and lover merge, and the journey in search of her is, as we suspected, a journey in search of himself.

What does Hurlebusch do with this quite interesting poem? Here is his setting:

In contrast to the Gräfe setting, where our first response was to be thrown off balance by the awkwardness of the phrasing, here we sense at once its rightness: not only the naturalness of the first two phrases and of the way the second answers the first, but their suitability to the words of the opening stanza. The drop of a fourth and the dying fall of the minor third are perfect for the inward-turning weariness of "Ich verschmachte"; similarly, the more assertive rise of a fourth and the descent of a major third at a higher level capture the assertive overtones of "Verlangen." And as the poetry explains the quality of the "Verlangen," the phrases grow more long-breathed and discursive—though some of the quality of the opening is retained by the echoing descent of a minor third at the beginning of m. 4. (Notice too that the long descending phrase in mm. 2-4 not only encompasses the octave defined by the song's highest and lowest notes so far but also circles back in mid-career to "embrace" its lower sixth—thus neatly catching the sense of "umarmen.")

The notes G-F# are then picked up from the minor-third descent, and ornamentally elaborated with a trill, to form the bridge to a new episode that takes us into the relative major. But although the tonality temporarily brightens, the downward contour of the initial, minor-key phrase is retained, and the D-F#-G opening to the phrase in mm. 6-7 recalls the beginning of the song. Thus we are prepared for the way in which the bass line, as soon as G major has been firmly asserted at the beginning of m. 8, immediately slips back down to D#, returning us to the dominant of E minor. Appropriately enough, this is just the point at which the rather hopeful injunction "Faule Stunden, eilet doch!" is turned round on itself to form the almost despairing plea for compassion: "Eilet doch, ihr faulen Stunden, / Und erbarmt euch meiner Noth!" After the song's opening two phrases are repeated (mm. 8-10), the harmony takes a surprising turn toward B minor. The phrases continue all to head downward, their initial notes sinking from E to D to C.

But Hurlebusch has one final surprise for us: in the antepenultimate bar the vocal line suddenly stands out nakedly, the accompaniment stilled—the first time a phrase has so begun. And instead of proceeding steadily downward, this final phrase jumps up a fourth to high E (the song's highest note) and then resolves stepwise down to low E (its lowest note). The whole compass is thus once again, just as in the long descending phrase in mm. 2-4, summed up. Why should this be so? If we look back at the text of the poem, we notice that in each stanza the last line, the one set by the phrase in question, sums up the content of the preceding seven lines by pushing just a little further dramatically—thus the sudden, dramatic nakedness of the vocal line in m. 14.

Viewed in the context of the first Berlin song movement, this song of Hurlebusch's seems rather old-fashioned, with its tight motivic organization, its air of nobility and high drama, its generally Baroque feel. There is none of the *galant* simplicity and "naturalness," the easy flow, that the Berlin composers usually sought. The bass line, far from retiring into the background along with the rest of the accompaniment, as was to be the rule, stands out in sharp relief, creating an active polyphonic contrast to the vocal line. And of course none of this is surprising. Hurlebusch was born only six years after Bach and Handel, and before he made his debut as a song composer in Gräfe's collections, he had achieved a certain modest reputation as a composer of concertos and suites in the High Baroque style. Bukofzer mentions him, along with Telemann and Graupner and others, as one of the imitators of Vivaldi's solo concertos.[19]

The third main contributor to the Gräfe collections, the mysterious de Giovannini, is also different from the general run of Berlin song composers—but in a quite different way. One can get an idea of his style—and also of what was wrong with the Sperontes songs—by comparing his and Scholze's settings of a poem that is attributed, in the appendix to the last Gräfe collection, to a poet identified only as "K." The poem, entitled "Sinne" in its Gräfe incarnation, is a kind of empiricist's declaration of faith. We need not examine it in detail; a glance at its opening and closing stanzas will do. While the versions of the poem printed in the Sperontes and Gräfe volumes differ considerably, the opening stanzas are, except for minor spelling differences, the same. Here is the Sperontes version:

> Alles, alles hör ich an!
> Es sei Wahrheit oder Lügen;
> Dennoch soll kein falscher Wahn

Meinen freien Sinn betrügen;
Denn ich glaube was ich kann.

The two versions of the final stanza, on the other hand, differ verbally:

Sperontes	Gräfe
Also leb' ich in der Welt.	Also leb ich in der Welt.
Wo ich mit Vernunft belache,	Wo ich mit Vernunft belache,
Was man oft für heilig hält;	Was man oft für heilig hält.
Denn ich prüfe jede Sache,	Denn mein Sinn prüft jede Sache,
Wie sie in die Sinne fällt.	Das verweis ich, das gefällt.

The Scholze setting, presumably taken from a preexisting instrumental piece, is characteristically ungainly:

Aside from the very awkward, unvocal phrases in m. 7, the vocal line is without profile or character, and the harmony is so dull as to be generic—except for that isolated, one-beat lurch into i and bVI^7 in m. 5.

De Giovannini's setting is quite a different matter:

What we see here, plainly, is the influence of Italian opera. De Giovannini has taken this very odd, pseudo-philosophical poem as the occasion to turn out a triumphant, dashing miniature cabaletta. Robust, ebullient, self-assured, and (above all) theatrical, this little song fairly begs to be sung from the stage, in celebration of love or victory in battle. For the first four bars the rush of eighth notes in the bass is nonstop, pausing only as the half-cadence is reached in bar 4. The vocal line begins with an assertive downward move from F to C, then unexpectedly (and exuberantly) jumps up to A to launch its own shower of eighth notes. The movement in tenths over the bass in bar 3, which will be repeated just before the end, is especially satisfying. The contrasting second section in the dominant, beginning in bar 5, is quieter in its melodic movement, and the bass complements this change by alternating quarter notes with its pairs of eighths. But at the words "meinen freyen Sinn" the melody unexpectedly (but most appropriately) leaps up an octave, and the bass once again moves into constant eighths.

The return to the tonic in bar 9 is marked by a stepwise melodic descent, in quarter notes, to the subdominant, which sounds as though it is beginning a new larger section that will play itself out and then be followed by a return to the opening. But no. After two bars de Giovannini echoes the run of tenths between melody and bass heard in bar 3, and in a flash the song is over. What sounded like the beginning of a new section now turns out to have been a decisive summing up, a positive, assertive dramatization of the words "Denn ich glaube, was ich kann." And the dancing eighth notes in the bass at bar 9 enforce the general air of triumph and jubilation.

It would be very strange to hear this little melody repeated, over and over, as the singer toiled through the five remaining stanzas of the dreadful poem, in which the operation of the various sensory faculties is laboriously examined. But de Giovannini, unlike Scholze, has provided a real piece of music—making the best, one feels, of a pretty ungrateful assignment. One can get a still clearer idea of his peculiar quality—and, by contrast, of what was coming to be the predominant north German song style—by seeing what he does with a far more distinguished poem that was also set by several of his contemporaries. The poem is by Hagedorn and is entitled "An den Schlaf"; here it is as it appears in the 1757 edition of Hagedorn's *Sämmelte poetische Werke*:

> Gott der Träume! Freund der Nacht!
> Stifter sanfter Freuden!
> Der den Schäfer glücklich macht,
> Wann ihn Fürsten neiden!
> Holder Morpheus! säume nicht,
> Wann die Ruhe mir gebricht,
> Aug' und Herz zu weiden.
>
> Wann ein Ehmann, voll Verdacht,
> Seine Gattinn quälet,
> Und aus Eifersucht bey Nacht
> Ihre Seufzer zählet,
> Mach im Schlaf sein Unglück wahr;
> Zeig ihm träumend die Gefahr,
> Die ihm wachend fehlet!
>
> Nimm auch itzt was dir gehört;
> Nur erlaub ein Flehen!
> Warte bis mein Glas geleert!
> Wohl! es ist geschehen!
> Komm nunmehr! O komme bald!
> Eil und lass mich die Gestalt
> Meiner Phyllis sehen!

Plainly, some commentary is called for before we go on to look at de Giovannini's setting.

One would expect a poem with this title, that begins as this one does, to be a dignified, celebratory catalogue of those gentle joys of which sleep is proclaimed the begetter. But Hagedorn immediately begins to play with the convention established (or at least suggested) by his opening two lines. The notion of the careworn prince envying the happy shepherd is of course familiar to us from centuries of pastoral poetry. But usually the stress falls on the shepherd's happiness rather than on the prince's envy. Not so here: the unexpectedly harsh word "neiden" cuts like a knife at the end of line 4. Moreover, "Wann" is an odd word with which to make the logical connection between the shepherd's happiness and the prince's envy. The shepherd, it appears, is happy when—and therefore because—the prince envies him, not because his shepherd's life is intrinsically happier than that of the prince. There is thus something just a little nasty in the shepherd's happiness. Stranger still, that happiness comes to the shepherd only in dreams: it seems not to be a feature of his everyday waking life. Without sleep, and the dreams sleep brings, he would, so far as we know, have no happiness. There is even, perhaps, the subversively witty suggestion that the shepherd has been reading a little pastoral poetry, and that his reading is the source of his glorious dreams. (One thinks of the modern tabloid press, which does a very good business by telling the poor how unhappy the rich and famous really are!)

In the stanza's last two lines, however, Hagedorn reverts (apparently) to the conventional stance of the opening. He prays, very formally, to Morpheus, asking that when he lacks rest the god not delay in feeding or nourishing his eye and heart. But the word "weiden" seems an odd one here. It can mean to feed, but normally means to feed a flock, to lead to pasture ("Weide"), and if used as a reflexive verb it means to feast one's eyes on, or to gloat. So the formal plea to Morpheus also turns a little odd at the end. The speaker is asking not just for rest and comfort but for a full belly, such as a grazing animal would crave—and of course the pastoral overtones of "weiden"/"Weide" throw our attention back to the shepherd of the earlier lines.

The subversion of pastoral convention and of the convention of poems to sleep that was initiated in the first stanza is carried further in the second. A new character, by implication parallel to the shepherd, is introduced: a married man who is filled with suspicion. Were this a conventional poem to sleep—gentle sleep, downy sleep, innocent sleep, sleep that knits up the raveled sleave of care—we should expect to hear next that a good night's sleep will lay his suspicion to rest. But after giving a vivid picture of how the man's suspicion leads him to torture his wife—with questions, presumably—by day, and by night to lie awake counting her sighs, in the hope that she will talk in her sleep and betray herself, the speaker once again prays to Morpheus, god of dreams. And this time his prayer is that the jealous husband's worst fears be realized, rather than allayed, by his dreams, that dreaming he may be forced to confront the terrible reality that haunts his thoughts but eludes him in waking life.

So the jealous husband is both like and unlike the shepherd of the first stanza. His jealousy ("Eifersucht") reminds us of the princes who envy ("neiden") the shepherd—or at least who do so in the shepherd's dreams—and the unsatisfactory waking life that is only implied in the shepherd's case (by comparison with his dream life) is made real in the case of the jealous husband. But while the shepherd obtains some relief—slightly tainted though it may be by the fact that it arises out of the perhaps imagined envy he awakens in others—it seems that the husband obtains no relief at all. Or does he? Is there perhaps a suggestion in the word "fehlet" (which answers to "gebricht" in the first stanza) that to encounter in dreams something that we fear in real life but do not encounter there is to have a lack supplied, is to gain a perverse sort of relief after all?

Finally, in the third and final stanza, the speaker turns directly to his own case. Take what belongs to you, he says to sleep—it is most interesting that he does not ask to be given rest or relief or indeed anything. But (he adds) just grant me this one plea: wait until I've emptied my glass! Suddenly strong drink seems to have entered the picture—though this is obviously no more a conventional Anacreontic lyric than it is a conventional poem to sleep or a conventional pastoral poem. He empties the glass instantly, and the urgency of his plea to sleep is stepped up: come now! come soon! hurry! Hurry and let me see my Phyllis—the conventional pastoral name once more reaches back to the opening stanza.

But what will this dream of Phyllis be like? The speaker is, we recall, not asking to be given something but rather telling sleep—with an air, almost, of angry resignation—to take what belongs to it, to take something from him rather than giving something to him. In the preceding two stanzas the poem has established—implicitly in the first stanza, explicitly in the second—a relation between the dreaming and the waking lives of the person under consideration. What is that relation here? When a poetic lover asks to dream of his beloved, he usually does so in joyous anticipation of some future time when he will actually be with her. But here there has been no talk of such a coming occasion—nor, for that matter, has there been any mention of Phyllis or even of love. The emotion that has increasingly occupied the speaker's attention is not love but jealousy. The reader is, in fact, surprised to find any mention of a lover coming into the poem at all—and especially to find it coming at the poem's climax.

Certainly we cannot read the ending, in the light of all that has come before, as a conventional lover's plea to dream of his beloved. But Hagedorn does not explicitly tell us how else to read it. Like his two principal poetic masters, Horace and Pope, Hagedorn is a complex and subtly ironic poet, fond of ironies created by juxtaposition rather than stated baldly. If we have read the poem attentively, and followed the speaker's thoughts as he works himself up to his final, almost despairing plea to see Phyllis (or at least her "Gestalt") in his dreams, we cannot fail to be troubled by the course those thoughts have followed. Why should he have approached his desire to dream of Phyllis by way of the shepherd who wants to be envied and the husband filled with (presumably groundless) suspicions of his wife? And why is he so insistent that his glass be drained before sleep visits him? Are we to feel that his dream of Phyllis will be altogether different—more pleasing, innocent, conventionally romantic—than those of the shepherd and the jealous husband, that it will enable him to transcend the rather unpleasant thoughts that have been building in his mind? Or are we to feel that he consciously or unconsciously knows that his dreams of Phyllis will be rather like those of the other dreamers? I don't think we can choose. Perhaps the most we can say is that Hagedorn has skillfully played upon the various poetic conventions alluded to in the poem in order to plant this rather disturbing ambiguity in our minds.

This poem was a popular one with the song composers. It appeared in Hagedorn's *Oden und Lieder* in 1740, and the next year received two settings, one from de Giovannini in the third volume of Gräfe's collection and the other from Telemann in his *Vier und zwanzig, theils ernsthafte, theils scherzende, Oden*. Let us look first at de Giovannini's setting:

As in the song of de Giovannini's that we looked at earlier, here too we feel the strong influence of Italian opera. Once again we have a song that is, in spite of its presumably slower tempo, robust, self-assured, theatrical. We see that influence first in the way the vocal line, complete with roulade and grace notes, boldly asserts itself before the accompaniment enters. Then, after the opening invocation, the line, still more boldly, rises in concert with the bass line. The fact that the next phrase, like the first one, begins on D makes us expect a reprise. But instead the rhythm and melodic contour are smoothed out to produce a gracefully curving phrase—sung a little softer, one would hope—that nicely dramatizes the words "Stifter sanfter Freuden." Only then do we get the repeat of the opening phrase—a fourth lower as we move into the dominant.

The fact that the phrase begins lower than the first one makes the wholly appropriate upward leap on "glücklich macht" a pleasant surprise. And one is also pleased (and surprised) by the way the echo at the beginning of m. 4 of the phrase at the beginning of m. 2 has a wholly different effect from its predecessor: the two assertive high A's that precede it—the highest notes in the song—and the trill that follows it give the phrase a triumphant air that perfectly suits those "Fürsten" who are said to envy the shepherd.

At this point we begin what sounds like the middle section of the song. The bass line steadies itself on low D, and the melody—except for the fine little burst of urgency on the upward arpeggio that sets the word "Säume"—traces a series of graceful downward-dropping phrases whose first notes gradually ascend (from C to D to E) in order to prepare us for the final surprise. Instead of having this section become a middle strain that will take us back to the beginning, de Giovannini cuts the Gordian knot by suddenly taking us back, at the end of m. 6, to the little upward rise in the middle of m. 1, and from there speedily to the end. There are other nice details to notice: the languorous, almost Richard Straussian move from D# to E over a C chord in m. 6 on the word "Ruhe"; and the touch of spice provided by the lombard rhythm (or Scotch snap) that begins the final bar.

So once again de Giovannini offers us a very well-turned little piece. What's missing, of course, is any hint of the darker, stranger meanings that become more pronounced in the second stanza of the poem but are beginning to be felt even in the first. The joyous little grace-noted trill on the word "neiden" has no relevance whatever to the word's meaning—de Giovannini is still thinking of those "Fürsten"! And one imagines that the song's triumphant air of high drama would grow less relevant to the text as it went on. Telemann's much better-known setting gives us more of the meaning of the poetic text:

What one notices first about this setting—especially coming to it from de Giovannini's—are the minor key and the restlessly moving bass line. The word "Trollend," which Telemann has chosen to express the tempo and expression he had in mind, is an odd one. Most modern dictionaries give meanings for the verb *trollen* that are confusing because they seem to contradict one another: to roll about, to loll, to trip, with "trolle dich!" meaning "be off!" Is the movement in question, one wants to know, slow (lolling) or fast (tripping)? The word, Kluge's *Etymologisches Wörterbuch der deutschen Sprache* tells us, is of uncertain origin, possibly related to *treppen*. It was apparently more common in Middle High German, and Kluge follows Lexer's *Mittelhochdeutsches Wörterbuch* in giving the basic meaning as to move in short steps—the speed now evidently not being the point at all. And so we can see how it applies to Telemann's restless bass line. His aim in using the term was perhaps merely to stress that the motion of the bass line must continue to be felt throughout, which would suggest a medium tempo, neither so fast as to obscure the motion nor so slow as to make us lose track of its direction.

As for the minor key, Telemann's choice of it suggests at once that he may be more in tune with the meanings that de Giovannini skirted. Of course there is the change, at the double bar, into the relative major, but the song ends as it began, in the minor. Kretzschmar tried to relate the song to Hagedorn's poem, and his comment is worth examining in some detail:

> The music approaches sleep with the air of a tired old man. But at the words "Holder Morpheus" the F minor changes to a bright A-flat major, becoming extraordinarily beautiful, hopeful, and grateful. One notes also that in this piece Telemann sharply criticized his poet, Hagedorn, who after the prayerful first stanza descended into frivolity ("Wann ein Ehmann voll Verdacht," etc.), by setting only the poem's first stanza to music.[20]

His remark about the music moving with the step of a tired old man suggests that Kretzschmar is assuming that Telemann wanted a slower tempo than we determined a moment ago. He approves the move to the major—but only, apparently, because of the words "Holder Morpheus": he does not comment either on the remaining words of the prayer or on the return to the minor. Kretzschmar seems to intend his words "extraordinarily beautiful, hopeful, thankful" to apply to the whole last half of the song. Therefore he views the song's change at midpoint from geriatric weariness to hope and thankfulness as Telemann's implicit criticism of Hagedorn's poem, whose second stanza he sees as falling off disastrously into mere frivolity after the prayerfulness of the opening stanza. Kretzschmar, in other words, sees no connection whatever between the poem's first and second stanzas, and since Telemann's setting works well with his conception of the first stanza's meaning but (or therefore) not with that of the second stanza, he assumes further that Telemann decided, as a conscious criticism of the poem, to set only the first stanza—even though all three were printed with his setting.

As will by now be clear, I think Kretzschmar is very much mistaken about Hagedorn's poem; and I think he is no less mistaken about Telemann's song. If the song is taken at the proper tempo, the almost constant bass motion expresses not weariness but just the sort of restless, disturbed energy appropriate, in different degrees, to all three stanzas of the poem. The motion, we notice, continues into the major-key section of the song, providing a continuity of feeling with what has come before. And when it does, rather dramatically, cease for a moment, it is to bring us back to the minor key of the opening—as well as to a renewal of motion. And in all three stanzas the line that is set by that break in the bass motion is suitably urgent: "Wann die Ruhe mir gebricht," "Zeig ihm träumend die Gefahr," "Eil und lass mich die Gestalt." It seems to me that Telemann has succeeded quite well in creating a setting that could, with appropriate slight variations by both singer and accompanist, be made to fit very well with all three stanzas of Hagedorn's poem.

Let us look more closely at the shape of the melodic line and its relation to the bass line. The first phrase describes a decorated descent from the fifth to the tonic, with a still more elaborately decorated descent from the tenth to the tonic beneath it in the bass. The second phrase, which takes us to a cadence on the dominant, seems almost to tread water, being caught up in the three scale steps between the fifth and the tonic, and ending indecisively on the second as the bass line seems to ask a question. As the song is performed, these two phrases are of course repeated each time. The beginning of the next phrase is curiously similar to the opening phrase—considering that it ushers in a new key and mode—but it too, like the second phrase, has an indecisive, water-treading feel to it, despite the fact that it takes us back to the keynote of the new tonic. Then come the short, broken phrases under which the bass ceases its motion.

This is the most dramatic moment in a song that, despite its shift from minor to major and back again, generally keeps quite an even tenor owing to the constancy of the bass motion. The harmony centers on Bb minor, which is to be the pivot chord in the modulation back to the minor: ii in Ab, iv in F minor. I have seen modern "realized" versions of this song in which the keyboard's right hand continues to play harmonies in concert with the vocal line right through these bars. But that seems to me a grave mistake. Surely the vocal line (perhaps reinforced by the keyboardist but not harmonized) should suddenly stand forth alone here, the harmonies coming only when the bass line calls for them. I have noticed that in playing this song I am always strongly tempted to render the melody at this point thus:

This of course makes for symmetry but also for a certain banality. As Telemann ends it, the little rise to Db at the end gives the effect of asking a question. The result is a slight increase in dramatic urgency, which is reinforced a moment later as the Bb-C-Db phrase is echoed in the bass. The melody then falls into a repetition of the end of the song's first phrase, completing the circle.

One more thing remains to be said about this excellent song. Why has Telemann barred it as he has? Surely it would have been easier and more "natural" to begin at the beginning of a bar rather than making the first two beats pickup notes. When we take the slightly "off" barring in the context of the virtually constant bass motion and the effect that the song gives of circling back, at the end, to its own beginning, I think we can see what Telemann was driving at. Viewed thus, the constant tension between the way the ear partitions off the phrases and the way they are organized for the eye on the page can be seen as contributing to the general impression of seamlessness, cyclical movement, a lack of distinct beginnings and endings. And this, surely, is one of the effects of Hagedorn's poem, as it moves, in its dreamlike, free associational way, from the shepherd to the jealous husband to the speaker himself.

In 1742, the year after Telemann's *Oden* appeared, his young associate Johann Valentin Görner published the first of his three volumes entitled *Sammlung neuer Oden und Lieder*. The other two volumes appeared in 1744 and 1752. In all there were 70 songs, all set to poems by Hagedorn. The 1744 volume contained Görner's setting of "An den Schlaf":

This has usually been thought to be something of an improvement on Telemann's setting. Friedlaender[21] refused to take sides. Having praised Telemann's setting, "with its fine melody and splendid bass line," he later praised Görner's, "with its noble, highly emotional melody, suggestive of Gluck," and went on to observe, somewhat enigmatically: "The comparison with Telemann's very differently conceived yet equally good setting of the same poem . . . is not without interest" (I/i, 82, 99). Kretzschmar, as we saw, liked Telemann's setting—though for rather odd reasons. Of Görner's he had this to say:

> Here Görner competes most effectively with Telemann, setting against the latter's serious, melancholy understanding of the text his own youthfully sociable, beautiful dreams. With magnificent urgency and intimacy Görner sings the plea in the second part: "Holder Morpheus! säume nicht," etc.
>
> [P. 223]

Though Kretzschmar does not expressly choose one setting over the other, the eloquence of his language here suggests that he prefers Görner's.

In 1917, six years after Kretzschmar's book appeared, the Telemann and Görner collections were edited for the series *Denkmäler deutscher Tonkunst* by Wilhelm Krabbe. In his introduction, Krabbe cites Friedlaender's remark that Telemann's melodies are often more instrumental than vocal. Friedlaender had implicitly regarded "An den Schlaf" as an exception to this generalization; Krabbe does so explicitly, praising "the charm of expressive song" that it exhibits and calling it "Telemann's best piece." But he nonetheless prefers Görner's setting of Hagedorn's poem. In fact, he prefers Görner generally as a song composer: "In sharp contrast to those of Telemann, Görner's melodies are vocally conceived throughout, and fully effective by themselves alone, even without accompaniment." Of the two settings of "An den Schlaf" Krabbe writes:

> For Hagedorn's poem "An den Schlaf" Telemann, as we have already seen, provided a most happy setting. Of Görner's composition one may confidently say that he has succeeded in surpassing Telemann. His comprehension of this text, especially beloved of musicians, stands in direct opposition to that of Telemann, against whose serious, melancholy, prayerful tune Görner sets a wonderfully tender song, which, even in its choice of key—B major—sets itself apart from the other pieces. The declamation, beautiful and expressive right from the beginning, becomes more intense at the words "Holder Morpheus, säume nicht." The plea grows ever more urgent, and in the final bars the melody assumes an irresistible warmth and intimacy. This example shows how superior Görner is to Telemann as a melodist; in the movement of his bass line, however, he is far surpassed by the older master.[22]

As opposed to Telemann's seriousness, Görner offers tenderness and beauty, "beautiful and expressive declamation," "warmth and intimacy." Krabbe seems to be assuming unquestioningly, and without a close look at the text, that these latter qualities will naturally be appropriate to a poem by Hagedorn, whose affection for Horace quickly got him pigeonholed as the cheerful, life-loving celebrant of comfort, wine, and good society—a categorization, one might add, almost as unfair to him as to his master.

In later writers this view of the two settings has taken on an added historical implication. In 1962 Lothar Hoffmann-Erbrecht compared them thus: "While Telemann's angular bass line, like the whole direction of his song, is indebted to the *Hochbarock*, Görner solves this problem with a simplified bass line of steadily repeated notes, chooses a smooth high major key, and allows the simple melody to flow gently along."[23] Telemann's setting is now not merely inappropriately serious but also inappropriately old-fashioned, a relic of the *Hochbarock*. Hagedorn demands rather the new simplicity, suppleness, and gentleness of the *galant* style—which is, indeed, the subject of Hoffmann-Erbrecht's essay. Sixteen years later, Lukas Richter, writing on Telemann's Hagedorn songs, cited Hoffmann-Erbrecht with approval. Richter, however, realizes that Hagedorn's poem is itself very serious, and he appreciates the expressive adequacy of Telemann's setting: "The composer set the fifth poem, 'An den Schlaf,' the only one of Hagedorn's serious lyrics in the collection, with such sureness of hand that the melodic garment clings to the body of the text as closely as a skin." But Richter's main interest is in seeing both Hagedorn and Telemann as pointing forward to the folksong revival later in the century. Görner thus becomes a more "advanced" figure than Telemann in the struggle to unify *Ton* and *Wort*: "Görner's compositions successfully carry forward Telemann's stylistic impulses, with a perhaps still closer relation between *Wort* and *Ton*, and with a more obvious inclination toward a pronounced homophony."[24] Finally, J. W. Smeed, writing in 1987, sees Telemann's setting as "stylistically very close to the chorale settings with figured bass included by [Johann Ludwig] Krebs in his *Klavierübung* of the same decade," and thus as evidence of a conservative tendency. Görner, on the other hand, is for Smeed "one of the liveliest and most individual of the early song-composers."[25]

I have cited the commentary on these two settings of Hagedorn's poem at length because it tells us something interesting and important. In Chapter Two, reviewing the accounts of the *liederlose Zeit* given by historians of the lied, we had ample opportunity to witness the powerful influence on 19th-century historical writing of Darwinian, "progressivist" ideas, and at one point I mentioned Sir Herbert Butterfield's *The Whig Interpretation of History*. One area of historical writing in which this progressivist view has stubbornly retained its hold is the writing about the arts in the 18th century. In a splendid, but unfortunately little-known, essay of over 20 years ago, "The 'Whig Interpretation' of Literary History," Henry Knight Miller made this case in regard to histories of 18th-century English literature. Butterfield had said that the Whig historian's goal, whether conscious or not, is "to produce a story which is the ratification if not the glorification of the present."[26] Miller argued that because the history of English literature only began seriously to be written in the mid-19th century, in the afterglow of the Romantic movement, "one local and present instance of a general phenomenon was elevated into the very archetype and model of all changes in literary taste." In other words, the present that the whig historian of English literature sought to ratify became (and has, until recently, remained) Romanticism. The 18th century thus became, in Miller's words, a "necessary negative type, or antithesis. Without it, the governing theme of nineteenth-century literary historiography—an inevitable progress through the ages toward the culmination of all values in its own age—was incomplete, made no dramatic sense."[27] Summing up all that seemed valuable to him in the neoclassical period, Saintsbury memorably wrote: "The port was the Fair Haven of Romanticism."[28]

Now of course this sort of crude teleological view of the 18th century could never be held generally of German and Austrian 18th-century music. The century of Bach, Handel, Haydn, and Mozart could not be dispatched so handily as the century of Pope, Thomson, Gray, and Johnson. Yet D. F. Tovey's essays prove how much work needed to be done, in the first half of the 20th century, to defeat the standard Victorian views of "Papa" Haydn and of Mozart, "delicate . . . child of the dying rococo age."[29] And when we approach a genre like that of the lied, which was not much cultivated by the Classical composers, and thus had to wait until the Romantic period for its full flowering, we encounter a good deal of whig history.

As we have seen, all the commentators cited above tended to view Görner's setting of "An den Schlaf" as more modern, more in line with the developmental course along which the 18th-century lied would evolve into the Romantic lied, than Telemann's. Only Richter gave a clear indication of realizing that the rather old-fashioned-looking bass line of Telemann's setting was there for an expressive purpose peculiar to this particular poem of Hagedorn's, and even Richter was primarily interested in seeing the two settings in relation to the approaching folksong revival. I think it is fair to say that the commentators all tended, to varying degrees, to prefer the Görner setting because of its undeniably later, more clearly *galant* stamp.

This seems to me clearly a mistake. Looking finally at Görner's setting, one is struck first by his expressive direction: "Sanft." And this word, perhaps suggested by the line "Stifter sanfter Freuden," perfectly describes the air of the song, from start to finish. The modest little melody, with its gently pulsating bass beneath, creates precisely the "prayerful" atmosphere that some of the commentators approvingly noted. Everything is handsome and orderly: the neat cadence described by the first two bars, the tasteful grace note, the downward march of melody and bass, a thirteenth apart, that begins the move to the cadence on V that ends the song's first section. The sudden upward jump of the melody and the promise of a move to the subdominant that open the song's second section suggest that things will become somewhat more dramatic—and this suggestion is followed up by the urgent little phrase in m. 6. It appears for a moment as though this phrase will be repeated a step higher in the bar that follows, increasing the dramatic pressure—but no. Instead Görner prettily varies the phrase-ending, instantly quelling any sense of drama and returning us to the unruffled surface of the opening. To paraphrase Dr. Johnson on *Lycidas*, where there is leisure for variation, there is little dramatic urgency. When the original phrase is in fact repeated at a step higher than it was first heard, in the next bar, it is too late: another downward march in the bass, carrying us to the final cadence, is already under way.

So all the words used by the commentators to describe Görner's setting apply perfectly: it is indeed beautiful, expressive, warm, inward, a lovely dream. The problem is that the poem it is supposed to be setting is, as we have seen, quite different. How will this music go with the stanza about the jealous husband? How will its sustained air of gentle reverie handle the poem's rather unpleasant ironies? Telemann has allowed for these by lending an air of mild disturbance to his song—mainly, as we saw, through the movement of the bass line.

It is, however, of some importance to make clear that this sort of old-fashioned bass writing, suggestive of the *Hochbarock*, is quite untypical of the 1741 collection of *Oden*. In employing it Telemann was not following the unanswerable dictates of his position as a composer caught between the *Hochbarock* and *galant* eras; he was, rather, making an intelligent compositional choice suggested by the nature of Hagedorn's poem. It is true, as Karen Zauft has pointed out, that Telemann's bass lines in the *Oden* are more complex, more interesting, and more frequently imitative of the melody than in his earlier songs, but it is also true that this development is not to be seen as a throwback to the *Hochbarock* but rather as the result of a heightened sensitivity to expressive possibilities:

> Here the common function of melody and accompaniment, to aid in the interpretation of the text, is still more clearly expressed. New expressive elements in the poem are brought to light in the accompaniment, and new relations between bass and melody are created.[30]

Telemann dedicated his collection of *Oden* to Scheibe, and in his dedicatory note he makes clear that he has tried to follow Scheibe's dictum that "the melody of a song must be free, flowing, pure, and completely natural." Though he modestly doubts whether he has yet learned "the art of writing in a low style" that he deems necessary for successful song composition, Telemann nonetheless makes it clear that he prefers a simply set song to the artful, drawn-out melisma, the "ha-ha-ha, he-he-he" of the opera singers. Taking a hit at the Sperontes and Gräfe collections, and perhaps also at Mizler's ill-starred 1740 *Sammlung auserlesener moralischer Oden*, Telemann insists that at least his own songs can be sung by all voices "since they travel neither as high as the wren nor as low as the bittern, but take the middle way."

The prefaces to Görner's 1742 and 1744 collections are not by him but rather by Hagedorn, who used them, along with a few additional paragraphs, to introduce the 1747 edition of his own *Oden und Lieder*.[31] The former preface is a lengthy essay on the folksong and folk poetry, in which words like *frey* and *natürlich* frequently pop up, just as they do in Scheibe and other contemporary writers on the lied. (Interestingly, about half of this essay is a translation by Hagedorn, who had spent some years in England, of No. 16 of *The Guardian*, which was published on Monday, March 30, 1713, and though ascribed to Steele, may have been written by Ambrose Philips, known as "Namby Pamby" for the affected simplicity of his pastorals.) In the brief 1752 preface, which apparently is by Görner, he sums up his goal in song composition thus: "In my melodies my aim has been to be pleasing, charming, witty, playful, amorous, and gay."

Now the concept of naturalness, as applied to songs, can have a number of meanings. For both Telemann and Görner a song that is natural (or *natürlich*) is one that is easily singable, vocal rather than instrumental in layout, and of limited compass. But for Görner naturalness in the desirable sense seems also to be necessarily associated with the particular qualities that he tells us in his 1752 preface he has striven for in his melodies. I do not think this is true for Telemann. Otherwise he could not have written so deliberately uncharming, undelightful, unlovable a song as his "An den Schlaf." Görner's "An den Schlaf," on the other hand, is charming, delightful, lovable. The problem of course is that the poem it purports to be setting is none of these things—or, at least, is none of them consistently or without irony.

Aside from being singable, vocal, and so on, a song can also be natural in the sense of perfectly suiting or fitting the poem that it sets—so that "the melodic garment clings to the body of the text as closely as a skin," as Richter nicely puts it. In this sense of the term, Telemann's setting is natural while Görner's is not. Kretzschmar felt that Telemann had—and in Kretzschmar's view quite justifiably—attended only to the opening stanza of Hagedorn's poem; but this accusation might more fairly be leveled against Görner. Despite the special, individual gift that made him able to produce charming, skillfully made songs like "An den Schlaf," we can see in his work that the idea that songs should be simple, natural, and flowing is beginning to harden into a mannerism. Charm and delight are all well and good, but only as means to an end: the expressive end of fitting the music of the song to the words of the poem. If charm and delight become ends in themselves, as they often did for Görner, they lead not to the cherished union of *Ton* and *Wort* but rather to its opposite.

To get a still clearer idea of what was to become the stereotyped manner of the songs produced by the first Berlin song movement, let us look quickly at one more setting of Hagedorn's "An den Schlaf." This one was written by an unknown composer, and it is contained in the second of the four volumes entitled *Lieder der Deutschen mit Melodien* that Karl Wilhelm Ramler and Christian Gottfried Krause published at Berlin in 1767 and 1768:

An den Schlaf.

Gott der Träume, Kind der Nacht,
Das, mit Mohn in Händen,
Gaukelnde Gestalten macht,
Sterbliche zu blenden,
Laß den kargen Lykabas
Diese Nacht ein ganzes Faß
Theuren Wein verschwenden.

　Wenn Ursindo, voll Verdacht,
Seine Gattin quälet,
Und aus Eifersucht bey Nacht
Ihre Seufzer zählet:

Mach im Schlaf sein Unglück wahr!
Zeig ihm träumend die Gefahr,
Die ihm wachend fehlet.

　Schlaf, den ich zu lang' entbehrt,
Höre jetzt mein Flehen: —
Warte, bis mein Glas geleert: —
Wohl! es ist geschehen.
Komm nunmehr, o komme bald!
Eil, und laß mich die Gestalt
Meiner Phyllis sehen.

I have printed the poem just as it appears in the Ramler-Krause collection, in order to call attention to the verbal changes in the text—changes that were, according to Friedlaender (II, 18), made by Ramler.

Clearly, this setting owes something to de Giovannini's. The lombard rhythm (or Scotch snap) that de Giovannini introduces, with admirable tact and restraint, just once, at the very end of his song, is everywhere to be found in this one. Also, the little three-note rising phrase that consisted, in de Giovannini's setting, of a dotted sixteenth followed by a thirty-second and a sixteenth, appears here three times as a dotted eighth, a sixteenth, and an eighth. Friedlaender too saw a relation between the two settings. "Giovannini's composition is a good example of the *galant* style," he wrote, "which is grotesquely distorted in the anonymous song of 1767" (II, 18). Without agreeing that de Giovannini's song is particularly *galant* in style, we can nonetheless join Friedlaender in seeing the one under consideration as a kind of caricature of it.

For this song has none of the drama, the theatrical high style that we noted in de Giovannini's. Repeated insistently, the Scotch snaps become an annoying, pert little mannerism, as does the briskly changing harmony, with its patly stereotyped bass line. As for the melodic line, it is nothing but a decorated descent from E to A, followed by one from F# to B, both of which are then repeated. This constitutes two thirds of the song. And it is just at this point, in m. 16, that things get even worse. Suddenly, in what feels like a desperate lurch toward variety, the melodic line takes off in pairs of rising sixteenth notes. I am at a loss to know what to make of the direction "Starkwünschend" that stands at the head of the song. Does it connote dramatic urgency (which would dictate a quick tempo) or intense steadfastness of purpose (which would dictate one rather slower)? In either case, it seems to me, the sixteenth notes will fall flat. They come out of nowhere, have no discernible relation to the content of the poetic text, and will be awkward to sing clearly. At a fast tempo they will sound rushed; at a more moderate one, labored. The little arpeggio with which each run ends, carefully outlining the harmony, seems fussy. Finally, for the last four bars, we return to material heard earlier: the Scotch snaps and a version of the three-note rising phrase.

So this is, musically, a very feeble effort indeed. What about its general relation to Hagedorn's text? As I noted earlier, what we are dealing with this time is not, strictly speaking, Hagedorn's text but rather Ramler's reworking of it. Except for its first three words, the first stanza is entirely different from Hagedorn's original. Morpheus, who is not addressed by name later in the stanza, is now only the child, not the friend, of night. The image of him holding in his hands the soporiferous poppy that creates the deceptive shapes of which dreams are made—perhaps by casting shadows on a wall when artfully manipulated by the god?—is a nice one, but seems to have been imported from somewhere else since it has little to do with the context here. "Sterbliche" functions effectively as a contrast to "Gott," however. Lykabas is probably a Germanization of Λυκώπας, the name of a character mentioned just once in passing by Theocritus (V, 62). There he is an uncharacterized cowherd whose name means bright-eyed (λεύκος + ὤψ, presumably formed on analogy with such Homeric epithets as βοῶπις/ox-eyed); here he is a miser upon whom the speaker wishes the ill fate that a whole cask of his expensive wine may vanish in a night.

The second stanza, by contrast, is almost exactly the same as Hagedorn's. The only change is that the name Ursindo is substituted for the generalizing descriptive phrase "ein Ehmann." The aim is surely to gain vividness and particularity. And of course this was part of the point in introducing Lykabas too—though one suspects that Ramler was mainly interested in avoiding the troubling questions raised by having the first stanza turn to focus on the speaker. Presumably Ramler got Ursindo from Calderón's popular comedy *Peor Está Que Estaba*, in which César Ursino, the main character, is not a jealous husband but rather a man who keeps postponing his marriage in order to carry on an affair with a mysterious veiled lady. The name, however, has the proper south European tang of comic intrigue and sexual machinations. Ramler probably added the *d* to make it clear to German-speakers that the accent was to go on the second rather than the first syllable.

The only change in the last stanza is the first line: Hagedorn's "Nimm auch itzt, was dir gehört" has become "Schlaf, den ich so lang' entbehrt." Though it is small, this change is characteristic. At every turn, Ramler has got rid of details that contributed to the complex and problematic ironies of the original poem. The shepherd, together with his implied relation to the speaker, has vanished from the first stanza; the use of the name "Ursindo" in the second stanza, in place of the generic "ein Ehmann," similarly prevents us from seeking to draw a relation between speaker and spoken about; and here in the final stanza we have lost Hagedorn's provocative suggestion that sleep, in coming to the speaker, is not so much giving him something as taking what rightfully belongs to it. Once again, recalling the mindless cheeriness of the anonymous setting, we also recall how Telemann strove to catch, in his setting, just those troubling ironies that have now disappeared from the text.

This comparison of four settings of Hagedorn's "An den Schlaf" demonstrates very clearly, I think, the transitional nature of the period that German historians of the lied refer to as the *Aufschwung*. De Giovannini, Telemann, and Görner are all, in their different ways, interesting individual song composers. And the great differences among their settings of this one poem show how many choices were open to the song composers during the *Aufschwung* years, how many compositional styles were available. Though only three years separate their two songs, it is a long jump from de Giovannini's stylish theatricality to Görner's rather cozy intimacy. Though the latter, rather than the former, was closer to what the song composers of the 1750s, 1760s, and 1770s were striving for, more often they ended up in the faceless, impersonally perky mode of the anonymous setting just examined.

If the *Aufschwung* may be said to have begun in 1736, with the first Sperontes volume, it may be said to have ended 17 years later, with the appearance of the first Ramler-Krause collection, the *Oden mit Melodien* of 1753. For this collection, which was published at Berlin, is usually said to have been the one that established the first Berlin song movement as a cultural fact. It was better than many of its successors, and there is no song in it so dreary as the anonymous 1767 setting of "An den Schlaf." Nor is there any song as haphazardly assembled as most of Gräfe's or as directly indebted to operatic tradition as de Giovannini's. The aim is clearly to create a brand of simple, singable, directly affecting *Hausmusik* that will meet the needs of the rapidly expanding population of musical amateurs.

The preface to the collection, apparently Ramler's work, has often been called the "manifesto" of the first Berlin song school. It is hardly that, but it is nonetheless a most interesting document. After the usual opening formalities, Ramler goes directly to the matter of the textual changes made in the poems that appear in the volume. The poets, he tells us, are famous enough so that they will not mind, and besides, they have written more beautiful poems than those assembled here. Of these more beautiful, unused poems Ramler writes:

> But they could not be used because they are too rich in images for music, and have too many complicated jokes and too much elegant moral instruction to be clearly expressed in musical sound. Musical sounds [*Töne*] are the language of the emotions. With them we can characterize quite clearly a particular degree of joy or sadness, of anger or mockery or wonder; but we can express only very indistinctly and ambiguously a field of Flora or a chain that descends from Jupiter's throne. The musician wants certain symmetries in the poetic stanzas so that the recurring melody will fit every stanza. But we know that this will not be true of the poems of a fiery poet who makes a point of breaking the rules of poetic form—who varies his caesuras, who writes run-on lines, who abandons his subject and loses himself in bold digressions. What poets are more beautiful than Horace and Pindar? And what poems are less suitable to being sung than theirs?

I have cited these words of Ramler's at length because they seem to me of great significance. Earlier critics had laid their stress on what music must do or be or become if *Ton* and *Wort* are to be as fully unified in the strophic song as they have been in the through-composed forms derived from Italian monody. But Ramler is laying down specifications for poetry. Moreover, he is not speaking only in the familiar way about the moods or emotions that are most desirable in poems that are to be turned into songs—though he too does in fact favor poems (and songs) that are gay, lighthearted, good-humored, and so on. He is speaking primarily in formal or mechanical terms. Poems that are too rich in imagery, or too elaborately witty, or too exact in their delineation of manners will not do because these sorts of things cannot be expressed clearly and precisely in music. "Musical sounds," he tells us, "are the language of the emotions." Therefore certain scenes or objects—that fair field of Enna where Proserpine gathered flowers, the *aurea catena Homeri*—are also beyond the scope of music to represent. The composer of a strophic song wants the pauses and the general contours of all stanzas to be the same, since one melody must fit them all. But any poet who is fiery or spirited can be expected to make a point of breaking such laws of uniformity, to vary his caesuras and enjambments from stanza to stanza, to stray from his subject and lose himself in bold extravagances. The point is clinched by mention of Pindar and Horace.

If the mountain will not come to Mohammed, then Mohammed had best go to the mountain. Since it is obviously impossible for one melody to fit equally well all stanzas of an interestingly varied poem, then such poems must be neglected by composers of songs. And such poems as are more suited to musical setting must sometimes be altered to make them still better suited. Composers must be willing to compromise, but poets—or at least poems—must meet them halfway. This is a most important admission (or requirement) that Ramler is making.

He concludes his preface by speaking admiringly of the French, "these born friends of the lied." Their songs are "so easily and naturally composed that the whole land has become full of song and harmony." In German cities, by contrast, one hears only opera arias:

> These arias, however, are not really *song*—of the sort suited to a light comic ballad that might issue effortlessly from every mouth and that could even be sung without the accompaniment of a keyboard or other instruments. If our composers compose their songs singing, without using a keyboard instrument and without thinking that a bass line should be added, then the taste for singing will become more common in our nation and will bring with it general joy and sociable happiness.

Ramler pictures the spread of songs throughout Germany as bringing with it an age of simplicity and joy, an almost pastoral culture of music and companionship. Yet if this age of song is something of a return to an imagined time of perfect harmony, it is also, as his frank envy of the French shows, an advance into the Enlightenment world already occupied by France and England. (In the preface to his and Krause's 1755 *Oden mit Melodien*, Ramler refers admiringly to Addison.) It is, therefore, part of that large general effort of modernization and reform referred to at the beginning of this chapter.

Since the Ramler-Krause *Oden mit Melodien* of 1753 marks the close of the *Aufschwung*, it will be fitting to close this chapter with a comparison involving a song from that collection. In order to refine still further our sense of how the songs of the fledgling first Berlin song school differed from those just preceding its inception, let us look at two settings of another Hagedorn poem, one from Görner's 1742 volume and the other, from the 1753 Ramler-Krause collection, by Krause himself. The poem is Hagedorn's "Der Lauf der Welt," which appears thus in the posthumous 1757 edition of his *Sämmelte poetische Werke*:

> Unzählich ist der Schmeichler Haufen,
> Die jeden Grossen überlaufen,
> So lang er sich erhält.
> Doch gleitet er von seinen Höhen;
> So kann er bald sich einsam sehen.
> Das ist der Lauf der Welt.
>
> Ein Dürftiger sucht seine Freunde;
> Doch alle meiden ihn als Feinde;
> Allein er erbet Geld.
> Sogleich erscheinen zehn Bekannten
> Und zehn entbehrliche Verwandten.
> Das ist der Lauf der Welt.
>
> Ein Schulfuchs hofft mit dürren Gründen
> Den Beyfall aller Welt zu finden:
> Allein er wird geprellt.
> Mein Mädchen macht oft falsche Schlüsse:
> Doch überzeugt sie mich durch Küsse.
> Das ist der Lauf der Welt.

Ein freyes Weib von zwanzig Jahren
Ist zwar in vielen unerfahren:
Doch, was sie sagt, gefällt.
Gebt ihr noch zwanzig Jahre drüber:
So hört man ihre Tochter lieber.
Das ist der Lauf der Welt.

Leander stimmet süsse Töne,
Und singt und seufzet seiner Schöne,
Bis ihr das Ohr fast gellt.
Allein, eh er recht ausgesungen,
Hat schon ein andrer sie bezwungen.
Das ist der Lauf der Welt.

Stax sucht am Montag Doris Küsse:
Am Dingstag findt er Hindernisse:
Am Mittwoch siegt der Held.
Am Donnerstag vergehn die Triebe:
Am Freytag sucht er neue Liebe.
Das ist der Lauf der Welt.

Cephise schwört: Sie will ihr Leben
Der stillen Einsamkeit ergeben,
Und höhnt was sich gesellt.
Drauf will sie sich zur Heirath adeln,
Und spricht zu allen, die sie tadeln:
Das ist der Lauf der Welt.

Ein Mädchen voller Weisheitsgründe
Hält jeden Kuss für eine Sünde,
Bis ihr ein Freund gefällt.
Hat dieser sie dann überwunden;
So sagt sie selbst in frohen Stunden;
Das ist der Lauf der Welt.

Wenn junge Wittwen traurig scheinen,
Und in dem Mann sich selbst beweinen:
So ist es unverstellt.
Doch keine sieht den Trauerschleyer
Mit grössrer Lust, als einen Freyer.
Das ist der Lauf der Welt.

Though less novel than "An den Schlaf," this poem is no less skillful. The whole point, of course, is precisely its lack of novelty: everyone knows that sycophants will forsake a rich man who loses his money, that (conversely) a needy man who is accustomed to rejection will discover all sorts of new friends and relations if he comes into money, that both men and women are fickle in matters of the heart, that vows of solitude and chastity are more easily made than kept, and so on. The joy of the poem lies all in the wit and invention with which the particular examples are selected and put on show. And these are qualities that Hagedorn possesses in abundance.

In the first stanza, notice how the graceful ease of "gleitet," the sly understatement of "bald," and the delicate formality of "kann er . . . sich . . . sehen" work together to give a new twist to the ancient theme of the slipperiness of high places. Or in the second stanza notice the magical swiftness of "Sogleich," the comic precision of the repeated "zehn," the fastidious coolness of "entbehrliche." In both the second and third stanzas the rather mild and casual adversative "allein" is used—in a short line!—to reinforce the swiftness and immediacy with which each reversal of fortune is effected. One could go on at some length: the suddenness with which the coarseness of "gellt" jars against the elaborate description of the sweetly singing Leander in stanza five, the mock-heroic depiction of the quite unheroic Stax in stanza six, the neat juxtaposition of "ergeben" and "adeln" in stanza seven, the unobtrusiveness with which "Das ist der Lauf der Welt" slips (in stanzas seven and eight) out of the mouth of the speaker and into the mouths of the characters, to become their justification of their behavior. Though the poem might well end here, it is brilliantly capped by its concluding stanza.

As befits a poem that has been showing that "der Lauf der Welt" is largely made up of changes of mind and changes of status, this concluding stanza dramatizes the tricky relation between illusion and reality. In mourning their husbands, the young widows mourn for themselves: their loved ones are dead, their lives are over. And this act is "unverstellt": unpretended, uncounterfeited, undisguised—in other words, sincere. Yet the speaker has already told us that they only seem ("scheinen") to be grieving. How then can their mourning be sincere? The answer lies in the adjective "junge." Their youth makes them idealistic enough to believe sincerely (at least for the moment) that all their happiness has died with their husbands. Yet it also makes them naive enough not to see that this is a delusion and attractive enough to capture new husbands. But in spite of the fact that their grieving is sincere ("Doch"), they do not take greater pleasure in the sight of the mourning veil than in the sight of a wooer—an ironic, backhanded way of saying that whether they know it or not, they are leaving their options open. "Doch keine sieht den Trauerschleyer / Mit grössrer Lust, als einen Freyer" is a difficult sentence. At first, one wants to reverse the genders of "keine" and "einen" so that it will read (with some cost to the meter): "Doch keiner sieht den Trauerschleyer / Mit grössrer Lust, als ein Freyer" ("But no man sees the mourning veil with greater pleasure than does a wooer"). And I would guess that Hagedorn had this far simpler misreading in mind. Its temporary presence in the reader's mind heightens his sense of pleasure when he grasps the complexity of the real meaning. This fine-spun web of ironies is completed by a pun on "Trauerschleyer," which can mean a pretense of grief as well as a mourning veil. The reader is once again pulled up short: then was their grief, after all, insincere? "Das ist der Lauf der Welt"!

Except for a few minor changes in punctuation and spelling (e.g., "Dienstag" for the obsolete Mittelniederdeutsch "Dingstag"), the entire poem is printed, unaltered, with Görner's setting:

Actually, there is not much to say about this setting. It seems to me a real gem, Görner at his best. The melody has a gay, insouciant swagger that precisely fits the casual shrug—"Das ist der Lauf der Welt"—with which each stanza ends. Wisely, Görner does not make any attempt to capture musically the various ironies that we noticed occurring along the way in our analysis of Hagedorn's poem. What is of central importance to Görner, and rightly so, is that all the stanzas exemplify the same truth, the one told and retold in their common last line.

Within this general mood of casual gaiety, there are many instances of elegant musical craftsmanship. In the first few bars, the melodic line emphatically descends to the tonic—and then wittily scampers back up to the fifth, its ascent humorously underscored by the contrary motion in the bass. After another emphatic little descent (mm. 3-4), this time beginning a step higher and in a syncopated rhythm, the run up to the fifth is repeated, in a slightly more elaborate form. And underneath, as if to make sure that we paid attention this time, the contrary motion in the bass starts somewhat more aggressively than before, in a syncopated rhythm matching those in the melodic line. The melody then moves, in almost childishly simple stepwise fashion, to the fifth as the harmony settles on the dominant, underscored by the pedantic-pompous C-G-E-G-C movement in the bass. There is then a change in texture as we move to the subdominant. The melody confines itself to a few notes closely adjacent to one another, while the bass line, in a tenor register, repeats itself, one note for each change in the harmony. It sounds as though a full-fledged middle section is beginning, and so we are surprised by the rest in the bass line after the first beat of m. 12. Then, with a pair of cadential movements in the bass line and a flashing octave descent in the melody, the song is over and the joke is on us.

Let us look now at the setting by Krause printed in the 1753 collection:

As with the anonymous 1767 setting of "An den Schlaf," I have given the poem just as it appears in the collection, in order to call attention to textual changes, again of course made by Ramler. Of the nine stanzas, only four are used, the central stanzas three through six. And just as in Ramler's reworking of "An den Schlaf," proper names are supplied in place of descriptive phrases: the "Schulfuchs" becomes Gryphinus; the "freies Weib von zwanzig Jahren," Lätitia. Both are common caricature names.

Gryphinus (which sometimes appears as Gryphus or Grypho) derives from Latin *grypus* and Greek γρυπός, which mean hook-nosed. Thus the name is usually given to an old man. Laetitia of course comes from *laetus*, the ordinary Latin word for happy or joyful. Having each of the four stanzas begin with a proper name gives the text a consistency that complements the compactness attained by the omission of the other five stanzas. As much is lost, so something is gained.

But what of the music that Krause has composed? The first surprise is that the song is in the minor mode—whereas the poem, especially in this cut-down and radically simplified version, would naturally seem to call for a song in the major. The second surprise is the complexity of the melodic line and the harmony. The melody is full of angular leaps and shifting rhythmic emphases, while the harmony changes constantly and oscillates frequently between major and minor. Played at the required "Lebhaft" tempo, the piece sounds intolerably cluttered, as though it were being rattled off and should be taken a good deal slower. And indeed, when it is taken slower it sounds rather noble and stately. The unaccompanied first bar has the same tone of high drama as the one in de Giovannini's "An den Schlaf," and the ever-changing harmony seems searching and exploratory. But at neither tempo does the song seem to have the faintest relevance to the poem it ostensibly sets. This is really a rather handsome little piece of music, but it belongs somewhere else. One is tempted to think that Krause borrowed it from another work, and speeded up the tempo in a vain hope of thereby gaining the cheeriness required by Hagedorn's poem.

There is much more that one could say about this setting of Krause's. But the important point is that although simplicity is the most frequently avowed goal of the north German song composers, an insistence on rapid and involved harmonic change has become a firm and established part of the Berlin song school, and will remain so for several decades to come.

This completes our survey of the songs of the *Aufschwung*, the songs that effectively accomplished the return to viability of the strophic lied in Germany after the various tremors of the preceding century. We have looked occasionally into the critical and theoretical literature that accompanied and aided the strophic lied's reinstatement. Because this body of literature is very important, and also because it has been widely misunderstood and misrepresented, we must now examine it in detail. In doing so, our aim will be to understand not only why and how the strophic lied regained its standing as a musical genre, but why the songs of the first Berlin school assumed the particular musical characteristics we have seen gaining in importance over the course of this chapter.

Chapter Four

Rationalist Aesthetics: Rules

It might at first seem more appropriate to speak of "re-creating" or "reinventing" rather than merely reinstating the strophic lied. For as we have seen, the fact that strophic songs used the same music, repeatedly, for words of at least potentially different significance and emotional weight threw the genre into disrepute in Germany for upward of 50 years. It would seem that something as radical as re-creation or reinvention would have to have taken place if the strophic lied were again to become, in Kross's term, "acceptable."

Yet as he and the other historians of the lied, back at least to Kretzschmar, remind us, many manuscript collections of strophic songs survive from the *liederlose Zeit*. The strophic lied did not cease to exist between 1680 and the mid-1730s, it just lost status. Moreover, we all know that many of the greatest songs written during the greatest period of the German lied, a century ahead, were in strophic form. And, as we saw in the preceding chapter, German composers mostly rejected not only the through-composed form common to Italian monody but also the convenient compromise offered by the strophic variation form. Germans, after all, had been composing and publishing strophic songs for centuries; one has the distinct feeling that they would have somehow found a way of doing so again, with or without theoretical justification.

Yet during the years of the *Aufschwung*, and for several decades thereafter, that justification was in fact provided, though somewhat indirectly and obliquely, by theorists of various sorts. Only a few of the historians whose work we reviewed in Chapter Two attempted to explain how and why strophic songs again became not only "acceptable" but extremely popular. And, as we saw, their explanations were rather vague: the complexities of the old polyphonic style gave way to a new "simplicity," which we can see exemplified in the strophic lied; the rise in musical literacy in the early years of the 18th century produced a large and sudden demand for *Hausmusik*, a demand made to order for the strophic lied. These and other, similar explanations of course have a good deal of truth in them. But they do not touch on the main problem, which has to do with musical form: what was it that made the repetition of the same music, over and over, for different stanzas of a poem seem not only acceptable but actually more suitable as the musical expression of a poem's meaning? To answer that question, we must understand the musical aesthetics of the time and, equally important, the ways in which it has traditionally been misrepresented.

I

In the preceding chapter I mentioned Henry Knight Miller's seminal essay, "The 'Whig Interpretation' of Literary History."[1] Miller was thinking mainly of English literature and, within English literature, of poetry and fiction. But the critical literature, and even the technical philosophy, not only of England but also of Germany and France, written during the late 17th and 18th centuries, has also been subjected to a "whig interpretation" that is still widely accepted as true. We can begin to get an idea of its nature if we briefly examine sections of the two books that have been most widely used by recent scholars interested in the theory and criticism that helped to reinstate the strophic lied, Hugo Goldschmidt's 1915 *Die Musikästhetik des 18. Jahrhunderts und ihre Beziehungen zu seinem Kunstschaffen* and Walter Serauky's 1929 *Die musikalische Nachahmungsästhetik im Zeitraum von 1700 bis 1850*.[2] Both are excellent examples of whig history.

For both Goldschmidt and Serauky, the two most important musical aestheticians of the first half of the 18th century are Gottsched and Charles Batteux. Gottsched's list of publications is almost incredibly long. For almost 40 years, from 1726, when he began publishing the first of the many German moral weeklies patterned on *The Spectator*, to shortly before his death, Gottsched waged a one-man (and largely successful) campaign to reform the language, literature, and theater of Germany.[3] For our purposes, his most famous work was *Versuch einer critischen Dichtkunst vor die Deutschen*, which was first published in 1730 and which we have had occasion to mention in earlier chapters. Batteux's most famous work was the 1746 *Les Beaux-Arts réduits à un même principe*, one of the classic expositions of the theory, deriving ultimately from Aristotle, that all the arts are essentially based on μίμησις or imitation. In 1747–1748 Batteux published *Cours de belles lettres*, in which he applied his theory to the various genres of poetry and the other arts. Both Goldschmidt and Serauky, however, are keenly (not to say defensively) aware of the powerful influence exerted by French writers on aesthetics upon their German contemporaries. Therefore both men deal with Batteux before coming to Gottsched.

Because the nature that art imitates is, according to Batteux, not nature as she is but rather nature as she might be, an idealized nature, Goldschmidt praises his book "as the first scientific attempt to soften the old objectivism and, thereby, the point of departure for the victory over the barren and fruitless imitation theory" (p. 69). Goldschmidt thus concludes: "Batteux shook the system of the rationalists to its core" (p. 69). Yet the work is not without its faults. "The book's weakness lies . . . in its lacking the courage to renounce the basic aesthetic assumptions of its time and nation" (p. 69). But then, Goldschmidt adds, in a burst of chauvinistic generosity, no Frenchman could have dared so much without turning all of his philosophical fellows against him.

Throughout his chapter on Batteux, Goldschmidt seesaws back and forth between praising him for his insights and blaming him for the failure of nerve, the "timidity and halfheartedness" (p. 74), that prevented him from drawing from those insights what Goldschmidt sees as their obvious logical implications. Batteux's book is a "transitional work" and, as such, admirable: "It holds something like the same significance for musical aesthetics as the poetics of the Swiss [i.e., J. J. Bodmer and J. J. Breitinger] holds for the history of German literature. For they too, in spite of the Gottsched-derived, rationalistic foundations of their thought, took a significant step forward, and thereby helped us to understand the importance of feeling in language" (p. 70). Though he sets taste above judgment, intuition above reason, Batteux can nonetheless pay lip service to the old *Affektenlehre*, a theory of which musical devices best express the various emotions, allegedly beloved of 17th-century thinkers. Yet precisely because his defense of the *Affektenlehre* arises out of piety rather than conviction, it is unconvincing: "Even as the author struggles to save the theory, it crumbles in his hands" (p. 75). Goldschmidt can therefore sum up Batteux's position as "this aesthetics that gives with one hand and takes away with the other" (p. 73). At another point, thoroughly exasperated with what he sees as Batteux's endless self-contradictions, Goldschmidt exclaims: "You would think you were reading Hegel" (p. 75).

This treatment of Batteux pretty clearly implies the judgment of Gottsched that follows in the next chapter. It is his fault that the Germans did not develop, in the early 18th century, a musical aesthetics that could encompass and explain the greatness of Bach and Handel, thus encouraging younger composers:

That it turned out differently, that the rationalistic theory once again prodigiously distended itself and had an unwholesome influence on the production of new music, is the fault of the monstrously wide dissemination of the artistic ideas of Johann Christoph Gottsched, that man who for 27 years, from 1723 to 1750, worked in the same community as Johann Sebastian Bach, the most powerful embodiment of the principle he [i.e., Gottsched] most hated and resisted, the principle of the freely creative imagination!

[Pp. 79-80]

Goldschmidt's almost personal dislike, even loathing, of Gottsched could scarcely be clearer.

Throughout his long career, Gottsched, according to Goldschmidt, remained "an unwavering standard bearer of the post-classical rationalism of the French" (p. 80). Lacking Batteux's insight into the ideal nature of artistic imitation, Gottsched sided "with the French theologians and haters of art" who preceded Batteux, seeing in poetry merely "the pronouncer of truth or, at best, an instructor in morals" (p. 80). A lifelong enemy of the freely ranging poetic imagination, the dryly literal-minded Gottsched took the opposite course from that of Batteux, firmly subordinating taste to the judgments of reason—judgments reached "by following rules that apply universally" (p. 81). "An aesthetics more hostile to music," concludes Goldschmidt, "is scarcely imaginable" (p. 81). It is, however, worth noting that Goldschmidt never once quotes directly from Gottsched: all his information appears to be secondhand, gathered from Gustav Waniek's 700-page *Gottsched und die deutsche Literatur seiner Zeit* (Leipzig, 1897).

Serauky's treatment of the two thinkers is basically similar to Goldschmidt's. He too argues that Batteux's *Les Beaux-Arts réduits à un même principe* is a transitional work, and he too finds it full of contradictions. But Serauky lays less stress on Batteux's novel and liberating insights, and more on his adherence to the French tradition stemming from Descartes and Racine: "On the whole, however, Batteux remains firmly committed to the basically rationalistic biases of French aesthetics" (p. 13). Even Batteux's treatment of the concept of genius, praised by Goldschmidt, for Serauky "breathes . . . a wholly rationalistic spirit" (p. 13). Serauky is therefore bothered by the weight that Batteux gives to what he calls "enthusiasm": "Batteux here gives a definition that is, in the fullest measure, characteristic of his eclecticism" (p. 14)—"eclecticism" being the term that Serauky reserves for the facets of Batteux's thought that cannot conveniently be branded as symptoms of "rationalism." To be fair, though, Serauky does occasionally praise Batteux: "His acknowledgment of the emotional elements in taste raises Batteux's definition high above the theses of the contemporary French aestheticians" (p. 15).

In marked contrast to Goldschmidt, Serauky finds that Batteux's concept of "beautiful nature," the idealized nature that it is the task of art to imitate, sometimes seems merely a throwback to earlier French neoclassicism: "this definition goes back to Boileau's formulation of nature as what is typical and universal, the world of appearances stripped of everything that is individual" (p. 15). At other times, though, this concept seems to imply something more elevated: "Here beautiful nature is identified with a perfection whose characteristics are unity, variety, symmetry, conformity to rule, and proportion" (p. 16). Yet the criteria that this completed or perfected version of "beautiful nature" must meet—particularly, perhaps, "conformity to rule"—are of course characteristic of rationalist aesthetics.

Though Serauky's treatment of Gottsched lacks the intense personal animus of Goldschmidt's, it is scarcely more complimentary. "The intellectual leader in Germany between 1730 and 1740," it begins, "was Gottsched, the born Enlightenment Man: sober, clear, and articulate as the aesthetic principles that he revered" (pp. 64-65). These principles, which formed the basis of Gottsched's many reforms, were "narrowly dogmatic, rationally systematic in the spirit of the philosophy of Christian Wolff, whose devoted follower he was" (p. 65). Upholding a simpler and more straightforward version of the imitation theory than Batteux, Gottsched, in a passage cited by Serauky from *Versuch einer critischen Dichtkunst*, asserts that "a poet is a skilled imitator of all natural things; and this he has in common with painters, sculptors, musicians, et al." (quoted p. 66). Unlike Batteux, Gottsched seems to see no difference whatever between taste and intellectual understanding. After citing a passage from Gottsched's 1754 *Auszug aus den Herrn Batteux Schönen Künsten aus dem einzigen Grundsatz der Nachahmung hergeleitet*, Serauky asks rhetorically: "Where, in this rationalistic definition of taste, is there a particle of difference between taste and intellect" (p. 67)?

In Goldschmidt's and Serauky's comments on Batteux and Gottsched, we get a fair encapsulation of the view of pre-Kantian or pre-Romantic aesthetics that has been adopted, more or less wholesale, by most recent musicologists writing about the 18th century. How can we generalize this view? The most important fact about it is of course that rationalism is the enemy, the dominant destructive force that needs to be—and that eventually will be—routed by the increasing power of an opposing emphasis on the role of imagination, intuition, and feeling in both the creation and the appreciation or judgment of art. Sometimes this process is seen in simply "whiggish" terms as the steady progress, out of the rationalistic darkness and into what Saintsbury called "the fair haven of Romanticism." At other times, there is talk of a "synthesis" of rationalist and intuitionist views that was achieved by Kant in the *Critique of Judgment*. But the point of this synthesis is usually taken to be that earlier, rationalist views were too rigid, too committed to classical ideas of decorum and the strictness of boundaries among artistic genres. Either way, the whole historical process is seen as the movement from something like what Saintsbury called "the Neo-classic creed," held in lockstep agreement by all existing critics as a kind of semi-religious orthodoxy, to a more generously tolerant view of art and artists, one that leaves plenty of space for the free operation of the artistic imagination and also for individual differences in critical judgment. Goldschmidt's and Serauky's counterpart to Saintsbury's "Neo-classic creed" is of course the *Affektenlehre*. Any time one finds, in a rationalistic critic, a deviation from the alleged critical norm, one chalks it up either to the encroaching forces of light and truth or to an unexplained and seemingly unmotivated "eclecticism."

II

We can see this general view of early 18th-century aesthetics powerfully at work in some rather recent American doctoral dissertations on the three practicing music critics who were most influential in Germany during the period of the strophic lied's reinstatement: Johann Adolph Scheibe, Christian Gottfried Krause, and Friedrich Wilhelm Marpurg. In these dissertations the political vocabulary common to American academic liberals during the 1960s and 1970s is used to characterize the changes in musical aesthetics during the 18th century. The rationalist aesthetics so disliked by Goldschmidt and Serauky is called conservative or reactionary (i.e., bad), while the intuitionist aesthetics that succeeded it is called progressive or liberal or radical (i.e., good).

Imanuel Willheim, writing about Scheibe, sees him as representative of the transition between the two sorts of aesthetics.[4] The rationalist aesthetics stemming from Descartes and conveniently codified in Boileau's 1674 poem *L'Art poétique* was "concerned not with originality but with clarity, not with complexity but with simplicity, not with emotional transport but with insight" (p. 7). But even during Boileau's lifetime (he died in 1711) "a dissatisfaction with the austerity of the rationalist world could be felt at times" (p. 13). While "Boileau had assumed that pleasure would be the automatic by-product of the formulation of a truth," with Fontenelle there entered "a new consideration: art was meant to please" (p. 13). Jean Baptiste Dubos (1670–1742), whose *Réflexions critiques sur la Poésie et sur la Peinture* appeared in 1719, was "The most radical exponent of this new attitude" since his "only standard of judgment is the degree to which the audience has been moved" (p. 13). The result was a "new pragmatic approach to the arts" that "led to a critical re-examination of rationalistic rules and categories" and "permitted a less prejudiced evaluation of works of art hitherto spurned for their non-conformity to rationalistic standards" (p. 14)—works, namely, by Shakespeare and Milton.

How does Scheibe fit into this shift from a rationalist to an intuitionist aesthetics? He entered the University of Leipzig in the fall of 1725, the first year that Gottsched lectured on the philosophy of Wolff. Scheibe soon became Gottsched's disciple, and, as we saw earlier, gave the journal that he began publishing in 1737 the title *Der critische Musikus* in conscious emulation of Gottsched's *Critische Dichtkunst* of seven years earlier. But in 1749, in the preface to his libretto for *Thusnelde*, Scheibe, Willheim tells us, declared "his admiration for Milton, Klopstock and Shakespeare," and thus "openly joined those apostate disciples of Gottsched who had accepted English aesthetic ideas either by direct contact with British literature or through the mediation of the Swiss" (p. 51). Scheibe was thus caught between older and newer views on many topics. For example, like Mattheson he "never consciously broke with the *Affektenlehre*," which might suggest "a reactionary point of view on Scheibe's part" (p. 98). Yet such a conclusion would be false, since "what draws our attention to Scheibe is not his adherence to the *Affektenlehre* principles, it is rather his deviation from these principles, his acceptance of 'feeling' in lieu of precise affections" (p. 99). Moreover, despite his general switch from Gottsched to Bodmer and Breitinger, Scheibe "appears to take an even more reactionary position than did Gottsched when he argues that taste is the ability of the faculty of understanding to judge what the senses record ('empfinden')" (pp. 114–115).

John Richard Edwards writes similarly of the changes taking place in aesthetics in his dissertation on Krause.[5] Krause, Edwards tells us at the outset, was "the founder of the First Berlin Song School," a distinction that he won through being coeditor, with Karl Wilhelm Ramler (1725-1798), of the 1753 collection *Oden mit Melodien*, for which his *Von der musikalischen Poesie*, published the preceding year, was "the preliminary aesthetic study" (p. 5). Edwards then traces the intellectual background of Krause's work in a chapter that focuses on the effects, mainly adverse, of French influence on German letters, beginning in about 1600.

It was Opitz who, according to Edwards, "introduced into the German language the French Alexandrine verse form" (p. 15), in his 1624 *Buch von der deutschen Poeterey*. Then came Descartes, with his famous "Cogito, ergo sum," which Edwards rather oddly takes to imply that "reason and existence are the same thing, or to put it another way, reason is self-sufficient" (p. 10). In the early 18th century, the poets attached to the court of the Elector of Saxony "adopted and slavishly followed the rules Boileau had set forth in his *Art poétique*" (p. 18). Meanwhile, in Leipzig, Gottsched, who "was in many ways very similar to Martin Opitz" (p. 20), was lecturing and publishing. "Although he taught that poetry should be an 'imitation of nature,' he based his work on the French works of Le Bossu and D'Aubignac, and these rules led back to writing mechanical verse" (pp. 20-21). But soon Johann Jakob Bodmer (1698-1783) and Johann Jakob Breitinger (1701-1776) initiated their opposition to Gottsched:

> Gottsched wished to reform literature from without by imposing rules upon it; Bodmer and Breitinger sought to reform it by studying the nature of poetic creation from within, by investigating how poetry arose in the mind of the poet, and what its effect was on the reader. Gottsched's defeat was inevitable, not so much because of the attacks of his opponents, but because of the spirit of the age in which they were living.
>
> [P. 21]

Where does Krause's thought, as expressed in *Von der musikalischen Poesie*, stand in relation to these developments? Edwards notes that in 1741, Krause commenced the study of the law at the University of Frankfurt an der Oder, and that subsequently "he attended the lectures of Alexander Gottlieb Baumgarten whose ideas later influenced Krause's own aesthetic concepts" (p. 30). But Edwards never tells us just how the thought of Baumgarten (1714-1762), who may fairly be termed the creator of philosophical aesthetics, actually did influence Krause. Moreover, his exposition of Krause's book is confusing and hard to follow.

He begins by paraphrasing Krause's preface to the effect that "sometimes composers devise rules in order to guide the poet in the preparation of texts for musical settings, but these rules may be detrimental to the nature of poetry" (p. 49). He then cites Krause (in English translation): "Everything rests on the true expression of the passions . . . the imitation of an emotional state and the depiction of feelings require equally approbation" (quoted p. 50). We think we know where we are: Krause is on the side of the angels, against rules and in favor of direct emotional expression—though by now the word "imitation" may strike us as a danger sign.

But then suddenly Edwards is insisting that it would be "hardly worthwhile" to provide a complete translation of Krause's book, "for as previously indicated the work is poorly organized, highly repetitious, and dates from an era when language and philosophy had meanings and stresses different from those they have today. This was the age of rationalism" (p. 51)—and a long quotation from Paul Henry Lang's *Music in Western Civilization*, explaining what the age of rationalism was, follows. A few pages later Edwards launches into a long account of Serauky's article on the *Affektenlehre* in the 1949 *Musik in Geschichte und Gegenwart*, by the end of which the implication seems to be that Krause is about as old-fashioned and rule-bound as Mattheson. The extensive paraphrase of *Von der musikalischen Poesie* that follows does not help much because Edwards never generalizes about the book's relation to the historical developments he has been tracing. Perhaps we are simply to conclude that Krause too was a transitional figure.

As a final example, take Howard Jay Serwer's dissertation on Marpurg.[6] Early in the biographical sketch that opens his dissertation, Serwer cites some letters written around 1780 by J. S. Bach's former student Johann Philipp Kirnberger (1721-1783) to Bach's future biographer, Johann Nikolaus Forkel (1749-1818). The letters concern Marpurg, with whom Kirnberger had been feuding for some 30 years, and Serwer cites them in order to demonstrate "the difference in taste between the conservative court"—at Berlin, where Kirnberger had long been in the service of Princess Anna Amalia of Prussia—"and the progressive leanings of men like Marpurg and the publisher Friedrich Nicolai" (p. 15). While Kirnberger was lamenting that no one any longer listened to Handel, Bach, Graun, and Hasse, Marpurg was soon to develop a love for Haydn and Mozart.

Yet Serwer is at pains to show also that Marpurg was no mere faddist. During the 1750s he became known not only as "the champion of Rameau's ideas," one of the many subjects about which he argued with Kirnberger, but also as "the defender of fugue long after it had become unfashionable" (p. 119). Thus it was Marpurg whom C. P. E. Bach called upon in 1752 to write a new preface for his father's *Die Kunst der Fuge*. Serwer immediately points out that this affection for a seemingly outworn form "is modern rather than conservative" on Marpurg's part, "for he requires that we judge such musical works solely on their compositional merits without regard to the currency of their style." Thus it was the same instinct that led Marpurg to support the harmonic ideas of Rameau, and later the music of Haydn and Mozart, that led him to remain interested in the fugue, "a genuinely historical attitude which calls for the judging of old works in the context of the age in which they were written" (p. 125).

In discussing the changes taking place in aesthetic theory during Marpurg's lifetime, Serwer too is consistently patronizing toward rationalist or neoclassic writers and consistently kind to writers who stress the need for music to move the heart. "For Marpurg and his contemporaries," writes Serwer, "rules in this context referred first of all to the Aristotelian requirements of unity of time and place in the drama. Such dicta were at once misunderstood and canonized by Corneille and later by Gottsched" (p. 204). Old-fashioned theories based on the *Affektenlehre* "tended to become systematized and rule-bound," and thus "held in themselves the seeds of their own undoing" (p. 176). The undoing was helped along by Dubos, who in his *Réflexions critiques* "had eliminated the intellectual elements from the perception of art, and in their place had postulated a kind of universal sixth sense which unthinkingly responded to the emotive content of art" (p. 175).

The particular triumph that Marpurg, with the aid of his "genuinely historical attitude," accomplished as he lived through this era of change and development was a personal synthesis of the best of both old and new music and ideas about music. Serwer quotes many passages from Marpurg's various magazines that convincingly show the nature of this synthesis—not only in Marpurg himself but also in some of the other writers he published. In one such passage Marpurg "observed that even if the compositions were quite regular in their harmony, melody, and rhythm, they would still be only mediocre for 'it is not possible to please and move [one's audience] with the rules alone'" (p. 205). In another he wrote that "if a composer wants to work at no other time but when he feels himself completely heated up by his object, then he should have his fire under such control that he never forgets the rules of art" (quoted p. 214)!

In his final chapter, Serwer makes a most interesting and provocative attempt to connect the synthesis that Marpurg forged for himself in the 1750s with the one that issued, 30 years later, in the formation of the classical style. Taking note of the various composers for whom Marpurg expressed strong positive or negative feelings, Serwer sums up thus:

> In short, Marpurg's comments and criticisms imply a continuum of modern musical styles, shading at one end towards the harmonically saturated contrapuntal style of J. S. Bach and at the other end towards the tuneful style of the "modern" Italians and their imitators. The synthesis that Marpurg sensed in a vague way in the 1750s was already in progress in Vienna and was to culminate, of course, in the mature works of Haydn and Mozart.
>
> [P. 266]

Yet even after this high praise of Marpurg as a sort of prophetic voice in music criticism, Serwer nonetheless feels that he must apologize, in his conclusion, for Marpurg's not having been quite so "progressive" as he might have been:

> That Marpurg was no advocate of the most modern musical styles in the 1750s should not be surprising. It is rare that a successful critic is radically modern in his views, and it is this very conservatism that makes the critic a useful recorder of popular taste.
>
> [P. 282]

So great is the desire, felt by the whig historian, that the figure who is the primary object of his attention should be revealed to have been in step with the upward and onward march of history.

III

We have thus seen how three major music critics of the first half of the 18th century have been placed, by scholars who have studied them closely, in relation to contemporary changes in musical aesthetics. Willheim saw Scheibe as a transitional figure, Edwards apparently viewed Krause's thought as bafflingly self-contradictory, and Serwer felt that Marpurg had successfully synthesized conflicting elements in the music (and the musical aesthetics) of his time. These are, I think, three ways of saying something like the same thing.

All three scholars assumed that the early 18th century was a time in which serious thought about music was gradually shifting from one extreme to the other, from an emphasis on the composition and the critical judgment of music as activities of the reason, as guided by statable (and systematizable) rules, to an opposing emphasis on these same activities as determined by feeling or emotion—as felt and captured in sound by the composer, and as thence transmitted to and re-created in the listener. Yet each scholar, compelled to inspect the figure who was the subject of his dissertation at close range and in great detail, found him to be (as he no doubt was) richly (which is to say humanly) complex. It is this complexity that was then seen in Scheibe as his transitional status, in Krause as self-contradictoriness, and in Marpurg as the ability to create a synthesis of old and new.

Why does all this sound so familiar? Why does the person or the age at the center of our investigation so often emerge as transitional or self-contradictory or synthesizing? The answer, I think, is that we all tend to see history as a story of movement from one extreme to another—simply because that kind of story is the most interesting kind there is. Whether we see the age in question whiggishly (or Darwinianly), as moving from worse to better, or, à la Spengler, as moving in the other direction, there is a strong temptation to view successive individual figures as more or less simple embodiments of the steps or stages or points on a smooth continuum that carries us from extreme to extreme. With figures that we only examine superficially, especially if they come during the earlier stages of the historical process, this can work fairly well. But figures that we examine in detail always prove to be disappointingly unclassifiable. Thus we resort (most frequently, I think) to the "transitional" gambit: every age is an age of transition, every figure worth examining closely is a transitional figure. I am not contending (as some historiographers would) that history is not a story, but simply that it is not (usually, at any rate) a relatively clear and simple story of a progression from bad to good or vice versa. We are thus forced to adjust our categories.

How are we to make this adjustment in the case of early 18th-century German musical aesthetics? Since rationalism is, both for Goldschmidt and Serauky and also for the three scholars whose dissertations we have examined, the great enemy, the force to be triumphantly overcome, we might begin by asking what, in the context of the thinkers we are dealing with, makes a particular view of the creation and the criticism of musical art "rationalist"? What, in a word, does *rationalism* (or *Rationalismus*) mean in the thinkers we are here dealing with?

As we saw repeatedly, the concept of rationalism, in relation to aesthetics, was widely assumed to be closely connected to an insistence on the necessary existence of rules of some sort—rules both for the creation of successful works of art and also for their meaningful or correct judgment by critics. The creation and the judgment of art, in other words, are both rule-governed activities. When we engage in them we are following rules, even though we may not be able to state those rules. One of the main aims, in fact, of aesthetics or critical theory is precisely to discover what these rules are and to state them—not just individually but systematically, making clear their logical relations to one another.

The notion of rules that we follow and yet cannot state—or state fully, completely, so as to account for everything we do in the course of following them—may seem a troublesome one. For when we think of rule-governed activities, we tend first to think of games. And of course the rules of chess or bridge or golf not only can be but commonly are stated in a brief yet adequate form. Yet knowing the rules, in the sense of having read and understood them, and perhaps also having committed them to memory, does not, in itself, make one a chess-player or golfer—or, certainly, it does not make one a good chess-player or golfer. Experience of actual play refines upon the simple rules we find in some updated version of Hoyle's. We learn tactics, we develop particular modes of attack and defense, and we learn when and when not to employ them. In other words, we internalize the rules, and in so doing, we refine them into other rules that are far too complex to be stated succinctly—or perhaps to be stated at all.

Or take a skill like playing the violin or driving a car or wood-carving. While there is no precise equivalent to Hoyle's for such activities, no "rulebook" in the ordinary sense, there are certain simple dos and don'ts that we can be taught first, and that will soon lead on to more subtle and complicated rules of thumb and ways of proceeding that, again, will soon grow too complex to be stated, and that must therefore be taught by example, master to student. It is always interesting, in the teaching of a skill, to observe the point at which words give out, even for the most articulate of teachers, and there is nothing the teacher can do but take the violin or steering wheel or knife in hand and demonstrate.

When the critics and literary theorists of the late 17th and 18th centuries insisted that there were rules for producing and judging works of art, whether musical or literary or pictorial, they did so because they thought of the various arts as being one rung higher on the ladder of rule-governed activities that begins with simple games and ascends to complex skills. That is, they assumed that just as one can tell the difference between a good and a bad chess-player or golfer, and between a good and a bad driver or wood-carver, so one can tell the difference between a good and a bad poet or composer or painter. And from this assumption another follows: that there must be differences, in theory somehow specifiable, between what a good poet or composer or painter does and what a bad one does, just as there are such differences in the case of games and skills. To put it another way, they were aware that not just anything can qualify as a successful or valuable poem or musical composition or picture. Therefore there must be something, some set of specifiable characteristics, that separates the successes from the failures, and both artists who are successful and critics who are respected for their judgments must, in some sense or other, know what these characteristics are.

Now ever since Wittgenstein's analysis, in the *Philosophical Investigations*, of the concept *game*, the assumption that all the objects to which a common noun correctly applies must have some characteristics in common has been called into serious question. "Consider for example the proceedings that we call 'games,'" writes Wittgenstein:

> I mean board-games, card-games, ball-games, Olympic games, and so on. What is common to them all?—Don't say: "There *must* be something common, or they would not be called 'games'"—but *look and see* whether there is anything common to all.—For if you look at them you will not see something that is common to *all*, but similarities, relationships, and a whole series of them at that. To repeat: don't think, but look!

After carrying on his examination of different sorts of games at some length, Wittgenstein then concludes: "the result of this examination is: we see a complicated network of similarities overlapping and crisscrossing: sometimes overall similarities, sometimes similarities of detail." Wittgenstein proposes that we call these similarities "family resemblances": "for the various resemblances between members of a family: build, features, colour of eyes, gait, temperament, etc. etc. overlap and criss-cross in the same way.—And I shall say: 'games' form a family." Finally, he compares the structure of such a concept to that of a thread that is made by spinning fiber upon fiber: "the strength of the thread does not reside in the fact that some one fibre runs through its whole length, but in the overlapping of many fibres."[7]

Most present-day aestheticians would, I think, prefer to treat *art* as a family-resemblance concept rather than as one whose application to a large group of seemingly disparate objects depended on the existence of one or more characteristics shared by all (and only) those objects. As William E. Kennick showed in a most important 1958 essay, "Does Traditional Aesthetics Rest on a Mistake?,"[8] all previous attempts to specify this characteristic shared by all works of art (and in virtue of possessing which they are works of art) have failed, and have in fact been logically doomed to failure. (Yet Kennick also argued that while it is not true to say that the essence of art is expression, or significant form, or the imitation of nature, none of these attempted solutions to the main problem of traditional aesthetics is simply wrong: they can all be shown to be revealingly insightful.)

Therefore we can say that the rationalist aestheticians of the late 17th and 18th centuries were wrong to believe that the presence of the same characteristic (or set of characteristics) makes one object a (good, successful) work of art whose absence makes another object a bad (attempt at a) work of art. But they were most assuredly not wrong in insisting that works of art are not randomly created, and should therefore not be randomly judged or evaluated. The qualities that make one Romantic lyric good and another worthless are quite different from the ones that make one Renaissance portrait or one 18th-century string quartet good and one worthless. Yet when we express a judgment that one work of art is better than another, we never just stop there: we always go on to give reasons, and we do so precisely by pointing to discriminable objective features of the work that reinforce our judgment. Of course no two people, if they talk about it long enough, ever perfectly agree in their judgment of a work of art. But that is simply another way of saying that we all have different minds and sensibilities. It does not in the least discount the fact that evaluating works of art must be in some sense a rational process since in doing it we naturally produce what we think are good solid reasons for our judgments.

That is to say, we explain our judgments of works of art. And it is often possible to convince another person that his view is wrong and ours is right—or to be convinced that his is right and ours wrong. The fact that we naturally ask for, and provide, such explanations, and that they can be convincing in something like the same sense in which other sorts of explanation can be convincing, is further evidence that at least the criticism (if not yet the creation) of works of art is in some sense a rational process.

Yet critical explanations are unlike most other sorts of explanations in a most important way. Usually we think of explanations as proceeding from the particular to the general, and as becoming more satisfactory as they become more general. If, for example, we are asked, on a cold winter day, why the pipes have burst, we should reply that they always do when the temperature drops below the freezing point of the water that they contain. If we are then asked why that should be so, we explain further that water (unlike many other substances) expands when it freezes, and that this expansion is what breaks the pipes. But why does water expand (rather than contracting, say) when it freezes? We should then attempt to explain the structure of the water molecule.[9] But the explanations we give, as critics or teachers, of our judgments of works of art are quite different from this.

Suppose, for example, that I express my admiration for this short poem of Wordsworth's:

> A slumber did my spirit seal;
> I had no human fears:
> She seemed a thing that could not feel
> The touch of earthly years.
>
> No motion has she now, no force;
> She neither hears nor sees;
> Rolled round in earth's diurnal course,
> With rocks, and stones, and trees.

The person to whom I express my admiration is puzzled, and asks why I think this a good—in fact, a great—poem. What sort of an explanation do I offer?

What I most assuredly do not do is to demonstrate (somehow) that the poem falls under or is an instance of increasingly powerful and general laws, ending with some lawlike statement of the criteria for good poems or good works of art. Instead I begin pointing to details of the poem's language, trying to get the other person to see them as I see them, and to see how they go together.

Plainly, this is a love poem that draws a sharp contrast between the speaker's state of mind when the loved one was alive and his state of mind now that she is dead. We feel this contrast first in the contrast in tense between the two stanzas. Oddly, the moment of the girl's death is not part of the poem: it falls in the white space between the stanzas. The more we read the poem over, the louder the silence of that blank white space becomes. It is also odd that the speaker refers to the girl as "a thing"—or, more precisely, as having "seemed" to him to be "a thing." We might have expected that the reason he could not imagine her death was that she was so vividly, so humanly alive. The irony of course is that now, when he has fully realized her humanity, she has indeed become a thing, "Rolled round in earth's diurnal course," bereft of independent motion or force, inanimate. Or almost so: we notice those "trees" at the end of the final line.

So this is a rather peculiar love poem. It is not really about the girl at all, but rather about the "slumber" that sealed off the speaker from her even as he loved her, or (to put it more generally) about the curious way in which the idealization that commonly goes with love can dehumanize its object—which is surely the last thing the lover consciously intends. The speaker of course sees all this quite clearly now. Yet there is no melodramatic self-condemnation, no tearing of hair or gnashing of teeth. Throughout, the poem maintains a tone of sternly reserved dignity that is one of the main sources of its power.

There is much more that one could say, but this is surely enough to make the relevant point about critical explanations. Rather than getting increasingly general as they proceed, they get more particular, more closely attentive to details. This fact is intimately related—though whether as cause or as effect I am not certain—to the fact, pointed out by Kennick, that the traditional attempts of aestheticians to discover some general criterion that must be met by any and all objects that are to qualify as works of art are doomed to failure. There are no such general criteria because that is not the sort of things that works of art are. This is a fact of nature that follows from the sorts of concepts we employ when we discuss works of art, and there is no changing it.

The first philosopher I know of who realized the peculiar nature of critical explanations was Wittgenstein. For several years in the early 1930s, the Cambridge philosopher G. E. Moore sat in on Wittgenstein's lectures and kept careful notes, which he published in 1954–1955, after Wittgenstein's death. At one point, after asserting that "the question of Aesthetics . . . was not 'Do you like this?' but '*Why* do you like it?,'" Wittgenstein, according to Moore, went on as follows:

> What Aesthetics tries to do, he said, is to give *reasons*, e.g. for having this word rather than that in a particular place in a poem, or for having this musical phrase rather than that in a particular place in a piece of music. . . . *Reasons*, he said, in Aesthetics, are "of the nature of further descriptions" . . . and all that Aesthetics does is "to draw your attention to a thing," to "place things side by side." He said that if, by giving "reasons" of this sort, you make another person "see what you see" but it still "doesn't appeal to him," that is "an end" of the discussion; and what he, Wittgenstein, had "at the back of his mind" was "the idea that aesthetic discussions were like discussions in a court of law," where you try to "clear up the circumstances" of the action which is being tried, hoping that in the end what you say will "appeal to the judge."[10]

This seems to me an extraordinarily accurate account of what actually goes on in critical discussions, and of how the logic of critical argument actually works. The legal analogy is also very provocative—though one wants to add that in the case of critical arguments (or what Wittgenstein calls "Aesthetics") there is no figure of authority comparable to the judge in a court of law. If two people cannot agree about a work of art—and, as I said earlier, if they talk long enough, disagreements are sure to emerge—then that is indeed "an end of the discussion."

The late 17th-century and early 18th-century critics and theorists we have been considering were well aware that criticism involves giving reasons for one's judgment, and is thus a rational activity. But they were unaware of the special nature of critical explanations, which they assumed were like ordinary, commonsense, quasi-scientific explanations, like the explanation of why water pipes sometimes burst in the winter. Critical explanations, they assumed, would also end in general lawlike statements specifying what qualities make a good play, a good song, a good portrait, and so on. This brings us back to the notion of rules, for these general specifications of the qualities necessary for artistic worth were what the critics had in mind when they spoke of rules. These rules they thought of as being known, unconsciously at any rate but perhaps consciously, by successful artists and reliable critics. For in addition to knowing that criticism involved giving reasons and rational argument, and was thus a rational activity, they also were perhaps more aware than we are that becoming an artist of any sort involves a long and demanding training. As Paul Oskar Kristeller has shown, the notion of the fine arts, as clearly distinguished from practical arts or mere crafts, came into existence in the 18th century, just shortly after the time we are discussing.[11] So it was natural that the critics and theorists of that time should have recognized, more clearly than we do, the amount of sheer craft that is involved in becoming an artist.

But what did these rules look like? What (to put it more formally) was their logical status? They looked, of course, rather like the sort of general specifications that Kennick, in his article "Does Traditional Aesthetics Rest on a Mistake?," showed were invalid—yet that could, when taken less literally, yield valid insights about art. For the whole purpose of the rules was to state something generally true about art or about a particular genre of one or another art. Yet the rules are somewhat different from those statements of the essence of art that Kennick had in mind—statements like "Art is imitation," "Art is expression," "Art is significant form," "Art is configurational coherence," and the like.

During the period we are considering, virtually everyone believed that art is imitation—in some sense or other of that extremely slippery term. But I do not believe that they thought of this as what they meant by a rule. It was rather, as the title of Batteux's book makes clear, a *principe*, a principle. Rules are more directly connected to what the artist or the critic actually does when performing his job—though, interestingly, they are not necessarily less general than grand principles like "Art is imitation" and the rest. In a later section of his article, Kennick argues vigorously (and I think successfully) against the commonly held notion—commonly held by aestheticians, at any rate—that successful (or even meaningful) criticism is impossible unless one holds the correct general theory about precisely what the essence of art is. In so doing, Kennick gives some examples of rules:

> Criticism has in no way been hampered by the absence of generally applicable canons and norms, and where such norms have been proposed they have either, like the notorious Unities in the case of tragedy, been shown to be absurd, or else, like the requirements of balance, harmony, and unity in variety, they have been so general, equivocal, and empty as to be useless in critical practice.
>
> [P. 331]

That is, some rules, like the alleged Aristotelian unities of place, time, and action, are so narrow as to be obviously wrong, while the others are so broad (or unclear) as to be of no help. Though I agree with everything else in Kennick's article, it seems to me that this judgment is wrong, or at least misleading.

To learn what the critics of our period actually meant by rules, it is necessary to see how they talked about them and how they put them into practice. Dryden, whom Dr. Johnson praised "as the father of English criticism, as the writer who first taught us to determine upon principles the merit of composition," is a good person to begin with. His lifetime (1631–1700) neatly covers the period during which the criticism based on rules took root in England and France, and since he was the most distinguished English poet of the time, his criticism was, as Johnson put it, "the criticism of a poet; not a dull collection of theorems, nor a rude detection of faults, which perhaps the censor was not able to have committed; but a gay and vigorous dissertation, where delight is mingled with instruction, and where the author proves his right of judgment by his power of performance."[12]

By the time Dryden began to write criticism, in the mid-1660s, he was already successful both as poet and playwright. He had celebrated Cromwell's memory in *Heroic Stanzas*, welcomed Charles's restoration with *Astraea Redux*, and scored his first dramatic success with the heroic play *The Indian Queen*, written in collaboration with his brother-in-law Sir Robert Howard. His first important work of criticism, the *Essay of Dramatick Poesie*, was written between the summer of 1665 and the late autumn of 1666, but was not published until late 1667 or early 1668. It is cast as a dialogue, carried on among four friends and separated into three arguments. The first concerns the relative merits of ancient and modern dramatists, the second the relative merits of French and English plays, and the third the question of whether plays should be composed in rhyme or in blank verse. Understandably, the rules are mentioned often. The ancients are praised as the source of the rules, and the defender of French plays over English ones bases his argument on the contention that the French have been more punctilious in their observance of the rules.

Howard, who by this time was already feuding with Dryden over other matters, took issue with Dryden's treatment of the rules in the *Essay of Dramatick Poesie* in the preface to his play, *The Great Favorite, or The Duke of Lerma*, which was also published in 1668. In fact Howard was dead against the very idea of attempting to give rules for literary composition or critical judgment. He spoke scornfully of "the unnecessary understanding of some that have labour'd to give strict rules to things that are not Mathematical," and declared that there was "not any thing more unreasonable to my Judgment than the attempt to infringe the Liberty of Opinion by Rules so little demonstrative." For Howard, the final arbiter in literary matters was not reason but taste: "for in the difference of *Tragedy* and *Comedy*, and of *Fars* it self, there can be no determination but by the Taste; nor in the manner of their Composure; and who ever wou'd endeavour to like or dislike by the Rules of others, he will be as unsuccessful as if he should try to be perswaded into a power of believing, not what he must, but what others direct him to believe."[13] This was, it almost goes without saying, a most unusual position to hold at this time, one that would surely have warmed the hearts of Goldschmidt and Serauky.

To be fair, Howard made one solid point. You cannot persuade someone, simply by citing rules, to like or dislike a work of art. There is indeed something involuntary and nonrational about aesthetic response—it is not without reason that the word "taste" came to be used metaphorically in books on aesthetics. But in all other respects, Howard's objections are wide of the mark, for he has utterly failed to see how subtly and interestingly Dryden was making use of the concept of rules in the *Essay of Dramatick Poesie*.[14]

In the second of the three arguments, after the defender of French plays has made his point about the greater punctiliousness with which French playwrights have observed the rules of the ancients, his opponent reminds him that the four disputants have earlier agreed on the following working definition of a play: "A just and lively image of human nature, representing its passions and humours, and the changes of fortune to which it is subject, for the delight and instruction of mankind" (p. 36). The defender of English plays then acknowledges "that the French contrive their plots more regularly, and observe the laws of comedy, and decorum of the stage (to speak generally), with more exactness than the English" (p. 67). Yet in doing so, they have contravened a more important rule, implicit in the agreed-upon definition of a play:

> For the lively imitation of Nature being in the definition of a play, those which best fulfil that law ought to be esteemed superior to the others. 'Tis true, those beauties of the French poesy are such as will raise perfection higher where it is, but are not sufficient to give it where it is not: they are indeed the beauties of a statue, but not of a man, because not animated with the soul of Poesy, which is imitation of humour and passions....
>
> [P. 68]

It is therefore clear that Dryden is not considering rules as the quasi-mathematical "demonstrative" propositions that Howard understood him to mean. Rather, rules are like laws within a legal system: under certain conditions, their violation is justified in order that a more important law may be obeyed.

We can see this conception of the rules at work as the argument about French and English plays continues. French plays, according to the defender of the English, are not only cold; they are also monotonous. He cannot see why his opponent and others of like mind "should cry up the barrenness of the French plots, above the variety and copiousness of the English":

> Their plots are single; they carry on one design, which is pushed forward by all the actors, every scene in the play contributing and moving towards it. Our plays, besides the main design, have under-plots or by-concernments, of less considerable persons and intrigues, which are carried on with the motion of the main plot: just as they say the orb of the fixed stars, and those of the planets, though they have motions of their own, are whirled about by the motion of the *Primum Mobile*, in which they are contained. That similitude expresses much of the English stage; for if contrary motions may be found in nature to agree; if a planet can go east and west at the same time, one way by virtue of his own motion, the other by the force of the First Mover, it will not be difficult to imagine how the under-plot, which is only different, not contrary to the great design, may naturally be conducted along with it.
>
> [Pp. 70-71]

In the earlier example, the rule that took precedence over the rule about unity of action was that the image or imitation of nature furnished by a play must be lively, not cold and rigid; this time the rule in question is the classical stipulation that works of art must combine unity and variety. Though he acknowledges that "the Unity of Action is sufficiently preserved" in the French plays, the defender of the English plays concludes that "our variety, if well ordered, will afford a greater pleasure to the audience" (p. 71).

In the third and final argument of the *Essay of Dramatick Poesie*, as to whether blank verse or rhyme is better for serious plays, the defender of rhyme naturally has his work cut out for him since classical poetry did not rhyme, and therefore there is no ancient rule recommending the use of rhyme. To make his case, he points out that with the birth of the modern European languages "a new way of poetry was practised" that "consisted in measure or number of feet, and rhyme; the sweetness of rhyme, and observation of accent, supplying the place of quantity in words" (p. 97). Therefore the use of rhyme in serious plays, though of course not practiced by the ancients, may be considered as established for the moderns "since the custom of all nations at this day confirms it, all the French, Italian, and Spanish tragedies are generally writ in it; and sure the universal consent of the most civilized parts of the world ought in this, as it doth in other customs, to include the rest" (p. 98). Yet Dryden does not want to make this rule absolutely binding: "no poet need constrain himself at all times to it. It is enough he makes it his general rule; for I deny not but sometimes there may be a greatness in placing the words otherwise; and sometimes they may sound better, sometimes also the variety itself is excuse enough" (p. 98). Once again Dryden is sensitive to the fact that other, conflicting rules, such as the need for variety, may under certain circumstances invalidate the rhyme rule.

We have seen, then, that although Dryden insists on the existence, and the need to honor, rules in literary composition (and, by implication, in literary criticism as well), he does not do so in blind obedience to the authority of the ancients and he does not see the rules as universally binding but rather as laws in a legal system, able under certain circumstances to prevail over one another. We can get a still clearer idea of what rules meant to him if we look briefly at his reply to Howard, "A Defence of an Essay of Dramatique Poesie," which he prefixed to the second edition of his play *The Indian Emperour*, also published in 1668.

After several pages of badinage, Dryden gets down to business, challenging Howard's contention that "there can be no determination but by the Taste" insofar as the differences between good and bad plays:

> The liking or disliking of the people gives the play the denomination of good or bad, but does not really make or constitute it such. To please the people ought to be the poet's aim, because plays are made for their delight; but it does not follow that they are always pleased with good plays, or that the plays which please them are always good.
>
> [Pp. 120-121]

Dryden is here merely appealing, by implication, to the fact that it is not self-contradictory to say of a play "The audience loved it, but it was bad" (or, for that matter, "The audience hated it, but it was good"). In fact, we do say such things all the time. That the audience liked or disliked a play can sometimes be adduced as a reason for judging it to be a good or bad play, but the audience's like or dislike is a different fact about the play from its being either good or bad, it is not another way of stating the same fact.

Dryden then attacks the more general question of whether or not it makes any sense to speak of rules governing the creation and critical judgment of plays (and, by extension, of other works of art). "I never heard of any other foundation of Dramatic Poesy than the imitation of Nature," he writes. From which he concludes: "if Nature is to be imitated, then there is a rule for imitating Nature rightly; otherwise there may be an end, and no means conducing to it" (p. 123). Notice that Dryden thinks of the general principle that drama is an imitation of nature as different from a rule, as the "foundation" on which not only the practice of dramatic art but the rules themselves are somehow based. (Though, as we saw earlier, in the *Essay of Dramatick Poesy* he treated the notion that a play must be a specifically "lively" imitation of nature as merely another rule.)

Picking up Howard's word "demonstrative," Dryden then writes:

> Hitherto I have proceeded by demonstration; but as our divines, when they have proved a Deity, because there is order, and have inferred that this Deity ought to be worshipped, differ afterwards in the manner of the worship; so, having laid down, that Nature is to be imitated, and that proposition proving the next, that then there are means which conduce to the imitating of Nature, I dare proceed no further positively; but have only laid down some opinions of the Ancients and Moderns, and of my own, as means which they used, and which I thought probable for the attaining of that end.
>
> [P. 123]

Dryden is here drawing a distinction, common in the philosophy of the time, between degrees of certainty. He believes that the logical relation between the principle that the foundation of poetic drama is the imitation of nature and the truth of some rule(s) or other for imitating nature (in the relevant fashion) is exactly as close as the relation between successive steps in a geometrical proof. But the logical relation between that principle and any particular rule for imitating nature that has been (or might be?) proposed is merely one of probability. Therefore he says "I dare proceed no further positively," using that word not just in its ordinary sense of confidently or explicitly but also in its technical sense of absolutely or unconditionally—a sense common in contemporary logical and legal writing. In other words, if we accept the principle, then we logically commit ourselves to the belief that there must be some rules or other that tell writers and critics how to go about imitating nature; but we do not commit ourselves to the truth or validity of any particular rule.

Howard had discovered and criticized what he foolishly took to be inconsistencies in the *Essay of Dramatick Poesie*, not realizing that it was a genuine dialogue rather than a simple, straightforward expression of Dryden's own views. Dryden's correction of this error offers him the opportunity to explain further the state of mind in which one can be committed to the existence of rules for the composition and criticism of literature and yet not finally committed to the truth of any particular rules:

> He is here pleased to charge me with being magisterial, as he has done in many other places of his preface; therefore, in vindication of myself, I must crave leave to say, that my whole discourse was sceptical, according to that way of reasoning which was used by Socrates, Plato, and all the Academics of old, which Tully and the best of the Ancients followed, and which is imitated by the modest inquisitions of the Royal Society.
>
> [P. 124]

Calling attention to the title of his work, he insists that it is genuinely an essay, an attempt or trial effort, "a dialogue sustained by persons of several opinions, all of them left doubtful, to be determined by the readers in general" (p. 124). And he reminds Howard (and the reader) that in the "Epistle Dedicatory" originally prefixed to the *Essay* he had spoken of the four characters in his dialogue as having "differed in their opinions, as 'tis probable they would; neither do I take upon me to reconcile, but to relate them" (pp. 124–125; cf. p. 27).

Dryden's emphasis on his own skeptical attitude toward the questions discussed in his *Essay* of course contradicts the implication that we noticed, again and again, in Goldschmidt and Serauky and also in the scholars whose dissertations we reviewed, that even to speak of rules in connection with the arts is to be rigid, dogmatic, not in tune with the freedom of imagination we grant to artists and the freedom of judgment we grant to critics. To see the creation and criticism of literary art as rule-governed, and therefore rational, activities is not necessarily to deny or minimize the influence of taste on both poets and critics. We can see how Dryden the rational skeptic set about reconciling an apparent clash between rules and taste in several of his later critical essays.

For example, in his brief essay "The Grounds of Criticism in Tragedy," appended to the Preface to his reworking of Shakespeare's *Troilus and Cressida* (1679), Dryden deals with the conflict between his own overwhelming sense of Shakespeare's greatness and the fact that Shakespeare knew little or nothing of the classical rules. The rule about tragedies having unity of action, Dryden insists at the outset, is founded on "natural reason": "two different independent actions distract the attention and concernment of the audience, and consequently destroy the intention of the poet" (p. 208). This rule, however, from which it follows that a tragedy "must not be a history of one man's life, suppose of Alexander the Great, or Julius Caesar, but one single action of theirs," would immediately disqualify "all Shakespeare's historical plays, which are rather chronicles represented, than tragedies; and all double action of plays" (pp. 207–208). But just as Terence constructed his plots by weaving those of two Greek comedies together, keeping one subservient to the other so as to preserve the essential unity of action, so this custom "has obtained on the English stage, to give us the pleasure of variety" (p. 208).

Having thus bent the rule about unity of action somewhat, Dryden proceeds to bend it still further—to include much of Shakespeare's tragic writing, though not without occasionally censuring the obscurity and extravagance of his language. While "it is not just that new rules should destroy the authority of the old" (p. 211), it is nonetheless true that "to instruct delightfully is the general end of all poetry" (p. 209), and therefore it is also a rule "to put nothing into the discourse which may hinder your moving of the passions" (p. 223). Though Dryden finds it true that "no man should pretend to write, who cannot temper his fancy with his judgment" (p. 222), and though he cannot deny of Shakespeare that "the fury of his fancy often transported him beyond the bounds of judgment" (p. 224), he also asserts that "Shakespeare had an universal mind, which comprehended all characters and passions" (p. 228). From the analysis of several passages, Dryden argues that these virtues outweigh Shakespeare's failure to abide by the letter of the unity of action rule.

In conclusion, Dryden apologizes for not having covered in his essay all the topics he intended to cover:

> It is, I confess, but cursorily written; yet the judgment, which is given here, is generally founded upon experience: but because many men are shocked at the name of

rules, as if they were a kind of magisterial prescription upon poets, I will conclude with the words of Rapin, in his *Reflections* on Aristotle's work *of Poetry*: "If the rules be well considered, we shall find them to be made only to reduce Nature into method, to trace her step by step, and not to suffer the least mark of her to escape us: 'tis only by these, that probability in fiction is maintained, which is the soul of poetry."

[P. 228]

It is evident, then, that the rules are empirical generalizations formed by observing what succeeded and what failed in poetry, and what is therefore likely to succeed and fail in the future. They are not more or less arbitrary regulations established by fiat, "magisterial prescriptions upon poets." The nature of poetry naturally changes with the passing of centuries: rhyme is now admitted in serious plays, Shakespearean double plots are permissible so long as the secondary plot remains clearly subservient to the primary one, and so on. But there is also the conviction that poetry will change only within certain limits: for poetry is, after all, written by and for human beings, and (as 17th- and 18th-century writers were fond of saying) human nature is everywhere and always the same. Though we cite Aristotle or Horace in referring to the rules, they are (to quote Rapin again) "founded upon good sense, and sound reason, rather than on authority," as is evident from "the ridiculous mistakes and gross absurdities which have been made by those poets who have taken their fancy only for their guide," for "if this fancy be not regulated, it is a mere caprice, and utterly incapable to produce a reasonable and judicious poem" (quoted pp. 228-229)—or, we might add, critical judgment.

IV

So-called rationalist aesthetics, then, was far from the "narrowly dogmatic" monstrosity it has usually been made out to be. As I indicated earlier, I would even argue against Kennick's contention that the rules were so narrowly restrictive as to be downright absurd (like the unities of time, place, and action) or (like the requirements of unity in variety, balance, and the like) were too vague to be of any real use to either critics or artists.

Take first the requirements of unity in variety, proportion, symmetry, harmony, balance, and so on. All these terms are, of course, vague in the sense that we do not immediately know whether or not to apply them in a given case. If someone shows us a poem or painting, or plays us a piece on the piano, and then asks whether or not the particular work has harmony or unity, he is not asking a simple empirical question. There is no direct, immediate procedure for making the test that will determine whether or not the term applies. And yet the question is not meaningless: terms like *harmony* and *unity* do, after all, have a certain aura of suggestion about them. Though there is no simple procedure, such as counting or measuring or weighing, that will immediately give us an answer to the question, the terms do suggest the direction in which we might look for answers.

These terms, and many others like them that we use in critical discussion—*graceful*, *somber*, *powerful*, *delicate*, *serene*, and so on—are thus vague and yet not totally vague. Their application is not governed by any set list of necessary and sufficient conditions, as is the application of terms like *square* or *isosceles triangle*. In his 1959 article "Aesthetic Concepts,"[15] Frank Sibley has argued that these terms that pop up so often in critical discussions are not condition-governed at all in their application, except perhaps negatively. Other familiar, everyday but non-aesthetic terms like *lazy* and *intelligent*, Sibley points out, do not depend for their application upon any list of *necessary* conditions being met, yet for the concepts such terms represent "there are a number of relevant features, A, B, C, D, E, such that the presence of some groups or combinations of these features is *sufficient* for the application of the concept" (p. 425). If, for example, we were told that someone had mastered three languages by the time he was seven, had stood at the top of his high school class, and had earned a Ph.D.

in physics from M.I.T. at age 20, we should probably be ready to agree that he was, in our ordinary sense of the term, intelligent. Moreover, the fact that somebody plays chess extremely well can only count toward, and not against, our judging him to be intelligent. But aesthetic terms and concepts are not like this.

There is, Sibley contends, no specifiable list of conditions that, if met, would put it more or less beyond question that a vase was delicate, a landscape serene. Moreover, the perceptual facts about a work of art do not count so clearly in one direction, either for or against the application of an aesthetic term. The art critic Harold Rosenberg once described Jackson Pollock's painting "Blue Poles" as being "attractive because of a degree of naturalistic grossness."[16] Aesthetic concepts, Sibley concludes, can be only negatively condition-governed: "If I am told that a painting in the next room consists solely of one or two bars of very pale blue and very pale grey set at right angles on a pale fawn ground, I can be sure that it cannot be fiery or garish or gaudy or flamboyant" (p. 427).

Therefore I think that Kennick is too harsh when he says that requirements of harmony, balance, and unity in variety, and the rules about the three unities, are too vague to be of real use to either artists or critics. Like other aesthetic terms, these too are not simply vague but are open-ended. They possess what the Viennese philosopher Friedrich Waismann (1896–1959) called *Porosität*, porousness, or (as it is usually rendered in English) open texture.[17] But, recalling that Dryden seemed to conceive of the rules rather the way in which we conceive of laws in a legal system that is constantly changing and evolving, we might note that many key legal concepts are also open-textured. Take, for example, *criminal negligence*. We all know (roughly) what the phrase means, and can give real or hypothetical examples of the offense it designates. Yet even though there are doubtless many statutes in existence that refine upon its meaning in particular circumstances, no one, not the most learned jurist in the country, can give an exact and exhaustive definition. We have to see what issues are raised by particular cases as they come up. Or take two such concepts much in the news just now, *sexual harassment* and *obscenity*. They too get progressively (though never finally, definitively) clarified as particular cases are tried and decided, but to ask for a final definition would be pointless. They are simply not that sort of concept. The Supreme Court Justice who recently said that he did not know what obscenity was, but knew it when he saw it, was not being either dense or evasive but just honest.

If indeed the rules that the critics and theorists we are considering were so concerned with are neither narrowly dictatorial nor hopelessly vague, then their relation to the concept of taste, which was gaining ground so quickly in the early 18th century, is not, as it has so frequently been said to be, one of simple opposition. For most of these thinkers, it was not a matter of rules (cold reason) versus taste (feeling, emotion): choose one, or work out some proportion between them. The whole point was to fuse or reconcile the two, for to almost everyone it was obvious that both play a vital role in the creation and the appreciation of art.

Chapter Five

Rationalist Aesthetics: Taste

The concept of taste (*goût*) does not appear as such in Boileau's *L'Art poétique* (1674), though he does at one point use the phrase "injustes dégoûts" (IV, 63) and at another a form of the verb *goûter* (IV, 183). The unadorned noun *goût* had apparently not yet established itself as the name for a faculty (or quasi-faculty) of the mind or sensibility. At this time the talk in France was rather of a mysterious something—indefinable, indescribable, inexplicable—called the *je ne sais quoi*, a quality of nature or art or human behavior that pleased us in a deeply personal and intimate way but that seemed to lie outside the standard, accepted categories or sources of pleasure. In 1671, three years before Boileau's poem, Father Dominique Bouhours published the fullest account of the *je ne sais quoi* as one section of his book *Entretiens d'Ariste et d'Eugène*.[1] In the course of this particular conversation the elusive *je ne sais quoi* is said to be "a grace which brightens beauty and other natural perfections," the very existence of which forces us to "give the lie to philosophers who have always maintained that knowledge precedes love; that the will can love nothing which is unknown to the rational faculty" (p. 184). It is also pointed out that "the *je ne sais quoi* is almost the only subject about which no books have been written and which the learned have never taken the trouble to elucidate. Lectures, dissertations and treatises have been composed on very odd subjects, but no author, as far as I know, has worked on this one" (p. 191). That situation would soon be remedied.

The *je ne sais quoi* was the source of both moral and aesthetic pleasure, and indeed in the 17th and 18th centuries the two were often blended together or actually confused with one another, as in the famous yet enormously tedious writings of Anthony Ashley Cooper (1671-1713), third Earl of Shaftesbury. Even before Shaftesbury, though, hints of an English version of the *je ne sais quoi* could be found in the writings of Lord Herbert of Cherbury (1583-1648), brother of the great poet George Herbert, and the so-called Cambridge Platonists of the late 17th century. The philosophers' attention shifted inward, from the external source of this mysterious, unclassifiable pleasure to the faculty that detected or recognized it, what Cambridge Platonist Henry More (1614-1687) called "the *Boniform Faculty of the Soul*":

> namely, a Faculty of that divine Composition, and supernatural Texture, as enables us to distinguish not only what is simply and absolutely the best, but to relish it, and have pleasure in that alone. Which Faculty much resembles that part of the Will which moves towards that which we judge to be absolutely the best, when, as it were with an unquenchable thirst and affection it is hurried on towards so pleasing an Object; and being in possession of it, is swallowed up in satisfaction that cannot be expressed.[2]

In the later writings of Ralph Cudworth (1617-1688), Locke, and others, this line of investigation led to the development, in vigorous opposition to Hobbes, of what is called ethical intuitionism, the view that our awareness of moral values is as immediate and intuitive as our knowledge of mathematical truths.[3]

In France, the same shift of attention produced a sort of conflation of the *je ne sais quoi* and *goût*, and, finally, a concentration on the latter. The first important writer seriously to discuss *goût* as a sort of sixth sense was apparently Jean Baptiste Dubos, in his 1719 *Réflexions critiques*, which was mentioned earlier.[4]

I

It is in Chapter xxii of Volume II of his work that Dubos makes his famous assertion that we judge whether or not works of art please us, not by rules but rather by attending to the promptings of a "sixth sense." Yet it is important to point out at once that this assertion of the primacy of sense in aesthetic judgment in no way diminishes the importance of the rules for Dubos. Throughout his first volume and the earlier chapters of the second, he has insisted that works must conform to the rules if they are to be successful—that is, to please and move their audience. Like Dryden, he knows that the rules for poetry passed down by the Romans "are nothing else in fact but the observations and practice of the best poets reduced to method" (I, 261), and he admits the difficulty of "positively" stating the rules: "let those, who have more confidence and resolution than I am master of, attempt to fix the limits between the probable and the marvelous, with relation to each kind of poetry" (I, 197). Yet these qualifications do not stop him from asserting, in his chapter on music, that since music, like poetry and painting, is an imitative art, "like these arts it must conform to the general rules with respect to the choice of the subject, the probability, and several other points" (I, 372). He realizes, as did virtually all contemporary critics, that conformity to rule is not a sufficient condition for artistic excellence: "'Tis impossible for either a poem, or picture, to produce this effect [i.e., to move the heart], unless they have some other merit besides that of the regularity and elegance of execution. The best drawn picture imaginable, or a poem disposed in the most regular manner, and written with the greatest accuracy of style, may prove frigid and tiresom" (II, 2). Still, there are good reasons why "eminent masters" produce works that "conform to rules": "not as the ultimate end of their art, but only as means for displaying beauties of a much superior nature. They conform to rules, in order to gain our minds by a continued probability; a probability capable of making us forget, that 'tis a mere fiction which softens our hearts" (II, 3-4).

In his chapter on the sixth sense, Dubos wants merely to insist that it is not the fact of a work's conformity to the rules that pleases or moves us:

> Now our senses inform us whether a work touches or makes a proper impression upon us, much better than all the dissertations composed by critics, to explain its merit, and calculate its perfections and defects. The way of discussion and analysis, which those gentlemen employ, is indeed very proper, when the point is to find out the causes why a work pleases or not; but this method is inferior to that of the sense, when we are to decide the following question: Does the work please, or does it not?
>
> [II, 237-238]

In other words, Dubos has nothing against reason and the rules so long as they know and keep their place: "Reason therefore ought not to intervene in a judgment which we pass on a poem or picture in general, except it be to account for the decision of our senses and to explain what faults hinder it from pleasing, and what charms are capable of rendering it engaging" (II, 238). In other words, the "decision" made spontaneously by the senses upon receipt of their "impression" of a work is logically prior to a rational explanation, probably offered in terms of the work's conformity or lack of conformity to various rules, of why and how it pleases or fails to please. Boileau would certainly not have disagreed, though his emphasis would have been different.

Dubos is less clear, however, about the precise status of this sixth sense in relation to the ordinary five senses. Directly after the passage just cited, he jokingly parodies an imagined hyper-rationalism by asking, tongue in cheek: "Do we ever reason, in order to know whether a ragoo be good or bad; and has it ever entered into any body's head, after having settled the geometrical principles of taste, and defined the qualities of each ingredient that enters into the composition of those messes, to examine into the proportion observed in their mixture, in order to decide whether the ragoo be good or bad" (II, 238)? No, of course not. This is similar to the point that Howard was making, in his argument with Dryden, about the impossibility of getting oneself to like or dislike something merely on the basis of someone else's rules.

Dubos is now prepared to unveil his sixth sense. The whole paragraph in which he does it is worth citing, since it is so confusing (and perhaps confused):

> We have a sense, which judges of the merit of works, that consist in the imitation of objects of a moving nature. This is the very sense, which would have judged of the object, that the painter, poet, or musician has imitated. 'Tis the eye, when we are to judge of the coloring of a picture. 'Tis the ear, when we are to decide, whether the accents of a recitative be moving, whether they agree with the words, and whether the music be melodious. If we are to determine, whether the imitation we are entertained with in a poem or in the composition of a picture, be capable of exciting our pity, and of moving us; the sense whose province it is to judge thereof, is the very sense which would have been moved, and have judged of the object imitated. 'Tis that sixth sense we have within us, without seeing its organs. 'Tis a portion of ourselves, which judges from what it feels, and which, to express myself in Plato's words, determines, without consulting either rule or compass. This is, in fine, what is commonly called sense or sensitive perception.
>
> [II, 239]

The problem of course is how the sixth sense differs, in nature and function, from the other five.

When we read the opening sentence of the paragraph, having some idea of what lies ahead, we surely assume that "this sense" refers to the sixth sense, whose operation is about to be defined. But then the point turns out to be that the same sense judges a particular aspect of a work of art that would have judged that aspect of whatever natural object the work of art imitates. Thus with the coloring of a picture, it is the eye—which would have judged the coloring of the natural scene shown in the picture. And with the emotional effect of the recitative (*récit* is Dubos's word), the ear will be the judge—though it is hard here to know exactly what is being imitated, what in nature would correspond to the coloring of the landscape in the previous example. The sentence that follows seems just a summary of what has preceded: the emotional effect of an artistic imitation will be judged by the same sense that would have judged the effect of the imitated original. But then suddenly this sense turns out to be the mysterious sixth sense, not the eye or ear or organ of any other ordinary sense. The reference to Plato, footnoted to Book X of the *Republic*, is singularly unhelpful. The passage Dubos has in mind is probably at 602-603, where Socrates and Glaucon contrast two functions of the soul. One, the superior function (which Plato terms λογιστικόν, skilled in calculation or reasoning), can see through the illusions created by artists; the other, which Plato contemptuously does not even name (but characterizes as base or trivial, φαῦλον), is taken in by the illusions of art. It is of course to this latter, despised function of the soul that Dubos compares his sixth sense! For unlike Plato, he regards the ability to calculate, at least in this context, as a liability, not an advantage.

It does not get any easier. Dubos also seems confused about exactly who possesses this sixth sense. "'Tis as rare to see men born without the sense here mentioned, as 'tis to meet with people born blind" (II, 240), he tells us. Thus virtually everyone would seem equally competent to judge artistic merit—just as everyone with normal color vision would perform about the same on a color identification test. And indeed the title of the chapter is "That the public judges right of poems and pictures in general. Of the sense we have to distinguish the merit of these works." But then Dubos casually remarks: "I do not mean the lower class of people by the public capable of passing judgment on poems or pictures, or of deciding the measure of their excellence. The word *public* is applicable here to such persons only, as have acquired some lights, either by reading or by being conversant with the world" (II, 245). But then again: "As the chief aim of poetry and painting is to move and please us, every man who is not absolutely stupid, must feel the effect of good verses, and fine pictures" (II, 247-248). Yet on the other hand: "The perfection of a great part of the beauties of a picture, for instance, that of the design, is not rightly perceptible but to painters, or *connoisseurs* who have studied painting as much as the artists themselves" (II, 249). The tangle seems hopeless.

Despite all his confusions, however, Dubos does make it clear that for him reason and feeling, rules and the sixth sense, are not opposed: they are, rather, complementary, reason stepping in and explaining exactly why a particular work of art has moved (or failed to move) us emotionally. This is also true in the next work to be considered, *An Inquiry into the Original of our Ideas of Beauty and Virtue* (1725) by the Scottish philosopher Francis Hutcheson (1694–1746).

II

The difference is that Hutcheson, a professor at the University of Glasgow, was an experienced thinker who had at his disposal the philosophical machinery developed by Locke in his *Essay concerning Human Understanding* (1690). Because Hutcheson generously dedicated his book to Shaftesbury, their names are always linked in histories of English thought during this period. But this is most unfair to Hutcheson. In fact, two writers could scarcely be more different: Shaftesbury the enthusiastic rhapsodist, careless of distinctions and more attentive to his self-preening prose style than to what he is saying; Hutcheson the careful, hardheaded reasoner, extending the advances made by Locke into philosophical territories that Locke had scanted. As its title suggests, Hutcheson's *Inquiry* is divided into two separate treatises, one on aesthetics and the other on morals. Hutcheson argues that in each of these areas a sixth sense, an "internal sense" or "sense of beauty" in the case of aesthetics and a "moral sense" (sometimes also called an "internal sense") in the case of morals, is the power that receives impressions and renders judgment. Only the first of Hutcheson's two treatises concerns us here.[5]

Hutcheson begins with a bow to Locke: "There is no part of *Philosophy* of more importance, than a *just Knowledge* of *human Nature*, and its various Powers and Dispositions. Our late Inquirys have been very much employ'd about our *Understanding*, and the several Methods of obtaining *Truth*" (p. iii). Yet while we all acknowledge that "the Importance of any Truth is nothing else than its Moment, or Efficacy to make Men happy, or to give them the greatest and most lasting Pleasure," the philosophers have failed to tell us "how it is that *Knowledge* or *Truth* is pleasant to us" (pp. iii-iv). So far as pleasures are concerned, all the philosophers have given us is "some bare Division of them into *Sensible*, and *Rational*, and some trite commonplace Arguments to prove the *latter* to be more valuable than the *former*" (p. iv). As a result, both sorts of pleasure have been sold short:

> Our *sensible Pleasures* are slightly pass'd over, and explain'd only by some Instances in *Tastes, Smells, Sounds*, or such like, which Men of any tolerable Reflection generally look upon as very trifling Satisfactions. Our *rational Pleasures* have had much the

same kind of treatment. We are seldom taught any other Notion of rational Pleasure than that which we have upon reflecting on our Possession, or claim to those Objects, which may be occasions of Pleasure; such Objects we call *advantageous*; but *Advantage*, or *Interest*, cannot be distinctly conceiv'd till we know what these Pleasures are which advantageous Objects are apt to excite; and what Senses or Powers of Perception we have about such Objects.

[P. iv]

The suggestion is clearly that there is something arbitrary and misleading about the philosophers' "bare Division" of pleasures into sensible and rational, that there is a good deal of commerce back and forth over the dividing line, and that there is perhaps an intermediate territory, hitherto ignored or dismissed as a kind of no-man's-land, that is worth investigating.

Hutcheson is not long in reaching it. "In reflecting upon our *external Senses*," he writes, "we plainly see, that our Perceptions of Pleasure, or Pain, do not depend directly on our Will" (p. v). That is, they are out of our control: we cannot will ourselves to reject or alter a sense impression. But, Hutcheson continues, "there are many other sorts of Objects, which please, or displease us as necessarily, as material Objects do when they operate upon our Organs of Sense" (p. v). As examples, Hutcheson lists: "a *regular Form*, a piece of *Architecture*, or *Painting*, a Composition of *Notes*, a *Theorem*, an *Action*, an *Affection*, a *Character*" (p. v). In these cases too the impression, whether pleasure or pain or something more complex, cannot be rejected or altered by an act of will: as surely as any simple impression of sight, smell, or touch, it just is what it is. Yet these objects are not material objects—despite the fact that the piece of architecture will be made of stone or wood, and the painting of canvas and bits of pigment. For in these cases "the Pleasure arises from some *Uniformity, Order, Arrangement, Imitation*; and not from the simple Ideas of *Colour*, or *Sound*, or mode of *Extension* separately consider'd" (p. vi). For the sources of pleasure are (to invoke Locke's distinction) not simple ideas but rather complex ideas, formed by the mind's act of combining together several simple ideas.

This then is Hutcheson's intermediate territory. The pleasure we derive from contemplating the order or harmony of a building, a painting, a musical composition, is as irresistible as a simple sense impression. Yet, as Hutcheson points out, it is also very different. For there are many people whose ordinary (or external) senses operate quite normally, yet who "relish no pleasure in Musical Compositions, in Painting, Architecture, natural Landskip; or but a very weak one in comparison of what others enjoy from the same Objects. This greater Capacity of receiving such pleasant Ideas we commonly call a fine Genius or Taste" (p. 8). "There is still something further necessary," beyond normally operating external senses, "not only to make a compleat Master in Architecture, Painting, or Statuary, but even a tolerable Judge in these Works; or to receive the highest pleasure in contemplating them" (p. 9). Therefore Hutcheson proposes that we call this special sense—or these special senses, for he suggests that there may be several of them, even in just the aesthetic realm—an internal sense.

He also offers another, quite interesting justification for adopting the phrase "internal sense" for the power that receives ideas of beauty, harmony, and the like. "In some other Affairs, where our External Senses are not much concern'd, we discern a sort of Beauty, very like, in many respects, to that observ'd in sensible Objects, and accompany'd with like pleasure: Such is that Beauty perceiv'd in Theorems, or universal Truths, in general Causes, and in some extensive Principles of Action" (p. 8).

But what is it, about the natural objects and works of art that give us these impressions of beauty, harmony, and order, that causes them to do so? What particular qualities in them enable them to do so? This important question Hutcheson answers with perhaps surprising ease:

> The Figures that excite in us the Ideas of Beauty, seem to be those in which there is *Uniformity amidst Variety*. There are many Conceptions of Objects that are agreeable

> upon other accounts, such as Grandeur, Novelty, Sanctity, and some others, that shall be touched at afterwards. But what we call Beautiful in Objects, to speak in the Mathematical Style, seems to be in a compound Ratio of Uniformity and Variety; so that where the Uniformity of Bodys is equal, the Beauty is as the Variety; and where the Variety is equal, the Beauty is as the Uniformity.
>
> [Pp. 15-16]

In fairness it should be added that in later editions of the *Inquiry*, Hutcheson considerably toned down the mathematical analogies.

Now of course "Uniformity amidst Variety" is just another of the rationalist rules. Yet Hutcheson is saying that this is what appeals to our sense of beauty. Therefore he too, like Dubos but in a much clearer and more suggestive manner, is bridging the gap between reason and emotion, thought and feeling: the rules and emotional response are two complementary ways of dealing with the same phenomenon. Most of the remainder of Hutcheson's first treatise need not concern us. It is devoted to reiterations of the theological argument from design; proofs of the universality among men of the internal senses (though of course Hutcheson, like others, has trouble with the problem of critical disagreements); proofs that the internal senses are innate and are not formed by custom or education; and speculation on the final cause, the importance to human life, of the internal senses. There is, however, one further remark worth citing because it bears out Hutcheson's desire to bridge the gap between reason and emotion by this discovery of the realm of internal sense. "As in our external senses, so in our *internal* ones, the pleasant Sensations generally arise from those Objects which calm Reason would have recommended, had we understood their Use, and which might have engag'd our pursuits from *Self-interest*" (p. 33).

It would be very interesting to know whether or not Gottsched had read Hutcheson's *Inquiry* either before or during the writing of *Versuch einer critischen Dichtkunst*. We know that he had read Shaftesbury, whom he cites admiringly in the preface to the *Versuch*, and he might well have been led to the *Inquiry* by Hutcheson's dedication of it to Shaftesbury. Since Gottsched cites Shaftesbury in English, and voices the hope that his works will soon be translated into German, we know that he kept in touch with English letters. In any event, his treatment of taste compares very interestingly with Hutcheson's.[6]

III

The passage from Shaftesbury that Gottsched cites in his preface in fact concerns taste. He has been explaining why he spoke, in his title, of a specifically *critical* poetics, and this has involved him in a discussion of the term and its overtones. Many readers, he fears, will take offense at the term, either because they think of criticism as mere "scholastic pedantry" (p. i) or because they understand perfectly well what real criticism is but are afraid of opening their own works to critical scrutiny and so have a bad conscience. There is, he admits, a lower class of so-called critics who concern themselves only with "Buchstaben und Sylben," letters and syllables—one is reminded of Pope's satirizing of dull, pedestrian philological critics in the *Dunciad*, the first version of which had been published in 1728, just two years before Gottsched's *Versuch*. But genuine criticism is far nobler: "Her name itself shows that she must be an art of exercising judgment that necessarily sets out to test or investigate something according to the basic rules appropriate to the object under investigation" (p. ii). Criticism in this elevated sense applies, however, only to the liberal arts, not to the sciences or geometry, which long ago attained demonstrative certainty: "According to this explanation, then, a critic is a learned person who has examined the rules of the liberal arts philosophically, and who is thus in a position to test rationally and judge correctly the beauties and defects of all masterpieces or works of art that come his way" (p. ii).

Gottsched then gives a brief intellectual autobiography, listing the books he read while in the employ of Professor Johann Burkhard Mencke, a Leipzig historian, whose children he tutored and who had the largest private library in Leipzig. It was this reading, together with his association with another Leipzig scholar, an historian and legal writer named Mascov, that gave Gottsched the idea for the *Versuch*: "I now seized the opportunity to prepare a first draft of a critical poetics, and to bring the thoughts and observations about poetry, which up to now had been disorganized, into a coherent system" (pp. vii-viii). The work would "certainly not be spun out of my brain, but rather assembled from all the aforementioned writers . . . and brought into an orderly arrangement" (p. viii). It is in this context that he cites Shaftesbury, to the effect that "*a Taste or Judgment*, 'tis supposed, can hardly come ready formed with us into the World":

> Use, Practice and Culture must precede the Understanding and Wit of such an advanced Size and Growth as this. A legitimate and just *Taste* can neither be begotten[,] made, conceiv'd, or produc'd, *without the antecedent Labour and Pains of Criticism.*
>
> [Quoted pp. xi-xii]⁷

It is thus no surprise that Gottsched considers the problem of taste quite early in his book, in its third chapter.

The opening chapter is devoted to the origins of poetry, in poems designed to move the passions, and the second to the character of the poet. Since he is to be "a skilled imitator of all natural things" (p. 83), the poet must develop "wide-ranging erudition": "No branch of knowledge is wholly excluded from his sphere" (p. 88). High on the list of a poet's necessary attainments stands, of course, "good taste."

Noting that taste has been much talked of recently, Gottsched says he will not discuss the history of the concept but will move immediately to explaining what he terms the rule that a poet must possess sound, highly developed taste. To do this, he examines the nature of what we mean by taste, beginning with its literal sense, as "the capability or gift of our tongue, to experience the various impressions produced upon it by food and drink, if they have affected and permeated it sufficiently" (p. 100). Gottsched then introduces a distinction that was becoming important in German philosophy, and would become still more so in the aesthetics of Alexander Baumgarten (1714–1762) and his pupil and popularizer Georg Friedrich Meier (1718–1777): "Further, one will readily grant that the concepts and ideas that we have of the taste of various foods, for all their distinctness [*Klarheit*], nonetheless have nothing intelligible [*deutliches*] in them" (p. 100). At first this seems puzzling: most non-native speakers of German are used to thinking of *klar* and *deutlich* as synonyms, as in Rosalinde's teasing question in *Die Fledermaus*: "Spricht denn diese Situation hier nicht klar und deutlich schon?" But this is clearly not the case here.

Gottsched immediately explains:

> When we are healthy, we are surely able to distinguish sweet from acetic, sour from bitter, etc., and to call each by its proper name: thus the concepts given us by these words are not completely obscure [*dunckel*]. Yet we are not able to answer the most trifling question of all: if someone should ask us how the sour taste differs from the bitter, or how the bitter differs from the acetic, the sharp, etc., and how we distinguish one from another. This shows that our ideas of these things are confused [*verwirrt*], and are just as unintelligible [*undeutlich*] as our concepts of the colors red, blue, green, and yellow. And it was because of this unintelligibility [*Undeutlichkeit*] that someone made up the proverb: one must not quarrel much about taste.
>
> [Pp. 100-101]

The distinction being drawn between *klar* and *deutlich* is the distinction between simple instinctive recognition or identification and recognition or identification of something that we can then go on to explain, to give some sort of account of. And of course this makes perfect sense when we consider the two words. *Klar* is from Latin *clarus*, which has the notion of brightness, and hence a visual metaphor, behind it, while *deutlich* is from *deuten*, to explain or interpret. Thus *klar*, taken strictly, means clear in the sense of being bright, shining, easily recognizable (the Latin word often means famous), while *deutlich* means verbally, conceptually explicable, interpretable. Thus our sensations of taste (in its original, literal sense) can be both *klar* and *verwirrt*, clear and confused, because we can distinguish them one from another on the tongue but cannot do so verbally beyond simply naming them. They are thus in a special, in-between realm, which may remind us somewhat of Hutcheson's efforts to delineate a similarly special realm, similar to and yet different from ordinary sense experience, in which aesthetic (and moral) experiences take place.

But Gottsched is not—or not yet, at any rate—talking about aesthetic experience: he is still dealing with taste in its common literal sense. Yet he certainly seems to be suggesting that ordinary experiences of taste—tasting sugar, vinegar, ragouts, and so on—occupy a different realm from that occupied by other ordinary sense experience—toothaches, for example, or the tingling we feel when our foot has fallen asleep, or the sense of butterflies in the stomach we may get before taking an examination. For the word that we use, metaphorically, to cover aesthetic experiences and our judgment of them is, after all, *taste*, which is confined, in its literal sense, to this very special group of sense experiences.

In any case, Gottsched arrives soon enough at the metaphorical use of *taste* in aesthetics. In his preface, we recall, he had pointed out that we only spoke of criticism in relation to the liberal arts, not to the sciences or geometry. He now notes that the same is true of taste, and he explains why this is true:

> Taste in poetry, rhetoric, music, painting, and architecture is all very well known; and likewise in clothes, gardens, furniture, etc. But I have never yet heard anyone speak of taste in arithmetic or geometry or in the other sciences where one is able to construct the strictest demonstrations from clearly [*deutlich*] known basic truths. But in those fields in which the intelligible [*deutliche*] and unintelligible, the proved and the unproved, are still mixed together, one still speaks of taste.
>
> [Pp. 101-102]

Thus Gottsched's intermediate territory does overlap with Hutcheson's: in addition to literal experiences of taste, it includes the metaphorical taste experiences, of the arts and also of natural objects and articles of clothing and interior decoration, to which Hutcheson's internal sense responds.

But the conditions for entry to Gottsched's intermediate territory are different from those for entry to Hutcheson's. Hutcheson's point, we recall, was that while our experiences of beauty, harmony, and the like are just as immediate and just as little under the control of the will as our experiences of sight and hearing, there are many people who have normal sight and hearing and yet who lack the sense of beauty or harmony. Though the internal senses are innate in the sense of being capabilities waiting to be trained and developed, they seem to be further extensions of our perceptual faculties. As Hutcheson puts it, "There is still something further necessary" beyond ordinary normal sense perception. Gottsched's point, on the other hand, is that the areas of experience in which we speak of taste, whether literally or metaphorically, are areas in which our concepts are *klar* but not *deutlich*, discriminable and namable yet not explicable or interpretable.

Gottsched gives several interesting examples to illustrate exactly how he is delineating this area to which the concept of taste properly applies:

> E.g.: I might well speak of a theological book that is to Mossheim's taste, a law of nature that is to Pufendorf's taste, an art of medicine that is to Boerhaave's taste. But here I would observe that one consults taste only in those parts of such disciplines as are still uncertain, and thus are still not completely definite. As soon as a thing gains

general applause and is regarded as having been demonstrated, then one also ceases to view it as being subject to taste. Thus astronomers will soon no longer be able to speak of the construction of the world according to Copernicus's taste, since this system is already known and accepted as the only true one.

[P. 102]

What is interesting here is Gottsched's selection of fields outside the arts to which he says the concept of taste can be properly applied: we do not in fact speak of someone's taste in theology, natural law, or the theory and practice of medicine. Why should Gottsched have chosen these rather odd, and surely borderline, examples?

The reason, I think, is that he conceived of these three disciplines as ones that had high hopes of becoming what he calls "demonstrated." If this seems strange to us, we need only recall that no less a thinker than Descartes envisaged, near the end of the *Discourse of Method*, the possibility of a demonstrative science of medicine, and that Pufendorf had more recently, in both the *Elements of Universal Jurisprudence* (1660) and *On the Law of Nature and Nations* (1672), expressed confidence in the possibility of a demonstrative science of law and of morals generally. Though Pufendorf had been dead for some 35 years when Gottsched was writing the *Versuch*, Mossheim and Boerhaave were still very much alive. In using their names, Gottsched was perhaps suggesting that they would soon raise the status of their disciplines to that which astronomy had attained since Copernicus—if not quite to that of geometry. For we notice that Gottsched speaks of the disciplines to which the concept of taste applies as being "still uncertain"—just as he had earlier spoken of "the intelligible and the unintelligible, the proved and the unproved" as being "still mixed together" in those disciplines, and of this as being the reason why one "still speaks of taste" in regard to these disciplines. Plainly, that repeated word *still* (*noch*) is meant to suggest that just as fields like medicine and morals may sometime attain a degree of certainty equal to that of astronomy or astrophysics, so too may the criticism of the arts. This was, after all, one aim of traditional aesthetics.

Gottsched therefore concludes "that the metaphorical taste, just like the literal one, deals only with concepts of things that are distinct [*klaren*], but not wholly intelligible [*deutlichen*], and distinguishes from one another such things as one judges merely by feeling" (p. 102). He then gives an example. A man wants a house built, and arranges for a builder to draw up several sets of plans. They are all different from one another, and though the man knows nothing of architecture, he chooses one plan over all the others. We say then that he has made his choice according to his taste. If anyone asks him why he has chosen this plan and not another, he can say nothing more than that it pleased him best—that is, he found it the most beautiful and the most perfect. But if we laid these plans before a mathematically trained connoisseur of architecture and asked him to choose one, he would make a thorough investigation based on the rules of architecture, and would finally select the one that possessed the most perfection according to the basic principles of the science.

Gottsched's point of course is that one decision is based merely on taste while the other is based on solid insight grounded in the rules. But the interesting thing is that Gottsched does not express this conclusion in a simple, straightforward manner:

> But here one would scarcely say that this connoisseur has chosen according to his taste. Rather, it would mean: he has tested the plans according to the rules, and is able to give a firm basis to his insight that the one chosen is the best.
>
> [P. 103]

In a writer who usually puts things quite straightforwardly, the qualifying words "scarcely" ("schwerlich") and "rather" ("vielmehr") would seem to indicate a degree of uncertainty as to just where taste leaves off and insight begins.

This example, Gottsched continues, shows that different degrees of knowledge can produce the same judgment of a situation. Of course the untrained customer and the learned connoisseur might choose different sets of plans—but then again they might not. What does all this prove? Three things:

> 1) That people who judge merely by taste may differ a great deal from each other; 2) that both judgments cannot be true since they are opposed; 3) that finally the judgment to be preferred is the one that agrees with the rules of architecture and with the opinion of a master in this science.
>
> [P. 103]

But then the note of slight uncertainty is heard again:

> The first two conclusions are incontestable; concerning the third, however, one also cannot have much doubt. For how would it be possible that that plan could be best that had been made in violation of all the rules of architecture? That would be as if a piece of music could be beautiful that violated all the rules of music.
>
> [P. 103]

The reluctance to pronounce the last of the three conclusions quite so certain as the other two ("cannot have much doubt") and the rhetorical question that immediately follows—only one of many in this convoluted, troubled paragraph—vividly give us the voice of a man dealing cautiously and scrupulously with very difficult matters about which he is not quite certain. Certainly the Gottsched we hear in these sentences is very far indeed from the "narrowly dogmatic" figure conjured up by Serauky.

But let us say we accept Gottsched's third conclusion, that the best judgment of the plans reached "merely by taste" will necessarily be the one that is also in accordance with the rules and is also reached by the connoisseur of architecture. Does this really say any more than that the best judgment is the one for which convincing reasons are (or can be) given? Though Gottsched talks about a judgment agreeing with the rules—as we might say that the color of a new car agrees with the manufacturer's color sample that we hold up to the car for comparison—his language makes clear that the real test is whether or not the maker of the judgment can then go on to explain why he made it. As we saw earlier, to give reasons for an aesthetic preference does not typically involve invoking this or that general rule with which the work being judged is somehow in agreement or accordance. Rather, it involves pointing to particular features of the work in an effort to get the other person to see (or hear or understand) it as we do. It seems to me that Gottsched is confused about this important issue, and that all he really means, in practical terms, when he speaks of a judgment that accords with the rules, is a judgment for which convincing reasons can be and are given.

Gottsched now declares himself ready to offer his definition or description ("Beschreibung") of good and bad taste:

> Good taste is when the intelligence [*Verstand*] correctly judges, on the basis of mere feeling [*Empfindung*], the beauty of an object of which one has no clear [*deutliches*] and profound knowledge. Bad taste, on the other hand, is likewise when the intelligence judges unclearly [*undeutlich*] known objects on the basis of feeling, but deceives itself in such judgments.
>
> [P. 104]

The thing to notice here, I think, is the presence of the two often opposed terms *Empfindung* and *Verstand*: plainly, Gottsched is insisting on the importance, to the concept of taste, of both feeling and intelligence or understanding. And each of these terms is carefully qualified in a way that stresses the separation between them: in a judgment based on taste (rather than rules and "clear and profound knowledge") the intelligence judges correctly, and yet it does so on the promptings of "mere," unassisted feeling.

Gottsched then goes on to explain in some detail where, in the scheme of human faculties, he locates taste and why he locates it where he does:

> I rank taste under intelligence [*Verstand*] because I can put it with no other power of the mind. Neither wit nor imagination nor memory nor common sense [*Vernunft*] can lay any claim to it. But the senses also have no right to it, so one would have to create a sixth sense for that purpose. I say, however, that it is a judging intelligence. For those who really employ it to make a discrimination of things, either externally or internally, make the declaration: this is beautiful and that is not. I contend further that this judgment is based upon mere feeling, which I understand to mean the inward impression of a beautiful thing, which either really exists outside us or else is produced by our own imagination—as, e.g., a painter can create, in thought, a draft of a painting, and can judge its beauty according to his taste.
>
> [P. 104]

It is especially important to be fully aware of the complexities of thought that make this passage worth citing at such length when one recalls Serauky's flippant question: "Where, in this rationalistic definition of taste, is there a particle of difference between taste and intellect?"

For Gottsched is of course not merely equating *Geschmack* and *Verstand*. He is saying that he finds himself forced to classify or categorize or rank taste as (a type of) intelligence because it does not seem to belong anywhere else. It is important to note that he sounds displeased (and perhaps even surprised) that this is true. But why is it true? Why does Gottsched find it impossible to class taste with wit, or imagination, or memory, or even with *Vernunft*—good sense or reasonableness? And why, moreover, does he seem unwilling to follow Dubos and Hutcheson in seeing taste as a special sort of sense? I think it is because he is keenly (and admirably) aware that to utter a judgment based on taste—"This is beautiful," "This is ugly"—is not merely to report that one feels pleased by the object or that one likes it or anything else of the sort. It is, rather, to offer a judgment, to make a claim about something in the real objective world—whether, as he later makes clear, the external world or the internal world of one's thoughts or imagination. That is, to say "This is beautiful" is more like saying "This is a horse" than it is like saying "This pleases me." The person who says "This is beautiful" is, in Gottsched's fine phrase, really making a "discrimination of things" rather than merely reporting on his own inner state. The much abused Gottsched is thus right where legions of 20th-century aestheticians have been dead wrong. He knows something about the logic of taste judgments that they have found it convenient to ignore by assimilating taste judgments to reports of inner states.

And one can sympathize with them. For to recognize this feature of taste judgments is to let oneself in for a great deal of trouble. But then, after all, who said that aesthetics had to be easy? One cannot help admiring Gottsched for purposefully striding, eyes open, right into the thick of the trouble. To make sure we understand him, he repeats that what he is calling a judgment of taste is grounded "upon mere feeling," by which he means "the inward impression of a beautiful thing." That is, the feeling we have that the object is beautiful is the basis of our judgment that it is beautiful, but to utter the judgment is not merely to report the feeling: it is, rather, to claim something about the real world. And this is true, he adds, whether the object about which we have this feeling is in the external world or the product of our own "imagination." In the latter case, both the object and the feeling would be features of our mental life, but they are to be clearly distinguished from each other.

We can say then that Gottsched stands up for the intellectual dignity of a judgment of taste, even though its basis is in feeling, by classing taste with *Verstand* rather than with some lesser power of mind or spirit. He diverges very sharply from Dubos in insisting that taste only decides whether or not a thing is beautiful, not whether it pleases us:

> For this alone is what taste is concerned with. One never uses it to decide another question, namely: whether something pleases us or not. The pleasure arises always from an idea or image of beauty—beauty that may be either real or imagined.
>
> [P. 104]

The pleasure, which Dubos insists comes first, is thus only an effect of the beauty, and (Gottsched seems to imply) we may be right about the beauty yet wrong about whether or not we are pleased. So sternly does Gottsched want to emphasize the objective content or significance of the feelings transmitted to us by taste.

Yet he still stresses that an object's beauty, as transmitted by our taste, "although very distinct [*klar*], will be experienced only unintelligibly [*undeutlich*], since he whom it pleases cannot say why it pleases him" (p. 104). As soon as the person becomes able to account for his feeling, everything of course changes:

> For as soon as one is able to show out of what perfections a particular beauty really arises, the taste for the object is transformed into a profound insight, as has been proved above. Finally I distinguish good taste from bad by the adjective "correct," as I apply it to a judgment. Whoever has good taste must judge correctly the distinctly [*klar*] felt beauty of an object—that is, he must regard nothing as beautiful that is not truly beautiful, and nothing as ugly that is not ugly.
>
> [Pp. 104-105]

What, we wonder, will be the criterion for deciding whether these judgments of beauty or ugliness are true or false? The answer is not long in coming:

> The touchstone for this judgment does not need to be sought far and wide. One finds it in the rules for perfection that govern each particular art of beautiful things—that is, buildings, paintings, pieces of music, etc.—and that have been clearly [*deutlich*] understood and proved by the real masters of those arts.
>
> [P. 105]

Yet at other times Gottsched appears to have mixed feelings about the rules. Earlier he has said of them:

> The rules that have been established in the liberal arts do not come from the mere willfulness of men but have their basis in the unchanging nature of things: in the unity of diversity, in order and harmony. These laws, which through long experience and much meditation have been sought out, discovered, and established, remain unbreakable and they stand fast—should anyone ever express a preference, according to his taste, for a work that has more or less offended against them.
>
> [Pp. 103-104]

But later, after describing how the rules were discovered by the Greeks and Romans, he suddenly asks, in seeming irritation, "Must one then always be burdened with rules, if one wants to have good taste" (p. 108)? His answer is that while it was Opitz who made known the rules to Germans, it was not through the rules but through reading his writings that the Germans became better poets. For finally the development of good taste depends not on learning the rules—as one learns, say, the seven great rivers of India—but rather on internalizing them, which can only come from the reading of great literature: "If anyone asks how one can help a young person to have good taste in poetry, I give this answer: from his youth on, give him only poets of good taste to read" (p. 109). There speaks Gottsched the practical reformer.

IV

Like Dubos, Hutcheson, and Gottsched, Batteux saw taste not at all as opposed to reason but rather as formed by the collaboration of reason and sentiment.[8] In fact he defines taste as "the knowledge of rules by sentiment" (p. 65). But his view of the relation of reason to sentiment in the formation and exercise of taste is precisely opposite to that of Dubos. Dubos, we recall, had the promptings of the "sixth sense" precede—whether temporally or logically or both is not clear—the explanations furnished by reason with reference to the rules. First we feel pleased, then we discover what qualities of the object in question have caused our feeling. After announcing that he will "leave to the profound researches of the metaphysicians to unfold the secret springs of the human mind, and to dive into the principles of its operations," Batteux says he will merely "set out upon a principle which no one will contest with me, viz.":

> The mind conceives, and this conception produces in it a sentiment. Conception is a certain light diffused over the mind. A sentiment is a certain motion actuating the mind. The one enlightens, the other warms it. The one points out the object, the other either inclines us towards it, or diverts us from it.
>
> [P. 38]

Taste in the arts, Batteux tells us, is analogous to knowledge in the sciences: "Knowledge considers objects as they are in themselves, according to their essence, and without any regard to us; taste on the other hand employs itself on those objects solely with regard to us" (p. 37). Marshall R. Schwartz, in a dissertation on Batteux, comments on this sentence as follows: "We see that Batteux, upon entering into the analysis of taste, begins the discussion of the subjective aspect of esthetics—human reactions to objects of art."[9] But Batteux's language, in what immediately follows, is decidedly objective:

> That knowledge is sound and perfect which sees without confusion, and distinguishes without error between truth and fiction, probability and demonstration; and that is a good taste, which, by a clear distinct impression, perceives the good and bad, the excellent and the indifferent, without once confounding them or taking the one for the other.
>
> So that I may define knowledge an aptitude of discerning truth and fiction, and of distinguishing them from each other; and taste, a like aptitude of perceiving the good, the bad and the indifferent, and distinguishing them with perspicuity [*sic*] and certitude.
>
> [Pp. 37-38]

Schwartz therefore immediately accuses Batteux of contradicting himself. But the accusation is unjust; Batteux is doing no such thing.

Batteux is indeed talking about "human reactions to art," but that does not mean that he is concentrating on "the subjective aspect of esthetics" in the sense of *subjective* that Schwartz intends, the modern sense in which it means what is peculiar to an individual mind—as in the phrase "merely subjective." As an 18th-century thinker, Batteux is interested primarily in what is common to all (normal) minds, not what is peculiar to this or that mind. And what is common to all minds is just as much a part of objective reality as is the world of external objects. Taste for Batteux is a sentiment, "a certain motion actuating the mind," but by locating taste in the mind Batteux is not speaking of it as peculiar to each individual mind, and hence as subjective in the sense that Schwartz has in mind, the sense that would conflict with Batteux's avowed objectivity. As he asserts: "There is but one sole and absolutely good taste" (p. 35).

The objectivity of taste, as conceived by Batteux, is ensured by the priority of conception to sentiment, to which he reverts again and again:

> Altho' this sentiment may appear to proceed from a sudden or blind sally of the imagination, yet it is always preceded by some glimmering or spark of light, by favor of which we are able to discover the qualities of the object.
>
> [P. 39]

"A proposition in geometry," he tells us, "once well conceived, naturally enforces our assent; and so in what concerns taste, we are guided as it were imperceptibly by our heart, and we find that nothing is so easy as to love what is formed to be loved" (p. 40):

> That taste which has art for it's objects, is not a forced taste [*un Goût factice*], it is a part of ourselves, it is born with us, and it's office is to determine us towards what is good. Knowledge precedes it like a torch to light it on it's way.
>
> [P. 40]

It is in fact the very strength and irresistibility of taste—the same qualities that led Hutcheson to his notion of internal sense—that lead Batteux to associate taste more closely with reason and the rules:

> A disposition in itself so remarkable and strong clearly proves that we are not guided by fancy or chance in our conceptions and taste. The whole is governed by immutable laws, every faculty of the mind has one determinate end, to which it must naturally tend to preserve it's proper order [*pour être dans l'ordre*].
>
> [P. 40]

V

Thus we have seen that for all of our four thinkers—Dubos, Hutcheson, Gottsched, and Batteux—the faculty of taste was not opposed to reason and the rules, as passed down by the ancients and refined upon by the moderns. While Dubos and Batteux were content with simply seeing taste as involving the complementary operation of reason and feeling, Hutcheson and Gottsched went further, and attempted to carve out a mental territory between reason and feeling in which they carried on this joint operation. There is of course no way of deciding who is right, since all four thinkers, along with their contemporaries, have put the question "What is taste?" in terms that make it insoluble.

The widespread and long-standing discussion of taste in the 18th century resulted from a sharpened awareness, on the part of thinkers of many different persuasions, that aesthetic (and usually also moral) judgments are special in a most important way. We are inclined toward such judgments by responses as spontaneous, immediate, and irresistible as the response of our hand when it happens to land accidentally on a hot stove, and yet we explain them, argue about them, and clarify them for ourselves in rational terms—we give reasons for them. Also, unlike the response to the hot stove, our response to a poem or a picture or a piece of music, no matter how immediate it may have been and how firmly we may have defended it, may well be altered by something someone else points out to us about the work under discussion. We may be argued out of it by the reasons the other person produces to defend his competing judgment.

All this is true, and the thinkers of the early 18th century were trying to explain important facts about our relation to art—they were not, as has so often been suggested, just spinning ridiculous theories that no sensible person could possibly hold. The problem is that they came at these facts from the wrong angle. They were actually trying to explain why we talk as we do about works of art, which is a conceptual or logical matter. But they thought they were trying to give a correct inventory of the various faculties of the mind and a correct account of their relations to one another, which is of course a psychological matter. Thus they produce these little quasi-allegories, in which feeling precedes reason in the operation of taste (Dubos) or reason precedes feeling (Batteux), in which taste is seen to be a new sort of sense (Hutcheson) or is, somewhat reluctantly, seen as primarily a function or offshoot of *Verstand* (Gottsched). The possibilities were endless.

The problem was that at least since Descartes, and the early years of the 17th century, the primary focus of serious philosophy had been inward and its principal method had been introspection. This was to change in the early 19th century, but it was a way of thinking about and doing philosophy that prevailed for a good 200 years, right through the period we are considering. When Descartes wanted to provide a firm foundation for philosophy by doubting everything that could possibly be doubted, he looked inward and found that the one thing he could not doubt was his own existence as a thinking being. From this fact he then worked outward to build up the world around him. And if we glance at the tables of contents of such important post-Cartesian philosophical works as Hobbes's *Leviathan* (1651), Locke's *An Essay concerning Human Understanding* (1690), and Hume's *A Treatise of Human Nature* (1739–1740), we see that they all begin by looking inward, to see how we have sensations and how we form ideas, and then work outward to their various goals—political in the case of Hobbes, religious in the case of Locke, moral in the case of Hume.

I think it is fair to say that in most medieval philosophy the mind or intellect was known primarily through its activities, above all through its investigation of the physical world. Knowledge of the mind itself was therefore secondary to knowledge of the world. In St. Thomas the important boundary between spirit and nature is not, as in Descartes, between thinking and extension, consciousness and mere mechanism, but rather between intellect and sense. But from Descartes on, for two centuries or so, it was natural to group intellectual operations together with volition, emotions, feelings, and sensations as distinguishing a thinking being, a *res cogitans*, from a mere machine. And, as Descartes's turning inward to discover himself as a thinking being makes clear, it was also natural to regard the internal as more immediately and surely known than the external, to see the self rather than the world as philosophy's proper point of departure.[10]

Thus it was natural for the aesthetic theorists we have been considering to assume that the answers to the questions they were asking concerning the roles of taste, feeling, and reason in aesthetic experience could only be found by turning inward, by ascertaining what the ways in which we experience and discuss works of art imply about our internal organization. From the way they write about it, one gathers that they thought of this sort of endeavor as fully empirical, as though one could (imaginatively) open up the mind and examine its structure, just as one can (literally) do with the body. Even Coleridge, writing well into the 19th century, talks about his supposed discovery that the fancy and the imagination are two separate faculties of the mind as though he had just discovered the spleen.

Therefore if we want to make sense of what our theorists are saying about taste and other questions, we must translate their answers from psychological terms into conceptual terms, from statements about the functioning of our various faculties into statements about the ways in which the concepts we employ in discussing works of art function in critical discourse. And it is important to make sense of what they are saying because they were all extremely intelligent men, and the only way to understand their historical significance is to get inside their arguments (so to speak), to figure out what questions they were really trying to answer and why. Not until we make this effort can we appreciate how unjustly the whole so-called rationalist movement in criticism and aesthetics has been treated by historians.

The familiar idea, which we saw in Goldschmidt and Serauky as well as in our three dissertation-writers, that reason and emotion are necessarily opposed, and that even to mention the place of reason or rules in artistic creation or aesthetic judgment is necessarily to disparage the creative imagination, comes later in the 18th century and does not belong to our period. Precisely because 17th-century philosophers, following Descartes, tended to group reason and emotions or feelings together as making up human consciousness, it was natural that the theorists and critics we are considering should have been attracted to an aesthetics that laid simultaneous and equal stress on both reason and emotion, that in effect saw them as partners. What is not natural—is, in fact, very mysterious—is that so little attention has been paid to the thinker who most powerfully influenced these theorists and critics. That thinker was the Roman poet Horace.

Chapter Six

Ars poetica

When historians of the aesthetics of the late 17th and early 18th centuries search for influences, they tend almost automatically to assume that the most powerful influences, the real prime movers, must have been the great philosophers, namely Aristotle and Descartes. Horace was merely a poet, and I think it seems to most modern historians quite unlikely that a poet could have had any deep or serious influence of a specifically theoretical sort. But Horace was a very special sort of poet, and anyway, in the 18th century the modern specialization and compartmentalization of intellectual life that rigidly separates poetry from serious thought had not yet sundered what Hume memorably called "the republic of letters."

I

So far as I have been able to gather, there is no book devoted to Horace's intellectual influence. Yet it is hard to see how anyone who read some of the writers whom we have been considering and will consider—Gottsched, Batteux, Baumgarten, and Krause, for example—could fail to see the strength and breadth of Horace's influence at this time. For one thing, they quote from his works constantly. In *Von der musikalischen Poesie*, Krause cites Horace at least 14 times—and on another occasion cites as Horace what is actually an epigram of Martial's.

More important, the title page of the first edition of Gottsched's *Versuch einer critischen Dichtkunst* bears the words: "In the place of an Introduction, Horace's *Ars poetica* [*Horatii Dichtkunst*] is translated into German verse and explained with notes." The German word *Dichtkunst* is thus Gottsched's translation of the title of Horace's longest and perhaps greatest poem, the epistle to his still unidentified friends the Pisos that in the manuscripts bears the title *De arte poetica liber* or (more commonly) *Ars poetica*. Not only did Gottsched think that an annotated translation of Horace's poem was the most suitable and helpful introduction to his own work that he could offer the reader; he had also titled his book in explicit homage to Horace. In the second (1737) and succeeding editions of the *Versuch*, Gottsched added Horace's Latin text, on facing pages, to his German translation. In a very similar gesture, Batteux, among the essays that he published, as a supplement to *Les Beaux-Arts réduits à un même principe*, in 1747-1748 under the title *Cours de belles lettres*, included his own 100-page annotated translation of the *Ars poetica*.

Perhaps somewhat more surprising, the two most important philosophical aestheticians of the time, Alexander Baumgarten and his pupil and popularizer Georg Friedrich Meier, are scarcely less devoted to and dependent upon Horace. Baumgarten, whose aesthetics was, in effect, an attempt to elaborate upon and systematize the implications of Gottsched's point about aesthetic responses being *klar* but *undeutlich*, cites or alludes to the *Ars poetica* some 35 times in his brief *Meditationes philosophicae de nonnullis ad poema pertinentibus* (1735). After noting over 20 citations to Horace, almost all of them to the *Ars poetica*, in the first 50 pages of Baumgarten's 600-page *Aesthetica* (1750, 1758), one soon gives up counting. One does not even begin to count the citations, all of which are helpfully translated into German at the ends of the volumes, in Meier's 1,650-page *Anfangsgründe aller schönen Wissenschaften* (1748).[1]

Why should all these thinkers have paid such extraordinary attention to Horace's *Ars poetica*? What was it about this ancient poem that made it suddenly seem more interesting, more relevant to present-day concerns, than it perhaps had ever done before? Unlike many great ancient works, such as Lucretius's *De rerum natura* or (to take an extreme example) the poems of Bacchylides, Horace's *Ars poetica* never had to be "rediscovered": it was there all the time—there are commentaries on it that date from the Carolingian age.[2] But what we think of as critical attention only began to focus on the *Ars poetica* in the 16th century.

In 1527 the Cremonese poet Marco Girolamo Vida published his avowedly Horatian *De arte poetica*, in Latin hexameters.[3] In many ways ahead of its time and enormously influential on later poets and critics, Vida's work was praised by the great Julius Caesar Scaliger, in his posthumously published *Poetices libri septem* (1561), as even better than Horace. The *Ars poetica* was first rendered into English by Thomas Drant, in 1567, but only as part of a complete version of Horace's satires and epistles. Far more significant was Ben Jonson's translation of the *Ars poetica*, which was published in 1640, three years after the poet's death. The references to Horace by Elizabethan critics had been mostly cursory and dutiful. The one exception was an elaborate listing of fifty-four "Cannons or general cautions of Poetry, prescribed by Horace," included by William Webbe in his *A Discourse of English Poetry* (1586), but these were merely translated from the Latin of the German philologist Georg Fabricius (1516-1571), in whose *De re poetica libri septem* (1560) they had earlier appeared.[4] Jonson was perhaps the first English poet whose classicism was not mere antiquarian "classicizing." It consisted, rather, in his effort (as F. R. Leavis once put it) to feel the ancient writers "as contemporary with himself; or rather, to achieve an English mode that should express a sense of contemporaneity with them," a mode "consciously urbane, mature and civilized."[5] Jonson's *Horace, His Art of Poetrie* is a poet's translation, a brilliant and suggestive achievement that points ahead to the translations and "imitations" of classical writers by Dryden, Pope, and others.

It is significant that Jonson's translation was published together with his short sketch of English grammar and his collection of critical remarks entitled *Timber: or, Discoveries*: clearly, he intended the three works to function as a kind of manual for the reform of the English language and English letters. His opposite number in Germany was Opitz, whose *Buch von der Deutschen Poeterey* (1624), a parallel attempt at reforming German poetry, was prefaced by an epigraph from the *Ars poetica* and a brief poem by Augustinus Iskra, dedicated to Opitz and based on a Horace ode. Seeking to modernize and standardize German poetic practice, Opitz recommended that archaisms be avoided, that the natural speech accent of words be made to coincide with the metrical accent, and that German poets restrict themselves to two meters, iambic and trochaic.

These and other recommendations of Opitz's had immediate results in the work of such poets as Paul Fleming (1609-1640) and Simon Dach (1605-1659). But as the 17th century progressed, some poets, particularly those of the so-called Second Silesian School, principally Hofmannswaldau and Daniel Casper von Lohenstein (1635-1683), turned to the Italian poet Giambattista Marini (1569-1625) for inspiration. As a result, their style became elaborate, heavy, and ornate—something like that of their English contemporaries, the later "Metaphysical" poets John Cleveland (1613-1658) and Abraham Cowley (1618-1667). Therefore in the early decades of the 18th century, the need for reform was felt again among German men of letters, and it took the form of a return to Opitz—and also to Horace.

One poet who continued to write in the more natural yet controlled mode recommended by Opitz, and who often declared his allegiance to Horace and Boileau, was Friedrich Rudolf von Canitz (1654-1699), a diplomat by profession. In 1727, just as the second poetic reform was getting under way, Johann Ulrich von König (1688-1744) brought out a complete edition of Canitz's poems, in which he included an *Untersuchung von dem guten Geschmack*, an essay later praised by Gottsched. König claimed that the influence of Marini had undone the good accomplished through Opitz's influence, and that Canitz represented the sort of taste that German poets should now attempt to emulate.

Only three years later, of course, came Gottsched's *Versuch*. In his second chapter, on the character of a poet, Gottsched expresses views similar to König's: "It is well known that Hofmannswaldau and Lohenstein also followed the Italian taste, and could not always control their passion" (p. 92). By contrast, Gottsched referred to "Opitz, Dach, Gryphius, Canitz and others of our best poets" (p. 94).

Prominent among the poets who followed more or less in Canitz's footsteps were Johann Christian Günther (1695-1723) and Friedrich von Hagedorn (1708-1754). Both, as we have seen, were important to the renewal of the strophic song. Soon Hofmannswaldau and Lohenstein seemed as out of date to these poets and their readers as Cleveland and Cowley did to Addison and Steele, whose *Tatler* and *Spectator* papers, as we have noted earlier, were often copied, or simply reproduced in translation, by the editors of German moral weeklies of the 1720s and 1730s. Just as Addison could speak disparagingly of Cowley's "Gothic manner in writing" (*Spectator* No. 70), so the German term for the Italianate excesses of Hofmannswaldau and Lohenstein became *Schwulst*, as in Hagedorn's poem addressed to Hofmannswaldau: "Jetzt kennt man deinen Schwulst und deine Fehler nur." Scheibe's famous (or infamous) comment about J. S. Bach in *Der critische Musikus*, we recall, was cast in the same terms:

> This great man would be the wonder of all nations if he had more charm, and if he did not deprive his pieces of naturalness by his bombastic and confused manner, and did not obscure their beauty by excessive art.[6]

Horace was connected still more closely with the second reform movement than he had been with Opitz's original reform. For in the meantime the two great modern imitations or counterparts of the *Ars poetica* had appeared, Boileau's *L'Art poétique* (1674) and Pope's *An Essay on Criticism* (1711). Like Jonson's translation, these two poems were written by men who felt (and made their readers feel) Horace as a contemporary who had important things to tell them about the writing of poetry. But what were these things? Boileau, Pope, and their German readers certainly did not turn to Horace for helpful little rules—those "Cannons or general cautions of poetry" cribbed by Webbe from Fabricius. Though Boileau was tagged *le législateur de Parnasse*, the words *règle* and *loi* actually appear less often in *L'Art poétique* than one would expect—much less often, in fact, than the words *rule* and *law* do in the English translation made by Dryden's friend Sir William Soames, revised by Dryden, and published anonymously in 1683.[7]

What they found, I think, first perhaps in Boileau and Pope and then, in an even more powerfully concentrated form in Horace, was a way of talking about the writing and the reading of poetry that simultaneously took account of the roles played by emotion and reason, imagination and craft, the instinctive response and the reasoned judgment—a way of talking, what is more, that was both studiedly casual, as informal as good conversation, and yet composed in strict Latin hexameters and crackling with unpretentious intelligence. Indeed, many people who study the *Ars poetica* in a sustained and concentrated manner come to think of it as perhaps the most intelligent poem they have ever encountered. As Pope put it in *An Essay on Criticism*, "*Horace* still charms with graceful Negligence, / And without Method *talks* us into Sense" (653-654).

Precisely because the *Ars poetica* is so purposefully composed "without Method," the only way to understand what its 18th-century readers saw in it is to look closely at the part of the poem they found the most important, the first 31 lines. It is an impossible poem to paraphrase—or rather, it is impossible to see what is valuable about it from a paraphrase. Pope's phrase "graceful negligence," which is often echoed by his contemporaries in their writing about the *Ars poetica*, shows that he and they were closer to understanding the poem than are the 20th-century classicists who patronizingly deplore Horace's lack of coherence and "system."

The *Ars poetica* begins, as Horace will later in the poem (148) commend Homer for having begun, *in medias res*, with a witty evocation of a painter who thoughtlessly slaps together details that do not belong together:

> Humano capiti cervicem pictor equinam
> iungere si velit, et varias inducere plumas
> undique collatis membris, ut turpiter atrum
> desinat in piscem mulier formosa superne,
> spectatum admissi risum teneatis, amici?
>
> [1-5]
>
> (If a painter wanted to join a horse's neck to a human head, and spread variously colored feathers over limbs collected from here and there, so that the beautiful woman up above would end below in a repulsively black fish, could you, my friends, permitted a view, restrain your laughter?)

The slapdash quality of the painter's act—and apparently also of Horace's poem, at least so far—is heightened, in a way that cannot be captured in English, by the Latin word order. Not until almost the end of the first line ("pictor") do we get any hint that this is a picture we are looking at, and not until the second line ("si") do we learn that the opening sentence is conditional. As C. O. Brink points out in his invaluable commentary on the poem, to place this many words before "si" in its own clause is not only very unusual but is also, itself, "a violation of the law of unity"—which is, of course, also being violated by the painter.[8] The language of the poem, that is, enacts what it is talking about—and not for the last time. Moreover, we notice that the word "varias" is right there, in line 2, to plant in our minds the idea of variety, the countervailing force to poetic or artistic unity.

Horace then assures us that this quite unacceptable, chaotic sort of variety can be found in books as well as in pictures:

> credite, Pisones, isti tabulae fore librum
> persimilem cuius, velut aegri somnia, vanae
> fingentur species, ut nec pes nec caput uni
> reddatur formae.
>
> [6-9]
>
> (Believe me, Pisos, very like this picture would be a book whose ineffectual notions had been shaped like a sick man's dreams, so that neither head nor foot could be assigned a form that would give it unity.)

Brink tells us that "nec pes nec caput" ("neither foot nor head") is—as we might have guessed from the shortness of its component words and the resulting snappiness of the phrase as a whole—a "metaphor proverbially applied to incoherence or inconsistency" (p. 90). "Reddatur," on the other hand, is a rather formal word, often used in legal language to speak of rendering or granting something to someone, giving someone his due. And of course *forma* comes from the technical language of literary criticism. The close juxtaposition of the colloquial and the formal is typical of the poem.

In fact it occurs again in the next lines, in which, as so often in Horace, an interlocutor suddenly and unexpectedly butts in—unnamed in this case, but perhaps intended to be one of the Pisos, addressees of the poem:

> "pictoribus atque poetis
> quidlibet audendi semper fuit aequa potestas"
> scimus, et hanc veniam petimusque damusque vicissim;
> sed non ut placidis coeant immitia, non ut
> serpentes avibus geminentur, tigribus agni.
>
> [9-13]

("Painters and poets have always had the right to dare anything." We know—and this indulgence we both claim and grant in return. But not so that savage should mate with tame, serpents unite with birds, lambs with tigers.)

As elsewhere in Horace, the other voice, coming in from nowhere, raises an objection that refers back to something that either was said before we tuned in on the conversation or is being assumed to be understood by all parties to the dialogue. Creative freedom, this voice insists, has always been accounted the right of both painters and poets—and now Horace is threatening this right. Horace's impatient, faintly scornful, dismissive reply, "scimus" ("Oh, of course we know all *that*"), leads to a rather pious affirmation that he of course perfectly shares the other speaker's views on this matter—and the legal language of claiming and granting (which picks up "reddatur" and the other speaker's talk of a right, "potestas") seems to give the agreement a kind of official finality. "Sed non" ("But not")—there is, after all, a catch to this bargain: of course I agree in principle, but not to the absurd extent you seem to be suggesting. And then the final two lines swiftly conjure up the alleged absurdities, taking us back to the fantastic language of the poem's opening.

The poem's principal speaker, whom we may just as well call Horace, then holds forth at length in defense of his views—but in a way that characteristically explores, in only a few lines, a wide range of tones and attitudes:

> inceptis gravibus plerumque et magna professis
> purpureus, late qui splendeat, unus et alter
> adsuitur pannus, cum lucus et ara Dianae
> et properantis aquae per amoenos ambitus agros,
> aut flumen Rhenum aut pluvius describitur arcus.
> sed nunc non erat his locus. et fortasse cupressum
> scis simulare: quid hoc, si fractis enatat exspes
> navibus aere dato qui pingitur? amphora coepit
> institui: currente rota cur urceus exit?
> denique sit quodvis, simplex dumtaxat et unum.
>
> [14-23]

(Works with portentous beginnings, and promising great things, often have one or another purple patch stitched on, which glitters far and wide—when Diana's grove and altar, and the course of the hastening stream through the pleasant fields, or the river Rhine, or the rainbow is being described. But this is not the place for such things. And perhaps you know how to draw a cypress. But what of it?—if you have been paid to paint a desperate man swimming away from his wrecked ship. A wine-jar begins to be formed—why, as the wheel turns round, does it come out as a pitcher? In short: whatever the work may be, let it at least be simple and one.)

The serious, rather schoolmasterly tone of the opening warning against great pretensions is immediately undercut by the famous purple patch—though the exact intended meaning of the metaphor is still debated, the point is clear enough, and is driven home by the wide separation of "purpureus" and "pannus." The texture of the verse loosens still further, as Horace begins to reel off examples of the sort of special scene that might invite such an excessively colorful burst of language—but then pulls himself (and his reader) up short with the simple, matter-of-fact declaration "sed nunc non erat his locus" ("but this is not the place for such things"). But then he is off again: what does it matter that you can draw a cypress, if you have been commissioned to paint a picture to which a cypress is inappropriate? Not only would a tree be inappropriate to a sea scene, but the cypress in particular, with its funerary overtones, would defeat the patron's purpose, which is to celebrate his courageous escape from the sinking ship. In the final example, the transformation of wine-jar into pitcher seems to take place almost magically, suggesting that in the very process of being created, works of art can take on a life of their own and get out of the supposed creator's control—as if it were not bad enough that you had to choose only subjects to which your special skills were suited!

Then finally, after enumerating all the pitfalls that threaten the artist, all the reasons he has to be constantly on his guard, Horace rounds off this section of his poem with one of his ringing generalizations: "denique sit quodvis, simplex dumtaxat et unum" ("in short: whatever the work may be, let it be simple and one"). We seem at last to have come out somewhere, and the reader breathes a sigh of relief: after all this confusing welter of detail, we finally have something solid to catch hold of. But his relief is short-lived, for he soon realizes the glaring contradiction between the simple, sweepingly general instruction Horace seems to be giving about how poems ought to be written and the poem that he himself is actually in process of writing. It is hard to think of a poem that, for its first 23 lines at least, has ever seemed less "simplex et unum," less straightforward and all of a piece, than this one.

From what we have so far seen of Horace's extraordinarily lively wit and free sense of fantasy, it certainly seems clear that he cannot seriously be recommending that poems or pictures or anything else be either simple or unified in any easy or obvious way. "Simplex" means, rather, something like all of the same general kind—as Brink puts it, "*simplex* makes *unum* more concrete. H. avoids abstract terminology; *unum*, 'one,' is insufficiently explained by the preceding verses, hence he adds *simplex* 'of one kind,' a thing which is not *varium*" (p. 104). But this leaves a great deal of room for the play of imagination needed to generate a work that, while it may (and indeed must) be unified, will be varied and various enough to command our unflagging attention and prevent us from being bored.

To combine unity and variety in just the right way is, of course, the artist's problem in a nutshell, so far as Horace is concerned. This is the point that we have been heading toward since that madly chaotic painting with which the poem opened. In the lines that follow, Horace goes on to explore the difficulties presented by the problem of unity and variety:

> maxima pars vatum, pater et iuvenes patre digni,
> decipimur specie recti: brevis esse laboro,
> obscurus fio; sectantem levia nervi
> deficiunt animique; professus grandia turget;
> serpit humi tutus nimium timidusque procellae;
> qui variare cupit rem prodigialiter unam,

delphinum silvis appingit, fluctibus aprum.
in vitium ducit culpae fuga, si caret arte.

[24–31]

(Most of us poets, father and sons worthy of the father, deceive ourselves with a mere semblance of correctness. Laboring to be brief, I become obscure. If one pursues smoothness, vigor and force are lacking. He who has promised the sublime is bombastic. Another, too cautious and frightened of the storm, creeps along the ground. While he who longs to vary a single subject prodigiously paints a dolphin in the midst of a forest or a wild boar among the sea waves. Avoiding a fault leads to error if art is lacking.)

Like the wine-jar that mysteriously emerges from the potter's wheel as a pitcher, any quality with which we set out to endow a work of art is in danger of turning into its opposite. As so often, Horace begins as though he were speaking impersonally, from a lofty position above the battle: his opening words, "maxima pars vatum," simply mean "the majority of poets"—as though he were not personally concerned in all this. And his formal address to the Pisos intercedes before we get to the verb. But when we do—and here again Latin can create effects that are impossible in an English translation—we find that it is not third-person, as we should have expected, but rather first-person plural: *those poets* has, in effect, become *we poets*. Horace too has these problems. And in the next clause he becomes still more directly personal, paring down the verb form to first-person singular: "Laboring to be brief, I become obscure." Having frankly and disarmingly implicated himself in what he is saying about the poet's problems, Horace then again moves outward to generalize: what you intend as smoothness can come out as mere insipidity, you aim at sublimity but wind up with fustian, the painter who tries to vary his picture wondrously or marvelously ("prodigialiter") produces a picture just as bad as the one the poem started with. *Prodigialiter*, it should be noted, is not necessarily a negative word. In fact it may not really be a Latin word at all, for as Brink points out, it is so exceedingly rare that it was "perhaps coined by H. for the occasion" (p. 114). In any case, the comic effect of this unfamiliar word that takes up six syllables of a sixteen-syllable line would surely not have been lost on Horace's audience.

This section of the poem concludes with another ringing generalization: "in vitium ducit culpae fuga, si caret arte." The statement sums up the artist's predicament, as the preceding lines have presented it, all the more succinctly because of the fact that the two words *vitium* and *culpa* are, as Brink tells us, "sometimes interchangeable . . . in literary contexts" (p. 115). To make a conscious effort to avoid a mistake leads to a mistake—if we translate the two virtual synonyms by the same word, we make still clearer the brutal injustice of the artist's plight. What it comes down to is that there simply are no rules that will guarantee success. This poem that pretends, from time to time at least, to instruct us in the art of poetry is now telling us that no instruction can, in itself, produce a good poem or picture. Every potential virtue in a work of art can so easily slip over the line and turn into a related vice—brevity into obscurity, smoothness into flaccidity, sublimity into bombast, prudence into timidity, variety into chaos—that there is nothing both general and illuminating that anyone can tell us that will ensure that we will realize our aims.

But we have forgotten the last three words of line 31: "si caret arte," if art or skill or craft (for they are not distinguishable in Latin) is lacking. So it all hinges on the instructee possessing the mysterious *ars*. Later in the poem (295ff., 408ff.) Horace will comment on the relation of *ars* to inborn talent (*ingenium*, *natura*), and though he has some fun at the expense of those who, like Democritus, thought genius was everything (and thus encouraged poets to go around with uncut nails and beards), he willingly agrees that both art and talent are necessary, that each should form a friendly pact ("coniurat amice") with the other. But for the moment it is *ars* on which everything hinges—and which Horace will go on to investigate in the portions of the poem immediately following.

In a poem so undogmatic and open-ended, it may seem crude to speak of a moral, but if the *Ars poetica*, with all its matchless dialectical complexity, does indeed have a moral, it is that anyone who thinks deeply and accurately about the nature of the arts soon finds himself caught in a thicket of contradictions. The most important of these, as we have seen, concern the psychological or epistemological status of the arts, as compared with our other activities. Since works of art are obviously not random creations, and since we argue about their character and worth more or less rationally (though the arguments are somewhat different from other sorts of argument), it would seem that creating and judging them are rule-governed activities. But then, if we try to state the rules, we run into trouble. The freedom and unpredictability of art, the wide variety of works admired by anyone with a reasonably catholic taste, the obvious role played in both creation and judgment by the unconscious—all these sit very uncomfortably indeed with the notion of a rule-governed activity. These are the problems that we have seen our aesthetic theorists struggling with, and I think the reason they turned so eagerly to Horace was that he faced these problems—antinomies, if you will—boldly and directly, and found poetic means of dealing illuminatingly with them. To do the job that Horace saw that it must do, the *Ars poetica* had to be a poem that constantly gives with one hand and takes away with the other, moving between pronouncement and example, detachment and involvement. There was no other way.

II

This is also true, though in a lesser degree, of the poems by Boileau and Pope that the *Ars poetica* inspired. The "*législateur de Parnasse*" label has distracted readers of the *Art poétique* from noticing how much it says about the need for emotional intensity in the kinds of poem to which emotional intensity is appropriate. In fact, those historians who, like the dissertation writers whose work we reviewed earlier, think of Boileau merely as the strict law-giver who thought that obedience to the rules ensured literary success and had no interest in emotional content seem to have forgotten that in 1674, the same year in which *L'Art poétique* appeared, Boileau also published the first good modern translation of the ancient critical work that most strongly advocates, and most extensively documents, emotional intensity in literature, the treatise Περὶ ὕψους, or *On the Sublime*, attributed to Longinus.

In fact, Boileau begins his poem with the claim that there is no conflict between poetry, even sublime poetry, and good sense:

> Quelque sujet qu'on traite, ou plaisant, ou sublime,
> Que toujours le bon sens s'accorde avec la rime:
> L'un l'autre vainement ils semblent se haïr;
> La rime est une esclave, et ne doit qu'obéir.

[I, 27-30]

Just so, Pope, quite early in *An Essay on Criticism,* advances a similar claim about the apparent conflict between wit and judgment, which, though they "often are at strife," are "meant each other's Aid, like *Man* and *Wife*" (82-83). Boileau tells us to choose "un censeur solide et salutaire" (IV, 71) to criticize what we write:

> C'est lui qui vous dira par quel transport heureux,
> Quelquefois dans sa course un esprit vigoureux,
> Trop reserré par l'art, sort des régles prescrites,
> Et de l'art même apprend à franchir leurs limites.

[IV, 77-80]

Of the ode, he writes: "Son style impétueux souvent marche au hasard. / Chez elle un beau désordre est un effet de l'art" (II, 71-72). Similarly, Pope, after telling us to learn "for ancient *Rules* a just esteem," immediately adds:

> Some Beauties yet, no Precepts can declare,
> For there's a *Happiness* as well as *Care*.
> *Musick* resembles *Poetry*, in each
> Are *nameless Graces* which no Methods teach,
> And which a *Master-Hand* alone can reach.
> If, where the *Rules* not far enough extend,
> (Since Rules were made but to promote their End)
> Some lucky LICENCE answers to the full
> Th' Intent propos'd, *that Licence is a Rule*.
>
> [141-149]

It is precisely because any intended poetic virtue can so easily turn into a fault that poems such as Horace's or Boileau's or Pope's so often offer—and offer intentionally, not negligently—paradoxical bits of advice: be cautious, yet not so cautious that you lose energy and fire; follow tradition and conform to decorum, yet not so strictly as to blot out your own individuality; imitate universal human nature, but don't be afraid of novelty and what Dr. Johnson called "the pleasures of sudden wonder"; follow the rules, but if not following one of them works—well, that way of not following the rules has just become a rule. If this sort of advice seems unsatisfying because paradoxical (or downright self-contradictory), that is because art itself is paradoxical—compared with other, simpler rule-governed activities.

As we have amply seen, the main opposition encountered in the first 31 lines of the *Ars poetica* is the one between unity and variety: unity is expressed by precept ("simplex dumtaxat et unum"), variety by example (the slapdash painter of the opening lines, Horace and the other, hypothetical poets of lines 25-30, who set out to create a specific poetic virtue and wind up instead with its opposing vice). As early as line 2 Horace plants the idea of variety (*varietas*) in the reader's mind by using the adjective "varias" to describe the feathers that the slapdash painter will apply as decoration. And then in line 29, "qui variare cupit rem prodigialiter unam," he juxtaposes the two adjectival cognates of *varietas* and *unitas*, the "unam" at the line's end picking up the "unum" of six lines earlier. Though other oppositions occur throughout the poem, it is the opposition of unity and variety, and the poet's need somehow to mediate or transcend that opposition, that shapes and controls Horace's vision, right down to the mad poet of the final lines, the poetic counterpart of the painter we met at the outset.

Moreover, it was this particular opposition, and the problems it raised for both artists and critics, that especially fascinated the critics and theorists of our period. Early in the annotated translation of the *Ars poetica* that Batteux included in his *Cours de belles-lettres*, he observes, of Horace's dictum "simplex dumtaxat et unum":

> *Simplex*, taken in a general sense, signifies the opposite to *duplex*, or *multiplex*. It may likewise signify either *one subject*, or *a subject not complicated*; i.e. that when a subject is not too much crowded with incidents, and that the action may be easily kept in view, it may then be called simple; and, in this sense, unity and simplicity are two different things. Thus we may say that Corneille's Heraclitus is one, and not simple, because the plot of intrigue is very complicated. . . . This sense is in itself very just. But it does not seem to be that of Horace in this place, who introduces a sort of general principle between what he has already said, and what he is going to say further on the head of unity: so as that this principle may serve at once as a consequence of what has

> preceded, and a foundation for what is to follow it. In this light we shall find *simplex* to have nearly the same signification as *unum*; and that both these words mean no more, than that every work of art should be free from any thing that is likely to break in upon the unity.[9]

This is very close to Brink's analysis of *simplex*, and shows that Batteux, with his eye on the more general point about unity and variety, is not tempted to take *simplex* as meaning simple in any sense that would exclude the variety needed to balance unity. Batteux in fact goes on to deal immediately with the extreme difficulties of striking this balance: "Nothing is more easy, than to exceed or fall short of the exact point of perfection in this rule" (p. 256). And he concludes his commentary on lines 1-37 of the poem—six lines further than our analysis carried us—by observing: "This passage is the richest and most important in Horace's Art of Poetry; and the rules it includes are equally applicable to eloquence, architecture, and all other polite arts" (p. 258).

But the problem of unity and variety was of paramount importance even to thinkers who did not mention Horace. Hutcheson, as we saw, singled out "*Uniformity amidst Variety*" as the one characteristic shared by all "Figures that excite in us the Ideas of Beauty" (p. 15). And though he admitted that "there are many Conceptions of Objects that are agreeable upon other accounts, such as Grandeur, Novelty, Sublimity, and some others," nevertheless "what we call Beautiful in Objects, to speak in the Mathematical Style, seems to be in a compound Ratio of Uniformity and Variety" (pp. 15-16). Yet Hutcheson neither quotes nor even mentions Horace or any other poet in the first treatise of his *Inquiry*—in marked contrast to his German counterparts of a few decades later, Baumgarten and Meier. He was, of course, steeped in the classics: several of his shorter works appeared only in Latin, and *A Short Introduction to Moral Philosophy* (1747) was his own English translation of *Philosophiae Moralis Institutio Compendiaria*, which had appeared two years earlier. Yet his works are free of the quotations from poets so common in the works of the Continental aestheticians. Hutcheson cited only philosophers: Locke, Leibniz, Descartes, Samuel Clarke, Aristotle, and (of course) Shaftesbury. His abstention from poetic citations was certainly not due to ignorance but probably to a commitment to "the Mathematical Style," a desire to seem rigorously modern and scientific.

Another work that shows no direct indebtedness to Horace yet has a great deal to say about variety within unity as the essence of beauty is the 1715 *Traité du Beau* of Jean-Pierre de Crousaz (1663-1750), the Swiss philosopher and theologian probably best known to readers of English literature for his wildly misdirected attacks on Pope's *An Essay on Man*. After having proven that beauty is not an illusory idea but rather an idea that consists in the apprehension of a certain relation, Crousaz then concludes his third chapter:

> Variety tempered by uniformity, regularity, order, and proportion is surely not a mere idle fancy; it is not a product of the imagination, nor is it determined by caprice. We have just established the real quality of the Beautiful, a quality founded in nature and in truth.[10]

In *The Philosophy of the Enlightenment*, Ernst Cassirer suggests that Crousaz's immediate source may have been Leibniz.[11]

Moreover, the whole notion of unity in variety, or variety in unity, was very much in the air because of developments in science. The laws of Kepler and Newton, to cite only the most obvious examples, had shown how the dazzling multiplicity of planetary motion and gravitation could be succinctly explained—that is, reduced to unity—by a geometrical diagram or a brief formula. Pope could describe Windsor Forest, in his poem of that title, as a kind of microcosm of the Newtonian universe:

> Here Hills and Vales, the Woodland and the Plain,
> Here Earth and Water seem to strive again,
> Not *Chaos*-like together crush'd and bruis'd,
> But as the World, harmoniously confus'd:
> Where Order in Variety we see,
> And where, tho' all things differ, all agree.
>
> [11-16]

And Batteux, in *Les Beaux-Arts réduits à un même principe*, could create a charming little allegory to explain "how the arts first rose out of nature" (p. 45):

> As soon as men became a little polished by society, and that they began to be sensible of the superiority the gifts of the mind have over those of the body; it is probable that some extraordinary person, inspired with a more than common genius, cast his eyes on nature. That magnificent order, joined to an infinite variety; that just conformity of means with their end, of parts with the whole, and of causes with effects, which he every where observed in her works, struck him with admiration.
>
> [Pp. 44–45]

After he had thus examined nature, this "extraordinary person" turned inward to examine himself. Having "perceived that he had an innate taste for the harmony he had observed in the dispositions of nature," he next decided that "the elegant order, beautiful variety, and exact proportion" that he had observed in nature "might be capable of lifting men up to the knowledge of the one supreme intelligent being," and "might even be considered as so many lessons for their conduct, and be improved to the advantage of society" (p. 45). Thus it was that the Greeks "rightly judged, that unity, variety and proportion should make the basis of all the arts" (p. 47).

The ideal of variety within unity, whether considered as classical or Newtonian, had an especially strong appeal to German critics and poets of the early 18th century, who, led by Gottsched, were, as we have seen, intent on reforming their literature by bringing it out of the Baroque age and into the Enlightenment. If we read a few of Hofmannswaldau's sprawling, ruminative poems—the ones addressed to "Flavia," for example—we can see why in a moment. To turn from Hofmannswaldau to the neatly turned, witty stanzaic poems—often, it should be noted, on the approved "Horatian" subjects of wine, women, and song—of Günther and Hagedorn is to step into another world.

In the chapters of the *Versuch* devoted to stylistic recommendations for poetry, the poets cited with approval by Gottsched are, almost without exception, those strongly influenced by Horace: Günther, Dach, Canitz, Fleming, and of course the earlier Opitz. In an effort to avoid "Lowenstein's bombastic style" (p. 213), Gottsched tells us, many poets have adopted a style that goes too far in the other direction: "As easy and comprehensible as it is, if they just stick to the rules of grammar, it is equally thin and watery. It has no fire, no spirit, no life, and is perfectly capable of putting to sleep anyone who hears or reads it" (p. 212). Horace, as he points out, has warned us against both errors: "neither to seek the empty air high above the clouds nor to crawl in the dust" (p. 214)—after which Gottsched cites lines 29-31 of the *Ars poetica*, from "Professus grandia, turget" through "si caret arte."

Throughout his treatment of the various decorative devices and rhetorical figures, Gottsched insists firmly that the great enemies are "Schwulst" (p. 228) and "Dunckelheit" (bombast and obscurity): "Certain people hide themselves so deeply in their metaphors that they themselves do not know what they want to say" (p. 234). The word order must be such that clarity is preserved, and a metaphor must not be "so far-fetched that it is not easily comprehensible" (p. 221)—one is here reminded of the very similar objections of Addison, Pope, and Johnson to the excesses of Donne and the later "metaphysical" poets. Yet Gottsched also insists eloquently that the standard rhetorical figures are "more than mere decorations. The whole strength of a discourse consists in their possessing a certain fire that also, by a secret art, casts a spark into the hearts of readers or listeners, and likewise sets them aflame" (p. 259). A page later, after citing a passage from Canitz, Gottsched exclaims: "Anyone who cannot grasp, from such a heart-rending passage, the expressive power of the [rhetorical] figures must possess little sensitivity or contemplativeness" (p. 260).

So ends Part I of the *Versuch*. It is in the opening chapters of Part II, in which Gottsched applies his theories to the various poetic genres, that he takes up the formal considerations that have direct bearing on the reinstatement of the strophic lied.

The first of these chapters is entitled "Von Oden, oder Liedern," and since both words could apply either to a poem—and particularly to the sort of poem suitable for musical setting—or to the musical setting of a poem, it is sometimes hard to tell just how Gottsched means them to apply. The chapter purports to be an historical account of how *Oden* or *Lieder* developed. Since Gottsched believes that music and poetry were born more or less simultaneously, the first poets producing only "musical texts" and songs thus being "the oldest kind of poetry" (p. 327), both terms initially apply to both genres. But as we read on, we realize that Gottsched's opening sentence—"We shall follow the order of nature" (p. 327)—is, albeit unintentionally, ambiguous. For Gottsched is not only following the order of nature in the sense of telling the story as it happened, chronologically; he is also building up the concept of song logically, from the ground up, as it were.

The oldest poets, he tells us, were also singers, who created in performance, simultaneously improvising both music and words, and not abiding by any fixed rules. Interestingly, Gottsched relates that he himself has heard such a performance:

> I myself have heard an old mastersinger, who was both a musician and a poet, sing a specially composed new song, to the delight of an assembled crowd. Both poem and song were improvised, as one could easily tell from the doggerel verses and from the melody. Thus we can imagine what the most ancient poets were like.

[Pp. 327-328]

One is reminded of Milman Parry, who verified his hypothesis about the oral-formulaic composition of the Homeric poems by visiting southern Yugoslavia in the 1930s, first alone and then in the company of Albert Bates Lord, and recording native bards who composed in a manner similar to the one Gottsched describes. So one feels that this is not only the most ancient sort of poetry but also, because it still survives in our (and Gottsched's) world, somehow the most basic sort.[12] Thus the temporal-logical ambiguity of Gottsched's opening declaration about following the order of nature.

Gradually these poet-singers learned to compose in a more regular fashion, and both the poetry and the music improved as a result:

> They contrived certain tunes that were very beautiful to the ear, and took the trouble not to forget them. The text was fashioned accordingly, and that was a song of one strophe. If the poet had more thoughts or ideas to express, he began his melody once more from the beginning, and because his verse had to be made to fit it, another strophe, similar to the first one, was born. And so it continued, until the song seemed long enough or the poet had nothing more to say.

[P. 328]

Thus the strophic song was born. Gottsched is puzzled by the choral odes in Greek tragedy and, especially, by the odes of Pindar, each of which would seem to require two separate melodies, one for the strophes and antistrophes, which are metrically similar to one another, and another for the epodes, which are all in a different meter. But, disregarding these aberrations, it is the more or less pure strophic song that has descended to us: "Even in our art music of today, the stanzas of a poem-to-be-set-to-music [*Ode*] must possess one certain length and number of lines if they are to be sung to one certain melody" (p. 329).

That last sentence is interesting because the repeated "certain" ("gewisse") each time gives the preceding "eine" the force of "one" rather than simply "a." Gottsched is insisting on the fact that even today, with our far more artfully contrived music, we, like those ancestors of long ago, prefer to create strophic songs. Therefore each stanza of a poem to be made into a song must have the same metrical arrangement as all the others so that the same melody will be suitable for them all. This is the beginning of a rhetorical stratagem that is to characterize Gottsched's rather complex argument in this and the following chapter: here and subsequently he will play forms of and compounds involving the word *ein* against words such as *verschieden* and *verändert* that have to do with variation or change. What he is doing, of course, is invoking Horace's notion of variety within unity as a sort of criterion for judging the forms of vocal music current at the time.

After citing a brief poem, presumably of his own composition, that is addressed to Pindar and that has, like a miniature Pindaric ode, a strophe, antistrophe, and epode, Gottsched comments:

> If the poems [*Oden*] are not made for singing, or are suited to being sung between two choruses, as a conversation, then one can alternate [*abwechseln*] stanzas of two different kinds with each other and set them to two different melodies.
>
> [P. 330]

After citing an example, from the poems of Christoph H. Amthor (1678-1721), Gottsched remarks: "If this sounds very pleasing, it surprises me that more such Wechsel-Oden, as one may call them, are not introduced into religious as well as secular pieces" (p. 330). This is somewhat surprising because until now, Gottsched had seemed to be an unquestioning supporter of the strophic song. But now, perhaps because of the degree of variety introduced by the "two different melodies," he is clearly advancing the *Wechsel-Ode* as an at least occasionally possible alternative to the strophic song.

Another thing about the ancients that seems to puzzle Gottsched is that even in poems where they retained the same metrical structure in every stanza, they often allowed the sense to run on from stanza to stanza, thus preventing the full close that one expects at the end of each strophe of a strophic song. Horace is the example adduced—but of course it seems ludicrous to us that anyone should have assumed that Horace wrote his four books of odes in the expectation that they would ever be set to music. (The *Carmen Saeculare*, however, was written to be sung publicly, at the festival staged by Augustus in 17 B.C., to celebrate the 500th birthday of the Roman Republic.) At any rate, Gottsched concludes against run-on stanzas: "Among us, however, it has been established with good reason, and certainly sounds twice as good, as if one had to look for the end of a sentence in the following stanza" (p. 330). But Gottsched does, interestingly enough, insist that the stanza endings not be neatly epigrammatic: "This would be too artificial, and would sound very forced" (p. 331).

Though all stanzas of a poem intended for a strophic setting must of course be identical in metrical structure, Gottsched emphasizes that the lines within the stanza should not all be of the same length—and again we feel the force of a desire for variety, to balance the unity gained by having one melody for all stanzas of the poem: "In the first stanza one can make all sorts of combinations of lines with one, two, three, four, five, even six feet, and need only consider whether it sounds well to the ear" (p. 332). Another way in which variety may be gained is through the now innumerable possible subjects for lyric poems. In the early days, Gottsched notes, there were only "sad, happy, and amorous songs" (p. 332). As evidence he cites lines 83-85 of the *Ars poetica*:

> musa dedit fidibus divos puerosque deorum
> et pugilem victorem et equum certamine primum
> et iuvenum curas et libera vina referre.
>
> (The muse gave to the lyre gods and the children of gods, the winning boxer and the horse first in the race, the love-pangs of youth and the freedom bestowed by wine.)

Yet, as Gottsched goes on to point out, Horace himself wrote satires, epistles, and didactic poems, proving that even in his time the range of subjects for the lyric poet was not restricted to heroism, sport, love, and the pleasures of drink. The chapter concludes with a survey of the subjects now available and the style appropriate to each one.

Gottsched then turns to deal with cantatas, which he refers to as "a new discovery of the Italians, of which the ancients knew nothing" (p. 358). He then specifies the advantages the cantata (which is, for him, the name for a type of poetry as well as for its expected musical setting) has over the ordinary strophic song. First, the disadvantages of the strophic song:

> Because in songs with only one sort of strophe the same melody must be retained throughout, men came to realize that the one would not suit all equally well. The first verse of a poem was, for example, sad, but toward the end this emotion ceased, indeed changed to joy. If the tune of the song fit well at the beginning, it fit all the worse at the end.
>
> [P. 358]

Gottsched continues to belabor this rather simple point for several more sentences, which suggests, as I believe is indeed the case, that the whole issue of the strophic problem had not (or at least not often) been raised so clearly and trenchantly before this time. Gottsched then explains how the cantata was devised to remedy this situation:

> Therefore men got the idea of no longer making songs so completely unified [*einträchtig*] or keeping all strophes the same, but of allowing lines of unequal length to run into one another in a casual manner, and then accommodating the music to the content of the poem throughout. Thus one would surely avoid the disadvantage of [strophic] songs, and each line of such a song would express the pervading emotion, and give to each word, in its proper sense, the tone and weight appropriate to it.
>
> [P. 358]

There are several interesting things about this passage. First, in its opening sentence "einträchtig" (unified, harmonious) is something of a surprise. Gottsched is, after all, talking about an ostensible fault in the strophic song: the requirement that all stanzas of the poem be set to the same music almost inevitably results in the music being inappropriate to some sections of the poem. We might therefore have expected him to use a negative adjective suggesting strictness or rigidity—*steif*, *streng*, or the like. But *einträchtig* is, so far as I can gather, wholly positive in its implications, being the adjective formed from *Eintracht*, which means harmony, unity, concord. Johann George Hamman's *Poetisches Lexicon* of 1737 tells us that the standard adjectives used with *Eintracht* are *stille, reiche, volkommene, feste, erwünschte*, and so on. One of the conventional representations of *Eintracht* was a woman crowned with olive branches, holding in one hand a vessel containing fire and in the other a cornucopia—obviously an image of the good things produced by political stability.

Thus Gottsched, even as he is telling us about something that was felt to be wrong with strophic songs, is making it clear that the attempted correction involved the sacrifice of something valuable, namely unity—which of course brings us back to Horace. Another interesting thing about this passage is that in later editions of the *Versuch* Gottsched altered the phrase "Thus one would surely avoid the disadvantage" to read "Thus one hoped." This change would seem to strengthen the implication of his choice of the word *einträchtig*: that while it is understandable that there should have been an attempt to improve on the strophic song by inventing the cantata, perhaps the cure was worse than the disease, the desired improvement merely a hope, not an accomplished fact.

In the pages that follow, Gottsched pursues this line of thought, and he uses the vocabulary of unity and variety to do so. The shift from the strophic song to the cantata was easily managed, he tells us: "The poets obtained more freedom and the composers a thousandfold opportunity to have their arts and musical ideas [*Einfälle*] appear at their best" (p. 358). This all sounds very nice—though when we recall Gottsched's rather tartly critical use of the word "artificial" ("gekünstelt") in connection with those epigrammatic stanza-endings he was disowning, his stress here on the composers' "arts" ("Künste") perhaps puts us on the alert, as does "Einfälle," which makes the composers' ideas sound a bit whimsical or haphazard, conducive to the wrong sort of variety (in place of the unity that has been sacrificed by the shift). And perhaps a "thousandfold opportunity" is too much freedom, reminding us of the slapdash painter at the beginning of the *Ars poetica*.

It gets worse. As he continues describing the effect on composers of the shift to the cantata, Gottsched—a far more lively and colorful writer than he is usually given credit for being—warms to his task:

> They now were at pains to express almost all the syllables of such a song through changes in the music, and to try out all possible variations. It was no longer enough for them to set a text to music all of one sort. Yet they did not have enough confidence in themselves to believe that they had found the very best sort of music. Therefore they repeated the same word two, three, maybe ten or twenty times, and always with new changes. They particularly felt themselves obliged, at certain places, to do whatever would allow them to employ all the tricks of their craft. Wherever there was the slightest trace of emotion, or any place that allowed for any degree of imitation through singing or playing, they had a grand time with it, often holding on to one line longer than they would formerly have done with a whole poem. Though the ear had much to listen to, the understanding had just so much less to think about.
>
> [Pp. 358-359]

The effect of all this feverishly exerted artfulness—all these "changes" and "variations"—is chaos, variety run amok. For composers are no longer satisfied with merely setting a text in a single uniform style: again the criticism is couched in the Horatian terms of unity vs. variety. But Gottsched's rage is beyond anything we find in Horace. The slowly building high satiric scorn of his prose reminds us rather of the final book of Pope's *Dunciad*, as does the clear implication that all this self-indulgent silliness is culturally quite dangerous. The ear is tickled, but the mind has nothing to feed on.

After a few digressive pages, Gottsched turns his attention from the composers to the poets, and asks how they could possibly have thus allowed themselves to become the composers' slaves. "But how would it be," he asks, "if a poet just once told his composer that he wanted his cantata set according to the guidance of nature and reason? Would this conform to the rules and examples of their so great—yet very unnatural—Italian masters" (p. 361)? If we examine cantatas as a species of song, Gottsched continues, it is obvious that they should not be passionless and soporific: "They will express one certain emotion, or be filled with sublime and fiery thoughts, magnificent or tender expressions; in short, they will have content that will give the composer enough opportunity for good ideas" (p. 361). As before, the pointed specificity of "certain" ("gewissen") gives the preceding "einen" a force that turns the sentence into an insistence on unity—as opposed to the chaotic variety of the bad cantatas—as well as on emotional intensity. And in this case, as opposed to the earlier one, the composer's "Einfälle" will not be whimsical or haphazard because they will be controlled and limited by the content of the poem—as, indeed, they should always be.

Yet Gottsched wants to stress that in regaining control of the cantata from the composer, the poet will not thereby eliminate all variety from the resulting work: "He will organize the pieces so that more than one person is speaking, and the exchange of many voices will introduce variety [*Mannigfaltigkeit*] into the song" (p. 361). But the poet will, quite reasonably, demand of the composer that he not repeat a line innumerable times, that he not stretch out single words to the point where the singer runs out of breath, that he not burden the listener and obscure the sense with his endless trills, and, finally, "That he preserve a certain oneness [*Gleichheit*] in the melody of an aria, and not set the beginning too artfully or the ending too simply" (p. 361). Once again, "eine gewisse" insists on artistic unity, and thereby strengthens the overtones of identity and self-consistency in "Gleichheit." The remainder of the chapter is spent in classifying the different sorts of cantata and fulminating against the Italians.

Thus Gottsched, writing six years before the first Sperontes collection clearly signaled the return in Germany to the publication of strophic songs, offered a sort of qualified approval of strophic songs that by no means implied a condemnation either of the compromise *Wechseloden* or, despite his strong chauvinistic distaste for Italians, of more or less through-composed cantatas. Let us turn now to the practicing music critics who immediately followed Gottsched, and see how they responded to what he had written and also to the ideas, mainly gathered from the *Ars poetica*, that led him to write as he did.

Chapter Seven

"Das *Unum* des Horaz"

We have already reviewed part of this material in Chapter Two, when we examined Lindner's comments on the *liederlose Zeit*. We may define the pre-Gottsched position on strophic songs as fairly represented by the two remarks cited there from Mattheson's journal *Critica musica*. First this, from 1722: "Many wish to maintain that songs are musical; but they should know that in all of music nothing can be more despicable, more tasteless, than to hear the same melody, often repeated over and over, to different words, which also occasionally contain quite contrary *incisiones*." And then this, from 1725: "To me, songs are not at all musical . . . My reasons are that those poems that one wants to turn into songs will never match well with the music and a good melody because of the different stanzas, except in the melismatic style, since all will be shorn with the same comb."[1] Nothing could be clearer than these two remarks—which of course is why they provide us with such a convenient point of departure. What changed? How did strophic songs not only come to be viewed, once again, as "musical" but also become the predominant form of 18th-century German vocal music?

The first thing to say is probably that the change happened neither so swiftly nor so neatly and clearly as is often implied. This, in fact, we saw from some of the passages cited by Lindner from Scheibe's *Der critische Musikus*, and have just now seen from the passages from Gottsched's *Versuch* that we have examined. The second thing to say is that Gottsched probably had a great deal to do with the change. For as Lindner implied, the first important critics to prepare the way for the reinstatement of the strophic song were two of Gottsched's students and disciples, Mizler and Scheibe. Scheibe is by far the more interesting of the two, both as a thinker and as a writer. But Mizler, though a terrible composer and a very quirky thinker, was a learned, enterprising, and influential man.

I

Lorenz Christoph Mizler von Kolof, to give him his full Polish title, was born in Franconia in 1711 and died at Warsaw in 1778. As a theology student at Leipzig University, which he entered in 1731, he attended the lectures not only of Gottsched but also of the philosopher Christian Wolff. After taking his bachelor's and master's degrees, he moved on, in 1735, to Wittenberg, to study law and medicine. But two years later he was back at Leipzig, as a lecturer on music. In 1743 he entered the employ of a Polish count, as secretary, librarian, and court mathematician. In 1747 he earned a doctorate in medicine from Erfurt University, but then moved back to Warsaw, where he became court physician. For his services he was awarded Polish nobility in 1768. It was during this period, between 1736 and 1754, that he produced his magazine, *Neu eröffnete musikalische Bibliothek*, which was his most important contribution to the musical life of his time.

In October 1738, in one of the early installments of Mizler's journal,[2] he reprinted and commented on Gottsched's chapter on songs. His mission, which was also Scheibe's, is to apply to music what Gottsched has said about poetry: "Indeed, the relation between these two sciences is so great that the rules of each one can be employed in the other" (I, v, 2). Like Gottsched before him, Mizler maintains "that the style of the composer must be similar to the style of the poet" (I, v, 4). But Mizler later adds a qualification to this rule:

> If all stanzas are to be sung to one melody, there is much to be considered. The main rule, from which all the other rules are derived, is this: The style of the composer must be similar to the style of the poet. But the composer, since he is striving to express the thoughts of the poet, must not be too diligent [*fleissig*] in the composition of a song, for the sake of the stanzas that follow.
>
> [I, v, 16-17]

That is, if the composer matches the style adopted by the poet in the poem's opening stanza too closely, the musical strophe that results may not fit the presumably different content of the other stanzas.

Mizler pushes a bit beyond Gottsched in a somewhat different way in responding to Gottsched's innocent statement that each of the passions has its own distinctive tone: "Sighing, groaning, threatening, lamenting, pleading, scolding, admiring, praising, etc. all fall differently on the ear, because each requires a different alteration of the voice." Mizler seizes this opportunity to ride a favorite hobbyhorse:

> That all particular alterations of voice fall differently on the ear has its basis in the various interrelations holding among tones. The tones that cause sadness have different relations among themselves than do those that cause joy, etc. Thus as soon as we know how to determine correctly the interrelations of tones that cause this or that emotion, we shall also be able to accomplish incomparably more with music than now, since even otherwise capable men who are most knowledgeable about music are stuck fast in a dangerous error about the experiencing of music, namely that mathematics has no use in the practice of music.
>
> [I, v, 7]

Mizler's great dream, one gathers through the fog of his prose, was to establish some sort of mathematical system of music—a dream shared in the 20th century by Joseph Schillinger and others. So great is Mizler's conviction that the discovery of music's mathematical basis is necessary to the perfection of the art that he leaps on Gottsched's remark that at the present time "music has risen to its highest point":

> No, it still falls very far short. We still have no proven rules. We still can produce no demonstrated system of music truths, etc.
>
> [I, v, 10]

A few months later, still in 1738, Mizler also reprinted Gottsched's chapter on cantatas. But this time he kept his comments to a minimum, having perhaps been taken to task by the master for the severity of some of his earlier remarks. More interesting is the fact that in a much later issue of the *Neu eröffnete musikalische Bibliothek* Mizler too joined the ranks of those who felt the need to supply an extended commentary on Horace's *Ars poetica*. But while the fact that he made such an attempt is interesting, his comments have almost no interest. He simply goes through the poem, recasting Horace's remarks about poetry and painting in terms of music. The fact that Horace devoted so much of the *Ars poetica* to drama has always puzzled Latinists, since in Horace's time the Roman stage was moribund. But Mizler seizes on the long sections on drama and translates them into a defense of opera. Despite the general vacuity of his comments, the very fact of their existence reminds us once again of what so many historians of the aesthetics of his period have ignored: that to be a follower of Gottsched was, *ipso facto,* to be a follower of Horace since a serious, revitalized attention to the classics was part and parcel of Enlightenment "modernism."

II

The same point is made more clearly, and to far better effect, in Scheibe's writings on these matters in *Der critische Musikus.* Or perhaps the plural, "writings," is inappropriate since in all the length and breadth of *Der critische Musikus*, which Scheibe published fortnightly in 1737-1738 and weekly in 1739-1740, there is really only one number devoted to songs, the famous No. 64, which appeared November 17, 1739. As we saw when we considered Lindner's treatment of Scheibe, No. 64, like Gottsched's chapters, favors the strophic song while showing an awareness of its problems and also while favoring *Wechseloden* and under certain circumstances, *Durchkomponierung*. But let us look more closely at Scheibe's argument in No. 64.[3]

His motive for writing is made clear in his opening sentence: "Songs are now becoming very popular, but experience shows that their true character is very little known. Therefore it is certainly appropriate that I devote a special page to them, in order to contribute something informative about what their essence consists in, particularly since they are not so easy to compose as people think, and as many song-composers may well imagine" (p. 583). This even precedes the attack, cited by Lindner, on those "certain great and sublime composers" who scorn the lied. In fact Scheibe seems less concerned with their disapproval than he does with the fact that the lied has once again, suddenly, become popular but that during the *liederlose Zeit* composers seem to have forgotten precisely what is involved in song composition.

When one considers the exact time at which this issue of *Der critische Musikus* appeared, Scheibe's attitude makes perfect sense. The *Tafel-Confect* volumes and the first of the "Sperontes" volumes had appeared, but the only real song collection that pointed to the future was the first of Gräfe's volumes, which came out in 1737—and about which, as we have seen, Scheibe had severe reservations. Yet it is interesting that he assumes he can clear up the subject of songs and song composition in only one issue of his journal—"a special page." Certainly the "parody" settings in the 1736 Sperontes volume, and even many of the songs in Gräfe's collection, would have given Scheibe the idea that people no longer knew how to take song composition seriously and needed to be reminded of its pitfalls. But he does not think the job will take long.

After his dismissal of the "great souls" who do not deign to appreciate mere songs "that are natural, flowing, and beautifully set" (pp. 583-584), Scheibe says that since Gottsched has so effectively handled the poetic side of *Oden* and *Lieder*, he himself will only speak here "of the musical make-up of songs" (p. 584). But then he too reiterates the business about how the sense in ancient lyrics runs on from stanza to stanza, from which he reaches a conclusion, more detailed than Gottsched's, not only about their musical settings but also about the nature of the poems themselves:

> We comprise one or at most two stanzas of a poem in the melody of a song. But this could by no means have been the case with the ancients, because the sense of various stanzas would have been distorted and unclear.
>
> [P. 585]

From the odes of Horace it is obvious that they could never have been sung as our lyric poems are sung—that is, strophically, with one melody for all stanzas.

From this Scheibe concludes that the ancients were more attentive to the thought and feeling inherent in their lyrics than are present-day men:

> Therefore I maintain that the Greeks, and after them the Romans, sang their songs more in accordance with the content of the words rather than being confined by the melody of the first stanza. For we also know that in antiquity they were much more concerned with the emotion and the content of their songs than with enclosing, within the narrow compass of a few tones, the entire tune of a far-ranging poem.
>
> [P. 585]

Though their music, as we know, was much less rich harmonically than ours, we also know that they cared too much for the emotional content and the sense of their lyrics to enclose them in one poor strophe of music: "It is far more likely that they sang each stanza to its own melody" (p. 586). In other words, the ancients practiced *Durchkomponierung*.

What is very interesting, however, is that while Scheibe is proposing that we follow the example of the ancients and establish the art of song composition on a rational basis, he does not advocate that his contemporaries write through-composed songs. Rather, he proposes that they write strophic songs, but in a more circumspect manner that reflects what they have learned from the ancients:

> Whoever wants to give a song an expressive, well adapted, and moving melody must attend not only to the first stanza [of the poem] or first strophe [of the song]. The whole poem, or whole song, must be viewed with consideration. This is the reason: the composer must form a clear and complete concept of the character of the whole poem before he gives it a melody.
>
> [P. 586]

Even poems that might at first seem to require a different melody for each stanza can, he implies, be treated in this way. The composer's job is to examine the poem until he discovers "what emotion, what state of feeling most governs the whole poem and which poetic style the poet has really followed" (p. 587).

Scheibe's assumption is clearly that in any poem—or any poem worth setting to music—there will indeed be one, and only one, overarching emotion. Otherwise, presumably, the poem would lack the unity required of a work of art. But of course the identity of this one unifying emotion will often, perhaps even usually, not be immediately obvious. To discover it, and then to express it musically, is, in the realm of song composition, to follow Gottsched's rule about matching the style of the music to the style of the poem. Yet this insistence upon unity, and especially upon a unity that is not immediately obvious because it is embodied in a variety of dissimilar poetic stanzas, of course reminds us of Horace. Once again: to follow Gottsched is necessarily to follow Horace—not, of course, literally or slavishly but creatively, by shaping his rules to apply to the situation at hand. Looking back, we notice that the epigraph to No. 64 of *Der critische Musikus* is taken from a poem by Neukirch: "Trachte den Verstand der Alten zu ergründen: / So wirst du, was du suchst, und was uns mangelt, finden."—in a word, follow the ancients.

Only after a composer has thoroughly examined (and internalized) the content of a poem in this very special way will he be able to furnish it with "a melody both natural and in conformity with the rules" (p. 587). Even Scheibe's pointed coupling of these two attributes reflects the Horatian influence—one recalls Pope's lines from *An Essay on Criticism*: "Those RULES of old *discover'd*, not *devis'd*, / Are *Nature* still, but *Nature* methodiz'd" (88–89). Even—or, more precisely, especially—if the stanzas of a poem are all quite similar to one another, the composer must still remain vigilant: "A composer cannot attend merely to the first stanza, even if all the other stanzas are similarly arranged; rather, he must expound his ideas in such a way that they will be equally well adapted to all stanzas" (p. 588). For even if the content and feeling remain pretty much the same throughout the poem, the way in which the phrases are divided may vary from stanza to stanza, and the poet cannot allow his melody to follow the phrasing of the first stanza alone. "One sees this mistake very often," adds Scheibe, "and even our best collection of German songs is not wholly free of it" (p. 588). He is speaking, of course, of the first (1737) Gräfe volume. As we saw, in 1745, when Scheibe prepared the whole of *Der critische Musikus* for republication in book form, he added a long footnote in which he said that now, with the appearance of Telemann's *Vier und zwanzig, theils ernsthafte, theils scherzende, Oden* in 1741, the best German song collection was indeed free of these errors. In the same footnote Scheibe also made clear how little he thought not only of the first Sperontes collection but also of Mizler's 1740 *Erste Sammlung auserlesener moralischer Oden*.

It is just at this point, after having gone to so much trouble explaining how we can, despite the differences between our lyric poems and those of the ancients, nevertheless follow them and so produce better strophic songs than we have done heretofore, that Scheibe, much to our surprise, comes out in favor of *Wechseloden* in which the two melodies are strongly contrasted: "Such *Wechseloden*, if all their attendant beauties are taken into consideration, are generally pleasing, and the alternating melody makes them far more grateful to the ear than those songs in which one repeats the melody of the first strophe through all the other strophes" (p. 593). He then immediately surprises us further by praising through-composed songs: "this way of singing songs should be better known and more common, because it is much more suitable to the content and the passion of songs than the usual way is" (p. 593). He does, however, add a qualification to his advocacy of the through-composed song: "yet one must, wherever possible, allow the melody of the first strophe, or the beginning, always to stand out" (p. 594). He does not tell us just how this is to be accomplished—presumably through some sort of motivic allusion. Later we shall see Bach managing it in the most famous of his few through-composed songs.

And so Scheibe arrives at last at the concluding paragraph of No. 64, in which occur the words most frequently quoted from it: "The melody of a song must be free, flowing, pure, and generally natural, so as to be singable, immediately and without special effort, even by one who is inexperienced in music" (p. 594). This sentence, taken out of context and viewed in isolation, has often been produced to portray Scheibe as a wholehearted advocate of a return to the simple strophic song—and even of the folksong movement that was not to occur until several decades later. Read in its full context, however, this sentence offers further evidence of Scheibe's indecision about the strophic song. After taking such pains to explain what a composer must do if he is to preserve both unity and variety in a strophic song, Scheibe seems suddenly to get cold feet—remembering how much more variety is possible in a *Wechselode* or through-composed song—but then to shift ground yet again, specifying that the opening melody of a through-composed song must be made somehow to predominate, in order to unify the variety achieved by writing a separate melody for every stanza of the poem.

This indecision, or even confusion, is further manifested in the fact that while Scheibe devoted only one issue of *Der critische Musikus* to songs, he devoted many to cantatas. As with strophic songs, both his praise for various sorts of cantata and his concerns about them seem to stem from his constant preoccupation with the problem of balancing unity and variety. A few examples will, I think, make this clear.

Though cantatas, with their alternation of aria and recitative, and their possibilities for solos, duets, and choruses, possess a degree of variety that is very attractive to Scheibe, in No. 17 he worries that this can get out of hand: "Religious cantatas, which throughout mingle chorales, Biblical passages, arias, and recitatives in no particular order, are not suitable for musical setting because the Biblical passages are generally too long, the arias are too often interrupted by the recitatives and chorales, and they possess not the slightest emotion or passion" (p. 164). Finally, at the end of the issue, Scheibe invokes *Eintracht*, the spirit or goddess of unity and harmony:

> But Unity, mother of earthly happiness, must also play a part in the performance of such music. A unanimity of spirit must join the musicians to one another. A harmony so perfect will make more certain the attainment of the goal of church music, and we shall thereby with one voice praise and celebrate the supreme being in the most rational and circumspect manner, yet we shall also glimpse a tender vision of the eternal and heavenly music.
>
> [P. 167]

If poet, composer, and performing musicians have achieved the necessary unity or harmony of spirit, the work they perform will also be unified and will grant them a vision of the heavenly music, one and unchanging, that all righteous folk will someday hear.

In No. 41 Scheibe, after remarking that "it is well known, and daily experience proves, how seldom one encounters good cantatas," expresses the following concern:

> Yet I must point out that in serious cantatas it is not good if the poet gives the composer an aria of more than one stanza. For one must either set such arias in the manner of songs, which is contrary to the character of such a cantata and generally has a bad effect in cantatas, or one must compose a special strophe for each stanza, which falls annoyingly on the listener's ear because it is never good that two or more arias should directly follow one another.
>
> [P. 384]

If the composer sets the aria of many stanzas "in the manner of songs," that is strophically, the lighter tone connected with the strophic song will disrupt the seriousness of the cantata. On the other hand, if he writes a through-composed setting, that will seem like a string of arias, unbroken by any recitatives, which will throw off the delicate balance of unity and variety necessary for the piece to make its effect. Scheibe then adds: "In so-called *galanterie* cantatas, which are either amorous or humorous, one can avail oneself of this freedom and insert songlike arias of that sort because one composes such cantatas in a songlike way" (p. 384).

Finally, in No. 52 Scheibe, who constantly exhibits his master Gottsched's penchant for classifying types and styles and genres of music, sets out to analyze "the first species of epic cantatas" (p. 487). In epic, as opposed to dramatic, cantatas, the poet himself speaks in his own person, either alone or joined by other speakers, the latter being the case here. Scheibe writes:

> Because these vocal pieces are sung by many people, the poet must take that into account in the writing of his poem. Thus there are as many precepts that he must observe in regard to the construction of the arias as in regard to the coherence of the whole piece; otherwise such a piece will turn out to be disordered and tasteless if it is to be sung by many people.
>
> [P. 487]

Obviously, having a number of different singers is a virtue in such cantatas: it helps to provide the desired variety. But Scheibe is anxious immediately to point out the dangers of this variety: like Horace, he is keenly aware how easily the variety you are aiming at can turn into the disorder of the painter portrayed at the beginning of the *Ars poetica*. But then in the next paragraph Scheibe leans back in the other direction: "The poet should give the composer the opportunity to set some arias as choruses, others as duets" (p. 487). The potential for variety thus offered to the composer by the poet is an opportunity, something to be praised. But then, a page later, Scheibe is once again cautioning his readers: "The coherence of this sort of epic cantata still demands some explanation" (p. 488). And the promised paragraph of further explanation directly follows.

Now of course I do not mean to imply that Gottsched, and through him Horace, gave these critics the bright new idea that works of art must possess both unity and variety: that idea was as old as the hills, and no one doubted its truth. But it was Horace's exceedingly sharp focus on the problem of unity and variety that suddenly made him seem so directly relevant to German men of letters who were trying to bring their poetry closer to the neatness and urbanity of the English and French, and also to discover a respectable theoretical justification for a return to the strophic song—not an exclusive return, as was to be more nearly the case later in the century, with the rise of the folksong movement, but a return in which the strophic songs would happily coexist with other sorts of songs as well as with cantatas and, *pace* Gottsched, even operas. It is interesting that the epigraphs to some of Scheibe's papers on cantatas are taken from Horace, while others are taken from Opitz and (of course) Gottsched.

III

Krause's *Von der musikalischen Poesie*, as I suggested earlier, is even more explicit in paying homage to Horace. Of Krause's 14 citations of Horace (not counting the passage from Martial wrongly attributed to Horace), 12 are from the *Ars poetica*. He also cites Boileau's *L'Art poétique* six times, Pope's *An Essay on Criticism* four times, and Opitz twice. Moreover, in a letter of August 3, 1748, to the poet Johann Wilhelm Ludwig Gleim, which accompanied a draft of his book that he was sending to Gleim for criticism, Krause listed the books he had been reading. Prominent among them was "Horace's *Ars poetica* with Dacier's extensive and to me very useful commentary."[4] André Dacier's *Remarques Critiques sur les OEuvres d'Horace, avec une Nouvelle Traduction*, published in 10 volumes at Paris in 1681-1689, in the wake of Boileau's poem, had an enormous influence not only in France but in England and Germany as well. The prose translation that accompanied the critical remarks was widely hooted at—for example by Wentworth Dillon, Earl of Roscommon, in his 1684 *Essay on Translated Verse*:[5]

> Serene and clear, harmonious Horace flows,
> With sweetness not to be expresst in *Prose*;
> Degrading *Prose* explains his meaning ill,
> And shows the *Stuff*, but not the Workman's skill . . .
>
> [41-44]

But the remarks themselves, especially those on the *Ars poetica*, became something of a critical classic—as indeed also did those in Dacier's 1692 edition of Aristotle's *Poetics*.

Krause, who was educated at the University of Frankfurt an der Oder, made his career in the law. But he was an enthusiastic and active musical amateur. In addition to writing *Von der musikalischen Poesie* and compiling several song collections, he composed songs, cantatas, a few instrumental works, and a *Singspiel*. It is not clear just when he began work on his book, but work was well advanced by the summer of 1747, and before the end of that year he could write Gleim that "my treatise on musical poetry is finished, but longer than I expected."[6] This draft was thoroughly revised but then set aside in 1749, while Krause studied for his legal examinations. It was ready for publication, and Krause was searching for a publisher, early in 1750. But it did not appear until late in 1752, published at Berlin by Johann Friedrich Voss—apparently no relation of the poet and editor Johann Heinrich Voss, who was born at just about this time and whom we shall meet in later chapters. It was a very successful book that continued to be important in German musical circles for almost the next half century.

But it is a rather confusing book. It has often been tagged as the "manifesto" of the first Berlin song school. Raymond A. Barr, for example, in his entry on Krause in *The New Grove Dictionary of Music and Musicians*, writes that the book's publication "marked the beginning of a new era in the lied, and the foundation of the first Berlin lied school," and that Krause "advocated a return to folklike simplicity." But to say this, as many historians of the lied have done, is to telescope two eras together. The folksong movement, or second Berlin song school, flowered somewhat later, under the influence of writers like Herder. Again we can see the anti-rationalist bias of the historians in the assumption that to talk about music as the expression of feelings, as Krause and his contemporaries surely did, and to rail against the artificiality of Italian "ornaments," as they also did, is also to advocate a return to folklike simplicity. And surely one cause of this error is the historians' failure to see how important the influence of Horace was on the theorists and practitioners of the first Berlin song school. The simplicity they sought in song was the effortless urbanity advocated (and exemplified) by Horace, not—or not yet, anyway—the simplicity of the *Volk*. Moreover, Krause's book is not mainly about songs at all. Far from being the prescient, clear-eyed justification of the strophic song that it has so often been made out to be, its main point is to defend the *opera seria* of Graun and Hasse. Most of what Krause has to say about songs is found in Chapters III-VI of the 11 chapters that make up his book.

Yet he does say enough about songs, and about cantatas too, for one to see how *Von der musikalischen Poesie* has come to be so misrepresented. For like Scheibe, Krause is both intrigued and confused by the question of what musical forms can best balance unity and variety, and his argument too changes direction a number of times and in surprising ways.[7]

Krause's reason for writing his book, he tells us immediately, is that composers frequently complain that they find it difficult to set many of the poems apparently intended for musical settings. The only ones that lend themselves to setting are those that merely consist of flowing and agreeable words:

> But one does not find there the richness, the nobility and strength of thought, and the vivid and novel expression, that make other poems so valuable. One is therefore led to think that a poem cannot have the characteristic poetic excellences if it is suitable for music; the poet who writes such verses becomes a slave of music; he sacrifices good sense to the convenience of the composer, and music's gain is poetry's loss.

[Pp. iii-iv]

Recently, however, both poets and composers have wanted to do a better job of making common cause, and to prove that despite the apparent differences in their aims, the poetry that is most compatible with music is also the best poetry:

> In a vocal piece, music and poetry unite in order to bring forth a sensuously perfect work through their combined powers. How poetry may be most suitable for the fulfillment of this intention, I have been at pains to demonstrate in the following treatise.

[P. vi]

Soon after this statement of faith that poems suitable for musical setting need not be brainlessly "beautiful," and that a true and meaningful unity between *Ton* and *Wort* is possible, Krause cites two lines from Horace's *Ars poetica*:

> Non satis est pulchra esse poemata; dulcia sunto
> et quocumque volent animum auditoris agunto.
>
> [99-100]
>
> (It is not enough that poems be beautiful; they must be
> delightful, and lead the soul of the listener wherever
> they wish.)

The contrast of course is between mere external attractiveness (the poems with flowing words that merely please the ear) and an inner quality that speaks directly to the heart—when *dulcis* is used of persons, it often means kind or friendly.

One further point remains to be made about Krause's brief preface. He closes by recommending that pieces of vocal music, and therefore the poems that will serve as their texts, should be either dramatic or historical, so that they may have a genuine plot or fable:

> Thus they can possess the two highest kinds of poetic imitation, the fable and the language of feelings. Descriptions and pictures should be present in poems only rarely.
>
> [Pp. viii-ix]

This opposition of music, as the language of feeling, to the description and pictorial imagery so often found in poetry strikes a new note, I think, in the intellectual history that we are tracing. A good deal more of this anti-painting talk creeps in as Krause develops his argument.

Chapter II is devoted to specifying just what sort of ideas music communicates—clearly, Krause had read Baumgarten's early *Meditationes philosophicae* (1735) and had perhaps also had time to look at the first volume of *Aesthetica* (1750) before sending his own book off to be printed. Of music, Krause writes:

> Every tone, and every combination of tones, sounds to our ears either pleasant or unpleasant. We feel a pleasure of the senses—because without hearing we would not have it. But this pleasure does not simply remain in the ears; it communicates itself to the soul, which to be sure is conscious of it but which nonetheless does not analyze intelligibly [*deutlich*] what takes place within it. Tones, melodies, music thus give sensuous ideas [*sinnliche Vorstellungen*] that are very delightful and, for the most part, moving.
>
> [P. 27]

This is of course very similar to what Hutcheson was saying, though cast in a different philosophical language. Krause's dependence on Baumgarten's language (even as Hutcheson was dependent on Locke's) becomes clear two pages later:

> The greatest connoisseurs of music, while listening to pieces that are very moving, often are thinking of nothing else. They are perfectly conscious of the ideas contained therein, but their soul is so overwhelmed that they cannot make them [i.e., the ideas] intelligible [*deutlich*] but only feel them clearly [*klar*].
>
> [P. 29]

Because music transmits only these "sensuous ideas," which are *klar* but not *deutlich*, it is in one sense—though not in all, for this is a question on which Krause wavers back and forth—inferior to poetry and rhetoric, which have words at their disposal.

A little later in Chapter II Krause states the causes of this inferiority somewhat more clearly:

> As useful and natural to us as the delights of music are, however, tones cannot excite in us anywhere near all the ideas that words can awaken. With these latter [i.e., words] we can combine general [*allgemeine*] as well as individual and particular concepts. Thus an orator can provoke not only satisfaction generally but my particular satisfaction with my circumstances. The musician, however, brings forth only general ideas in me. An *Adagio* makes me grieve; an *Allegro,* rejoice—but I do not know why or over what.
>
> [P. 40]

Thus is raised the problem discussed in Chapter One, which was to become so vitally important in musical aesthetics, of music's *Unbestimmtheit* or indeterminacy. Music that has words to help it along, the argument runs, will inevitably be more precise in its emotional or expressive content than mere instrumental music. In time this idea would lead to a new and more complex recognition of music's special artistic nature—one thinks particularly of Schopenhauer and Wagner—but one can still, even today, find expressions of it that are not very different from Krause's. Of a passage from Haydn's *Lord Nelson Mass*, Peter Kivy writes: "The text, with its intentional context, has given the music the specificity of expressiveness that, as pure instrumental music, it lacks." A few pages later Kivy generalizes this perception: "the expressive character of music alone is rough-hewn in comparison with the fineness of distinctions possible in characterizing the expressions of human beings, or the expressive character of linguistic utterance . . . music alone makes rough, but palpable distinctions which texts and titles refine."[8]

But if this *Unbestimmtheit* of music makes it—sometimes, at any rate—inferior to poetry so far as Krause is concerned, it or other qualities associated with it help to make music superior to painting. Of painting he writes:

> The painter imitates what our eyes present to us. This sense is the judge of its imitations. In a certain sense he also strives to make the invisible visible. He gives his painting details that suggest merriment, cunning, pleasure, anger, sadness, simplicity, and the like. But whether the original was an honest man, he cannot express—as the orator, the historian, and the poet can.
>
> [P. 51]

We are reminded of those lines from Horace that Krause cited in his preface: poems can (and therefore ought to) possess more than mere external beauty, and can speak directly to the heart. The reason they can do this is that they can show not only the external surfaces shown by painting, but also the emotions and attitudes that lie behind these surfaces. Krause then cites a poem by Opitz to his friend Strobel, a painter, that praised Strobel precisely for being able to show us all a man's emotions through showing us the look in his eyes. Breitinger, early in his *Critische Dichtkunst*, had also cited this poem, and had gone on to take issue with it: "But for all his celebrated skill, the painter cannot clearly represent more than one or two sides of a thing at one time, or show it in more than one position; his colors cannot capture the invisible except insofar as it makes itself visible in the body through tell-tale signs."[9] Krause then goes on to apply this observation to music.

After paraphrasing Breitinger's remarks, Krause writes:

> If one considers the soul, the movement and swiftness of the feelings, the origin, energy, and disorder of the passions—neither the painter nor the sculptor can imitate any of these. Yet it is possible for the musician and the poet. The musician has his ear

as his instrument of feeling. As he now finds, in his art, tones that are suited to the depiction of a storm, ones that paint the ripple of a brook and the whisper of a zephyr, he delights the listener with these imitations. But aside from these, he also produces, by means of skillful manipulation of our aural nerves, such movements in the soul as are not based merely in the perceived agreement with a bodily archetype, but ones through which our spirit is swept away by violent passions. And this is the true and highest end of music.

[Pp. 52-53]

I have cited this interesting passage at length because it seems important to catch the growing excitement in Krause's tone as he launches into his praise of all the things music can do, reaching even into a sort of primitive physiology.

A few pages later he will repeat, rather dutifully one feels, his praise of poetry as superior because it, alone among the arts, uses words and hence can furnish "not only concepts that are delightful and moving but ones of almost all sorts" (p. 54), and is not confined to "general ideas" (p. 56). But he keeps returning to music's power to speak directly to the soul: "To our heart the musician says only: this is pleasant, this is moving. Since the soul is wax, and capable of taking all impressions, it immediately participates, and allows itself to be moved by the accumulation of such images" (p. 56)—immediately after which he cites a line-and-a-half of the *Ars poetica*:

> Format enim natura prius nos intus ad omnem
> fortunarum habitum &c.
>
> [108-109]
>
> (For nature in advance shapes us within to conform to
> every condition of fortune.)

That is, nature has fashioned the human mind or soul or spirit so that it reacts appropriately to the conventionally accepted ways of expressing various emotions. Horace is discussing dramatic portrayal through language, but Krause has in mind the still more direct relation—the directness nicely captured in the metaphor of the wax—between wordless musical expression and the responsive soul.

This feeling that while both music and painting, as wordless arts, are inferior to poetry in an important sense, and that music is superior to painting because it can show the insides of things and people, and can communicate that knowledge to the inner being of a sensitive listener, is most important. It is expressed enthusiastically by Krause but is not really placed in coherent relation to the rest of his thought. Later, however, as thinkers become preoccupied with the externality of painting's vividness, the stanza-by-stanza, word-by-word fidelity of a through-composed piece of vocal music to its text will come to seem rather vulgar, akin to all those Italian ornaments. Conversely, the idea that any poem worth setting to music will, *ipso facto* as it were, be unified by one "herrschendes Affekt," and that the composer's duty is to discern that guiding emotion and capture it in a strophe of music that will therefore suit all stanzas of the poem, will come to seem far more appropriate to the directness and inwardness of music as an art than will the dogged fidelity of *Durchkomponierung*. But this is certainly not all in Krause; one can see it coming only with hindsight.

In Chapter V Krause divides musical poems into odes and cantatas:

> The musical poems are either odes or cantatas. I take the latter word here in the sense
> of comprehending all poems for singing whose form consists of recitatives and arias.
> It is customary not to make more than one melody for all the stanzas of the poem; but

in the arias the musician repeats the words in which the stress lies, and sets different passages and movements of tones to the same poetic expression.

[P. 112]

The ode, he then goes on to explain, is the far older form. However, the convention that all the stanzas of an ode must make do with one and the same melody caused problems for poets and, in turn, for composers:

> The poets, however, could not confine themselves, in composing an ode, to placing the same caesuras and the same emotion at the same points in all stanzas. Therefore a lively thought that the composer happened to have in the first stanza often encountered, in the stanzas that followed, a melancholy or less spirited expression by the poet, and also the other way round. Moreover, a pause that the composer placed at a caesura in the first stanza often stood in the middle of a word in the other stanzas.

[P. 113]

Krause therefore views what would later be called the *leiderlose Zeit* as a natural, even inevitable, result: "Thus after our poets learned from the Italians how to compose cantatas, odes were almost completely supplanted by these poems for singing [i.e., cantatas]" (p. 113).

Yet he goes on to note that in a neighboring nation—France, no doubt—there is still a good deal of "Liedersingen," by which he must mean specifically the singing of strophic songs. Spitta, we recall, noted that Scholze had perhaps got the idea for the "parody" use of preexisting instrumental numbers as vocal settings from such French collections as the 1695 *Parodies bachiques, sur les Airs et Symphonies des Opera*. These attempts, Krause adds diffidently, could be imitated by Germans, and in fact have recently begun to be: "Some attempts at this have already appeared among us, although to speak generally, the taste in songs/poems [*Liedergeschmack*] in Germany is still not good, and especially with regard to music—since people mostly demand operatic melodies—it is not defined [*bestimmt*] enough" (p. 113). *Liedergeschmack* here must mean taste both in poems suitable for musical setting and in the settings themselves, with the emphasis especially ("sonderlich") on the latter.

Scheibe, as we saw, seemed simply to assume, in No. 64 of *Der critische Musikus*, that since poems must, as works of art, possess some sort of unity, and since the language of poems suitable for musical setting is, like music itself, the language of feeling(s), the unifying agent in such poems must be one *Affekt* or *Gemüthsbewegung* that governs or controls ("herrschet") the entire poem. Krause arrives at this same conclusion by a clearer logical process, indicating that in the decade or more that had elapsed since Scheibe's No. 64, the idea of just how a strophic song could be made a suitable musical expression of a poem with many contrasting stanzas had become more firmly established in the minds of critics and composers:

> Since music mainly has to do with feelings, sentiments, and emotions, all odes that are to be set to music must be moving; and since each stanza will not be set to a separate melody, the only poems [*Lieder*] that are musical are those that depict not more than one emotion.

[P. 114]

There is none of the groping tentativeness that we saw in Scheibe's advance toward something like the same conclusion. Krause's clipped and orderly prose suggests that he feels himself to be stating a generally accepted truth.

Krause is of course well aware of the requirements that this truth imposes upon poets: the sense of each stanza must be complete in itself, without the runovers we find in classical poets such as

Horace; the caesuras should come at the same point in all stanzas; the lines must be short, in order to save the singer's breath; there should not be too many stanzas, in order that the repetition of the melody may not become boring. Correspondingly, composers must make their melodies very easy, so that they may be readily memorized. But Krause is not so certain as Scheibe that composers can, with properly close and sustained attention, usually discover a way to extract and express the principal emotion from a poem of several stanzas. He therefore rather suddenly and surprisingly shrugs off the whole business, and recommends that composers go ahead and write more than one melody if that seems called for:

> The fewer stanzas a poem [*Lied*] has, the more possible is it for the composer to make the outward shape of the melody conform to the outward shape of the poem. But if the emotion changes in an ode, so that one stanza is happy and another sad, the composer should always write different melodies for them since his style should always match the style of the poet, and a single melody cannot adapt itself to either one or the other emotion.
>
> [P. 116]

This rather gives the game away, and Krause's falling back, in the last sentence just cited, on the old Gottschedian chestnut about the style of the composer matching that of the poet seems like a real failure of nerve. Yet a moment later Krause makes it clear that if the composer does indeed write a melody to fit each stanza, then the resulting composition will no longer be, properly speaking, an ode: "But in case the thoughts change in each stanza, and one wants to make different melodies for them all, then it will no longer be an ode but a string of ariettas" (p. 116).

The reader is at a loss how to take this statement. Would that be a good or a bad or a neutral thing—to have composed a series of ariettas rather than, as one had set out to do, an ode? Rather than making a clear value judgment one way or another, Krause takes refuge in terminological hair-splitting. After a little more consideration of this problem, he writes:

> From what has been noted here it can surely be seen that odes are not the most perfect kind of musical poetry. Music, for its part, can neither express the emotion vigorously and strongly, nor depict the content of the words through a felicitous imitation in tones, nor take notice in the melody of the stress of each thought, the accent of each word, the rhetorical pauses.
>
> [P. 118]

So he, like Scheibe, after investigating the problems associated with the strophic song in a way that suggests to us, reading of course with hindsight, that he is going to emerge as its champion, backs away and discovers that cantatas are, after all, superior.

Krause's reason for preferring cantatas, however, is most interesting:

> Music, however, has become a separate art. It therefore deserves that when it is united with poetry one does not produce light, ode-like melodies but ones that show special diligence and particular skill, especially since these beauties and perfections of music contribute so uncommonly much to the delight and emotion of vocal pieces. Now instead of one and the same melody's being composed for several words, expressions, and stanzas in odes, in perfect musical texts special and different melodies are written for identical words and expressions. These texts are cantatas.
>
> [Pp. 118-119]

The striking announcement "Music, however, has become a separate art" takes us by surprise. To modern ears it rings almost like a battle cry. For we are urgently aware of the paradox underlying 18th-century writing about music and its relation to the other arts: that with all the parallels drawn between music and rhetoric, the 18th century was in fact the time when music finally did step forth as a separate and independent art, the century in which instrumental music for the first time detached itself from verbal texts.[10] And we seem to hear—or perhaps only wish to hear—a precursor of that detachment in Krause's words. But no.

We know already that like most of his contemporaries, he considered music inferior to poetry and rhetoric because it could furnish only general ideas. Yet as we also saw, despite this official position, Krause did from time to time betray a keen enthusiasm about music's special power to touch the heart and reveal the essences of things. So perhaps it is not entirely wrong to hear something of the prophet in that grand pronouncement. Be that as it may, however, his point is that music has risen in dignity to the point where it deserves that composers, when they are setting texts, should not produce merely those simple, trifling melodies one commonly finds in strophic songs but rather melodies that demonstrate the distinctive industry and skill characteristic of the best present-day composition. And in the sentence that follows, Krause makes it clear that one thing that makes these melodies better is that they are not required to set a variety of words, as are the melodies of strophic songs.

There is much more that is puzzling about Krause's book. But it does seem clear that here he is saying that cantatas are superior to strophic songs precisely because they are through-composed rather than repetitious, and can therefore demonstrate music's expressive powers more effectively. So it is certainly wrong to treat Krause as purely (or even primarily) a champion of the strophic song. It would, however, be equally mistaken to ignore the part he played in its reinstatement. We must always remember that in dealing with writers like Krause and Scheibe, we are dealing with men for whom the alternatives that are so clear to us were far less clear. As Krause's language strongly suggests, it is the greater variety obtainable in cantatas that draws him to them, while it is the notion of a strophic song capturing, in its one melody, the variety of a poem that draws him to songs. Like Gottsched and Scheibe, he feels pulled in several different directions. And indeed there is nothing wrong in this. Most of us feel, at one time or another, that one particular musical genre is superior to the others—but then quickly change our minds when confronted by a different, and equally vivid, musical experience. The point is merely that the reinstatement of the strophic song was not accomplished quickly or easily, and it was not an intellectually direct and simple matter.

Even for cantatas, with all their alluring variety, Krause's requirement of unity still holds:

> Meanwhile, although the poet and the musician bring the most moving expression into the arias and the accompanied recitatives, which are considered as arias in respect to emotion, the recitatives connect the emotions with one another, and must therefore not be soporific but rather composed in a fiery and lively style. The whole substance of a cantata [*Singgedichts*] is moving, and since, according to general aesthetic rules, the unity of the fable, of the action, the *unum* of Horace is to be observed and everything should finally lead to a certain definite idea and feeling, the heart must remain continuously in the emotional state required for that end.
>
> [Pp. 137–138]

In fact, by specifying "das *unum* des Horaz," and thus alluding to line 23 of the *Ars poetica,* Krause makes it clear that the sort of unity he has in mind is one that coexists with, and is balanced by, a certain degree of variety. A few pages later, Krause uses the phrase again. He is discussing the composition of an aria that dramatizes a series of intense passions: shame, repentance, hope, shock, and so on: "A musical poet who wants to achieve his aim in this way and to take the *unum* of Horace into consideration is therefore most careful to see that the ease and convenience with which this or that emotion may be expressed in music, as well as other circumstances, do not mislead him into writing an aria about an emotion that contributes nothing to the main purpose" (p. 140). Krause then cites a couple of examples of recent librettists who have failed, in one way or another, to preserve the sort of overarching emotional unity he is advocating.

IV

As will already have become clear from our consideration of Serwer's dissertation on him, Friedrich Wilhelm Marpurg was a fascinating, many-sided character. In addition to being a composer, editor, critic, and theorist, he was director of the Prussian state lottery from 1766 until his death in 1795. In the mid-1740s he served as secretary to a diplomat based in Paris, where he became friendly with Voltaire, D'Alembert, and other French men of letters. Though his compositions included several sonatas and other instrumental works, he devoted himself mainly to songs—as we shall see, he was one of the better composers generally included in the first Berlin song school. Perhaps even more important, in the years 1756-1759 he edited seven collections of songs. To all but one of these he contributed at least half the songs himself; to that one he contributed one third.

The first of his three magazines was *Der critische Musikus an der Spree* (1749-1750), the title of which registered both Marpurg's homage to Scheibe and the fact that he himself was at that time dwelling either near Berlin's river or actually on one of its islands. The magazine's 50 weekly issues contain nothing that bears significantly on the reinstatement of the strophic song. A course in music theory is outlined in several issues, there are discussions of the relations among the various national styles of the time, and two French works on the subject of taste are presented in translation: *Essai sur le bon goust en musique* by Nicolas Rogot de Grandval (1676-1753) and *De la corruption du goust dans la musique françoise* by Louis Bollioud-Mermot (1709-1793).

There is somewhat more to catch hold of in Marpurg's second magazine, *Historisch-Kritische Beyträge zur Aufnahme der Musik* (1754–1762, 1778).[11] For in the years between the last issues of *Der critische Musikus an der Spree* and the first ones of this new journal there had appeared not only Krause's *Von der musikalischen Poesie* but also his and Ramler's 1753 *Oden mit Melodien*.

As we saw earlier, the preface to that collection, apparently by Ramler, is a most interesting document. After noting that some of the verses have had to be changed, either by their authors or by himself, in order to be suitable for musical setting, Ramler tells us that some of the poems have been imitated from earlier, non-German poems, but assures us that this is nothing to be concerned about but is in fact perfectly natural and even necessary:

> Our poets have taken some of the devices used in their poems from foreigners. This has been done in all ages by those great people who have introduced polite literature among their countrymen. They have translated, imitated, and improved upon their predecessors until at last they themselves have become creators and their works originals, until they have learnt the art of drawing on a thousand sources and making from them an artistic whole. For man does not live long enough to take everything from Nature for himself; he must artfully join together a thousand pieces that others have prepared if he is not to leave behind him remembrances of his spirit that are all too few and imperfect.

This leads Ramler to his contrast between the ways in which songs and song-singing are cultivated in France and Germany—to the disadvantage of the Germans. The French, he tells us, are born "Liederfreunde": "They have paid more, and more frequent, attention to the melodies of their songs, and indeed have made many that are so easy and natural that the whole land has become filled with song and harmony." He then paints this charmingly idealized picture:

> It is a very beautiful sight for an unbiased citizen of the world and general friend of man, to see, among these people, a countryman, with his grapes or his onion in his hand, singing and happy; or to see how the middle-class city people drive away troubles from their supper-table with a song, and how the inhabitants of the *haut monde,* the refined ladies and the talented gentlemen, refresh their parties and their promenades with songs and mingle their wine with wit and singing.

In Germany it is quite different: "We Germans now study music constantly; yet in many great cities one hears nothing but opera arias."

It is important, however, to notice that the idealization involved in Ramler's image of the song-singing French is not that of the adherents of the folksong movement of a few decades later. Just as the doctrine of imitation of earlier works is upheld, in order to produce poems that are "artful," so Ramler is not suggesting that the French all dress up like peasants and sing peasant songs. We are still some years distant from Marie Antoinette's pastoral entertainments. Ramler's vision is of a society in which all classes joyously sing the songs that happen to be congenial to them, and in which the lives of countrymen, members of the bourgeoisie, and the finest ladies and the most talented gentlemen are all made happier through song. There is no talk here of "leveling down." The mere act of singing, as "easy and natural" as the songs themselves, will beautify life; there is no need for any pretended or actual breaking down of class barriers.

Thus in his recommendations for the Germans, Ramler does not specify that the desiderated songs be drawn directly from the folk; he merely asks that they be joyous, easy to understand, and well enough written so that they can stand on their own, without accompaniment:

> If our composers compose their songs singing, without using the clavier and without thinking that a bass part is still to be added, then the taste for singing in our nation will soon become more common, and will bring with it pleasure and sociable merriment everywhere.... But people will not sing serious songs, for the reason they get together is to break off being serious. Yet these songs must not be so licentiously amorous that the ladies are ashamed to sing them and the men will be derided. They should not mislead anyone, or provide an opportunity for foolish jokes. They are to be polite, elegant, naive. Not so poetic that the lovely songstress cannot understand them, but not so light and flowing that no clever person will bother with them.

Though Ramler does not say so in so many words, it seems clear that the only songs that would fit his description would be strophic songs. Of the 31 songs contained in the 1753 Ramler-Krause *Oden mit Melodien*, all but two of those that set poems of more than one stanza are in fact strophic songs; the two exceptions are songs by C. P. E. Bach.

In the preface to *Historisch-Kritische Beyträge*, which is dated April 1, 1754, Marpurg, in the course of summing up the current musical situation in Germany, notes: "Yet we still lack a manual of the art of singing; for those pamphlets that explain nothing more than solmization or the details of notation cannot be dignified by that title" (I, ii). Such books, he adds, are scarcely adequate to the job of producing tolerable choristers—let alone accomplished solo singers. Those who are in charge of vocal music in the large cities, where more good voices are available, should use these singers to spread their teaching methods to places less richly endowed with vocal talent. Like Ramler, Marpurg praises the singing of Germany's southern neighbors and looks to them for aid: "It would unquestionably make a skilled German singing teacher deserving of the world's praise if he shared his method, prepared in accordance with the best Italians of the time, and put his countrymen in the position gradually to free themselves from the reproach of bellowing, levelled against them by arrogant foreigners" (I, ii-iii).

That Marpurg was at this time in direct touch with both Ramler and Krause is also suggested by the fact that the very first piece to appear in the first volume of *Historisch-Kritische Beyträge* was a German translation, with copious notes, of a letter on the differences between Italian and French music, addressed to an anonymous "M. le marquis de B.***," that Krause had written in French and published in 1748 (I, 1-46). More important, a little further on in the first volume of the periodical Marpurg listed the contents of the 1753 Ramler-Krause *Oden mit Melodien*, giving the names of the poets and composers, which had not appeared in the original volume (I, 55-57). Marpurg introduced his listing thus:

> The present collection of new songs has already been so celebrated in so many public papers, and received by so many connoisseurs with such approbation, that it needs no more praise. We wish to do no more here than to provide those who do not yet own it with a catalogue of the pieces it contains, and those who already know it with the names of the poets and composers; we do this with the presumed consent of the editors.
>
> [I, 55]

And Marpurg appends to his list the good news that another Ramler-Krause collection will soon appear: "I hear that the editors are making arrangements to publish a second part, to meet the demands of the public" (I, 57).

The first *Stück* of the first volume of *Historisch-Kritische Beyträge* closes with a little song of C.P.E. Bach's (I, 88-89). Marpurg's interest in the growing popularity of strophic songs is attested by the fact that almost all of the *Stücke* that make up the first two volumes of *Historisch-Kritische Beyträge* end with a song—though after Volume II the practice is abandoned. Volume III also contains a prose work of Bach's, "Einfall, einen doppelten Contrapunct in der Octave von 6 Tacten zu machen, ohne die Regeln davon zu wissen" (III, 167-181). When Marpurg begins, in Volume IV, actually to review collections of songs, he discusses the settings of Gellert's *Geistliche Oden und Lieder* by Johann Friedrich Doles and the volume, which Marpurg edited and to which he contributed half the songs, entitled *Geistliche Oden, in Melodien gesetzt von einigen Tonkünstlern in Berlin*, both of which were published in 1758 (IV, 188 and 563-564). Since Bach's *Sechs Sonaten fürs Clavier mit veränderten Reprisen* is also reviewed (IV, 560-561), it is surprising that Marpurg did not also mention Bach's own volume of Gellert settings, which, as we shall see later, was immensely popular.

Krause and Ramler also continue to figure in the later volumes of *Historisch-Kritische Beyträge*. Krause contributes a selection of "Vermischte Gedanken" (III, 523-543), in which he gives voice to a good many of the key ideas of *Von der musikalischen Poesie*. Once again he praises his favorite composers of opera: "Have not Graun and Hasse enriched the music of the Italians with priceless beauties" (III, 527)? Once again present-day composers are upbraided for believing "that only verses that are light, flowing, and not burdened with thoughts are suitable for music" (III, 528), and Horace is invoked as an authority. After paraphrasing parts of Seneca's *Hercules Furens*, Krause goes so far as to suggest, a few pages later, that it would make a suitable song text for those who complain "that they cannot find many serious German songs for serious Germans" (III, 533). There is more on the differences among national musical styles and further insistence that music is, and has been since the time of the ancients, a language of emotion: "It is said of the ancient musicians that they created emotions, and not just empty melodies; hence the admiration of Arion, Amphion, Orpheus, Apollo, Mercury" (III, 542). As for Ramler, he contributes to the journal's final volume an elaborated paraphrase, with special application to music, of the opening chapters of Batteux's *Les Beaux-Arts réduits à un même principe* (V, 20-44). At the end a continuation is promised for a future issue, but there was none.

Songs were treated most extensively in Marpurg's *Kritische Briefe über die Tonkunst* (1759-1763).[12] It began as a weekly but Marpurg, as usual, fell behind, and so only 142 issues (or *Briefe*) appeared between June 23, 1759, and September 17, 1763. In this journal Marpurg adopted a somewhat lighter tone. The issues were shorter, any topic that demanded extended treatment being strung out over several *Fortsetzungen*. As a model, Marpurg, like many others before him, took *The Spectator* of Addison and Steele. The opening letter of *Kritische Briefe über die Tonkunst*, like the opening two numbers of *The Spectator*, introduces us to the members of the imaginary "club" whose doings are to make up the substance of the journal. In this third and last of Marpurg's journals, the emphasis is more strongly on criticism than in the others. In *Historisch-Kritische Beyträge* the few reviews of song collections were little more than mere notices of publication, while in *Kritische Briefe über die Tonkunst* comparisons are drawn and judgments are made. *Historisch-Kritische Beyträge* really stopped in 1762; the final *Stück* of its final volume was added in 1778 merely to fill out the book. There were no more journals after 1763 because it was at just about this time that Marpurg went to work for the lottery, which at that point was under the directorship of Raniero de Calzabigi, who also served on several occasions as Gluck's librettist.

Letter No. 3 is addressed to Krause by Marpurg, who signs himself as "Amisallos." The name is taken from a very rare Greek word for unsociable, and its bearer is the oldest member of the "club," a learned, well-traveled, and highly critical man.

Marpurg begins by asking Krause a provocative question about the ways in which songs are treated in the contemporary music literature: "Do you not find that some people make too much fuss about the nature of a music poem while others make too little" (I, 17)? He then illustrates what he means by citing two prefaces to recent song collections. The author of one preface, also the composer of the songs that it introduced, stresses the enormous difficulties of song composition as an art:

> It is not so easy as many believe to set to music the sort of poems that will satisfy both connoisseurs and amateurs. It demands precise artistic correctness; an especially flowing melody; a superabundance of beautiful ideas; a rigorous assembling and clever choice of ideas, to express the emotion of the poem in the most natural and lively way. Passages that are unexpected yet unforced, refined, and tender must be conspicuous in works of this kind if one does not want to fall into pedestrian dullness.
>
> [I, 17]

I have quoted at length because it is important to catch the wit of the passage. The speaker that Marpurg creates here, his clauses growing ever longer and more eloquent as he is swept away by pride while explaining the extreme difficulty of his craft, reminds one of Dr. Johnson's Imlac, in Chapter X of *Rasselas*, seized by an "enthusiastic fit" as he explains the difficulties of being a poet.

Having brought this splendid creature into being, Marpurg urbanely dismisses him with a wave of his hand: "what he has told us of the difficulties of songs is far too general, and anyway applies to the composition of any sort of vocal piece" (I, 18). Marpurg then notes, somewhat more soberly, that the author of the preface also comments on the special problems of writing strophic songs: "He makes a postscript, in which he reports that if a song does not have many strophes, one will be able to get the expression of the words into the melody with greater precision and vigor; but since one must only consider the principal emotion and certain especially beautiful places, it is no wonder that the melody does not create the same effect for all the verses" (I, 18).

The other preface-writer, by contrast, insists that he has gone to no particular bother in composing his songs. He is all for spontaneity, and "believes that the less he has sweated over his songs, the fewer people who hear, or sing and play, them will yawn" (I, 18). No friend of rules and regulations, he has, he confesses, broken a musical law here and there: "He has thought freely; he has tried to express the character and the passions according to his ability, and has generally followed the newest taste more than any other" (I, 18). That is, he has sought to be pleasing without being shallow or tasteless, to be sublime without losing naturalness and flow, or becoming (the hated word) *schwülstig*.

Both these writers are mistaken, Marpurg tells Krause. It is true that there are worthless songs—but that does not condemn the genre. "I know music-lovers," he tells Krause, "who would rather hear a song by Capellmeister Graun than an entire opera by Galuppi" (I, 19). Anyhow, short works are, in general, in no way inferior to long ones:

> Whoever does not know how to reveal himself as a master of his art within very narrow bounds will do so still less when the racecourse is extended. . . . A song, at least a well-made one, must run its course in a very confined space, from beginning to end and with no head start, yet with appropriate liveliness. As the Spectator says, the composer must emulate the chemist, who knows how to concentrate the strength of a whole drink in a few drops.
>
> [I, 19-20]

The passage from *The Spectator* Marpurg has in mind comes in a paper of Addison's, No. 124. The motto of the paper is the famous phrase of Callimachus, Μέγα βιβλίον, μέγα κακόν—that is, a big book is a big evil—but Addison is discussing the special problems that beset a writer of periodical essays, like himself. "The ordinary Writers of Morality prescribe to their Readers after the Galenick Way," he writes; "their Medicines are made up in large Quantities. An Essay Writer must practise in the Chymical Method, and give the Virtue of a full Draught in a few Drops."[13]

You and I, Marpurg tells Krause, have often discussed the nature and constitution of a good song, agreeing on some points and differing on others. Permit me to share my thoughts with you now; reply to me whenever it is convenient. Warming to his subject, he enlarges upon this genial invitation to Krause:

> Perhaps our opinions will agree, and do you not believe that friends of harmless fun will be grateful for our efforts, even if we do not instantly gain the applause of certain morose persons? And some of those same people, who are kindly disposed only to very portentous affairs—scores with 24 staves, fugues with three or four subjects (in both ordinary and retrograde motion), and other, similar artistic elaborations against which, in their place, I have no objection whatever—may perhaps learn taste.
>
> [I, 20]

Again the wit is worth noting: the pedantry of those who admire only scores with 24 staves and fugues with three or four subjects is parodied in the sentence's labored and elaborate syntax, and then, just as Marpurg has generously pardoned them, the word "taste" drops ironically into place. "To each his own pleasure," he concludes.

The nature of songs, and what differentiates good ones from bad ones, will, it is clear, be a major preoccupation of this new periodical. For evidence in deciding these questions Marpurg will examine the song collections that have been published during recent years, ever since the strophic song reestablished itself as an acceptable genre: "I have thus decided to mix together the remarks for the poet and the composer, and to set them down as they occur to me. I can do nothing more useful than to use as a guide the various song collections with which we have been presented over the past 18 or 20 years" (I, 20).

Regarding the current controversy over the meanings of the terms *Ode* and *Lied*, Marpurg declares that he will use them interchangeably to signify what the French call a *chanson*—be it secular, spiritual or moral in nature. He then makes it clear that his interest will be only in strophic songs:

> Therefore neither the irregular songs, in which the strophes are not all similar to one another in rhythm and meter, nor the regular ones in which each strophe has been

given its special melody and setting, are relevant here. . . . In the songs we shall be dealing with here, all the different strophes will be sung to one and the same melody.

[I, 21]

The point could scarcely be made more clearly. In order to aid music historians, then, Marpurg will systematically review, in chronological order so far as possible, all the collections of strophic songs published since the first of Gräfe's four collections appeared, in 1737. As though warning Krause (and the reader) of the difficulty and seriousness of this task, Marpurg observes: "It is no small thing to bring a whole heap of collections into some sort of order" (I, 22).

Krause begins his reply, in Letter No. 22, by remarking that "Der Herr Amisallos" seems to ridicule the first preface-writer's notion that songwriting is not an easy business, and by suggesting that Marpurg ought to be even more critical of those songwriters who are convinced that they have surmounted all difficulties if they have merely followed all the rules strictly—though they have not given a thought to melody and expression. He then cites Batteux to the effect that works in even the humblest genres must be composed with inspiration: "Therefore it is not to be doubted that inspiration is required even in the smallest musical pieces" (I, 168).

Though he does not know the identity of Marpurg's first preface-writer, Krause says he agrees with him that there are special difficulties connected with the composition of songs. First, they must be composed with more correctness ("Kunstrichtigkeit") than other sorts of pieces:

> Songs are made for everyone in the musical community. But how can they please everyone without correctness? Many other pieces survive without this quality, and because of an ornamental texture or forceful orchestration or beautiful voices and instruments they manage to render those lapses of correctness unnoticeable. But I would take it almost as a basic principle that no one can easily learn by heart an incorrectly written song.

[I, 168]

For the same reason a flowing melody is absolutely necessary to a song, but not to other sorts of vocal pieces: "There are many cases in which the melodic flow may be ignored in order to give the piece other excellences. An artistic singer can exhibit these excellences; but [strophic] songs are for everyone to sing, and therefore they must have a flowing melody" (I, 168). One might think that the fact that ordinary strophic songs are composed for everyone, talented and untalented alike, and that they must therefore be simple, would make their composition easy. But no: the simplicity turns out to be a kind of nakedness, resulting from the absence of the airs and graces of more sophisticated vocal pieces; and the ordinary singer's lack of talent makes him or her unable to provide the delightful distractions that would conceal the absence of that necessary basis of all song, a flowing, natural tune.

The composer's task in setting an *Ode* to music, Krause agrees, is to express the principal emotion of the poem "very naturally and vigorously." But this too is more difficult than in other sorts of vocal piece because of the formal requirements of the strophic song:

> The composer has only a few notes, with which to portray it [i.e., the emotion]. He cannot count on an ornamented texture, which especially with tender feelings can often take the place of the emotion. No instrumental accompaniment is there to help him make it vivid. What inner life must there be in the emotion itself, where there is no recourse to these and all other aids with which the composer of an opera aria can put on a great show—with the help of a gifted singer and a well-equipped orchestra!

[I, 169]

Moreover, all beautiful works of music, Krause asserts, possess what he too, echoing Marpurg, terms "unexpected yet unforced passages" (I, 169)—one is reminded of Tovey's famous remark that "nothing in Haydn is difficult to follow, but almost everything is unexpected."[14] The problem is that it is difficult to discover such passages "within the narrow bounds of a song to be sung by everyone" (I, 169).

The conclusion of Krause's reply takes as its point of departure the postscript written by the first of the two preface-writers:

> What is the point of saying that "if a song does not have many strophes, one will be able to get the expression of the words into the melody with greater precision and vigor; but since one must only consider the principal emotion and certain especially beautiful places, it is no wonder that the melody does not create the same effect for all the verses"? In songs with many strophes, the expression of each and every word, or at least of most of them, does not matter. If the principal emotion of the song is caught, and so expressed that the singer can easily combine the words with the tones, that is enough. For who demands that the melody, with a view to the musical portrayal in the words of the poem, should have the same effect for all verses? In a song of one strophe, besides the emotion, all the turns in the poet's thought, the caesuras of the text, the topics of each clause, and of every word in them, are strictly observed. With a song of many strophes, however, all this is almost completely ignored.
>
> [I, 169-170]

I have cited this passage at length because Krause's view of strophic songs turns out to be surprisingly complex, and interestingly different from Marpurg's.

At first, we recall, Krause chided Marpurg for mocking the first preface-writer's lengthy recital of the difficulties of song-composition. He then pointed out several of these difficulties: though they are very short, songs too demand inspiration of the composer; the fact that they are directed at a general audience that includes inexperienced amateurs means that songs must be more "correctly" written than other sorts of vocal music, and thus makes them harder, rather than easier, to compose. Krause agrees that the song-composer's most important task is to express the poem's principal emotion—but he notes that this is especially difficult to do in so short a composition. But then, in his long concluding statement Krause more or less dismisses the most commonly lamented difficulties of the strophic song, those mentioned by the first preface-writer in his postscript. These are, of course, the difficulties associated with what I have called the strophic problem. Once the poem's principal emotion has been successfully embodied in the song, Krause feels, the rest will take care of itself. No need to worry about every slight change in content from stanza to stanza, line to line, word to word, or the shifting of caesuras. If the emotional thrust of the music is generally right for the poem—and, it goes without saying, if the song is well sung—the listeners will be involved to the point where the niggling little worries of the theorists will not bother them. This seems to me an admirably clear and realistic point of view.

Krause's reply to Marpurg, appropriately enough, is sandwiched between the first two installments of Marpurg's promised systematic examination of published song collections. There are various other sequences of letters in *Kritische Briefe über die Tonkunst* that deal with songs and text setting: a group, addressed to Lessing, that duplicate much of the material contained in Marpurg's 1758 *Anleitung zur Singcomposition*; some *Anmerkungen* quarreling with the preface to a 1761 volume of *Oden mit Melodien*, in which a theory of song composition was outlined; and some papers on recitatives. But these are mostly occupied with rather niggling technical matters. Marpurg's examination of the actual song collections, in which his theoretical views emerge in particular critical judgments, often buttressed by musical examples, is more to the point here.

Letter No. 21, which contains the first of Marpurg's reviews of song collections, begins with a spirited defense of song-composers that echoes some of the points made in the letter to Krause. "Every good song-composer is a miniaturist [*Künstler im Kleinen*]," he writes, immediately making it clear that this is no insult:

> The greatness of an artist does not depend on the excellence of an art, considered in itself, but rather on the quality of work that he demonstrates in that art. Is Herr Simon of Swabia a great artist because he has published a dozen fugues? No more than Telemann or Bach is a lesser one because they have composed melodies to songs.
>
> [I, 159]

The Herr Simon referred to is presumably Johann Caspar Simon (1701-1776), who published collections of fugues, fughettas, and chorales set in fugal form. Educated at Jena, in 1731 he became organist and director of music at St. George's Church in Nördlingen. But in 1750, when his brother-in-law died, Simon inherited a drapery business in Leipzig, gave up his Nördlingen post, and spent the rest of his life as a merchant. Marpurg's tone suggests that by 1759 poor learned Simon may have become something of a joke in the music business.

Marpurg's first group of reviews begins with Gräfe's four-volume *Sammlung verschiedener und auserlesener Oden*, published in 1737-1743: "Although Gräfe's collection is 20 years old," writes Marpurg: "it has long been treasured for the many good songs it contains, along with a few bad ones" (I, 160-161). In the five-volume *Neue Sammlung verschiedener und auserlesener Oden*, published at Leipzig in 1746-1749, however, Marpurg finds "very few good pieces," and he adds: "many melodies appear not to have been composed for the texts beneath them, but the texts appear to have been forced under the melodies" (I, 161). In *Das deutsche Lied im 18. Jahrhundert*, Friedlaender tells us that Spitta, in his groundbreaking article on Sperontes, had conjectured that these collections too had been prepared by Scholze—which makes sense if the songs look like "parodies." But Friedlaender discovered a contemporary review by Johann Adam Hiller, evidently unknown to Spitta, that identifies the editors as two men named Fritsch and Gerstenberg.[15] Of the Sperontes volumes themselves Marpurg has little to say, closing with the scornful words: "We will not stop any longer over this foul collection" (I, 162). Mizler's three volumes (1740, 1741, 1743) also draw Marpurg's scorn:

> Non omnia possumus omnes. Herr Mizler forgives practical musicians for seldom understanding the theory of music; and they forgive him, that he has not been more fortunate in his practice.
>
> [I, 162]

Finally, there is Telemann's 1741 *Vier und zwanzig, theils ernsthafte, theils scherzende, Oden*, which earns the highest marks from Marpurg: "Among all the possible song collections, this is the only one that contains true songs [*Oden*]. In all other collections, the character of this sort of composition is too much disregarded, either consistently or sporadically, and when the composers fail to achieve it, they have brought into the world either little keyboard pieces or opera ariettas" (I, 163).

It seems clear that Marpurg thought of this first piece as a sort of introduction to his own standards for songs. With so many collections to catch up on, he could have picked many other ones than these. But these five offered him a good spectrum of material on which to demonstrate his own likes and dislikes. Plainly, the "parody" technique of Sperontes and the five Leipzig volumes will not do: text and music must be intended for each other and be matched as perfectly as possible, given the admitted inconveniences of the strophic song as a genre. Nor will Mizler's pedantically theoretical approach fill the bill: real "inspiration," of the sort he could never provide, is necessary as well as "correctness." The Gräfe collections come first because they marked a real breakthrough over the

Sperontes volumes, even though they were admittedly uneven. Finally, there is Telemann's collection, which Marpurg, like Scheibe, considers the best of the early song volumes.

From here on the reviews are much more loosely ordered—if indeed one cares to think of them as ordered at all. It is clear from the later criticism written about the song collections of C.P.E. Bach and others that in this series of papers Marpurg either established or at least ratified what came to be considered the canon of the first Berlin song school. It will therefore be useful first to see which collections he particularly praised—though he less often gives reasons for his praise than for his condemnation.

Of the three volumes of settings of Hagedorn poems by Görner (1702-1762), entitled *Sammlung neuer Oden und Lieder* (1742, 1744, 1752), Marpurg writes:

> This song collection would be perfect if so many errors in harmony had not escaped the composer's notice, and if he, in his otherwise flowing and pretty melodies, had done more to accommodate the capability of most voices. This latter comment, however, applies to only a small number of songs.
>
> [I, 170-171]

He also praises the two Ramler-Krause collections of *Oden mit Melodien* that appeared in 1753 and 1755. (Marpurg gives the date of the latter volume as 1754, however, which is odd, since its preface is dated April 22, 1755.) Of the songs they contain he writes: "They occupy the middle ground between the overelaborate, fancy style and the flat dull style of various other collections; they are appropriate to the content of the well chosen poems, which cause neither a blush nor a yawn, and are as good for singing alone as with keyboard accompaniment" (I, 243). Of the volume of C.P.E. Bach settings of Gellert's *Geistliche Oden und Lieder* (1758), Marpurg makes only the rather tantalizing remark: "Since the subjects of Gellert's muse are somewhat more elevated than wine and love, the renowned composer had no choice but to turn aside from the usual style of song composition, and who could expect, from the divine art of a Bach, anything but what is extraordinary and always excellent" (I, 250)? This was, as we shall see, the collection in which Bach first found his distinctive voice as a composer of songs, and one has the feeling, from Marpurg's rather vague language, that he was a little flummoxed by it.

Marpurg is more specific, and therefore more illuminating, in his praise of the volume of Gellert settings by Johann Joachim Quantz (1797-1773), Bach's associate at Frederick's court, that appeared in 1760. Quantz entitled his collection *Neue Kirchen-Melodien zu denen geistlichen Liedern des Herrn Professor Gellerts*, and he made it clear in his preface, from which Marpurg quotes extensively and with approval, that he has set Gellert's poems to be sung "by whole congregations at sacred service," and that this has to a great extent determined their mode of composition:

> For this reason I have deliberately abstained from all ornaments and graces, which anyway are heard only in polyphonic music and never in choral song, except for an occasional indispensable appoggiatura.
>
> [Quoted I, 497-498]

Marpurg's judgment on the collection is very much in line with his point about an artist's greatness often revealing itself in small details and in the lesser genres: "The hand of a master betrays itself even in the smallest pieces, and this collection of 22 religious songs, which contains the most moving melodies, with figured bass set beneath them, is proof of this" (I, 498).

Clearly, Marpurg was attracted (and moved) by the willed simplicity of Quantz's approach and by its obvious appropriateness to the content of Gellert's poems. (Which helps to account for his apparent puzzlement at the very different way in which Bach approached Gellert.) It is not surprising, therefore, that he had reservations about the settings of Gellert by Johann Friedrich Doles (1715-1797), published in 1758, for Doles's settings, though in chorale form, were elaborately (yet unevenly) ornamented. After a little cautious praise, Marpurg wrote:

> The composer's intention was to write easy and artless chorale melodies, and in this intention he has not failed. We only wish either that the descant melody had not been embellished with so many gay ornaments of every sort, or that all the parts had been ornamented in proportion. For otherwise the three lower voices make an astonishing contrast with the upper voice.
>
> [I, 251]

It is clear, then, that Marpurg is rather suspicious of ornamentation. When he reviewed Doles's earlier *Neue Lieder nebst ihren Melodien*, published in 1750, he again had only qualified praise:

> A collection of 25 pieces, dominated by refined taste and song that does not need to borrow its charm from the accompanying clavier; yet all the pieces possess all the possible qualities of good small keyboard pieces.... What one can object to about the song collection of which we are speaking is that not all the pieces are for everyone, partly because of the exaggerated ornaments and partly because of the wide range, which here and there stretches to a twelfth or more.
>
> [I, 252-253]

What Marpurg plainly is looking for in all these collections is some version of the style that he praised in the Ramler-Krause collections, a middle style that is neither so simple as to be flat and dull nor so tarted up with ornaments as to be inappropriate to strophic songs that are, after all, directed at "everyone."

Occasionally he will censure a collection for erring on the side of plainness. For example, in his review of the second (1760) printing of *Lieder mit Melodien fürs Clavier*, originally published anonymously at Leipzig in 1759 but the work of Johann Adam Hiller (1728-1804), Marpurg writes:

> It seems to us as though the easy, natural song has gone a bit sour on this composer. He seems to want to compensate for this mishap through certain harmonic changes. But too often he fails to be correct. Because the melodies are not made to be sung alone, and are therefore not provided merely with a figured bass, why has he not here and there, for example where the bass and the descant form an open fifth, improved the resulting emptiness in the harmony by adding a third?
>
> [I, 356]

Most of Marpurg's complaints, however, and virtually all of his musical examples are in response to the opposite fault, overelaborate ornamentation or some other sort of fussiness. Though he is certainly no advocate of the kind of *volkstümlich* simplicity that would be so popular a couple of decades later, Marpurg is far more suspicious of a desire to be modish, of those who breathlessly follow what he referred to in his letter to Krause as "the newest taste." Thus he comes down hard on Friedrich Gottlob Fleischer (1722-1806), composer of *Oden und Lieder mit Melodien* (1756, 1757):

> Since he is proficient in all styles, and is as well acquainted with the simple, artless musical language that is well adapted to every throat as with elaborate, ornamented, and difficult song, why has he not written his songs in that simple manner? ... Herr

Fleischer can atone for his sin in no other way than by laying before the world a dozen arias in the simple style of Telemann's songs, with syllabic underlaying of the text.

[I, 246]

And by the *Musikalische Gemüthsbelustigungen* (1761) of Georg Gottfried Petri (1715-1795), he is forced to these dire generalizations:

Harmony and phrasing [*Bindung*] are things unknown to most of (the Muses will forgive me this expression!) the composers of our time. With melody increasingly bungled from day to day, and all rhythmic and harmonic organization disintegrating, what wondrous things we have to expect from the future! . . . Is this disease of fashion not capable of bringing scholars and other artists to the delusion that in music everything is confused and uncertain [*unbestimmt*]?

[II, 51-52]

Yet of *Lieder zum unschuldigen Vergnügen* (1757) by Johann Heinrich Hesse (c. 1712-1778), he can write: "This collection contains 18 pieces that would all be of the same high quality if in some certain old-fashioned [*altväterische*] mannerisms, . . . and in others certain harmonic errors, had been avoided" (I, 245). Toward mistakes that are old-fashioned rather than modish, Marpurg's tone is almost affectionately indulgent.

It is perhaps difficult for us to realize how necessary and useful a service these reviews of Marpurg performed. Unlike Marpurg and his contemporaries, we have behind us the great flowering of the German song in the 19th century. It would never occur to us that anyone would seriously put together the words and the music that we find in example after example adduced by Marpurg. One gets a sense of composers groping in the dark, wondering how to meet the special challenges offered—or, perhaps better, forced upon them—by the requirements of the strophic song. To bring *Ton* and *Wort* together to form an intelligible and plausible unity has never been easy. Its difficulties were vastly increased by the requirement that the composer somehow intuit, and then capture in musical sound, the *Hauptaffect* or *Hauptempfindung* of a poem in one brief strophe in such a way as at least not to do outright violence to the meaning of any of the poem's various stanzas. By establishing the canon of song collections in which this challenge was successfully met, and by pointing out, along the way, the various pitfalls that lay in wait for the unwary or inexperienced composer, Marpurg, perhaps more than any other single figure, showed the way to the reinstatement of the strophic song.

The Songs

Chapter Eight

Bach's Earliest Songs

The most familiar post-Baroque 18th-century music is of course the music of the Viennese Classical composers. Therefore we shall begin our attempt to isolate what was special and characteristic about Bach's early songs by comparing three of them with settings of the same poems by Haydn and one other Viennese composer of the Classical period. We shall then compare two more Bach songs with settings of the same poems by north German contemporaries. Finally, we shall examine one of Bach's very few through-composed songs in the light of a revision of it proposed by another north German contemporary.

I

Bach's first surviving song is entitled "Schäferlied." Probably composed in 1741, it appeared first in that year's volume (the third) of J. F. Gräfe's *Sammlung verschiedener und auserlesener Oden*, and subsequently in Bach's own 1762 *Oden mit Melodien*. The text is by Christina Mariana von Ziegler (1695-1760), a well-known poetess who in 1725 had supplied texts for nine of J. S. Bach's cantatas. The poem embodies the message that an unnamed shepherdess is asking her fellow-shepherds to carry to her beloved, Thyrsis:

>Eilt, ihr Schäfer, aus den Gründen,
>Eilt zu meinem Thyrsis hin,
>Und, so bald ihr ihn könnt finden,
>Sagt, dass ich ihm günstig bin;
>Sagt, was er mir mitgenommen,
>Nennt die Freyheit und mein Herz;
>Sagt, er soll auch wieder kommen;
>Denn man treibt damit nicht Scherz.
>
>   Ach! wie stellt sein holdes Wesen
>Sich mir in Gedanken vor;
>Thyrsis bleibet auserlesen,
>Unter unserm Schäferchor.
>Ich vergesse Flur und Heerde
>Ja, ich kenn mich selbsten nicht,

Weil ich ganz bezaubert werde,
Wenn man nur von Thyrsis spricht.

Denk ich noch, geliebte Seele!
An der Stunden schnelle Flucht,
Wenn ich sie zurücke zähle,
Die mein Geist vergeblich sucht?
Denk ich auch der zarten Liebe,
Die mein Thyrsis blicken liess,
Und der fromm- und reinen Triebe,
Da er mir mein Herz entriss!

Sitz ich unter Tann und Buchen,
Fällt mir auch mein Thyrsis ein;
Diesen will ich nur da suchen,
Ach! frag ich, wo mag er seyn?
Da lauf ich durch Flur und Auen,
Ob mein Schäfer sich versteckt?
Doch ich kann der Spur nicht trauen,
Weil mich alles Wild erschreckt.

Nichts kann mir mehr Freude stiften,
Als wenn ich oft ganz allein,
Auf den buntbeblümten Triften,
Darf mit meiner Heerde seyn.
Fliegt die Taube mit dem Haufen,
So bleibt sie doch stets gepaart:
Keine wird vom Gatten laufen;
Das ist treuer Seelen Art!

Mir ist weiter nichts geblieben,
Als dies, dass ich sagen muss,
Ewig will ich Thyrsis lieben;
Ewig ist mein fester Schluss.
Schöner Wechsel! süsses Leiden!
Thyrsis! ach du hörest nicht!
Ich will auf den Auen weyden,
Wo ich seh dein Angesicht.

Leg ich mich des Abends nieder,
Spiel ich auf dem Haberrohr;
Bleibt der Inhalt meiner Lieder
Thyrsis Name, wie zuvor.
Ach! du wohnst in meiner Hütte,
Wenn du gleich entfernet bist,
Denn ich spür auf jedem Schritte,
Dass mein Thyrsis bey mir ist.

Soll ich mich mit deinem Schatten,
Weil mein Schicksal widerspricht,

Unterdess im Traume gatten?
Wohl? ich weigre mich auch nicht.
Endlich schlägt die frohe Stunde,
Endlich kömmt der frohe Tag,
Da ich dich aus Herzensgrunde
Wiedersehen und küssen mag.

This is, of course, a pastoral. Like all pastorals, it depends for its effect upon the attribution of delicate, complex sentiments (and alterations of sentiment) that could, in reality, be felt and delineated only by people who were highly civilized, to people who live a life of rural simplicity–to, in short, shepherds and shepherdesses. The elaborate pretense behind this ancient and appealing poetic mode is–as Wordsworth, who did not think it a pretense, wrote in 1800–that in the condition of "humble and rustic life . . . the essential passions of the heart find a better soil in which they can attain their maturity, are less under restraint, and speak a plainer and more emphatic language."[1] But if pastoral is to attain its desired effect, if it is not to turn into mock-pastoral or burlesque of the *Shepherd's Week* or *Beggar's Opera* sort, the poet (through the speaker of his poem) must not reveal his consciousness that the pretense is indeed a pretense.

In the opening lines of Ziegler's poem, the shepherdess's urgency–felt first of all in the repetitions of "Eilt . . . Eilt" and "Sagt . . . Sagt . . . Sagt" but also in the openness and naked vulnerability of "die Freyheit und mein Herz"–is nicely balanced by the reserved, almost courtly quality of "günstig" and by the grave indirection of "man treibt damit nicht Scherz." As she (no doubt literally) warms to her task, we feel the urgency being stepped up as we move from stanza to stanza. First there is the self-forgetfulness of stanza 2, then the suspicious bitterness of "blicken liess" and the sudden violence of the final "entriss" in stanza 3, the conflict in stanza 4 between the overpowering desire to run distractedly "durch Flur und Auen" in search of Thyrsis and the equally overpowering terror of "alles Wild," the self-created illusion in stanza 6 that "mein Thyrsis bey mir ist," and finally, in stanzas 7 and 8, the simile of the "stets gepaart" dove elaborated into the shepherdess's fantasy of remaining forever joined to Thyrsis's shadow "im Traume"–since fate forbids any more fleshly conjunction.

Though it is surely too long, and drags somewhat toward the middle, the poem is, in its way, quite effective. How does Bach handle it? Strophically, in an AABB form, with each of the two repeated segments lasting 8 bars. The time-signature is 3/4 and the tempo direction, both in the Gräfe volume and in Bach's *Oden*, is "Pastorella," to which Max Friedlaender, reprinting the song in *Das deutsche Lied im 18. Jahrhundert*, adds the words "Nicht schnell":

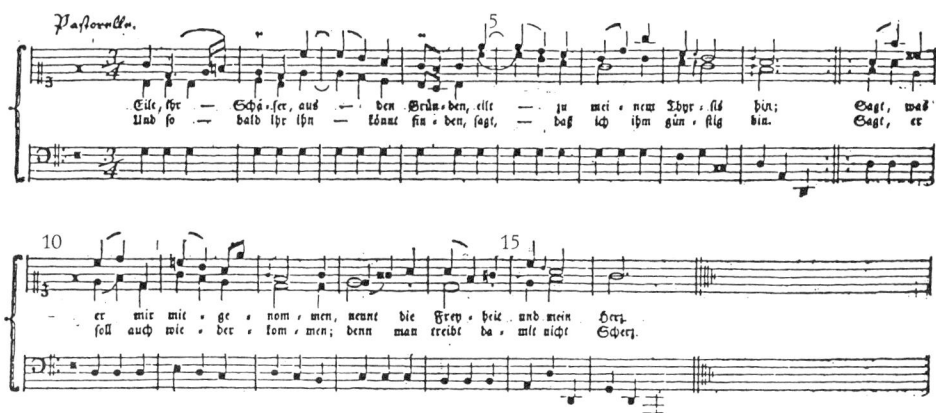

In the A segment we notice immediately the insistent pedal point on the tonic G—no doubt intended to suggest the drone bass traditionally associated with pastoral. Only in the penultimate bar does the G in the bass yield to the leading-tone F#, as the movement to the dominant cadence begins. And it is only in that bar that we at last get a hint of dominant—and just a hint: a triad on VII. Up to that point the harmony over the tonic pedal point has been strictly tonic and subdominant. The strong subdominant presence is of course also a common pastoral element, as are the parallel thirds and sixths in the keyboard's right hand. But what is interesting is the very individual way in which Bach uses these pastoral conventions to catch the rather peculiar dramatic situation of Ziegler's poem.

The urgency that we noted in the opening lines of the poem seems belied by the calm, even progress of the music, with its pedal-point bass line and rather tame melody. After the gentle drop of a fourth in bar 1, the motion is mainly stepwise and downward, broken only by the two upward skips in bars 2 and 4, and by the ascending arpeggio and downward skip in bars 6-7. The skips, we notice, are all to notes firmly in the harmony. Thus there seems nothing angular, abrupt, irregular. But then we notice the little push given by the turning figure at the end of bar 1, and the syncopations at the ends of bars 2 and 4. The syncopations not only intensify the subdominant presence essential to the pastoral mode; they also extend, in a decorous and rather guarded way, the push given by the little turning figure in bar 1. We thus have precisely the balance of urgency and reserve that we noted in the poem.

Segment B begins just at the point where the text of the first stanza becomes explicit about the loss the shepherdess feels she has incurred at Thyrsis's hands. The upward skip of a sixth in bar 9 echoes the earlier upward skips in bars 2 and 4, but the heightened emphasis that Bach gives this later skip by moving it to the beginning of the bar dramatizes the increase in the shepherdess's urgency. The slight clash of the melody's two C#'s against the pedal-point D in the bass also helps to step up the emotional intensity, as does the upward skip of a seventh in bars 10-11.

At this point the song begins to pull together, to fill out its form, as the bass, for the first time, starts to move in an orderly, stepwise manner, in concert with the melody. But its progress is stalled in bar 13 as it comes to rest on C, returning us momentarily to the subdominant as the melody moves sinuously up from E through G# to A, and from there around through F# to G. The keyboard's lower right-hand voice, moving first downward away from the melody and then up to join it in a closing unison, ceases to be a mere harmonization and unobtrusively takes on a life of its own.

It would be tedious to pursue in detail, stanza by stanza, the relation between text and music in this song of Bach's. But we might note that the progression we have traced in the music—a gradual rise in emotional intensity over the A strain that is pushed a bit further at the beginning of the B strain and then withdrawn as the strain comes to a close—would counterpoint nicely against the steadily rising emotional intensity that we observed over the course of the poem. The effect, I should think, would be to create an increasing gap between the comparative restraint of the music and the growing abandonment of the text, and thus to heighten our sense of the shepherdess's conflict—and of the sensitive way in which she keeps that conflict partially concealed, as a well-bred (though of course suitably countrified) pastoral heroine should. Though the poem is stanzaic, one can imagine a *durchkomponiert* setting, from the 19th century perhaps, that steadily increased in intensity along with the text. Such a setting would be more suited to Romantic taste, but it would run the risk of breaking the fine decorum of the pastoral mode, so carefully preserved by Bach.

Haydn's setting of the same poem—or something like it—appeared in the first of his two collections of German songs, published by Artaria in 1781. While the poem's opening stanza is the same, the others (there are only two) are quite different:

> Eilt, und sagt dem lieben Hirten,
> Dass ihn Doris nicht mehr neckt,
> Nicht mehr zwischen jenen Myrten
> Sich verrätrisch ihm versteckt.

Sagt, dass ich in jene Rinde
Schmerzen meiner Liebe schnitt,
Dass ich alles nun empfinde,
Was für mich der Arme litt.

    Ach, an meinem jungen Leben
Zehret schon der Liebe Gram.
Sagt, er soll mir wiedergeben,
Was er mir so grausam nahm,
Soll mich länger nicht mehr kränken;
Denn ich könnt' am nächsten Baum
Voll Verzweiflung mich erhenken,
Aber sagt ihm—nur im Traum!

The shepherdess has picked up a name: she, like so many of her kind, is a Doris. And the conventionality of the name—stamping her, as it does, with the all-too-familiar conventionality of the coyly playful pastoral heroine—robs her of the mystery, and thus of the capacity for emotional complexity, possessed by Ziegler's original unnamed shepherdess. We are therefore not surprised that her part in the relation is quite different from that of her unnamed counterpart. This Doris has teased her Thyrsis and hidden "verrätrisch" from him amongst the myrtles—though of course she has also, like the lover in Schubert's (and Wilhelm Müller's) "Ungeduld," found some relief by carving up the bark of a few trees.

    It is hard to take her "Schmerzen" very seriously. And so when the language of the last stanza suddenly becomes grotesquely melodramatic—"Zehret," "Gram," "grausam," and the astonishing penultimate line—we are primed to believe that it is, after all, just a big joke, more of the teasing that she had earlier promised would now cease. And the final "nur im Traum!" makes it clear that this is indeed the case.[2] This "Traum" is, then, utterly different from the very serious (and pathetic) one of Ziegler's concluding stanza.

    Here then is Haydn's setting, which bears the title "An Thyrsis":

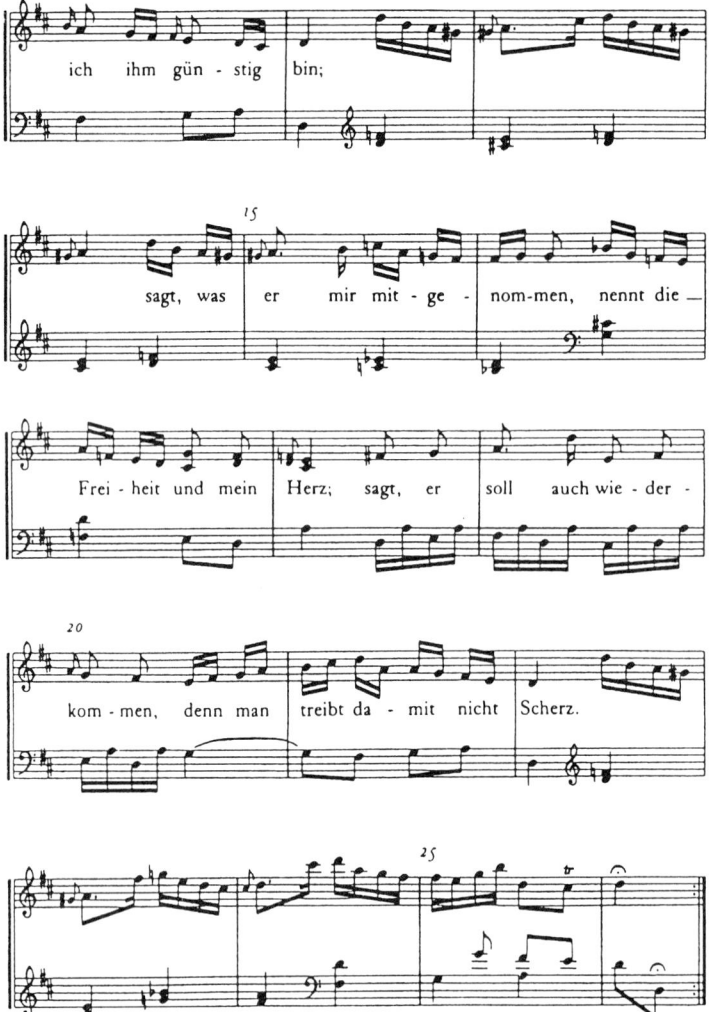

The first thing one notices about this setting is that it has a keyboard introduction. This is, of course, not unusual for Haydn. Of the 46 songs contained in Volume XXIX/1 of the new Haydn edition, only eight lack a keyboard introduction. Bach, on the other hand, avoided keyboard introductions almost completely in his ordinary solo songs—though he employed them in his few brief cantatas and in the few songs he called arias. Certainly this contrast has something to do with the fact that Haydn was deeply influenced by the Italian opera aria—was himself, in fact, a far more distinguished composer of operas than is generally realized. Often the keyboard introductions to his songs—and one thinks here particularly of the marvelous late setting of the Shakespearean "She Never Told Her Love"—add a decidedly theatrical air to the proceedings, bowing the main character onstage, as it were. Not only did Bach compose no theatrical music; in his songs he was, unlike Haydn, very pointedly writing *Hausmusik*, for the rapidly growing number of musical amateurs to play and sing in their homes.

In the introduction to "An Thyrsis," the gay, springing rhythm of the left-hand sixteenth notes, the upward-thrusting first phrase, and the clear tonic-dominant opposition combine to create an atmosphere utterly different from that of Bach's song. And this atmosphere is not only sustained but is also elaborated when the voice enters, turning the keyboard introduction into the antecedent of an eight-bar antecedent-consequent sequence. What, exactly, is this atmosphere? Charles Rosen's fine phrase "the discipline of comedy" comes to mind.³ Just as with the Bach song, we are of course dealing here too with pastoral. But we are worlds away from the rather sober, contemplative pastoral mode we found there. What we have here is the witty, sociable pastoral mode that Haydn, in the later symphonies and quartets—and, less often recognized, in the great late masses—was to extend and expand into the unique mix of intelligence and high spirits, sophisticated knowingness and sweet innocence, that characterizes not only his finest work but also the Classical style itself.

Therefore when, after the first eight-bar phrase, the keyboard part moves through a pensive diminished chord, we know that the disturbance is not to be a serious one. The voice, picking up the keyboard phrase, moves it down stepwise. But after this mock-serious deployment of minor sonorities, the return to the major is accomplished with a wink as we move from the appoggiatura F-natural on the first beat of bar 18 to the F# on its second beat.

This is a straight AA¹BA¹ song, and so after the little minorish interlude we return, via the F/F# juxtaposition, to a restatement of the second four-bar phrase. But Haydn is not done with us yet. Just as the keyboard part bowed the singer onstage, so it must bow her off. And this Haydn accomplishes with characteristic Haydnesque dispatch. The first phrase of the little interlude is repeated—almost as though we might be thoughtfully returning to that (ostensibly) more thoughtful part of the song—but then Haydn, as so often in his greater music, simply cuts the Gordian knot: the whole phrase is transposed up a fourth to give us a progression that we hear as iv-I and that leads us directly into the concluding cadence. What could be neater—or (one wants to add) more brusquely and wittily dismissive of any pretensions to high seriousness that the text initially seemed to possess?

As it happens, there is another setting of the revised text of Ziegler's poem, by a lesser Viennese composer, rather in the style of Haydn's setting.⁴ Josef Anton Steffan (1726-1797) lived and worked in Vienna from age 15 until his death, but since he was born in Bohemia, the *New Grove* lists him as Josef Antonín Štěpán. While still young he became a favorite pupil of Wagenseil's, was connected with the court until 1775, and spent his last years composing and teaching privately. He was one of the first Viennese composers to specialize in the lied.

Oddly enough, considering that the shepherdess's name had by then been clearly established as Doris, Steffan's setting is titled "Chloe an Thyrsis":

Immediately, we are reminded of Haydn's setting. Steffan too begins with a pickup beat, and starts his melody on the third, rising to the fifth. And the lively sixteenth-note motion in the keyboard's right hand recalls the pervasive sixteenth-note motion in the left hand in Haydn's setting. The song is by no means as subtle or as finely wrought as Haydn's, but the general tone is similar. Like Haydn, Steffan has caught the witty note struck by the revised version of Ziegler's poem.

In the opening bars the emphatic low G at the beginning of the first full bar immediately anchors the upward-thrusting melody—and then itself moves swiftly upward, through the widely spaced octave D's, into the melody's range. A few bars later this effect is repeated, with still greater emphasis: not only is the low G doubled at the octave, the *p*-to-*f* dynamic marking (where there had been none before) also suggests a heightening of drama. This suggestion is carried a step further in bar 6 when the left hand, instead of pausing lamely on the second beat as in bar 2, takes up the sixteenth-note motion and presses upward. But the conclusion to each four-bar phrase is rather limp, and the melody itself is unmemorable.

In the following phrase, where Haydn had created a substantial shift in tone by introducing a brief keyboard interlude that strayed into the minor, Steffan simply moves, through V/V, to the dominant. Yet the melody's leap of a tritone (from G to C#) is effective—before the playful "chasing" of the downward-moving melody by the left hand in the latter half of bar 10 and bar 11. In the next four-bar phrase (the final one for the voice), one feels the song pulling together as the left hand breaks into a dance rhythm, the sixteenth notes at last returning. In the keyboard coda, the *sforzando* octave D in the left hand at bar 17, where we expected a G, formalizes the close by slightly postponing it, only to have it then playfully hastened by the right-hand triplets in bars 18 and 19.

All in all, then, not a very impressive song—though certainly pleasant enough. Since Steffan's and Haydn's settings were published in the same year, and since there is (so far as I know) no record of any direct personal or professional relation between the two men, there would seem to be no question of influence one way or the other. The similarities between their two settings are accounted for simply by the fact that they were both Viennese composers working within the particular version of the pastoral mode closely associated with the developing Classical style.

Interestingly enough, C. P. E. Bach's next song, composed in 1743, was also to a poem that was set almost 40 years later by Haydn. "Der Zufriedene" appeared in 1743 in Gräfe's fourth and last volume, and was reprinted in the 1762 *Oden*. The poem, by a poet named Stahl who is apparently otherwise unknown, runs as follows:

> Entfernt von Gram und Sorgen
> Erwach ich jeden Morgen,
> Wenn ich vorher die Nacht

Vergnügend zugebracht.
Die Freyheit meiner Seelen
Ist mir das höchste Gut;
Und, ohne mich zu quälen,
Bleib ich bey gleichem Muth.

    Mich blenden keine Güter,
Der Fallstrick der Gemüther,
Die sich um sie bemühn,
Und Kummer an sich ziehn.
Mich foltert keine Liebe,
Mich nimmt kein Ehrgeiz ein,
Ich wünsche, solche Triebe
Mir unbekannt zu seyn.

    So bring ich meine Jahre,
Da ich die Grillen spare,
In einer stolzen Ruh
Vergnügt und munter zu.
Geschick, dem ich ergeben,
Wenn ich im Sterben bin,
So nimm mir zwar mein Leben;
Nur lass mir diesen Sinn.

This is, in a sense, a retirement poem since it extols the virtues of a life that is simpler than that of most people—a life lived "Entfernt von Gram und Sorgen." But it is not a pastoral since it does not specifically associate that simpler life with the countryside, as opposed to the city or the court. Love, which plays such a major role in pastoral poetry, is dismissed along with ambition, which would seem to suggest the city or the court, as one of those delusive goods that ensnare the soul and keep it from its true happiness. As the last stanza makes clear, this is a religious poem: the particular state of proud and cheerful serenity that characterizes the speaker as "Der Zufriedene" will persist even after death.

Here is Bach's setting:

Two things stand out immediately: its heroic, almost martial air and its unusual length, 20 bars. Though it is less interesting musically than "Schäferlied" (even as its text is less interesting than that of the earlier song), there is still a good deal to be said about "Der Zufriedene."

The vocal line, probably enforced by the keyboard's right hand, launches out immediately on its own, presumably without harmonic underpinnings but clearly defining the tonality for us by its assertive upward leap of a fourth. What is interesting is that the word set by this bold gesture is "Entfernt"! It is thoroughly characteristic of Bach's quirkily thoughtful approach to his texts that it would have occurred to him to set a word meaning distant or remote by a musical gesture that represents a leap into the fray—or, at the very least, a triumphant declaration of independence. Reading the first line of the poem, one might rather have expected some sort of lulling quietude. But as one reads (and listens) on, it becomes clear that this initial paradox embodies, in miniature, the paradox of the whole poem: that real satisfaction, real life if you will, is to be found precisely where most people do not search for it. Neither love nor ambition nor the various other "Triebe" and "Grillen" that occupy most other people's time and mental energy will bring one to this desired state.

And yet, surprisingly, there is nothing withdrawn or inward about this state of true satisfaction—we are not dealing with "Ich bin der Welt abhanden gekommen"! Indeed, many of the words used to describe this state—"Freyheit," "stolz," "vergnügt," "munter"—are words commonly associated with the ordinary forms of worldly happiness. And, as was suggested by the song's opening gesture, the whole manner of both poem and song is very public, very outgoing, not at all contemplative or reflective. It is in complementing this brisk outgoingness that the song's formal peculiarity comes into play.

The song, we noticed, is a rather unusual 20 bars long. After the firm assertion of the tonic in bar 1, the harmony, spelled out by the striding bass line, swings momentarily to the dominant in bar 2 and then back to the tonic in bar 3. Naturally, we expect another bar of tonic, rounding out the four-bar opening phrase. But instead the vocal line immediately launches out once more at the end of bar 3, reiterating its initial assertion. And once again the phrase is completed in three bars, by the end of bar 6, the two curiously awkward three-bar phrases creating a sense of thrusting urgency.

At this the vocal line marches up the scale, does a turnaround in bar 8, and then heads back down for the cadence on the dominant in bars 9 and 10, which is enforced by the vigorous bass line. At last we have been handed a satisfyingly regular four-bar phrase. But then the restless bass line, moving down from A to F#, helps to carry the harmony to a comparatively remote V/ii. The song threatens for a moment to become reflective after all.

But our sense that we are wandering far afield—and how appropriate it is that the word just here is "Freyheit"!—is controlled and qualified by the bass line, which in bar 12 echoes the striding figure of bars 2 and 5. We are still, at least partially, in the briskly energetic world of the song's opening. And there are other reminders of the first six bars of the song. The vocal line of bars 11-13 echoes that of bars 1-3 and 4-6—though the pitches are slightly different and the bass line moves stepwise as well as striding. And the vocal line of bars 15-16 is a decorated version of that of bars 2-3 and 5-6, again with a stepwise rather than a striding bass line.

We might say that the song exhibits two different sorts of texture: declarative and discursive. The former, found in bars 1-6 in its pure form, is characterized by aggressive leaps in the vocal line, a striding arpeggiated bass line, simple tonic-dominant alternation in the harmony, and irregular (three-bar) phrases. The latter, which sets in with the pickup to bar 7, is characterized by orderly stepwise motion in both vocal and bass lines, harmonic movement to the slightly more remote V/ii, and regular phrases. But Bach has no sooner introduced the discursive texture than he begins allowing the declarative to interpenetrate and overlap with it. Besides the reminiscences of the vocal line already noted, one might mention the uncertainty about phrase-boundaries in the song's second half. Bars 7-10 are a clear four-bar phrase, contrasting with the two three-bar phrases that have preceded. But where does the next phrase end? The last four bars of the song are clearly one phrase, but how are we to divide bars 11-16? Judging purely by the vocal line and the harmonic motion, we want to say that bars 11-14 form a four-bar phrase, landing us back on the dominant. But if we go by the text of the poem, the break comes rather after bar 13, resulting (once again) in two three-bar phrases.

I think that this establishment and subsequent mingling of the two different textures, along with the concision and even compression produced by the telescoping of the first two phrases, are responsible for the song's tightness and cohesiveness. I do not think it would be forcing a point—since we are, after all, dealing with a very thoughtful and intelligent composer—to see this mingling of textures as a sort of musical counterpart, or dramatic enactment, of the poem's fusion of worldly and otherworldly language.

But there is one last formal surprise in Bach's song. As the vocal line descends G-F#-E in bar 17, one expects it to continue down to D and then C#, for a half-cadence, probably to be followed by a capping restatement of the opening melody to fill out a rough ABA[1] form. But instead the vocal line brilliantly o'ertops itself by pushing still further upward to A, the highest note of the song. The bass line ceases for a moment, and the vocal line is left on its own, as it begins the joyous proclamation that leads to the song's lightning-swift conclusion.

As it has been throughout, so it is here. Bach's formal concision heightens the most interesting fact about the poem: the state of satisfaction that it celebrates and dramatizes, while not to be sought in the ordinary world of affairs, has nothing monkish or escapist about it but in fact possesses all the energy, vitality, and joy that most people—quite wrongly, the poem is telling us—suppose may be found only in that world of affairs. And this state, of course, has the further advantage of transcending death. One can, it turns out, have it all ways at once.

Once again, the version of the poem that Haydn set has the same opening stanza as that set by Bach but then goes its own way, the other stanzas supplied by an unknown hand. Those stanzas run as follows:

>   Hier ruh' ich und ergötze
> Mich an des Bachs Geschwätze,
> Der, halb in Busch verhüllt,
> Leis aus dem Felsen quillt;
> Hör', wie in blauen Lüften
> Das Chor der Lerchen singt,
> Indess auf Blumentriften
> Das muntre Lämmchen springt.
>
>   Seh' ich bei Fledschalmeien
> Das Landvolk sich erfreuen
> Misch' ich mich in die Reihn
> Der Dörferinnen ein
> Und heb' im leichten Schwunge
> Mein Dirnchen flink empor;
> Mir tut's kein Bauernjunge
> An Mut und Lust zuvor.
>
>   So fern von Harm und Neide
> Scherz' ich bei Lieb' und Freude
> Mit unbewölktem Sinn
> Froh meine Tage hin.
> Mir blühet nie vergebens
> Ein Blümchen auf der Flur,
> Ich nütz' die Zeit des Lebens:
> Denn einmal lebt man nur.

It is worth noting that Haydn's setting, and presumably the version of the poetic text that he employs (if it was ever published separately), bears the title "Die Landlust." For the transformation of the text that Bach set is even more radical in this case than in that of the Ziegler poem. There we had one sort of pastoral changed into another sort; here we have a religious retirement poem changed—beyond recognition, really—into a pastoral.

The unnamed reviser wastes no time putting all the familiar pastoral appurtenances on display: the babbling brook, the choir of larks, the "muntre Lämmchen" gamboling on the "Blumentriften," the peasants with their rude "Feldschalmeien," the gay competitive dance. A reader of English poetry recalls Goldsmith's vanished Auburn and Blake's "Echoing Green." The concluding stanza of the revised poem more or less rehashes the opening stanza that it shares with the version set by Bach, but it does so in unambiguously secular terms: "Ich nütz' die Zeit des Lebens: / Denn einmal lebt man nur." We have indeed come a long way from Stahl's original poem.

The revised poem, then, is a pretty lame thing. Not only is it packed with clichés; one also has to wonder at the ear that produced "misch' ich mich"—one is reminded of Wagner at his worst; e.g., "Des Schweigens Herrin heisst mich schweigen: fass' ich, was sie verschwieg, verschweig ich, was sie nicht fasst." The most important point, however, is that the paradox that gave Stahl's poem what interest it possessed, and that Bach captured so tellingly, the paradox of a transcendent happiness that was nonetheless energetic and vital, has vanished. What do we find when we look at Haydn's setting? Here it is:

At first glance, this seems quite disappointing. The first three two-bar phrases all have exactly the same rhythm—except for the left hand's eighth-note lead-in to the fourth phrase—and it looks as though the fourth phrase will too, until the right hand unexpectedly cuts loose with its arpeggio in bar 8 and extends the pause between phrase-groups with its little interlude. Moreover, the first three phrases all end with a melodic "dying fall" of a half- or whole step. And we think that the fourth will too—moving from F# to A and then dropping to G—until the vocal line lands squarely on G so the right hand can begin its arpeggio. The harmony for the first eight bars (and indeed for the whole song) is similarly monotonous and predictable. And the lack of a keyboard introduction, taken in light of what was said earlier about Haydn's preference for them, seems to suggest that he did not take this song very seriously, that he was kidding the poem rather than setting it.

But, as so often with Haydn, one should not jump to conclusions. The little offbeat accentuation initiated by the keyboard's right hand in bar 9 is picked up in bars 11 and 13 by its left hand, which "chases" the vocal line. This serves to give a bit of tongue-in-cheek variety to the melody, which maintains the same rhythm and the same "dying fall" closes as in bars 1-8. Further variety is provided at the end of bar 16 by the left hand's "push-off" into the song's final section. This is an abbreviated version of the opening eight bars, with the keyboard given a chance to repeat its arpeggio (in bar 20) and then (in bars 22-24) to elaborate it into a full-scale, and very witty, conclusion. After all the rhythmic monotony, the burst of sixteenth notes is just as liberating as Haydn knew it would be. This is by no means as interesting a song as "An Thyrsis," and Haydn does, finally, seem to be treating the text a bit ironically, yet it is a rather more interesting song than it seems at first.

What have we learned from our examination of these five songs, set to competing versions of two different poems? First of all, I think, that the approach taken to the pastoral mode by Haydn and his Viennese contemporaries was quite different from that taken, at least in these two songs, by Bach. Rosen and others have, quite rightly, made much of the role played by the pastoral in the development of Haydn's art and of the Classical style generally. For ways of thinking and feeling traditionally associated with pastoral were surely one of the prime sources of the wit, the drama, the "discipline of comedy" (to recall Rosen's phrase) that so largely inform the great Classical masterpieces. After speaking of Haydn's symphonies as marked by "that combination of sophisticated irony and surface innocence that is so much of the pastoral genre," Rosen writes:

> The pretension of Haydn's symphonies to a simplicity that appears to come from Nature itself is no mask but the true claim of a style whose command over the whole range of technique is so great that it can ingenuously afford to disdain the outward appearance of high art. Pastoral is generally ironic, with the irony of one who aspires to less than he deserves, hoping he will be granted more. But Haydn's pastoral style is more generous, with all its irony: it is the true heroic pastoral that cheerfully lays claim to the sublime, without yielding any of the innocence and simplicity won by art.[5]

No one has ever written better about Haydn. And yet Rosen's generalization about the almost necessary connection between pastoral and irony is troubling. Certainly the connection is there not only in Haydn but also in the writers cited by Rosen: Marvell, Goldsmith, Johnson, Sade, Voltaire. But these are all writers of the Enlightenment. Pre-Enlightenment pastoral is often quite free of irony. One need not go back to Bion's lament for Adonis or Virgil's *Eclogue* IV ("Pollio") to find pastorals that are more reflective than ironic, pastorals in which the disjunction between the present age and the Golden Age—and, in the case of *Eclogue* IV, the imminent return of the Golden Age: "magnus ab integro saeclorum nascitur ordo"—is not made a subject for wit. What about *Lycidas* by Milton, Marvell's greater contemporary who was in some ways as behind the times as Marvell was ahead of them? Or Spenser's *The Shepheardes Calendar*? Or Sidney's *Arcadia*? Or the poems in a Renaissance miscellany such as *Englands Helicon*? Even without that very convenient child in *Eclogue* IV, whose birth ushers in a new Golden Age, it was natural that the pastoral mode should, over the centuries, become thoroughly Christianized, the gap between past simplicity and present complexity (or confusion) yet another testimony to man's fallen state. Thus Puttenham, in *The Arte of English Poesie* (1589), insists that "the Poet deuised the *Eglogue* . . . not of purpose to counterfait or represent the rusticall manner of loues and communication: but vnder the vaile of homely persons, and in rude speeches to insinuate and glaunce at greater matters," and thus "to containe and enforme morall discipline, for the amendment of mans behauiour."[6]

Though C. P. E. Bach is a man of the middle and late 18th century, his approach to pastoral has more in common with Puttenham's than with Haydn's. Pastoral, that is to say, is for Bach, as it was for his father, a more directly Christian-didactic mode than it was for the Viennese Classical composers. This fact is of no small importance not only for understanding Bach's work as a composer of songs but also for placing him generally in the history of 18th-century music more satisfactorily than he has so far been placed.

As we saw earlier, ever since the mid-19th century, music historians have attempted to place—and thus to vindicate or justify—Bach as a sort of middle term or missing link between Baroque and Classical forms and styles. As we also saw, this direction of interest led them to concentrate on his instrumental music and to ignore his songs. As recently as 1952 Ernst Fritz Schmid, in the "Vorlagenbericht" to his edition of the three quartets (Wq. 93-95; H. 537-539) composed during Bach's last year, declared that these works give "the impression of a complete breakthrough, of an almost Beethovenian character, into the Viennese Classical style."[7] Though there are plenty of surprises in these fine works, it is precisely the absence of anything like the wit that Rosen correctly connects to Haydn's approach to pastoral that marks them as distinctly un-Classical. Whatever C. P. E. Bach may have accomplished in his long career— and I think he accomplished a great deal—it was not a "breakthrough" to the Viennese Classical style. The special approach to pastoral that Rosen singles out in Haydn is just as important to the formation of the Classical style as Rosen says it is, and it is—no doubt along with many other factors—Bach's quite different approach to pastoral that makes him definitely not a Classical or pre-Classical or proto-Classical composer but a composer of quite a different sort.

It is most significant that the poems by Ziegler and Stahl were altered before being set by the Viennese composers. We have no information as to who altered them or why. But it does not seem overly speculative to assume that the two poems, in their original form, must have seemed utterly unsuitable to the Viennese. The pastoral or retirement poem had come to be so firmly associated with cheery sociability and light romance that the original poems' darker, more serious didactic and even religious overtones probably made them seem so hopelessly old-fashioned (and perhaps provincial) as not to be worth considering for musical treatment. It is, after all, easier to leave a poem as it is than to get somebody to change it, and so there must have been ample reason why these two poems both seemed to require changes—and changes of roughly the same sort—before becoming palatable to Haydn and Steffan.

There are other comparisons that might be made between Bach songs and Viennese songs of the Classical period that set the same poems. But the results would be roughly the same as those produced by the ones we have made. Even where the poem being set is not a pastoral, similar differences hold: the Viennese settings tend to be public and outward-turning in their theatricality and their wit, painted (so to speak) with a broad brush; Bach's, on the other hand, tend to turn inward, to concern themselves with the sensitive moment-to-moment inflection of nuance, the fine delineation of ambivalences and ambiguities of feeling.

II

But how do Bach's songs look when compared with those that were being written by his north German contemporaries? In 1756 he composed a song called "Der Morgen" that was first published that year in Friedrich Wilhelm Marpurg's *Neue Lieder zum Singen beym Claviere* and that was subsequently included in the 1762 *Oden*. It is an interesting song for many reasons, not the least of which is the fact that it is one of only two surviving Bach songs set to poems by Friedrich von Hagedorn. Hagedorn, as we have seen, was a disciple of Horace and of Horace's slightly earlier modern disciples Boileau and Pope, and was noted for the grace and elegance, the symmetry, balance, and aphoristic point of his verse, for his unique ability to mix wit and *Empfindung*. "Der Morgen" is a fair sample of his work:

    Uns lockt die Morgenröthe
In Busch und Wald,
Wo schon der Hirten Flöte
Ins Land erschallt.
Die Lerche steigt und schwirret,
Von Lust erregt;
Die Taube lacht und girret,
Die Wachtel schlägt.

    Die Hügel und die Weyde
Stehn aufgehellt
Und Fruchtbarkeit und Freude
Beblümt das Feld.
Der Schmelz der grünen Flächen
Glänzt voller Pracht;
Und von den klaren Bächen
Entweicht die Nacht.

    Der Hügel weisse Bürde,
Der Schaafe Zucht,
Drängt sich aus Stall und Hürde
Mit froher Flucht.
Seht, wie der Mann der Heerde
Den Morgen fühlt,
Und auf der frischen Erde
Den Buhler spielt.

    Der Jäger macht schon rege,
Und hetzt das Reh
Durch blutbetriefte Wege,
Durch Busch und Klee.
Sein Hüfthorn giebt das Zeichen:
Man eilt herbey;
Gleich schallt aus allen Sträuchen
Das Jagdgeschrey.

    Doch Phyllis Herz erbebet
Bey dieser Lust.
Nur Zärtlichkeit belebet
Die sanfte Brust.
Lass uns die Thäler suchen,

> Geliebtes Kind,
> Wo wir von Berg und Buchen
> Umschlossen sind.
>
> Erkenne dich im Bilde
> Von jener Flur!
> Sey stets wie dies Gefilde,
> Schön durch Natur;
> Erwünschter als der Morgen,
> Hold wie sein Strahl;
> So frey von Stolz und Sorgen,
> Wie dieses Thal.

This is a very handsome and complex poem. Perhaps the first thing one notices about it is the delicacy of its metrical pattern: each eight-line stanza is composed of four pairs of lines, in each of which a three-stress line is followed by a two-stress one. Moreover, while each two-stress line is a straight iambic dimeter, each three-stress line has an extra syllable at the end, creating what used to be called a weak or feminine ending by (in effect) substituting an amphibrach for the final iamb. That extra unstressed syllable makes the ear expect the line to continue—we await the stressed syllable that will carry us on into a tetrameter or pentameter line. The unstressed syllable that begins the following line, by disrupting this expectation, repeatedly gives us a gentle let-down, to which the unexpected brevity of the line adds a sense of quiet finality.

Against this very elegant (and effortlessly sustained) stanzaic pattern, there is a good deal of change in perspective and, toward the end, dramatic change. In the first stanza we are on the ground, being lured into the shrubbery and the forest by the glow of morning and the shepherd's seductive piping. But then we rise with the charmingly enumerated birds—a reader of English poetry is here reminded of the "whirring Pheasant" and "mounting Larks" of Pope's *Windsor-Forest* (lines 111 and 133), which Hagedorn too would surely have known. The quasi-personification of the birds—"erregt, lacht"—is also charming, and plays wittily against "schwirret" and "girret," two prominently placed and rhymed words that depict specifically nonhuman sounds.

Thus in the second stanza we are looking down on the valley from far above. We can see the hills and the pastureland clearly, lit by the rising sun. But "aufgehellt" does not only mean literally made clear, illuminated; it also means made clear intellectually or conceptually, elucidated or explained. The sun not only shows the valley clearly to our physical vision; it also makes clear the symbolic or even allegorical significance of the valley, preparing us for the turn that the poem will take in the penultimate stanza. Thus it is not just literal, visible "Fruchtbarkeit" that we see when we look down at the wildflowers but also "Freude." While both "Schmelz" and "Flächen" are words that emphasize the surface finish of the landscape, this surface gleams from within with "Pracht," splendor or magnificence, almost a moral quality. And the brooks are not merely made clear by the coming of sunrise: it is from the already, essentially "klaren Bächen" that the night escapes or flees, as from an enemy superior in native force.

In the third stanza we focus first on what is first referred to, proleptically, as the hills' white burden—an initially puzzling phrase explained by the next phrase, which is in apposition to it: "Der Schaafe Zucht." The primary meaning of "Zucht" of course is flock, but it also has overtones of order, discipline, good breeding. Therefore there is a pleasing surprise in the verb "Drängt sich," as there also is in the mildly oxymoronic phrase "froher Flucht"—flight not usually being a happy affair. The vivid reference in the first line to the flock as seen from above is proleptic because they have not yet forced their way out of the stall or pen.

In the second half of the third stanza we focus for the first time on a human being, the expected shepherd. "Seht," Hagedorn enjoins us—but what is it that he would have us look at? Not, as we should expect, some particular physical scene or action, the shepherd at some characteristic task. We are to look, rather, at how he *feels* the morning—surely an odd request, which once again indicates that there is an inner meaning to be exacted from this external scene. As it turns out, we are to infer his feelings from the way in which he acts the part of a lover, a gay blade, to some unnamed maiden—and notice how neatly the adjective "frischen" both literally describes the earth and figuratively characterizes his attitude and (unspecified) actions.

In the fourth stanza the human focus becomes still sharper and more detailed. For the first time we begin not with a detail of the landscape but rather with a person: "Der Jäger." As we encounter him, he is already ("schon") in action, tracking his deer "Durch blutgetriefte Wege, / Durch Busch und Klee." The vision of the blood-besprinkled ground, the sounding of the horn, and the raising of the hunters' triumphant shout all seem to happen at once ("Gleich")—the effect is something like what Eisenstein meant by montage. We are never actually told that the deer has been shot or has fallen or is dead: we simply have the ground, the horn, the shout—telescoped into a single moment. The violence that must have gone into the action is nowhere to be found in the verse. The detailed description of the deer's path "Durch Busch und Klee," coupled with the absence of any clear violent act, make us for a moment reverse Beckmesser's error and hear "blut-" as "blüt-": the drops of blood seem as decorative as the wildflowers of stanza two. The ease and grace of Hagedorn's verse make this violent scene seem a perfectly natural part of the peaceful, glowing landscape of the valley.

It is just at this point that the poem surprisingly changes direction: "Doch Phyllis Herz erbebet / Bey dieser Lust." Who is Phyllis? Perhaps the maiden courted by the shepherd in stanza three? Or are we even supposed to ask that question? I think that her value to the poem may lie wholly in her total unexpectedness, in our inability to identify her. And that effect of course involves a sly joke, on Hagedorn's part, about the mechanical, faceless application of the standard pastoral names—something we saw a good deal of in the poems we looked at earlier. But what then is "dieser Lust"?—or, to put it more clearly: how wide is the extension of "dieser"? Does it refer only to the hunt described in the preceding stanza? Since Hagedorn so completely glossed over the violent side of the hunt, stressing the cheery horn—which, we notice, "schallt," rather as "der Hirten Flöte" in the first stanza "erschallt"—and the joyous shout of triumph, "Lust" is not an inappropriate word for the hunt. But of course it also could apply to everything that has been viewed and discussed in the preceding stanzas: the sun's glow, the birds, the hills and flocks, the shepherd as would-be gallant. It is only tenderness, we are told, that animates Phyllis's gentle breast, and we have not really had any of that in the preceding stanzas. So "Lust" seems set against "Zärtlichkeit."

Addressing her as "Geliebtes Kind," the speaker of the poem then suggests that he and Phyllis survey the valley, in which they are "Umschlossen"—surrounded but also with the overtone of embraced—by mountain and beech tree. He then enjoins her to recognize herself as pictured or represented ("im Bilde") in the fields and meadows, to assume the desirability of the morning, the purity of the sun's rays, the whole valley's freedom from pride and care. He is asking her to be, as he puts it, "Schön durch Natur." The key word in this phrase is "durch," which I take to mean not only through in the sense of by means of or owing to—she will be beautiful because she has recognized her image in the natural world around her—but also something like throughout: as she takes on the desirable qualities of all of nature, so too, reciprocally, various aspects of her beauty will be reflected throughout the natural world. "Natur" is perhaps also ambiguous, meaning not only nature in the ordinary sense, the nonhuman natural world, but also her own nature—which is, more or less *ex hypothesi*, at one with that larger, more general nature.

From what we have seen of Bach's tendency toward inwardness, reflection, and contemplation, we should not expect him to take to an urbane, witty poet like Hagedorn—and indeed, it cannot be an accident that he set so few of Hagedorn's poems. Here is what he made of "Der Morgen":

In view of what was said earlier about Bach's general avoidance of keyboard introductions, this one is particularly striking. For it is neither a mere "vamp" nor (as in the first of the two Haydn songs) the music that will immediately be heard again as the singer's first phrase. Rather, it immediately sets a distinctive mood: the horn-call imitations—given first in the upper voice and then answered in a lower one—and the galloping rhythms tell us that this is to be a hunting song. This impression is corroborated by the first phrase of the vocal line and also by the insistence with which the keyboard's left hand pounds out the galloping rhythms—notated in octaves, which is unusual for songs of this period. The excitement of the chase is also captured by the tricky rhythmic effect of having each succeeding voice enter on a sixteenth note—with a sort of lurch forward, as it were. As we look quickly over the remainder of the song, we see that hornlike melodic figures and galloping rhythms continue right to the end.

But this is not a hunting song. The only mention of a hunt comes more than halfway through, in the fourth of its six stanzas, and the hunt is not specifically mentioned after that stanza. So why should Bach have made these descriptive effects, which were of course very familiar to his contemporaries, dominate the song? Plainly, he saw the stanza about the hunt as perhaps even more of a turning point in Hagedorn's poem than we did in our reading of it. Hence he wanted the hunting music to be heard—puzzlingly, perhaps, to his listeners—right from the beginning and continuously throughout the song. The reason would only become clear when the singer reached the fourth stanza—if, indeed, then. For what Bach has done is really quite subtle, an excellent example of a composer very pointedly making musical choices that throw a particular aspect of a poem into unexpectedly sharp relief, and thus more actively offering a personal interpretation of the poem than composers usually do when they turn poems into songs.

Though the hunt music of the song's opening persists until its end, Bach constantly varies the texture in interesting and amusing ways. After the heavy insistence given to the first phrase by the keyboard's left hand, the song immediately lightens, the galloping rhythm passing to the vocal line and the keyboard's left hand dropping out altogether for almost a bar. Then it reenters for a long and playful chase through six bars and over the course of just over two octaves. The vocal line does not, as we might have expected, rise on the word "steigt," but delays a moment, letting the bass line do the rising, and then suddenly jumps to high G—a fine surprise. From there, the rhythm of the vocal line evens out to straight eighth notes—Bach perhaps sensed the danger that the dotted rhythms would grow monotonous—and gradually descends to the tonic, the dotted rhythms returning for a moment at the very end. The swiftness with which the conclusion arrives is felt in the close juxtaposition of D# and D-natural in the antepenultimate bar of the bass line. The harmony throughout is appropriately simple—we are, after all, dealing with natural horns. To generalize, we can say that the mood of the song is gay and playful, in keeping with the elegance and grace of the poem, the tempo marking "In der Bewegung der Reveil" indicating a moderate *Allegretto* with an easy swing to it.

A far more "orthodox" north German setting of Hagedorn's poem appeared in 1744, in the second part of Johann Valentin Görner's *Sammlung Neuer Oden und Lieder*. As we saw earlier, Görner, unlike Bach, was a composer perfectly suited by temperament to set the poetry of Hagedorn. Görner was not a member of the Ramler-Krause group usually credited with initiating the first Berlin school. Sometime in the 1720s he settled in Hamburg, where he became director of music at the cathedral in 1756. He was in some way associated with Telemann, who of course had become director of music at Hamburg's five parish churches in 1721—a job he held until his death, upon which he was succeeded by C.P.E. Bach—and in 1729 Görner contributed two harpsichord pieces to Telemann's *Der getreue Music-Meister*. Telemann, as we have seen, was very important in the history of the early 18th-century German lied. Aside from the two songs he contributed to *Der getreue Music-Meister*, he composed 48 for inclusion in his *Singe- Spiel- und Generalbass-Übungen* (1733-1734), and in 1741, only a year before Görner's first collection, he published *Vier und zwanzig, theils ernsthafte, theils scherzende Oden*. His eminently singable melodies fully satisfied Scheibe's specification, in *Der critische Musikus*, that "the melody of a song must be free, flowing, pure, and generally natural," and most subsequent historians—though not, interestingly enough, Scheibe—have felt that Telemann found in Görner what Hermann Kretzschmar termed "a talented surrogate."[8] W. K. von Jolizza wrote of Hagedorn's poems, as set by Görner: "These light, happy poems, full of joy and the love of life, found their echo in Görner, and are in no small degree responsible for the fact that his compositions—with their refreshing melodies, singable declamation, warm feeling, and homely simplicity—compare very favorably with those of his contemporaries."[9]

Here then is Görner's setting of Hagedorn's "Der Morgen":

The differences with Bach's setting could scarcely be greater. Where Bach had an introduction, Görner has none; where the sixteenth-note entries of the various voices in Bach's introduction gave the rhythm an exciting, slightly "thrown off" feel, Görner's rhythm, throughout his song, is solidly square and even; where Bach, for the first two pairs of lines in the poem's stanza, changed the song's rhythm to correspond to that of the poem, Görner does not do so; and, perhaps most important, where Bach dramatically prefigured the turning point of the poem by beginning with hunting music, Görner does nothing of the kind—his setting, we feel, could work just as well for a poem on a quite different subject. The general air of Görner's setting—and in this it is characteristic of the songs written by Bach's north German contemporaries, though it is certainly more skillful and more finished than most of them—is one of brisk, neat cheerfulness, even pertness or self-satisfied complacency. (Leafing through the Berlin, Hamburg, and Leipzig song collections of the 1730s through the 1760s, one is struck by the extraordinary frequency with which words like *zufrieden* and *vergnügen* turn up in titles and first lines or are otherwise prominently placed.) In addition to the only very slightly varied rhythmic regularity of the melodic line, the constant contrary motion of melodic and bass lines contributes to this sense of overall neatness. The downward jump of an octave on the words "Die Lerche steigt" is just possibly a touch of wit, but I rather doubt it. Finally, in comparing the two settings, while also thinking back to the other songs of Bach's that we have looked at, one is struck by the fairly rapid rate of harmonic change in Görner's setting. As we saw in Chapter Three, this too is typical of the north German songs—though not of Bach's.

Unlike Scheibe, Marpurg approved of Görner's three volumes. Writing in *Kritische Briefe über die Tonkunst* for November 17, 1759, he characteristically pointed out "some too obviously visible offenses against the rules of harmony," but praised the songs' "otherwise very flowing and pretty melodies."[10] And most of Marpurg's own songs are very similar to the Görner song just examined. Therefore it will help to compare one of his settings to one of Bach's of the same poem—especially since the Marpurg song is well above the level he usually achieved.

The poem is by Ewald Christian von Kleist (1715-1759), great-uncle of the more famous Heinrich, and is, once again, a pastoral lament. It is titled "Amint" and runs as follows:

> Sie fliehet fort! Es ist um mich geschehen!
> Ein weiter Raum trennt Lalagen von mir.
> Dort floh sie hin; komm, Luft, mich anzuwehen;
> Du kommst vielleicht von ihr.
>
> Sie fliehet fort! Sagt Lalagen, ihr Flüsse,
> Dass, ohne sie, der Wiese Schmuck verdirbt;
> Ihr eilt ihr nach, sagt, dass der Wald sie misse,
> Und dass ihr Schäfer stirbt.
>
> Welch Thal blüht jetzt, von ihr gesehen, besser?
> Wo tanzt sie nun ein Labyrinth? wo füllt
> Ihr Lied den Hayn? welch glückliches Gewässer
> Wird schöner durch ihr Bild?
>
> Nur einen Druck der Hand, nur halbe Blicke,
> Ach! einen Kuss, wie sie mir vormals gab,
> Vergönne mir von ihr: dann stürz, o Glücke,
> Mich, wann du willst, ins Grab!
>
> So klagt Amint, die Augen voll von Thränen,
> Den Gegenden die Flucht der Lalage;
> Sie schienen sich mit ihm nach ihr zu sehnen,
> Und seufzten: Lalage!

The lovers' names perhaps demand a word of explanation. Amint (or Amynt, as the name is spelled in Marpurg's setting) is just a German version of Amyntas, a shepherd's name found in Theocritus and Virgil—though there was also a real Amyntas who was king of Galatia and one of the commanders at Philippi, and the Amyntas mentioned obscenely by Horace in *Epode* 12 may or may not have been real. His most important Renaissance incarnation was as the eponymous hero of Tasso's 1573 pastoral drama *Aminta*. In none of these writers, however, is he paired with Lalage—his beloved in Tasso's play is called Silvia.

Lalage is a name that does not appear in Theocritus or Virgil or the other classical bucolic poets, but does appear in two of Horace's odes. The famous references are in *Ode* 22 of Book I ("Integer vitae scelerisque purus"). The poem's first two stanzas seem at first to be grandly moralistic: he whose life is untainted and who is free from vice needs no weapons, but may travel freely and in safety over the burning sands of the Sahara or the savage wastes of the Caucasus. (These stanzas have, indeed, been pressed into service as a Protestant hymn!)[11] But, as so often with Horace, the moralizing turns out to be tongue-in-cheek as he describes how, while he was wandering in the woods one day and singing of his Lalage, a wolf fled from him, even though he was unarmed. And so, concludes the poem, "dulce ridentem Lalagen amabo, / dulce loquentem" ("I will go on loving sweetly laughing, sweetly talking Lalage").

Apparently the name was coined, whether by Horace or by someone else, from the Greek word λαλαγή, an onomatopoetic word meaning prattle or nonsensical talk that comes from the verb λαλαγέω, to babble or (of birds) to chirp. Commentators on Horace enjoy pointing out soberly that while "Integer vitae scelerisque purus" is indeed witty and playful, it is also serious: what keeps the wolf away is the fact that Horace, a poet after all, is singing—i.e., making poems. But this alleged seriousness is somewhat undone by the fact that he is singing about an empty-headed girl who apparently can do nothing but smile and talk sweetly (though that seems to be quite enough). I do not know when or why a connection was made between Amint and Lalage. In another 18th-century German poem, by Johann Samuel Patzke (1727-1787), that is also titled "Amint" and was set to music by Christoph Nichelmann (1717-1762), there are the familiar Doris and Phyllis but no Lalage. An answer does suggest itself, however. Theocritus only mentions Amyntas once, in *Idyll* VII, at line 132. He only uses the verb λαλαγέω twice, and one of these uses occurs just seven lines after the mention of Amyntas. Can this be a coincidence? My guess would be that once Horace (or whoever) had coined the name Lalage from λαλαγή, some wag decided, as a sort of pastoral poet's in-joke, to team up Amyntas (or Amint) and Lalage.

There is really very little to be said about Kleist's poem. It is conventional in the bad sense, merely a string of clichés common to pastoral laments in several languages, ancient and modern. There are filler lines, in which many syllables are occupied to say very little: "Ein weiter Raum trennt Lalagen von mir." And there are embarrassingly awkward lines: "Welch Thal blüht jetzt, von ihr gesehen, besser?" The first two of the five stanzas are taken up with lamenting the absence of Lalage from the landscape with which she, like any good pastoral heroine, has been so closely identified, and which therefore now languishes—along with the unfortunate Amint. The third stanza asks on what place she is now lavishing her favors—where she dances, where she sings. In the fourth Amint proclaims his willingness to die—if only he could be granted one kiss (which of course seems unlikely). And in the fifth the plodding narrator quite unnecessarily sums it all up for us. One looks in vain for distinction of either language or thought.

But Marpurg's setting, especially considering the triteness of most of his songs, is quite stunning. It appeared in the third (1763) volume of *Berlinische Oden und Lieder*, a collection edited by Marpurg:

After the quiet resignation of the simple descending phrase with which the song opens, over the bleak minor third in the bass, the melodic line suddenly leaps upward on the word "fort," and continues to rise dramatically as the harmony becomes slightly more complicated—the D#/E clash at the beginning of bar 3—and then resolves as the line again descends. The C-major triad heard (in first inversion) at the end of bar 4 as the second phrase begins sounds momentarily consoling. But the bass immediately drops out, and the melodic line descends chromatically to A#, the bass line mimicking its motion and arriving at D# (which in a moment will be the third of an incomplete dominant triad) just early enough to form a very disturbing sonority with the A# and C# above—though the harmony rights itself as those two notes resolve to the octave B and we move to the E-minor triad in the next bar. But once again the bass drops too early—this time much too early—to a note (A#) that creates a downright clash with the B above. And there the bass stubbornly remains, until in the next bar the upper voices move to fill out the diminished chord that was wanted all along to lead to the cadence in bar 8.

From this point on the song begins to pull together, starting with the orderly upward motion of the bass in bars 8 and 9, repeated in sequence a step lower in bars 9 and 10. Meanwhile the vocal line loosens and softens, and the harmony continues to move, now somewhat rapidly, in an orderly fashion. Varied by octave leaps, the bass line moves steadily upward from F# to C at the beginning of bar 14, where it is joined above by the same D# and F# that earlier, in bar 7, created that disturbing vii^6_4 chord with the A# in the bass. The cadence is clear and orthodox. Thus the song moves from a quiet though tentatively disturbed opening through increasing pain and harmonic disorder to a climax at the midpoint, and gradually works its way back to order in its second half. Throughout, the harmonic motion is quite rapid, just as in the Görner song—though of course with entirely different effect. The daring harmonies early on capture Amint's anguish far better than anything in the poem does, and the gradual return to a sad tranquillity works well with the gentle falling off provided by the short line at the end of the poetic stanza. All in all, this seems to me most effective.

Now let us see what Bach does with the same poem. His setting was first published in the Ramler-Krause *Oden mit Melodien* of 1753, and was later included in Bach's 1762 *Oden*:

The mood is certainly different from that of Marpurg's setting. In the first place, Bach's is firmly in the major: the first three notes of the melodic line outline the tonic G triad. Taken at the moderately slow tempo probably implied by the direction "Mit Affect," this seems an inappropriately calm, even sedate opening, given what the text is saying. It is interesting that while Marpurg had his vocal line leap upward on the word "fort," as we might have expected, Bach saves his upward leap for the next line, in which Amint declares that Lalage's departure has undone or finished him. Clearly, Bach is more interested in the registering on Amint's consciousness of Lalage's departure than he is in the departure itself. Still, however, there is no painful clash in the harmony: Amint's plaint, "es ist um mich geschehen!" is strikingly restrained and dignified—we are reminded of the first of Bach's songs we looked at, "Schäferlied." The harmony has been so square and simple that at the beginning of bar

4 we expect a return to the tonic. Instead we get a deceptive cadence on vi, but a surprisingly mild and (once again) restrained one. And in the next bar we are back in the major, heading for the dominant. The movement of the upper voices in thirds continues melodiously through the cadence on V, but the bass begins to grow more active, joining in the motion of the melodic line as the second half of the song begins.

The melodic line recalls the very opening, but this time carries its G arpeggio a step further, to high D. The phrase that follows also duplicates the corresponding phrase in the first half of the song, but pitched a step higher and with slightly more emotional intensity owing to the F-natural that eventually clashes gently with the E in the bass. In the concluding four bars the melodic motion slows, and we have a simple, dignified cadence on the tonic. There is none of the harmonic strife that characterized Marpurg's setting, only the slightest increase in emotional pressure as we move into the song's second half—which is then dissipated at the close. The setting seems to me effective, but in an oblique, indirect way: as in "Schäferlied," it is the pathos of the protagonist's calmly dignified reaction to the lover's departure that engages us, not, as in Marpurg's setting, the departure itself.

In particular, we notice the slow pace of the harmonic motion in Bach's setting: most of the time the harmony changes only at the bar-line. Interestingly enough, this fact was noticed (and severely criticized) by a contemporary of Bach's whom I mentioned a moment ago, Christoph Nichelmann, who was not only a composer but was also, like Bach, a harpsichordist at Frederick's court. In 1755 Nichelmann published a treatise called *Die Melodie nach ihrem Wesen sowohl, als nach ihren Eigenschaften*. Despite its title, however, the book is really more about harmony than melody—or, to put it more exactly, about the primacy of harmony over melody. The principal influence is of course that of Rameau, whose dictum that melody has its roots in harmony Nichelmann begins by asserting in a very general form: "Every sound is already a harmony."[12] It was in the 1750s that former supporters of Rameau such as Rousseau, Diderot, and d'Alembert began to break from him, and when the arguments about harmonic theory reached Germany, Marpurg was quick to establish himself as Rameau's German champion. Nichelmann evidently was acquainted with Marpurg, for also in 1755 he contributed a brief autobiography to Marpurg's *Historisch-Kritische Beyträge*.[13] Though Nichelmann's interpretation of Rameau differs somewhat from Marpurg's, it nonetheless seems probable that Marpurg's work on Rameau's behalf stimulated Nichelmann's interest in the French theorist.

Like many moral and aesthetic writers of the 17th and 18th centuries, Nichelmann—whether consciously or no—acts on an assumed analogy between the physical world as described by Newton and the world of human intellectual and perceptual activity. Just as motion is the natural condition of matter, so harmonic motion is the natural condition of musical sound. One result of or evidence for this fact is that we all have an innate craving for harmonic change: "The basis of the delight that music gives us lies, above all, in the gratification and satisfaction of our innate demand for changing or varied harmony" (p. 5). To satisfy this craving is in fact music's *raison d'être*: "The principal and general purpose of every composition is to allay our innate demand for harmonic variety; thereby the soul is kept from weariness, and is restored to her natural happiness and activity" (p. 11).

Adopting a pair of terms from the 17th-century theorist and composer Wolfgang Caspar Printz's book *Phrynis Mitilenaeus, oder Satyrischer Componist* (1676-1679), Nichelmann calls the type of music in which harmony and melody are closely related in a satisfactory manner *polyodisch* and the type in which melody predominates at the expense of harmony (and of its relation to melody) *monodisch*. The terms, however, are misleading since the distinction they denominate has nothing to do with the number of voices employed in the piece or pieces involved. Nichelmann also uses the terms *polyodist* and *monodist* to denote the types of composers corresponding to the two types of music. "A *polyodisch* composer," explains Nichelmann, "writes for many or few voices; yet he tries to form and construct the different sequences of tones, in each particular voice, so that the different chords of the harmony are genuinely connected and united with one another" (p. 37). On the other hand, "A monodist is satisfied if he can just make the main sequence of particular tones, in one particular voice, so attractive and so splendid, through the use of all sorts of ornaments and harmonic decoration, that it will please and gratify the senses" (p. 35).

What it amounts to is that Nichelmann dislikes music in which the composer's (and hence the listener's) attention is all on the superficial beauties of an elaborately ornamented melody, and the harmony is merely a pallid backdrop; in the music he favors, melody and harmony work together satisfyingly, the harmony changing in rich and surprising ways that complement the inflections of the melodic line. Though he is a doggedly, hopelessly repetitious writer, hammering home his points time after time for a full 175 pages, one must admit that Nichelmann has a real point. Against the superficiality of much merely decorative music, particularly vocal music from Italy and France, he is groping his way toward expressing a preference for a deeper unity of musical elements that makes a fuller use of music's true power, a unity for which Romantic thinkers of a half century later would use organicist metaphors.

If Nichelmann's book remained on this general level, it would, though praiseworthy perhaps, have little interesting to tell us today. What makes it interesting is that he endlessly cites chapter and verse, producing passages from works by his contemporaries, telling exactly how they fail to fulfill his demands, and then (in many cases) actually rewriting the passages in a more satisfactory form—complete with fundamental basses, learned from his reading of Rameau. And one of the pieces on which he does a bit of rewriting is the song we just examined, C. P. E. Bach's setting of "Amint."

Nichelmann wants rapid and constant harmonic change, with modulations if possible, and is even impatient if a melody note is repeated too often. For he feels it necessary that a melody constantly exhibit its dependence upon its underlying harmony. In Chapter 47 of his book he writes:

> The value of a melody is the greater, the more it is dependent upon its harmony and subordinate to it; . . .
>
> This is so true that every melody, whether single or of many parts, pleases us more or less depending upon how clearly or unclearly it manifests the different basic chords, or harmonies, from which it is constructed.
>
> [P. 112]

He then cites the first three-and-three-quarters bars of Bach's "Amint":

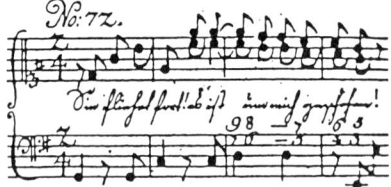

The citation is accompanied by a general pronouncement and a rhetorical question: "The successful imitation of nature is the source, and the sure indication, of all true beauty. Why does this particular song please us, and arouse just such feelings as should be aroused given the circumstances?" (p. 112).

As we might expect, Nichelmann is quick to answer his own question:

> The succession of particular tones in an effective melody, and still more its harmony, brings to our ears such relationships as are in conformity with the [melody's] main effect, as it is communicated to us. The $\frac{9}{4}$ [sic] chord in the third bar makes that impression which, according to the nature of the circumstances, it ought to make, and this impression is still more firmly established in the fourth bar, which immediately follows, when the composer, instead of moving, as expected, to the tonic, brings in the completely unexpected chord on the sixth.

All these various harmonies are also indicated completely clearly by the melody, and one needs to have heard them only once to be able to recall them when the song is repeated.

[Pp. 112-113]

As before, some of Nichelmann's statements—that such-and-such an effect or impression is just what is demanded by the circumstances, and so on—seem utterly vacuous. But I think he is onto something interesting here. He likes the suspension at the beginning of bar three to which, in the example, he correctly gives the figure $\frac{9}{7}$ but which he calls $\frac{9}{4}$ in the body of his text. If I understand him correctly, his reason for liking it is that E in the melody subtly prefigures the deceptive cadence on E minor a bar later. He admires the cadence itself because it is a surprise ("completely unexpected"), yet the fact that the melody has, in a sense, predicted it renders it a coherently understandable part of the whole. Thus it can be held in the (unconscious?) memory and recognized with pleasure the next time the piece is heard.

We might again recall Tovey's remark that almost everything in Haydn is unexpected yet nothing is difficult to follow. This is, as we have seen, what neoclassical (or "rationalist") aesthetics was all about: fusing the novel and the familiar in a surprise effect that almost immediately makes rational sense and hence is memorable—rather than merely shocking and forgettable, as randomly achieved effects are. This is also what Pope had in mind when he followed his famous (and much maligned) dictum that "*True Wit* is *Nature* to Advantage drest, / What oft was *Thought*, but ne'er so well *Exprest*," with the less famous but more illuminating lines: "*Something*, whose Truth convinc'd at Sight we find, / That gives us back the Image of our Mind."[14] For as Nichelmann's preceding statement about "The successful imitation of nature" shows, he values this sort of rational or comprehensible surprise because it is by such surprises that nature herself works, and to provide them in art is one important way in which the artist can imitate nature.

But the second phrase of Bach's song does not please Nichelmann at all. He duly cites it, through the cadence that ends the first half of the song:

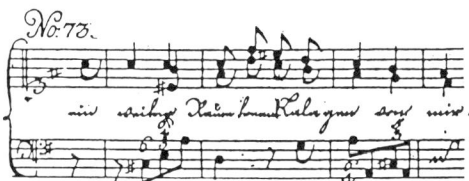

And he then asks another rhetorical question: "Why, on the contrary, does this bit of melody, when it appears, not yield a similar pleasure?" (p. 113). Once again his answer is worth citing and examining in some detail:

> It appears to interfere with the variety of the harmony, or with the harmonization itself, and manifests the fundamental chords of the harmony on which the melody depends only very obscurely, and ambiguously. Nevertheless, the A-major chord, as the subdominant triad of the preceding E chord, fits very well, and indicates very clearly the special aim of the composer, which was to give an image or idea of great distance; but the fourfold repetition, in the upper voice, of one and the same note leaves us in doubt as to which root it is really dependent upon, whether the ubiquitous A is itself a root or only a part of the harmony, and if, and at what point, whether on the upbeat or downbeat of the measure, it is one or the other?
>
> For the A that is the second quarter note in the fifth bar can just as well be the fifth of the root D as the octave of the fundamental tone A. Likewise, one can tell just

as little from the bare melody whether the first eighth note of the sixth bar is a root or a fifth.

[P. 113]

The A chord spelled out by the bass line in bar 5 is perfectly all right in itself: as the subdominant of the E-minor chord in the preceding bar, it suits its context well enough. But the melody's insistent dwelling on A leaves us in doubt, says Nichelmann, as to the relation between that pitch and the harmony: both the A on the second beat of bar 5 and the next A can be heard as either the root of the A chord that is just giving way or as the fifth of the D chord that is taking its place. This sort of ambiguity is intolerable to Nichelmann.

Therefore he rewrites these bars as follows:

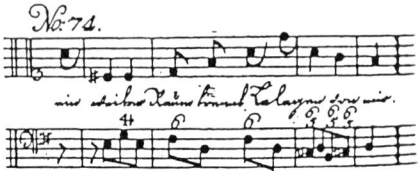

Instead of dwelling on A, the melodic line now jumps downward to the unambiguous C# while the bass line busily fills in not only the fifth but also the seventh of the chord. In the next bar the melodic line alters decisively with the harmony and then proceeds to outline the whole chord, the voice exchange with the bass line on the first beat adding a touch of the neatness the Berliners so much admired. This is how Nichelmann explains the change:

> One now makes the melody subordinate to the harmony, without however undertaking any further change than subordinating the melody to one or the other voice of the harmony or to the root. . . .
> Not only would the monotony of the melody thus be avoided; there would also be a more natural alteration of tones, and more expression would be introduced into the melody.
>
> [P. 113]

The main point is of course that the melody has been subjugated to the harmony—brought to heel, as it were—and yet without changing the harmony, without making any "further change." Thus three separate but related goals have been achieved: the monotony of the repeated A's in the melody has been eliminated, the changing (or succession?) of (melodic?) tones is now more natural than before, and the song is more expressive.

I find it difficult to see what bothers Nichelmann about the passage as Bach wrote it. It seems obvious that the A that ends bar 5 is the root of the chord while the A that begins bar 6 is the fifth of the new chord. Perhaps the trouble lies with Nichelmann's concept of "dependent." Just how temporal (or time-bound) a concept is this for him? He seems to have trouble with the idea that the same melodic note, coming just before and just after a change in harmony (and with no intervening notes) could at one moment be in one relation to the root of the chord and at the next moment in a different relation to it. Because the melody note itself does not change, the relation cannot (or ought not to) change. Moreover, that melody note is a member of the triads of both the earlier and the later chord—as the C# with which Nichelmann replaces the offending A is not: that is why the C#, unlike the A, is unambiguous and therefore satisfactory. Perhaps what Nichelmann really means by saying that a melody ought to be subordinate to its harmony is that the melody alone, viewed in isolation, should immediately make perfectly clear the harmony underlying it. It thus seems to him not only monotonous but also downright unnatural for the melody note to remain the same and yet to change its relation to the harmony as the harmony changes. But what is this phrase expressing in the first stanza of Kleist's poem? The "weiter Raum" that now separates Amint from Lalage. It seems to me that the repeated A, sounded on quarter notes, effectively dramatizes how far this distance stretches out in poor Amint's mind as he thinks about it.

Nichelmann's view of what music ought and ought not to do is thus highly abstract—he seldom considers what the text the music is expressing may be saying. Yet Nichelmann spoke for the composers who initiated the first Berlin song school. The busy and constantly changing harmony he advocated is a characteristic feature not only of his own songs but also of those found in the most important anthologies of the late 1730s through the 1760s and in the collections by such important individual forerunners of the first Berlin song movement as Telemann and Görner. Before Nichelmann's book appeared, the powerful Marpurg called his readers' attention to it in his journal *Historisch-Kritische Beyträge*, in very flattering terms, as having "a subject that deserved to be treated by a pen which, like his, has long displayed itself in the most beautiful and tasteful practical tests, to the world's applause" (I, 147-148). And the following year, after the book had been published, Marpurg printed in the same journal an extensive review that paraphrased Nichelmann's argument at length, breaking off after seven pages with the excuse that "this short abstract is sufficient to convince the reader of the author's reasonable mode of thought" (II, 268).

Marpurg's review concluded, however, with the news that Nichelmann had been replaced at Frederick's court by the young Carl Fasch (1736-1800). We do not know whether Nichelmann left Frederick's service of his own volition or was forced out, but two letters in which he asks for help in finding a new position, one of them to Telemann, survive from early 1756. Although he may fairly be said to have given a theoretical justification for the practice, especially the harmonic practice, of the Berlin songwriters—C. P. E. Bach always being an exception—Nichelmann's criticisms not only of Bach but also of such other colleagues at Frederick's court as Agricola and C. H. Graun must have stirred up a good deal of personal animosity. Indeed, one of the many replies to Nichelmann's book, *Gedanken eines Liebhabers der Tonkunst über Herrn Nichelmanns Tractat*, published in 1755 under the pseudonym "Caspar Dünkelfeind" ("Enemy-of-Conceit"), is often attributed to Bach himself. Besides, Nichelmann's preference for rich and varied harmony was not in accord with the taste of his monarch, who had no interest whatever in the developing German lied and tended to favor just the lighter sort of French music that Nichelmann abominated.

In any case, the *pièce de résistance* of Nichelmann's book is his extensive criticism, and complete bar-for-bar recomposition, of one of Bach's few through-composed songs, "Die Küsse." We shall still better understand Bach's relation to his songwriting contemporaries if we examine the song in the light of Nichelmann's complaints.

III

The poem is by Nicolaus Dietrich Giseke (1725-1765), and it runs as follows:

>Dass ich, bey meiner Lust durch keinen Zwang mich quäle,
>Und meine Küsse niemals zähle,
>Das straft Philet, der schon zu alt zum Küssen ist.
>Die Alten, lehrt er mich, die pflegten auch zu küssen;
>Allein nicht aufzuhören wissen,
>Allein, so viel, wie du, zu küssen,
>Das Laster war noch nicht bey ihnen eingerissen.
>Ich habe selbst weit sparsamer geküsst.

So soll ich denn, wann ich, Neära, dich umfange,
Und trunken von der Lust, an deinem Halse hange,
Wann mein entzückter Geist, der gern sich selbst vergisst,
Auf deinen Lippen stirbt, mich erst mit Zweifeln plagen,
Ob auch die Leute sagen,
Dass ich zu viel geküsst?

Neära hörts, und lacht, und klopft mir sanft die Wangen,
Und giebt mir einen Kuss voll jugendlicher Glut,
Dergleichen Mars von Venus nicht empfangen,
Wenn er in ihrem Arm von Siegen ausgeruht:
"Für wessen Urtheil denn, sagt sie, scheut Thyrsis sich?
"In dieser Sache wider dich,
"Ist ja kein Richter, als nur ich."

Looking at this charming poem with an eye to its possible musical settings, one is struck first by the fact that it is not a strophic poem: the three stanzas all differ from one another both in number of lines and in rhyme scheme. Therefore it will not admit of a strophic setting but only of one that is through-composed. Since this is unusual in the lyric poems (and thus in the songs) of this period, one might well want to ask why Giseke has chosen this unusual form.

The poem is, of course, yet another pastoral. Thyrsis is by now a familiar figure, and Neara is the name of a country girl mentioned by Virgil in *Eclogue* III. Philitas (sometimes spelled Philetas) was an Alexandrian grammarian who is supposed to have been the teacher of Theocritus. In *Idyll* VII (line 40) Theocritus uses the name to represent an honored older shepherd-singer. The name appears, in the accusative, in the manuscripts as φιλήταν, but was emended in the 19th century to φιλίταν—presumably to correspond to the usual spelling of the historical personage's name. It would of course have been the former spelling that Giseke knew and from which (hence) he derived his Philet.

The poem begins with a high-flown, strung-out "Dass"-clause that seems perfectly to catch the youthful ardor and recklessness of this youth who never counts his kisses. But then in line 3 we are pulled up short by "Das straft Philet." This Philet, like Theocritus's, is older and (the as-yet-unnamed speaker of the poem assumes) wiser. Those of Philet's generation also were given to kissing, he learns, but—and the force of the qualification is strongly felt in the repeated "Allein . . . Allein"—among them the vice (and "Laster" is an unexpectedly harsh word here) of doing it to excess, as the "du" being addressed apparently does, had not yet taken hold.

In the second stanza the speaker addresses Neära directly by name. "Should I then—" he begins to ask, in what at least pretends to be a serious request for advice. But at that point his syntax again becomes tied up in itself as he imagines kissing and embracing her. In his vivid evocation of the scene he forgets himself even as he is saying that that is what his spirit loves to do—until we are again pulled up short by the words "mich erst mit Zweifeln plagen." Are we or are we not to believe that this amorous youth who so easily loses himself in fantasy can really be all that worried about whether "die Leute" will disapprove of him for his excessive kissing? The finely poised wit of the poem leaves the question open.

After all this syntactic—and (perhaps pretended) emotional—complication, the easy, colloquial rhythms of the third stanza's opening line bring relief, as does the playful humor of Neära's gently cuffing him on the cheek. But then her kiss only sends him off into a high-flown mythological parallel. She brings the poem back down to colloquial rhythms (and common sense) as she simply asks why he is concerned since she alone is the judge of his kissing. The legal metaphor of judge and verdict, with its appeal to the larger public world, plays neatly against the fact that what she is stressing is, after all, the privacy of lovemaking, its inaccessibility to that public world represented by "die Leute" and "die Alten" and, indeed, Philet. The same mix of public and private can be seen in the fact that although Neära here refers to her lover by name, she does so in an impersonal third-person construction before addressing him directly, as "dich."

As to why Giseke might have chosen this unusual form for his poem, it would seem that he wanted a more fluid patterning of long and short lines than any conventional stanza could offer, and that he wanted the patterning to change in order to mirror the changes in the dramatic situation. It is indeed hard to imagine how the long high-flown speeches of Thyrsis and the more simple responses of Neära could have been captured in an ordinary stanzaic form that stayed the same throughout the poem—but I am not a poet, and this explanation does not really satisfy me. Suffice it to say that the fluidity of form, whether absolutely necessary or not, plays an important part in giving the reader a sense of Thyrsis's extreme malleability.

C.P.E. Bach's setting, first published in 1753 in the first of the two Ramler-Krause *Oden mit Melodien* volumes, was reprinted by Bach in his 1762 *Oden*:

The initial mood is one of serene, inward-turning reverie—we are reminded, perhaps, of the first Bach song we looked at, "Schäferlied." Here too we have a melody in $\frac{3}{4}$ time that moves mainly in quarter notes over a repeated tonic pedal. But after the first phrase—which, we notice, is dreamily extended to five bars—the bass line carries up an octave, and the melody, also placed higher, begins to move with greater urgency as Thyrsis turns from describing his lack of compulsion to mentioning the kisses that (he assures us as the phrase falls gently) he does not count. The words "Das straft Philet," which pulled us up short in our reading of the poem, do not do so here. Instead of producing the jolt we might have expected, they are set to a calmly ascending F arpeggio, after which the melody drops, rises, and then descends gracefully. The harshness that the word "straft" suggests is completely absent. Instead, Bach directs our attention to the unexpected D-minor cadence at m. 13, and the pause, for a full bar, on "alt." This gives the word a certain poignancy, and Philet emerges a far more sympathetic character than in the poem. But he is in no way pitiable: the reassertion of power and authority in the *forte* melody and bass line of m. 14 (after the delicate *piano* of the preceding bar) makes this clear. In fact, the comically gruff ascending bass arpeggios in mm. 15-16 and 18-19 may be heard as a whimsical suggestion of his voice as he kindly instructs Thyrsis.

Thyrsis's report of the instruction continues until m. 21, in the same calm mode as the phrase that led up to the D-minor cadence. At the word "Allein," Bach makes a major break in mood and texture that (once again) we could not have predicted from our reading of the poem. There is a note of drama, even of pathos, in the two downward arching phrases that set the two appearances of

"Allein," and the move into C minor. But the music works its way efficiently back to B-flat, and in mm. 30ff. the instruction continues with calm, unanswerable logic—again we are surprised at the absence of harshness, this time the harshness suggested by the word "Laster." Bach is letting us feel the regret that crosses Thyrsis's mind as he thinks of the intensity of Neära's kissing—which Philet is, by implication, telling him he must reject. The first stanza ends, appropriately, in the relative minor.

The music setting the poem's second stanza begins with an elaborated reprise of the song's opening: the first phrase is stated twice, and the second is varied. It is as though Thyrsis is taking special pains, as he explains to Neära what Philet has told him, to get it exactly right. It is interesting to notice that in the varied reprise of the song's second phrase (mm. 53ff.), the harmony in the keyboard's left hand is just a little fuller, more elaborate. As Thyrsis finally gets to the point—that his doubts will plague him (mm. 62ff)—the melody again takes on a note of pathos, almost of yearning or complaint. But we feel Thyrsis regaining his resolution as the music of the stanza's closing three bars (mm. 68-70) forcefully echoes the music earlier (mm. 12-15) associated with Philet's kindly lecture. And as we did there, so we end here in the dominant, F major.

Bach leads us into the poem's final stanza with a very unusual bar of descending keyboard octaves marked *staccato* (m. 71). There is no dynamic marking in either of the early prints, but it would seem that the combination of *staccato* attack, downward sweep, and minor key (for we are back in D minor) was intended to imply a certain forcefulness for the singer's entry. The first two bars, in fact, are quite dramatic, even ominous: Bach means us to be taken in, to imagine (along with Thyrsis) Neära's adverse reaction to what he has just told her. "Neära hörts"—and what will she say? Perhaps that Thyrsis is using Philet as an excuse to pull away from her, that he no longer loves her, and so on. But no: she merely laughs—her laughter mimed by the downward-tripping eighth notes in the next bar (m. 74)—and gives him that gentle knock on the cheek. She is, it turns out, far ahead of him in sophistication and understanding.

As Thyrsis begins to describe the kiss she gives him (mm. 78ff.), the ardent rising phrase from earlier in the song (cf. mm. 6 and 53) reappears, and is duly imitated in the bass. Bach turns the mythological excursus about Mars and Venus into a real production number, with elaborate suspensions in the melody and inexorably descending bass line (mm. 81-85) leading, in mm. 85-86, to a reminiscence of mm. 68-69, near the end of the preceding stanza—a passage that was itself an echo of mm. 12-13, the music associated with Philet and his teaching. The bars that follow (mm. 87-92) also echo, in a more approximate manner, Philet's teaching (mm. 19ff.) and the concern it causes in Thyrsis (mm. 65ff.). Thus the mythological flight of fancy is musically as well as verbally tied to the situation of Thyrsis, Philet, and Neära. Even the descending eighth-note arpeggio in the bass at the D-minor cadence (m. 92) is a sort of humorous inversion of the ascending ones that earlier suggested Philet's voice (mm. 15-16 and 18-19).

So we are back in D minor, and just as at the beginning of this stanza of the poem, there is a moment of pathos and doubt as the bass breaks off and the voice enters, high and alone: "Für wessen Urtheil denn" (mm. 93-94). But once again, just as there, Thyrsis's fears prove groundless. Neära's laughter returns with the descending eighth notes as she proceeds sensibly to resolve matters and bring the song swiftly to its close. Once again Bach creates an insightful musical connection by having the music to which she sings her triumphant, joyous "als nur ich, als nur ich" (mm. 101-105) closely echo that to which Thyrsis, at the end of the poem's first stanza, declared that he had become more frugal in his kissing since listening to Philet (mm. 36-40). Neära has taken the situation in hand and turned it right around—from G minor to B-flat major.

The song seems to me a brilliant performance on Bach's part, a demonstration of what he could do with a through-composed song that for a moment makes us sympathize with the 19th-century music historians' complaint that he did not write more of them. The extraordinary amount of musical allusion back and forth throughout the piece gives the interrelations of the three protagonists a far greater richness than in the poem—and, as we saw, Bach makes Philet a more sympathetic figure, more a part of the young people's lives, than he is in Giseke's poem. But what did Nichelmann have to say about this extraordinary production? A great deal more than he had to say about any of the other pieces of music he discussed. For he plainly viewed his analysis (and recomposition) of "Die Küsse" as the capping demonstration by which his theories would stand or fall.

He first mentions the song in a chapter on the inadequacies of "Monodie." He has been arguing that harmonic motion, once established in a piece, should be consistently maintained. He then cites the first five bars of "Die Küsse":

and as he does so he asks rhetorically: "Who is not struck here by the failure of the harmony, or of the tonic chord, to progress, and by the monotony that results from this failure?" (p. 85). His reasoning for this judgment will by now be familiar to us—though we perhaps could not have predicted its application to this particular passage:

> The progress or movement of the changing harmony is here firmly established in quarter notes, so that in two bars there are six changes. Now if the tonic and dominant chords were also used too much in these two bars, it is unthinkable that we could experience either one of them, at the beginning of the third bar, without a secret disgust or loathing. We are greedy for harmony that is varied and progressive. Thus the composer ought to have provided a change of harmony on the downbeat of the third bar. . . .
>
> [P. 85]

Bach, however, has not provided the required change of harmony: the third bar of the song begins on the tonic. Therefore Nichelmann recommends a change to the subdominant, which so far has not been used, thus:

In conclusion, Nichelmann asks how on earth Bach could have failed to see that his way would end in monotony rather than the desired variety, and as usual his answer is a rhetorical question cast in a curiously moralistic mode: "What else could it have been, other than that he believed himself to have discharged his duty, in regard to this composition, by composing, for himself and without a view to the harmony, a particular series of single tones in a single voice, without having to think about satisfying our hunger for a varied, richly-diversified harmony?" (p. 85). Here and elsewhere, Nichelmann's use of the word "single" in such contexts makes clear that he thinks there is something positively selfish (or at least self-absorbed) about a composer who lavishes all of his attention on a sequence of individual melodic tones as an end in itself, rather than on the organic—though he would not have used that word—unity of harmony and melody that constitutes the true, quasi-communal essence of music.

Nichelmann returns to "Die Küsse" some 30 pages later, shortly after his comments on Bach's "Sie fliehet fort." He has just been making a point very similar to the one that prompted him to bring up the song earlier, but making it by using a new (and rather interesting) metaphor: "As in music, so in all the other arts, after the first step nothing is arbitrary but everything is bound together, as in a chain, and must hang together; not only must the following progression of the harmony be based in what has preceded, but each succeeding progression must contribute to the aim of the whole, and serve the ultimate purpose which it was summoned to serve by the demand of circumstances" (pp. 116-117). But in bringing up "Die Küsse" again he adds to his argument a new dimension that makes his whole view of musical necessity and possibility not seem quite so abstract as it had done before: "The various chords of a passage of harmony must always necessarily have a relation to the tonic; but this connection becomes still greater when the sense of the words of a text, to which the music is set, demands of the harmonies a particular relation" (p. 117).

Nichelmann picks up "Die Küsse" at exactly the point where he had left it 30 pages earlier. Then he had corrected the harmony of the phrase that began in m. 3 and ended in m. 5; now he cites the words that are set in mm. 6-9, "Und meine Küsse niemals zähle," and notes that since these words are only separated by the conjunction "und" from the words preceding them, the move into the dominant that Bach makes just at this point "is far too remote for words that are so closely connected to one another" (p. 117). The momentary landing on V/V in m. 9, which Nichelmann actually refers to as a "modulation," is of course still worse. Moreover, since mm. 6-9 are, for Nichelmann, the "answer" to mm. 1-5, it is wrong of Bach to have abandoned the basic quarter-note rhythmic movement established in mm. 1-5.

Nichelmann agrees, however, that the move into D minor at m. 13 is wholly appropriate to the word "alt," because "this progression in this sequence of tones has something old-fashioned about it" (p. 118). But he finds Bach's setting of the words "Die Alten, lehrt er mich" (mm. 16-18) too drawn out—and for a very interesting reason: "Despite the fact that the generally low tones selected for the melody very naturally depict the seriousness of old Philet in the delivery of his lecture, I must not leave unnoted the fact that the composer pauses too long over the interpolated words *lehrt er mich*, and thereby not only obscures the sense of the words but also makes the melody wholly inappropriate." Both the drawing out of the word "lehrt" and the move into the subdominant in m. 17 make it seem to Nichelmann "as though the old Philet wanted to teach his pupil to know and understand the older generation, which is not at all the poet's meaning" (p. 118). Nichelmann has here caught the same note that we caught when we said that there seems less harshness in Philet's speech than we should have expected from the poem. This does indeed seem a genuine (and important) part of Bach's interpretation of the poem—but need it be a completely incorrect one? Is there perhaps not room (and evidence) for this interpretation as well as the more obvious one? I think it not only makes the poem more interesting but also works well with the other touches of psychological complexity in the treatment of the characters.

Nichelmann likes the way in which Bach's setting of the first occurrence of the word "Allein" sets that word off from its context, but then finds that the harmony in the next few bars "is much too broken up, and has too little life and movement, and therefore maintains neither the natural activity of the soul nor the type of movement that has been established" (p. 118). Once again, the harmony does not move quickly enough for him. And it is this lack of movement that dominates the music up to the move into G minor (mm. 38ff.)—though Nichelmann finds that move, like the earlier one into D minor, appropriate to the character of Philet. Once again he finds that the lack of both rhythmic and harmonic movement gives the closing bars of the first stanza "the emotional force more of tenderness than of seriousness" (p. 119). Like his earlier comment about Bach making it seem as though Philet wants Thyrsis to understand the older people's point of view, this one too seems perceptive but arbitrarily condemnatory: why can't we hear something of tenderness as well as (mild) severity in Philet's speech?

Nichelmann's main criticism of Bach's setting of the poem's second stanza is that the series of six three-bar phrases that extend from m. 53 through m. 70 create a "new meter" that has "no relation to any of the parts that have come before" (p. 119). But this is not true: the second phrase of the song (mm. 3-5) and those two phrases that Nichelmann had objected to, in which Thyrsis describes Philet's teaching ("Die Alten . . . auch zu küssen," mm. 16-21), are important three-bar phrases. Anyway, even if true, the objection would be hopelessly arbitrary—what, one wonders, would Nichelmann have made of Haydn's playing with phrase-lengths? Equally arbitrary is Nichelmann's next objection, that at the beginning of the third stanza Bach has set the opening line in a four-bar phrase even though he used a five-bar phrase for the opening line of each of the preceding two stanzas: "Now although the poet has retained the same number of syllables at the beginning of this stanza, the composer has nonetheless changed his meter" (p. 119). This has, Nichelmann seriously believes, disrupted "the necessary similarity of the parts within the whole" (p. 119).

There are a number of other, localized objections before Nichelmann arrives at the end of "Die Küsse." Of mm. 76ff. he writes: "Not only is the prevailing movement of the harmony in quarter notes disrupted at the words *und giebt mir einen Kuss*, etc.; but this dissimilarity is increased in what follows because the meter is altered and disrupted by the repeated slowing of the harmonic rhythm" (p. 119). But of course the rhythm of the phrases in question alludes first to that of mm. 16-21 and 29-35, and then to that of mm. 6-9 and 53-59. And, as we have seen, Bach uses such allusions to make points related to the content of the poetic text. Nichelmann also finds that "an annoying monotony" (p. 120) results from Bach's using the same harmony for "Wangen" (m. 75) and "empfangen" (m. 86)—even though far greater monotony would result if one followed his stipulations about maintaining harmonic rhythm as strictly as he seems to want Bach to have done. And he objects to Bach's having disrupted the meter once again, in mm. 85-92, by having written a six-bar phrase.

Generally, Nichelmann finds that the large number of "secondary chords" and the swiftness of the ending obscure the clarity of the tonic's primacy. "A composition consists of either many or few parts," he writes, "but the tonic must stand out, and must especially be established so firmly before the end that one feels unambiguously from which tone the piece has emerged, and at the end nothing more is demanded" (p. 120). Another cause of confusion and lack of clear tonal coherence is the fact that the cadences are unequally spaced: the first one is the F cadence in m. 15, which is followed 27 bars later by the G-minor cadence in m. 42, which is in turn followed 28 bars later by the F cadence in m. 70, the D-minor cadence another 21 bars later in m. 92, and finally the concluding B-flat cadence another 13 bars later in m. 105. These are Nichelmann's numbers, but they add up to 104, not 105, bars. He either miscounted between his third and fourth cadences or (more likely) decided not to count the transitional m. 71, the descending keyboard scale in octaves that leads into the final stanza of the poem.

So how did Nichelmann deal with these various difficulties in his rewriting of Bach's song? It is interesting that while he printed out all 111 bars of his version, he did not think it necessary to print any more of Bach's original than the first five bars. Evidently he thought that Bach's song was familiar (or at least accessible) enough to his readers that he could bring it back to their minds by furnishing just those five bars. But he proudly printed out every bar of his revised version, and did so on three staves, the bottom one of which contained, as a gesture of homage to Rameau, the "fundamental bass" of each chord. There is certainly no need to work through Nichelmann's version, bar by bar; a few illustrative comparisons with Bach's original will show clearly enough how he put his theories into practice.

Take first the song's opening. Here, once again, is Bach:

Earlier we noted that the change in texture at m. 6–the move to a higher register, the speeding up of the melody–captured the increasing urgency in Thyrsis's voice as he turned from describing his lack of compulsion to actually mentioning his kisses. But Nichelmann objected that the phrase ending in m. 5 and the one beginning in m. 6 are joined only by the movement of the earlier phrase. He therefore rewrote the first nine bars thus:

Though he insisted on moving to the subdominant in m. 3 in order to avoid monotony in the harmony, he created rhythmic and melodic monotony in mm. 6-9 by retaining the quarter-note movement and having the bass echo it in mm. 6-7. More important, Nichelmann's steadily plodding version completely misses Thyrsis's heightened urgency.

Generally speaking, this difference is typical of those between Bach's original song and Nichelmann's recomposition. Though most of Nichelmann's book is taken up by endless repetitions of the need to create harmonic variety and diversity, at least as much of his energy is spent on preserving textural uniformities of various sorts. Thus his music is far less responsive to the moment-to-moment inflections of the poem than is Bach's.

Another example is provided by the two composers' handling of the two lines of Philet's little sermon that begin with the word "allein." Here, once again, is Bach's version:

Here too, as we saw earlier, we have a sudden break in texture–though one that we might not have predicted from the text of the poem. The two gracefully arching unaccompanied phrases that set "allein," the high thin harmony, and the move into C minor all bring out the tenderness and regret– rather than the harshness the poem leads us to expect–with which Philet delivers his sermon. But Nichelmann, as we saw, characteristically finds that the harmony lacks "life and movement." Therefore he adds some that is both thick and busy:

This of course utterly wrecks the quiet, contemplative moment created by Bach—but then, as we saw, Nichelmann's interpretation of Philet and his message differed from Bach's.

But the most spectacular (and unexpected) change Nichelmann made in Bach's song comes at its end. Bach, we recall, made the ending quick and witty, to express the good-humored efficiency with which Neära resolves the situation:

For once—one would have thought—the harmony is varied enough, and changes quickly enough, to please even Nichelmann. But no. As we saw, he reserved his severest reproaches for the ending of "Die Küsse." The tonic must be firmly and unambiguously established at the end of a piece, and Nichelmann feels that both the speed of Bach's ending and the large number of "secondary chords" he employs interfere with this process. Here then is Nichelmann's revised ending:

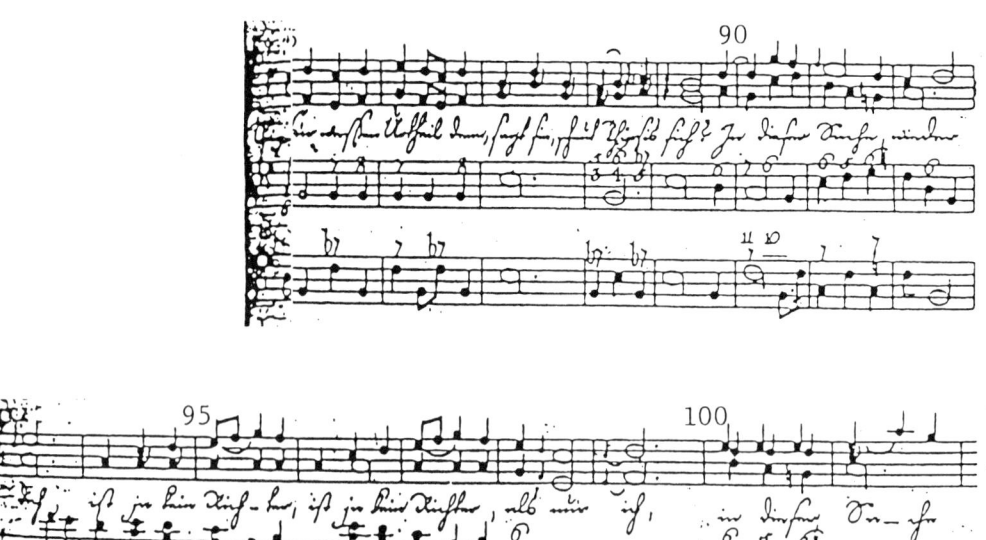

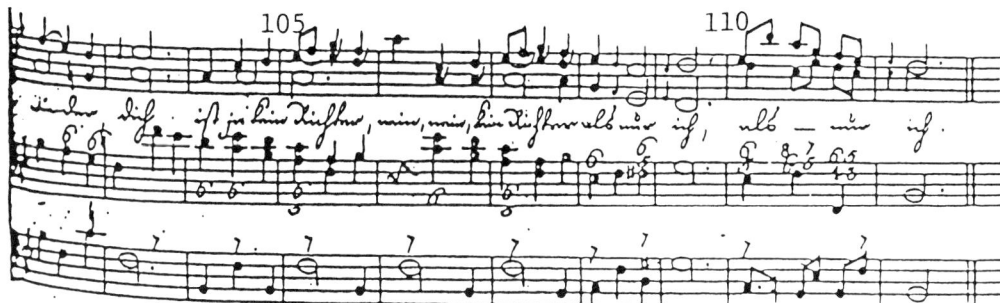

This seems to me not just odd but quite mad. Nichelmann has taken 27 bars, almost exactly a quarter of his 111-bar song, to set the last three lines of a 21-line poem. Quite aside from the dullness and repetitiousness of the music, the excessive length of the passage is so out of proportion with the rest of the song as to dislocate completely any expressive relation between *Ton* and *Wort*. Once the appropriate adjustments of scale have been made, the ending to Beethoven's Fifth looks modest and understated by comparison. Why should Nichelmann, apostle of constant and rapid harmonic change, have chosen to end this song, the principal demonstration piece of his book, by harping so unremittingly on the tonic and a couple of other closely related chords?

Precisely because he was the apostle of harmonic change, and because he too had come under the influence of Horace's doctrine of the need for works of art to balance or reconcile unity and variety. The tonal system can be viewed as a machine for unifying pieces of music. It offers the composer a hierarchy of chords that enable him to depart from, and then return to, his chosen tonal center in a satisfying way—to create, in short, what Parry called "harmonic design." But unity and design, as we all know, can become boring if unrelieved by variety, novelty, and surprise. Nichelmann, for reasons of his own, fixed obsessively upon harmony as the great and necessary source of this variety. What then was to furnish the unity? Obviously, the other musical elements: rhythm, phrasing, and so on. Thus, as we saw, he repeatedly (and quite arbitrarily) found fault with the frequent changes in texture that Bach made, in response to what he took to be the constantly changing expressive demands of Giseke's poem.

Nichelmann is of course an extreme case. Yet he is useful because he reinforces our sense of what made Bach, as a composer of songs, very different from his north German contemporaries. Even in as skilled a composer as Görner, we can see that the harmony changes more quickly, and the rhythm and phrasing tend to be more uniform, than in Bach. For some of the same reasons that he was more inward-turning and less theatrical than the Classical song-composers of a couple of decades later, Bach also tended to take a more relaxed approach to harmonic rhythm than the so-called Berlin composers, to be more concerned with expressing the moment-to-moment changes in a poem—insofar as one could do this in a strophic song—and less content to surrender to the abstract musical considerations of change and continuity that drive the work of a composer like Görner as well as the theories of Nichelmann. Let us turn now to Bach's 1758 settings of Gellert's *Geistliche Oden und Lieder*, the collection in which he found his true voice as a composer of songs.

Chapter Nine

The Gellert Songs

At the beginning of Chapter Two we noted that C. P. E. Bach not only waited until he was in his late 20s to begin composing songs, but that he also took a long time to become accustomed to the genre—during the years 1741-1755, we recall, he wrote only about nine songs. Meanwhile, his output of instrumental works increased at an astonishing rate. Therefore while he made a distinctive contribution to the north German song literature during the period when the first Berlin song school was establishing itself, what stands out is how small, quantitatively, that contribution was. This situation changed suddenly and dramatically when he encountered the *Geistliche Oden und Lieder* of Christian Fürchtegott Gellert.

I

According to Gudrun Busch, that encounter probably took place in early 1756.[1] By then Gellert (1715-1769) was a famous and most popular author. Born in Saxony, he came to Leipzig in 1734 to study at the university. But after four years the poverty of his family forced him to break off his studies and go to work. In 1741 he returned to Leipzig, where he soon came under the influence of Gottsched. As he was completing two degrees, he published his first works: *Lieder* (1743), a collection of anacreontic lyrics; and two pastoral plays, *Das Band* (1744) and *Sylvia* (1745). He then assumed the post of university lecturer in poetry and rhetoric. His next works were a series of prose comedies: *Die Betschwester* (1745), *Das Loos in der Lotterie* (1747), and *Die zärtlichen Schwestern* (1747); two collections of fables (1746, 1748); and a highly acclaimed "novel of sensibility," *Das Leben der schwedischen Gräfin von G**** (1747-1748). In these, his most famous works, the influences operating on him were Horace, Pope, and La Fontaine—the same influences operating on his friend Hagedorn—and, in addition, Richardson (*Pamela* had appeared in 1740). But shortly after this there was a dramatic change in Gellert's life.

The details are not clear, but Gellert's friend and first biographer, Johann Andreas Cramer, tells us that from the summer of 1752 on, "the terrible malady, hypochondria" made Gellert's life "one of permanent misery." Cramer's moving account continues:

> He suffered constant chest pains, and in all his activities the powers of his soul were oppressed by the most burdensome physical listlessness. He seldom experienced the happiness that tends to accompany the free and healthful circulation of the blood and other bodily fluids. An extreme sadness and an insurmountable depression spread from the hidden source of his sick life over his whole spirit.[2]

At some point during this period Gellert's university appointment was extended to cover morals as well as poetry and rhetoric, and gradually the man whose books of fables had been the most widely read collections of poetry in Germany, the man whose verses had made all classes of German readers laugh, turned his attention to moral instruction and became the sickly, dour, pathetic figure described by Cramer. *Lehrgedichte und Erzählungen* appeared in 1754, and the posthumously published *Moralische Vorlesungen* (1770) became the book upon which Gellert's subsequent reputation was based.

That reputation had nothing to do with his earlier, completely different one; nor indeed had it anything to do with art or his artistic gifts. For during his last years and after his death Gellert was celebrated—canonized, almost—as a moral teacher and exemplar, the perfect embodiment of the virtuous Christian life, a sort of Pietist saint. As his first and middle names attest, Gellert was the son of a pastor. But he had no known connection with Pietism before he was stricken with hypochondria and, in the fall of 1757, with a serious lung ailment that was never to leave him. It was also in 1757 that he published his *Geistliche Oden und Lieder*.

In 1751, as Gudrun Busch shows, Ernst Samuel Jacob Borchward (1717-1776), a government official residing in Berlin who was a friend of both Gellert and C. P. E. Bach, invited Gellert to visit him. It may have been during that visit, Busch conjectures, that Gellert and Bach met. In 1753 Gellert was again invited to visit Berlin, this time by the aesthetician and lexicographer Johann Georg Sulzer (1720-1779). Whether or not the visit took place is apparently not known; poor Gellert's characteristic response, in a letter to Sulzer, rather makes one doubt it:

> If I can attain, this winter, only some degree of the happiness from which I have relapsed, then I shall respond personally, during the coming spring, to your most kind invitations, your love, and the compassion of your Wilhelmine. May God grant that I once again taste this joy![3]

Soon after this Gellert began work on the *Geistliche Oden und Lieder*, and in the spring of 1755 he sent drafts of 31 of the poems to Cramer for criticisms.[4] On October 24 of the same year he sent the same 31 poems to Borchward, remarking "I have sent these to no one but Cramer and Gärtner" (*Sämmelte Schriften* [1839], VIII, 146)—Gärtner being Karl Christian Gärtner (1712-1791), a school friend of Gellert's who was editor of *Neue Beiträge zum Vergnügen des Verstandes und Witzes* (1745-1748), the journal of the "Bremer Beiträger." In a letter of December 22 Gellert thanked Borchward for his criticisms, complained about his own failing powers—"For me everything is hard, very hard" (VIII, 153)—but promised to send 20 more poems soon. Though he had specifically asked that no copies of the poems be made, Gellert learned that they were now being discussed in Berlin drawing rooms, and in a letter of the following June 3 he complained about it to Borchward. Gudrun Busch sums up the situation: "Thus despite his precautions, Gellert's religious poems were known in Berlin in early 1756, and Bach might have encountered them at the house of either Sack or Borchward" (p. 61). (August Heinrich Wilhelm Sack was a prominent Berlin churchman.)

Whenever or however Bach got to know Gellert's *Geistliche Lieder und Oden*, they must have made a strong impression on him. For while Gellert's poems would be set by many composers over the following half century, right down to Beethoven's *Sechs Lieder von Gellert* of 1803, Bach was, I believe, the only one to provide a setting for every poem in the book. Gellert wrote 54 poems; Bach, dividing one of the poems in half, wrote 55 songs. In his preface he tells us explicitly how this came about: "For my part, I was so struck by the quality of the sublime, instructive thoughts with which these poems are filled, that I could not restrain myself from writing melodies for all of them, without exception." This from a man who had not yet produced a dozen songs in his whole career! Moreover, he must have worked quite quickly. Gellert's book appeared in April 1757; Bach's preface is dated February 1, 1758.

Before we turn to his settings, it will be helpful to look at Gellert's own preface, which is a most interesting document—especially in light of the reputation as a sort of patron saint of sensibility that was to engulf him immediately after his death. Though he often complained in his letters of failing powers, his preface exhibits a sharp mind working at top form, a mind accustomed to the dialectic of academic essays and lectures, a mind (what is more) peculiarly revealing about literary and intellectual currents in mid-18th-century Germany.

To begin with, the preface is unexpectedly long: a little over seven pages of closely reasoned prose in the standard editions of Gellert's works. He first insists upon what he sees as the contemporary poet's duty to religion. But he is careful to do it in an elaborately roundabout manner, in order to protect himself from accusations of being a narrow fanatic interested only in poetry's paraphrasable content and insensitive to its other, specifically poetic, qualities:

> If the language of poetry is especially capable of animating the imagination, engaging the understanding in an agreeable manner, and lightening the work of memory; if it is capable of setting the heart in motion and arousing, or maintaining, feelings of joy, love, wonder, sympathy, and pain: then it is undoubtedly one of the great duties of poets to dedicate this power of poetry above all to the truths and the feelings of religion.
>
> [*Sämmelte Schriften,* II, 61]

Gellert's listing, in his first clause, of the various functions of poetic language, moves gradually from the purely artistic to the everyday, from enlivening the imagination through engaging the understanding to easing the work of memory. The last stage is a little puzzling—we are not yet sure just what sort of relief he is saying poetry affords the memory—but the faculties are arranged in a clear "outside-in" sequence, precisely the reverse of the "inside-out" order in which they were always dealt with in books of empiricist epistemology or psychology, such as Hobbes's *Leviathan*, Locke's *Essay concerning Human Understanding*, and Hume's *Treatise of Human Nature* and *Enquiry concerning Human Understanding*. For the philosophers saw it as their task to build up a picture of man's mental functioning by beginning with memory, which merely stores sense experiences, and moving through reason, which performs such operations as abstraction upon them, to imagination, which arranges them in new combinations. But Gellert wants to move back home, from the far-flung poetic imagination to the prosaic memory.

In his second clause, he first pays homage to poetry's power to move the heart—a phrase very common at the time, as we have seen—and then enumerates the various emotions poetry is commonly held to arouse: joy, love, wonder, sympathy, sorrow. Then at last, after the carefully placed colon, Gellert is ready to make his great claim: that in light of everything that has been said, it is unarguably the duty of poets to devote the power of poetry first and foremost to the truths and—please note—the feelings of religion. Gellert neatly tucks the word "Empfindungen" into that last phrase as one final bit of insurance against any reader's taking him for the sort of narrowly literal-minded Christian who wants to reduce poetry to a barren restatement of mere "Wahrheiten."

In the sentences that follow, he reinforces this emphasis by continuing to speak the language of feeling and taste:

> Since, moreover, song has great power over our hearts, and is just as natural an expression of certain feelings as are the looks and movements of the face, one should especially consecrate to religion that sort of poetry which can be sung.
>
> [II, 61]

Because the addition of music intensifies the emotional power of poetry, just as facial expressions and gestures intensify the impact of speech, it is the further duty of poets to consecrate to religion the sort of poetry that is suitable to be set to music. This is what Gellert has sought to provide in the present collection. If, he tells us, still speaking the language of feeling and taste, he has managed "to further the edification of the reader, to increase the taste (*Geschmack*) for religion, and to inspire in hearts feelings of piety" (II, 61-62), this success will mean more to him than would the fame of the greatest heroic poet or the most eloquent philosopher. Just as Scaliger said he would rather have written a certain ode of Horace's than been king of Aragon, so Gellert says he knows certain old "Kirchengesänge" that he would rather have created, along with their melodies, than all the odes of Horace and Pindar.

It is worth recalling that only four years earlier Ramler had asserted, in the preface to the 1753 *Oden mit Melodien*, that certain poems were "too rich in images," possessed "too many complicated jokes and too much elegant moral instruction," and were too varied in their formal structure to suit the requirements of music. What poets, he had asked, are more beautiful, and yet less suited to musical setting, than Horace and Pindar? One cannot help wondering—especially since Gellert later uses the nominal form of Ramler's somewhat unusual adjective "bilderreich"—if he is here alluding, though rather obliquely to be sure, to Ramler's preface and, by implication, the whole first Berlin song movement. For Ramler had taken the odes of Horace and Pindar as the examples *par excellence* of poems that are too fine, too supremely poetic, to be set to music. Gellert seems to be saying that there is no such conflict between poetry and music—or at least between the sort of poetry and the sort of music that interest him. The musical setting is merely the completion of the poem's expressive work.

This sort of poetry and music—for both are combined in his phrase "geistliches Lied"—is, he admits, at present not valued highly. It is this fact that has led poets to neglect the duty that Gellert has just outlined and that he has taken upon himself in preparing this collection. But what is responsible for the prevailing low opinion of sacred poetry and music? It is this question that Gellert next addresses.

Many sacred songs—and at this point Gellert shifts to the word "Gesänge"—are indeed bad, he admits. For many men who have attempted this sort of work, while pious and honorable, have no gift for poetry. And, Gellert insists, it is not enough merely to be pious: "a pious man, merely by virtue of being pious, will not meet with success in poetry if he is not acquainted with her rules and is not gifted with any poetic genius" (II, 63). What is interesting here is the careful balancing of "Regeln" and "Genie": neither knowledge of one's craft nor native talent is, by itself, enough; one must have both to be a poet. Moreover, the required knowledge is knowledge of rules. This, of course, comes straight from Horace and is characteristic of neoclassical aesthetics. As we saw in Chapter Four, however, the word *rule* has had somewhat the same effect on many historians of aesthetics as a red cape usually has on a bull. They have concluded that any use of the concept of a rule in talking about art suggests that merely learning a list of rules or specifications is enough, that no native talent is necessary.

A good neoclassical thinker, however, is usually quick to provide a context that will head off this sort of misreading—and that is precisely what Gellert now proceeds to do:

> One can have a good heart, along with understanding and knowledge, and yet have terrible taste. One can express oneself unnaturally, incorrectly, and strangely when one speaks of the holy truths in the language of poetry, and yet mean [*meynen*] well.

[II, 63]

Like his master Gottsched before him, Gellert very clearly distinguishes the taste that is (by implication) necessary for an effective understanding and application of the rules of poetry from both knowledge and understanding in the ordinary senses of those terms. In his next sentence Gellert seems to go a step further. One can, he tells us, express oneself unnaturally, incorrectly (so much, it would seem, for rules!), and strangely when one is speaking in poetic language of the truths of scripture, and yet ("doch") one can have good intentions and/or convey his meaning effectively. The problem, of course, is *meynen,* which has the same central ambiguity as the English word *mean*: both words can refer merely to an intention to communicate or signify something or to a successful act of communication or signification. It seems to me that Gellert does not want merely the sense of intend here—otherwise he would not have used "doch." For from what he has so far said, it is perfectly obvious that one could express oneself unnaturally, incorrectly, and oddly or quixotically yet still have good intentions. For the adversative force of "doch" to make sense, "meynen" must mean more than simply intend. Under certain circumstances, perhaps brought about here by the very special nature of the religious truths Gellert is considering, the rules—or what had formerly been taken for rules—may be jettisoned without damage to the resulting poem. If this seems odd or self-contradictory, that is only because historians of aesthetics have inclined us to take an unfairly limited and disapproving view of neoclassical criticism and aesthetics. Gellert, it seems to me, is only saying here what Pope had already said more fully and clearly in the passages cited earlier from *An Essay on Criticism*.

Gellert's third explanation of how and why one can go wrong in writing sacred poetry is of less interest: "If one is not accustomed to wearing the chains of poetry, and to overcoming the multitude of her difficulties, one can write devotional poems that are forced, miserable, and cold, and yet nonetheless be a good, yes, even a great, orator" (II, 63). Gellert is doubtless thinking of preachers famed for their pulpit eloquence who turn their hand to poetry. It is interesting, however, that as our point of view shifts, rules once again assume a vital importance, becoming now "the chains of poetry," the emblems of a formal discipline necessary if one is not to produce poems that are cold and contrived. For Gellert as for Pope, rules can be seen as necessary or as dispensable, depending upon the swing of the dialectical pendulum.

It is only now, having made it clear that "it does not depend merely upon our good heart, not merely upon understanding and erudition, not even upon eloquence alone if we wish to compose religious poems" (II, 63), that Gellert reaches the heart of his argument:

> Another reason why we in our day should perhaps work harder on behalf of religious poetry is that the taste in poetry and eloquence has changed very much during our century. Much that was allowable, customary, and inoffensive in the language of our fathers, and in their way of thinking, no longer is so in our day.
>
> [II, 63]

It is not, then, simply that the composition of sacred poetry is in itself a difficult task: recent changes in taste have made it still more difficult—and therefore still more urgently necessary to undertake. In the long paragraph that follows, Gellert repeatedly harps on the word "Väter," until the changes of taste that have taken place in the first half of the 18th century are made to seem volitional acts of filial ingratitude—if not outright patricide.

Though Gellert recognizes clearly that German taste in poetry and rhetoric has improved in recent years owing to the reforms undertaken by Gottsched and his disciples—of whom, we must not forget, Gellert himself was one—he nonetheless has a haunting sense that while something has certainly been gained, something has, perhaps, been lost: "when our manners become more elegant, we are disgusted by a negligent, indiscriminate, flat style of writing" (II, 64). And just as he has done throughout, Gellert is careful to express his feelings about this matter in a way that prevents the reader from classifying him as a reactionary by immediately making clear his ambivalence: "I do not wholly approve of this disgust; yet I also do not approve of the fact that we are not more eager to resist it" (II, 64). But as he goes on, the ambivalence gradually hardens into a clear sense that the loss has been more significant than the gain.

Do we not still have among us, he asks rhetorically, a large number of good old preachers? Why then should we automatically approve only what is new? "The taste in oratory has changed and improved; and many people can no longer tolerate the rough and disordered language, and the careless expression, of our fathers" (II, 64). Still more emphatically: whoever rejects the sacred songs of Lutheran tradition, "in order to support only those that are newer, is behaving ungratefully to our fathers, and coldly toward the edification they created" (II, 64). After citing a couple of examples of these old hymns, Gellert comes fully into the open; of one such passage he writes:

> It has much that is harsh, judged by our present dialect, and inversions that are strange to us; and yet, who can sing or read it without being moved, without feeling his soul pierced by thanks and humility? It is worth more than the whole volumes of new songs that have no other virtue than that they are pure. And why is this passage, despite its harshness, so beautiful? Because the expression is strong and powerful, because the content of the thought is great, and yet the thought is not over-extended; because the brevity and the vigor excuse the harshness; because the inversions do not interfere with clarity but rather heighten one's attentiveness.
>
> [II, 65]

A reader of English literature is reminded of such almost exactly contemporary works as Thomas Warton's *Observations on the Fairie Queene of Spenser* (1754), the first volume of his brother Joseph Warton's *Essay on the Writings and Genius of Pope* (1756), and Richard Hurd's *Letters on Chivalry and Romance* (1762). The English writers too were made uneasy by the extreme polish and correctness of contemporary manners and letters, for they too had a feeling that something important from the past had been lost in the process of attaining all this quite admirable civilization. But there is an important difference. Gellert looks back longingly to the clarity, brevity, directness, even roughness of the verse of Luther and those who followed him. The English, on the other hand, yearn for the imaginative freedom and extravagance of Spenser's great allegory and Shakespeare's tragedies and romances, the grandeur and sublimity of Miltonic epic. Thomas Warton saw the English poetry of the preceding half century as a poetry "in which imagination gave way to correctness, sublimity of description to delicacy of sentiment, and majestic imagery to conceit and epigram," while Hurd closed his book with the famous lament: "What we have gotten by the revolution, you will say, is a great deal of good sense. What we have lost, is a world of fine fabling."

For the English writers, the enemy is common sense, prosiness, and (in a very vague sense) science; they want a more elaborately fanciful and more richly ornamented poetry. But for Gellert the enemy is precisely richness of ornamentation, the grand manner affected by poets who have read their Horace and Pindar, and have trafficked with a courtly society:

> Religious songs must be dominated by a certain strength of expression that is not akin to the splendor and ornamentation of poetry but is rather the language of feeling, the language of the thinking mind. Neither richness of imagery [*Bilderreiche*] nor lofty and splendid figures of speech can be well sung and easily transformed into feeling. They fill the imagination so full that the heart receives nothing.
>
> [II, 66]

The language that must predominate in sacred poetry and song is for Gellert not the language of fanciful invention but the language of Luther's translation of the Bible, "this inimitable language, full of divine loftiness and delightful simplicity" (II, 66). One could not ask for a better illustration of the difference between the German and English 18th centuries.

It is, incidentally, in elaborating his view of the sort of language he desiderates in sacred poetry and song that Gellert at last clears up a question he had earlier raised in our minds. In the opening paragraph of his preface, we recall, he had spoken of the ability of poetic language to animate the imagination, engage the understanding, and ease the work of memory—and the precise significance of that last phrase had not been clear to us. He concludes his praise of Luther's translation of the Bible thus: "often it most irresistibly calls back the truths, teachings, promises, and threats of religion to the memory, or renews our conception of them in the understanding in the most lively and effective manner" (II, 66). This too is standard neoclassical doctrine. Even the simplest and most familiar truths of morals and religion, precisely because they are so simple and so familiar, are easy to forget or to lose track of mentally, so that we cease to act on them as we should. Therefore they need constantly to be rekindled, to be given fresh life in our minds and hearts—and this is what poetic language, especially when reinforced by music, can do.

In the preceding chapter I mentioned Pope's famous lines: "*True Wit* is *Nature* to Advantage drest, / What oft was *Thought*, but ne'er so well *Expresst*" (*An Essay on Criticism*, 297-298). They are easy lines to make fun of because they seem to reduce poetry precisely to that bland restatement of accredited sentiment that Gellert is at pains to say it is not. Even Dr. Johnson made fun of them, noting in the "Life of Cowley" that "Pope's account of wit is undoubtedly erroneous: he depresses it below its natural dignity, and reduces it from strength of thought to happiness of language." But to say this is to ignore the couplet that immediately follows, and that explains Pope's meaning more precisely: "*Something*, whose Truth convinc'd at Sight we find, / That gives us back the Image of our Mind." (299-300). This is just what Gellert has in mind when he speaks of poetic language easing the work of the memory: the poet has the power to fuse strength of thought with happiness of language so as to provide an image that is irresistible because it combines the familiar and the new, presenting the familiar truth we have let slip away from us in a new guise that recalls the truth to us—i.e., "gives us back the Image of our Mind." Johnson, it is worth recalling, praised *The Rape of the Lock* above Pope's other poems because "In this work are exhibited, in a very high degree, the two most engaging powers of an author. New things are made familiar, and familiar things are made new."[5]

This talk of sacred poetry's function as a religious and moral teacher leads Gellert to distinguish between two kinds of sacred poems: "Lehroden," in which instruction predominates, and "Oden für das Herz," which are dominated by feeling. Each has its own style: "In *Lehroden* clarity and brevity must be predominant; in the other sort, the language of the heart, language that is lively, urgent, fiery, and yet always comprehensible" (II, 66). For understanding or intelligence ("Verstand") must, Gellert insists, be present in both sorts of odes if they are to perform their educational function. It is because instruction counts more, and pleasure at least somewhat less, than in other sorts of poetry that sacred songs can tolerate some of the seeming stylistic imperfections noted in the "old songs" cited earlier:

> Since religious songs do not have pleasure as their main purpose, as do other sorts of poetry, one should be less concerned about beautiful sound than about energy and power. Let the ear be hurt by a little harshness, by a dropped *e,* by an imperfect rhyme—so long as the heart gains thereby. A small error, without which a greater beauty could not be attained, ceases in that context to be an error.
>
> [II, 67]

Once again one is reminded of *An Essay on Criticism*:

> Great Wits sometimes may *gloriously offend,*
> And *rise* to *Faults* true *Criticks dare not mend*;
> From *vulgar Bounds* with *brave Disorder* part,

> And *snatch* a *Grace* beyond the reach of Art,
> Which, without passing thro' the *Judgment*, gains
> The *Heart*, and all its End *at once* attains.
>
> [152-157]

In other words, the end justifies the means.

Finally, Gellert concludes his preface, somewhat surprisingly, by saying that he has already picked out the musical settings for the majority of his 54 poems:

> For most of these poems I have thought of chorale melodies, of which I have appended a catalogue at the end of the book; as the declamation of an orator gives life to his speech, so it is often the melody that first gives a poem its full power. A great deal can become more affecting and more gentle through song than it was in the reading; and many poems must be considered mainly from this point of view. If not all of the present poems are well adapted to musical setting, it will be sufficient recompense for me if they can be read with edification.
>
> [II, 68]

And sure enough, when one turns to the end of the *Geistliche Oden und Lieder*, one finds that Gellert has assigned, with some duplication, 26 traditional chorale melodies to 33 of his 54 poems. But is this really surprising? Though he has, throughout the preface, striven (and quite successfully) to sound like a modern, feelings-oriented theorist of poetry, Gellert's main thrust, the undercurrent of his preface as it were, has been that tradition must, at least in the area of sacred poetry and song, be preserved and revitalized to meet the challenges posed by the new age of sensibility and refinement. Considered in this light, his having chosen traditional melodies for the majority of his poems seems perfectly justified.

But what are we to make of his final sentence? Is he merely being modest in suggesting that perhaps certain of his poems—presumably the 21 for which he did not choose melodies were those slated for exclusion—are not really suited for musical setting? Or is there a veiled attempt to force any prospective composer's hand, by suggesting that only traditional chorale tunes (or perhaps new ones formed on their model) will do for these poems? Gellert was certainly aware of the burgeoning first Berlin song movement, and one would expect him not to look too kindly on its highly secular, wine-women-and-song character—an expectation that would be borne out if indeed he was, on the occasions mentioned, alluding to Ramler's preface to the 1753 *Oden mit Melodien*.

One can gather a few hints of his feelings in the matter from his letters. On June 3, 1756, in the letter in which he complained to Borchward that news of his songs had spread in Berlin, Gellert touched on the question of musical settings:

> I have now and then added melodies to which the poems may be sung, but I have often omitted to do so since none occurred to me; but many, if they are indeed to be sung, must first be given their harmony by the hand of a competent composer. This service I hope to obtain easily—if it has to be.
>
> [VIII, 145]

Apparently, he had been experimenting with already existing melodies, but had had no success in fitting them to his poems. He had then concluded that it would take a clever composer indeed to give him just what he wanted. But his final sentence suggests that the thought that the task of finding such a composer might only add to his already heavy burdens has suddenly depressed him into shrugging off the whole idea of musical settings ("if it has to be").

II

Bach's settings, as we should by now expect and as we shall soon see, were very far indeed from chorale tunes. How then did Gellert react to them? On March 25, 1758, probably very soon after receiving an early copy from Bach, Gellert wrote to his sister:

> Bach, a chamber musician in Berlin, has set all of my poems to music, and has recently sent me a copy. Herr von Zedtwitz and Herr von Schönberg played some of them, and the gracious lady sang. They are beautiful, but too beautiful for a singer who is not musical.
>
> [VIII, 247]

Of Gellert's reaction as he expressed it directly to Bach, we have only a rather cryptic fragment that Christian Friedrich Daniel Schubart included in his *Deutsche Chronik auf das Jahr 1774*: "The best poem [*Lied*], without the melody that belongs to it, is a loving heart lacking the wife who animates his feelings and in whom he awakens hers."[6] Max Friedlaender takes this as unequivocal praise: "Very warm indeed are Gellert's words of thanks to Bach, whose settings of his poems delighted him."[7] But this judgment seems to me questionable. Without more of a supporting context, I think it is impossible to say whether this is high praise or sly evasion. Gellert, after all, is here merely repeating in metaphorical form what he had already said quite clearly in his preface: an appropriate melody is the expressive completion or complement of a poem. He is not saying, at least in the fragment we possess, whether or not Bach's melodies are appropriate to his poems.

Gudrun Busch's judgment seems closer to the mark: "Soft tones of consternation are mingled with Gellert's joy; he expected chorale melodies rather than pretentious songs that are 'too beautiful'" (p. 64). In fact, I am tempted to go a step further. Gellert's deepest concern, in his preface, was with sacred song as a tool of public religious education ("Erbauung"). This would suggest, at the very least, that he wanted musical settings simple enough to be sung in the home by ordinary, not necessarily "musical," believers. But it might very well suggest further that he envisioned chorale settings that would render his poems suitable for congregational singing during sacred service.

Certainly that was what Gellert's friend Johann Friedrich Doles thought he wanted. Doles (1715-1797) had been a student of Johann Sebastian Bach's. During his student years he had briefly been director of the Leipzig Grosses Konzert, which would later become the Gewandhaus Orchestra, and in 1744 he had become Kantor at Freiburg. In 1755, upon the death of Johann Gottlieb Harrer, J. S. Bach's successor as Kantor of the Leipzig Thomaskirche, Doles applied for the job and was chosen unanimously and without audition over a group of applicants that included C. P. E. Bach, who had also applied five years earlier, after his father's death. Doles assumed his post on January 30, 1756, and apparently became acquainted with Gellert soon thereafter. One of his first official acts was to ask Gellert to provide the text for a Passion to be performed on Good Friday. The two men remained close friends until Gellert's death thirteen years later.[8]

Doles's preface to his settings of Gellert's *Geistliche Oden und Lieder* is dated April 16, 1758, two-and-a-half months after Bach's, and seems to have been written with Bach in mind. Even before he gets to his preface, Doles is eager to show that he has produced settings that match Gellert's wishes and intentions. On his title page Doles proudly proclaims that Gellert's poems have "not yet been provided with chorale melodies [*Kirchenmelodien*]," and that his settings—unlike others, namely Bach's, is the clear implication—are suitable for both "private and public devotion." In the preface itself Doles elaborates: "That which first gave Professor Gellert the idea of writing these poems, and which was his pious muse during the completion of his project, has also been my principal aim: namely, to serve the cause of private, and perhaps also public, devotion." Just as Gellert sought to attain his object by writing poems in which "a gentle, artless feeling was predominant," so he, Doles, has provided "easy and artless melodies," which may be sung either by a four-part chorus or by a single voice, with keyboard accompaniment. Moreover, Doles stresses that he has followed Gellert's wishes to the letter, by setting only the 21 poems for which the poet did not supply suggested chorale melodies.

As we have seen, the composers of the first Berlin song movement thought of themselves as modernists, participants in Gottsched's Horatian reform of German arts and letters. The chorale idiom demanded by Gellert must have seemed to them both old-fashioned and provincial. Yet Gellert's *Geistliche Oden und Lieder* was one of the most important and popular midcentury books of German poetry—and therefore one of the most potentially profitable ones for composers on the lookout for texts to set. Thus it presented the composers with something of a challenge. The best way to appreciate the very special quality of Bach's settings is to look at a number of settings of the same poem by different composers, beginning with Doles, who made the greatest effort to meet Gellert's demands, and ending with Bach, whose settings are the most remote in style from the chorale idiom Gellert had in mind.

One of the most frequently set Gellert poems, and also one that gives a clear idea of what sort of a poet he was, is "Busslied":

> An dir allein, an dir hab ich gesündigt,
>   Und übel oft vor dir gethan.
> Du siehst die Schuld, die mir den Fluch verkündigt;
>   Sieh, Gott, auch meinen Jammer an.
>
> Dir ist mein Flehn, mein Seufzen nicht verborgen,
>   Und meine Thränen sind vor dir.
> Ach Gott, mein Gott, wie lange soll ich sorgen?
>   Wie lang entfernst du dich von mir?
>
> Herr, handle nicht mit mir nach meinen Sünden,
>   Vergilt mir nicht nach meiner Schuld.
> Ich suche dich; lass mich dein Antlitz finden,
>   Du Gott der Langmuth und Geduld.
>
> Früh wollst du mich mit deiner Gnade füllen,
>   Gott, Vater der Barmherzigkeit.
> Erfreue mich um deines Namens willen;
>   Du bist ein Gott, der gern erfreut.
>
> Lass deinen Weg mich wieder freudig wallen,
>   Und lehre mich dein heilig Recht,
> Mich täglich thun nach deinem Wohlgefallen;
>   Du bist mein Gott, ich bin dein Knecht.
>
> Herr, eile du, mein Schutz, mir beyzustehen,
>   Und leite mich auf ebner Bahn.
> Er hört mein Schreyn, der Herr erhört mein Flehen,
>   Und nimmt sich meiner Seelen an.

This poem's manner and method are quite characteristic of *Geistliche Oden und Lieder*. One is immediately struck by the chaste compression and almost shocking directness of the language, by the mix of intimacy and reserve, powerful authority and self-abnegating humility, clear-eyed realism and intense religious fervor. After reviewing some of the bombastic, lachrymose odes, filled with "high flights of pathos," that were inspired by Gellert's death, Carsten Schlingmann,[9] the poet's most sympathetic recent critic, asks rhetorically: "What have these self-dramatizing, holy-heroic bards to do with the moderation and skepticism of the highly esteemed Saxon man of the Enlightenment" (p. 16)? And a few pages later, Schlingmann once again perceptively pits the real Gellert against the darling of the Gellert-cult, the patron saint of "Empfindsamkeit":

> Only up to a certain point can one classify him as the herald or forerunner of *Empfindsamkeit*. He is not really the "sentimental" but rather the "sensitive" Gellert. For him the border of sentiment is at the point where ecstatic infatuation [*Schwärmerei*] begins.
>
> [P. 28]

Much of the special quality of Gellert's language, here and elsewhere, depends on its complex and intimate relation to the language of Luther's Bible. As Schlingmann remarks of "Busslied," "There is scarcely a line that does not show borrowings from the Psalms" (p. 171).

In *Untersuchungen zu Chr. F. Gellerts Geistlichen Oden und Liedern*, Emil Werth has shown exactly how this dependence on the Bible works.[10] Arranging the biblical passages to which Gellert alludes in the order in which they appear in the poem, one comes out with this:

> An dir allein hab ich gesündiget und übel vor dir getan. [Ps. 51:6]
> Siehe an meinen Jammer . . . [Ps. 25:18]
> Derr Herr höret mein Flehen. [Ps. 6:10]
> . . . mein Seufzen ist dir nicht verborgen. [Ps. 38:10]
> Ich habe . . . deine Tränen gesehen. [Is. 38:5]
> Wie lange soll ich sorgen . . . [Ps. 13:3]
> Er handelt nicht mit uns nach unsern Sünden und vergilt uns nicht nach unserer Missetat. [Ps. 103:10]
> Suchet den Herrn, weil er zu finden ist. [Is. 55:6]
> "Ihr sollt mein Antlitz suchen." Darum suche ich auch, Herr, dein Antlitz. [Ps. 27:8]
> Gott aber der Geduld . . . [Rom. 15:5]
> Reichtum seiner Güte, Geduld und Langmütigkeit. [Rom. 2:4]
> Fülle uns frühe mit deiner Gnade. [Ps. 90:14]
> Gelobet sei Gott, . . . der Vater der Barmherzigkeit. [2 Cor. 1:3]
> Erfreue uns nun wieder. [Ps. 90:15]
> Um deines Namens willen Herr, sei gnädig. [Ps. 25:11]
> Tue mir kund den Weg, darauf ich gehen soll. [Ps. 143:8]
> Lehre mich deine Rechte! [Ps. 119:12]
> Lehre mich tun nach deinem Wohlgefallen, denn du bist mein Gott. [Ps. 143:10]
> . . . ich bin dein Knecht. [Ps. 143:12; cf. Ps. 116:16]
> Eile, mir beizustehen, Herr, meine Hilfe! [Ps. 38:23]
> Herr . . . mein Schutz. [Ps. 18:3].
> . . . dein guter Geist führe mich auf ebener Bahn. [Ps. 143:10]
> Herr, . . . vernimm mein Flehen . . . erhöre mich. [Ps. 143:1]
> . . . und hörete mein Schreien. [Ps. 40:2]
> . . . niemand nimmt sich meiner Seele an. [Ps. 142:5]

It perhaps comes as something of a shock to a modern reader that anyone would bother to write a poem with so much of its language directly lifted from the book that most of his readers would be likely to know better than any other book. At first glance, the tabulation of biblical passages just given looks like a rather hasty set of notes that someone might have taken while listening to Gellert's poem being recited. But only at first glance. Perhaps the first sharp divergence we notice is between the last of the biblical citations, "niemand nimmt sich meiner Seele an," and Gellert's last two lines: "Er hört mein Schreyn, der Herr erhört mein Flehen / Und nimmt sich meiner Seelen an." What in Psalm 142 is a direct expression of blank despair—"no man cares for my soul" in the words of the King James Version—has in Gellert's poem become a cry of triumph. And as we trace the comparison back, we notice further disparities: the prayerful imperatives of the psalms ("vernimm," "erhöre," "hörete") have become the strongly positive indicatives of the poem ("hört," "erhört"). Yet we notice that the poem does begin exactly in tune with Psalm 51; how then does the dramatic process of change that carries us to Gellert's quite different conclusion come about?

The first two lines of the opening stanza are nothing but a rhetorical elaboration of the line from Psalm 51: the phrase "an dir" is repeated for emphasis, and "oft" is inserted primarily for metrical reasons. The final line of the stanza is also just a rhetorical elaboration of the phrase from Psalm 25, but in the third line Gellert has provided a dramatic and logical link between the first two lines and the final one by introducing the word "Schuld." The speaker's guilt, the outward and (to God at any rate) visible sign of the sin to which he has just confessed, is already known to God; he then begs God to look deeper, to see also his "Jammer," the misery that flows from his sense of guilt.

In the second stanza the three key terms of the biblical phrases—"Flehen," "Seufzen," and "Tränen"—are smoothly combined in a statement that both opens and closes with the word "dir." It is to God that the speaker's plea is directed, from God that his sighing is not concealed, because of (and in the presence of) God that the speaker weeps. In their original contexts, however, the plea had been said to have been heard by (rather than directed at) God, and the tears had been spoken of reassuringly, by God himself. The third line is again a simple rhetorical elaboration of the biblical phrase, but in the final line Gellert deftly ties the whole stanza together with the word "entfernst": alienation from God has indeed been the subject of the preceding lines.

The third stanza rounds off the first part of the poem. The sentence from Psalm 103 has been put into the mouth of the speaker as an imperative—but the tone here is commanding rather than pleading, as with the earlier imperatives, and the word "Schuld," which reaches back to the first stanza, feels very different here from the way it felt there. The biblical imperative "Suchet den Herrn," on the other hand, becomes the firmly assertive "Ich suche dich"—the speaker having taken control—and God is addressed almost familiarly, even confidently, as the God of forbearance and long-suffering found in Romans 2:4. An especially fine touch is the word "finden." One might have expected "Lass mich dein Antlitz sehen," or perhaps even "Lass mich dein Antlitz rühren." But the open-endedness of "finden"—finding or discovering something can imply or even presuppose a search or quest of indefinite length—suggests that the speaker, with all his gradually accumulated confidence, perhaps still has a long way to go. Moreover, a face is an oddly familiar and concrete thing to speak of finding: the verb (quite appropriately) makes this particular face seem both familiar (the speaker will recognize it when he finds it) yet also monumental (like the faces on Mount Rushmore). The juxtaposition of "Antlitz" and "finden," in short, is strangely moving.

This is the turning point of the poem—Beethoven, in his setting, at this point changed from A minor to A major. The psalmist's urgent plea "Fülle uns frühe mit deiner Gnade" has become the speaker's self-assured "Früh wollst du mich with deiner Gnade füllen." And the familiar phrase "um deines Namens willen" in line three is given concreteness and clarity by the speaker's having addressed God, in the preceding lines, as "Vater der Barmherzigkeit." It is most interesting that here there is no direct biblical source—besides the request "Erfreue uns nun wieder"—for the stanza's last line: "Du bist ein Gott, der gern erfreut." The three preceding stanzas have ended with either a plea or a question. But this one ends with a firm flat statement that this is a God who gladly makes us glad, a statement of the speaker's own creation, without literal sanction in the poem's biblical sources. The dramatic action of the poem so far has been the speaker's gradual pulling away from the various biblical contexts to which his words were originally attached; with these words he steps out confidently on his own, his hard-won victory assured.

Both of the poem's concluding stanzas also end with firmly assertive statements that depart sharply from the original contexts of the words that compose them. The plea from near the end of Psalm 143, one of the darkest of the so-called penitential psalms, "Lehre mich tun nach deinem Wohlgefallen, denn du bist mein Gott," uses the fact that this God is the speaker's God as a sort of argument or even justification for the preceding request that He teach the speaker to do His will. But in the last line of the poem's fifth stanza, "Du bist mein Gott, ich bin dein Knecht," the phrase "Du bist mein Gott" has an air of triumphant possession that is rescued from being arrogant by the balancing phrase "ich bin dein Knecht." And as we noted at the outset, the last line of the concluding stanza converts the imperatives of the psalm to indicatives, the psalmist's despairing pleas to a cry of triumph. Finally, it is interesting to note that in the final two lines the speaker no longer addresses God directly but turns to us, speaking of "Er" and "der Herr": after his transforming penitential experience, he returns to himself, as it were, and both acknowledges and celebrates his newfound strength.

What kind of poem is this? Surely it belongs in the centuries-long tradition of Christian meditative poetry, perhaps most familiar to readers of English poetry from the poems of the great 17th-century devotional poets: Herbert, Vaughan, and Crashaw. Obviously, the close and pervasive dependence on the language of the Bible makes it impossible for such poems to be "original" in the radical sense that the Romantics taught us all poems—all works of art—should be. Indeed, a major part of the impact of such poems depends on their readers' knowing and recognizing, in the very act of reading them, their biblical sources. In reading (or watching) a Shakespeare play, we may either know or not know the relevant passages in Plutarch or Holinshed—indeed, it makes little difference to our understanding and enjoyment of the play. But to read Gellert or Herbert without being sharply aware, at every turn, of his dependence on particular biblical passages and of exactly what he is doing with those passages is to miss the poem he intended us to read.

For while it is impossible for meditative poems to be "original" in our ordinary sense of that term, it is certainly not impossible for them to embody that other great Romantic value, "self-expression." But the self that is expressing itself in a poem like Gellert's "Busslied" does so by consciously setting itself in a dialectical relation to selected passages from the Bible. Out of these resonant fragments of common knowledge is created a new, personal drama of private religious experience. As we saw, while some of the biblical passages are incorporated into the poem more or less as they originally appear, many are subtly altered, and—especially toward the end of the poem—the implication and even the plain sense of some are virtually reversed. "Busslied" is a poem of hope that shows a Christian speaker creating, out of the remembered bits of biblical language, his own personal, inner movement from abject penitence to triumphant self-assurance that his act of contrition has reestablished him in God's grace.

But precisely because the biblical language is not only common knowledge to all Christians but also their common property, the speaker's movement from misery to confidence is not his alone: it belongs to any Christian who can follow him in using the Bible in this way—which is, of course, the way in which it was meant to be used. There is thus a tension created between the personal and the public, the individual and the universal, the particular situation and experience of this particular speaker and the timeless situation and experience of all Christians. It is in this tension, this dialectical relation, that the poet's self-expression in a poem like "Busslied" resides. No other, similar poem will have the particular, individualizing touches that this poem has—and that stand out all the more clearly against the background of familiar biblical language: the logical and dramatic functioning of the word "Schuld," the way in which "entfernst" focuses the progression of the first two stanzas, and that splendid "finden."

Let us look now at the setting provided for "Busslied" by Doles. Like all his Gellert settings, it is printed in two forms: as a four-part vocal chorale at the top of the page, and as a two-stave "Klavierlied" at its bottom. Here are the two settings:

Stripped of its ornaments, Doles's chorale would be a perfectly suitable, indeed quite expressive, setting of Gellert's poem. The overall construction, in which irregular three-bar phrases alternate with regular two-bar ones, nicely catches the speaker's pained, uneasy relation to God—at least in the opening stanzas of the poem. The very conventional opening does not prepare us for the anguished leap of an octave and sudden spreading out of voices at the end of m. 1 on the very effective $\frac{6}{5}$ chord. It is as though the speaker, after mouthing the words "an dir"—a conventional enough opening for a prayer—suddenly realized their full significance in the light of what is to follow: the octave leap italicizes the phrase, as it were, brings it into sharp relief. The extension of the phrase into m. 3 heightens our sense of his pain, and the Db/B clash on the second beat twists the knife. Then the second phrase—regular, orderly, stepwise, symmetrical, in the relative major—offers temporary relief. The third phrase, again irregular, takes us back into F minor with a cadence that echoes the earlier Db/B clash, but the sustaining of the stepwise motion makes the pain less than in the first phrase. The final phrase rather uninterestingly closes the proceedings.

But with all the ornaments dutifully observed, this chorale would of course sound grotesque. They are, I suppose, less wildly inappropriate to the setting for keyboard and solo voice. But there are so many of them, and they are so indiscriminately applied, that it would still be hard to integrate them into the melody. Moreover, the very square, quarter-note movement of both melody and accompaniment would quickly become monotonous in a solo song.

Doles's setting (or settings), then, has the worst of all possible worlds. But Doles was not an unaccomplished or ignorant musician. He seems to have been thrown into confusion by the nature of Gellert's poem, at once intimate and, because of the dependence on biblical language, public. He undoubtedly thought he was realizing Gellert's intentions by composing a chorale setting, but perhaps felt that something extra, some "modern" touch, was needed—and provided it in the form of ornamentation. One interesting incidental suggestion does, however, emerge from an examination of Doles's paired settings for this and the other Gellert poems. It is often said that in performing 18th-century songs notated on two staves, we should assume that the ornaments were intended only for the keyboardist's right hand and not for the singer. But the fact that Doles retains all the ornaments from the solo setting for the soprano voice in the four-part chorale setting suggests the opposite. And if he could have expected the ludicrously complex ornaments of his settings to be scrupulously performed by a solo singer, it would seem that other song composers could have expected the same of their more infrequent and tactfully applied ornaments. We need say no more, I think, about Doles's Gellert settings.

In 1760 Gräfe published a song collection with the following title page:

Fünfzig

Psalmen, geistliche Oden und Lieder

zur

privat und öffentlichen Andacht

in

Melodien mit Instrumenten

gebracht,

von

Johann Friedrich Gräfen.

The "geistliche Oden und Lieder" were, of course, by Gellert, while the psalms were the translations by Gellert's great friend and biographer Johann Andreas Cramer, which had begun to appear in 1755 and many of which Bach would later set. Cramer (1723-1788) was not only a poet but also a prominent Protestant theologian who served first as professor and later as chancellor at the University of Kiel. Gräfe gave the two genres practically equal billing: there are 26 of Cramer's psalms and 24 of Gellert's poems.

In his preface Gräfe tells us that he has been made aware of the demand for "geistliche Lieder" by the appearance of two recent publications that have used earlier melodies of his own as settings for specially written religious poems. The songs are notated in the ordinary way, on two staves, but Gräfe, like Doles, does not want his work confined to solo performances accompanied by keyboard. As his title page makes clear, he envisions performances accompanied by various instruments for the purposes of both private and public devotion. This is his way of fulfilling what he sees as Gellert's, and in this case also Cramer's, intentions:

It is intended not only for the youth and for beginners in music but also for small groups that enjoy accompanying their songs with instruments, even for churches in small cities where there is only one singer and a few instrumentalists, and where the frequently repeated [yearly] cycles [of music] grow wearying to the listeners.

The middle and lower voices of the keyboard accompaniment, he points out later, may be allotted to singers if there is a chorus available, and the performances may be lengthened by having whole choruses played by instruments alone. At the end of the volume Gräfe provides parts for first and second violins; and since he mentions oboes in his preface, he probably intends these parts to be played by oboes if there are no violins available.

In his setting of "Busslied" Gräfe marks each cadence with a fermata, apparently in an attempt to suggest the mood and movement of a chorale. Here is his setting:

Like Doles, though using very different means, Gräfe seems to be trying for a sort of compromise between a chorale setting and a conventional north German solo song. Though the marking of each cadence by a fermata—which, incidentally, Gräfe does not do in most of his Gellert settings—is certainly meant to suggest a chorale, the $\frac{3}{4}$ meter is of course very un-chorale-like. As in the Doles setting, here too the two halves of the song are similarly constructed. But here the effect is not of moving from an irregular to a regular segment, but rather of segments of increasing length. The song is 18 bars long, each of its two halves possessing 2+3+4 bars.

Though Friedlaender scornfully dismisses this collection—"Among these extraordinarily weak compositions there is scarcely a single ray of light" (I/i, 95)—it seems that Gräfe has improved considerably as a song composer during the almost 20 years since the last of his four earlier volumes. Besides suggesting a chorale, the fermate also give an air of tentativeness to the song—as though the speaker/singer were working out his thoughts as he went. In the very simple first phrase—the fifth rising to the upper third, which then descends to the tonic—this air of tentativeness is increased by the late entry of the bass line. The second phrase, twice repeating the first phrase's descent at ever higher pitch levels, seems to be elaborating on its predecessor, but then sinks back down toward the F# from which we began, leaving us hanging on the G# fermata. At first, the steadily upward-moving bass line gives a sense of resolution, but this is dissipated at the end of the phrase, the urgency lost. The third phrase is altogether different. The sinuously chromatic melodic line seems to be struggling to rise—and then falling back ineffectually. There is a sense of sinking into oneself that is wholly appropriate to the first stanza's confession of evil often committed.

The second half of the song begins unexpectedly (and soothingly) in the relative major, and moves to its subdominant. This time the rise of the melodic line, buttressed a third below, is steady and successful. As in the first half, the second phrase extends and elaborates on the first. But this time there is no sinking back: the third phrase begins on the highest note of the song, and then makes an extended and dignified descent to the tonic.

"Busslied" is of course a poem that raises very acutely the old problem of strophic settings: how indeed can one short stretch of music adequately express each and every stanza of a poem that moves from misery to triumph? And in fact Gräfe grumbled a little about this old problem in his preface. Of the composers that he singled out as the judges of whether he had succeeded with his settings or not, Gräfe wrote: "These men will know how confined and cramped one feels, in writing such small melodies, by the short stanzas, by the unequal lengths of the lines, by the alterations in the many passions that occur all at once in a poem, by a change in the punctuation marks, the verse types, etc., and by how often one must leave out the best thoughts, merely because they do not accord with the following stanzas." Yet Gräfe did quite well—certainly far better than Doles. For although Gräfe's setting ends in the minor, as it began, its general movement is in the direction of reassurance and consolation. One can imagine the singing of the successive stanzas being varied in a way that would accent the poem's movement toward triumph.

In 1758 Marpurg published anonymously a volume entitled *Geistliche moralische und weltliche Oden, von verschiedenen Dichtern und Componisten*, which contained a setting of "Busslied" by Friedrich Christian Rackemann (b. 1735).[11] Here it is:

From what we have learnt so far, it is easy to classify this as a typical, mediocre north German or Berlin song of the period. Even when one follows the tempo direction, "Langsam," the harmony marches forward steadily, boringly, ensuring the "Mannigfaltigkeit" so highly valued by Nichelmann and others. The composer's attention seems more firmly fixed upon this, and upon making melody and bass line proceed in contrary motion wherever possible, than on expression. The languishing air of the first phrase is immediately spoiled by the upward march of the bass line (joined at the tenth by the under voice in the keyboard's right hand) and the flaccid cadential pattern. The one moment of harmonic life comes at the beginning of m. 3, when the melody's unexpected shift from C to C# (with A beneath it) makes it sound for a moment as though we have gone from A minor to A major. But then, with the entrance of the bass line on F, it becomes apparent that the C# was only a leading tone to the D that defines the key for the rest of the bar as D minor—a nice moment of defeated expectation. The effect is quickly spoiled, however, by the extraordinarily limp cadence on C in m. 4—topped off, inappropriately (considering the text), by the neat, flippant, off-beat octave jump in the bass. This jump is immediately reversed—again with inappropriate (but wholly characteristic) neatness and briskness—at the beginning of m. 5, as the bass begins its imitation of its pattern two bars earlier. The cadence and upward bass march in m. 6 are just as feeble as those they echo in mm. 2 and 1 (respectively), and the final two bars are no better.

Marpurg himself contributed a better setting of "Busslied" to another of his collections, *Geistliche Oden, in Melodien gesetzt von einigen Tonkünstlern in Berlin*, which was also published in 1758:

This is the first of our settings to begin in the major. But the sweetness of the first-inversion Ab chord with which the song opens only serves to sharpen the pathos of the bass line's slide downward—as though the bottom were dropping out of everything. Pathos is also the effect of the melodic line's insistent downward appoggiatura on the third beat. Like all the phrases of this song, the first phrase has three bars, and the vague sense of truncation—the cadence on G beginning in the second half of the first bar, earlier than we expect it—heightens the pathos. Both the upward skip of a fourth with which the song began and the downward half-step appoggiatura unobtrusively become motifs—or at least elements of design. The second phrase begins by jumping upward from G to C, and immediately elaborates upon the appoggiatura, then dramatically jumps upward another fourth, from C to F, as the harmony broadens out and the bass line completes its octave descent from C to C.

The third phrase opens by repeating the C-F skip and then further elaborates the appoggiatura. But in m. 7 the bass line interrupts its downward course, becoming more independent and then, in m. 8, being richly filled out by a tenor voice a third above it as we cadence on Ab. The fullness of the harmony, the more conventionally cadential motion of the bass line, and the swing to the major combine to give a feeling of reassurance. But this is only momentary. The Db-C with which the third phrase ended is picked up at the beginning of the fourth, but given a different meaning—closer to that of the earlier appoggiaturas—because of the harmony, which is returning us to C minor. But the return to the pathos of the opening is not quite complete: the bass line does not drop away step by step, but completes a conventional cadential turn around Eb as it moves up to G, drops an octave, and centers on C. Yet its earlier inexorable downward motion is given to the right hand's inner voice, and we end on the rather bleak, spare octave C.

This seems quite effective. Many of the same Berlin conventions that we encountered in Rackemann's setting are found here too—but not so baldly and not for their own sake: they all serve an appropriate expressive function. Thus the harmony changes steadily, the cadences are varied, there is a reasonable amount of contrary motion between melody and bass line, and certain melodic figures are picked up and given motivic significance. But as we saw, everything serves to express what Marpurg sees as the content of the words. And here, as in the Gräfe setting, the general movement is toward a slight qualification of the initial bleakness—that reassuring fullness in the third phrase—and so one can imagine the setting solving the strophic problem set by a poem that moves in the direction of affirmation, as this one does.

Finally, then, we arrive at C.P.E. Bach's setting. I have postponed it this long in order to give as full an idea as possible of the ways in which other composers saw Gellert's poem, and of the compositional choices that their respective visions of the poem caused them to make. Here is Bach's setting:

The first thing that we notice is the variety of texture exhibited within the song's scant eight bars. The highly inflected melody with steady quarter-note accompaniment (mm. 1-2) suddenly gives way to a steady beat of quarter notes in the melody accompanied by pulsing eighth notes (m. 3), and then to a combination of the two textures that takes us to the cadence on V that ends the song's first half (m. 4). But the two halves are linked by a slurred bass line phrase—quite unusual in songs of this period. The pulsing eighth-note accompaniment returns (mm. 5-6), and then we revert, in the penultimate m. 7, which melodically echoes m. 1, to the original texture—except for the eighth-note bass lead-in to the final bar, which again is more carefully phrased than bass parts in these songs usually are.

Moreover, within this variety there is further complication. The tenor C# in m. 1 sounds as though it wants to resolve upward to D, producing something like this:

But of course we get nothing so ordinary. The tenor does not resolve at all, but just drops out; the alto does not drop to F#, but stays on G; and the bass drops only a half-tone, to D#. The result is to give us, for a moment on the third beat, an extraordinary D# major triad! Similarly, in m. 2, when the pattern in the left hand is repeated, we expect the B introduced on the second beat to resolve upward to C, thus:

But once again the tenor drops out, the alto stays put, and the bass drops only a half-tone instead of the expected whole tone. In both cases, not only are odd, unexpected sonorities provided; we are also made sharply aware of how painfully slow the harmonic motion is—as though the speaker's confession were giving him great anguish.

The melodic movement in these opening two bars is at first syncopated and broken, in a way that complements the odd and fragmentary disposition of voices, and then grows more fluent. But in m. 3, after the odd, angular double appoggiatura, the melodic line suddenly becomes simple and insistent, sternly declamatory against the excitedly pulsing accompaniment. And as the melody simplifies, so does the harmony. The bass line, jumping an octave, continues its chromatic downward course, but the conventional cadential pattern is very different from the odd and uncertain harmonic movement of the opening two bars. The effect of the little slurred bass phrase leading from m. 4 into m. 5 is to link the two halves of the song seamlessly. It is as though the speaker/singer, having managed to break out of his initial self-entrapment into the clear declaration of guilt in m. 3, could now continue more easily than before.

The voice enters high and plaintive at the beginning of m. 5, with a phrase that nicely suits not only "Du siehst die Schuld" in stanza 1 of Gellert's poem but also the parallel phrases in succeeding stanzas: "Ach Gott, mein Gott," "Ich suche dich," "Erfreue mich," and so on. The phrase that sets the second half of line 3 of each stanza, which begins at the end of m. 5 and leads into m. 6, echoes the phrase in mm. 1-2 that sets the rhyming second half of line 1, reaching up to high F-natural and then dropping stepwise. But this time the descent is in steady eighth notes and goes only to C, not all the way to A. Moreover, the simplification of the harmony that began in mm. 3 and 4 is continued: we now get the A-minor chord we expected but did not get in m. 2, and it is approached in the most orthodox way imaginable: by way of E-minor and E^7 chords. This simplified echoing of earlier phrases is continued in m. 7, which takes us back to m. 1. Here, just as earlier, the bass line sinks chromatically, but the descent is swifter, the chords less startling and painful. The rather surprisingly urgent eighth-note rise in the bass at the end of the bar takes us into the final cadence.

How well has C.P.E. Bach succeeded in creating a strophic setting for Gellert's poem? Certainly the song is arresting and deeply moving in its highly expressive use of harmony and textural variety. But it does seem too thoroughly "Traurig" to capture much suggestion of the poem's move toward eventual joy and triumph. As we saw, Gräfe and Marpurg both gave their settings middle sections that strongly suggested reassurance and consolation, and thus provided the singer with ways of emphasizing the dramatic change as the song moves into its later strophes. And perhaps Bach may be said to provide something similar in the growing openness and regularity of the vocal line and the simplification of the harmony that we have noted. But that does not seem enough.

That Bach was thoroughly aware of what I have called the strophic problem is clear from his preface to the volume of Gellert settings. After duly paying tribute to Gellert's poems and to the "fromme Absicht" that inspired them, Bach writes:

> In composing the melodies I have, as far as possible, considered the whole poem. I say "as far as possible" because everyone who understands music knows that one cannot demand too much of a melody that is to be sung to more than one stanza. The diversity of punctuation marks, of monosyllabic and polysyllabic words, also often of the subject matter, etc. makes a great difference in the musical expression. From my work one will observe that I have sought in various ways to avoid many of these inequalities.

The tone and terms of this little apologia are so similar to those of the one contained in Gräfe's preface of two years later, which we looked at above, that direct influence does not seem unlikely. For Gräfe would surely have known of Bach's settings.

But what is really interesting about Bach's rather defensive comments on the strophic problem is their relation to what he has to say about Gellert's "pious intention." After noting that the warm reception accorded Gellert's poems renders further praise unnecessary, Bach nonetheless bestows some: "One especially cannot thank him enough for imparting this collection to us because one is completely persuaded by the exceptional use for which he created it." It is, we recall, the "quality of the sublime, instructive thoughts" contained in these poems that made Bach unable to stop until he had set every one of them. Then, picking up Gellert's distinction (in his preface) between the two kinds of sacred poems, Bach writes:

> One knows that *Lehroden* are not so well adapted for music as are *Lieder für das Herz*; but when the former are as beautiful as those written by Herr Gellert, one feels a pleasant compulsion to contribute as much as possible toward realizing the intention behind them and toward making their use more common.

> It is this pious intention alone that has occasioned my melodies. I have especially wished to make the use of these poems more common among music-lovers and, thereby, to give them the opportunity to attain edification.

The paragraph on the difficulties of writing strophic songs follows immediately. Bach closes his preface with one more reference to intentions: "Finally, I also wish for this effort the applause of connoisseurs that has honored my previous works, and I shall count myself fortunate if my good intentions are realized."

Bach is clearly bending over backward to justify himself for not having provided the sort of chorale-like settings that Gellert explicitly demanded. After saying that praise is unnecessary, he praises Gellert especially because the exceptional use that Gellert has in mind for his poems is one with which he (Bach) is so fully in agreement. This use is, of course, the religious edification (*Erbauung*) that Gellert said was his ultimate aim and that he thought would best be achieved if the songs received traditional chorale-like settings. Bach then compliments Gellert further, asserting that the beauty of the *Lehroden* in his collection imposes the pleasant duty of doing everything possible to make certain that his intention in writing them is fulfilled and that the use for which he has intended them thereby becomes more common than it is at present. This pious intention, Bach then adds, has been the only begetter of his melodies, and he hopes to make Gellert's poems more commonly used among music-lovers so that they may achieve edification ("sich . . . erbauen"). Bach thus not only emphasizes that he is fully in accord with Gellert's intentions (all appearances to the contrary notwithstanding!); he also harps on the utilitarian nature of these intentions and even picks up Gellert's term *Erbauung* in its verbal form. Finally, Bach speaks yet again of "my good intentions"—by which point we are to understand that these are the same as Gellert's.

Yet it is of course precisely the familiar limitations of the strophic song, as pointed out in detail by Bach, that make a strophic setting—in which the composer will, to recall Gräfe's phrase, be forced to "leave out" many of those precious "thoughts"—of questionable value in helping readers (or singers) achieve the desired *Erbauung*. Of course chorale-like settings would be strophic, too; but the whole tone would be different, and more appropriate to direct religious instruction. As Gellert himself implied, settings that are "too beautiful for a singer who is not musical" would run the risk of obscuring the content of his poems as settings to a traditional chorale tune (or reasonable substitute) would not.

There is one more paragraph of Bach's preface that demands our attention. Immediately after his comments on the strophic problem, he writes:

> I have added the necessary harmony and ornaments to my melodies. In this way I have taken into account the desires of a confirmed figured-bass player, and the pieces can be used also as *Handstücke*.

At first glance, this is merely a clear declaration of what seems to have been Bach's usual intention in regard to the performance of his songs: he has included all the necessary harmony and ornaments, and he wants little or no filling out or other improvisation added by the keyboard accompanist. But the final, almost throwaway clause is perhaps of even greater interest. Because everything has been fully notated, these pieces may also be used as "Handstücke"! The *New Grove* tells us that *Handstück* was "a term used by D. G. Türk for a didactic keyboard piece suitable for the development of a student's technical proficiency," a term superseded in the 19th century by *étude*. One could scarcely conceive of a more purely "musical" use, one that so clearly says that despite all Bach's earlier (and later) protestations, his intentions are not exactly the same as Gellert's. Now we know why the protestations seemed excessive: Bach is trying to have it all ways at once.

But if Bach's feelings about Gellert's collection of poems were complex enough to call forth all this backing and filling, what was it about these poems that inspired him to take the most unusual step of setting every last one of them? The songs he wrote prove that his intentions were really very far from Gellert's—despite all the protestations of his preface. For there could be no question of Bach's songs ever being "used" in the ways that Gellert expressly had in mind. They are far too involuted, too complex in expression, too personal, too "musical" to create the communal religious illumination Gellert had in mind. What then did Bach find in *Geistliche Oden und Lieder*?

III

It is, once again, important to recall how few songs Bach had written before he tackled Gellert's book—but how much music of other sorts he had written. In much of this music—the "Prussian" and "Württemberg" Sonatas, the early symphonies, the keyboard concertos—Bach made a point, particularly in the slow movements, of experimentally probing and imaginatively elaborating odd and extreme emotional states. The 1750s was the great decade of treatises dealing with both music and general aesthetics. And Bach, in the first volume of his own *Versuch über die wahre Art das Clavier zu spielen* (1753), had laid great stress on the emotional nature and content of music. As songs came back into favor, it was natural that he should also try his hand at this way of communicating and awakening emotions through music—a way, unlike the others he had tried, that called in words to the aid of musical sound. But until he encountered Gellert's poems, Bach had obviously not found his proper subject as a composer of songs.

Every one of the 15 or so songs that Bach had composed before his Gellert songs was, like the ones we analyzed earlier, secular in nature. And while the poetry of a Hagedorn could elicit fine and suitable settings from Bach, after "Morgen" (1756), he composed only three more songs to Hagedorn poems: "An die Liebe" (1768) and "Alster" and "Harvstehude," both of which were composed very late in Bach's life and neither of which has survived. Plainly, though Hagedorn was the most popular poet of the time, his subjects did not offer Bach the opportunities he was seeking. Nor, for that matter, did those of Klopstock, who succeeded to Hagedorn's position of preeminence but only a handful of whose poems were set by Bach. And Klopstock was, of course, the poet of emotion par excellence—and also the poet to whom Bach, later in his career, was most often compared.

The inescapable conclusion, I think, is that in order to explore the emotional states that most interested him, Bach needed religious poetry. And not just any religious poetry, for of course Klopstock, aside from *Der Messias*, wrote several other, shorter religious poems. But it is impossible to imagine Bach setting a rambling free-form rhapsody like "Dem Allgegenwärtigen" or "Die Glückseligkeit Aller," both of which are almost exactly contemporary with Gellert's collection. No—what Bach seems to have needed was religious poetry like Gellert's, which not only is written in strict stanzaic forms but also is very closely bound to religious tradition, as embodied in Luther's translation of the Bible. Bach was of course a very different sort of artist from Gellert. But his deep sympathy with the conservative side of Gellert's art evidently allowed him to use it as a springboard for his own far more experimental and radical works. Robert Frost once described writing free verse as like playing tennis without a net: one can easily imagine how the constraints of Gellert's forms and the conservative bent of his imagination provided Bach, himself in many ways a very conservative man, with the net, the court, the ground rules he needed to allow his own imagination free play.

Another reason that Gellert's poems may have held a special appeal for Bach is that so many of them, unlike "Busslied," are basically undramatic. As one can see from their titles, many of them—"Gelassenheit," "Demut," "Geduld"—are elaborated descriptions of a particular emotion or state of mind important to the religious life. Others—"Preis des Schöpfers," "Gottes Macht und Vorsehung," "Die Ehre Gottes aus der Natur"—discuss or celebrate a particular aspect of the divine nature. Still others—"Passionslied," "Osterlied," "Weihnachtslied"—are relevant to a particular event in the church year. Unlike a personal meditative poem such as "Busslied," none of these types of poems requires a dramatic development of the speaker's experience. Thus the strophic problem that Bach showed an awareness of in his preface, and that gave him some trouble in his setting of "Busslied," is minimized.

Often in these poems the stanzas will all share a common structure—a situation made to order for a strophic setting. Take for example "Bitten"—which, incidentally, Beethoven set strophically:

> Gott, deine Güte reicht so weit,
> So weit die Wolken gehen;
> Du krönst uns mit Barmherzigkeit,
> Und eilst, uns beyzustehen.
> Herr, meine Burg, mein Fels, mein Hort,
> Vernimm mein Flehn, merk auf mein Wort;
> Denn ich will vor dir beten!
>
> Ich bitte nicht um Ueberfluss
> Und Schätze dieser Erden.
> Lass mir, so viel ich haben muss,
> Nach deiner Gnade werden.
> Gieb mir nur Weisheit und Verstand,
> Dich, Gott, und den, den du gesandt,
> Und mich selbst zu erkennen.
>
> Ich bitte nicht um Ehr und Ruhm,
> So sehr sie Menschen rühren;
> Des guten Namens Eigenthum
> Lass mich nur nicht verlieren.
> Mein wahrer Ruhm sey meine Pflicht,
> Der Ruhm vor deinem Angesicht,
> Und frommer Freunde Liebe.
>
> So bitt ich dich, Herr Zebaoth,
> Auch nicht um langes Leben.
> Im Glücke Demuth, Muth in Noth,
> Das wollest du mir geben.
> In deiner Hand steht meine Zeit:
> Lass du mich nur Barmherzigkeit
> Vor dir im Tode finden.

In saying that the stanzas all have the same structure, I am of course not speaking simply of meter and rhyme scheme—that would go without saying. I mean, in addition, that they have the same rhetorical shape.

The overall rhetorical structure of the poem is very simple: in the first stanza the speaker addresses God formally, saying that he wants to pray; in the other three stanzas, he makes a series of detailed requests of God. It is easy enough to see the rhetorical similarities among the last three stanzas: in the first four lines of each, he tells God what he does not want; in the last three lines he tells what he does want. In the two middle stanzas this difference is clearly pointed by the contrast between the common beginning, "Ich bitte nicht," and the positive stress immediately felt in "Gieb mir" and "Mein wahrer Ruhm." The final stanza is a little different. Its opening is more formal, as befits a conclusion: "So bitt ich dich, Herr Zebaoth, / Auch nicht ..." And the shift from negative to positive emphasis is made by the striking line: "In deiner Hand steht meine Zeit"—striking because the sudden concreteness of "In deiner Hand steht," coming after the preceding run of abstract nouns, prepares us for a concrete subject, instead of which we get "meine Zeit." The image of God's (presumably vast) hand both is and is not there since it is holding something we cannot imagine to ourselves. The first stanza, of course, is even more different. Still, we can feel a shift in something like the same direction as we move from the glorifying yet still somewhat matter-of-fact statements of the first four lines to the firm, impassioned insistence of "Herr, meine Burg, mein Fels, mein Hort." In a strophic setting of "Bitten," therefore, we should expect something interesting to happen at the beginning of the fifth line.

Thus what we have here is not a steadily evolving drama, as in "Busslied." The situation of the speaker's offering a prayer to God is set up in the first stanza and elaborated in the following three. It is therefore of interest that the relation of poem to biblical text here is quite different from what it was in the case of "Busslied." There, we recall, almost every line of the poem could be found somewhere or other in the Bible, though as we progressed through the poem we became increasingly aware of the growing distance between the original contexts of the biblical passages and the ways in which Gellert was using them in order to form his drama of a speaker moving from abject humility to triumphant self-assurance. In the case of "Bitten," however, virtually all the direct borrowings from the Bible, most of them from Psalms, come in the first stanza, which, as was the case with the whole of "Busslied," can virtually be reconstructed from the relevant biblical passages:

> Herr, deine Güte reichet, soweit der Himmel ist, und deine Wahrheit, soweit die Wolken gehen. [Ps. 36:6]
> ... der dich krönet mit Gnade und Barmherzigkeit. [Ps. 103:4]
> Eile, mir beizustehen! [Ps. 38:23]
> Herr, mein Fels, meine Burg, mein Erretter, mein Gott, mein Hort ...
>   [Ps. 18:3]
> Herr, vernimm mein Flehen [Ps. 143:1]
> ... merke auf mein Wort. [Prov. 4:20]
> Denn ich will vor dir beten. [Ps. 5:3][12]

We even have two passages here that were also used in "Busslied": "Eile, mir beizustehen!" and "vernimm mein Flehen." But there is only one other firm reminiscence of the Bible. Apropos of line 12, "Gieb mir nur Weisheit und Verstand," Werth notes (p. 44) several places at which the conjunction of "Weisheit" and "Verstand" occurs, but there seems nothing to choose amongst them, no one context that Gellert had in mind more than the others. The only other direct citation of a particular biblical passage is the line we found so striking earlier: "In deiner Hand steht meine Zeit." At Ps. 31:16 we find: "Meine Zeit stehet in deinen Händen."

This is evidently a literal translation of the Hebrew. In the English Bible, where it appears in Ps. 31:15, the passage reads: "My times are in thy hand." But Gellert's shift from plural to singular makes all the difference. The original plural signifies merely the dates of birth and death, which are, in the words of *The New Jerome Biblical Commentary*, assumed "in the ancient Near Eastern view" to have been "fixed by the gods."[13] Of course one of the senses of "Zeit" in this context is time of death or time of delivery—the speaker has, after all, just said that he is not asking for a long life. Moreover, this use of the word is common in the New Testament, especially in the utterances of Christ—for example, "meine Zeit ist hie" (Matthew 26:18). But the open-endedness of the word, enhanced by its close juxtaposition to the concrete "Hand" and "steht," forces us to read it more generally. Not only my beginning and my end, the speaker is saying, but everything about every moment of my time on earth (and hereafter) is in your control. This breadth of implication makes all the more moving the neat return of the word "Barmherzigkeit" in the poem's penultimate line. In the first stanza, "Barmherzigkeit" was singled out as the virtue with which God had crowned humanity: not only has he shown his compassion by creating man in his image; he has also granted man the ability to be compassionate to his fellows. At the poem's end, having shown his clear awareness of the immense power God has over him, the speaker asks only ("nur") that a similar compassion be shown him in the judgment rendered at his death.

Once again, comparisons will be useful in appreciating C. P. E. Bach's setting of this fine poem. Here is what Gräfe made of it:

Gracious, charming, and neatly constructed, this song has only one problem: it has little or no connection with the words of Gellert's poem. The $\frac{3}{4}$ meter, the prettily decorated descent of the melody in thirds, and the drone bass all suggest the pastoral mode we encountered in earlier chapters. There is (so to speak) not a hair out of place: the tidy little descending scale in the bass that joins the two opening eight-bar strains, the little circle-of-fifths bridge passage that follows, and the conclusion—pleasingly varied by a dash of syncopation—all complete the picture. But where are the power and urgency of Gellert's verse?

Marpurg did a good deal better in this setting, taken from the 1758 *Geistliche, moralische und weltliche Oden*:

As with Gräfe, we notice at once the characteristic Berlin neatness: the upward curve of the melody, in thirds, and its return to its starting point exactly mirrored in the bass line of mm. 1–4. Yet the appoggiaturas of m. 2 give the melody just the right touch of pathos to achieve the tender devotion specified in the tempo direction. And in the four bars that follow, the slight complications of rhythm and voice-leading heighten the intensity of feeling. As the eight-bar strain is repeated, we notice that the descending bass line is now harmonized, and that when it begins to ascend it is doubled at the lower octave. The poem's speaker seems to be gathering self-assurance.

At this point, which we earlier singled out as the stanza's turning point, Gräfe could think of nothing better than his tired little circle of fifths. But Marpurg pushes the speaker's self-assurance still further by having the melody, triadically harmonized, start on F#, the highest note in the song and one earlier heard merely as a glancing appoggiatura. Accustomed as we have become to the almost steady movement of the bass line in eighths and sixteenths, we are somewhat taken aback when, in m. 19, it suddenly begins to move in quarters. And we are still more surprised when, in m. 21, the bass begins to pound insistently in octaves against the harmonized rising A arpeggio in the melody. This steadying insistence effectively captures the urgency of the penultimate line in each of the poem's four stanzas: "Vernimm mein Flehn, merk auf mein Wort"; "Dich, Gott, und den, den du gesandt"; "Der Ruhm vor deinem Angesicht"; "lass du mich nur Barmherzigkeit." And the way in which the return of harmony to the keyboard's left hand softens the last six bars seems equally effective in catching the humility of each stanza's final line.

Let us now look at Bach's setting:

The first thing we notice is that this setting, in contrast to those by Gräfe and Marpurg, is in the minor—an interesting and surprising choice for a poem that begins with straightforward, heartfelt praise of God. And the music of the opening bars utterly lacks the sweet, secure assertiveness of the other two settings. Instead, Bach makes the speaker sound sensitive, hesitant, awed by the grandeur he praises. The rather weak and yielding quality of the first phrase, the sudden dropping out of the bass on the first beat of m. 2, the pathos of the rising and falling melodic phrases in mm. 4-5 and 5-6 as the bass again drops out, but this time for more than a bar—these and other details combine to suggest a relation between God and the speaker that is less intimate, shakier even, than we might have expected. The sliding eighth notes that close the eight-bar phrase seem for a moment to be heading us off in a new direction, but then the opening phrase begins again—rather doggedly, as it were—with added ornamentation and a new bass dropout (m. 9).

We are thus completely—or almost completely—unprepared for the very sudden and extreme change of direction taken with the pickup to m. 17. Suddenly the melody is being declaimed, *forte*, first on D and then on B, in an insistent repeated rhythm as the two lower voices move in fluid eighth notes. The insistence reminds us of Marpurg's setting, and indeed Marpurg may well have picked up the idea from Bach. But the difference between the initial tentativeness and this very firm, almost desperate declamation is far more dramatic than anything in Marpurg. As the melodic line drops from D to B, and the tonality shifts back to the minor, the speaker seems to be backing off somewhat. The last four bars, with the rather surprising downward melodic leap of a fifth into the cadence, are *pianissimo*.

Bach has done something quite wonderful here. As we saw earlier, "Bitten," unlike "Busslied," does not have a steadily evolving drama, and is therefore better suited to strophic setting. But we also saw that there are real differences between the poem's first stanza and the three that follow it. The most important of these differences is that there seems to be less of a shift in tone in the fifth line of that stanza than there is in the others. We might therefore have expected Bach to compromise by minimizing the shift of tone at the fifth line. But what he has done instead is to accentuate it, to make it more dramatic than we could have predicted from our reading of the poem—and thereby to give us a new reading of the first stanza's first four lines. There now seems something shy, dubious, even wary about the speaker's initial praise of God's goodness. He seems to feel unworthy of all this beneficence—until he bursts forth with his impassioned plea to be heard.

Another Gellert poem about prayer that is easy to set strophically is the one entitled simply "Das Gebet." Like "Bitten," it is a sustained, undramatic meditation on its chosen subject; moreover, it is so long that a non-strophic, quasi-dramatic setting would be out of the question. In fact, it is doubtful that the composers who set this and some of Gellert's other quite long poems ever intended that every stanza would be sung. Though C.P.E. Bach does print every stanza of every poem with his settings—perhaps because Gellert's book was still quite new—Gräfe simply prints as many stanzas as will fit on his page, and then refers the reader to Gellert's collection for those he has omitted.

Nor need we examine every one of the 14 eight-line stanzas that make up "Das Gebet." Assuming a Christian reader who has fallen away from the habit of prayer out of laziness or (interestingly enough) shame or embarrassment, Gellert begins by earnestly enjoining him to take it up again:

> Dein Heil, O Christ, nicht zu verscherzen,
> Sey wach und nüchtern zum Gebet!
> Ein Flehn aus reinem guten Herzen
> Hat Gott, dein Vater, nie verschmäht.
> Erschein vor seinem Angesichte
> Mit Dank, mit Demuth, oft und gern,
> Und prüfe dich in seinem Lichte,
> Und klage deine Noth dem Herrn.
>
> Welch Glück, so hoch geehrt zu werden,
> Und im Gebet vor Gott zu stehn!
> Der Herr des Himmels und der Erden,
> Bedarf der eines Menschen Flehn?

Sagt Gott nicht: Bittet, dass ihr nehmet?
Ist das Gebetes Frucht nicht dein?
Wer sich der Pflicht zu beten schämet,
Der schämt sich, Gottes Freund zu seyn.

Sein Glück von seinem Gott begehren,
Ist dies denn eine schwere Pflicht?
Und seine Wünsche Gott erklären,
Erhebt dies unsre Seele nicht?
Sich in der Furcht des Höchsten stärken,
In dem Vertraun, dass Gott uns liebt,
Im Fleiss zu allen guten Werken,
Ist diese Pflicht für dich betrübt?

The phrase "Bet oft" runs like a refrain through the 11 stanzas that follow, beginning many of them and also recurring within the stanzas to heighten the speaker's urgency. The various comforts and benefits of prayer are painted with moving directness yet in quite conventional terms. As Werth shows (pp. 45-47), "Das Gebet" is a chrestomathy of passages, gathered from all over the Bible, concerning the relation between man and God; though it has the touching directness and immediacy characteristic of Gellert, Schlingmann is perfectly fair in characterizing it as "an extended *Lehrode* on the meaning of prayer; of little artistic interest" (p. 168).

Once more Gräfe's setting can help to set off what is special about Bach's. Here is what Gräfe made of "Das Gebet":

As with his setting of "Bitten," we note that this one too is neatly constructed. Its form is AA^{1}BC. The four strains are linked to one another by their rhythmically similar openings, the B strain is divided into two closely matched halves, and the differences between A and A^1 yield a pleasing variety. There are some awkward moments—for example, the sudden F major of m. 18, which we do not yet know will flower into the dominant of B-flat minor in the bar following. The text gives no justification for this abrupt shift, and in fact the stanzas of "Das Gebet," unlike those of "Bitten," do not have a rhetorical turning point. Thus Gräfe was right to make his setting an almost uniform lament, firmly held together by the almost continuously pulsing eighths in the left hand.

But once again Bach saw more in the poem, and produced a more interesting and insightful setting. Here it is:

After the sustained uniformity of Gräfe's setting, we are here struck first by the constant irregularities: the stopping and starting of the rhythm, the angular broken phrases, the mix of scalar passages and odd unexpected melodic leaps. The form is AA^{1}BB^1, each segment being only four bars long.

After the initial unaccompanied upward leap of an octave, the melody is immediately involved in a rather complicated polyphonic context, the bass rising to meet it with the momentary suspension on Ab pointing up the Bb-G voice exchange between melody and bass. After the cadence in m. 2, the melody once again leaps upward, but this time with a supporting undervoice that continues to descend a sixth below it as the bass unexpectedly vaults upward and then drops back. Coming just after the incomplete Eb-minor triad on the second half of the second beat of m. 3, the Db and F in the two upper voices, when heard for the first time, suggest Bb minor—but then the bass enters and the harmony softens, resolving on Ab in the following bar. In the repeat of the A section, only the first half is varied. This time the melody, pushing higher than before, has undervoices from the outset—but they drop away for an instant on the second beat of m. 5. And the little voice exchange in the second half of m. 5 is pointed up still more strongly by the grace notes in the melody and by the Gb/F dissonance on the third beat. In the following bar, the melody is again higher and more urgent than before, its fall longer and more dramatic.

The B strain begins with a melody that is rhythmically similar to that with which the A strain ended, thus tying the two strains together. As the melodic line attempts to rise higher, the little Bb-A phrase to which it falls back is echoed by the octave Gb-F in the bass. When it finally achieves its high point, the bass line rises to meet it as it begins its long descent. This time it is the second half of the melody that is varied in the repeat of the strain, though the bass line is different in the first half: instead of the echoing octaves, we have vaulting phrases that remind us of those in mm. 3 and 7. The pathos of the melody's long descent at the end of the strain is complicated this time by a sinuously chromatic phrase—reminding us of the beginning of the repeat of the A strain—that is twice imitated in lower octaves as the song moves down to its conclusion.

What has Bach seen in the poem that Gräfe did not, and why is his setting more interesting and insightful than Gräfe's? Gräfe, we recall, set the poem as a straightforward lament about the difficulties of prayer and the infrequency with which it was practiced—difficulties in which, by implication, the speaker himself was not involved. But the jagged, sinuous phrases of Bach's setting make it clear from the outset, by movingly dramatizing these difficulties, that they are also experienced by the speaker: the situation he laments and seeks to correct is one in which he too is deeply involved. This involvement gives his lament more authority as well as more emotional weight.

Another song in which Bach employs a highly inflected, rhythmically restless melodic line to gain a sense of tortured inwardness is the setting of one of the two poems in Gellert's book called "Passionslied," the one that begins with the line "Erforsche mich, erfahr mein Herz." This poem, like

"Das Gebet," is too long to permit (or require) complete citation, consisting of 11 ten-line stanzas. Addressing Christ directly, the speaker imaginatively re-creates the scene of the crucifixion:

> Erforsche mich, erfahr mein Herz,
> Und sieh, Herr, wie ichs meyne.
> Ich denk an deines Leidens Schmerz,
> An deine Lieb, und weine.
> Dein Kreuz sey mir gebenedeyt!
> Welch Wunder der Barmherzigkeit
> Hast du der Welt erwiesen!
> Wenn hab ich dies genug bedacht,
> Und dich aus aller meiner Macht
> Genug dafür gepriesen?
>
> Rath, Kraft, und Friedefürst und Held!
> In Fleisch und Blut gekleidet,
> Wirst du das Opfer für die Welt,
> Und deine Seele leidet.
> Dein Freund, der dich verräth, ist nah.
> Des Zornes Gottes Stund ist da,
> Und Schrecken strömen über.
> Du zagst, und fühlst der Höllen Weh:
> "Ists möglich, Vater, o so geh
> "Der Kelch vor mir vorüber!"

He first asks God to examine his heart, to ascertain his state of mind. Then he describes that state of mind as it concerns Christ's passion, stressing first his sadness at Christ's suffering and then his joy that this suffering is offered to him personally as a blessing ("sey mir gebenedeyt") and to the whole world as a miracle of compassion. But then, suddenly overcome by sadness once again, he turns on himself for not having thought of this often enough and for not having praised God accordingly. Over the course of the second stanza, he gradually identifies himself with Christ, ending finally by citing the familiar words from Matthew 26:39: "O my father, if it be possible, let this cup pass from me." With only very slight changes, made for reasons of meter and rhyme, the passage is cited almost exactly as it appears in Luther's translation: "Mein Vater, ist's möglich, so gehe dieser Kelch von mir." And of course this is not the only direct reference to the Bible in the second stanza. The only biblical reference in the first stanza is in the first two lines, which are taken from the penultimate verse of Psalm 139: "Erforsche mich, Gott, und erfahre mein Herz; prüfe mich und erfahre, wie ich's meine." But the second stanza is almost completely made up of such direct references—as Werth (pp. 56–57) shows:

> . . . er heisst Wunderbar, Rat, Kraft, Held, Ewigvater, Friedefürst.
>   [Isa. 9:6]
> Meine Seele ist betrübt bis an den Tod. [Matt. 26:38]
> Siehe, der mich verrät, ist nahe. [Mark 14:42]
> Siehe, die Stunde ist hie, dass des Menschen Sohn in der Sünder
>   Hände überantwortet wird. [Matt. 26:45]
> Schrecken ist um und um. [Jer. 46:5]
> . . . und fing an zu trauern und zu zagen. [Matt. 26:37]
> Angst der Hölle hatte mich getroffen. [Ps. 116:3]
> Mein Vater, ist's möglich, so gehe dieser Kelch von mir. [Matt. 26:39]

And this is pretty much true of the remaining nine stanzas of "Passionslied," which in this respect is similar to "Busslied."

For all their differences from each other, however, the first and second stanzas have something important in common: both rise in emotional intensity at the fifth line and then decline in the last three lines. The first stanza begins with the speaker's earnest, humble plea that God understand his grief at Christ's sacrifice, becomes suddenly (and powerfully) hopeful at "Dein Kreuz sey mir gebenedeyt!", and then retreats into itself for the concluding three lines of self-accusation. The second stanza speaks of Christ's suffering in its first four lines, then suddenly shifts to the drama of Judas's betrayal, then concludes with the pathos of Christ's fear and grief—made all the more immediate by the direct quotation from Matthew.

Most of the other stanzas have the same emotional rhythm—for example the sixth:

> Ein Opfer, nach dem ewgen Rath,
> Belegt mit unsern Plagen,
> Um deines Volkes Missethat
> Gemartert und zerschlagen,
> Gehst du den Weg zum Kreuzesstamm,
> In Unschuld stumm, gleich als ein Lamm,
> Dass man zur Schlachtbank führet.
> Freywillig, als der Helden Held,
> Trägst du, aus Liebe für die Welt,
> Den Tod, der uns gebühret.

After the suspended syntax of the first four lines, the fifth begins with the welcome thrust of the long-postponed verb ("Gehst du den Weg"), producing a burst of energy that is immediately balanced by the simile of the innocent lamb—just as in the biblical source, Isaiah 53:7. (Chapter 53, incidentally, is one of the famously "pre-Christian" chapters of Isaiah, the source also of "He was despised and rejected" and "All we like sheep have gone astray" from Handel's *Messiah*.) The last three lines again taper off in emotional intensity.

Or take the ninth stanza:

> Du neigst dein Haupt. Es ist vollbracht.
> Du stirbst! die Erd erschüttert.
> Die Arbeit hab ich dir gemacht,
> Herr, meine Seele zittert.
> Was ist der Mensch, den du befreyt?
> O wär ich doch ganz Dankbarkeit!
> Herr, lass mich Gnade finden!
> Und deine Liebe dringe mich,
> Dass ich dich wieder lieb, und dich
> Nie kreuzige mit Sünden!

The short, broken sentences of the opening lines, taken directly from John 19:30, express weariness and resignation. Lines two and three, on the other hand, take accusing words that in Isaiah 43:24 are spoken by God—"Ja, mir hast du Arbeit gemacht in deinen Sünden, und hast mir Mühe gemacht in deinen Missetaten"—and turn them into words with which the speaker accuses himself of making Christ's sacrifice necessary through his sins. This self-accusation leads to the stanza's climax, the despairing outburst of the fifth line: "Was ist der Mensch, den du befreyt?" In the concluding lines the tone again becomes quieter as the speaker asks for God's love.

Of course this common rhetorical shape shared by most of the stanzas of "Passionslied" is most convenient for the composer of a strophic setting. And of course it is no accident—it is, in fact, almost predetermined by the rhyme scheme that Gellert has chosen: ABABCCDEED. The fact that lines five and six are a couplet, preceded and followed by quatrains, immediately calls attention to them and makes them stand out. But in most stanzas the emotional climax of the stanza lasts for three lines, including the first line of the concluding quatrain and thus making a smooth transition to the slackening of emotional tension in the final lines.

With all this in mind, let us now look at C.P.E. Bach's setting of Gellert's "Passionslied":

Like "Das Gebet," this song too begins with the vocal line striking out on its own. It is thus allowed to establish its rhythmic pattern of short-long-short (eighth-quarter-eighth) before the accompaniment joins in with its contrastingly steady quarter notes. This rhythmic contrast is maintained over the first four bars, as the harmony completes its i-iv-V-i circuit. But in the latter half of m. 4 there is a slight harmonic surprise: the first-inversion E-flat chord suggests that we may be moving toward B-flat. But then, as the melodic line rises beseechingly to D, the harmony beneath it retreats to a first-inversion D-minor chord, and the promised major resolution slips away. As the melodic line rapidly descends, the phrase ends hurriedly, and rather wearily, a bar early, in m. 7.

The total effect is one of initial depression rising slightly to hope and then sinking back upon itself. And this effect is repeated, as the whole phrase is heard again. Then suddenly, with the pickup to m. 15, the promised B-flat arrives at last. The melodic line is firmly declarative, giving way after a bar to follow the descent of the harmony beneath it. When it returns to A-flat, in m. 17, for a second, less energetic descent, the harmony softens toward the subdominant. But then yet another descent, beginning higher this time, brings us, in m. 21, to a moment of stasis: three bars of dwelling on the dominant of B-flat.

We have thus had a series of slightly irregular phrases: a seven-bar phrase followed by its repetition, and then a six-bar phrase (three plus three) followed by a three-bar holding pattern (as it were). We notice that the melodic line shifts from restless indecision to firm insistence at precisely the point (the pickup to m. 15) where the singer arrives at line five of Gellert's stanza, the rhetorical climax. But by keeping his phrases irregular, as well as by the graciously softening move to the subdominant in mm. 17–18, Bach almost immediately begins the tapering-off effect we noticed in Gellert's poem, deflating the emotional force of m. 15 almost before it has a chance to make itself felt. The three bars of stasis on the dominant neatly complete the process, bringing us to the withdrawal of the final three lines.

In m. 24 the bass line begins its descent—one of Bach's characteristic bottom-dropping-out-of-everything effects. The melodic line in mm. 26–27 is a harmonized version of that in mm. 3–4 and

10-11, reinvoking the sadness and weariness of the song's first strain as the bass, rising from D to G, gives a sense of closure. For once, the phrases seem to have regularized into two-bar units, and the apparent drift toward the flat side of the tonal spectrum in mm. 28-29 suggests that we are moving to a quiet conclusion. But at this point Bach suddenly and dramatically alters the emotional movement of Gellert's stanza as the vocal line jumps, with a desperate flourish, up a tritone, to C#, heard over a bleak, insistently pounding A-E open fifth in the keyboard's left hand. The effect is that of a stab at the heart. Wrenched around, the harmony begins its approach to the tonic from the sharp side, interrupting the orderly sequence of two-bar phrases. The passive regret with which Gellert's stanzas regularly conclude has become a *frisson*.

Looking back over Gellert's poem, I think we can understand why Bach wanted to end his song in this way. While the overt emotional intensity of Gellert's stanza does tend to fall off in the final three lines, he often uses these lines to raise an issue that is quite highly charged emotionally for Christians, the issue of original sin. The climactic fifth line of the second stanza, as we noted earlier, is "Dein Freund, der dich verräth, ist nah." Since the speaker of the poem has been conjuring up for himself the scene of the Crucifixion, this betraying friend is, obviously, Judas. But reading the line in context, one does a double-take. For in addition to conjuring up the scene of Christ's passion, as one would do in a religious meditation, the speaker is stressing his own personal relation to Christ's act. He speaks of it, we recall, not only as a "Wunder der Barmherzigkeit" offered to the world, but also as a personal blessing offered directly to him: "Dein Kreuz sey mir gebenedeyt!" Therefore when we read "Dein Freund, der dich verräth, ist nah," we hear it as also referring to the speaker himself, the point of whose meditation is precisely to bring him nearer to Christ and his passion.

That this is not merely a fanciful interpretation becomes clear in the fourth stanza:

> Du trägst der Missethäter Lohn,
> Und hattest nie gesündigt;
> Du, der Gerechte, Gottes Sohn!
> So wars vorher verkündigt.
> Der Frechen Schaar begehrt dein Blut,
> Du duldest, göttlich gross, die Wut,
> Um Seelen zu erretten.
> Dein Mörder, Jesus, war auch ich;
> Denn Gott warf aller Sünd auf dich,
> Damit wir Friede hätten.

In comparison with the three lines that precede them, the stanza's last three lines are low-pitched and matter-of-fact in tone. Yet "Dein Mörder, Jesus, war auch ich," precisely because it is stated so calmly and matter-of-factly—a fact, as it were, that everyone would of course acknowledge—shocks us. And yet of course it follows perfectly logically from what has preceded: that the speaker can look upon Christ's passion as a personal benison is a direct result of—or, perhaps better, merely another way of stating—the fact that Christ has died for his sins, and therefore that he is Christ's murderer. With this recognition we recall the earlier ambiguity of "Dein Freund, der dich verräth, is nah"—and everything falls neatly into place.

All this comes back down to original sin, for it is only because we are Adam's progeny, and because our souls are damaged by his sin, that we too are sinners requiring to be restored to wholeness by Christ's sacrifice. In the two stanzas that we singled out earlier as sharing the general rhetorical shape characteristic of the stanzas of "Passionslied," stanzas six and nine, we can also notice that Gellert has quietly slipped in references to original sin. In both stanzas the vivid evocation of Christ on the cross is followed by a quieter turn inward, as the speaker reminds himself (and us) of his (and our) responsibility for the Crucifixion. In stanza six, after picturing Christ traversing the *via dolorosa*,

"In Unschuld stumm, gleich als ein Lamm," the speaker concludes by speaking of his death as "Den Tod, der uns gebühret." Again, the small word "uns" enters so easily and naturally that it shocks us. And in the ninth stanza, after a still more dramatic evocation of the scene—"Du neigst dein Haupt. Es ist vollbracht. / Du stirbst!"—the speaker closes with the wish that he may not only love and be loved by Christ but that he may also never (again) crucify Christ with (his) sins ("und dich / Nie kreuzige mit Sünden!"). I think that it was Bach's recognition of the importance of original sin to the endings of a number of the poem's stanzas that led him to give the unexpectedly sharp dramatic twist to the end of his song.

While it is true that the greatest benefit offered C.P.E. Bach by Gellert's *Geistliche Oden und Lieder* was the chance to express complex emotional states, and that the most important songs, aesthetically and also for Bach's development as a composer, are those in which the poetic speaker turns inward, I do not want to leave the impression that those are the only good songs in Bach's collection. For he is also excellent at the poems that turn outward to offer wholehearted praise of God and his works. Therefore before closing this chapter, it will be useful to look at one of these outward-turning songs.

Interestingly enough, the poems that turn outward are generally shorter than those we have just been investigating. One of the best examples is "Die Ehre Gottes aus der Natur," which in its entirety reads thus:

> Die Himmel rühmen des Ewigen Ehre,
>   Ihr Schall pflanzt seinen Namen fort.
> Ihn rühmt der Erdkreis, ihn preisen die Meere;
>   Vernimm, o Mensch, ihr göttlich Wort!
> Wer trägt der Himmel unzählbare Sterne?
>   Wer führt die Sonn aus ihrem Zelt?
> Sie kömmt und leuchtet und lacht uns von ferne,
>   Und läuft den Weg, gleich als ein Held.
> Vernimms, und siehe die Wunder der Werke,
>   Die die Natur dir aufgestellt!
> Verkündigt Weisheit und Ordnung und Stärke
>   Dir nicht den Herrn, den Herrn der Welt?
> Kannst du der Wesen unzählbare Heere,
>   Den kleinsten Staub fühllos beschaun?
> Durch wen ist alles? O gieb ihm die Ehre!
>   Mir, ruft der Herr, sollst du vertraun.
> Mein ist die Kraft, mein ist Himmel und Erde;
>   An meinen Werken kennst du mich.
> Ich bins, und werde seyn, der ich seyn werde,
>   Dein Gott und Vater ewiglich.
> Ich bin dein Schöpfer, bin Weisheit und Güte,
>   Ein Gott der Ordnung und dein Heil;
> Ich bins! Mich liebe von ganzem Gemüthe,
>   Und nimm an meiner Gnade Theil.

After its two magnificent opening stanzas, this poem falters badly, becoming tiresomely repetitious, often rhythmically clumsy—"Ich bins, und werde seyn, der ich seyn werde"—and awkward in its final wrenching shift from the endless recital of God's power to the concluding invitation: "nimm an meiner Gnade Theil." Werth (p. 47) finds eleven biblical reminiscences, but many are too generic to be convincing. Besides the line just cited as rhythmically clumsy, which is taken verbatim from Exodus 3:14, the only significant ones are of the opening verses of Psalm 19 ("The heavens declare the glory of God"), upon which the opening two stanzas are heavily dependent.

Yet this was one of the Gellert poems most frequently set to music and it remains today his best-loved religious lyric. Doles provided one of his awkward, overornamented chorale settings, which Quantz imitated (but without the ornaments) in his 1760 *Neue Kirchen-Melodien zu denen geistlichen Liedern des Herrn Professor Gellerts*; the unquenchable Gräfe did one; and Marpurg did not one but two: a straight voice-and-keyboard solo song and a four-part (but not at all chorale-like) setting. Of these the only ones worth looking at briefly before we turn to Bach's are Gräfe's and Marpurg's solo setting.

First Gräfe:

This is the sort of thing that Gräfe does quite well: a cheerful, active piece that serves well enough to convey the poem's enthusiastic praise of God and his works. But it seems more an instrumental than a vocal piece. Playing the first few bars, one feels oneself at the beginning of a *galant* sonata or other chamber piece. And this sense is borne out by the prominent role that Gräfe has allotted to the two violins. In the other pieces of his that we have looked at, the violins were not really necessary but merely provided reinforcement for the keyboard part. But here are the two violin parts for "Die Ehre Gottes aus der Natur":

Clearly, the violin flourishes are an integral part of the piece not only at the end, where Gräfe felt impelled to superimpose them on the keyboard part, but all the way through. But the piece has many admirable things about it. The unexpected change of direction in m. 3, for example, where the urgent forward motion of the opening bars is suddenly dissipated for some bars in a burst of high-spirited foolery; or the equally unexpected renewal of the forward motion in m. 8, leading to the concluding flourishes. It does, however, remain a question whether the overall mood is quite appropriate to the seriousness of Gellert's poem.

Now Marpurg:

Though this at first looks like a familiar sort of $\frac{6}{8}$ dance movement, Marpurg's tempo indication "Mässig langsam" (as against Gräfe's "Munter") clearly indicates that he wants it to have a stately air, more in keeping with the dignity of the subject. But the unvarying, somewhat mechanical quality of both the melody and bass lines makes the piece seem an exercise rather than a spontaneous expression of dignified joyousness. Though Gräfe is further from the mood of the poem, he has written a more interesting piece of music.

Here, finally, is Bach's setting:

What strikes a listener first is the combination of the stately ("Prächtig") melody, declaimed in harmonized half notes, and the exuberant eighth-note arpeggios that surge up from the bass. Once encountered, it seems precisely right for Gellert's poem, dignified yet uninhibitedly joyous. And when one looks more closely, one sees much more to admire.

There is, first of all, the way Bach varies the pacing of his song without ever losing the momentum so stunningly set up at the outset. We are surprised when the bass suddenly comes to rest on a subdominant $\frac{6}{4}$ chord in m. 3. The vocal line waits just long enough before setting things going once again with its gracefully shaped descending eighth-note phrase. (It is also interesting how Bach ties the song together by having the vocal line, over a quite different harmony, allude to this bar in m. 16, as the song is coming to a close.) In m. 5 the bass again pauses for a moment, and when it begins to move again Bach emphasizes its voice-leading function (rather than just having it statically run an upward arpeggio in each bar) as we approach the cadence on B major in m. 8: amidst the running eighth notes we hear a line: E#-F#, D#-E, A#-B. At the same time, the melody moves with more fluidity than initially: the upper and lower voices are thus brought closer together rhythmically.

Second, one notices the ingenuity with which Bach uses the distinction between even eighth notes and paired dotted eighths and sixteenths to express Gellert's text. (And one problem in choosing the proper tempo for this song is surely to pick one fast enough to give those initial bass arpeggios thrust and buoyancy yet slow enough to leave the distinction between a pair of even eighths and a dotted eighth and sixteenth unobscured.) The spontaneity of the eighth-note arpeggios is somewhat compromised when one begins to notice that they have also taken on a voice-leading function. Then in m. 9, as we move into the dominant, Bach has the keyboard's left hand suddenly begin pounding out groups of octaves, connected by descending arpeggios, in a dotted-eighth-sixteenth rhythm. The music immediately becomes more martial, more organized-sounding: the ebullience and exuberance of the opening have, as it were, become official policy as the praise of God has spread from the heavens to the earth to the sea.

Third, one notices how Bach again creates a sort of synthesis at the end of the song. In m. 13 the keyboard's left hand suddenly breaks off, and the vocal line enters alone, with a grandly simple phrase in even eighth notes. But the dotted-eighth-sixteenth pattern gradually reenters in the bass, to be replaced by a version of the initial left-hand arpeggios as the song closes. The largeness of effect characteristic of the song is increased by a three-bar extension that Bach inserts into the final phrase as the two rhythms coalesce. If we jump from the end of m. 13 to the beginning of m. 17, we can hear how square-cut the song would have sounded without this extension.

The final thing to notice about "Die Ehre Gottes aus der Natur" is how comparatively virtuosic Bach's keyboard accompaniment has become. This increase in virtuosity tends to occur, for obvious reasons, in the other Gellert songs that are what I have called outward-turning—in "Die Güte Gottes," for example. It will be something to watch in the songs that follow.

There is much more that one could say about Bach's Gellert songs. There are, for example, many songs that are quite unspectacular yet beautifully made, satisfyingly adequate to the poems they set—for example, the first of the two songs entitled "Weihnachtslied" (No. 5), the first and second of the three entitled "Osterlied" (Nos. 10 and 22), "Morgengesang," the second "Abendlied" (No. 32), and "Am neueren Jahr." There are also a few dull, routine songs—but only a few. Suffice it to say that *Geistliche Oden und Lieder* was not merely an important step forward for its composer but also a song collection that offered a great deal to its intended audience.

It is therefore no surprise that critical praise was both immediate and enduring, and that the collection went into four subsequent editions in Bach's lifetime: the second in 1759, the third in 1764, the fourth in 1771, and the fifth in 1784. To the third and subsequent editions Bach added an *Anhang* comprising settings of twelve poems by authors other than Gellert, most of whom remain, to this day, unidentified.

Soon after the collection appeared, the reviewer for the Leipzig *Bibliothek der schönen Wissenschaften und freyen Künste* found that Bach had advanced Gellert's goal of religious edification:

> The religious poems of Herr Gellert were written for edification—and, indeed, for edification through song. Therefore they seem hampered by the lack of melodies, and they could not easily have received them from a worthier hand than that of Herr Bach, who has long been accustomed to uniting the noblest expression with the secrets of his art, and his characteristic concision with flowing song.[14]

As we saw in Chapter Seven, Marpurg, writing in 1758 in *Historisch-Kritische Beyträge*, was rather coy about Bach's collection, noting only: "We do not venture to praise the compositions of Herr Bach as they deserve."[15] The coyness is perhaps accounted for by the fact that notices directly follow of Marpurg's own two Gellert collections of that year, *Geistliche Oden, in Melodien gesetzt von einigen Tonkünstlern in Berlin* and *Geistliche, moralische und weltliche Oden, von verschiedenen Dichtern und Componisten*. Marpurg probably wanted to avoid putting them into direct competition with Bach's collection, which of course offered settings of all Gellert's poems, and yet of course he had no desire to offend or be unjust to Bach. As we also saw, Marpurg was more enthusiastic two years later, in *Kritische Briefe über die Tonkunst*:

> Since the subjects of Gellert's muse are somewhat more elevated than wine and love, the renowned composer had no choice but to turn aside from the usual style of song composition, and who could expect, from the divine art of a Bach, anything but what is extraordinary and always excellent?[16]

Far from seeing Bach as naturally fitting in with, and carrying further, Gellert's declared aim of religious "Erbauung," Marpurg is interested in the sublimity of Gellert's poems, which he rightly sees as having led Bach to write in a quite different style from his songwriting contemporaries.

In 1765 the *Allgemeine deutsche Bibliothek* published the following review of the collection's third edition, which had appeared the previous year:

> Even in these melodies one does not fail to discover the fiery and inventive spirit of our Herr Bach. To be sure, they seem to be designed more for playing at the keyboard than for singing. Nonetheless a voice that is sufficiently prepared through rigorous studies will find here abundant opportunity to become more skillful and secure in the performance of ornaments, in the execution of various difficult sequences of tones, and, generally, in expression. This third edition makes it clear enough why these songs have gained the well-deserved applause of the public. Twelve other religious songs by the same composer have been added as an Appendix.[17]

J. F. Reichardt, writing in 1782, shortly before the fifth edition of Bach's Gellert collection appeared, lamented that "our finest religious poems lack musical settings, or as good as lack them," a state of affairs he blamed on both composers and the public:

> The blame rests not only on the composers; the public also bears a share of it. Bach's compositions to Gellert's poems, which should by rights be in every hand, are little sung, except in the land where Bach and Gellert themselves have lived, and his splendid settings of Cramer's Psalms have not had another edition since 1774. Some of the songs in these masterly collections are nonetheless still common songs of edification.[18]

Finally, C. F. D. Schubart, probably writing in 1784 or 1785, just about the time the fifth edition of Bach's Gellert songs did appear, gave them pride of place when praising Bach as a song composer: "His cantatas, his chorales, for which he chose Gellert's, Cramer's, and Klopstock's texts, are full of pathos, full of novelty in the course of their melodies, unique in their modulations—in short, true music of the spheres."[19]

Bach's settings of the psalm translations of Johann Andreas Cramer, whom we encountered earlier in this chapter as Gellert's friend and first biographer, were the composer's next major song project. But these songs, which Bach apparently did not begin working on until about 1773, were not published until 1774. In the chapter that follows, we will examine the songs that he composed between his settings of Gellert and those of Cramer.

Chapter Ten

From Gellert to Cramer

Gellert's *Geistliche Oden und Lieder*, and the various collections of songs based on them, were published at an especially difficult time in the Seven Years' War. Indeed, their immense popularity has often been traced to that fact. Though the Prussians, under Frederick, had won some important battles early in the war, by 1757 their hopes for victory were dim. Austria had France, Russia, and (most recently) Sweden on her side, while Prussia had only England, from whom she was getting scant aid. By that summer Frederick found himself hemmed in, fighting the Russians in the east, the Austrians in the south, the French in the west, and the Swedes in the north. But then on November 4 he scored a great victory over the French at Rossbach. A month later he defeated the Austrians at Leuthen, and it seemed as though the tide had turned.

I

It was in this overheated climate that the well-known poet Johann Wilhelm Ludwig Gleim published his collection *Preussische Kriegslieder in den Feldzügen 1756 und 1757 von einem Grenadier*. Included were musical settings of eight of the poems, all or most of them probably by Krause. C.P.E. Bach, who had been forced to remove his family for some months from Berlin to Zerbst, 70 miles to the southwest, had been among those asked to contribute songs. But his contribution arrived too late for the publication date of July 1758.[1] The song that he submitted, which in fact dealt with the Rossbach victory, was the first of four that he placed alongside those he had published in earlier collections to make up the collection of 20 that he published in 1762 as *Oden mit Melodien*.

Though slight, the song is interesting as a sign of things to come in the years that separate the publication of Bach's Gellert collection from that of his settings of Cramer's psalms. Here is Gleim's poem, "Herausforderungslied vor der Schlacht bey Rossbach":

> Heraus aus deiner Wolfesgruft,
> Furchtbares Heldenheer!
> Heraus zum Streit in frische Luft,
> Mit Muth und Schlachtgewehr!
>
> Wir kleiner Haufe wachen schon,
> Und singen Schlachtgesang,
> Und wecken dich mit Kriegeston:
> Mit Lärm und Waffenklang.

> Was schlummerst du? Die träge Rast,
> Schickt die für Helden sich?
> Wenn du gerechte Sache hast,
> Warum verkriechst du dich?

Certainly this seems a straightforward enough call-to-arms. The members of the small elite corps who have been standing watch are summoning the rest of the force out to battle. The last stanza is a challenge, offered in the spirit of hearty male camaraderie often found in such poems: Why are you still sleeping? Is this indolent repose appropriate to heroes? If you're made of the right stuff, why are you slinking off like this?

But here is what Bach did with it:

The song is mainly built out of simple fanfare figures, punctuated by assertive pairs of full chords at the cadences and relieved by the up-and-down scalar movement in m. 6. The fanfares at the end of the first strophe loop back to the beginning of the second. But after the third and final strophe we end not on the tonic but rather on the first-inversion diminished triad that we so often meet in recitatives, functioning as a rootless secondary dominant (here a V/V). And this is followed by the unaccompanied voice repeating, softly and slowly, the poem's last words, "verkriechst du dich?" in a phrase that Deryck Cooke has identified as "one of the immemorial cadential clichés of German operatic recitative, when a character asked a question, going back to Mozart, and probably earlier."[2] The final low E in the keyboard's left hand—and one wonders whether or not Bach would have wanted it harmonized; probably not—signals that we end on the dominant.

So something is to follow—but nothing does. We are left hanging on the question—as Gleim certainly did not intend us to be. Strangely enough, this extraordinary moment has received virtually no attention from those who have written on C. P. E. Bach's songs. Of the 19th- and early 20th-century historians of the German lied, only E. O. Lindner mentions it, and then only as one more example to reinforce his contention that the songs in Bach's *Oden mit Melodien* are characterized by "comprehensible declamation," lack warmth, and have melodies that are angular and charmless.[3] And while both Gudrun Busch, in her masterly dissertation on the songs, and Hans-Günter Ottenberg, in his recent biography of the composer, discuss the song at length, neither one of them considers its ending.

But surely something very interesting is going on here. Writing from a Marxist viewpoint, Ottenberg notes that "many bourgeois artists, trapped in narrow political attitudes, praised Frederick's aggressive policies lavishly," and singles out Gleim's collection as "a typical instance of such triumphalist tendencies." But he sees nothing special about Bach's setting: "Given that C. P. E. Bach set one of these poems to music, . . . it may be concluded at least that his attitude towards such apologetic literature was unreflecting."[4] This seems to me dead wrong. We do not know precisely what Bach's attitude toward the Seven Years' War, or toward matters of war and peace in general, was; but the pointedly querulous ending to a setting of an ostensibly chauvinistic and bellicose poem surely is evidence of some sort of reflection on his part. The most one can say, I think, is that his intense absorption in Gellert's poetry, and the very powerful influence that Gellert's religious thought had upon his development as a composer of songs, forced Bach to an ironic (or at least deeply ambivalent) view of some of the conventional subject-matters of secular songs.

It may perhaps also be significant that Bach placed "Herausforderungslied vor der Schlacht bey Rossbach" last in his collection of 20 secular songs: for by 1762, when *Oden mit Melodien* was published, Frederick and the Prussians were once again in desperate straits. Their cause was saved only by the sudden death of Tsarina Elisabeth of Russia and the subsequent withdrawal of Russia from the war ordered by her successor, Peter III, who was a great admirer of Frederick. Bach may have meant to leave his audience questioning the war.

The three other songs that Bach composed after 1758 for inclusion in *Oden mit Melodien* are "Doris" and "Die Tugend," to poems by the Swiss poet Albrecht von Haller, and "Der Traum," to verses by an unknown poet. Of these, "Doris" is the most interesting. It is, in itself, an excellent song, complex and quite dramatic, and has the further significance for Bach's development as a composer of songs that in 1775 or 1776 he returned to Haller's poem and this time gave it a *durchkomponiert* setting.

The poem, consisting of 24 six-line stanzas, is much too long to quote in its entirety. It was written by Haller in 1730, and first appeared in 1744, in the second edition of his *Versuch Schweizerischer Gedichten*. Before Bach's *Oden* appeared in 1762, "Doris" had already received at least two published settings, by Marpurg (1756) and Kirnberger (1760). It would receive many more in the years that followed, and had evidently been turned into a song by someone as early as 1750, for Klopstock records having heard it sung then, both in letters and in his poem of that year, "Der Zürichersee."[5] Haller (1708-1777) was not merely (or even primarily) a poet. He was also an anatomist, physiologist, botanist, and doctor, who served from 1736 to 1753 as professor of all these subjects at the University of Göttingen. Even after he astonished the learned world by resigning his professorship and retiring to serve, for the remainder of his life, in a modest municipal post at Bern, Haller continued to do research and to publish in his various fields, as well as to write and publish poetry. Like Leibniz before him, he was known, even in his own time, as "the last universal genius."

It is thus no surprise that Haller's poems are filled with the most minute, detailed, quasi-scientific analyses of people and objects. "Doris" is certainly no exception. Since many of Gellert's poems also analyze the emotional states proper to certain religious doctrines and events with comparable minuteness, this may have been part of what drew Bach to "Doris." Its opening stanza is a conventional enough bit of romantic scene-setting—but very well done:

> Des Tages Licht hat sich verdunkelt,
> Der Purpur, der im Westen funkelt,
> Erblasset in ein falbes Grau;
> Der Mond zeigt seine Silberhörner,
> Die kühle Nacht streut Schlummerkörner,
> Und tränkt die trockne Welt mit Thau.

The faintly ominous first line is nicely balanced by the majesty ("Purpur") of the sunset; the dim and washed-out "falbes Grau" of line three becomes suddenly transformed by the fairy-tale magic of the moon's silver horns and the sleep-inducing grains of sand mysteriously strewn by the cool night (not, we notice, by the familiar figure of the Sandman); the grandly universal act of giving the whole dry world a drink is effortlessly performed by the delicate dew.

But then, in the second stanza, something odd begins to happen:

> Komm, Doris, komm zu jenen Buchen,
> Lass uns den stillen Grund besuchen,
> Wo nichts sich regt, als ich und du.
> Nur noch der Hauch verliebter Weste
> Belebt das schwanke Laub der Aeste,
> Und winket dir liebkosend zu.

Why "*jenen* Buchen"? Is this a scene that the speaker and Doris have visited before, and is he attempting to relive some past rendezvous, or is he merely pointing out the beech trees to her as he speaks? One cannot tell for sure. A similar question is raised, I think, by "*den* stillen Grund." It all seems somehow familiar, as in a dream, and this just slightly eerie, dreamlike feeling is enhanced by the speaker's stress on the absolute silence of the place, and perhaps also by the way in which the wind and the leaves seem to cooperate with his plan (though this could be merely conventional).

A couple of stanzas later, however, the poem grows still odder as the speaker delivers another injunction to Doris:

> Sprich Doris! fühlst du nicht im Herzen,
> Die zarte Regung sanfter Schmerzen,
> Die süsser sind als aller Lust?
> Strahlt nicht dein holder Blick gelinder?
> Rollt nicht dein Blut sich selbst geschwinder,
> Und Schwellt die unschuldsvolle Brust?

He apparently wants Doris to speak, to tell him exactly what she is feeling. But then he immediately goes on, in his series of increasingly anxious and excited questions, both to prevent her from replying—and she never does speak, not once in the 24 stanzas—and also to make it clear precisely what she ought to be feeling. At this point we are forced to ask: Is Doris there at all? Is she in fact real or only a figment of the speaker's overheated imagination (and perhaps memory)?

As the poem goes on, the speaker, frequently addressing her as "Mein Kind," repeatedly asks Doris what she is feeling or tells her what to do and how to feel about it. The opening lines of a few stanzas will make this clear: "Ich weiss, dass sich dein Herz befraget," "Du staunst; es regt sich deine Tugend," "Mein Kind, erheitre deine Blicke," "Wie? sollte dich die Liebe schrecken!" and so on. But all the while he is charting and/or commanding every slight variation in her feelings, real or imagined, the speaker is also, *sub rosa* as it were, delivering the familiar message of seduction poems: Gather ye Rose-buds while ye may, Old Time is still a flying. Finally, in stanza 14, he begins to come a little more out into the open:

> Du seufzest, Doris! wirst du blöde?
> O selig! flösste mein Rede
> Dir den Geschmack des Liebens ein.
> Wie angenehm ist doch die Liebe?
> Erregt ihr Bild schon zarte Triebe,
> Was wird das Urbild selber seyn?
>
> Mein Kind, geniesse deines Lebens,
> Sey nicht so schön für dich vergebens,
> Sey nicht so schön für uns zur Quaal.
> Schilt nicht der Liebe Furcht und Kummer,

> Des kalten Gleichsinns eckler Schlummer
> Ist unvergnügter tausendmal.
>
> Zu dem, was hast du zu befahren?
> Lass andre nur ein Herz bewahren,
> Das, wers besessen, gleich verlässt.
> Du bleibst der Seelen ewig Meister,
> Die Schönheit fesselt dir die Geister,
> Und deine Tugend hält sie fest.
>
> Erwähle nur von unsrer Jugend,
> Dein Reich ist ja das Reich der Tugend,
> Doch, darf ich rathen, wähle mich.
> Was hilft es lang sein Herz verhehlen?
> Du kannst von hundert edlern wählen,
> Doch keinen, der sich liebt, wie ich.

One feels that T. S. Eliot, had he known this poem, would have liked it. It is reminiscent of the Marvell and Herrick poems praised by Eliot not only in its theme but also in its possession of "a tough reasonableness beneath the slight lyric grace," which Eliot singled out, in his 1921 essay on Marvell, as characterizing the wit of the Caroline poets. (One also suspects that Eliot, as the author of "La Figlia che Piange," would have appreciated the element of fantasy in Haller's poem that makes the speaker simultaneously fill the roles of participant, spectator, and stage-manager in relation to the poem's action.)

Up to this point the constant, anxious following of Doris's moods has reminded us, in its obsessiveness, of the dead earnestness of a novel such as Richardson's *Clarissa*. But now, gradually, it all turns out—or does it?—to be a sort of elaborate joke. In the four stanzas just cited one can feel the speaker slowly tightening the screws of his argument as he by turns titillates ("Was wird das Urbild selber seyn?"), threatens ("Des kalten Gleichsinns eckler Schlummer / Ist unvergnügter tausendmal"), and flatters ("Und deine Tugend hält sie fest") poor Doris. Then, after generously urging her to choose a lover from the "Reich der Tugend" which she rules, he suavely adds: "Doch, darf ich rathen, wähle mich"—modestly adding that while she could of course choose hundreds who are nobler, none would love her as he does. This seems to me masterly.

The poem could well end here, but of course it does not. In the six stanzas that follow, he elaborates at length on his superiority to her other possible lovers, and once again we feel the reality of Doris slipping away from us, out of the poem. Then, after he declares "Ein einig Wort ist gnug zum Lohn," we have the poem's concluding stanza:

> Was siehst du furchtsam hin und wieder,
> Und schlägst die holden Blicke nieder?
> Es ist kein fremder Zeuge nah:
> Mein Kind, kann ich dich nicht erweichen,
> Doch ja, dein Mund giebt zwar kein Zeichen,
> Allein dein Seufzen sagt mir Ja.

And so that "einig Wort" never comes, and we are left merely with Doris's by now familiar sigh. Or perhaps not even with that. For after the climactic stanza in which the speaker actually puts himself forward as a candidate for Doris's love, we seem to lapse back into solipsism, a dream or fantasy of a relationship in which the speaker has the barren satisfaction of pulling all the strings.

Of course no strophic setting could even begin to do justice to the richness of this poem. And yet that richness, in particular the elaborate psychological complexity, must surely have played a part in what made Bach want to set it—and not just once, but twice. Here is his setting:

What first strikes one about this song is its relentless urgency. No sooner is the first phrase finished off with a tight little flourish at the beginning of m. 2 than the second phrase begins—with the same three-note descending group that began the first one. Similarly, the third phrase begins right on the heels of the second one, in m. 4, with a slightly altered version of the original three-note descending group. And in all three cases the bass marches in parallel with the three descending pickup notes of the melody. After the cadence on V in m. 6, the first phrase of the song's contrasting second section begins with an inversion of the three-note group—but we notice that the bass once again moves down, in a neat voice-exchange. At the end of m. 8, the rhythm loosens a bit as the vocal line begins the next phrase with a descent not in eighth notes but rather in sixteenths. But the same sense of urgency, of not allowing the music to breathe, is still there. (And the three-note descent in eighth notes is still there too, in thirds in the bass line in m. 9.) As the phrase ends in m. 10, the vocal line again jumps right in, taking us without pause to the final cadence.

Why has Bach set the poem in this way? What about the poem was he endeavoring to capture? Along with the urgency, the constant, anxious pushing forward that we have noticed, we notice also that the phrases, taken individually, are gracious, pleasing, and well turned. A tension is thus set up between the well-mannered address of the speaker/singer and the disturbing (and disturbed) restlessness that lies beneath his external poise. This is not precisely Eliot's tension between slight lyric grace and tough reasonableness, but it is, I think, akin to it. The compulsive way in which the poem's speaker dwells on Doris's constantly changing emotional states is, at any rate, effectively suggested.

Shortly after publishing his *Oden mit Melodien*, Bach wrote three songs that were published in 1765, together with a number of keyboard pieces, as *Clavierstücke verschiedener Art von Carl Philipp Emanuel Bach. Erste Sammlung*. Two of these were pastorals (or mock-pastorals); the third and most interesting, set to an odd satirical poem by N. D. Giseke, is called "Das Privilegium." Here is Giseke's poem:

>Ihr Brüder, zankt nicht mit den Thoren,
>Sie haben einen Eyd geschworen,
>Den halten sie, und bleiben dumm.
>Sie werden euren Spott ermüden,
>Und bleiben doch mit sich zufrieden,
>Das ist ihr Privilegium.
>
>Ein jeder Mensch hat seine Freude,
>Und denkt wohl, dass man ihn beneide;

Der Thor denkts auch, denn er ist dumm.
Wollt ihr ihm seine Freude nehmen?
Soll er sich seiner Weise schämen?
Er hat sein Privilegium.

Zwingt Narren nicht, euch hoch zu achten,
Sie sind befugt, euch zu verachten;
Denn ihr seyd klug, und sie sind dumm.
Die Herren wissen auch zu leben.
Und loben die, die sie erheben;
Das ist ihr Privilegium.

So oft ihr Gecken kommen sehet,
So weichet aus, bückt euch, und gehet;
Sie weichen nicht, denn sie sind dumm.
Könnt ihr von Narren das begehren?
Ja, wenn sie keine Narren wären!
Das ist ihr Privilegium.

Vergebens bleicht man einen Mohren;
Vergebens straft man einen Thoren;
Der Mohr bleibt schwarz, der Thor bleibt dumm.
Das Bessern ist nicht meine Sache,
Ich lass die Narren seyn, und lache;
Das ist mein Privilegium.

First published in 1748 in *Sammlung vermischter Schriften*, this poem reminds one of Swift—even to the point of being in Swift's favorite tetrameter meter. Though barbed, the wit is also playful, and the speaker remains in the background, anonymous, with none of the vigorous self-dramatization so often found in Pope's satires.

Don't bother to quarrel with fools, he tells us. And then there is the pleasant fantasy about their all having sworn a solemn oath to remain forever stupid. They will only exhaust your mockery and remain contented with themselves—so why bother? That is their privilege. Every man enjoys thinking he is envied by others, and the fool is no exception—for he is, we recall, stupid. Would you deprive him of his joy? It's his privilege. And so the poem goes on. Don't try to make fools respect you for they are authorized ("befugt")—the legal term neatly picks up the oath metaphor—to despise you for your cleverness. Whenever you see fools, it is better simply to withdraw and surrender the field to them; to punish them for their stupidity (in hopes of changing them) is as futile as trying to make a blackamoor white. Such improvements are none of my affair: I let the fools be and laugh—that's *my* privilege!

There are many other fine touches along the way, but perhaps the finest of all is the title. *Privilegium*, it turns out, has never really been a German word. It means, of course, privilege in the legal sense, and it can be found in medieval German legal documents as *prîvilêgjum*, but in non-official contexts it becomes *prîvilêgje, prîvileige*, or *prîvileie*.[6] Even Grimm's magisterial dictionary does not have an entry for it. So to use it in the mid-18th century was not simply to use a slightly archaic synonym for *Vorrecht* but was to evoke a whole context of legal observance—as when we use a phrase like *habeas corpus*. Moreover, in the mid-18th century the context in which the term *privilegium* arose in Roman law was better known to readers of poetry than it is today. For the history of Roman law of course played a far larger part in legal education then than it does today. Moreover, in Germany a legal education was one of the principal routes to what we think of as a liberal education, and many men who had no intention of ever becoming lawyers, C.P.E. Bach for example, were trained in the law. Therefore they would know that in Roman law the term *privilegium* had a most interesting history.

It is, of course, merely *privus + lex*, a law that is private in the sense of applying only to one person in particular rather than generally. But at least through Cicero's time it meant a law passed against (rather than in favor of) an individual. One of the surviving fragments of the Twelve Tables, the earliest Roman code of laws, supposedly drawn up in 451–450 B.C., declares: "Privilegia ne inroganto"—no law may be passed against an individual. Legislative procedures, that is, may not be used to penalize individuals who have not broken a general rule of the community. Parsing this famous phrase in the chapter of his *Historical Introduction to the Study of Roman Law* devoted to the republican constitution, H. F. Jolowicz writes: "An example of a *privilegium* would be an English 'Act of Attainder,' i.e., an Act of Parliament ordering a particular person to be executed, such as was used for instance by Henry VIII to get rid of his minister Thomas Cromwell."[7] Scarcely what we mean when we speak of a privilege!

In the early years of the empire *privilegia* could be either favorable or unfavorable, depending upon the will of the emperor. But in his *Institutes* (c. A.D. 161) Gaius is interested in *privilegia* only in connection with the acquisition of property—i.e., only in the favorable sense. While C.P.E. Bach and his fellow-students would have known Gaius only in fragments (since the manuscript of his complete work was not discovered until 1816), they would doubtless have known the famous tag from the Twelve Tables and the relevant works of Cicero. They would therefore have been in a position to appreciate the joke neatly encapsulated in Giseke's choice of a title for his poem.

Looking back at the poem armed with this knowledge, one finds the wit even sharper than before. The repetition of the word "Privilegium" at the end of the last line of each of the first four stanzas (neatly answering "dumm" at the end of each stanza's third line) sounds at first mock-generous: the speaker is broadmindedly allowing the fools to go their way, complacent in their foolishness, and (as it were) wishing them well. But of course all this changes once we know the double meaning of the term *privilegium*. Without losing its generally playful tone, the poem picks up something of a sting: the wit becomes more complex. Should we also extend the negative meaning of *privilegium* to the final stanza of the poem, and discover that the speaker is turning his wit against himself? No—that would be going too far in our search for complexity and ambivalence. This is, surely, a completely lighthearted poem.

Of C.P.E. Bach's setting Gudrun Busch remarks: "Even in the secular song Bach increasingly moved away from the Berlin school. Thus, for example, 'Privilegium,' from the 1765 *Clavierstücke*, surpasses . . . Kirnberger's melody of 1758, with its compressed declamation" (p. 399). I quite agree that the comparison between Bach's and Kirnberger's settings of the poem does indeed show how individually Bach was now also treating secular subjects in his post-Gellert songs; but I would put the point rather differently from the way Busch does.

Here is Kirnberger's setting, which appeared in Marpurg's 1758 collection, *Geistliche, moralische und weltliche Oden*:

Certainly it has all the familiar earmarks of the standard Berlin song of its time: a generally perky air, neatly turned phrases, harmony that moves quickly and in an orderly fashion, a midsection in the dominant. Beyond this, one can note features that stamp it as a typical drinking song: the octave unison in mm. 10-12 that is repeated in the tonic at the close (mm. 21-24), the numerous internal repetitions. It is free enough from developmental complications to allow for group singing. Let us now look at C.P.E. Bach's setting:

This song is not only witty: it positively sparkles. For the first time, we have a Bach song that reminds us of the Viennese Classical composers. The first melodic phrase is genial and gracious, accompanied by the easy swing of the downward bass arpeggios. The second phrase is a slightly bolder variation of it, beginning higher (with an arpeggio that answers those in the bass) and ending lower. Then suddenly everything is disrupted: forward motion stops as we pause on a dominant first-inversion chord that sounds as though we had landed in the midst of an accompanied recitative. (And surely it is no coincidence that the first time this long-held note occurs, the singer is intoning the word "halten"!) The emphatic, fully harmonized cadence on the phrase that ends each time with the word "dumm" perfectly catches the self-satisfied air of the fools—stupid and proud of it!

Notice how skillfully Bach sets the song in motion again after this climactic point, having the bass move to D and giving to the vocal line repeated eighth notes that are then passed on, in the next bar, to the bass line. The phrase ending in m. 15 recalls the endings of the song's first two phrases, and the rising arpeggio in the bass neatly balances the descending ones heard earlier. As the melodic line moves gracefully toward the end of the song, the bass begins to perform comic leaps that sort themselves out under the vocal line's sixteenth-note descent (m. 22) to the cadence. But just when we think all is over, Bach wonderfully has the stanza's last line (ending of course each time in "Privilegium") repeated insistently, *fortissimo*, on A to the accompaniment of a boisterous cadential sequence. Again the pomposity of the declaration is perfectly caught—and we appreciate Bach's slapstick tactics all the more if we recall the double meaning of *privilegium* and if we note the graceful arpeggio that links the first ending back to the beginning of the next stanza, making its opening phrase sound like a response.

II

The songs of this period cannot be dated very precisely, but it was probably about the same time that Bach was working on the three songs for the *Clavierstücke verschiedener Art*, the early 1760s, that he also was working on the twelve songs for the Appendix or *Anhang* to be added to the third (1764) edition of his Gellert songs. It is traditional to criticize these *Anhang* songs as not being up to the level of the Gellert ones, but I am not at all sure that this is fair. At any rate, the *Anhang* songs are mostly quite experimental in nature, and show very clearly the directions in which Bach was now moving in his song composition.

A good contrasting pair to examine first is two songs that set poems that share a common title, "An Gott," and that are by the same author, Anna Louisa Karsch (1722–1791), known to her contemporaries as "die Karschin." She is a most interesting figure, one of those uneducated, evidently inspired poets who seemingly arose out of nowhere, warbling their native woodnotes wild, and were so popular in the mid-18th century. Born into miserably poor circumstances, with a mother who hated her because she was ugly, Karsch, like Cinderella, was reduced to being a slave to her younger stepsisters after her mother remarried. She married, also miserably, at 15, and bore child after child before the marriage ended—only to give way to another just as bad. But all the time she was reading—and writing poems.

Her stirring patriotic poems written during the Seven Years' War brought her to the attention of the Berlin literary circle, and no less a figure than Moses Mendelssohn pronounced her an "uncommon genius." She became the darling of the salons, and was befriended by Sulzer, Ramler, and (especially) Gleim, for whom she nourished a long-standing, unrequited love. It was Gleim who dubbed her "the German Sappho." But the desperate days of 1762 left her once again in poor circumstances. She sought and gained an audience with Frederick the Great, who promised her a house and pension but failed to keep his promise. With a growing family to take care of, mere survival once again became an issue, and she wrote and wrote—to mixed reviews as her novelty wore off.

The poems set by Bach show both her strong and weak points, her oddly original way of thinking of common religious subjects and the banality that her lack of education allowed her often to slip into. Here is the shorter of the two poems entitled "An Gott":

> Erheb auf mich dein Angesicht,
> Und lass mich deine Güte schmecken,
> Gott, der mich schuf! Es mag auch Dunkel oder Licht,
> Vor meinem Auge dich verdecken;
>
> O Herr! es mag ein Feuermeer
> In tausend Strömen dich umgeben;
> Verkleide dich im Sturm, und lasse rings umher
> Die Welt von deinem Wetter beben;
>
> Lass deinen Blick, voll Gottes Macht,
> Den Berg, die Felsen niederblitzen;
> Verhülle deine Stirn mit Zorn, und lasse Nacht
> Wo sonst der Tag regierte, sitzen;
>
> Doch betet meine Liebe dich
> Gott Schöpfer! an, tief unter Waffen,

Die dich umrauschen Herr! zum Leben hast du mich,
Und nicht zum Untergang, erschaffen!

The speaker begins, in a naively childlike way, by asking God to be allowed to see his face and (thereby) to taste his goodness. But the formulaic mention of the fact that God is her creator ("der mich schuf") starts a new train of thought, and she begins to dwell on God's awesome power. The God of infinite goodness that she asks to show himself to her is also the mysterious hidden God, the *deus absconditus*, of the Old Testament and the church fathers, able to conceal himself from her either by darkness or dazzling light. So she begins to ask for the "shows" of God's power so common in a book like Exodus. Since he could, if he chose, surround himself in a sea of flame, perhaps he might clothe himself in a storm that would cause the world to shake with fear. Or allow the lightning of his divine gaze to shatter the rocks and mountains. But then she suddenly remembers her own place in all this, and humbly begs him—out of her love, not as before out of mere awe of (and vicarious identification with) his naked force—to remember that he has created her for life, not for the total destruction her overheated imagination has just conjured up.

Like the holy sonnet of Donne's beginning "At the round earth's imagined corners," this poem dramatizes a religious meditation gone wrong. But whereas Donne's meditation is that of a learned priest who has lived so long with the eschatological machinery of the last day that he dreams himself into the position of God summoning the forces to the bar of judgment, hers is that of the naive, largely untaught but intensely sincere Pietistic Christian that she was. The poems are alike, however, in that in both of them the speaker recollects, perhaps just in time, his/her own place in the grand scheme of things. "But let them sleep, Lord, and me mourn a space," says Donne as he repents the sin of pride that led him temporarily to play God; Karsch returns to the concept of God as creator ("Schöpfer," "erschaffen") with the realization that creation is a positive, life-giving act, not a mere demonstration of power.

Very interestingly, Bach in setting this song writes a sort of chorale—which, as we have seen, he pointedly refused to do with Gellert's poems despite the fact that Gellert all but demanded chorale-like settings:

Though this is meant as a solo song, the word "kräftig" in Bach's direction suggests that singer and accompanist should cooperate to provide something like the direct, unified force provided by a congregation singing a traditional chorale in church. Thus the first phrase moves in simple harmonies and even quarter notes, the rhythm yielding a bit only at the cadence. But the second phrase, introduced by the emphatic octaves in the keyboard's left hand, immediately thins in texture as the chords are widely spread and the melody makes leaps. Also, the phrase, instead of ending in its second measure like its predecessor, is extended a bar and ornamented at its end to give a sort of lingering effect. The stanza's third (and longest) line is divided into two short phrases. In the first, the melody rises boldly, step by step, once again in granitic quarter notes but with more dramatic harmony than before; in the second, the texture again thins as the bass descends chromatically and the harmony expresses pathos (the incomplete minor seventh and German sixth chords at the beginning of m. 7). The final phrase has the vocal line making, and this time continuing, the same determined rise that it began in mm. 5-6 with the bass line this time descending in orderly contrary motion. The melody's successful attaining of high F is pointed up by the emphatic left-hand octaves for the keyboard. Only then, at the very end, can the rhythm loosen to permit the left-hand syncopations, giving the song a softer, more yielding resolution.

What about the poem is Bach trying to express here? This is one of those songs in which he "solves" the strophic problem by making the song recapitulate in miniature the arc of feeling manifested by the poem as a whole. The steadfast, resolute, very chorale-like music of mm. 1-2, 5-6, and 8-10 alternates with the somewhat more tentative, vulnerable-sounding music that prepares us for the softening of the ending. Thus the beginning and end of the song are rather like the beginning and end of the poem, but the steps along the way are quite different in the two cases. By associating this alternation of resolute and tentative music with traditional chorale style and a style less direct and focused, a style closer to that of solo song, Bach has dramatized the speaker's feeling as oscillating between traditional and more personal forms of worship.

Karsch's second poem entitled "An Gott" is a good deal longer (11 quatrains), and we need not quote it here in its entirety. Once again it is God's specifically creative power that intrigues her, but she sees it very differently in this poem. It begins with the speaker saying she thinks of God each morning upon awaking:

> Wenn ich erwache, denk ich dein!
> Du Gott, der Tag und Nacht entscheidet,
> Und in der Nacht mit Sonnenschein
> Den finstern Mond bekleidet.
>
> Er leuchtet königlich daher,
> Aus hoher ungemessner Ferne,
> Und ungezählt, wie Sand am Meer,
> Stehn um ihn her die Sterne.

God's first creative act was of course precisely to separate day from night by speaking the word "light" and therefore bringing it into being. The poem begins as it does because each morning when we open our eyes to the day, we replicate, in miniature, that act. One can see Karsch's characteristic mix of originality and banality quite clearly in these two stanzas. To think of God as clothing the moon in sunshine seems at first peculiar—but of course it is perfectly accurate. Moreover, to do so "in der Nacht" is of course once more to separate day from night by juxtaposing them in the night sky. But to describe, yet again, the stars as being like the sands of the sea without number is pretty lame.

As the poem goes on, Karsch continues to play with these ideas of light, creation, and verbal utterance:

> Welch eine Pracht verbreitet sich!
> Die Dunkelheit geschmückt mit Lichte
> Sieht auf uns nieder, nennet dich
> Mit Glanz im Angesichte.

The night sky, in which day and night, light and dark, are clearly separated by (paradoxically) being placed side by side, looks down on us and (thereby) speaks of or praises God, its face all splendor. Or so it would seem, but here are the stanzas that follow:

> Du Sonnenschöpfer! wie so gross
> Bist du im kleinsten Stern dort oben!
> Wie unaussprechlich nahmenlos!
> Die Morgensterne loben
>
> Dich miteinander in ein Chor
> Geschlossen, wie zu jener Stunde,
> Da aus dem Chaos tief hervor
> Ein Wort aus deinem Munde
>
> Allmächtig diese Welten rief,
> Am Firmament herum gesetzet.
> Du sprachst, das Rad der Dinge lief,
> Und läuft noch unverletzet.

To begin the stanza by exclaiming "Du Sonnenschöpfer!" is precisely to name God, to give him the name he deserves as creator of light and the world. Thus it is suggested that "nennet" in the preceding stanza means that the stars and sky were not just speaking of God or praising him but were, by the very act of shining so splendidly, naming him—even as God named light in the act of bringing it into being. And the speaker is joining them in this act. Looking back at the preceding stanza, we also now notice that the last line is ambiguous: does it refer to the night sky or to God? Or perhaps it does not matter, since God is in the smallest star: they are, in a word, identical.

Despite the fact that the speaker, directly after giving God his name, says he is "unaussprechlich nahmenlos," the poem goes on to dwell on the swelling chorus of praise, which is explicitly compared to the moment when one word from God's mouth, emerging out of the surrounding chaos, called into motion "das Rad der Dinge," which still turns, unimpaired by time. Particularly fine, I think, is the way in which these three stanzas run on one to another, dramatizing the intimate connection between that first moment of creation and this—and, by implication, every—instant of the world's existence, which glorifies God and thus re-creates his creation. As the speaker will say, several stanzas later:

> Ich lese, grosser Schöpfer! dich
> Des Nachts in Büchern, aufgeschlagen
> Von deiner Hand. O lehre mich
> Nach deinem Lichte fragen.

The book, of course, is the book of nature, which unlike other books can be read in the darkness of night—even as one is learning from it that God is the creator of light, the "Sonnenschöpfer." After all this, the concluding stanza is somewhat anticlimactic:

> Sey meiner Seele Klarheit, du
> Regierer der enstandnen Sterne!
> Und blicke meinem Herzen zu,
> Dass es dich kennen lerne!

Even as she reads God in his creation, so she asks God to look at, to read, her heart—not, however, that he may learn from it but that it may learn to know him.

All in all, a most interesting poem despite its occasional lapses. Here is Bach's setting:

Of course the first things we notice are the very odd dynamic markings right at the beginning. Why would Bach mark the vocal and right-hand pickup notes and the first left-hand half note *piano* and then instantly shift to *forte* for the melody and bass notes that immediately follow? From our reading of the poem, I would guess that he wanted to recapture, in each stanza, the effect of God's saying "Let there be light" (the soft notes) followed immediately by light itself coming into being (the loud notes). It is interesting that he provided no further dynamic markings for the remainder of the song: he evidently counted on singer and accompanist to arrive at what he wanted on the basis of the music—as of course they could not possibly have done for the song's beginning.

Once the *forte* level has been suddenly attained, it should probably be kept for the remainder of the first phrase, perhaps tapering off a bit in m. 4. For the distance between the right hand's melodic thirds and the low single notes in the bass—half notes at first, then quarters—creates a sense of naked, austere majesty. The two hands seem to encompass a world between them; it would be a great mistake to play left-hand octaves or to attempt to fill in the harmony in any way. The slight clashes between the two hands—at the beginnings of mm. 2 and 4—only emphasize this feeling of majesty and power.

But the rhythm does loosen a little at the end of the first phrase (m. 4), and the second phrase is quite different in character—more compliant, as it were. We can feel this compliance in the way the vocal line, for the first time, moves out on its own a little, and also in the graceful syncopation in the last half of m. 5. The bass line also seems less formidable and commanding. So it would be a good idea gradually to reduce the dynamic level coming into the second phrase. And one would want to reduce it still more for the last phrase, letting the song fade away. The carefully slurred pairs of eighth notes in the vocal line, the rest on the first beat of the penultimate bar followed by the unprecedentedly high left-hand harmonies, and the gentle closing cadence are plainly meant to express the humility of the plea for illumination that closes the poem. Once again Bach has attacked the strophic problem by making the beginning and end of his song match the poem's beginning and end, and then fashioning intervening music that acts as a natural transition from one to the other.

Finally, we might consider from the *Anhang* songs one that combines the chorale idiom used in the first "An Gott" setting with the care for dynamics seen in the second one: a setting of Psalm 88 in a verse translation by an unnamed author. This psalm, which in the King James version begins "O Lord God of my salvation, I have cried day and night before thee," is one of the psalms of lamentation, a desperate plea for deliverance from illness. The translation is into six-line tetrameter stanzas with ABBACC rhyme scheme. Mostly the translation sticks fairly close to Luther, but there are some most interesting divergences.

Since the psalm is a plea for deliverance from personal pain, most of the language is very personal in nature: almost every verse of Luther's translation is studded with "ich" and "mich" and "mein." But there is one passage in which the psalmist turns momentarily from his own case and asks some general questions of God, verses 11-13 in Luther (10-12 in the King James version):

> 11. Wirst du denn unter den Toten Wunder tun? Oder werden die Verstorbene aufstehen, und dir danken? Sela.

> 12. Wird man in Gräbern erzählen deine Güte? Und deine Treue im Verderben?
> 13. Mögen denn deine Wunder im Finsterniss erkannt werden, oder deine Gerechtigkeit im Lande, da man nichts gedenket?

The first ten verses of the psalm are a direct appeal for help to an apparently uncaring God by a man so miserable that he feels he has already been placed among the dead: "Ich liege unter den Toten verlassen, wie die Erschlagenen, die im Grabe liegen, deren du nicht mehr gedenkest und sie von deiner Hand abgesondert sind" (verse 6). Then, after declaring once more that he has repeatedly cried out to God for help, in verses 11-13 he bitterly asks God a series of general rhetorical questions: Will you do wonders among the dead? Will they arise and praise you? Will they tell of your goodness in the grave? The answer to all of these questions is of course no. The psalmist is ironically supplying God with a reason for having ignored his pleas: he is indeed among the dead, and God does not bother with them.

But the verse translation of the psalm used by Bach for his setting renders these key stanzas rather differently. Here are stanzas 6-8 of the verse translation:

> Mein Aug erstirbt vor langer Pein.
> Vergeblich such ich dein Erbarmen
> Mit immer aufgestreckten Armen.
> Soll ich erst Staub und Asche seyn,
> Und aus dem Moder auferstehen,
> Um deine Thaten zu erhöhen?
>
> Wie sollte wohl mein Dankgesang
> Die Huld und Stärke meines Helden
> In Fäulniss und Zerstörung melden?
> Wie sollte wohl mein Untergang,
> O Vater! deine Treu bewähren,
> Und deiner Gnaden Ruhm erklären?
>
> Wer wird in jener Dunkelheit,
> Darinn wir unser selbst vergessen,
> Die Wunder deines Heils ermessen?
> Ich schrey zu dir bey früher Zeit,
> Dass mir dein Trost noch Kraft ertheile,
> Eh das Verderben mich ereile.

It is interesting, first of all, that these three verses, which stand apart from the body of the psalm in Luther's translation (and, one assumes, in the Hebrew original), are embedded in stanzas of the verse translation that also contain material preceding and following them. For the second half of stanza 6 of the poem corresponds to verse 11 of Luther, stanza 7 corresponds to verse 12, and the first half of stanza 8 corresponds to stanza 13. Moreover, it makes sense that this should be so because the verse translator has made the general rhetorical questions of the original just as personal, just as filled with first-person pronouns, as what precedes and follows them. And this has resulted in an important change in tone—not only of these verses but of the entire psalm.

The desperate bitterness of the original has vanished, and in its place we have an almost calmly reasonable series of questions perfectly in tune with the generally humble, pleading tone of the rest of the poetic version. The speaker is no longer assuming that he really is already among the dead, and that this is why God has not answered his prayers. He is instead asking whether he must first be reduced to dust and ashes, and then resurrected, in order to praise God's works, and how he can possibly express his gratitude to God amidst the filth and ruin of the land of the dead. How, he asks further, will destroying me prove your fidelity (to those who worship you) or spread the news of your grace? Who, in that dark world in which we lose even our selves, will appreciate the wonders of salvation? The ardently inserted "O Vater!" in the third of these four questions helps to establish a tone of devoted (though rather bewildered) love.

What we have here is of course a Christianization of a sternly Old Testament document. But the psalm has not merely been Christianized, it has also been thoroughly personalized. It is not praise of God and his works by just anyone that the speaker asks about, it is his own ability to praise and love God that he is emphasizing: if God continues to treat him in this abominable fashion, he will not be able to fulfill his mission as a Christian of spreading the good news of Christ's sacrifice for mankind. One is reminded of those wonderful words from the requiem mass: "Recordare, Jesu pie, quod sum causa tuae viae." Here, as also in those words, is the hope born of pride in being one of those for whom Christ died.

But all this is standard, ancient Christian doctrine. In this poetic rendering of the psalm, with its constant, sustained stress on the importance of the speaker and his experience, we also see evidences of what Jaroslav Pelikan, in *Christian Doctrine and Modern Culture (since 1700),* the final volume of his splendid *The Christian Tradition*, has called "The Theology of the Heart." From the beginnings of the Pietist movement in the late 17th century until late in the 18th century, there were many Lutherans who tended to make what Pelikan has termed an "affectional transposition" of traditional church doctrine, discovering a subjective correlative (to invert Eliot's famous phrase), a translation in terms of personal, inner experience, for each point of church doctrine. "The argument from morality to religion and from the subjective experience of the soul to the reality of God," writes Pelikan, "was no less legitimate than the traditional cosmological arguments for the existence of God." In 1747-1748 Nikolaus Graf von Zinzendorf published his *Ein und zwanzig Discurse über die Augspurgische Confession*, which recast the classic 1530 Lutheran statement of faith in terms of inner experience. Whereas Melancthon had declared in the original document that "no faith is firm which does not show itself in confession," Zinzendorf replaced the criterion of external public confession with one of private feeling: for him faith was "not in thoughts nor in the head, but in the heart, a light illumined in the heart." As Pelikan points out, this "dichotomy between internal and external worship corresponded in many ways (though by no means in all) to a dichotomy between the individual and the church."[8] So throughout the 18th century, Lutheran theologians endeavored mightily to avoid the two extremes of formalism and authoritarianism (on the one hand) and enthusiasm and fanaticism (on the other), with every possible position between these extremes receiving eloquent support at one time or another.

This theological conflict is of interest to us not only because it turns up in the poems that Bach set, but also because it may well have had something to do with his choice of musical idioms. As we saw in the preceding chapter, when he was faced by Gellert's poems, for which their author all but demanded chorale settings, Bach protested (rather too much) in his preface that his religious aims were precisely the same as Gellert's—and then went ahead and produced settings that were deliberately personal and subjective, utterly lacking in the suggestion of public, communal worship that had for centuries been intimately connected with the chorale style. Yet in these *Anhang* songs, even when setting a poem by Karsch, a very different sort of poet from Gellert, Bach could turn to the chorale idiom. And three of the 12 *Anhang* songs actually set translations of psalms, thus getting us one step closer to scripture, the established church, public worship. As we shall see in the next chapter, Bach's next major song project was to set 42 of the psalm translations of Johann Andreas Cramer. One cannot help wondering whether, during these years, Bach's religious views, or at least his views on the relation between music—or anyway his music—and religious devotion had altered somewhat.

The setting of Psalm 88 in the Gellert *Anhang*—for there is quite a different one in the Cramer collection—is an absolutely splendid piece that brings together many of the concerns that are new in Bach's post-Gellert songs. Here it is:

At the slow tempo Bach prescribes, the first phrase, with its full voicings and steadily rising bass line, is heavy with grief, very straight and old-fashioned-sounding. The second phrase begins similarly, but the octave leap of the bass line in m. 3 lightens the texture, and the Neapolitan sixth at the beginning of m 4. (as the bass returns to the lower register) is something of a surprise. Moreover, the cadence on V is given an odd, personal twist by the lingering repetition of the diminished chord and the little ornament. Because the opening phrase so thoroughly and decisively establishes a "choralmässig" atmosphere, these small details are enough to make us feel that the idiom is changing in the direction of personal, subjective expression appropriate to the solo song.

In the next phrase or two—depending upon where you mark the phrase-boundaries, and the fact that this suddenly becomes a question is part of the point!—Bach plays back and forth brilliantly between the two idioms. The unexpected beat of rest at the beginning of m. 5 and (once again) the lightening of texture steer us toward personal expression and the solo song, but the neat contrary motion between vocal and bass lines as we approach the A-minor cadence in m. 7 once again evokes the world of the communally sung chorale. But then that A-minor cadence turns out not to be a resting-place at all—here is where the phrase-boundary problem enters. For while the singer sustains A, the undervoices continue to move. It is just at this point that Bach begins to be very fussy about dynamics. The music of the wordless undervoices begins softly, as a sort of afterthought. But then as the bass begins to move downward with an inexorability that recalls (even as it inverts) the song's opening, and as it is joined in m. 9 by the vocal line, the volume gradually increases from *piano* to *mezzo piano*, then from *mezzo piano* to *forte*, gathering strength as it goes. We are led to expect a cadence on G minor, but the music marches right past G minor to land on a root-position Neapolitan—which is immediately hushed from *forte* to *piano* as we move into the delicately decorated cadence on B-flat. (It is interesting that in many of the poem's stanzas the three syllables that are sung during these first three beats of m. 10 form words that are crucial to the poem's developing meaning: "meine Thränen," "jämmerlich," "deine Hand," "deine Macht," "Grabes-Haus," and so on.)

The next phrase recapitulates in brief the movement of its predecessor. Beginning at *mezzo forte*, it moves up to *forte* and then *fortissimo*, and then suddenly down to *piano* for the cadence on A, decorated similarly to the one preceding. This time the inexorability is in the vocal line, rising chromatically to high G (the high point of the song so far) and remaining there insistently until descending for the cadence; and this time it is the bass that follows the vocal line's lead, by spreading into octaves at the loudest point.

For the concluding phrase the texture once again lightens as the vocal line rises higher than ever for its climactic pronouncement. But what appears to be a direct approach to the expected concluding D-minor cadence is marred by the B-flat in the bass line on the last beat of m. 14—surely, we think, it has arrived at B-flat a beat early: the note should be A. But no. This clash in the midst of what appears to be an orderly concluding progression is Bach's way of alerting us to further surprises. And in the next bar the vocal line, descending stepwise, unexpectedly lands on E-flat rather than the E we expect. As with the preceding clash, we have a chord that can be read (and heard) in two ways: either as a minor chord that would have been perfectly in place (D minor in the former case, G minor in the latter) but that has had a flatted sixth added to it; or as a major seventh chord on the flat side of the tonal spectrum (B-flat in the former case, E-flat in the latter). But then, we have already spent a good deal of time on the flat side: remember the Neapolitans and the cadence on B-flat in m. 10. If the vocal line had landed on E (rather than E-flat) in the midst of m. 15, we would have had an ordinary G-minor sixth chord (iv) that would lead nicely to an A seventh (V^7) and so back to the D minor tonic. And even with the odd flatted sixth, we can still hear the chord as a rather unorthodox subdominant ready to move to a dominant. But Bach treats it as though it were itself a dominant seventh (with a D-flat rather than a D in it) and resolves it (if that's quite the word) to an A-flat chord that is emphasized heavily by the reappearance of the bass octaves. Only then do we get the V^7/iv (on D, a tritone away from the A-flat!) that leads us into a proper concluding cadence.

The power and poignancy of this ending, and indeed of the whole song, are stunning. They work in tandem with the artfully contrived interplay between the chorale and solo song idioms to create a deeply moving realization of this almost despairing psalm. And the way in which Bach has combined all the elements we have noticed in this song clearly shows him exploring new expressive possibilities in his song composition.

Bach was also exploring new possibilities during this period by writing short cantatas, which allowed him more space and more expressive variety than the strophic song afforded. Between about 1760 and 1775 he composed six of these: (1) "Freude, du Lust der Götter und Menschen" (Wq. 202/A; H. 688), which appeared in *Drey verschiedene Versuche eines einfachen Gesanges für den Hexameter* (1760), along with works by C. H. Graun and Agricola; (2) *Phillis und Thirsis* (Wq. 232; H. 697), composed in 1765 and published the following year, for either one or two sopranos, 2 flutes, and continuo; (3) "Der Frühling" (Wq. 237; H. 723), an expanded version of "Freude, du Lust der Götter und Menschen," composed 1770-1772 and existing only in manuscript, scored for tenor, two violins, viola, and continuo; (4) "Die Grazien" (Wq. 200/22; H. 735), composed in 1774 and published in 1789 in Bach's posthumous *Neue Lieder-Melodien*; (5) "Selma" (Wq. 236; H. 739), composed c. 1775 and existing only in manuscript, for soprano, two flutes, two violins, viola, and continuo; and (6) "Selma" (Wq. 202/I/2; H. 739.5), a cut-down version of the preceding for solo voice and keyboard, composed in 1775, classified by Helm as a cantata but referred to by Gudrun Busch as a "through-composed song" (pp. 362-363). It will be noticed that several of these works were written after 1768, when Bach assumed the position of director of music for the five principal churches of Hamburg and embarked on his series of major choral works, which included many cantatas and thus enabled him to continue and broaden his experiments with form in vocal music. There is also one more work to be mentioned in this connection, *Der Wirth und die Gäste* (Wq. 201; H. 699), composed and published in 1766, for four solo voices and keyboard, which Bach termed "eine Singode" and which C. H. Bitter has nicely described as being "midway between a cantata and a song."[9]

III

Before he left for Hamburg, however, Bach composed nine songs that would eventually be published in the *Neue Lieder-Melodien* of 1789, which he apparently lived long enough to prepare for the press. These songs too show him experimenting—not only in formal ways (there is one through-composed song) but also in respect to what we mentioned, earlier this chapter, as his newly ironic view of some of the conventional themes for secular poems and songs—a view apparently shared by some contemporary poets.

Take first a song called "An den Schlaf," to a poem by J. H. Röding that reads as follows:

> Komm, süsser Freund der Müden,
> Dich grüss ich gähnend schon,
> Du bist für mich hienieden
> Des Schweisses bester Lohn.

In meinen matten Blicken
Schaust du dein sanftes Bild;
Komm, Schlaf, mich zu erquicken,
Weil mich die Nacht umhüllt.

In deinem stillen Schoose
Ist mir so wonniglich,
Dich wünscht so mancher Grosse,
Vergebens wünscht er dich.
Du deckst mit deinen Schwingen
Umsonst ihn manche Nacht,
O Schlaf, dich zu erzwingen,
Hilft nicht des Reichtums Pracht.

Du wallest leise nieder
Auf manches klagend Herz,
Und bald entfliehst du wieder,
Verscheucht durch Gram und Schmerz.
Wie mancher würf die Sorgen
In deinen Schoos dir gern,
Und ist bis an den Morgen
Mit seinem Joch dir fern.

In schmutzigen Gewühle
Wälzt sich der Thor herum,
Er sucht im Schwarm und Spiele
Nur sein Elisium.
Zu diesem schwarzen Glücke
Dringt er berauscht hinzu,
Und flieht mit trübem Blicke
Dafür die süsse Ruh.

Man lass die Thoren machen,
Ich mach es nicht wie sie,
So Nächte durchzuwachen
Ist meine Sache nie.
Entfernt von Spiel und Schwärmen,
O Freund, erwart ich dein!
Verscheuch mir Gram und Härmen,
Und stärke mein Gebein.

Wie du in niedern Hütten
Um gute Menschen schwebst,
Und nach so manchen Schritten
Den Wandrer neu belebst;
So schweb auch um mein Bette,
So werd auch ich erquickt,
Bis früh die Morgenröthe,
Mein helles Aug erblickt.

260 ∞ Chapter Ten

This does not seem a very good poem. The tone is at first uncertain: Is "Dich grüss ich gähnend" meant to have any comic overtones? Or is "des Schweisses bester Lohn" meant to be ironic? It seems not, from the way the first stanza concludes. And what is the logical relation between the first two lines of the second stanza and the two lines that immediately follow? Or between the two pairs of lines that conclude the third stanza? From the moment that the stock figure of the "Thor" (with whom we are becoming rather familiar) appears, the poem seems clear enough—but why did Bach choose it?

Probably because it offers—whatever its obscurities may be—a view of sleep quite different from the traditional one. Sleep, in this poem, seems both unwilling to perform its accustomed function and rather easily discouraged. It spreads its wings over the great ones of this world, but to no effect—apparently because it resents being ordered about ("dich zu erzwingen, / Hilft nicht des Reichtums Pracht"). It settles down upon the suffering only to be frightened off by their "Gram und Schmerz." Though it pays its obligatory visit to the huts of the lowly, the outcome in relation to the speaker of the poem—despite his bold declaration "Nächte durchzuwachen / Ist meine Sache nie"—seems far from assured, as we can tell from his concluding plea.

That Bach wanted to write a song to which that sort of view of sleep, rather than the conventional one, would be appropriate, is clear from his setting:

There are three essential things to notice about this slight, haunting, extremely effective song. First, it is in a minor key. Second, each of its four phrases (AABB) contains seven bars. Third, its motion never stops: there is rhythmic movement of some sort on every single one of its 83 beats. These three facts combine to produce a sense of restlessness, of uneasiness that is, however, kept from being downright painful by the relaxed, gentle movement and the thin two-part texture. There is nothing threatening or alarming here—but neither is there any comfort or peace. The slight variations within the repeats of the two strains are very artfully done, and help to keep us from developing a sense of security.

Let us look at one more of the *Neue Lieder-Melodien* songs, "Auf den Geburtstag eines Freundes"—not so much because of what it is in itself as a work of art as because of what it represents in Bach's development as a song composer. For here at last we get a through-composed song. The only one Bach had written before this was "Die Küsse," which we examined earlier and which, we recall, had to be through-composed because of the strophically irregular nature of the poem. This poem by C. D. Ebeling, however, cries out for an ordinary strophic setting:

> Holde Freude, senke dich
> Von dem Himmel heute nieder!
> Töne Glück in unsre Lieder:
> Sie erschallen feyerlich.
> Wünsche für des Freundes Leben
> Fühlt mein Haus mit mir, sie heben
> Froh vom Herzen sich empor.
> |: Werden ein Gesang, ein Chor :|
>
> Singt dem besten Manne Heil!
> Jede Seligkeit der Erden
> Soll von ihm empfunden werden!
> Jede Wonne sey Sein Theil!
> Seine segensvollen Tage
> Lächeln heiter, ohne Klage,
> Sanft, wie seiner Gattin Blick.
> |: Beyder Lebenslauf sey Glück! :|

This seems a standard bit of celebratory doggerel, with nothing interesting enough in it to demand comment and certainly with no difference between its two stanzas of the sort that would suggest to a composer that a through-composed setting was demanded.

Yet this is what it got from Bach:

As we have had ample opportunity to see in this and the preceding chapters, C.P.E. Bach was a composer who was wonderfully alive to poetic nuance and extremely creative in finding appropriate musical means for expressing it. Yet here we have a song that seems virtually to run free on its own, regardless of the poem it ostensibly sets. Its two parts, differing both in tempo and time-signature, seem almost as different as the slow introduction and the following *Allegro* in a Haydn first movement. What is it in Ebeling's poem that motivates such large distinctions between the parts of the song?

The first part has a solemnly ceremonial air, fitted for an important public occasion. The dotted-eighth-and-sixteenth rhythm suggests a slow march, despite the $\frac{3}{4}$ time signature, and the runs of eighth notes at the cadences are almost operatically florid. Perhaps one can read the first few lines of the poem as implying such an occasion. But why, at m. 9, should we become still more solemn, moving into E minor? The poem is merely continuing the friendly good wishes with which it began. The stately unison at mm. 16–17 can, I suppose, be justified by the proposal "Ein Gesang, ein Chor," but the change of tempo and time-signature is very difficult to account for.

Once into the faster tempo, Bach begins to write something that looks far more like an instrumental piece than a song. Notice, for example, the play with bass offbeats that begins in mm. 27–28 and the way it is wittily repeated under the descending half notes in thirds in mm. 31-32 on the word "sanft," and then the contrasting way the word "sanft" is handled when it reappears in mm. 38-39. These seem to me clearly instrumental effects—as does the little burst of energy in the final four bars.

So Bach has written a through-composed song, yet not for any reason motivated by his text, but (as it seems) just because he wanted to, to try his hand at it. He was not to wait long before he tried again—and with much greater success. But at just about this time he was also continuing to experiment in a direction opposite to that represented by the through-composed song: the conservative direction represented by the chorales included among the Gellert *Anhang* songs.

The Counts of Wernigerode, in the province of Anhalt about 50 miles northwest of Leipzig, were staunch Pietists, and had long been in the habit of publishing collections of sacred songs in the tradition of the Freylinghausen and Schemelli songbooks of the early 18th century. Such collections had appeared in 1738 and 1752, and the Counts were preparing another, to be published in 1767. They were not only friends of poets such as Gleim (who had gone to school in Wernigerode), Karsch, Klopstock, and (somewhat later) Herder; they were also themselves poets, especially Count Heinrich Ernst, whose reign did not begin until 1771, when his father, Count Christian Ernst, died. Gleim had introduced Karsch to the Counts, who had given her a small yearly stipend and subscribed to her works—generous acts that she repaid with a deluge of poems. It was probably either Gleim or Karsch or both who involved C. P. E. Bach in the project of the 1767 songbook. At any rate, when *Melodien zu der Wernigerödischen Neuen Sammlung geistlicher Lieder* appeared at Halle in 1767, it contained (without attribution) 10 chorales composed by Bach to poems by Count Heinrich Ernst (H. 842) as well as reworkings of two of the Gellert songs and one of the Gellert *Anhang* songs.[10] And this was only the first of three rather old-fashioned collections of sacred chorales to which Bach was to contribute.

Soon after Bach arrived in Hamburg at the end of March 1768, he became acquainted, through the mathematician Johann Georg Büsch, with the poet Christoff Daniel Ebeling, who would later translate Dr. Burney's *The Present State of Music in Germany, the Netherlands, and United Provinces* into German. Bach was also soon collaborating with the poet Daniel Schiebeler on the oratorio *Die Israeliten in der Wüste*, which was completed in 1769 though not published until 1774. Since both poets were closely associated with the Hamburg magazine *Unterhaltungen*, it was probably through their influence that Bach published 13 songs in the magazine between 1768 and 1770. They are a mixed lot, but several are excellent, including one that (if we stretch the term a little) may be considered through-composed.

That song is "Phyllis," set to an exceedingly unpretentious poem by Ewald Christian von Kleist, whom we encountered earlier as the poet of Bach's song "Amint." Here is Kleist's "Phyllis":

> Ich will nicht mehr der Liebe fröhnen,
> Ich will sie fliehen, sie verhöhnen;
> Sie füllt mit Furcht und Angst das Herz,
> Macht kurze Freude, langen Schmerz,
> Es mag ein Thor der Liebe fröhnen,
> Ich will sie fliehen, sie verhöhnen.
>
> Viel lieber bin ich treu der Tonne,
> Aus ihr strömt lauter Freud und Wonne,
> Der Wein macht Freundschaft, stärkt das Herz,
> Schafft länger Wollust, keinen Schmerz.
> Dir, Bachus, weih ich meine Lieder—
> Doch Phyllis kommt, ich liebe wieder.

This is a perfectly simple, conventional love-vs.-wine ballad, with the usual turnaround at the end: the beloved appears, and all previous resolutions are null and void. The wit of the poem—what wit there is—lies in the dogged repetition of the terms in which the speaker casts his resolution, which at first suggest forthright manliness but, in light of his easy capitulation, seem merely signs of his own silliness.

But what a splendid miniature comic *scena* Bach makes of this fairly unpromising material! Here is his setting:

The direction, "Hurtig und entschlossen," swiftly and resolutely, is perfect: for we have here a speaker who has reached a firm decision, but has apparently reached it rather hurriedly—and, as it turns out, ill-advisedly and only temporarily.

Right from the beginning, the song has a bracingly dramatic, even operatic air. The defiant announcement, "Ich will nicht mehr der Liebe fröhnen," is belted out, straight from the shoulder, all on one note (except for a little flourish at the end). And the accompanist responds with a celebratory riffle of fanfares in octaves, descending portentously to the bass. The announcement is then repeated a third higher, and itself turns into a kind of fanfare as the accompanist joins in. The music has an Italianate dash and flair that remind us of the songs in the Gräfe collections by the mysterious Giovannini. The keyboard fanfares in m. 6 end in a descending scale passage that takes us to G-sharp, and the melody suddenly becomes plaintive as the poem speaks of the "Furcht und Angst" produced in the heart by love. But Bach wittily overplays the moment just slightly: we expect the high G-sharp in the keyboard's left hand at the end of m. 7 to resolve upward to A, but Bach postpones the A-minor resolution for a whole bar as we dwell on the V/ii chord and the melody melodramatically repeats its plaintive little phrase. A small touch but (once again) exactly right! As the singer moves toward his declaration that only fools will serve love, the music takes on an almost heroic tone, with the rising arpeggios in the bass and the rising sequence in the vocal line.

As we reach the cadence in m. 16, another round of keyboard fanfares takes us into a repeat. But the repeat, in which the singer declares his preference for drink over love, lasts only five-and-a-half bars. Then the music takes us into D minor, and heavy seriousness, as he praises the masculine pleasures of friendship yielded by wine—notice, however, that when he gets round to "Wollust," Bach slips us back into the major! As the singer formally declares his lasting homage to Bacchus, there are more fanfares—until the music suddenly and radically changes direction, on cue from the little word "doch."

All at once we are in the midst of a ceremonial accompanied recitative, as the accompanist repeats loud dominant chords and the singer announces the coming of Phyllis—almost as though she were a royal personage. And then, in this song of surprises, Bach has one more for us. As the singer repeats, over and over again, his return to love—the word "liebe" occurs five times!—the music, now in $\frac{3}{4}$ time, becomes slow and languorous, the chromatic passing-tones in the melody suggesting that we (and the singer) are being taken into delightful new realms. The volume dwindles, from *piano* to *pianissimo*, and there is one final point of emphasis (the *forte* G-sharp in m. 42) before the final cadence and sweetly soothing keyboard epilogue.

In contrast to "Auf den Geburtstag eines Freundes," Bach has here made real use of the through-composed form in capturing—and considerably extending and enriching—the poem's meaning and dramatic action. It is perhaps worth pausing a moment to consider the extension of the term "through-composed." In her indispensable dissertation on Bach's songs, Gudrun Busch uses it in what to me is a surprisingly narrow and restrictive way. She is willing to call "Auf den Geburtstag eines Freundes" "Completely through-composed" (pp. 363-364), but for "Die Küsse" and "Phyllis" she prefers the title "modified strophic song." And of course the latter two songs do have a good deal of repetition in them. But would she, one wonders, be willing to call "Gretchen am Spinnrade" or "Der Erlkönig" merely modified strophic songs rather than through-composed? It seems to me that creating extra categories muddies the waters in this case. Generally, I think it is useful to employ the term "through-composed" of any song in which the music is significantly modified to take account of the poem's dramatic action. Though even here one cannot insist too much on precision: it would, for example, be absurd to speak of "Herausforderungslied vor der Schlacht bey Rossbach" as through-composed, even though the question phrase added at the end of its third strophe certainly does shape the meaning of the song and add something to the meaning of the poem.

IV

In an earlier chapter, discussing Bach's setting of Friedrich von Hagedorn's poem "Der Morgen," we noted the oddity of the fact that it was one of only two surviving Bach songs that set Hagedorn poems. (Two others, "Die Alster" and "Harvstehude," composed shortly before Bach's death, are lost.) Though Hagedorn was an exceedingly popular poet, his aphoristic, urbanely Horatian mode may not have appealed to Bach. The other surviving Hagedorn-Bach song is "An die Liebe," which also appeared in *Unterhaltungen*. The poem is extremely short, elegant, and suggestive:

>   Tochter der Natur,
>   Holde Liebe!
>   Uns vergnügen nur
>   Deine Triebe.
>   Gunst und Gegengunst
>   Geben allen
>   Die beglückte Kunst
>   Zu gefallen.

It was conventional enough, in the poetry of the period, to address love as "holde Liebe," but what Hagedorn does, with superb concision and grace, in these eight short lines is to give that overused adjective real substance. If the poem had ceased after its fourth line, it would have seemed merely pretty: it is the last four lines that make it into something special.

There are of course many ways in which the impulses that originate from love give us pleasure or gratify us. Hagedorn's particular interest in this poem becomes evident in the ceremonial, almost courtly phrase "Gunst und Gegengunst." It is in the exchange of affection, kindness, grace (with perhaps a suggestion of divine grace) that the beneficial, civilizing effect of love lies. For it is from this exchange that all can learn the happy or blessed (again perhaps with a slight religious overtone) art of pleasing. Like the English verb to please, the German verb *gefallen*, used intransitively, can mean merely to practice the easily learned social art of making oneself pleasant and attractive to others. But used as it is here, very generally and open-endedly, with a vast penumbra of implication surrounding it, it of course means far more. Hagedorn is, I think, very deftly and concisely suggesting the links between human love—social, companionable, sexual—and the mutual love between God and man. One is reminded of the songs and masque from *The Tempest*.

When we looked earlier at Bach's setting of "Der Morgen," we found it helpful to compare it with Johann Valentin Görner's setting in the second (1744) volume of his *Sammlung neuer Oden und Lieder*; it will be equally helpful now to look at Görner's setting of this poem, whose title he prints merely as "Die Liebe," before going on to look at Bach's. Here is Görner's setting:

The one word "Reizend" really says it all: Görner sees this poem of Hagedorn's as no more than a charming trifle. The first phrase, with its triadic rise and stepwise fall, is echoed with just enough variation in the second phrase, when the harmony changes to the subdominant. And the surprise beat of rest at the end of m. 2—for we should surely not fill it up as the eager *D.D.T.* editor has done in his realization of the keyboard part—is balanced by the vocal line's emphatic entrance on "Gunst" at the end of m. 4. The third phrase duplicates the rhythm of the first one, and everything is neatly wrapped up by the little two-bar ending, vocal line and bass line in impeccable tenths ("and a partridge in a pear tree"!). So much for Görner.

Here is what Bach made of "An die Liebe":

As we have noted before, Bach's songs very rarely have keyboard introductions. And indeed, the two bars that precede the entry of the voice at the beginning of this song are not, properly speaking, an introduction. They don't, in any conventional way, set the stage for the singer's entry; rather, they seem to embody the silent thought out of which the spoken thought of the singer's first line naturally grows. The direction "Zärtlich und etwas langsam"—what a contrast with Görner's "Reizend"!—perfectly suggests the appropriate mood of rapt contemplation. The lightening of texture in mm. 6-9 seems just right for the invocation of "holde Liebe"—especially given what we said earlier about the importance of that adjective in the total experience of the poem. And just right too is the bare open fifth (B-flat/F) at the beginning of m. 8, which projects the chaste feelings to be associated with "holde Liebe." With the talk of the gratification offered by love, the music grows solider, more weighty as the first half of the song ends.

We finish, conventionally enough, in the dominant, and the little passage that leads to the second half seems at first just a dominant recapitulation of the music with which we began. But then in m. 15, instead of the resolution to B-flat that we expect, the melody stays put on A while the bass moves up to D-flat. A beat later the melody does resolve to B-flat, but the octave E in the bass and the G in the melody form a diminished chord, creating momentary tonal confusion. The bars that follow, in

F minor, are tortuous and convoluted, with wide melodic skips and inner parts moving in syncopation, the bass octaves on E heard in m. 15 not resolving to octaves on F until m. 18. Of course this is just where the whole matter of "Gunst und Gegengunst" begins to be taken up in the text. In the poem, as we noted earlier, the words came naturally enough—yet they altered, and began to define, everything that had come before. What Bach is giving us is the mental effort that goes into that act of definition, what I referred to earlier as the penumbra of implication that we feel surrounding the rather bare and simple words of the poem's second half.

Bach has the phrase "Gunst und Gegengunst" repeated in mm. 18-21, and this time the vocal line simply descends, without convolutions and to a simple harmonic background: the issue, we feel, has been satisfactorily worked out. At m. 22, leading into "die beglückte Kunst," the texture again grows thick and solid, in a manner reminiscent of mm. 10-11. But "zu gefallen" is again a difficult notion that demands some working out and working through. The first time the words are sung, the texture is bare, open, chaste—as in mm. 8-9 earlier (note the open fifths at the beginning of m. 25). But the second statement (mm. 26-27) begins with a gracious downward skip of a sixth and continues serenely as the other voices join in. The third statement, delivered *forte* (mm. 28-30), is still fuller, more self-assured. Yet—and this seems to me a truly wonderful touch—the voice completes its statement at the end of m. 29, before the resolution to E-flat! As the song began in silent thought, so it ends in silent thought.

This is surely one of Bach's finest achievements so far. Sober, technically unpretentious, yet every note expressive of something going on in or around and behind the words of Hagedorn's fine poem. There are other fine songs among the *Unterhaltungen* group: the witty "Der Unbeständige"; "Am Communion-Tage," in which the somber F-sharp minor setting belies the rejoicing of the poem's opening stanza to anticipate the more complex feelings with which Christ's sacrifice is contemplated in the later ones; "Auf die Auferstehung des Erlösers," with its virtuoso keyboard accompaniment; the dramatic and harmonically adventurous "Klagen einer Schäferinn"; and the oddly haunting "Passionslied," in which vocal and instrumental lines intertwine. But this will have to do.

Bach's only other song project before the settings of Cramer's psalms was a group of six songs, composed in 1772-1773, that he contributed to *Dr. Balthasar Münters . . . erste Sammlung geistlicher Lieder. Mit Melodien von verschiedenen Singkomponisten*, which was published at Leipzig in 1773. Other contributors included Scheibe, Bach's brother Johann Christoph Friedrich (the "Bückeburg Bach"), Georg Benda, and Johann Adam Hiller. Münter (1735-1793) was born in Lübeck, and early gave evidences of poetic talent. He studied theology at the University of Jena, and was appointed to the philosophy faculty there before deciding to become a pastor. In 1760 he moved to Gotha, where he became a famous preacher, publishing his sermons in 1765. It was in that year that he was called to Copenhagen, to be head pastor of the Petrikirche there. In Copenhagen, owing to the influence of Klopstock and Cramer, who became close friends, Münter returned to poetry. His *Erste Sammlung geistlicher Lieder* appeared in Leipzig in 1772. It was followed not only by the volume to which Bach contributed but also by *Zwote Sammlung geistlicher Lieder* in 1774 and, also in that year, a second collection of song settings, all of them by J. C. F. Bach. In the 19th century Münter's poetry was valued more highly than Gellert's because of the former's stress on personal feeling—"Poetry must speak the language of feeling" was one of his most frequently quoted sayings. But Eduard Emil Koch, in his *Geschichte des Kirchenlieds und Kirchengesangs des christlichen*, remarks perceptively of Münter's poems: "But all of them lack a certain something—and that is: the specifically Christian element."[11]

Bach's Münter songs are a disappointing lot—especially when we compare them with "Phyllis" and "An die Liebe." Several are quite mechanical, and the only one that deserves mention here does so mainly on technical rather than expressive grounds. This song is "Communionlied," the text of which we need not examine in detail. As in the first line—"Zitternd, doch voll sanfter Freuden, komm ich, Herr, auf dein Gebot"—Münter throughout speaks "die Sprache der Empfindung" and, specifically, links belief closely to feeling, as in Zinzendorf's *Discurse*—and, indeed, the whole Pietist movement. A later stanza begins: "Herr, dies glaub' ich, und empfinde / Freudigkeit und Zuversicht." The poetry is undistinguished, a rehearsal of familiar sayings and sentiments, and one could easily shuffle the order of the stanzas without doing much damage.

Certainly, we do not detect in Bach's setting the intense involvement with the subject matter and the very words of the poetry that we did in his settings of Gellert and of some of the poets dealt with in this chapter. His mind seems to be on something else. Here is his setting:

It seems to me clear that Bach was less interested in Münter's words, and the evolving poetic structure they form, than he was in seeing how tightly he could bind his song together through the development of little motifs made up, like the opening phrases in both melody and bass line, of rising half-steps. Particularly interesting, I think, are the reappearance of the motif (beginning on D-sharp!) to "spoil" the C-major cadence in m. 8, its use to link the 3-bar phrase with which the song's second section begins (mm. 17-19) to the phrase that follows, and the thorough working-out that it receives as the song nears its end. It is also interesting that some of the other portions of the song—the approach to the two C-major cadences (mm. 7-8 and 15-16) and the very beginning of the second phrase (mm. 17-18)—seem lame and static by comparison with the points at which Bach is developing his motif. Of course the rather somber, A-minor, chromatic feel of the song is not in any way inappropriate to the subject of the poem; but one feels no intimate link between song and poem.

This brings us to the end of our review of the Bach songs that span the interval between the publication of the Gellert settings in 1758 and that of the settings of Cramer's psalm translations in 1774. As we have seen, the deeply probing investigation of the strophic songs and its expressive possibilities that Bach carried out in assembling his triumphantly successful collection of Gellert songs led to a decade-and-a-half of searching experimentation in many directions: he continued to grapple with the strophic problem, tried his hand at cantatas, and attempted a few through-composed songs. Moreover, he experimented not only with form but also with idiom: after having pointedly declined to compose chorale settings for Gellert's poems, he contributed to the Wernigerode chorale book and used modified versions of the chorale idiom in some of his original settings. During this transitional period, Bach's relation to secular poetic texts seemed to be a rather uneasy one. Either he picked texts that viewed the familiar secular subjects in a slightly skewed or jaundiced light, or he himself added musical touches that placed the texts in such a light. In the chapter that follows, we shall see how all this experimentation paid off when he tackled the psalm translations of Johann Andreas Cramer.

Chapter Eleven

The Cramer Psalms

Johann Andreas Cramer (1723-1788), 42 of whose free, hymnic psalm translations provided C. P. E. Bach with texts for his next important songwriting project, was a man of considerable parts who led an interesting and varied life among some of the leading literary and intellectual figures of his time. It is therefore surprising that more has not been written about him. In 1910, Adolf Blümcke published a doctoral dissertation, *Beitraege zur Kenntnis der Lyrik Johann Andreas Cramer's (1742-1761)*, that remains the most extensive discussion of Cramer's life and work.

I

Born in the Saxon *Erzgebirge*, Cramer was the son of a pastor and the oldest of three brothers. At 13 he was sent to school at Grimma, about 50 miles northwest of Dresden. Though his father wanted him to study theology and also to become a village pastor, Cramer immediately fell in love with the literature and mythology of classical antiquity. The family was dealt a hard blow in 1740, when Cramer's father died suddenly, but Cramer managed to remain in school until graduation two years later. He then traveled on foot to Leipzig, with only five gulden in his pocket.

He immediately enrolled as a theology student at the university, but was soon deeply involved in Leipzig's flourishing literary life—which was of course dominated by Gottsched and his followers, one of whom Cramer promptly became. He contributed poems praising and influenced by Gottsched to Johann Joachim Schwabe's short-lived (1741-1745) monthly magazine *Belustigungen des Verstandes und des Witzes*.

But even as Gottsched was preparing the revised and increasingly expanded editions of his 1730 *Versuch einer critischen Dichtkunst* that would appear in 1737, 1742, and 1751, opposition to him was brewing. Most of this opposition came, of course, from Switzerland. Johann Jacob Breitinger's two-volume *Critische Dichtkunst* (with a preface by Johann Jacob Bodmer) and his *Critische Abhandlung von der Natur, den Absichten und dem Gebrauche der Gleichnisse* were both published at Zurich in 1740. Almost immediately Johann Elias Schlegel produced two important essays on the doctrine of imitation that criticized both Gottsched and Breitinger, and that also showed the influence of Baumgarten:[1] *Abhandlung, dass die Nachahmung der Sache, der man nachahmet, zuweilen unähnlich werden müsse* (1741) and *Abhandlung von der Nachahmung* (1742).[2] Meanwhile Bodmer published two contributions to the increasingly popular theory of the Longinian sublime, *Critische Abhandlung von dem Wunderbaren* (1740) and *Critische Briefe* (1746). It was also 1746 that saw the publication of Charles Batteux's widely influential *Les Beaux-Arts réduits à un même principe*, a book that was of course much discussed in Leipzig literary circles before the appearance, in 1751, of its German translation,

Einschränkung der schönen Künste auf einen einzigen Grundsatz, by Johann Adolph Schlegel—who had by that time become a close friend and associate of Cramer's.[3]

Thus change was in the air, and Cramer was right in the thick of the writing and the discussions that were leading to it. This change—or, more properly, these changes—in aesthetic doctrine was not the black-and-white shift from an aesthetics of reason to an aesthetics of feeling that it has usually been said to have been. It was more a shift of taste and emphasis—which of course took different forms in different thinkers. But it was most important nonetheless, though of only peripheral interest to us here.

Not surprisingly, Cramer too joined the shift away from more or less strict adherence to the doctrines of Gottsched, which had come to seem rather constricting and literal-minded. In 1744 he joined forces with Johann Adolph Schlegel and Karl Christian Gärtner in founding and editing *Bremer Beiträge*, which remained the principal organ of opposition to Gottsched until its demise, in 1748.[4]

Cramer had arrived in Leipzig penniless. So the first thing he did was to get himself hired by Bernhard Christoph Breitkopf to help with the translation of Bayle's *Dictionnaire historique et critique*. It was this post that led to many of his intellectual and literary friendships. But neither his work for Breitkopf nor his writing and editing kept him from his theological studies. Through these studies he became acquainted with Gellert, who had been teaching philosophy at the University of Leipzig since 1742. Cramer first worked as an aide to Gellert, and then in 1745 was himself made a teacher and lecturer in philosophy. Along with Johann Adolph Schlegel and Gellert, Cramer's closest literary friend during his Leipzig years was Klopstock, with whom he also worked closely, helping to get the first three cantos of *Der Messias* published in *Bremer Beiträge*.

There seems in fact to have been virtually no one of literary and intellectual importance in the Leipzig of the 1740s who did not know, respect, and like Cramer. Hagedorn, Gleim, Giseke, Ebert, Rabener—they, in addition to the writers mentioned earlier, were all friends and coworkers of Cramer's. But in 1748 he received an appointment as pastor to the village of Cröllwitz, slightly to the west, and so he left Leipzig—though not his friends, who visited him often in the years that followed.

While in Cröllwitz, Cramer was evidently a model village pastor, on one occasion ringing the church bell to save his parishioners from drowning in a flood occasioned by a ruptured dike. But he also contrived to produce a translation, with commentary, of the works of St. John Chrysostom, fourth-century Patriarch of Constantinople, that was published—in 10 volumes!—at Leipzig, 1748-1751.

Cramer remained in Cröllwitz until 1750, when he was offered a more prestigious pastoral appointment in Klopstock's hometown of Quedlinburg, about 60 miles northwest of Leipzig. Here too, in addition to his pastoral duties, Cramer took on a major literary project: a translation, with commentary, of Bossuet's 1681 *Discours sur l'histoire universelle*. Publication of this massive work began in 1756, but was not completed until 1786, two years before Cramer's death. He also kept writing poems, including of course the psalm translations upon which Bach was later to draw. Some of these translations had been published in magazines during Cramer's Leipzig years; but it must have been at about this time that he began systematically assembling them for book publication. They would appear in four volumes, published by Breitkopf in 1755, 1759, 1763, and 1764. They were popular enough to merit a second edition in 1764 and a translation into Dutch in 1768.

In 1752 King Frederik V of Denmark had granted Klopstock an annual income and leisure to complete *Der Messias*. It was through Klopstock's influence that Cramer obtained, in 1754, an appointment as court preacher in Copenhagen. He had enormous admiration for King Frederik, whom he considered an ideal monarch, and remained in Copenhagen until 1771, five years after Frederik's death. In addition to writing poems and continuing his work on Bossuet, Cramer began publishing his sermons and once again became an editor, this time of a monthly magazine, *Der Nordische Aufseher*, that appeared between 1758 and 1761. In 1765 he was made Professor of Theology at the University of Copenhagen, and in 1767 he was granted a doctorate.

Cramer left Copenhagen only after it had become clear to him that Frederik's successor, his son Christian VII, was unfit to be king. Though highly intelligent, Christian had been brutally treated as a child and had been given no conception of the duties of royalty. At the age of 17, when he assumed the throne, he was already thoroughly debauched and was probably also what we should call a schizophrenic. He had no interest in public business, and so the court degenerated into a chaos of intrigue and corruption, power eventually devolving upon a physician named Johan Friedrich Struensee. Struensee, who soon also became the lover of Queen Matilda, was a freethinker and social reformer. Even if his morals had been impeccable, such a person would obviously not have been to the taste of a thoughtful, religious man such as Cramer. Though his friends counseled him against doing so, Cramer courageously spoke out against the abuses he saw going on around him. As Eduard Emil Koch memorably wrote, "His friends trembled for him; he trembled not at all."[5] Cramer was forced to leave Denmark in September, 1771.

He was successful in securing a minor post at Lübeck, but the following year the political situation in Denmark changed radically once again. Though Struensee had effected some reforms of genuine worth, his excessive zeal and relentless self-seeking had managed to offend Danes of every class. Early in 1772 a conspiracy of nobles forced Christian to sign orders for the arrest of both Struensee and the Queen. That April Struensee was tortured and beheaded; the Queen was saved through the intervention of her brother, George III of England, but was deported. From 1772 to 1784, when Christian's son, the Crown Prince, would come of age and be able to be installed as regent for his now hopelessly insane father, the government was in the hands of Queen-Dowager Juliane Marie, Frederik V's widow; her younger son Frederik; and his tutor Guldberg, who had become secretary to the Cabinet. In 1774 this new regime appointed Cramer Prochancellor of the University of Kiel and Professor of Theology.

Cramer remained at Kiel for the remaining 14 years of his life. He lived to see both his sons serve as professors at the University, and shortly before his death he was appointed its chancellor and curator. Thus ended the remarkably interesting, active, and productive life of Johann Andreas Cramer. Posterity, however, has not judged his writings very kindly. Indeed, there were complaints even while he was alive. Blümcke, the most sympathetic of biographers, was forced to admit:

> Cramer's tendency to write too much, to allow all his utterances to be published without first submitting them to a critical revision, was condemned, even by his contemporaries, as improper. For such a voluminous production could not avoid being monotonously repetitious. His "factory-like mass production" of religious poetry often resulted in work that was superficial and tasteless, work that dishonored the dignity of his subjects.[6]

How then did C.P.E. Bach, a highly literate man with excellent taste in poetry, come to choose Cramer's verses for his next big song project?

Johann Gottlob Immanuel Breitkopf had taken over the family business from his father in 1745, while Cramer was still an employee. They had become friends, and so Breitkopf had personal as well as professional reasons for wanting to see Cramer's psalm translations set to music:

> As early as 1756 Breitkopf had hoped, with Marpurg's help, to persuade a Berlin composer to take on the assignment, but nothing had come of the plan.[7]

So wrote Hermann von Hase in 1911. But while Breitkopf's idea of bringing out, under the Breitkopf imprint, a full collection of Cramer psalm settings did not at once bear fruit, composers were responding to Cramer. Marpurg's *Geistliche, moralische und weltliche Oden* and *Geistliche Oden, in Melodien gesetzt von einigen Tonkünstlern in Berlin*, both of which appeared in 1758 (and both of which we glanced at in our survey of Bach's Gellert settings), contained settings of Cramer psalm translations. The former contained Krause's setting of Psalm 31, the latter settings of Psalms 10, 13, and 22 by Schale, Agricola, and Krause, respectively. And in Gräfe's *Fünfzig Psalmen, geistliche Oden und Lieder* of 1760 (which we also looked at earlier), there were, along with the 24 settings of Gellert poems, settings of 26 of Cramer's translations: those of Psalms 1, 3, 5, 6, 11, 12, 13, 15, 17, 18, 23, 25, 28, 30, 31, 32, 34, 36, 38, 39, 42, 43, 47, 51, 63, and 70. The reason Gräfe did not attempt any of the later psalms is that by 1759 only Psalms 1-82 (plus Psalm 119) had appeared, in the first two Breitkopf volumes.

It appears that somewhere around this time Marpurg contacted Bach and asked for some Cramer settings. For in the second collection of Marpurg's *Musikalisches Allerley*, issued in 1761, there are Bach settings of Cramer's translations of Psalms 2 and 4. The former is for four-voiced chorus a capella, while the latter is a duet for soprano and alto with figured bass accompaniment. The same volume also contains two Cramer settings by C. F. Fasch, of Psalms 1 and 5. The former is for four-voiced chorus and the latter is a duet for two sopranos; both have figured bass accompaniment. The obvious parallelism between the two pairs of settings prompted the following comment from Gudrun Busch: "The similarity in the lay-out leads one to suppose that Bach and Fasch had here set themselves a specific compositional problem."[8]

Bach did no more with Cramer's psalm translations for 12 years, until he set about preparing the 1774 collection. In his book on Bach's chamber music, Ernst Fritz Schmid cites at length a letter written on December 5, 1767, by Heinrich Wilhelm von Gerstenberg to Friedrich Nicolai. In the course of praising Bach as a "Singcomponist," Gerstenberg tells how he has obtained excellent results by underlaying some of Bach's instrumental pieces with texts of his own devising—and by putting a paraphrase of Hamlet's "To be or not to be" soliloquy to Bach's keyboard Fantasia in C minor (the last movement of the Sonata Wq. 63/6; H. 75).[9] He then remarks that he has in his possession Bach's "Gellert songs (in which, almost all the way through, I have replaced Gellert's text with a Psalm by Cramer or another poem with moral content)." Schmid then adds, in a footnote just below: "perhaps the genesis of Wq. 196 (the Cramer Psalms, 1774) can be traced back, indirectly, to Gerstenberg's instigation."[10] And Gudrun Busch accepts this interpretation, noting appreciatively: "Schmid is right that it was probably Gerstenberg who redirected Bach's attention to the Cramer-Psalms."[11] But this seems to me an unjustifiable elevation of what was offered only as a conjecture into a solid probability—if not an established fact. Gerstenberg is only saying that he has found that the text of a Cramer psalm or some other "poem with moral content" will work just as well with Bach's Gellert songs as the poetic texts for which they were designed.

However Bach came once again to be interested in Cramer's psalm translations, the following notice appeared in the *Allgemeine deutsche Bibliothek* in 1768:

> An anonymous person [*ein Ungenannter*] has written to Herr Music Director Bach, imploring him to set the Cramer Psalms to melodies like those he provided for Gellert's religious poems, and has also demanded that he read the answer to this request in the *Allgemeine deutsche Bibliothek*. Herr Bach takes this occasion to make it known that if a suitable publisher were found, he would not be averse to carrying out the request.[12]

Busch hypothesizes that the unnamed person may have been Gerstenberg, noting that Bach mentioned the matter to Matthias Claudius, who wrote a detailed description of his visit with Bach in a series of letters to Gerstenberg. Here, from a letter that is undated but was probably written in the autumn of 1768, is the relevant passage:

> I mentioned Klopstock's bardic poems to him, but he seemed either not to understand or to be cold toward anything that would not pay well—which he himself said in regard to the Cramer Psalms, and also added something about a letter from an anonymous person [*eines Anonymi*] on this subject and, as you know, an answer to it.[13]

Now the phrase "as you know" might indeed indicate that Gerstenberg had been the unnamed person, and that Claudius knew this. But it might instead indicate that the notice in the *Allgemeine deutsche Bibliothek* had already appeared, that both Gerstenberg and Claudius had read it, and that they had discussed it. In this case, which seems to me the more likely one, the *Allgemeine deutsche Bibliothek* notice would be merely a trial balloon, floated anonymously by Bach himself, to see if there were any favorably inclined publishers out there. The mysterious unnamed person would then be merely a fiction, invented by Bach to minimize appearances of ambition and aggressiveness on his part, and to make it look as though a setting by C.P.E. Bach of Cramer's psalm translations would be merely a response to (probably widespread) public demand. Why, after all, should Bach go out of his way to mention the matter to Claudius? To float another trial balloon.

A favorable publisher, however, was nowhere in sight. Yet Bach would not compose without a solid financial basis. Gerstenberg, writing in the *Neue Hamburger Zeitung* of December 28, 1769, lamented the lack of a volume of Bach settings of Cramer that would match his earlier Gellert collection:

> Aside from this use [i.e., of Cramer's Psalms], we wish for them another: that like the Gellert poems, with melodies by our inimitable Bach, they may encourage domestic edification. We regret that his Psalms have not already attained this important advantage.

And so the years passed. In September 1772, Claudius reported to Gerstenberg that he had attempted to prod Bach into composing some Cramer settings but had failed, "because the ability to move Bach to composition is not granted to mere mortals":

> Already for half a year I have been giving him pages of Cramer's imitations of the Psalms, he wanted to write melodies for them, yesterday he sent them back to me—and he has written no melodies.[14]

Finally, in the summer of 1773 Bach began to consider publishing the settings himself, on a subscription basis, the printing to be handled by Breitkopf. On June 24 he wrote to Johann Breitkopf, outlining his plans for the book and adding that he considered it "the companion to my Gellert."[15] By October Bach had begun work on the settings, and the *Hamburger unparteiische Correspondent* that month carried the following announcement, signed by Bach and dated October 18:

> As soon as my Gellert songs were published, my friends expressed the wish that I might also publish melodies to be sung to keyboard accompaniment to Herr Doctor Cramer's Psalms, for private edification. This wish is now fulfilled insofar as a selection of these Psalms, equal in volume to my Gellert songs, will appear in print, along with a prospective Easter mass. In composing these Psalms I have had in mind amateurs [*Liebhaber*] of varying abilities, and therefore they are easier to perform than the Gellert songs, without, I trust, doing any damage to the special magnificence of these Psalms.[16]

The notice concluded with details as to how one might subscribe to the Cramer settings.

There are several interesting things about this notice. First, one notes the firm insistence that Bach's friends have been asking for these settings ever since the publication of the Gellert collection. While there was of course some truth in this claim, when we take it in the context of the curious business about the "Ungenannter," it does raise the question of why Bach should have been so eager to insist, repeatedly, that his setting of the Cramer psalm translations was in response to popular demand rather than simply because he found them worth setting. His preface to the Gellert collection, we recall, was devoted to praise of the poems, complaints about the "strophic problem," and a rather defensive insistence that he really did share Gellert's aim of encouraging "Erbauung"—despite the fact that he had not provided the chorale settings that Gellert plainly wanted. Here too, however, Bach makes it clear that "Privat-Erbauung" is his aim in setting these poems.

Second, we notice that he is anxious to reassure prospective purchasers that these songs will be "easier to perform than the Gellert songs." Perhaps he had somehow got wind of Gellert's comment, in his letter to his sister, that he found Bach's settings "beautiful, but too beautiful for a singer who is not musical." Or perhaps, especially since he had undertaken the publication of the Cramer settings himself, Bach was merely trying to ensure as wide a sale as possible—as his comment about having taken into consideration the varying abilities of "Liebhaber" would suggest. This surely is why he bothers to mention that the size of the volume is equal to that of the Gellert collection. For in his letters of the preceding month to Breitkopf, Bach had insisted that the Cramer volume be no thicker—and therefore no more expensive—than the Gellert volume. In his letter of June 24, 1773, for example, amidst talk of paper costs and the subscriber list, Bach writes: "The collection should be *at most* as thick, and not thicker, than the Gellert songs."[17] In the event, while the Gellert collection had had 63 pages, including the title page, preface, and table of contents, the Cramer had 62, including title page, dedication, preface, and subscription list.

Further light on Bach's motives is perhaps cast by his dedication and preface to the Cramer settings. The volume is dedicated to Friedrich, Duke of Mecklenburg-Schwerin:

> I make so bold as to dedicate to Your Serene Highness the present collection of Psalms by the Royal Poet, which I have set to melodies for singing, because I know that Your Highness particularly values among musical pleasures one of the noblest goals of the musical art, the propagation of religion and the promotion of edification of our immortal souls, and know also that you reward with your most gracious approbation the works of men who apply their talents to the attainment of this end.

The dedication was well placed. This prince, known as "Friedrich the pious," swam against the current of the Enlightenment in a way that would naturally have appealed to both Bach and Cramer. In his *Geschichte Mecklenburgs*, Ernst Boll writes:

> Until 1756 the symbolic-ecclesiastical orthodox party was in the ascendancy in Mecklenburg. But when in that year Duke Friedrich attained power, a new page turned. The Duke, averse to rigid orthodoxy and also to rationalism, favored the biblical-theological conviction, which at that time had its seat at Halle. . . .[18]

Friedrich's father, Christian Ludwig II, had been a worldly man fond of music, theater, and dance, a prominent collector of paintings. Friedrich too was very fond of music, but (in the words of Karl Schmaltz) "he did not have his father's lighthearted nature." Schmaltz continues:

> He too took pleasure in art, music, and paintings; he had a passion for building things, and his particular love was mechanics. But everything he did had a certain air of pedantry, which showed itself in the minute conscientiousness with which he performed his duties. The strain of impetuosity that ran in his family urged him to create, but he was conscious of this urge, and had learned to master it. He soon fell under the influence of Pietism.[19]

Friedrich, however, was childless, and when he died, in 1785, he was succeeded by his nephew, Friedrich Franz I. Though Friedrich had had charge of the young prince's education, Friedrich Franz proved to be more like his grandfather than like his uncle, and the religious climate of Mecklenburg reverted to the times of Christian Ludwig II.

In his dedication, Bach refers to the "Psalms of the Royal Poet," since by the time he was writing—the dedication is dated March 28, 1774—Cramer had been restored to his official position by the new Danish administration. (Though Mecklenburg is always considered a German duchy, it had had close dynastic and political relations with Denmark ever since being conquered by Canute IV in 1183.) It is interesting that in Bach's preface, however, the word *Dichter* is never applied directly to Cramer.

Bach begins by once again referring to the collection as having been demanded by his friends: "At last I have the pleasure of acceding to the request made of me long ago by my patrons and friends, and providing them with melodies to Herr Doctor Cramer's Psalms." He then explains why he has published the volume himself, expresses the hope that it will match his Gellert collection in popularity, and speaks of the common aim of the two collections:

> Since these latter [i.e., the Gellert settings] have, as I have often been assured, brought about so much edification, I firmly believe that these Psalms will be of even greater usefulness because their divine content is so full of majesty that nothing ever written by the greatest poets of this kind can match them. I am not competent to judge the translation of these Psalms, the work of one of our greatest theological scholars [*Gottesgelehrten*], as it deserves; any praise of that sort that I could offer would be merely superfluous; I can only appeal to what I myself felt as I was composing these melodies.

Bach then repeats his assertion in the *Hamburger unparteiische Correspondent* announcement, that in setting Cramer's translations he has provided "short melodies to be sung at the keyboard, for amateurs who are not yet highly skilled performers," in order to gain a wide audience. But this point leads him into complaining once again about the "strophic problem" and almost apologizing for the necessary expressive limitations of strophic songs: "But anyone who knows the constraint that is unavoidable with melodies designed for more than one strophe, and who also knows how small and constricted a field, so far as modulation is concerned, this leaves to the composer, will not be too demanding, but will rather, as I hope, honor me by being satisfied with this work of mine." He concludes his preface by saying that he has set only those psalms that seemed of contemporary relevance, that were especially suited "to general edification," and that had no more than one meter, and also by calling attention to the stylistic variety of this collection: "The great number of Psalms of praise, with their majestic content, has forced me to think about variety of expression, in order to avoid bringing forth only one kind of thoughts; to please some of my friends I have given certain Psalms chorale melodies; at times I have also dared to do some contrapuntal writing and to make frequent modulations: all these circumstances give this collection greater variety than one encounters in my Gellert songs, and I hope that I will not thereby lose the approbation of my friends."

There are many interesting things about this preface, especially perhaps the way Bach refers to Cramer and his poems. Bach believes that these poems, when set to music, will be even more useful in stimulating *Erbauung* not because of Cramer's poetry but rather because of the divine content of the original psalms, a content that for sheer majesty has never been matched by even the greatest poets. And when he comes to refer directly to Cramer, he does not use the term "Dichter" but rather "Gottesgelehrte," or theological scholar. Since he has just used "Dichter" in the sentence preceding, the contrast stands out boldly. We are still more struck by it once we know that Bach had begun the preface to his Gellert settings not by explaining that his friends have, in effect, selected the poems he is using, but rather by praising Gellert as a poet: "It would be superfluous to say anything in praise of the renowned author of these poems; the general approbation that has everywhere been accorded his work is far too well known." Gellert is praised for his art, Cramer only for his learning—the implication being that the majestic spiritual content of the psalms exists independently of any particular verbal rendering of it, and that it is, in effect, indestructible. Thus Cramer's role of poet-translator shrinks to that of a mere reflecting surface.

This seems to me important because it helps to explain Bach's repeated references to the friends who have demanded that he set Cramer's translations—there were no such references in the Gellert preface because Gellert stood on his own as a poet—and also, perhaps, the curious business of the mysterious (and, I believe, fictional) "Ungenannter." Bach was a highly intelligent man of taste who mixed habitually with literary figures of the stature of Lessing and Klopstock. But Cramer, considered as a poet, was well below the level of those whose verses Bach usually set. Understandably, he did not want to go on record as praising Cramer's poetry in anything like the terms he had used about Gellert's. But why then set Cramer's psalm translations? There were certainly other versions to have chosen. In fact, Bach had chosen one (or more) of them for the texts of the psalm settings he included in the Gellert *Anhang*. Yet for this major song collection he chose the translations of a poet whose poetry, in his preface, he explicitly refused to judge, pleading incompetence.

I think Bach chose Cramer's psalm translations because he felt a spiritual kinship with the man, whom he had come to admire. Bach was a very reticent man, and his letters tell us little about the precise nature of or alterations in his religious or moral beliefs. But Bitter notes the importance that the Gellert settings held for Bach, and observes of the time between their appearance and that of the Cramer settings: "Meanwhile the direction of his whole life, of his spirit and his artistic activity, had inclined toward subjects and thoughts of a religious and ecclesiastical nature. And so one finds him, in Hamburg, testing his powers anew, in this direction, within the area of the German song."[20]

Naturally this growth in religious interest was connected with his assumption of his Hamburg post in 1768—though whether as cause or effect or both is not yet clear. But I think it is evident even before 1768. As we have seen, by 1767 at the latest he was working on his contributions to *Melodien zu der Wernigerödischen Neuen Sammlung geistlicher Lieder*. Three of the 12 songs in the 1764 Gellert *Anhang* had been marked "Choralmässig," and had mingled the idioms of chorale and solo song. Equally important perhaps was the fact that in 1765 Bach had edited a collection of 100 of his father's four-part chorales. In his preface to the collection he praised "the singular deployment of the harmony and the natural flow of the inner voices and bass line by which these chorales are particularly marked."[21] The publisher, F. W. Birnstiel of Berlin, issued another volume of 100 chorales in 1769—but without informing C. P. E. Bach of the fact. Bach in turn issued a public protest that the volume was full of mistakes, and publication of J. S. Bach's chorales was not completed until the 1780s.

Thus Bach had both redirected his interest from secular to sacred songs and had begun experimenting with chorales well before he came to Hamburg. It was probably three years after his arrival there, in 1771, that he first met Johann Andreas Cramer. Cramer, accompanied by his son Carl Friedrich, had come to Hamburg to visit Klopstock. So far as is known, Cramer never offered a judgment of Bach's settings of his translations. In 1774 Carl Friedrich Cramer, by then a student at Göttingen and a member of the so-called Göttinger Hainbund, came to Hamburg and met with Bach, Claudius, Ebeling, and other friends.[22] These were just the years during which Cramer courageously stood up against the abuses at the Danish court, was banished, and was then reinstated after Struensee's execution and the installation of the Crown Prince as regent. Bach's dedication of his collection to Duke "Friedrich the pious" suggests that his religious views were roughly the same as Cramer's. He would therefore probably have viewed Cramer's actions with regard to the corrupt Danish court not only with approval but with admiration as well. Moreover, it was just as Bach was preparing his settings of Cramer's psalms that Cramer was preparing his biography of Gellert, which, like Bach's collection, was published in 1774, five years after Gellert's death. This too would probably have endeared Cramer to Bach.

Thus we can understand how Bach came to be so enthusiastic about setting Cramer's psalm translations and why he treated the whole project so oddly. It is time now to look at some of the poems and to see what Bach made of them. Since Bach's growing interest in the chorale idiom is one of the significant developments in his songwriting of this period, it will perhaps be appropriate to begin with the psalms for which he provided chorale settings.

There are nine of these: Psalms 6, 25, 38, 42, 86, 91, 103, 121, and 130. And of course the first question one wants to ask is why it is these particular psalms that were chosen for chorale settings. Any answer to this question can of course be only speculative. Yet it surely cannot be simply a coincidence that the first five of these nine psalms are all laments, prayers either for healing from sickness or for deliverance from enemies. Psalms 6 and 38 in fact belong to the group of seven known as the Penitential Psalms, perhaps the darkest of the 40 laments found among the 150 psalms. Of these initial five psalms, however, the last two, Psalms 42 ("As the hart panteth after the water brooks") and 86, are rather more hopeful and praising of God than are the first three. This upward turn of mood is continued in Psalms 91 ("He that dwelleth in the secret place of the most High shall abide under the shadow of the Almighty"); 103, a prayer of thanks for deliverance from sickness; and the buoyant 121 ("I will lift up mine eyes unto the hills, from whence cometh my help"). But then the final psalm to receive a chorale setting, Psalm 130, is the famous "De profundis clamavi" ("Out of the depths have I cried unto thee, O Lord"), another of the penitential psalms.

What can we make of this? Perhaps the most we can say is that for Bach the chorale idiom, at least so far as this work is concerned, is associated with the austere side of Christian life, the unending cycle of trouble, turning to God for help, the granting of help, praise of God, and the return of trouble—which of course begins the cycle once again. Of the 42 psalms in Bach's collection, the ones with chorale settings are numbers 3, 9, 13, 14, 19, 22, 28, 34, and 36. Even as the Book of Psalms itself begins ("Blessed is the man that walketh not in the counsel of the ungodly") and ends ("Praise ye the Lord. Praise God in his sanctuary") in unstinting, unalloyed praise of God and his goodness, so does Bach's selection of psalms. The chorale settings are spread unevenly throughout the collection so as to depict that austere side of Christian life, to provide a realistic reminder of the inevitable pain and stress of postlapsarian earthly existence within the initially and finally joyous and exultant promise of God's goodness and love.

Now of course an immense range of emotion, religious and otherwise, can be expressed in the chorale idiom. And no one knew this better than the son of J. S. Bach, who also happened recently to have edited his father's chorales for publication. Yet quite apart from the content of the particular psalms that C. P. E. Bach chose for chorale setting, the sort of chorales he wrote shows that in assembling the Cramer collection he was taking the very special and limited view of the chorale idiom suggested above. For these are not fully realized four-part chorales that demonstrate that natural flow of inner voices and bass line so eloquently praised by C. P. E. Bach in his preface to the collection of his father's chorales. They are, rather, simple melodic lines, usually in even half notes, over a figured bass. On the page they look bare and (if one does not read the figures too closely!) even primitive, as though Bach were pointedly, even willfully, denying himself the expressive possibilities of the various complex and luxuriant musical idioms that he had by this time thoroughly mastered—and that are deployed elsewhere in this collection more elaborately than in any of his earlier songs.

Bitter found at least two of the chorale settings, those of Psalms 6 and 130, to be "masterworks, vocally and artistically"[23]—a judgment that one finds it difficult to agree with, at least at first glance. Though Bitter prints the two chorales pretty accurately, there are a few minor errors in the placement and spacing of the bass figuration, to which printers of the 1860s were probably no longer accustomed. Therefore I give them as they appear in the original 1774 print. First, Psalm No. 6:

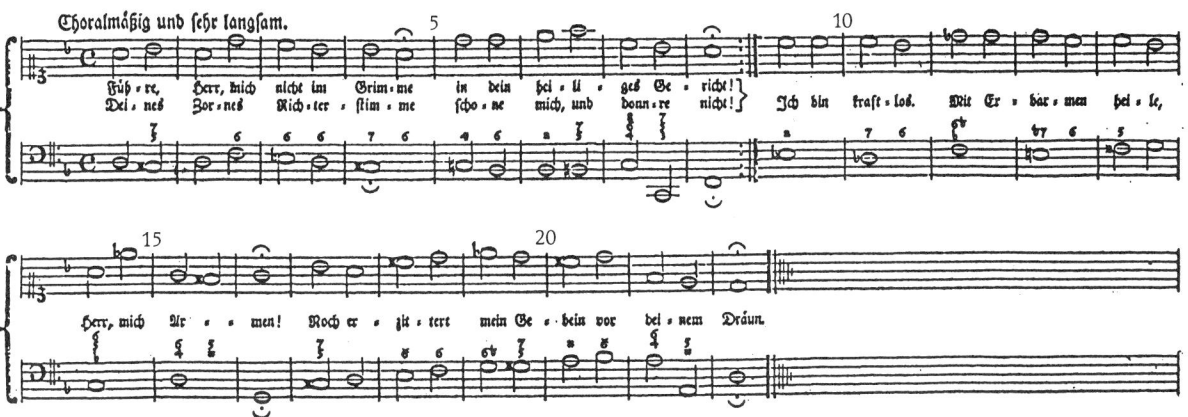

Certainly this is a fine, straightforward piece, well suited to its text: "O Lord, rebuke me not in thine anger, neither chasten me in thy hot displeasure." And we are struck by the way in which Bach suddenly halts the march of the bass line at the words "Ich bin kraftlos," pointing up the expressive sighs in the melody. Here is Psalm No. 130:

This too is rather starkly straightforward, yet also finely expressive. We notice the octave leap that enacts the leap of prayer "Aus der Tiefe"; the insistently repeated C's over changing harmony that set the words "höre, Gott"; the haunting harmonization of "meiner Stimme Flehen." Yet when we recall the variety, complexity, and expressive range of some of the songs surveyed in the last two chapters, Bitter's word "masterwork" scarcely seems justified.

We must, however, recall that Bitter had earlier written a book on J. S. Bach and that he was living and writing during the palmy days of the Bach revival: the Bach-Gesellschaft edition was well under way, and Spitta's great biography would soon be published. There is thus every reason why he should have been strongly inclined to praise, even perhaps to overpraise, C.P.E. Bach's chorales, to celebrate the continuing presence of the father in the work of the son. This tendency is all the more interesting in light of what else Bitter has to say about Bach's Cramer Psalms. For he begins his review of the collection by discussing not the seemingly "conservative" chorale settings but rather some of the most elaborate and experimental "advanced" ones.

After citing Bach's entire preface, Bitter notes that while Bach clearly expected this collection to be an advance ("Fortschritt") over his Gellert songs, he still felt constrained to provide mainly strophic settings, specifically avoiding the psalms cast in more than one meter, which "would have led him, through a more perfected mode of composition, to be forced to take yet a further step [*Schritt*] on his path." This lack of daring, Bitter felt, was due to Bach's concern for his public, who he feared might not be up to dealing with the difficulties of songs in more complex forms. While this worry over sales may have been "prudent" on Bach's part, Bitter cannot bring himself to approve of it from an artistic standpoint: "a freer treatment, on a larger scale, of what these psalms already offer, in their constricted form, would have resulted in an extraordinary achievement" (II, 65).

Bach has, nonetheless, achieved greatness and perfection—even operating, regrettably, in this rather cramped and constrained manner. Bitter then proceeds to praise a number of settings that especially evince this achievement. First of all comes Psalm No. 8, which is "completely through-composed"—a phrase that makes clear what is really at stake here. Strophic form is perfectly acceptable to Bitter if it is employed in the venerated chorale idiom; but once that idiom, with its special and historically justified constraints, is abandoned, Bitter, a mid-19th-century man acquainted with the songs of Schubert, Schumann, and the early Brahms, sees only artistic disadvantages in strophic form. He wants chorales or through-composed songs, with nothing in between. In the setting of Psalm 33 he notes appreciatively the imitations between right and left hand in the accompaniment, which make it "a contrapuntal masterwork." In Psalm 67, which is really a sort of mini-cantata, he praises the alternation of solo voice and chorus, and in Psalm 93, which is printed on three staves with the vocal line completely separate from the keyboard's right hand, the elaborately figured accompaniment. He concludes by observing, a little lamely, that in some of the other songs, though they are of restricted range, the thoughts are of unusual purity: "The melody thereby attains a distinctive character, one might say an intensity, which is scarcely found even in the best songs of modern times" (II, 66). Plainly, it is by mid-19th-century standards that these 18th-century songs are being judged.

Contemporary reviews of the Cramer Psalm settings single out some of the same settings for praise, but do so in quite different terms. The *Hamburgischer Correspondent* reviewer noted first of all "the originality of our Bach, the strength of his expression, the novelty and boldness of his thoughts, and the often unusual and surprising course of the harmony." What struck him about Psalm 8 was not that it was through-composed but rather that the choral harmony was magnificent and the Prophet's song full of high seriousness. And in the setting of Psalm 33, where Bitter had singled out the imitations between the two hands for special praise, the *Hamburgischer Correspondent*'s man rather anxiously reassures his readers: "the contrapuntal writing is not, in itself, damaging to the song." Whereas any sign of.contrapuntal activity is most welcome to Bitter, the reviewer of the mid-1770s and his readers automatically assume that such activity will interfere with the directness and simplicity of a song—and the reviewer hastens to point out that this particular case is exceptional. In Psalm 67 the *Hamburgischer Correspondent* reviewer, like Bitter, praises the mix of chorus and solo voice—but not until after he has called attention to the "very gentle melodies" of that setting and of the setting of Psalm 65. And like Bitter, he notes, in Psalm 93, "a special accompanying voice for the keyboard."[24]

The review in the *Neuer gelehrter altonaischer Mercur* begins by repeating the statements made by Bach in his preface about the principles governing his selection of psalms: that he has chosen those of particular relevance to the present time and particularly well suited to general religious edification, that he has omitted those in which the meter changes, those which seemed too long, and those with too much variety of content to be satisfactorily encompassed in a song. The reviewer then remarks that anyone setting out to review the collection, after having played through it, must first give himself time to get over his enthusiasm and achieve critical distance. Of Psalm 8 he, like his colleague at the *Hamburgischer Correspondent*, notes the "splendor and artistry" of the accompaniment. And of Psalm 93 he writes: "The melody is simple, and full of dignity and majesty; and the accompaniment, which is wholly composed of broken chords, contributes not a little toward making this song of praise as fiery and splendid as the content demands."[25]

It is most interesting that while the *Neuer gelehrter altonaischer Mercur*'s reviewer refers in passing to the fact that some of the settings are in chorale form, neither he nor the reviewer for the *Hamburgischer Correspondent* appears to attach any particular value judgment, or even any importance or interest, to this fact—which was, as we saw, of great importance for Bitter. Like Bitter, the 18th-century critics admire some of the collection's more elaborate and highly wrought settings, but they (necessarily!) do not do so because such settings point the way to the through-composed song of the 19th century; in fact, they are at pains to make it clear that such elaboration is praiseworthy only when it does not interfere with the directness and simplicity expected of the (strophic) song. What neither they nor Bitter do is to take any notice whatever of the cumulative effect of Bach's Cramer settings. None of them, for example, notices that the four elaborate settings Bitter singled out for praise—the mini-cantatas Nos. 8 and 67, the free and operatic yet very polyphonic No. 33, the brief but splendidly wild No. 93—all are placed either immediately after or immediately before a chorale setting. Since this accounts for almost half of the nine chorale settings, it suggests that Bach had in mind some sort of ordering that would set up a significant relation between his simplest and his most elaborate settings. What can he have had in mind?

As we saw when we considered his Gellert settings, the songs do not occur in that collection in anything resembling the order that their poems do in Gellert's *Geistliche Oden und Lieder*. But Bach says explicitly in his preface to the collection that he has presented the songs "in the order in which I wrote them." Here he says nothing about the order. And of course there was, in a sense, no need for him to do so. For the settings are in exactly the same order in which their psalms are found in the Book of Psalms. But whereas he set all of Gellert's poems, Bach has set only 42 of the 150 psalms. Moreover, he has, as we have seen, gone to some trouble to state the principles on which his selection was based. But he has not really explained those principles in terms of the content of particular psalms chosen and rejected: his only guiding principle so far as content—as opposed to length, metrical structure, or form—is concerned has been the rather vague one that the chosen psalms should be those "which are well adapted to the present time and which serve the cause of general edification." We still do not know just how this principle was put into practice.

We can begin to get a clearer idea of what Bach may have had in mind by seeing how the range and distribution of content of the psalms he chose compare to the range and distribution of content throughout the Book of Psalms as a whole. The following helpful table appears on page 231 of *The Psalms: Their Structure and Meaning* (Montreal: Palm Publishers, 1965), by Pius Drijvers, O.C.S.O.; I have encircled the psalms set by Bach:

Psalms of Praise	Psalms of Thanksgiving		Psalms of Petition					Pilgrim Psalms	Processional and Enthronement Psalms	Royal Psalms
	Priv.	Commun.	Priv.	Commun.	of Trust	against Judges	on the Righteous and Sinners			
			3		(4)		(1)			2
			5							
			(6)							
(8)	9		7				10			
							11			
			13				12			
(19)	18		(17)		16		14	(15)		20
	22b		22a							21
	(23)		(25)					24a	24b	
			26							
			27							
29	(30)		28							
(33)	(32)		31							
	34		35							
			36				37			
			(38)							
			39							
	40a		40b							
	41	(46)	(42) 43	44					(47)	45
		48	51				49	50		
							52			
			54				53			
			55							
			56							
			57			58				
			59	60						
	63		61		62					
		(65)	64							
	66b	66a								
		(67)	69						68	
			70							
			71	74			73			72
		76		77			75	78		
				79						
				80		82		81		
				83				84		
			(86)	85				87		
			(88)	89						
	92			(90)			94	(91)	(93)	
								95	(96)	
									(97)	
									98	
(104)	(103)		102					(100)	(99)	101
105	107			106						
			108a	108b						
(111)			109				112			(110)
113										
114	(116)			115						
117	118		120				(119)	(121)		
		124		123			125	122		
				126			127			
		129	(130)		131		(128)	133	132	
135								134		
136	138		(139)	137						
			140							
			141							
			(142)							
(145)			143							144
(146)										
147										
(148)										
(150)									149	

Drijvers's categories perhaps require a few words of explanation and comment. In the first place, not all scholarly writers on the psalms would agree with them. It is perhaps more common to find many of Drijvers's "Psalms of Petition on the Righteous and Sinners" and some of his "Psalms of Thanksgiving" classed as "Wisdom Psalms"—i.e., didactic psalms concerned with specifying the rules for a just and correct life. In the second place, while such categories as "Psalms of Praise," "Psalms of Thanksgiving," and "Psalms of Petition" are clear from their titles and familiar to every reader of the Bible, Drijvers's other three categories might seem a little puzzling. Their titles—"Pilgrim Psalms," "Processional and Enthronement Psalms," and "Royal Psalms"—reflect what has undoubtedly been the most important development in 20th-century psalm scholarship: the attempt to interpret the psalms in the light of what is now known (or assumed) concerning the cultic ritual practices of early Israel.

This approach, pioneered by Hermann Gunkel (1862-1932), and extended in the work of his student Sigmund Mowinckel (1884-1965), is still hotly disputed but nonetheless must be seriously considered by any modern psalm scholar. Certainly it seems strange at first to a layman who has grown up thinking of the Book of Psalms as a collection of individual laments. Indeed, as Drijvers's table makes clear, over a quarter of the psalms are individual laments, and it is perhaps significant that in order to make his (and Gunkel's) case Mowinckel finds it necessary to argue, in *The Psalms in Israel's Worship*, that many psalms that have traditionally been taken to be individual utterances are really communal ones.[26] One is reminded of the strenuous attempts, early in the 20th century, to establish the ritual origins of ancient Greek drama.

Once all this has been said, we may turn to what Drijvers's table reveals to us about Bach's choice of psalms. Of those 40-odd individual laments, Bach has set just ten, less than a quarter, which make up just less than a quarter of his 42 settings. On the other hand, he has set about half of the psalms of praise and of the processional and enthronement psalms, and about a third of the psalms of thanksgiving. Thus the individual laments make up a slightly smaller proportion of Bach's collection than of the Book of Psalms, while the psalms of thanksgiving make up a slightly larger proportion, and both the psalms of praise and the processional and enthronement psalms bulk almost twice as large in Bach's collection.

As we saw earlier, of the nine chorale settings, the first five and the last set individual laments (Psalms 6, 25, 38, 42, 86, and 130), while the sixth and eighth, setting what Drijvers calls "Pilgrim Psalms" (91 and 121), flank the setting of Psalm 103, a psalm of thanksgiving. The movement within the chorale settings is thus from a sustained period of depression gradually upward to the gratitude of Psalm 103 and then back down to the deepest depression of all in Psalm 130. On the other hand, the elaborate settings praised by Bitter and the contemporary reviewers—of Psalms 8, 33, 65, 67, and 93—are all psalms of praise, thanksgiving, or procession and enthronement.

When one plays through the entire set of Cramer settings, each of the complex, rather experimental settings praised by the reviewers—of Psalms 8, 33, 67, and 93—is seen to function as the climactic resolution of a preceding sequence, each of which contains one or more chorale settings. (The setting of Psalm 65 acts as a kind of lead-in to that of Psalm 67.) This is also true of the settings of Psalm 110, a bravura tour de force in which the keyboard plays in octaves throughout, leaving the vocal line on its own, and Psalm 145, which has another of Bach's adventurous accompaniments. The final three settings form a kind of coda of praise.

So what Bach has given us in his collection of settings of Cramer's psalm translations is not simply another volume of separate songs, as in his preceding collections. He has, rather, given us a single work of art—loosely organized, to be sure, but organized nonetheless. Each of the six brief sequences of songs explores the various attitudes that the psalmist takes up in relation to God, climaxing in a song of joyous praise. The collection is thus a sort of selective critical reading of the whole Book of Psalms, containing both Psalm 1 and Psalm 150, the alpha and omega. Just what circumstances of performance Bach envisaged for this very strange work he has not told us, but the presence of a chorus in several of the settings suggests that he had church performance in mind for at least sections of it. What did he mean by saying in his Preface that he had chosen psalms of special relevance to the present time? Though the Seven Years' War had been over since 1763, much of Germany was still devastated. And though Bach was now settled and financially secure in peaceful and prosperous Hamburg, his memories of his own experience of the war may well have made him feel that Germans stood in need of the consolation his reading of the psalms could offer.

II

Let us begin by analyzing the first of these six sequences. Perhaps in order to help us get the drift of his work, Bach has made this sequence shorter than those that follow; it contains only four settings: of Psalms 1, 4, 6, and 8. Here is the setting of Psalm 1, familiar to English readers as "Blessed is the man that walketh not in the counsel of the ungodly":

We are immediately struck by the contrast, in the first two bars, between the straight, firmly declarative insistence of the descending melodic line and the joyously vaulting bass line. Since the C in the keyboard's left hand on the last half-beat of the first bar is not (as we expect it to be) immediately followed by another left-hand note at the beginning of the second bar, it seems to act as a kind of pickup to the right-hand chord, the large, exuberant leap of an eleventh between the low C and the F in the chord adding to the buoyancy of the music. (In fact, it works well to play that F with the left hand rather than with the right thumb.) In bar three the rhythm of the melodic line loosens playfully as the music hurries to a cadence a bar early, the bass line (again unexpectedly) not resting but pushing on urgently to the next phrase, which also contains only three bars. But instead of returning to the tonic in bar six, we have a quick deceptive cadence followed by a one-bar coda in which the melody speeds down the octave, met at the conclusion by the rising arpeggiated bass line. The whole song is, as Bach's direction specifies, "Munter"—an added pleasure is that there is no fermata over the left hand's low F on the third beat of the final bar: the arpeggio is to be played following the last stanza too.

But the psalm itself, as it appears in Luther's translation of the Bible, is not so simply "Munter." Here it is:

1. Wohl dem, der nicht wandelt im Rat der Gottlosen, noch tritt auf den Weg der Sünder, noch sitzt, da die Spötter setzen,

2. sondern hat Lust zum Gesetz des Herrn und redet von seinem Gesetz Tag und Nacht.

3. Der ist wie ein Baum, gepflanzet an den Wasserbächen, der seine Frucht bringet zu seiner Zeit, und seine Blätter verwelken nicht, und was er macht, das gerät wohl.

4. Aber so sind die Gottlosen nicht, sondern wie Spreu, die der Wind verstreuet.

5. Darum bleiben die Gottlosen nicht im Gerichte, noch die Sünder in der Gemeine der Gerechten.

6. Denn der Herr kennet den Weg der Gerechten, aber der Gottlosen Weg vergehet.

The psalm's six verses are divided evenly between the good man and the godless man, with the break clearly announced at the beginning of verse 4: "Aber so sind die Gottlosen nicht." And even the final verse, which initially reverts to mentioning the way of the righteous, does so only in order to firm up the concluding, loftily scornful dismissal of the way of the ungodly. The final effect is one of balanced, impartial judgment.

Cramer's verse translation, though filled with verbal echoes of Luther, yields a quite different effect:

> Heil, Heil dem Manne, der dem Rath
> Der Frevler sich entzieht;
> Dem Manne, der den krummen Pfad
> Der Uebertreter flieht!
>
> Der, wo der Gottheit Spötter lacht,
> Die fromme Seel entfernt;
> Sich Gottes Recht zur Freude macht,
> Und Tag und Nacht es lernt!
>
> Er grünet, wie am Bach ein Baum
> Von seinem Segen schwillt,
> Sich hebt, und einen weiten Raum
> Mit seinem Wipfel füllt.
>
> Er trägt, wenn seine Zeit kömmt, Frucht,
> Stets unentlaubt und grün;
> Er tröstet den, der Schatten sucht;
> Der Wandrer segnet ihn.
>
> Das ist der Fromme! Was er macht,
> Wird Segen und erfreut.
> Der Sünder ist, der seiner lacht,
> Spreu, die der Wind zerstreut.
>
> Der, der sich gegen Gott empört,
> Besteht nicht im Gericht.
> Und wo ein Volk ist, das Gott ehrt,
> Blühn die Verbrecher nicht.
>
> Der Herr verklärt die edle Bahn,
> Die der Gerechte geht.
> Er schaut im Zorn den Sünder an:
> Des Sünders Weg vergeht!

The opening "Heil, Heil" creates a celebratory mood, quite different from Luther's dryly clinical "Wohl dem." And instead of being pictured negatively as not taking the advice of the godless, not walking in the path of the sinners, not sitting with those who mock God, the good man is said positively to withdraw, to flee, to distance his "fromme Seel" from their company. He is not driven by an irresistible "Lust zum Gesetz" to speak compulsively of it day and night; rather, he gains joy from his eager study of the law. Cramer's addition, to the image of the tree, of the "Wipfel" that fills a large space gives the good man a kind of personal grandeur, a nobility that is enhanced by the details added at the end of stanza four: this man is not only good himself; he also comforts those who seek respite from the world, and is in turn blessed by them.

Perhaps even more important, at the beginning of stanza five, corresponding to the point where Luther shifts from the good man to the ungodly one, Cramer keeps the good man before us by summing up the preceding stanzas: "Das ist der Fromme!" And when he does get around to the ungodly man, Cramer defines him by his attitude toward the good man—"Der Sünder ist, der seiner lacht"—rather than merely by Luther's contemptuous image of the chaff blowing in the wind. Though the penultimate stanza does deal, very much in the manner of Luther's original text, with the ungodly man, Cramer subtly keeps the good man in our field of vision with the line "Und wo ein Volk ist, das Gott ehrt"—which is more elaborate and (again) celebratory than Luther's rather flat "in der Gemeine der Gerechten." Finally, in the first line of Cramer's last stanza, there is that magic word "verklärt": God not only knows the way of the righteous, as in Luther; he transfigures it; it becomes the shining path to eternal life, heaven's pavement of trodden gold.

With all this in mind, we can see why Bach gave Cramer's translation of Psalm 1 an unalloyedly joyous musical setting that would, perhaps, be quite inappropriate for Luther's dour and powerful version. Here is Bach's setting of Psalm 4 ("Hear me when I call, O Lord of my righteousness"):

This psalm, we recall, is one of the two of which Bach published settings in 1761. That earlier setting is virtually identical with this one; the two right-hand voices are allotted to the soprano and alto, with the keyboard given only a figured bass line. The most interesting difference between them comes at the very beginning. In the 1761 version the first four bars run as follows:

Instead of having the bass line start together with the upper voices and proceed downward in steady quarter notes, accenting their syncopation, Bach has now allowed the upper voices to venture out alone, the bass only joining on the second half of the first beat of the first bar and then creating its own syncopations against those of the upper voices. The underlying steadiness is gone; in its place is a note of tentativeness and indecision.

That this note is quite appropriate to the rest of the song soon becomes clear. After the cadence in bar four, the harmony turns to C minor, and at the end of bar six we expect that when the bass drops back to D at the beginning of bar seven it will be at the bottom of a $^6_4$ chord that will take us to another cadence on G minor. But suddenly the harmony veers to B-flat. The words of at least the first stanza make this credible: the psalm, in Cramer's translation, has opened with talk of the psalmist's anxiety in approaching God; but then at the B-flat cadence he is suddenly speaking of the celestial height from which God will (he hopes) answer his prayer. But musically the change to the major still sounds odd—another instance of indecision. Immediately thereafter, though, we are back in the minor, with an elaborately ornamented vocal line and two poignant clashes: the melody's C against the bass's C-sharp in bar nine, and the undervoice's A-flat against the bass's G appoggiatura in bar ten.

The growing harmonic complication makes these bars sound like a sort of midsection, after which we will return to the opening (or something like it) to round off the piece. But instead Bach just tacks on an extra bar and swings back to G minor. The piece seems to have ended too quickly, almost arbitrarily. What we expect is, rather, something like this:

The song's odd, peremptory ending, cheating us of that closing phrase, perfectly fulfills the promise of wavering tentativeness extended by the change Bach made in the opening bars when he revised his earlier version.

But what has this tentativeness to do with Cramer's poem? Its first two stanzas are addressed directly to God:

> Wenn ich zu dir in meinen Aengsten flehe,
> Antworte mir, o Gott, von deiner Höhe;
> Gott meiner Frömmigkeit,
> Wenn ich dich rufe, sey nicht weit!
>
> Der du mir Raum machst, wenn der Feind mich beuget,
> Und mir kein Weg aus meiner Angst sich zeiget,
> Erhöre mein Gebet,
> Womit mein Herz um Hülfe fleht!

The speaker immediately announces that he is praying to God while surrounded by dangers and distresses ("in meinen Aengsten"), and he contrasts this depressed status with that of God ("von deiner Höhe). He then turns suddenly—and, given his depressed state of mind, rather improbably—to haranguing the enemies who have brought him to this pass, and whom he addresses as "ihr Mächtigen auf Erden." The harangue, which focuses on their vanity, guile, and anger, goes on for four stanzas and concludes with him enjoining them, rather in the manner of an evangelist preacher, to turn to God: "Lasst allein / Den Höchsten eure Hoffnung seyn!" In the last three stanzas he himself returns to addressing God. He still sees himself as besieged and put upon—he begins by speaking of "viel Thoren, die mich hassen"—but concludes by asserting that he now feels secure in God's hands:

> Ich liege, Gott, von deiner Hand beschirmet,
> Und ruhe ganz im Frieden, wenn es stürmet.
> Du nimmst dich meiner an,
> Damit ich sicher wohnen kann.

The poem is thus filled with violent oscillations between the speaker's sense of powerlessness and a conviction of his own moral authority and high standing in God's eyes, oscillations which are nicely captured by those of Bach's setting.

Again, Luther's text is rather different. Since it is quite brief, I give it in its entirety:

> 1. Ein Psalm Davids, vorzusingen auf Saitenspielen.
> 2. Erhöhe mich, wenn ich rufe, Gott meiner Gerechtigkeit, der du mich tröstest in Angst; sei mir gnädig und erhöre mein Gebet!
> 3. Lieben Herren, wie lange soll meine Ehre geschändet werden? Wie habt ihr das Eitele so lieb und die Lügen so gerne! Sela.
> 4. Erkennet doch, dass der Herr seine Heiligen wunderlich führet! Der Herr höret, wenn ich ihn anrufe.
> 5. Zürnet ihr, so sündiget nicht! Redet mit eurem Herzen auf eurem Lager und harret. Sela.
> 6. Opfert Gerechtigkeit und hoffet auf den Herrn.
> 7. Viele sagen: Wie sollt' uns dieser weisen, was gut ist? Aber, Herr, erhebe über uns das Licht deines Antlitzes!
> 8. Du erfreuest mein Herz, ob jene gleich viel Wein und Korn haben.
> 9. Ich liege und schlafe ganz mit Frieden; denn allein du, Herr, hilfst mir, dass ich sicher wohne.

Here, although the speaker is of course asking God for aid, a certain amount of solid confidence is present from the beginning. Rather than immediately emphasizing his own distress, he refers to God as one who has comforted him in distress, and asks God to be gracious to him—with the clear implication that God has been so many times in the past. The elaborate self-pity of Cramer's talk about God having made room for him when the devil afflicted him, and when there seemed no way out of his distress, is reduced to the simple and straightforward phrase "in Angst." And with that the speaker turns immediately to address his tormentors. The King James Version has him addressing them as "ye sons of men," and the New Revised Standard Version simply as "you people"; therefore, in my ignorance of Hebrew, I can only assume that Luther's trenchantly ironic "Lieben Herren" is his own splendid invention. Behind those words stands the confidence that the speaker has already expressed; the somewhat improbable mood swing of Cramer's speaker is nowhere in evidence.

The rest of Luther's translation continues to exhibit the same confident scorn of those whom the speaker is addressing. His firm sense of how God has comforted him in past troubles earns for him the authoritative tone in which he commands the "Lieben Herren"—which also carries the social or class implications of Cramer's "ihr Mächtigen auf Erden"—to recognize God's power and cease from sin, and in which he restates his absolute trust in God. The rather melodramatic shifts in Cramer's version, mirrored in Bach's setting, are not a part of the original psalm but would seem, rather, to result from the Lutheran (and, more generally, the Reform) view of the Book of Psalms as law rather than gospel, as embodying a more sternly Augustinian view of man's sinfulness than most late medieval Roman Catholic thinkers had found there.

It is time now to see how Bach's setting of Psalm 6, which we glanced at earlier in passing, looks when set in its context and viewed in relation to Cramer's whole poem and Luther's psalm. Here first is Luther:

    1. Ein Psalm Davids, vorzusingen auf acht Saiten.
    2. Ach, Herr, strafe mich nicht in deinem Zorn und züchtige mich nicht in deinem Grimm!
    3. Herr, sei mir gnädig, denn ich bin schwach; heile mich, Herr, denn meine Gebeine sind erschrocken,
    4. und meine Seele ist sehr erschrocken. Ach, du Herr, wie lange!
    5. Wende dich, Herr, und errette meine Seele; hilf mir um deiner Güte willen!
    6. Denn im Tode gedenkt man dein nicht; wer will dir in der Hölle danken?
    7. Ich bin so müde von Seufzen, ich schwemme mein Bette die ganze Nacht und netze mit meinen Tränen mein Lager.
    8. Meine Gestalt ist verfallen vor Trauern und ist alt worden; denn ich allenthalben geängstet werde.
    9. Weichet von mir, alle Übeltäter; denn der Herr höret mein Weinen,
    10. der Herr höret mein Flehen, mein Gebet nimmt der Herr an.
    11. Es müssen alle meine Feinde zuschanden werden und sehr erschrecken, sich zurückkehren und zuschanden werden plötzlich.

As in Psalm 4, we again have a speaker who is imploring God for aid, yet who immediately manifests a certain confidence and dignity—felt here first of all in the measured repetition of "Herr" throughout the first several verses. (One is reminded of the opening of Hopkins's great sonnet: "Thou art indeed just, Lord, if I contend / With thee, but, Sir, so what I plead is just.") Even after the anguished outburst "Ach, du Herr, wie lange!" the speaker can turn and remind God that it is not only to his own but also to God's interest to help him: "hilf mir um deiner Güte willen!" For if God's goodness is to be known in the world, it must be made manifest in and attested to by his human worshippers. Similarly, the next verse—"Denn im Tode gedenkt man dein nicht; wer will dir in der Hölle danken?"—expresses not only the speaker's fear of losing, in death, his relation to God, but also his desire to let God know that the knowledge of divine mercy and providence can only be spread by living human witness. This sense of one's own worth and usefulness in relation to God persists even through the following two verses' starkly matter-of-fact description of the speaker's tears and bodily wasting away. Therefore when he commands evildoers to avoid him because God has heard his prayer, and concludes by assuring himself and us of his enemies' destruction, there is not the abrupt, puzzling change of tone that some scholars have found in the Hebrew.[27] The assurance has been there all along, and it is nicely enforced by the concluding punch of Luther's "plötzlich."

Cramer's version is, again, rather different:

    Führe, Herr, mich nicht im Grimme
    In dein heiliges Gericht!
    Deines Zornes Richterstimme
    Schone mich, und donnre nicht!
    Ich bin kraftlos. Mit Erbarmen
    Heile, Herr, mich Armen!
    Noch erzittert mein Gebein
    Vor deinem Dräun.

>   Deine Schrecken, Gott, durchschüttern
> Die betäubte Seele noch.
> Ach wie lange soll sie zittern!
> Wenn erfreuest du mich doch?
> Hör, um deiner Güte willen;
> Lass den Sturm sich stillen!
> Gott, erbarme meiner dich,
> Und rette mich!
>
>   Weil ich noch mein Leben habe,
> Wende, Tröster, dich zu mir!
> Denn dein Ruhm wohnt nicht im Grabe:
> Und wer dankt im Staube dir?
> Ach ich bin vom Seufzen müde!
> Gieb mir, gieb mir Friede!
> Doch mein thränenvoll Gesicht
> Bemerkst du nicht!
>
>   Ungezählte Thränen quellen,
> Wo ich Armer ruhen soll:
> Täglich strömen sie und schwellen
> Jede Nacht mein Lager voll.
> In der Nacht, die mich umziehet,
> Hat mein Lenz verblühet.
> Elend durch des Grams Gewalt,
> Klag ich mich alt.
>
>   Weicht von mir, ihr Uebelthäter,
> Denn mein Weinen dringt zum Herrn.
> Thränen sind zu starke Beter;
> Meine Seufzer hört er gern.
> Schmach und Schrecken müsse fassen
> Alle, die mich hassen.
> Plötzlich breche Schmach und Pein
> Auf sie herein!

Though the two versions share many of the same words and phrases, there is a great difference between their modes of address to God and the ways in which the speaker sees himself. The powerful, matter-of-fact plainness of "Herr, sei mir gnädig, denn ich bin schwach," and "mein Gebeine sind erschrocken, und meine Seele ist sehr erschrocken" seems worlds away from the self-pitying, almost cringing language of Cramer's opening stanzas, with all their shaking and trembling, their stress falling on "mich Armen"—rather than on a dignified being who can directly ask God to be gracious to him because he is weak (as though ordinary fairness or decency demanded such treatment). The soul of Luther's speaker is not, one feels, "betäubte": to be weak, frightened, exhausted is quite different from being deafened, confused, stupefied. The very directness and force of Luther's speaker rule out these latter afflictions. Though Cramer dutifully repeats "um deiner Güte willen," it loses its point, buried amongst the metaphors with which Cramer has elaborated Luther's language—the storm and the life that has withered like a flower—and the fulsome repetitions ("quellen," "strömen," "schwellen").

Therefore after the monosyllabic debility of "Klag ich mich alt," the command to the evildoers really does come as a shock. The self-assurance it demands has not been earned by the rest of the poem.

Here, once again, is Bach's setting:

Earlier we noted the song's straightforwardness, and in particular the way in which, while keeping the melody moving after the double-bar, Bach suddenly halts the marchlike movement of the bass line, pointing up the pathos of "Ich bin kraftlos" by a series of sighs in the melody. What can we now note in addition, having analyzed both Luther's translation of the psalm and Cramer's verse elaboration?

After the starkly D-minor harmony of the opening bars, relieved only by the passing B-flat chord in bar 3, we surprisingly turn toward a rather hopeful F-major cadence. It is only after this first strain has been repeated that the bass line halts its motion and we get the forceless, deflating effect of the melodic sighs. And even in the midst of those there is the small surprise of the first-inversion D-flat chord in bar 11. (Given the melody, we might rather have expected the bass to move to an E-natural, under a diminished seventh, and then, in the next bar, to an F, under a second-inversion B-flat-minor chord and then a root-position chord in F-minor.) This is followed by the fine pathos of the minor $^6_5$ chord on C and the cadence on G minor.

At this point, however, the bass line begins its steady rise, the melody rising along with it, and the music seems to have taken on a new energy and sense of purpose. Then comes the finest touch of all: instead of letting the melody continue its rise as the phrase fills out its expected eight-bar length, Bach suddenly cuts the song short, dropping the melody a sixth as the harmony swiftly completes a D-minor cadence. The effect is one of utter exhaustion. On purely musical grounds, disregarding for a moment Cramer's text, we might have expected something like this:

292 ～ Chapter Eleven

But instead the final phrase is abruptly truncated, and the melody not only drops a major sixth, the largest interval in the song—the second largest, the minor sixth just before the G-minor cadence, perhaps foreshadows the effect of the ending—but also drops to a note lower than any heard previously (and keeps on dropping!). Yet Bach does not give us this effect of exhaustion and debility without having earlier given us—through the steady movement of the bass line and the forward thrust of the mainly stepwise melody—a good deal more of Luther's strength and dignity than we get in Cramer's rather namby-pamby verse. (Compare the doggerel of Cramer's concluding lines with the hard determination of Luther's final verse!)

We are therefore better prepared for the extraordinary outburst of Bach's through-composed setting of Psalm 8, which it will be just as well to look at immediately, even before we analyze the psalm as we find it in Luther and Cramer:

This is, to say the least, a very strange piece of music. Nothing we have encountered so far, even in the through-composed songs we examined at the end of the preceding chapter, has prepared us for this. In the first place, the keyboard, at least for the first portion of the piece, has two staves to itself and does not duplicate the vocal line. The music, with its harmonically determined vocal line and keyboard fanfares in octaves, reminds us at once of the accompanied recitatives in Bach's oratorios. In fact, the dotted-sixteenth and thirty-second figures that we see here were a favorite device of his when he was dealing, as he is here, with divine power and majesty. In the accompanied recitative for bass, "O Freunde, Kinder," No. 21 in *Die Israeliten in der Wüste*, the same figures appear as soon as the text predicts Christ's eventual victory over sin. And they are found in three similar contexts in the *Auferstehung und Himmelfahrt Jesu*: the bass recitative No. 3, "Judäa zittert"; the latter portion of the bass recitative No. 14, "Dort seh' ich aus den Toren"; and, less prominently, the tenor aria No. 18, "Mein Herr, mein Gott." In the two former cases, the figures are carried over into the arias following the recitatives.

But the first section of Psalm 8 is different from an accompanied recitative in that the elaborate fanfares do not punctuate the vocal line but actually accompany it. Moreover, the vocal line is not rhythmically free, as is usual in recitatives accompanied or unaccompanied, but is in strict meter. It is as though an accompanied recitative had been condensed or telescoped. But of course the subject here too is divine power and majesty. The portion of Cramer's text that this music sets runs as follows:

> Wer ist so würdig als du, von uns bewundert zu werden,
> Du, unser Beherrscher, o Gott?
> Wie stralet dein Name so herrlich auf Erden,
> So weit umher, Herr Zebaoth!

> Wer schaut zu deinen Himmeln hinan,
> Sieht deine Majestät im Glanze jeder Sonne,
> Und jauchzet nicht dir und betet voll Wonne
> Nicht, Urquell aller Wunder, dich an?

There seems little point in analyzing this music point by point in relation to its text: in both music and text the mood is set and maintained; there is little change or inflection in either. What is remarkable, in fact, is the way in which Bach sustains the trumpets-and-drums keyboard part through 30 bars.

At this point both text and music change. We revert to Bach's accustomed two-stave format for (in effect) a strophic song consisting of a seven-bar strain (3 + 4), which is repeated, and a twelve-bar one (6 + 6). So in a sense this piece is not completely through-composed after all. Actually, however, neither music nor text changes that much. The text, though its meter changes, is still straightforward praise of God; here are the four stanzas that are set by the strophic song portion of the piece:

> O welch ein Lob bereitest du
> Dir aus dem Munde schwacher Kinder!
> Dir jauchzet selbst der Säugling zu,
> Und straft die Bosheit stummer Sünder.
> Ihr Lob, das weit umher erschallt,
> Verkündigt deines Arms Gewalt,
> Beschämt der Widersacher Heere,
> Und rettet deines Namens Ehre.
>
> Mein aufgeklärtes Aug erblickt
> Zahllose Wunder deiner Stärke,
> Die Himmel prächtig ausgeschmückt,
> Jehova, deiner Finger Werke!
> Wie glänzt der Mond mir, dessen Licht
> Des Nachts von deiner Grösse spricht!
> Wie stralen in der hohen Ferne
> Mir deine Herolde, die Sterne!
>
> Gott, wie unendlich wirst du mir!
> Was ist der Mensch, das du sein denkest?
> Was ist des Menschen Sohn vor dir,
> Das du ihn suchst und dich ihm schenkest?
> Geringer wird, als Engel sind,
> Dein Auserwählter, Gott, dein Kind;
> Doch bald nach seinem kurzen Leiden
> Wirst du in Majestät ihn kleiden!
>
> Dann betet ihn die Schöpfung an;
> Du willst, dass sie dein Zepter küsse.
> Du hast ihm alles unterthan,
> Zum Schemel unter seine Füsse:
> Den stolzen Stier, der muthig brüllt,
> Das sanftre Schaf, das freye Wild,
> Das Volk der Luft, und in dem Meere
> Die Fisch und alle seine Heere.

The music, though it has the appearance of a conventional strophic song, is almost wantonly untuneful. As in the earlier portion of the piece, the vocal line, except for the descending scale in the opening bars, is harmonically determined, mainly a series of arpeggios. Hence the declamatory, very public air of the opening section is maintained despite the change of format. After these four stanzas are sung, we return to the opening portion, which ends at the fermata in bar 19.

With Psalm 8, which is really a sort of mini-cantata, our sequence of four settings comes to a close. We have seen the straightforward joyous exuberance of Psalm 1 give way, in turn, to the tentativeness and indecision of Psalm 4, the spiritual exhaustion of Psalm 6, and now, most surprisingly, the wild clamor and public pronouncement of Psalm 8. In this context, as we saw, the austere chorale setting of Psalm 6 looks a good deal more interesting than it did when we viewed it initially, standing on its own. And the increasingly intimate, personal quality of the three preceding settings makes the almost official impersonality of the Psalm 8 setting seem both justified and brilliantly effective. Something like this same spiritual journey, from simple joy or satisfaction through doubt and confusion to depression and then suddenly to ecstatic praise, will be retraced in each of the five similar sequences of settings that follow. But there is still more to be said about this one.

Cramer seems to have intended his setting of Psalm 8 to be turned into an even more ambitious cantata than Bach made of it. For he has headed the first four lines of the opening section "Erstes Chor" and the second four lines "Zweytes Chor." The strophic song, on the other hand, bears the heading "Der Prophet," while the concluding repeated portion of the opening section is allotted to "Beyde Chöre." Bach's collection reproduces these settings in the poem as quoted following the music of the setting. And yet, as the layout of the vocal part (and the word "Singstimme" at the beginning) seem to indicate, Bach had in mind a single voice for the whole piece. Yet surely the textural difference between the accompaniments to the two sections was intended to evoke the difference between choral and solo song.

Interestingly enough, this was not the original form in which Cramer set Psalm 8. His first two volumes of psalm translations were published in 1755 (Psalms 1-41) and the second in 1759 (Psalms 42-48 plus Psalm 119). The last two appeared in 1763 (Psalms 83-116) and 1764 (Psalms 117-150). But in the meantime the ever-industrious Cramer had republished the two early volumes and had revised some of his translations—including that of Psalm 8. The new first volume (Psalms 1-41) appeared in 1763, labeled "Zweyte verbesserte Auflage," and the new second volume also in 1763 (Psalms 42-82), labeled merely "Zweyte Auflage." Bach set the revised, 1763 version of Psalm 8; the 1755 version, though different in detail and simpler in conception, also seems intended to be a cantata text.

In the 1755 version, the opening section is assigned only to "Chor," and is half as long as that in the 1763 version:

> Wie ist dein Name so gross! Mit welchem Ruhme geschmücket,
> Herr, unser herrscher, voll Weisheit und Macht!
> Der Erdkreis weis es und staunt; von deinem Namen entzücket,
> Frohlockt er über seine Pracht.

Of the four stanzas of the strophic section, the last two are almost the same as in the 1763 version, but the first two are quite different:

> Die Himmel, über die er geht,
> Und aller deiner Himmel Heere
> Sind voll von deiner Majestät,
> Sind voll von deines Namens Ehre.
> Dich lallt das schwache Kind mit Lust,
> Und selbst der Säugling an der Brust
> Wird, wenn dich deine Hasser schänden,
> Stark und dein Lob in deinen Händen.

> Die Nachbegierigen vergehn,
> Und wer dich hasst, durch ihre Stärke.
> Ich werde deine Himmel sehn,
> Jehova, deiner Finger Werke!
> Ich will den Mond sehn, dessen Licht
> Des Nachts von deiner Grösse spricht,
> Und deine Welten in der Ferne,
> Herr, deine Herolde, die Sterne.

Though the four stanzas of this section bear no heading in the 1755 version, the repetition of the heading "Chor" before the concluding section, which this time is identical to the whole first section, makes it clear that Cramer intended the four intervening stanzas to be sung or chanted by a single voice.

But what about Luther's translation of Psalm 8? Here it is:

> 1. Ein Psalm Davids, vorzusingen auf der Githith.
> 2. Herr, unser Herrscher, wie herrlich ist dein Name in allen Landen, da man dir danket im Himmel!
> 3. Aus dem Munde der jungen Kinder und Säuglinge hast du eine Macht zugerichtet um deiner Feinde willen, dass du vertilgest den Feind und den Nachgierigen.
> 4. Denn ich werde sehen die Himmel, deiner Finger Werk, den Mond und die Sterne, die du bereitest.
> 5. Was ist der Mensch, das du sein gedenkest, und des Menschen Kind, dass du dich sein annimmst?
> 6. Du wirst ihn lassen eine kleine Zeit von Gott verlassen sein. Aber mit Ehren und Schmuck wirst du ihn krönen.
> 7. Du wirst ihn zum Herrn machen über deiner Hände Werk; alles hast du unter seine Füsse getan:
> 8. Schafe und Ochsen allzumal, dazu auch die wilden Tiere,
> 9. die Vögel unter dem Himmel und die Fische im Meer und was im Meer gehet.
> 10. Herr, unser Herrscher, wie herrlich ist dein Name in allen Landen!

Though this is a famously eloquent psalm of praise, it is a far more modest production than we might expect, coming from Cramer's poem and Bach's setting.

It had, of course, been common, at least since the time of Athanasius, to discover foreshadowings of Christian truth everywhere in the Old Testament, but especially in the Psalms—indeed, to read the Book of Psalms as a sort of allegory of Christ's coming and eventual triumph. Psalm 8 was especially open to such a reading. Luther, in a commentary based on a sermon delivered on All Saints' Day, 1537, referred to Psalm 8 as "a glorious prophecy about Christ, where David describes Christ's person and kingdom and teaches who Christ is; what kind of kingdom He has and how it is formed; where this King rules, namely, in all lands and yet in heaven; and the means by which His kingdom is founded and regulated, namely, only through the Word and faith, without sword and armor."[28] Thus we can understand why Cramer provided such a grandiose dramatic elaboration of Psalm 8, complete with two choirs and a Prophet to speak these words.

Perhaps the main reason Psalm 8 invites such an interpretation is the occurrence of the innocent-looking Hebrew phrase *ben adam*, which literally means son of man, in the verse that Luther numbers 5 but that is counted as 4 in the King James Version: "What is man, that thou art mindful of him? and the son of man, that thou visitest him?" "Son of Man" was, of course, one of the main ways in which Christ referred to himself and is referred to by others in the New Testament. Yet the Hebrew phrase means no more than man's progeny—it is translated "mortals" in the New Revised Standard Version. This verse of Psalm 8 and the two verses following, however, had been picked up and applied directly to Christ in Hebrews 2:6-8. Thus there was strong scriptural justification for taking them as also applying to Christ in Psalm 8. It is, however, interesting that while Luther, in both of his commentaries on Psalm 8, takes *ben adam* as meaning Christ, his translation does not, as we should expect (and as it does in the Hebrews passage), read "des Menschen Sohn" but rather the more neutral "des Menschen Kind."

III

We now have an idea of how Bach arranged the psalms he chose to set in sequences, each of which dramatizes a spiritual journey or progress through various emotional states to a culminating, joyous acknowledgment and celebration of God's goodness and power. There is therefore no need to examine any of the other sequences so closely as we have that comprising Psalms 1, 4, 6, and 8. The relation that we have noted between Luther's translation and Cramer's poetic elaborations continues, generally, to hold true throughout: where Luther is tough and succinct, Cramer is verbose, personal, a little soft at the core—very much, in other words, in tune with the Pietist Movement. And Bach manages to mediate between them, maintaining Luther's economy while also doing justice to Cramer's *Empfindsamkeit* sensibility, which he of course shared (though without the softness at the core). We can best fill out our idea of Bach's Cramer settings by looking at the fourth sequence of settings, which includes those of Psalms 86, 88, 90, 91, and 93. First, however, it will help to look very briefly at Bach's setting of Psalm 67, which concludes the third sequence.

Psalm 67 is the one that begins, in the King James Version, "God be merciful unto us, and bless us; and cause his face to shine upon us." It is usually classed as a "Psalm of Thanksgiving," and the penultimate verse—"Then shall the earth yield her increase; and God, even our own God, shall bless us"—strongly suggests that it is either a prayer for a good harvest or a song in celebration of one. As with Psalm 8, Cramer has divided Psalm 67 into solo and choral portions. After each of the poem's three stanzas, there is a choral refrain of praise and thanksgiving.

As with Psalm 8, here too Bach marks the change from solo voice to chorus indicated in Cramer's text with a change in tempo, texture, and time signature, even though the whole song is apparently for solo voice alone:

There is, I think, no need to analyze this piece in detail. The first, 16-bar section is unmitigatedly cheerful and lively, rather in the manner of a ballad about hunting or country life. The keyboard's left hand alternates between joining in to support the melodic line (in either thirds or sixths) and pushing the song along with its little arpeggiated figures. But the second section is quite spectacular. Under the simple, forceful melody the keyboard's left hand keeps up a continuous explosion of arpeggiated sixteenth-note figures that finally end in the two bars of runaway triplets (for so they should be felt and accented) in tenths with the melodic line and in the octave unison with which the piece closes. There is little more to be said.

From the joyous heights of the setting of Psalm 67, we return suddenly to the depths with the one of Psalm 86, a straightforward lament. Cramer, as so often, makes it rather more melodramatic than it is in Luther. From the outset, Luther's speaker has his usual dignity: "Herr, neige deine Ohren und erhöre mich; denn ich bin elend und arm. Bewahre meine Seele; denn ich bin heilig." Cramer's is considerably weepier and more self-pitying:

>Herr, erhöre meine Klagen!
>Schaue her auf meine Plagen,
>Elend bin ich; arm bin ich.
>Ich bin dir allein ergeben;
>Rette deines Knechtes Leben;
>Hilf mir, denn ich trau auf dich!

In his second stanza Cramer adds a bit of pathos about a ray of light from God's countenance breaking through to the speaker before he resumes his plea for help:

>Ach es leucht ein Stral des Lichtes
>Deines Vaterangesichtes
>Dem, den du gebeugt hast, mir!

Täglich ruf ich: Hilf dem Knechte
Deiner Wahl, mit deiner Rechte:
Denn mein Herz verlangt nach dir!

This is pretty poor stuff—none of the self-possession, even in the midst of deep need, so cleanly embodied in Luther's "denn ich bin heilig."

The remaining seven stanzas of Cramer's poem are no better. And indeed this poem did not call forth anything very remarkable from Bach; here is his setting:

A 24-bar chorale consisting of six four-bar phrases, the sixth virtually an echo of the third, thus neatly dividing the piece in half. The cadences are quite usual for a piece in C minor: Eb, G, C minor, Ab, G, C minor. The only interesting moment occurs in the fourth phrase, with the unexpected turn to the extremely lush Db ninth chord in m. 15. But nothing is made of the effect, as the harmony immediately reverts to the expected Ab. There is nothing special about the fourth lines of Cramer's stanzas that would seem to invite the extra lushness, so perhaps Bach was merely striving for variety.

The next setting, of Psalm 88, is considerably more interesting. In the preceding chapter, we recall, we looked at an earlier setting Bach had done of another, anonymous translator's poetic version of this psalm. It was, as we saw, one of Bach's attempts to combine the traditional, public chorale idiom with the more private, subjective idiom of the strophic song. The gravity and weight of the former coalesced with the tentativeness and lighter textures of the latter to produce a song of rare power and poignancy. This setting is very different:

Though Bach has marked it to be performed sadly, very slowly, and with the notes sustained, the initial impression is nonetheless one of languishing grace—especially when we recall the declamatory force of the opening bars of the earlier setting of Psalm 88.

All along the way there are small harmonic surprises, little unexpected glints of light or dark that suddenly cast the meaning of the text, and the speaker's relation to God with which it is concerned, into doubt. The first four bars, with their gracefully curving melodic line, seem to be governed by the bass line, which rises steadily, in even dotted half notes, taking us from the irresolution of the opening diminished seventh to the security of A-flat major in m. 4. And as the bass line turns down to Gb, we confidently expect a D-flat major chord at the beginning of m. 5. But instead we get D-flat minor, which not only darkens the landscape considerably but also makes us feel, more decisively than the major would have done, a pull to the flat side of the harmonic spectrum. But no: at the beginning of m. 6 Bach surprises us again by not giving us a Db in the bass but rather a D-natural. And from there we are pulled back toward the sharp side, with a quite orthodox cadence on C minor, the v of the (apparent) home key, F minor. Both times m. 8 ends with an eighth-note phrase that, like the opening, suggests graceful resignation.

The second section begins by recapitulating the first, a fourth higher, but soon strays. The C-flat first-inversion chord in m. 11 is another surprise, an unexpected moment of repose. But the following bar, instead of carrying us through B-flat minor to a cadence on F, as we expect, abruptly—note the rhythm—reverses the two expected chords, giving us a cadence on B-flat minor. After another graceful little linking phrase, the bass line and the harmony above it once more evoke the song's beginning. But the very dark G-flat minor of m. 15, which slips immediately into the major, is another unsettling development.

The final eight bars begin with yet another reminder of the opening, as the bass line, calling attention to itself by entering a beat early, echoes the four-note descent of the melody in mm. 1–2. After the firmly declared F minor at the end of the descent, we seem to be moving to B-flat minor—but once again we are surprised when the appoggiatura Eb moves not to Db but rather to D-natural, giving us a sudden hint of hope or consolation. And the move up a half-step in the next bar to C-flat is also a surprise. But from there on the bass line moves inexorably down in a steady, repeated rhythm, taking us into the final cadence. All that remains to be remarked is the left hand's linking phrase—like the others, graceful and subdued—that takes us back to the beginning for the next stanza.

This is, then, a far more wistful and delicate reading of Psalm 88 than Bach gave us in his previous setting. And surely part of the difference can be attributed to Cramer's poem. The two opening verses of Luther's translation read: "Herr Gott, Mein Heiland, ich schreie Tag und Nacht vor dir. Lass mein Gebet vor dich kommen; neige deine Ohren zu meinem Geschrei!" But in Cramer's poem the scream has given way to a sigh:

> Tag und Nacht, du Heil der Frommen,
> Seufz ich, Herr, mein Hort, zu dir;
> Lass mein Seufzen vor dich kommen;
> Neige, Gott, dein Ohr zu mir!

Also, Cramer, despite his usual desire to personalize the content of the psalms by attributing directly to his speaker what in the psalms is vaguely attributed to the world at large, does not follow the anonymous translator in personalizing those central verses in which the psalmist asks God a series of rhetorical questions—as to whether the dead will know and praise his wonders and his goodness. These are left in the impersonal form. Thus we can see why Bach chose this time to write a personal but rather subdued, wistful, understated, and finally ambivalent—those harmonic surprises!—setting of this psalm.

Also, Bach was writing this setting in the context of other psalm settings, some of which are actual chorales. Therefore he did not need to incorporate more than one idiom into any one of his settings. He could depend on the rather bleak chorale setting that preceded that of Psalm 88 and, as we shall see, the thoroughly cheerful one of Psalm 90 that follows it. Indeed, one can see the setting of Psalm 88 as mediating (or modulating) between those two settings.

Psalm 90 is one of the psalms that most makes one regret one's ignorance of Hebrew, for it is obviously a splendid poem. At first the relentless good cheer of Bach's setting seems surprising. For this is, on the face of it, not an altogether cheerful psalm. Its superscription attributes it to "Moses, the Man of God," but this is a late addition to the text, to be taken merely as evidence that the poem was regarded most highly—worthy indeed of Moses—in ancient times. It begins happily enough—in the King James Version: "Lord, thou hast been our dwelling place in all generations. Before the mountains were brought forth, or ever thou hadst formed the earth and the world, even from everlasting to everlasting, thou art God." But it goes on to dwell mainly on God's wrath, and on the immense disparity between his eternal existence and the extreme brevity of man's life. Yet there is not a breath of complaint. The poem is characterized throughout, rather, by a bold and clear-eyed realism that reminds one of Homer—of the moment in Book III of the *Iliad*, for example, when Helen, sitting by Priam on the wall of Troy and identifying the Greek heroes for him, misses her two brothers Castor and Polydeuces and characteristically attributes their failure to join the Greek forces to their shame at her conduct; to this the poem replies: "Thus she spoke, but the nourishing earth already covered them there in Lacedaemon, dear land of their fathers." Mowinckel and others have labored to discover a communal or cultic origin for this superb psalm, the 20th century's updated version of primitivism resting on the curious notion that ancient poets could accomplish nothing great on their own but only as speakers for their communities.

Cramer's version of Psalm 90 is far from what one can gather of the original from Luther, the King James Version, and various modern, presumably quite literal translations of the Hebrew. Luther speaks repeatedly and frankly of God's wrath:

> 7. Das macht dein Zorn, dass wir so vergehen, und dein Grimm, dass wir so plötzlich dahin müssen.
> 8. Denn unsere Missetat stellest du vor dich, unsere unerkannte Sünde ins Licht vor deinem Angesichte.
> 9. Darum fahren alle unsere Tage dahin durch deinen Zorn; wir bringen unsere Jahre so wie ein Geschwätz.

But Cramer, though he does use the word "Grimm," prefers to speak of God's "Eifer" and of God as an "Eifrer":

> Dein strenger Eifer schilt, und wir, o Gott, verderben:
> Wie könnte, wenn du schiltst, der Staub vor dir bestehn?
> Dein aufgebrachter Grimm gebietet uns zu sterben,
>   Du dräuest nur, und wir vergehn.

And Cramer prefers to speak of man's death not as quick or sudden, as Luther does, but as easy. "Du willst: Wir sind. Dein Hauch beseelet unsre Glieder; / Wie schnell erstarren sie, des Todes leichter Raub." And again: "Du strömst die Menschen weg; ihr Leben, Herr, vergehet / Schnell, wie ein leichter Schlaf." And while Luther contemptuously speaks of man's life as a "Geschwätz," Cramer has a nicer word for it:

> Geschwinder, als ein Bach, verfliessen unsre Tage,
> Wie ein Gedank so schnell, weil du ein Eifrer bist;
> Und unsre Jahre sind vor dir wie eine Sage,
>   Die man kaum anhört und vergisst.

"Lass für uns das Grab der Klugheit Schule seyn!" begs Cramer's speaker; "Lass deine Gegenwart uns endlich noch geniessen." It is thus left open whether we are to learn wisdom from the thought of the grave (*respice finem!*) or in the grave itself, in the afterlife, while we are enjoying God's eternal presence. As always, Luther is refreshingly tough and to the point: "Lehre uns bedenken, dass wir sterben müssen, auf dass wir klug werden."

So the poem that Bach set is quite another thing than the magnificent Psalm 90 of the Old Testament. Softer, gentler, with everything prettied up, it does not return at its end to the joyful praise of its beginning after traveling far, as the original Psalm 90 (apparently) does; rather, Cramer's poem seems never to have left off its genial praise of the Lord. So Bach had reason to set Cramer's poem as he did:

The first thing one notices is that virtually every phrase in this song moves downward. Beginning in thirds at a moderate rate of speed, the downward movement is soon taken up by the bass line as well, leading into the first cadence. Then the one significant upward-moving phrase in the piece, the curiously harmonized little pronouncement that bridges mm. 2 and 3, leads to quicker descending phrases, in sixteenth notes, and the second cadence. Finally there is a joyous little bout of imitation between melody and bass line (mm. 5 and 6), and the bass line, inverting in thirds the opening phrase of the piece, ushers in its repetition in the melodic line, which leads to the final cadence—and the little descending phrase that links strophes of the song.

This seems to me an entertaining little song, but certainly not one of Bach's memorable ones. Next comes a chorale—but one in a major key that sets Psalm 91: "He that dwelleth in the secret place of the most High shall abide under the shadow of the Almighty." Why, we wonder, would Bach have chosen the chorale idiom, so far usually reserved for psalms of total or comparative pessimism, for a psalm with such a cheering message?

One answer, it seems to me, might be that at least the last three verses of the 16 that make up this psalm seem to come from the mouth of God. In the King James Version, these verses read:

> 14. Because he hath set his love upon me, therefore will I deliver him: I will set him on high, because he hath known my name.
> 15. He shall call upon me, and I will answer him: I will be with him in trouble: I will deliver him, and honour him.
> 16. With long life will I satisfy him, and shew him my salvation.

Bach may have thought that words seemingly coming directly from God demanded the solemnity of the chorale idiom, that the comparative looseness of an ordinary song would have been unsuitable.

Moreover, this change of speakers is neither abrupt nor very clear. It seems to me that the preceding verse might also be spoken by God: "Thou shalt tread upon the lion and adder: the young lion and the dragon shalt thou trample under feet." In fact, for some verses previous to this the psalmist has, through his gradually mounting confidence in his faith, been speaking words that only an occasional pronominal reference to God as "he" prevents us from taking as God's own. These verses include the familiar reassurances about the terror by night and the arrow that flieth by day, the pestilence that walketh in darkness and the destruction that wasteth at noonday. In fact the whole psalm is delivered in a tone of authority that we are clearly meant to interpret as resulting from the direct contact with God that the speaker attains through his unquestioning faith. This is true even of the famous opening verse: "He that dwelleth in the secret place of the most High shall abide under the shadow of the Almighty." Therefore it makes sense that Bach should have chosen the rather solemn and elevated chorale idiom for his setting.

But what about Cramer's version, the words Bach was actually setting? Here are his first three stanzas:

> Wie selig ist, der Gott vertraut,
> Der in des Höchsten Zelte sitzet;
> Der, dem vor keinem Wetter graut,
> Von ihm umschattet und beschützet!
> Der freudig zu dem Höchsten spricht:
> Herr, meine Burg und Zuversicht;
> Mein Gott, auf den ich hoffe!
>
> Er weiss mich, wenn ein Sturm mir dräut,
> Dem Untergange zu entrücken;
> Der Herr bewahrt mich, und befreyt
> Mein Leben von des Jägers Stricken.
> Weil sich mein Herz auf ihn verlässt,
> Errettet Gott mich von der Pest
> Weitwürgendem Verderben.
>
> Dich wird der Schutz des Herrn umfahn;
> Dich werden seine Flügel decken.
> Vertrau' ihm nur; kein Unfall kann
> Dich unter seinen Fittig schrecken.
> Er kann nicht lügen; er erfüllt,
> Was er verheisst; dein Helm und Schild
> Ist deines Gottes Treue.

These stanzas answer to the first four verses of the psalm, which stand thus in Luther's translation:

> 1. Wer unter dem Schirm des Höchsten sitzt und unter dem Schatten des Allmächtigen bleibt,
> 2. der spricht zu dem Herrn: Meine Zuversicht und meine Burg, mein Gott, auf den ich hoffe!
> 3. Denn er errettet mich vom Strick des Jägers und von der schädlichen Pestilenz.
> 4. Er wird dich mit seinen Fittichen decken, und deine Zuversicht wird dein unter seinen Flügeln. Seine Wahrheit ist Schirm und Schild.

While Luther celebrates God's power, Cramer is more interested in celebrating its beneficiary. Luther dismisses him with a quick "Wer" to get right to God and his protective force: the two parallel phrases "dem Schirm des Höchsten" and "dem Schatten des Allmächtigen" are what command our attention in Luther's first verse. But Cramer keeps us firmly focused on the faithful believer, and on the favored position that his faith gains for him—"Der in des Höchsten Zelte sitzet" sounds almost like a description of a courtier close to the throne. "Zelte," rather than "Schirm," seems the point.

Moreover, the whole relation between God and the believer is described in the language of ordinary human emotional relations. The believer is happy or blessed, he trusts God, he is (once again) happy as he addresses God directly, his protection from harm consists in God's "Treue," his faithfulness or loyalty—a virtue human beings too are capable of possessing. Luther, on the other hand, tells us nothing whatever about the believer's feelings or state of mind, for they are of no interest to him (or, it would seem, to the Hebrew poet). The only salient fact about the believer is that he is under God's protection, and that he achieved that position not by virtue of God's fidelity or trust or good feeling toward him but rather through God's truth. Whereas "Treue," like the happiness experienced by the believer, is a mere state of mind or feeling, truth or "Wahrheit" is objective fact: "deines Gottes Wahrheit" refers to the objective fact that the God of the Jews is the real and true creator and ruler of the universe, a fact that also makes the believer's faith in him objectively true. Neither the believer's faith nor God's reciprocal trust and protection is a matter of mere human "Treue."

Here as so often in Cramer's versions, there are many verbal reminiscences of Luther, but everything is personalized, emotionalized. In Luther's translation, and (it would seem) in the Hebrew original, the only time the addressee of the poem is heard from is in the psalm's second and third verses—and we note that Cramer expands this brief utterance to cover nine lines, the last two of the first stanza and all of the second. Moreover, later in his poem Cramer inserts a little three-line speech, for the believer's "fromme Seele," into his sixth stanza, which corresponds to the ninth and tenth verses of the psalm. Here is Luther's translation of those verses:

> 9. Denn der Herr ist deine Zuversicht, der Höchste ist deine Zuflucht.
> 10. Es wird dir kein Übels begegnen, und keine Plage wird zu deiner Hütte sich nahen.

Here is Cramer's sixth stanza:

> Denn deine fromme Seele spricht:
> Mich wird der Arm des Herrn bewahren;
> Der Höchst' ist meine Zuversicht,
> Und meine Zuflucht in Gefahren.
> Kein Unfall überwältigt dich,
> Und keine Plage nahet sich
> Zu deiner sichern Hütte.

Once again our focus is not, as in Luther, on the plain objective fact that God will keep evil and the plague far from the believer, but rather on the latter's state of mind, his assured self-satisfaction as heard directly in the voice of his "fromme Seele." Finally, the last words spoken by Luther's God embody his promise to continue his protection of the believer: "Ich will ihn sättigen mit langem Leben und ihm zeigen mein Heil." Those of Cramer's God, on the other hand, return the focus to the acts and feelings of the believer: "Dann betet er mich dankbar an, / Und preiset meine Hülfe."

Bach's little chorale setting preserves the dignity and austerity of the chorale idiom while sensitively adding a warmth and intimacy appropriate to Cramer's distinctly humanized and personalized reading of the psalm:

The austerity is felt not only in the steady half-note march of the rhythm but also in the occasional minor chords—each one of which gives way, usually somewhat unexpectedly, to a warm and reassuring major chord or a turn into the major. The E-minor chord in m. 2, given an added pathos by the appoggiatura in the melody, soon moves to an E-major seventh chord that leads us into the dominant as the melody, which had been heading downward, makes a sudden upward jump of a fourth—a gesture, one feels, of hope and reassurance, enacting the meaning of the words "der Gott vertraut." The second phrase too begins on an E-minor chord, but again we immediately turn back toward the major as the harmony takes us, unexpectedly, into the subdominant. We expect to cadence there, but the phrase gets extended by a bar as the melodic line keeps rising and we turn back toward the tonic. The effect is formal and ceremonial yet also warm and (once again) reassuring.

The song's second section begins on an A-minor chord and, after all this warmth and mellowness, we feel we must be heading toward a contrasting episode in the minor. But no—the A-minor chord instantly gives way to its relative major and we now get the cadence on the subdominant that we had expected earlier. Both of the two final phrases also begin with a turn into the minor. But in each case the harmony immediately begins heading, through a series of major chords, toward a cadence on the tonic. The string of descending quarter notes in mm. 14–15, the longest break in the march of half notes, conveys a special intimacy. Hearing this somber, lovely little piece inevitably calls to mind the word *Trost* (consolation, solace), so important in Lutheran theology.

This sequence of pieces is rounded out by Psalm 93, a brief, triumphantly exuberant celebration of God's kingship that in the King James Version begins with the words "The Lord reigneth, he is clothed with majesty." Luther's translation is short enough to be cited entire:

> 1. Der Herr ist König und herrlich geschmückt; der Herr ist geschmückt und hat ein Reich angefangen, so weit die Welt ist, und zugerichtet, dass es bleiben soll.
> 2. Von dem an stehet dein Stuhl fest; du bist ewig.
> 3. Herr, die Wasserströme erheben sich, die Wasserströme erheben ihr Brausen, die Wasserströme heben empor die Wellen.
> 4. Die Wasserwogen im Meer sind gross und brausen greulich; der Herr aber ist noch grösser in der Höhe.
> 5. Dein Wort ist eine rechte Lehre. Heiligkeit ist die Zierde deines Hauses ewiglich.

The psalmist moves easily back and forth between speaking of God in the third person and addressing him directly, so that the poem seems at once addressed to God himself and to the world at large—as though there were no difference between them, God and the world being equated. The only act that God is said to commit is the act of creation ("angefangen, . . . zugerichtet"); the only other verb used in connection with him is the verb *to be*. God, that is, is not characterized at all except as the performer of the supreme act of creation. Otherwise, the poem implies, he transcends human characterization: he simply is. As he says to Moses, "I am that I am" (Exodus, 3:14). The poem has about it an air of hypnotically incantatory repetition—"erheben . . . erheben . . . heben"—that seems perfectly appropriate to its mysterious subject.

In Cramer's version everything gets fleshed out and, if not explained, at least elaborated upon in a way that destroys the power and the mystery that Luther captures so well. Here is the first of Cramer's four stanzas:

> Jehova herrscht, ein König über alle,
> Geschmückt mit Majestät und Pracht.
> Damit sein Name die Welten durchschalle,
> Bewaffnet sich der Herr mit Macht.
> Der Herrscher, umgürtet mit Hoheit und Stärke,
> Hat grosse herrliche Wunder gethan.
> Er baute die Welten, gewaltige Werke,
> Davon nicht eins erschüttert werden kann.

To fill out the verse, the synonymous pairs accumulate: "Majestät und Pracht," "Hoheit und Stärke," "herrliche Wunder" and "gewaltige Werke." This God is not simply that he is: he is armed and girded round, the image of a warrior. His name and fame resound through the worlds he has built. It is all too much: more is less. And, later in the poem, God is not simply greater or more powerful than the stormy waters: the voice of the waters is "fürchterlich," yet he is twice said to be "Gefürchteter." Something is lost in the move from Luther's simple statement of God's absolute power to the positing, in the minds of his subjects, of fear or awe at his power. This is, for Cramer, a very mild example of the personalizing we have seen throughout his poems, but it is an example nonetheless.

Bach's setting is quite unexpected and, in its way, brilliant:

This is not just exuberant: it is downright wild. The first thing we notice is that the vocal line is completely independent of the keyboard part (and vice versa). The song is divided into four sections, AABB, each of which begins, in the vocal line, with an insistent, aggressive three- or four-note phrase. The keyboard part, in the meantime, is made up solely of cascading triplet arpeggios, with the two hands sometimes moving in the same direction and sometimes in opposite directions. These arpeggios, it seems clear, are both fanfares celebrating God's power and also representations of the mighty, undulating waves to which his power is compared. The melody, taken by itself, is utterly unremarkable—except perhaps for the unexpected landing on E-flat in the third phrase of the B section (mm. 13 and 17). The keyboard's only departures from its arpeggios come at the beginning of mm. 3 and 8, when it plays quarter-note chords (with the F's in the bass clashing with the E's in the right hand) that echo the vocal line's insistence. There is really little else to be said about this splendidly abandoned little tour de force—except perhaps to note how unusual it is for Bach to write a piece this straight-ahead and free of moment-to-moment inflection.

IV

At the conclusion of the preceding chapter we noted that in the songs written during the years separating the Gellert collection of 1758 from the present Cramer collection, Bach had done a good deal of formal experimentation. Having found his basic voice, as we may call it, as a composer of strophic songs in the Gellert songs, he extended his range by experimenting with cantatas, chorales, chorale-like settings, and through-composed songs. In the Cramer collection he extended his range still further. Not only did he employ all the forms with which he had experimented in the post-Gellert years; he also selected psalms and grouped settings so as to give the collection a special sort of organization—which we have been tracing in this chapter. But where did he get the idea for doing this?

In the third and final volume of his definitive *A History of the Oratorio*,[29] Howard E. Smither draws a distinction between the dramatic oratorio and the lyric oratorio: "In German-speaking lands from the mid-eighteenth century to at least the early nineteenth two concepts of oratorio existed side by side: the traditional Baroque, Italianate, dramatic oratorio paralleled the development of the new, lyric, *empfindsam* oratorio" (p. 331). Even as the older, dramatic oratorio was historically linked to the opera, so this new, lyric oratorio developed out of the church cantata, and was considered suitable for performance at divine service. "In accord with this view," notes Smither,

> the term *Oratorium* began to designate works with texts emphasizing the religious feelings aroused by familiar Biblical stories, primarily those relating to the major

feasts of the church year and thus to Jesus as the Messiah: mainly Christmas, the Passion, Easter, and Ascension. Rather than presenting the external events of the story in a connected, dramatic or narrative-dramatic text, as the traditional Baroque librettist had done, the poet assumed the listener's knowledge of the story and wrote a contemplative, lyric drama with personages who are usually unnamed and "idealized," and who express their sentiments about the story's events.

[P. 336]

C.P.E. Bach wrote three major oratorios: *Die Israeliten in der Wüste*, composed in 1769, soon after Bach's arrival in Hamburg, and published in 1775; *Passions-Cantate* (also known as *Die letzten Leiden des Erlösers*), also composed in 1769 and published, in an incomplete vocal score, in 1789; and *Carl Wilhelm Rammlers Auferstehung und Himmelfahrt Jesu*, composed in 1774–1780 and published in 1787. Of these, the first is a conventional dramatic oratorio while the other two are lyric oratorios. His preparation of the volume of Cramer settings, in 1773 and 1774, thus fell between his two lyric oratorios, just as or shortly before he began work on the *Auferstehung und Himmelfahrt Jesu*.

Die Israeliten in der Wüste begins with a halting, broken chorus of lamentation, punctuated by outcries to God, asking why he has forsaken his people. In a recitative and aria, an Israelite woman first decides that God is actually enjoying their suffering, but then vacillates between thinking this cannot possibly be true and mourning those who have already died. Aaron steps forward to reassure her, in a wheedling, not altogether convincing aria, that God will indeed take care of his people. But a second Israelite woman asks why they ever left Egypt, and then, in a graceful and florid aria, first evokes the pleasures of Egypt but then, in the aria's second section, angrily laments their loss. Again Aaron steps forward to give reassurance, but this time he is interrupted by a brief, majestic little overture that introduces Moses, who protests the people's lack of faith. There is an exchange of accusations. And so it goes, event by event, until the water pours from the rock (Exodus 17:6), ending the first part of the oratorio.

The openings of the *Passions-Cantate* and the *Auferstehung und Himmelfahrt Jesu* could scarcely be more different. In both cases the major event, the Crucifixion, has already happened and is known to all the characters. So the question is not what has happened but what it means and how to feel about it. The action therefore takes place in the emotional or psychological space of the various characters rather than in the external world in which they dwell.

Take the *Auferstehung* as an example, since it is the richer and more complex work. It opens with a very brief introduction, somber and enigmatic, for lower strings in octaves. This is followed by a chorus, stately and grieving yet emphatically insistent that God will surely not allow Christ's soul to remain in hell or otherwise to suffer corruption. It seems clear, then, not only that the Crucifixion has already occurred but also that Christ's tomb has already been found to be empty. The next number is a bass recitative, accompanied by timpani and by strings playing an insistent dotted rhythm. He describes how the mountains of Judea tremble as Christ stands on the rock and declares that he still lives, Michael rolls the stone away from the mouth of the tomb, and the Roman guards flee in terror. The same dotted rhythm carries over into the bass aria that follows, in which the singer tells us that his spirit also trembles, that he is caught between fear and joy as he laments Christ's sufferings even as he beholds him liberated, in glory. We are then taken by surprise by a straightforward choral celebration of triumph: suddenly, out of all this ambivalence, has come clarity. The point of view shifts once again as the tenor tells of the women who visit the tomb and start back in dread, only to be reassured by an angel. The aria that follows is not, as we should expect, by the tenor but rather by a soprano—apparently one of the women mentioned in the recitative preceding. Though she lamented, she now sheds tears of joy. Then the bass, in a recitative, tells of Mary Magdalene's visit to the tomb, where Christ appears to her and tells her to send Peter to him. This is followed not by an aria, by either the bass or (as we might now expect) a soprano, but rather by a duet for soprano and tenor, a quiet, rather mournful prayer of thanksgiving for God's compassion and forgiveness. Next comes a tenor recitative that tells of still more women visiting the tomb and of Christ's appearing to them and saying he will see them in heaven. This time the following aria is by the tenor but it has only an indirect connection with the preceding recitative: it is a joyous, spirited declaration, complete with trumpets, of the singer's intention to follow Christ. The first part of the oratorio concludes with a chorus celebrating Christ's victory over death.

It is impossible to make clear here, without much fuller reference to both text and music, how frequent and subtle are the changes in perspective required of the listener. Speaking of the difference between dramatic and lyric oratorio, Smither writes: "The absence of personages' names in the libretto involves the reader-listener in an active role. Rather than being an observer of a drama, he more readily identifies with the poet or the unnamed personage who experiences the feelings expressed in the text" (p. 336). I agree perfectly that the listener to lyric oratorio, or at least to Bach's lyric oratorios, does indeed become active. But I think that his activity consists not so much in "identifying" with the unnamed characters as in trying to make sense of the often rather bewildering juxtapositions of music, language, and point of view that confront him. It is, I should say, something like the activity engaged in by the first readers of Eliot's *The Waste Land*.

It is also like the activity we have been engaged in while tracing the relations among psalm settings that make up the various sequences of which Bach's Cramer collection is composed. Just as in the *Passions-Cantate* and the *Auferstehung*, so with the Cramer collection: we have repeatedly seen the same theological topic addressed from different points of view and in different musical idioms in each sequence of settings, culminating in a usually quite experimental final setting. We have no way of knowing whether Bach set out consciously to employ something like the methods of lyric oratorio in selecting the Cramer poems he set and in then arranging them in his collection. But it seems to me that the methods are strikingly similar. Instead of moving from recitative to aria or duet to chorus, as in the oratorios, he moved in the Cramer collection from one to another of the various song or song-like forms he had recently been experimenting with, and so carried the experiment a step further by seeing how they might work in juxtaposition one to another. The effect, as in the oratorios, is to explore, more fully than would be possible in a single short piece, the possible points of view from which an issue or event might be regarded.

C.P.E. Bach's *Herrn Doctor Cramers übersetzte Psalmen mit Melodien* is, then, a very special, probably unique, sort of artistic product—which we suspected all along. The only question remaining is how Bach imagined it, or parts of it, being performed. Certainly the separate songs could be sung in the home, just like his other songs. But the chorales probably would have seemed a bit odd, taken out of context, this late in the 18th century. And the fact that Bach retained Cramer's specifications for two choruses and a character called "Der Prophet" in Psalm 8 strongly hints that he might have envisioned these settings—not all of them on any one occasion, of course—being performed, as lyric oratorios frequently were, at divine service. We shall probably never know the answer. One way or another, the Cramer psalms are a fascinating collection that show us, once again, Bach's restlessly experimental nature at work.

Chapter Twelve

Folksongs for Voss

After the publication, in 1774, of his settings of the Cramer psalms, C.P.E. Bach allowed six years to elapse before he produced another collection of songs. In fact, he wrote only 20-odd songs from 1774 to early 1780, when he turned his attention to the poems of his friend Christoph Christian Sturm, pastor of St. Peter's, one of the five Hamburg churches whose music it was Bach's job to supervise. The two collections of Sturm settings, each comprising 30 songs, were published in 1780 and 1781.

During those six years, Bach of course composed a good deal. The most important works of this period are the four "Hamburg Symphonies" (Wq. 183; H. 663-666) and two major choral works, the oratorio *Auferstehung und Himmelfahrt Jesu*, to a text by Ramler, and the brief but stunning *Heilig*. Other instrumental works include two keyboard concertos, almost 40 solo keyboard pieces, 13 sonatas for chamber groups involving keyboard, and six violin sonatas. Though some of these wound up in the six *Kenner und Liebhaber* collections of solo keyboard works and in the three collections of chamber works published by Breitkopf and by Bremner in the mid-1770s, the majority are still in manuscript. Much of Bach's time, however, went to the preparation of the many passions, cantatas, and other occasional church choral pieces demanded by the everyday requirements of his job.

Of the songs that he did write during this time, almost all were either reserved for the posthumously published 1789 *Neue Lieder-Melodien* or were written more or less to order for Johann Heinrich Voss's *Musen-Almanach* volumes. Voss, as editor first of the *Göttinger Musen-Almanach* started by Heinrich Christian Boie and then of his own Hamburg *Musen-Almanach*, was an important tastemaker whose voluminous correspondence has survived in surprising bulk. It will be useful to examine briefly his life and his relations with Bach.

I

Voss was born in the Mecklinburg-Schwerin village of Sommersdorf on February 20, 1751, the son of an innkeeper. His grandfather had been a wheelwright, but his father had higher cultural aspirations. He got himself educated, after a fashion, and entered the service of a Lübeck canon who also served as ambassador in Berlin. He enjoyed writing poetry and often said that he wished his oldest son, Johann Heinrich, to become a poet like Brockes, whom he very much admired. After his marriage, the Easter after Johann Heinrich was born, the elder Voss settled in Penzlin, a small village of scarcely 2,000. He knew something of the law, and in addition to his innkeeping he functioned as a notary. Four other children were born, but only one of them, a daughter, survived into adulthood, and she died at 24, For a while the family did fairly well, but the Seven Years' War impoverished them, and the younger Voss's childhood was hand-to-mouth.

School was his haven. He had an extraordinary memory, and was in fact a sort of prodigy. Brave and aggressive though not physically strong, he was also stubborn, exceedingly ambitious, materialistic, and skeptical to a degree that rendered him immune to religious feeling. He also had a compulsive desire to read that his 19th-century biographer, Wilhelm Herbst, describes as "almost pathological."[1] Since Greek was not taught at his school, he taught it to himself, and also made an attempt at Hebrew—though he found its guttural sounds unbecoming to the supposed language of Paradise. At 15, in the fall of 1766, he moved on to the City School in Neubrandenburg. Here he remained for three years, studying hard, taking music lessons, and developing a love for poetry in spite of the school's exceedingly dry and pedantic teaching methods. Not only Virgil and Horace but also Hagedorn, Haller, and Uz became his familiars, and it was here that he discovered Klopstock, who was always to remain his favorite and who would soon become his lifelong friend.

In September 1769, his schooling at Neubrandenburg at an end, Voss went home to Penzlin, where he spent six months with his parents. He then took a job as tutor to the three children of a rich man who lived at Ankershagen, to the southwest of Penzlin. The lady of the house was, he wrote home, a "fury," and Voss's inbred (and now highly developed) love of freedom and resistance to authority soon brought them into conflict with each other. He also contracted a serious, even life-threatening illness that Herbst refers to as "bilious fever" and that caused him to spit blood and led to the beginnings of jaundice. He went home and told his father he had to leave his position. This experience, Herbst insists, laid the groundwork for Voss's lifelong hatred of the nobility: "Voss's incentives were not theories and doctrines, the airy dreams of poets or the fantastic utopias of Rousseau, not even revolutionary impulses to overthrow the throne and nobility, but rather the real, wounding experiences of his own life" (I, 48). When the French Revolution arrived, Voss greeted it with enthusiasm, but with the rational enthusiasm of an Enlightenment Man pleased to see abstract justice done at last, not with the ardor so familiar to us from the Romantics—"Bliss was it in that dawn to be alive." All his life Voss would be firmly against the Romantic movement, which for him was connected with a sentimental nostalgia for feudalism and the Middle Ages rather than with revolution and social justice.

In time he returned to his post at Ankershagen, where he stuck it out for two more years. He was forced to play the piano for visitors, and, as house poet, to compose odes for special occasions. Yet he managed, in his exile, to read Hesiod and Homer, and in time he met the man to whom he would write, many years later: "You were my first friend."

An hour's distance from Ankershagen lay the village of Gross-Vielen. Voss became acquainted with the local pastor there, whose name was Fabricius. When Fabricius died, in 1771, he was succeeded by a man only five years Voss's senior, Ernst Theodor Johann Brückner. The two immediately hit it off. Brückner had studied theology at the University of Halle, and was a very modern sort of pastor, interested in philosophy and anthropology, who had determined that his goal would be "to study the human heart." In later years he would suffer for his heterodoxy. It was Brückner who introduced Voss to Shakespeare, and together they also read Klopstock, Ramler, Gessner, and (in translation) Milton and Young. Brückner too wrote poetry, and he encouraged Voss to keep doing so. The friendship lasted until Brückner's death in 1805.

At Easter 1771 a man named Kessler offered to pay for Voss's education at the Hochschule at Halle, and Voss quit his position at Ankershagen—cheated, as he later wryly remarked, out of some of his wages by his wealthy employer. But somehow or other the Kessler deal fell through, and poor Voss was caught, having burned his bridges and with no solid prospects. It was at just this time that Boie's *Göttinger Musen-Almanach* fell into his hands. In July he sent three poems to one of the *Almanach*'s editors, Boie judged that they showed the required signs of "Genie," and he accepted them for the 1772 edition. Voss's career was launched.

Boie arranged for Voss to attend the Hochschule at Göttingen, one of the best in all Germany, and he took up the study of theology and philology in May 1772. The former was speedily dropped—"God did not intend me to become a pastor," he wrote to Brückner—and he decided to concentrate on philology, also reading history and philosophy. His principal teacher was the famous classical scholar Christian Gottlob Heyne (1729-1812), who was also a close and perceptive reader of poetry. Though Voss's willfulness sometimes led to conflict between them, Heyne played an important role in shaping Voss's taste. It was in Heyne's seminars that Voss met the young poet Ludwig Christoph Heinrich Hölty (1748-1776), who was also to be a close friend for the few remaining years of his brief life.

It was mainly as a classical philologist and a translator of classical poetry that Voss was to make his mark in the last 40 years of his life—with which we have no concern here. He ended his career as a professor at Heidelberg, a post he assumed in 1805, and at his death in 1826 he was probably best known for his 1780 translation of the *Odyssey* into German hexameters. He also produced translations of Virgil, Horace, Hesiod, Aristophanes, and (with the help of his sons) Shakespeare. But he was a special sort of classicist—and that is of concern to us here. For he was, from the beginning of his studies, interested in somehow combining the ancient with the immediately contemporary. Klopstock he saw as Pindar *redivivus*, and among his quasi-Theocritan Idylls are some in *plattdeutsch*, the dialect of his native Mecklinburg-Schwerin. The classical world was to him not at all remote, but was felt as the immediate (and still present) source of the rationalism, democratic convictions, and high ethical standards that he espoused all his life.

During the portion of his life with which we are concerned, however, Voss was perhaps known primarily as an original poet. For it was soon after his settling in Göttingen that the so-called Göttinger Hainbund, which figures in every history of German lyric poetry, was formed, with Voss as one of the charter members. On the evening of September 12, 1772, a group that included Voss, Hölty, and Johann Martin Miller met in a woodland setting and solemnly declared themselves dedicated to furthering the cause of lyric poetry in Germany. Their patron saint was Klopstock, and it was from Klopstock's ode of five years earlier, "Der Hügel, und der Hain," as well as from the physical surroundings of their meeting, that they took their name. At first, however, they spoke of their group as either the "Bund" or—a grove necessarily consisting of a number of trees growing close to one another—the "Hain." The term "Hainbund," more frequently seen today, was evidently a later coinage.[2]

Voss has left the following charming description of their meeting:

> The evening was serene, and the moon full. We completely surrendered to the beauties of nature. We ate supper in a peasant's hut and then walked in the fields. Soon we came upon a small stand of oaks, and it immediately occurred to us all to swear an oath of friendship beneath these sacred trees.[3]

It was decided that the group would meet weekly, and that minutes of the meetings—which, fortunately, have survived—would be kept. Soon the members present at that first meeting were joined by others: Boie, J. F. Hahn, Christian and Friedrich Leopold von Stolberg, J. A. Leisewitz, and Carl Friedrich Cramer, son of Johann Andreas Cramer. Moreover, there were other poets who never became official members of the "Bund" but remained close to its members and its operations. Besides Klopstock, the principal ones were Matthias Claudius and Gottfried August Bürger.

Voss's connections with the Göttingen Hochschule, with the "Bund," and with Boie's *Musen-Almanach*, all formed so quickly, completely altered his life. Herbst's judgment does not seem an exaggeration: "Transported, as by a stroke of magic, out of the almost friendless surroundings of his home and into the most engrossing intellectual society, he was forced to live as though in a new world" (I, 83). It was the last of these three connections, that with the *Musen-Almanach*, that proved most important to Voss's career.

Boie had originally started the *Musen-Almanach* in 1769, shortly after matriculating at the Göttingen Hochschule. He got the idea from the *Almanach des Muses*, which had been published yearly in Paris since 1765. With a fellow-student, Friedrich Wilhelm Gotter, as his assistant and Johann Christian Dieterich, a local bookseller, as publisher, Boie brought out his first *Almanach*, the 1770 edition, in January of that year. (Later, when the *Musen-Almanach* became a going concern, each installment would appear the fall preceding the year whose number it bore.) By the second installment, that of 1771, the *Musen-Almanach* was attracting widespread critical attention, and gave signs of becoming what Boie wanted it to be: a sort of clearinghouse for new work that would give, each year, an overview of the German poetic landscape. Almost immediately the work of Klopstock began to appear alongside that of older-fashioned (though not much older) poets such as Ramler and Gleim. And by the 1774 *Almanach* the work of the "Bund" members was prominently displayed. Also, the work of Herder and Claudius struck a "Volkston" note that would be heard more loudly as the years passed. The motto of both the *Musen-Almanach* and the "Bund," frequently expressed both in private letters and in public prose and poetic pronouncements, ran: "For God, Virtue, and Fatherland"—with "Freedom" sometimes thrown in for good measure. The enemy, denounced with increasing frequency, was Christoph Martin Wieland, friend of Goethe, Herder, and (later) Schiller, and editor of the rival *Der Teutsche Merkur*, whose love of all things French had earned him the sobriquet "the German Voltaire" as well as the hatred of the ultra-nationalistic "Bund" members.

In the summer of 1774 Boie left Göttingen to accompany a rich young Englishman named Vaughan, whose private tutor he had been, on a journey to Spaa, where Vaughan's parents were vacationing. It was time to assemble the 1775 *Musen-Almanach*, and since it would have been cumbersome to do it from such a distance, Boie turned the editorial duties over to Voss, who was now in love with Boie's sister Ernestine, whom he would marry three years later. Voss made it clear at once that he wanted not only good poems but strongly moral ones. Indeed, the last stanza of a Goethe lyric, "An Christiane N." (later known as "Christel"), so offended him that he rejected it—it was published in Wieland's *Teutsche Merkur* in 1776. Thus the 1775 *Musen-Almanach* was still more uniform in tone than its predecessors because of the now overwhelming predominance of "Bund" members. The increasingly brutal treatment of Wieland and his ideas so offended Boie, who was friendly with Wieland, that he vowed to sever his connection with the *Almanach*, which he did in October, upon his return to Göttingen.

Meanwhile Voss, always a difficult man to get on with, was having troubles with his publisher Dieterich, and he began looking for another place to bring out the *Musen-Almanach*. In Boie's absence, the influence of Klopstock upon the *Almanach*'s specific content and general ideological slant had grown still more powerful, and since Hamburg was Klopstock's home base, Hamburg was the city to which Voss decided to move the *Almanach*. Hamburg was also, of course, the city of C.P.E. Bach, and on his first visit to the city, which took place in the spring of 1774 and lasted three months, Voss visited both men. The letters he wrote to Brückner, Miller, and Ernestine excitedly describe these visits, and give a vivid picture of Hamburg as a cultural center. They also enable us to learn a good deal about the circumstances under which some of the songs Bach wrote during this period came into existence and how they were judged by his contemporaries.[4]

II

Writing to Miller "und den Bund" on March 30, just shortly after his arrival in Hamburg, Voss tells of a discussion with Klopstock "about the rhythm and the music of prosody," and adds that Klopstock is completely happy with two settings of his poems by Gluck, just published in the 1774 *Musen-Almanach*. Voss then notes: "The others, e.g. *das deutsche Mädchen*, pleased him not completely, but more than Bach's composition" (Suchalla, p. 374). That is, the other Gluck settings of Klopstock poems—for example, that of "Vaterlandslied" (which begins with the words "Ich bin ein deutsches

Mädchen")—have not fully pleased Klopstock, but Gluck's "Vaterlandslied" setting has pleased him more than the setting of the same poem composed by Bach, also in the 1774 *Musen-Almanach*. The Paris *Almanach des Muses* had paid little attention to music, but Boie had from the beginning wanted music to play a significant role in his *Musen-Almanach*. The 1774 edition, with songs by both Bach and Gluck, the two most famous German composers of their time, marked a musical as well as a literary high point. In a letter that he wrote to Brückner on October 17, 1773, just about the time the 1774 *Musen-Almanach* was coming out, Voss expressed his enthusiasm for its high musical quality:

> The Ritter Gluck in Vienna has set some of Klopstock's Odes splendidly. Two appear in the *Almanach*. Klopstock has sent us the others. At last we are getting some lyrical composers.[5]

In a letter that Bach wrote to Voss on August 5, 1774, after Voss's departure from Hamburg, he encloses two songs. Suchalla's note on this letter in *Briefe und Dokumente* (p. 429) says that these songs are probably Bach's settings of Klopstock's "Vaterlandslied" and of J. M. Miller's "Der Bauer." But this has to be wrong. For both of these songs appeared in the 1774 *Musen-Almanach*. What Bach is sending to Voss, as Busch's account (pp. 124–125) implies, is his settings of Klopstock's "Lyda" and Voss's own "Die Schlummernde," both of which will appear in the 1775 *Almanach*, which was being prepared at this time.

"Vaterlandslied" is usually dismissed as one of Klopstock's simple, nationalistic poems, hearty and inspiring but short on complexity:

> Ich bin ein deutsches Mädchen!
> Mein Aug' ist blau, und sanft mein Blick,
> Ich hab' ein Herz,
> Das edel ist, und stolz, und gut.
>
> Ich bin ein deutsches Mädchen!
> Zorn blickt mein blaues Aug' auf den,
> Es hasst mein Herz
> Den, der sein Vaterland verkennt!
>
> Ich bin ein deutsches Mädchen!
> Erköre mir kein ander Land
> Zum Vaterland,
> Wär' mir auch frey die grosse Wahl!
>
> Ich bin ein deutsches Mädchen!
> Mein hohes Auge blickt auch Spott,
> Blickt Spott auf den,
> Der Säumens macht bey dieser Wahl!
>
> Du bist kein deutscher Jüngling!
> Bist dieses lauen Säumens werth,
> Des Vaterlands
> Nicht werth, wenn du's nicht liebst, wie ich!
>
> Du bist kein deutscher Jüngling!
> Mein ganzes Herz verachtet dich,
> Der's Vaterland
> Verkennt, dich Fremdling! und dich Thor!

> Ich bin ein deutsches Mädchen!
> Mein gutes, edles, stolzes Herz
> Schlägt laut empor
> Beym süssen Namen: Vaterland!
>
> So schlägt mir's einst beym Namen
> Des Jünglings nur, der stolz wie ich
> Auf's Vaterland,
> Gut, edel ist, ein Deutscher ist!

According to Karl Kindt, this is the only Klopstock poem of which the poet also wrote a *plattdeutsch* version, in 1775, five years after the original version. This fact, however, does not justify Kindt's offhand description of the poem as "the . . . very simple 'Vaterlandslied.'"[6]

Quite the contrary, in fact. That Klopstock went to the trouble of composing an alternate dialect version of "Vaterlandslied" implies that it meant something special to him—as, indeed, does the fact that the poem originally bore the dedication: "For Johanna Elisabeth von Winthem to sing." She was the niece of Klopstock's first wife, Meta, and would in 1791 become his second wife. Moreover, at this particular moment in German literary and musical history, when there was widespread interest in the great monuments of Middle High German poetry and the "Volkslied" craze was taking hold, to write a poem in dialect or "im Volkston" was not a way of implying that it was merely simple or homespun but rather a way of insisting that sorts of complexity worth a sophisticated reader's attention might be concealed beneath an apparently simple surface. We recall the example of Voss's *plattdeutsch* allusions to Theocritus. What we have here, of course, is yet another version of pastoral—though quite a different one from the ones we met in our examination of some of C.P.E. Bach's early songs.

Where is the complexity in Klopstock's "Vaterlandslied"? Certainly the first stanza—all that is usually cited in references to the poem—does seem simple enough: the sort of idealized German maiden that might, today, smile out at us from a tourism poster, delivers an inventory of her qualifications. The blue eyes, the pure and noble heart—she has it all. If there is anything that surprises us a bit, once we look a little more closely, it is the gentleness or mildness of her glance. This seems to go somewhat against the firmly declarative tone of the first stanza—and as our eye quickly travels down the page, we note that every stanza except the last one begins with a similar declaration, capped with an exclamation point. We should expect her glance to be direct, clear-eyed, unblinking rather than gentle.

And so it suddenly becomes in the second stanza—a surprise for which the faintly off-key "sanft" has, so to speak, set us up. Suddenly those mild eyes are ablaze with righteous anger and even with hatred. And the force of her emotion is driven home by the subtle way in which Klopstock uses his rather odd stanza form. He unexpectedly breaks off the relative clause begun at the end of the second line, allowing the speaker to correct herself by intensifying her account of the emotion inspired in her by anyone who is less patriotic than herself. The increase in intensity, as we have noted, is from mere anger to hatred. But it is further emphasized by the switch from a noun ("Zorn") to a verb ("hasst"), by the heavy accent on "hasst," by the concentration of the short third line, and by the way in which the second "Den"—in contrast to the first, which comes at the end of a line—strikes like a hammer blow at the beginning of the stanza's final line.

She would not, she tells us in stanza three, choose another fatherland even if she were given the chance to do so. And in the fourth stanza that glance of hers—now elevated to "Mein hohes Auge"—unerringly seeks out and scorns anyone who would even hesitate in the face of such an opportunity.

Up to this point in the poem the maiden seems to be speaking to no one in particular, merely delivering a declaration of faith. Though the "den" in stanza two gathered force through repetition and change in placement, it did not become more definite in its reference but seemed still to point not to a particular person but simply to anyone lacking in patriotic feeling. At the beginning of stanza five, precisely at midpoint, this changes. Suddenly she is turning on someone who has, evidently, been there all along: "Du bist kein deutscher Jüngling!" The hesitation mentioned in the preceding stanza was not, as it seemed, merely hypothetical: the youth being addressed has actually been guilty of it, and the poem is her direct response to this fact. He is not worthy of the fatherland if he does not love it as she does. As her rage rises still further, in the next stanza, she tells him she despises him and denounces him as an alien and a fool.

Her attention then returns to herself: "Ich bin ein deutsches Mädchen!" she reasserts, adding that her noble heart beats loudly at the very mention of the fatherland's sweet name. And here the poem could well have ended. But of course it does not. Klopstock's final stanza makes all the difference.

Her heart, she tells us, picking up the thread of the preceding stanza, would (or might possibly) also beat just as loudly upon hearing the name of a youth who loved the fatherland as much as she loves it, who was (thereby) as good, as noble, as German as she is herself. But that paraphrase does damage to the tact and subtlety of Klopstock's line "So schlägt mir's einst beym Namen," for he does not use a modal auxiliary equivalent to English "would" or "might" but simply a third-person singular present: "schlägt." "Einst" can refer either to a single past occasion, whether definite or indefinite, or to an indefinite, even hypothetical future occasion. With a verb in the past it means "once," but with a present-tense verb it means "someday," "sometime," "at some point in the future." If Klopstock had written "schlug"—and had gone on to alter the stanza's other verbs accordingly—the final stanza would have completed the maiden's bitter denunciation of the youth: "Once my heart also beat loudly at the sound of your name—when you loved the fatherland as much as I do." But the present-tense "schlägt," together with the other present-tense verbs that follow, delicately leaves open the possibility that if he recants, if he reaffirms his patriotic feeling, then she will love him as before—and, what is more, love him as she loves the fatherland.

All of which, of course, wittily takes us back to that slightly puzzling "sanft" in the opening stanza. Everything we have been told of the maiden's eyes and her glance since then has made them out to be anything but gentle. Yet, as it turns out, that word was doing more than simply setting us up for the surprise of the second stanza. We can now look back and see that it carries a hint of the possibility of forgiveness left open in the poem's final stanza. With all her perfectly sincere patriotic feeling, it is, quite naturally, not only her country that she is capable of (and interested in) loving.

She thus turns out to be a rather more complex, three-dimensional person than we took her to be at first. But this does not imply that Klopstock intends to satirize her patriotism or wants us to believe that it is merely a cover for half-understood sexual feelings. Klopstock, after all, is not a 20th-century poet. He was, rather, a deeply nationalistic poet at a time of rising nationalistic feeling in Germany—this was a large part of his attraction for the younger Göttingen poets, as we have seen. Moreover, unlike most 20th-century poets of comparable stature, he was secure enough in his patriotism to be able to use it in poetically complicated ways.

Similarly, the fact that Bach wrote a rather witty setting of the poem should not make us look for doubt or corrosive irony in his frequent declarations of love for his country. After his first meeting with Bach during his visit to Hamburg in the spring of 1774, Voss wrote to his friend Brückner:

> I have visited him once, and had the good fortune to please him since I, as he sees, am a German patriot. He is proud to be a German since they have the only genuine, serious music.
>
> [Suchalla, P. 381]

Here is Bach's setting:

Like Klopstock's poem, and with somewhat more justice, this setting has usually been dismissed as simple. Certainly the unison of the opening bars suggests the simplicity of some of Bach's earlier settings of drinking songs and the like. But that simplicity sets off all the more sharply the surprising abruptness of the first phrase, which is only three bars long. The direction "Stolz" suggests a medium-fast tempo, perhaps leisurely enough to give a hint of pomposity, and so the opening bars of unison would sound measured, even stately—but then the sixteenth notes in m. 3 throw it all away. While the vocal line pauses for breath, the bass line presses on, carrying us into the next phrase, which begins with a sort of imitation of the opening—with the bass line this time moving actively rather than in sedate unison—but then suddenly softens in mm. 6-7. It is, we notice, just at this point that the poem's first stanza mentions the maiden's gentle glance. The bass line, however, remains active below, responding humorously to the brief moment of lyricism in the melody. In the final four bars the melody and bass line once again fall into step with each other and move inexorably to the cadence—indeed, the last phrase, though it contains a reminiscence (m. 9) of the preceding phrase, is little more than an elaborated cadence.

Bach has solved the strophic problem in this case by forcing us to hear, with each stanza of the poem, those two lyrical bars in the middle of his song. We are thus continually reminded of the gentleness of the maiden's glance, which wins out in the end by allowing her to extend to the youth a promise of forgiveness. But the abruptness of that first, three-bar phrase also repeatedly reminds us of the charming impetuosity that allows the maiden to entangle her feelings of patriotism with her affection for the youth. I cited Bach's setting of "Vaterlandslied" above as it originally appeared, in the 1774 edition of the *Göttinger Musen-Almanach*. But it is now accessible only in Otto Vrieslander's *Carl Philipp Emanuel Bach, "Lieder und Gesänge"* (Munich: Drei Masken Verlag, 1922). It is worth pointing out that Vrieslander prints the opening of Bach's setting thus:

It is extraordinary how much damage this regularization of the opening three-bar phrase into a four-bar phrase does to the song. The impetuous rush into the second phrase is lost, and m. 3 becomes a rhythmic dead spot that sets up a plodding pace from which the song, short as it as, can never recover. Bach's "Vaterlandslied" thus became, in Vrieslander's hands, the "very dryly declamatory composition" that Ernst Otto Lindner once claimed it to be.[7]

Gluck's setting of "Vaterlandslied," in contrast with Bach's, has continually been accessible ever since its composition. The seven settings that Gluck made of Klopstock's poems are his only songs to German texts. It is not known exactly when he began working on them, but three of them were published in the *Musen-Almanach* volumes of 1774, 1775, and 1785, and some appeared in song collections even before they were first all published together, at Vienna by Artaria, in late 1785 or early 1786. The most recent edition was published by Breitkopf und Härtel in 1917, and contains an excellent introduction by Gustav Beckmann. As we might expect, Gluck's "Vaterlandslied" is quite different from Bach's:

Gluck too is interested in capturing the maiden's impetuosity, but he does it by beginning not at the beginning of the bar but with a rhythmically somewhat complicated pickup phrase that thrusts us into the song before we have a chance to become oriented rhythmically. The dotted-quarter-and-eighth figure that dominates the pickup phrase soon becomes regularized into a series of sequences, its thrusting motion complemented by the steady rise in the melodic line as well as by the rising triplet figures in the accompaniment. (How orchestral this setting is, in contrast to Bach's!—it is easy to hear those triplet figures being tossed from strings to winds and back.) In the second four-bar phrase the rhythm gradually simplifies itself as we approach the cadence, but the music retains its aggressively martial air.

In the four bars that remain, the familiar rhythm is taken up by the keyboard accompaniment— but with the rising triplets reduced to grace notes. Moreover, the dynamic markings indicate that the two two-bar subphrases are to get louder and then softer, ending on a first-inversion B-minor chord. Though the tempo has not diminished, the "Feurig" quality demanded at the outset is qualified by a kind of pensiveness. It is as though the maiden had suddenly withdrawn into herself to think things over. Of course she returns at the beginning of each stanza, "Feurig" as ever, but the little four-bar postlude establishes sufficient dramatic tension to make her into a vividly conflicted (though miniature) theatrical personage.

Why did Klopstock prefer Gluck's setting to Bach's? Perhaps because Gluck directs our attention primarily to the maiden while Bach directs it to the affectionately, genially witty way in which he himself is handling her. It would be pleasant to know what Klopstock thought of Bach's other setting of one of his odes, "Lyda," which appeared in the next edition of the *Göttinger Musen-Almanach*, that of 1775. The poem was originally known as "Edone," but appeared, with only a couple of slight verbal changes, as "Lyda" in the *Hamburgische Neue Zeitung* in 1773,[8] and thus in the *Almanach*:

> Dein süsses Bild, o Lyda!
> Schwebt stets vor meinem Blick;
> Allein ihn trüben Zähren,
> Dass du es selbst nicht bist.
> Ich seh' es, wann der Abend
> Mir dämmert; wann der Mond
> Mir glänzt, seh' ich's; und weine,
> Dass du es selbst nicht bist.
>
> Bey jenes Thales Blumen,
> Die ich ihr lesen will,
> Bey jenen Myrtenzweigen,
> Die ich ihr flechten will,
> Beschwör' ich dich, Erscheinung,
> Auf, und verwandle dich!
> Verwandle dich, Erscheinung,
> Und werde Lyda selbst!

The "Edone" versions of the poem have "Edone" in line 1 in place of "o Lyda," and "werd' Edone" in line 16 in place of "werde Lyda." Both versions, in all the editions I have seen, read "wenn" rather than "wann" in lines 5 and 6, and are divided into four four-line stanzas rather than two eight-line ones, as in the *Almanach* printing.

Karl Kindt classes "Edone," along with "Vaterlandslied," as one of Klopstock's poems written "Im Volkston." But here too there is more than meets the eye at first glance. The concreteness of the word "Bild" in the opening line leads us to assume, momentarily, that this is one of those poems written to a missing loved one as the lover gazes yearningly at her picture. But "Schwebt," prominently placed at the beginning of the second line, suddenly changes all this. The phrase "schweben vor," used with the dative "mir" or (as here) some form of the pronoun "mein" and a noun such as "Auge" or "Blick," is the standard German idiom for having an image before one's mind's eye. But used literally, "schweben" means to hover or to float, with overtones of indistinctness, indecision, lack of clarity, and, often, possible danger or disaster. And suddenly, in the third line, Klopstock alerts us to these literal meanings by having the speaker tell us that tears are now troubling or disturbing or dimming his look or glance. Moreover, the use of the pronoun "ihn" to refer back to "Blick" effectively separates the speaker from his look, much as the curtain of tears now separates him from the indistinct image of his beloved. And of course the cause of the tears is the realization that the insubstantial image is not the beloved herself. Fittingly, this image comes to him at times when the light of sun or moon is indistinct or unclear, at twilight or on a moonlit night, thus carrying forward the implications of "Schwebt." In contrast to all this vagueness, he now says outright "ich . . . weine"—whereas earlier he had used the poetic word "Zähren" (rather than the ordinary word "Thränen") to refer to his tears—and numbly, despairingly repeats his earlier plaint: "Dass du es selbst nicht bist."

In the second stanza the distance between speaker and beloved is enforced by the fact that he now uses the third-person pronoun "ihr," rather than the second-person pronouns "du" and "dein," to refer to her. He is no longer gazing at her image, but is invoking the pastoral landscape in which, we now assume, their relation took place. By the valley's flowers, which he would gather for her, by the myrtle branches, which he would plait for her (presumably to hold the flowers in a pastoral queen's crown)— where is this sentence taking us? After the straightforwardness of the preceding stanza's last lines, this rhetorical elaboration is unexpectedly (and puzzlingly) formal. And then the answer comes: "Beschwör' ich, dich, Erscheinung, / Auf, und verwandle dich!" Like an enchanter, he is conjuring up his mental image of her—now, however, called not a mere picture but an "Erscheinung," a vision or apparition—and commanding it to transform itself. Into what? Into "Lyda selbst," of course. It is now the vision that is referred to as "dich," and the vague hints of magic and enchantment that traditionally cluster, in a pleasing and harmless way, around the edges of a pastoral landscape have taken on an eerie and disturbing power. He no longer addresses Lyda herself but rather his vision of her, which has, terrifyingly, become an end in itself. His self-absorption is confirmed by the ritualistic repetition of the magic words "verwandle dich!"

Here is Bach's setting of "Lyda":

This time I give the song as it appears in Vrieslander's collection because it seems to be closer to Bach's intentions than the *Almanach* printing.

In a famous letter that he wrote to Voss on September 9, 1774, just as the 1775 *Musen-Almanach* was being readied for the press, Bach requested a textual change in "Lyda":

That is, instead of

which is evidently how mm. 2-3 of the song had read in the manuscript that Bach had earlier sent to Voss, Bach now wanted to substitute

Voss, however, made the substitution only partially. Here is how those bars stand in the 1775 *Musen-Almanach*:

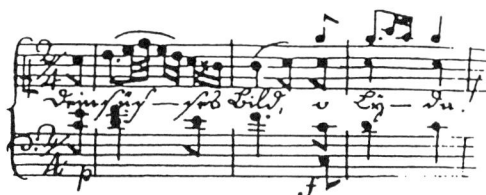

While Voss has corrected m. 3 as instructed, he has left the low C, together with its *"f"* dynamic marking, sticking out like a sore thumb at the end of m. 2. Vrieslander, on the other hand, has carried out Bach's instructions—though, as we shall see, there are problems about the dynamic markings in even the corrected version.[9]

The first graceful, lamenting little phrase bespeaks frustration, ending on the same note on which it began and thus moving, as it were, in a circle. As we have seen, Bach originally intended to follow this with an angry, emphatic outburst. But he decided—happily, surely—to save the melodrama for later and to sustain the weary pathos of the first phrase a bit longer. The effect of the change is perfectly complemented by the emptiness of the stacked open fifths at the beginning of m. 3. The syncopations in the melodic line in mm. 4-5, at the beginning of the second phrase, catch the sense of shifting and hovering inherent in "Schwebt." The third phrase (mm. 8-10) is a sort of simplified variant of the first phrase, ending an octave lower. Like the first phrase, it is three bars long. As we go through the song, we gradually become aware of the way the mix of three- and four-bar phrases also contributes a sense of unease and restlessness that goes back to the implications of "Schwebt."

Until this point the whole song has been *piano*, as directed at the beginning. But the fourth phrase begins (m. 11) with just the sort of dramatic outburst Bach had originally planned for m. 3. Here we confront the problems about Bach's intentions, so far as dynamics are concerned, that I mentioned earlier. For the *forte* that he had originally planned for the pickup to m. 3 (and that still appeared, through Voss's error, in the *Almanach* print) was apparently meant to last through the first two phrases, until the pickup to m. 8. Only at this point is it canceled by a *"p"* in the *Almanach* print:

This *"p"* does not, of course, appear in the Vrieslander print cited above, since there has been no *"f"* in m. 2 that needed canceling. But when one examines the *Almanach* print closely, one cannot help asking whether Bach can really ever have intended the second phrase, which begins with those wavering syncopations in the melodic line, to have been played *forte*. I have no answer.

At any rate the outburst in m. 11, with which the fourth phrase begins, is most effective. The third phrase has just died away on the word "Zähren" with the bittersweet dissonance between the grace-note G in the melodic line and the G-sharp in the bass line. Suddenly we have the loud octave F's in the keyboard's left hand, followed immediately by the assertively rising eighth notes, bare and unharmonized, in the melody. But instead of continuing its brave rise, the phrase suddenly drops a sixth as the harmony subsides into a gentle cadence in the relative major. The speaker's momentary rage at his own tears gives way to sadness at their cause: the fact that the image is not Lyda herself.

But he immediately regains heart as the boldly descending arpeggio that opens the fifth phrase (pickups to m. 14), immediately echoed by the striding bass line, declares "Ich seh' es"—he does, at least, actually see her image. Yes, but it is only an image: and so once again the harmony softens in m. 16. But once again boldly declarative octaves are heard in the bass as the melodic line, this time harmonized a third below, repeats the little three-note rise it began in m. 11 and this time completes it on high G, extending the fifth phrase to five bars.

Immediately, however, the music once more retreats into itself as the soft little two-bar phrase, in sighing eighth notes, tells us of his weeping. But then, in the seventh and last phrase, the octave F's are heard again, *forte*, as he repeats "Dass du es selbst nicht bist"—not at all wearily or despairingly, as in the poem, but defiantly.

One cannot help admiring the mastery with which Bach has made his music follow each twist and turn of feeling possibly discoverable in Klopstock's stanza while all the while tying the song together through repeated phrases and motifs. But how does it work for the poem's other stanza? Very poorly, it seems to me. For although the two stanzas have the same underlying meter, they are quite different in rhythmic detail—not to say meaning.

There is trouble immediately, in the song's first phrase. While it makes sense to stretch out the word "süsses" over the long turning phrase in m. 2, it makes no sense whatever to do so with "jenes." Still worse, the upward leap of a fifth falls naturally in the first stanza, between "Bild" and "o," but in the second stanza it awkwardly splits the word "Thales." The syncopations at the beginning of the second phrase, as we saw, perfectly suit the ideas behind "Schwebt"; but they make the second stanza's line, "Die ich ihr lesen will," seem labored and unduly drawn out. There are many other bad fits between Bach's music and the words of Klopstock's second stanza, but perhaps the worst two come in m. 15, where the eighth-note F-sharp at the end of the bar is now made to bear the burden of the conjurer's "Auf" in the line "Auf, und verwandle dich!" and in mm. 18–20, where the softly sighing descending phrases that went perfectly with "und weine und weine," are utterly inappropriate to the forced repetition of the challenging—and not at all softly sighed—word "Erscheinung."

I cannot recall another example of a song in which Bach has so completely given up on solving the strophic problem. It is as though he had read only the first stanza of Klopstock's poem—and then, it must be admitted, done a masterly job of setting it. Unlike "Vaterlandslied," "Lyda" (or "Edone") seems almost to cry out for a through-composed setting. And, interestingly enough, it was given one that appeared alongside Bach's setting in the 1775 *Musen-Almanach*.

The composer was Johann Friedrich Reichardt. Reichardt was then 24, and had recently published *Über die Deutsche comische Opera* and the first volume of *Briefe eines aufmerksamen Reisenden die Musik betreffend*. In both of those books, as we saw, he eloquently praised the music of Bach, whom he had met in his travels, and more praise followed in Reichardt's *Musikalisches Kunstmagazin* (1782–1791) and in the autobiography that he wrote, late in his life, for the *Allgemeine musikalische Zeitung*. For a while relations between the two men were cordial, but by 1780 they had soured to a point where Voss could assert, in a letter of May 29 to Goecking, that Bach actually hated Reichardt. J. G. Meusel, in his 1783 *Miscelaneen artistischen Innhalts*, wrote: "J. Fr. Reicherdt [*sic*] has a special talent for speaking of things he does not understand. C.P.E. Bach calls him the musical windbag" (Suchalla, *Briefe und Dokumente*, p. 649). And Reichardt, for his part, could write, in 1796 with Bach safely dead, the following about the latter's vocal compositions:

As a vocal composer, our Bach need only have composed *Heilig* in order to be counted among the greatest masters of authentic church music; in all his other vocal works, however, he appears more as a great instrumental composer, to whom the study of language and poetry, fine and deep feeling, and that taste for nobly simple beauty that issues from the whole being of the inner man are simply lacking.[10]

That final phrase suggests something about Reichardt's significance for developments in song composition in the Germany of the last two decades of the 18th century. For it was precisely the search for "nobly simple beauty" that materialized in the folksong movement in which Reichardt, Voss, and Voss's frequent collaborator Johann Abraham Peter Schulz were to play leading roles. Shortly after he received Bach's setting of "Lyda" in August 1774, Voss wrote a letter to his fiancée Ernestine Boie in which he compared it with Reichardt's setting:

> Last Monday I received a letter from Bach, with melodies for Klopstock's "Lyda" and my "Die Schlummernde." They are both excellent. For "Lyda" I now have two compositions, both of which I must print. Reichardt's is also fine, and I would insult him if I turned it down. But Bach's is incomparable, so deeply felt, so moving!
>
> [Suchalla, P. 431]

Voss sounds almost reluctant to publish Reichardt's setting, while his admiration for Bach's is unstinting; as we shall see, there is reason to believe that a few years later his preference might well have gone the other way.

Here is Reichardt's setting of Klopstock's "Lyda":

There is certainly nothing very remarkable about this song. Its one virtue is that Reichardt, unlike Bach, at least saw that the poem's second stanza called for different music. But the music he provided for both stanzas is, for the most part, woefully conventional. The first part, taken at the medium slow tempo implied by the direction "Sanft schwermüthig," sounds like a hundred lover's complaints of the period. Rather than following, moment to moment, the flow of the poem's emotions, the music falls neatly into chunks: four bars in the tonic ending in a half-cadence, four bars in the parallel minor ending in another half-cadence, and eight bars taking us through the subdominant to the relative minor and through a full cadence. The dull stamp of the left hand's eighth notes, set against the predictable scalar and arpeggiated movement of the melodic line's sixteenths, very quickly becomes wearying. The change at m. 5 from major to minor is appropriate to what is going on in the poem, but only in the most general way. And in the final eight bars Reichardt makes no attempt to dramatize the oddness of the landscape or the complexity of the speaker's response to it.

The talk of flowers with which the second stanza opens causes Reichardt to shift, automatically as it were, into his cheery pastoral mode. The time signature changes to $\frac{6}{8}$, the direction specifies "Etwas lebhafter," and the rhythm falls into the "Here-we-go-gathering-nuts-in-May" pattern so beloved of 18th-century composers for pastoral finales. (For a distinguished, witty example, see the finale of Haydn's great D-major cello concerto.) Worth noting, however, are the way the melodic and bass lines suddenly begin to move together at m. 23 ("die ich ihr flechten will") and the harmony goes quickly through the subdominant and back to the tonic; the emphatic push (against a rapidly ascending bass line) given the word "Auf!"; and the use of the ♭VI, twice, to set off the command "verwandle dich!" (mm. 28 and 32). But just as in the song's first section, the appropriateness of music to text is very general, not at all accurately or tellingly imagined.

The other song that Bach sent Voss along with his setting of "Lyda" was a setting of a strange, difficult, and rather interesting poem by Voss himself, "Die Schlummernde":

>   Eingewiegt von Nachtigallentönen,
>   Schlummert sie, die Königin der Schönen!
>   Frischer blüht der Thron der Königin;
>   Weste wehn die Opferdüfte hin.
>
>   Lächle sanft! Mit hohen Engelminen
>   Ist die That des Tages dir erschienen.
>   Strecke froh die schönen Händ' empor!
>   Denn sie hält dir ihre Palme vor.
>
>   Aber war's ein zitterndes Verlangen?
>   Lächelt Lieb' auf diesen Rosenwangen?
>   Und bin ich, bin ich die Traumgestalt,
>   Die bethränt dir jetzt vorüberwallt?
>
>   O so schweigt, ihr Nachtigallenchöre,
>   Dass kein Laut den schönen Traum zerstöre!
>   Oder wählt den Laut, durch den besiegt,
>   Näher stets das blöde Weibchen fliegt.

This is, plainly, the sort of dream poem that used to be called pre-Romantic, but, together with its counterparts in the visual arts, was a not uncommon product of 18th-century sensibility.

The mysterious queen of beauty, presented to us as though we should know who she is, lies sleeping, lulled by nightingales and resting not on a bed but rather on a throne that the verb "blüht" suggests is somehow alive. Some sort of homage is being paid to her, since the fragrance of the sacrificial offering floats toward us—and toward the west, perhaps suggesting sleep, trance, even death. Smile gently, the speaker tells some as yet unidentified listener and spectator. And he enjoins this person to reach up his hands to meet that of the sleeping queen, which is now extended toward him. It seems to be a ritualistic exchange. The speaker further assures the spectator that whatever it is that is going on—and he uses the purposely vague and mysterious phrase "die That des Tages"—will in due course be revealed through some sort of angelic aura, or perhaps by a choir of angels.

With the third stanza, everything seems suddenly to change. But was it (merely) a tremulous or fearful demand or claim?—the speaker asks, apparently now addressing himself. Does love smile on these rosy cheeks? The cheeks must belong to the sleeping queen, and the "it" that may now be a demand rather than a gentle, seductive invitation, is probably the whole dream scene, as described in the first two stanzas. Finally the speaker asks whether he himself is not the dream figure who is wandering past this scene. It is interesting that the "dir" in line 8 seems to be the former queen, now that the dream figure whom the speaker was earlier addressing has turned out—as so often happens in dreams—to be the speaker himself. It is also interesting that the speaker/dream figure is now in tears—presumably in the face of this disillusioning revelation.

The final stanza is perhaps most difficult of all. The speaker tells the chorus of nightingales to be quiet, so that no sound may disturb the beautiful dream—though this certainly seemed to be disturbed in the preceding stanza; but perhaps it was possible, between stanzas, for the speaker to banish the third stanza's doubts and return to his earlier, blissful state? At any rate, in the poem's last two lines he gives the nightingales another alternative: or choose (to continue) the sound, overcome by it (or by the dream?); the stupid little woman rushes ever nearer.

Whatever else may be unclear about this fascinating poem, the coarsely contemptuous final line makes it clear that what seemed to be an idealized vision of beauty has been merely the demand for love (and presumably marriage)—a demand all the more repulsive for being made nervously or tremulously—of an extremely ordinary human female: the supposed "Königin der Schönen" stands revealed as "das blöde Weibchen." I give Bach's setting as it appears in the *Almanach* (Vrieslander prints the keyboard right hand's half-note C in m. 2 as a B-flat and at two points alters the slurring of the bass line):

At first glance, this looks very simple. But the more one plays it, the more one becomes impressed by its air of eerie silence—which seems wholly appropriate to the dreamlike setting and atmosphere of Voss's poem. The evenness and imperturbability of the melody, together with the constantly drumming eighth notes of the keyboard's left hand, create a gentleness too perfectly sustained to be quite of this world. And then one begins to notice fine details of the right hand's voice-leading—for example, in m. 2, which is spoiled by Vrieslander's misprint. Or notice the F in the keyboard's right hand on the last beat of m. 9: it would have been just as easy to have repeated E, but the F not only leads smoothly to the G that will become the melody note in the next bar, it also gives a momentary tint of subdominant sweetness—for we have been in C major and A minor—that perfectly complements the air of unreality created by the song as a whole. Though the poem's tone and content change from stanza to stanza, the confusion of dream and reality that is its subject finds its ideal expression in the song's perfect, unchanging decorum.

III

During this period, Bach set a number of poems by other "Bund" members besides Voss. And not all of the resulting songs appeared in the *Musen-Almanach*; some were saved for publication in the *Neue Lieder-Melodien*. There was a setting of J. M. Miller's "Der Bauer," along with the compulsory drinking songs, to texts by Voss and Hölty. More interesting, however, is "Der Frühling," to this poem by Miller:

> O seht! die liebe Sonne lacht;
> Die Wiese kleidet sich in Pracht;
> Zerronnen ist der Winterschnee;
> Und Blumen dringen aus dem Klee.
>
> Auf blauen Veilchen sammeln sich
> Die kleinen Bienen emsiglich;
> Der bunte Buttervogel freut
> Sich über sein bemaltes Kleid.
>
> Die Lerche schwingt sich hoch empor;
> Im Hain erschallt der Vögel Chor;
> Vor allen aber tönt der Schall
> Der lieben kleinen Nachtigall.
>
> Von dir, O Liebe! schallt ihr Lied,
> Und das geliebte Weibchen flieht
> Zum Männchen hin, und inniglich
> Schmiegt sie an seine Seite sich.
>
> O hätt ich, liebe Nachtigall,
> Wie du, so reinen, süssen Schall!
> Dann käm mein Rösgen auch zu mir,
> Und freuen könnt ich mich mit dir!

This is of course a characteristic 18th-century Horatian love poem. Indeed, the final two lines of the first stanza are practically a translation of the opening lines of one of Horace's most famous poems: "Diffugere nives, redeunt iam gramina campis / arboribusque comae" (*Odes,* IV, vii). The difference from Horace comes with the twist at the end: amidst all this joyous, busy return to life and love, the speaker, separated from his beloved, is somehow prevented from joining in. But there is no real pain—in this poem at least—and we do not feel that the gap between the speaker and the happy natural world around him is unbridgeable. This sense of cautious optimism is somehow encouraged by the charming smallness of everything: the bees, the nightingale, even the "Weibchen" and "Männchen."

Here is Bach's setting of Miller's poem:

The first thing that strikes us is the juxtaposition of the direction, "Munter," and the minor key. At a slightly slower tempo than the direction suggests, the first bars would sound quite sad, a sort of noble lament. The bold upward leap of a fourth (imitated in the bass) gives way to a general droop in the melodic line, and in particular we notice how eighth-note pairs falling a tone or semitone begin to assume importance: first in m. 2, with the little accompaniment figure in sixths; then in the next bar, as the bass line's A-G is repeated and passed upward into the melody, and then repeated as the phrase ends in m. 4.

The second half of the song begins by wittily combining the rising fourths (in the bass) with the falling eighth notes in the melody, each pair preceded by a pickup note. As we traverse the circle of fifths, it sounds very much as though we are heading toward a cadence in the relative major, and thus a "happy ending." But Bach scotches this expectation by having the bass line return to E at the end of m. 6. The melody then goes on to rise higher than ever before as the combination of rising fourths in the bass line and falling eighth-note phrase in the melody is extended, leading to the final cadence in E minor. The effect is to insist, quietly yet forcefully, on the dominance of the minor.

This song seems to me one of Bach's fine small successes. At the proper tempo, the music continues to lilt throughout. And the circle-of-fifths passage beginning at m. 5 not only suggests that we are heading for an ending in the major but also, in its humorously exaggerated neatness, tells us that the world of the song (and poem) is well ordered, a place for everything and everything in its place. And so it is. Yet the return to the minor, the pushing upward of the melodic line in the penultimate bar, and the corresponding push forward of the bass line are all just slightly disturbing. This is an excellent example of what it means to solve the strophic problem: by playing the general sunniness of the world described in the poem's first three stanzas against the graceful regret of its last two, Bach has imaginatively—not, we note dramatically, for the effect is of fusion rather than process—caught Miller's tone perfectly.

Another interesting song on a "Bund" member's poem is Bach's setting of Hölty's mordantly witty poem, "Todtengräberlied," which is known today mainly because Schubert set it in 1813, a couple of weeks before his sixteenth birthday. Here is Hölty's poem:

    Grabe, Spaden, grabe!
    Alles, was ich habe,
    Dank' ich, Spaden, dir!
    Reich' und arme Leute

Werden meine Beute,
Kommen einst zu mir!

Weiland gross und edel,
Nickte dieser Schädel
Keinem Grusse Dank!
Dieses Beingerippe,
Ohne Wang' und Lippe,
Hatte Gold und Rang!

Jener Kopf mit Haaren,
War vor wenig Jahren
Schön, wie Engel sind!
Tausend junge Fentchen
Leckten ihm das Händchen,
Gafften sich halb blind!

Grabe, Spaden, grabe!
Alles, was ich habe,
Dank' ich, Spaden, dir!
Reich' und arme Leute
Werden meine Beute,
Kommen einst zu mir!

Like the gravedigger in *Hamlet*, this one too sings not only at his work but also about his work. "Alles, was ich habe, / Dank' ich, Spaden, dir!" of course means literally that he owes the spade his livelihood, and thus without it he would have nothing. But the literal meaning of the statement immediately gets expanded and elaborated upon: he owes the spade not only his livelihood but also his entire experience of life and society.

Rich and poor alike, he tells us first, will sooner or later become my prey, my spoil, my prize. The word *Beute,* cognate with English "booty," is usually used only of hunted animals or material goods, and has a ring of coarseness when applied to human beings. (Wagner, with a similar effect in mind, has Hagen ironically apply it to Siegfried in the final act of *Götterdämmerung*.) And the gravedigger's language coarsens further in the next stanza. Perhaps again alluding to *Hamlet*, Hölty has him turn up a skull as he digs—which he then proceeds to comment upon. This particular skull belonged not to a fellow of infinite jest but rather to a man so high and mighty that he never needed even to nod in acknowledgment of another's greeting. (One is reminded of the old poem about Boston, "Where the Lowells talk to the Cabots, / And the Cabots talk only to God"!) Then, turning his attention to a whole skeleton—whether or not it belongs to the skull is unclear—the gravedigger remarks that although it now has neither cheek nor lip, it once had gold and rank, class, quality. The word "Gold" of course means primarily money, wealth, but coming between the vividly imaged skeleton and the abstract noun "Rang," it inevitably takes on concrete meanings as well: the image of the skeleton draped in golden baubles also plays a part in the line's effectiveness.

As if this weren't bad enough, in the next stanza the gravedigger points out not a skull or skeleton but a more recent acquisition, a head, presumably that of a woman, that still has its hair. And he now seems consciously to enjoy the coarseness of his own language as he tells us of the angelic beauty the face once possessed, and of the thousand fops who licked the lady's hands and gaped at her beauty until they were half-blind—not wholly blind, as they will be when they come to him. The poem's final stanza circles back to its beginning.

One can best appreciate what Bach did with this poem by first looking briefly at what Schubert did with it. Schubert's setting is, as we should expect, through-composed, and is specifically for bass voice. Schubert immediately enforces upon us the sharp distinction between the associations we have with gravedigging and the way in which this gravedigger sees his job by having the first line of the poem delivered as a slow prologue, to an E-minor arpeggio, and then sending the gravedigger off on a merry little tune in G major:

After a few closing comments from the piano, the second strophe begins in C major, the subdominant, becoming thoughtful as it shifts briefly into A minor for the lines about the skeleton and then returning to C for the majesty of "Gold und Rang":

334 ~ Chapter Twelve

But the third strophe of Schubert's setting is the most remarkable of all, and therefore needs to be cited in its entirety:

After a bar of silence, Schubert then returns to the first strophe of his setting, which he repeats with only minor changes for the final stanza of Hölty's poem.

Our first sign that something quite new is going on in the third strophe of Schubert's setting is the way in which he pushes right past the line ending after "Jahren" (m. 43), ending the phrase on the first word of the next line, "schön," and thus throwing it into sharp relief. The crescendo and the rise of the vocal line to high E make clear the gravedigger's excitement at the idea of the head's recent beauty. After a bar of quiet piano vamping, to think it over, he rapturously completes the line: "schön, wie Engel sind." At this point the piano accompaniment breaks out of its rather countrified oom-pah pattern as the right hand begins to play smooth and elegant sixteenth-note broken chords over the left hand's quarter-note octave leaps (mm. 47ff.). The line about the young fops licking the beauty's hands is then sung, not once but twice. Each time the phrase is sung *dolce*, and softly, then finished off with a burst of boisterous heartiness. And each time we feel the gravedigger lose himself in visualizing the elegant court scene—and then come out of it with a laugh. A seven-bar piano interlude eases us back to the repetition of the little E-minor prologue that begins the song's final strophe.

C.P.E. Bach's strophic setting, which at first looks far more simple, turns out to be both more original and closer to the intent of the poem:

The first two bars are noncommittally pretty, and could come from almost anywhere. But the omission of the first beat in the bass in the following two bars makes us feel the gentle pressure of a dance rhythm, which is enforced by the corresponding omission at the half-cadence (m. 6). The unvarying rhythm into which the melodic line has fallen continues into the second half of the song as the bass, in thirds, steadily descends, with every other bar missing its first beat. What was pretty at the beginning has become monotonous, clunky, dead at the center. Gudrun Busch identifies the dance evoked by the song as a mazurka (pp. 202, 334, 404). I am not sure we need to be (or indeed can be) that specific, but I fully agree with her that we should not, in any case, take the dance rhythm as a "Totentanz" (p. 202). It is, rather, a lumpish version of the sort of dance the gravedigger associates with the high life summoned up for him by the skull, the skeleton, the head of still luxuriant hair.

In what sense is this setting both more original and closer to the intent of the poem than Schubert's? Schubert, by following so closely the course of each stanza of the poem, loses what ties the poem together: the shrewd, ironic, yet still severely (and necessarily) limited sensibility of the gravedigger. The evocation of high life in strophe three of Schubert's setting is vivid and elegant—the real thing. Hölty's (and Bach's) gravedigger is not nearly so imaginative. Schubert's gravedigger is more like the Hamlet of *Hamlet* V, i than he is like Shakespeare's gravedigger. To have given us the mazurka (or whatever it is) as filtered through the gravedigger's sensibility, at secondhand as it were, and to have retained that throughout the song as its unifying force, was a master stroke on Bach's part. Moreover, his success demonstrates an important truth about strophic, as opposed to through-composed, songs: a strophic song is, of course, necessarily a compromise struck by a composer with a poet and his poem; but it is a compromise by which not only the resulting song but also the original poem can gain concentration, unity, and expressive force.

IV

Before we close, there is one last song we should look at. Appropriately enough, it is a setting of a poem by Johann Heinrich Voss, with whom we began this chapter, that appeared in the 1781 edition of Voss's Hamburg *Musen-Almanach*.

The poem is entitled "Tischlied":

Gesund und frohen Mutes,
Geniessen wir des Gutes,
Dass uns der Grosse Vater schenkt.
O preist ihn, Brüder, preiset
Den Vater, der uns speiset,
Und mit des Weines Freude tränkt!

Er ruft herab: Es werde!
Und Segen schwellt die Erde,
Der Fruchtbaum und der Acker spriesst;
Es lebt und webt in Triften,
In Wassern und in Lüften,
Und Milch und Wein und Honig fliesst.

Dann sammeln alle Völker:
Der Pferd'- und Rennthiermelker
Am kalten Pol, von Schnee umstürmt;
Der Schnitter edler Halme;
Der Wilde, welchen Palme
Und Brotbaum vor der Sonne schirmt.

Gott aber schaut vom Himmel
Ihr freudiges Gewimmel
Vom Aufgang bis zum Neidergang:
Denn siene Kinder sammeln,
Und ihr vereintes Stammeln
Tönt ihm in tausend Sprachen Dank.

Lobsinget seinem Namen,
Und strebt ihm nachzuahmen,
Ihm, dessen Gnad' ihr nie ermesst:
Der alle Welten segnet,
Auf Gut' und Böse regnet,
Und seine Sonne scheinen lässt!

Mit herzlichem Erbarmen
Reicht eure Hand den Armen,
Wess Volks und Glaubens sie auch sein!
Wir sind (nicht mehr nicht minder!)
Sind alle Gottes Kinder,
Und sollen uns wie Brüder freun!

During this time, when the poetry of "Geselligkeit" was so popular, the title "Tischlied" was frequently used—the most famous instance being perhaps Goethe's early lyric beginning "Mich ergreift, ich weiss nicht wie, / Himmlisches Behagen." Voss's charming though not particularly distinguished poem, on the other hand, begins as a simple grace said at table, and then spreads—rather too schematically, perhaps—to all the peoples of the globe, whom God is watching over. There are few surprises or real points of interest, and the poem does not, I think, demand detailed comment.

More to the point is to see what Bach made of it:

A pleasant enough little song, certainly, and one that perfectly fulfills Bach's direction: "Vergnügt." The decorous first phrase, with its even eighth-note rhythm and orderly descent, mostly stepwise and neatly ornamented at its end, through an octave exudes exactly the contentment the direction demands. And nothing in the phrases that follow—leading into the dominant, in the dominant, and leading back through ii to the tonic—does anything to disturb that contentment. Everything is neat, pleasing, with just enough variation along the way to keep the listener interested without offering any distraction.

Though one might wonder, in this case as in the earlier one of "Lyda," whether Bach had bothered to read all the way through the poem he was setting—there is no hint of the geographical scope of Voss's lyric—the music certainly catches effectively the faintly self-satisfied piety associated with this sort of effort. As we noted earlier, Voss, in the letters he sent back to Göttingen from Hamburg in the spring of 1774, frequently expressed his admiration for Bach, both as man and musician. He even found Bach's admittedly problematical setting of "Lyda" preferable to Reichardt's. We therefore should expect him to have been pleased, only six-and-a-half years later, when he published it, with Bach's setting of "Tischlied." But he was not, and the reasons why he was not are of some historical interest and importance.

In October 1780, Voss sent two copies of the just published 1781 *Musen-Almanach* to the composer Johann Abraham Peter Schulz (1747-1800), with whom he had only recently struck up a correspondence but who would soon become his closest friend and collaborator. Schulz had two settings in this volume of the *Musen-Almanach*, the first of many to which he would contribute. After praising Schulz's settings for their "pure expression of feeling . . . with no concessions to fashionable taste, no empty virtuosity," Voss writes:

> Bach, in whose praise I join wholeheartedly, was surely tricked by a lying spirit when he set my "Tischlied" to music. I recognize nothing in it as correct. When I wrote the poem, I was not feeling like a man delighted with his well-filled stomach, but was rather serious.[11]

Evidently that air of contentment that we found in Bach's setting was a little too sensuous, even visceral, to suit Voss's notion of what he was up to in writing "Tischlied."

Shortly after this Schulz was preparing the first of his three collections entitled *Lieder im Volkston*, which would be published at Berlin in 1782. One of the songs he composed for inclusion in this volume was a setting of Voss's "Tischlied." This time Voss was very much pleased. On March 4, 1782, he wrote to Schulz:

> The melody for "Tischlied" is excellent. Good old Bach had so disfigured my child that I was angry with it. Now I hardly recognize it, so beautifully does it float in the airy garment of your light and expressive music.

[P. 19]

The sentences that immediately follow are also of interest, for they make clear the goals of the folksong movement as conceived by Voss and Schulz:

> I cannot praise you; but a heart that hates all pomp and frippery, without however longing for the half-savage sheepskin or beggar's rags, will not feel indifferent toward you. I consider you to be the man who will lead music—which now does stunts like a tightrope-walker, now creeps along in affected simplicity, without power or charm—back to her high destiny, and—without regard for the distinctions clever people make between old taste, new taste, Italian taste, fashionable taste, and whatever else—will fix your gaze steadily on the note struck by nature: the sharpest and liveliest expression of every passion or feeling.
>
> [P. 19]

Reading these words, we recall the anti-aristocratic fury that Voss developed as a result of his early experience. And we can perhaps understand how, despite the admiration that he still retained for Bach, Voss, who had preferred Bach's setting of "Lyda" to Reichardt's precisely because he found Bach's "so deeply felt, so moving," could now be led, by his increasing passion for simplicity and directness of feeling, to find the easy urbanity of Bach's "Tischlied" setting somewhat mannered and artificial. For C.P.E. Bach was in no sense a representative of the "Volk" but rather an honored member of what we should now call the German musical and intellectual establishment.

As for Schulz, his two great musical heroes had always been Bach and Kirnberger, whose help in launching his musical career he had sought while still in his teens. It was through Bach that he had got to know Kirnberger, with whom he studied for several years and who recommended him for his first position, as accompanist and music teacher to a Polish princess. In a letter to Voss of July 13, 1780, Schulz spoke of Bach as "the *non plus ultra* in music," adding:

> I am frightened when I think of how little I am beside him; and also beside Kirnberger, though not wholly so. For one can approach him in some respects; but Bach in none. That is surely true; and all the composers today, who know his works as I know them, must say the same, or else they lie. On that I'll swear an oath.
>
> [P. 15]

Yet Schulz's setting of "Tischlied" was indeed very different from Bach's, making it clear that he saw the poem very differently from the way Bach had seen it:

Plainly, what we have here is a hymn—which is fair enough, considering the content of Voss's text. But the ponderous triadic (and even unison) solemnities are unrelieved by any sign of rhythmic or harmonic life. It is curious that Voss singled out the melody for particular praise, since there is virtually no melody here, merely a top part to the simple, sluggish harmony. The congregation that Schulz evokes as singers of this hymn are surely not about to be tempted by "pomp and frippery," but they do not seem much interested in music either. This is not pastoralism but primitivism—of an almost baby-talk variety. One is reminded of the very worst poems contributed by Wordsworth to the 1798 *Lyrical Ballads*: "I have a boy of five years old; / His face is fair and fresh to see"—and the like. And yet Schulz's volumes, which were very popular, contain many such songs. Even before Schulz's three volumes appeared, in 1777 and 1778, the Berlin writer and editor Friedrich Nicolai had brought out a two-volume satirical collection of mock-"Lieder im Volkston" entitled *Eyn feyner kleyner Almanach Vol schönerr echterr liblicherr Volckslieder*. Looking at Schulz's setting of "Tischlied," one can see his point.

In Chapter One we saw that while the idealization of folksongs by Herder and others dramatically raised the prestige of songs in general, it hurt the critical reputation of C. P. E. Bach's songs. For as Heinrich W. Schwab has pointed out:

> As a composer of songs, Bach—apart from a few exceptions—did not attempt to realize that ideal of the song that was characterized by such concepts as "singableness" and "popularity." This holds for his secular as well as for his religious songs. The "harmonist" Bach saw himself as quite obviously unable to obey such demands as seemed absolutely necessary to the creation of a *Lied im Volkston*. In general, of course, as Bach consciously distanced himself from contemporary tendencies toward simplification, he created for himself the hypothesis that he might, also in his writing of songs, forge a path to "connoisseur's music," and thereby strive for "originality" in a genre in which that quality had for a long time not been expected.[12]

This is all very well as far as it goes, but I think that those exceptions alluded to by Schwab perhaps deserve more stress than he gives them. As we have seen, Bach did not fight against the "tendencies toward simplification" that led to the folksong movement of the 1770s and 1780s. On the contrary, he consciously simplified his style, in the songs he wrote for Voss and also in many of the ones that he reserved for his *Neue Lieder-Melodien* of 1789.

Voss's stern disapproval of Bach's setting of "Tischlied" marks the moment at which the folksong movement's drive toward simplification passed beyond what Bach could or would provide. The popularity of the inane songs of Schulz and others was the result. Yet, as we shall see, Bach did not stop experimenting, in his shorter songs, with a simplified style that was more or less in tune with his times. As we shall see in the next chapter, however, during this same period he was also working on his most ambitious and elaborate through-composed songs.

Chapter Thirteen

A Cantata for Gerstenberg

The shorter of the two through-composed songs from this period is especially interesting because it is another setting of a poem that Bach had earlier set strophically, Albrecht von Haller's "Doris," which Bach has retitled "An Doris." As we saw in Chapter Ten, the poem, with its 24 stanzas, is not only extremely long but also extremely complex psychologically. It seemed, we recall, impossible to decide how much or which parts of the poem Bach had had directly in mind when he wrote his twelve-bar strophic song. When Bach composed his new setting, he printed out with it only eight stanzas of Haller's poem, the ones that stood in the 24-stanza version as numbers 1-4, 6, 10, 21, and 24. (By the fifth edition of his poems, published in 1762, Haller had relegated the penultimate and antepenultimate stanzas of the long version to a footnote, producing a poem of 22 stanzas; it has thus been printed ever since.)

I

The 8-stanza "An Doris" that Bach used for his through-composed setting also has, as we shall see, an important textual change, apparently made by Bach himself, for it is contained in no later printing of the poem that I have been able to locate. Here then is the poem:

Des Tages Licht hat sich verdunkelt,
Der Purpur, der in Westen funkelt,
Erblasset in ein falbes Grau.
Der Mond zeigt seine Silberhörner,
Die kühle Nacht streut Schlummerkörner,
Und tränkt die trockne Welt mit Thau.

Komm, Doris, komm zu jenen Buchen,
Lass uns den stillen Grund besuchen,
Wo nichts sich regt als ich und du.
Nur noch der Hauch verliebter Weste
Belebt das schwanke Laub der Aeste,
Und winket dir liebkosend zu.

Die grüne Nacht belaubter Bäume,
Führt uns in Anmuthsvolle Träume,

> Worinn der Geist sich selber wiegt.
> Er zieht die schweifenden Gedanken,
> In angenehm verengte Schranken,
> Und lebt mit sich allein vergnügt.
>
> Ach, Doris! fühlst du nicht im Herzen
> Die zarte Regung sanfter Schmerzen,
> Die süsser sind, als alle Lust?
> Strahlt nicht dein holder Blick gelinder?
> Rollt nicht dein Blut sich selbst geschwinder,
> Und schwellt die Unschuldsvolle Brust?
>
> Du staunst; es regt sich deine Tugend;
> Die holde Farbe keuscher Jugend
> Deckt dein verschämtes Angesicht.
> Dein Blut wallt von vermischtem Triebe,
> Der strenge Ruhm verwirft die Liebe,
> Allein dein Herz verwirft sie nicht.
>
> O könnte dich ein Schatten rühren
> Der Wollust, die zwey Herzen spüren,
> Die sich einander zugedacht!
> Du fordertest von dem Geschicke
> Die langen Stunden selbst zurücke,
> Die dein Herz müssig zugebracht.
>
> Mein Feuer brennt nicht nur auf Blättern,
> Ich suche nicht dich zu vergöttern,
> Die Menschheit ziert dich allzusehr.
> Ein andrer kan gelehrter klagen,
> Mein Mund weiss weniger zu sagen,
> Allein mein Herz empfindet mehr.
>
> Was siehst du furchtsam hin und wieder,
> Und schlägst die holden Blicke nieder?
> Es ist kein fremder Zeuge nah.
> Mein Kind! kann ich dich nicht erweichen?
> Doch ja, dein Mund giebt zwar kein Zeichen,
> Allein dein Seufzen sagt mir Ja!

The elaborate scene-setting discussed in Chapter Ten is all retained in this version, but the very odd turn that we noted at the beginning of the fourth stanza—"Sprich Doris!"—is missing: this is the important textual change I mentioned above. Instead we read, simply, "Ach, Doris! fühlst du nicht im Herzen"—and so on. The oddity, as we noted in Chapter Ten, derives from the fact that Doris, who in fact never speaks throughout the 24-stanza version of the poem, is being commanded to speak, and is then being told precisely what she is to say (and feel). Here the oddity is gone. Instead of the extraordinary demand of the earlier version, we now have, thanks to a stroke of Bach's pen, merely a quite ordinary lover's plea: "Oh, Doris, *don't* you feel"—and so on. Moreover, the omitted stanzas contained much of the obsessive psychologizing about what the ever-silent Doris might be or ought to be thinking or feeling that made the speaker seem so oddly self-enclosed, to the point where we were led to wonder whether Doris was a real person or merely a figment of his overheated imagination. Also omitted is the whole elaborate seduction drama in which he compares himself with the other possible suitors that inhabit the "Reich der Tugend" over which she rules.

In place of the extremely involved poem we encountered earlier, we now have a relatively straightforward love poem. The climax now comes right at the middle, just as it should, with the opening of the new fifth stanza: "Du staunst; es regt sich deine Tugend." Haller, a Swiss whose nervousness about his German impelled him to make alterations in this and other poems, attached to the word "staunst" the following note, which was retained in 19th-century editions of his poems: "I have made a point of retaining this old Swiss word. It is the root of *erstaunen,* and means *rêver,* a word for which there is no other equivalent."

It is a little difficult to see why he went to so much trouble. In modern German the verb *staunen* does have a slightly different sense: to be astonished or amazed. And one can see why Haller might well have wanted here a less melodramatic, spectacular word, one with the senses of dreaming, pondering, and yearning that attach to the French verb *rêver*. But these senses would not have been far to seek in other German verbs that would fit the meter: why not, for example, "Du träumst," or "Du sehnst"? Perhaps Haller, having committed himself to "staunst," which he liked for reasons he has not managed to make clear, simply wanted to explain to German readers that he was using it in a sense slightly different from the one they were accustomed to. To say, however truly or falsely, that no other word will do so well as the word one has become fond of in a given context is a frequent dodge of poets.

At any rate, after his analysis, in the fifth stanza, of Doris's maidenly blush, the speaker returns to soulful longing in stanza six and then, in the final two stanzas, rallies his forces for what appears to be his ultimate triumph. It is in the jump to these last two stanzas—the jump from stanza 10 to stanzas 21 and 24 of the long version of the poem—that we feel the awkwardness brought on by Bach's selectivity.

In the song, however, Bach brings off successfully the dramatic rise embodied in the final half of the shortened version of the poem. Since the setting is 155 bars long, it will be better to cite and analyze it in sections than as a whole. Here is Bach's setting of the first three stanzas:

The opening is calm and earnest, with a kind of gentle urgency felt in the joint upward movement of melody and accompaniment. After the cadence in m. 4, however, things immediately become a little more complicated—the eighth-note movement in the bass, the sudden turn toward A minor—but then quickly resolve themselves in (a little surprisingly) another C-major cadence. The complication in the music continues to grow, however, complementing that of the text, which is now telling of the moon's silver horns and the "Schlummerkörner" strewn by the night. A particularly nice touch is the little upward leap of a fourth, from C to F, in m. 8, which perfectly catches the cool freshness of the night air. (This upward leap will in fact become a sort of motif in the song as we go along.) Other nice touches are the unexpected landing on E-flat (against F-sharp and A in the accompaniment) at the beginning of m. 10, which gives an air of mystery and poignancy to the night's action, and the way in which the word "tränkt" is stretched out over almost two bars, comically enacting the long time it takes the night to give the whole dry world a drink. The first strophe ends with a graceful descent, in sixths, to an F cadence.

The second strophe begins playfully as the speaker turns to Doris and invites her to follow him, the vocal line (and its harmony a third below) cut loose from the bass line's moorings. But in m. 17, as the poem speaks of the "stillen Grund," the music becomes calmly intimate once more, just as at the beginning of the song. The cadence on C echoes the one that came at the corresponding point in the first strophe. The renewed quiet intimacy of the strophe's second half is charmingly broken in mm. 24–26 by the little sixteenth-note figures that depict the breeze's secret beckoning to Doris. Haller's phrase is "Und winket," but Bach, calling special attention to it, not only repeats it but gives it at first in its more common short form "und winkt," so that the repetition, "und winket," also becomes an opportunity for elaboration. The passage, we notice, begins with a downward jump from F to C and ends with an upward one. As at the halfway point in the strophe, the final cadence, with its descending sixths, is similar to that of the opening strophe.

The two opening strophes thus form a sort of unit, dominated by a gentle intimacy of tone increasingly broken by little signs of life or playfulness embodied in Bach's use of the high C-F figure.

The third strophe, however, is quite different—which surprises us because there is no marked change in tone in the opening lines of the poem's third stanza. The night and the leafiness of the surrounding trees are invoked once again. But Bach has his eye on that word "Träume" at the end of the second line: this time the night and the trees are said to lead us into gracious, charming dreams. Therefore we begin in B-flat, the subdominant, with a sustained bass and gently lulling eighth-note figures in the voice and the keyboard's right hand, ending in a graceful downward curve to the keyword "Träume." In the next phrase (mm. 34–36), which contains an allusion to the little turn at the beginning of m. 18, the poem tells us that in these dreams the spirit or soul rocks itself—into a sort of sleep-like trance, presumably.

But at just this point the music bursts out *forte*, with yet another leap upward from C to high F! The poem is elaborating upon the trancelike self-enclosure produced by the dreams brought on by the night. Indeed, it is stressing the ever more narrowed space into which the soul's wandering thoughts are being compressed. But the music has about it a positive air of triumph: exultation has replaced the earlier dreaminess. This seems very strange indeed until we recall such early songs of Bach's as "Der Zufriedne" ("Entfernt von Gram und Sorgen"), in which otherworldly withdrawal was treated joyously and robustly. The idea that we must lose ourselves in order to find ourselves, must indeed die to the world in order to live, is of course an important article of traditional Christian belief—one thinks of the Eliot of *Four Quartets*—and one that has often been applied as well to human love.

The triumphant outburst at m. 36 is followed by an assertive descending phrase in sixths ("in angenehm") that is immediately echoed *piano* ("verengte Schranken"), thus giving us, in a nutshell, both sides of the paradox: the intense pleasure of the self-enclosure depicted in the poem, and also its great distance from what we ordinarily think of as the world. Immediately, however, the bass line enters, once again *forte*, with a little springing figure that sets off another joyous C-to-F leap in the melodic line and takes us into the headlong descent into the final cadence.

Here is Bach's setting of the poem's next three stanzas, embracing the climax mentioned earlier:

 The beginning of the fourth stanza, we recall, is the point at which Bach (presumably) has substituted "Ach, Doris!" for Haller's "Sprich Doris!"—thus creating, as we said earlier, a lover's plea instead of a demand. Therefore the first bars are soulful, the voice answered by the repeated accompaniment figure in mm. 43-44. We descend to the expected G-minor cadence. And when the vocal line starts in again, on high E-flat, our ears are ready for a more elaborate variation on the initial G-minor plaint. But instead of descending, as we expect, from the pickup G and B-flat to F-sharp and A, the keyboard's left hand moves to F and A-flat, carrying us suddenly into the lush and comforting flat side of the tonal spectrum, appropriate to the tender impulse of gentle sorrows spoken of in the text. Not until the word "Schmerzen" does the harmony turn back toward D/G minor, the sharpest pain being felt (paradoxically) on "süsser," as the vocal line's C-sharp rubs against the E-flat in the bass.

 The second half of the strophe begins with a four-bar sequence that seems becalmed, almost static, the earlier pain suddenly nowhere to be felt—again Bach has his eye on the last word in the line: "gelinder." But the verb "Rollt" at the beginning of the following line instantly changes all that: we feel the imagined motion of Doris's blood in the eighth-note phrases exchanged between vocal line and bass line. Similarly, the word "schwellt" in the stanza's final line carries the melody upward stepwise before it finally settles into the G-minor cadence in mm. 64-65.

At this point Bach does something we could certainly not have predicted from the text, and something that we do not ordinarily encounter in a song of this period: he changes tempo. This makes the piece seem suddenly like a sort of miniature cantata. More than that, we also change key (though without a change in signature) and general mood. Suddenly we are in a fast, triumphant E-flat, with arpeggiated melody and bass line that suggest trumpet calls. Why?

This is of course the point at which the debated word "staunst" enters; certainly Bach does not seem to be taking it in the sense of *rêver!* In fact, he seems to be attending rather to "es regt sich deine Tugend": at the mention of Doris's suddenly aroused sense of virtue and modesty, we immediately enter into her sensibility (rather than that of the speaker)—or, one might perhaps say, we experience his sudden identification with her momentary flare-up. The arpeggiated phrases suggest a sort of call to arms. But then, just as suddenly, pleading phrases that remind us of the preceding strophe appear, *piano* though still at the new and faster tempo, and we seem to be back in his mind, regretting, even as he understands and perhaps even admires, her self-righteous withdrawal from him—for it does seem to be that.

The second half of the strophe begins *forte*, with the vocal line launching out boldly on its own. But though the line is assertive and positive, the harmony is, once again, minor. And if we look at the poetry, we can see why: "Dein Blut wallt vom vermischtem Triebe," Doris's withdrawal from him is caused by her mixed emotions. This is upsetting—hence the minor—because her sense of outraged virtue is driving her from him. But on the other hand, her emotions are mixed: that is, they are not entirely negative. The stanza concludes: "Dein strenge Ruhm verwirft die Liebe, / Allein sein Herz verwirft sie nicht." What was formerly spoken of as her virtue, her "Tugend," has now been slightly reduced to her "strenge Ruhm," her (perhaps excessively or even absurdly?) strict concern for her reputation, her good name. Her heart, which could not so easily be separated from her "Tugend," responds differently. Thus in m. 80 the harmony moves back to E-flat, and now it is the speaker who sounds triumphant, pushing forward in his self-assurance as the bass line rises steadily through mm. 81–84. He has managed, with some effort to be sure, to make a kind of reassuring sense of her response to him.

But his confidence immediately collapses as we return, in the next strophe, to the original slow tempo, a minor key, and soft dynamics. The pleading phrases take us back to the strophe before the E-flat outburst, not only melodically but also in the layout of the accompaniment—note the similarity of m. 88 to mm. 54–56. If only, he wishes, just a shadow of that sensual delight that two hearts can discover together might touch Doris—then, he tells her, she would demand back from fate hours her heart has so idly wasted. The harmonies that lead to the cadence on G at the halfway point in the strophe (m. 95) bespeak his weakness and lack of conviction—the Neapolitan at m. 94 has a cloying sweetness about it. Though the next lines ("Du fordertest von dem Geschick," etc.) are delivered *forte* and make a show of forcefulness, the E-flat/E dissonance at the end of m. 98 gives him away. The final bars, ending with a descent in sixths that takes us back to the first two strophes, are wholly submissive.

But the submissiveness does not last. Here is Bach's setting of the poem's final two stanzas:

Even before the last bar of the preceding section is completed, the bass line, soon joined a sixth above by the keyboard's right hand, begins a downward rush of eighth notes, *forte*. In a firm D minor, with the bass rising determinedly in thirds, the speaker announces: "Mein Feuer brennt nicht nur auf Blättern." It is this line that is rendered puzzling by the omission of the preceding ten stanzas of the poem. Those stanzas, as was suggested in Chapter Ten, are extremely elaborate in a specifically literary way; so by this point in the poem we have a strong suspicion that the speaker is a poetic lover—and indeed, as we saw, that "Doris" may be his creation rather than a real girl. But our puzzlement soon vanishes as, his tone softening with the conciliatory, pliant phrases of mm. 109-110, he declares that it is not his intention to deify her, to put her on a pedestal after the manner of traditional poetic lovers. No, he tells her, growing increasingly quiet and lyrical, it is her very humanness that draws him to her.

The second half of the strophe begins with pleading, coaxing phrases reminiscent of mm. 43ff. as he tells Doris, modestly, that another lover could more learnedly and eloquently lament the (apparent) futility of his suit to her, that—as the phrases fall in pitch and their rhythm grows more broken—he is unable to say much. And then, as the dynamic level descends still further, from *piano* to *pianissimo*, he says that only his heart—but at that he suddenly takes courage and repeats the words "mein Herz" *forte*—feels more (than any of those more eloquent lovers could possibly feel for her). It is interesting, and characteristic of the closeness and fineness with which Bach is following the suggestions of the poem's language, that those last words, "empfindet mehr," are once again sung *piano*, creating a sudden sense of awed intimacy.

The setting of the final stanza begins with a stirring upward arpeggio in the vocal line that is answered two bars later in the bass. The speaker is asking Doris why she glances fearfully to and fro, and one might have here expected more of Bach's searching inwardness. But no: the speaker is clearly taking charge, and he now has his own "call to arms," reminiscent of those connected with Doris's aroused sense of virtue earlier (mm. 66ff.). It is interesting that here, just as at the beginning of the previous strophe, the bass line rises in thirds—and to the same notes. But now we are in B-flat rather than D minor, and so we hear both difference and similarity. Why does she cast her eyes down?—he asks further; and the music suddenly sounds like the triumphant moment in an operatic recitative, complete with the traditional upward-turning question formula at the sentence's end. He grows more urgent as he reassures her that no strange (and potentially hostile) witness is near, and we note that Bach slightly alters the poem: "Es ist kein fremder Zeuge nah," writes Haller; but Bach adds a breathless, excited "kein Zeug' ist nah."

Bach also has the singer repeat "Mein Kind" at the beginning of the poem's next line. The lulling effect is increased by the shift to *piano* and by the generally slower melodic movement. But then suddenly—"kann ich dich nicht erweichen?"—the speaker once again seizes control, addressing Doris loudly and insistently.

This through-composed song, with its finely gauged mix of drama, humor, poignancy, and suspense, seems to me a triumph, a real milestone for C.P.E. Bach as a composer of songs. As we have seen, Bach complained about the inevitable limitations of the strophic song in several of his prefaces; yet about 95 percent of the songs he actually wrote are strophic songs. As we have also seen, however, he was experimenting, though infrequently, with non-strophic songs right from the beginning of his career as a song composer. He did not have to choose Giseke's poem "Die Küsse," which demanded a non-strophic setting because of its peculiar form, nor did he have to compose such non-strophic settings as those of "Phyllis" and "Auf den Geburtstag eines Freundes." Moreover, he made a point of revisiting Haller's "Doris" just so he could give it a non-strophic setting. And surely the peculiar way in which he grouped the settings of the Cramer psalms into extended semidramatic episodes was yet another attempt to escape the limitations of strophic form. Finally, there were his secular cantatas, which we mentioned in passing earlier but which now become of pressing importance.

II

The first of these cantatas, to Wieland's poem "Der Frühling," was composed in about 1760 and published in that year, along with two works not by Bach, in *Drey verschiedene Versuche eines einfachen Gesanges für den Hexameter*. In the early 1770s Bach rearranged it for tenor voice, strings, and continuo, providing a more elaborate introduction and dropping the key a whole tone; this version was published in 1990 by the English firm King's Music. In 1765 he composed the delightful, and comparatively well-known, *Phillis und Thirsis*, a conventional pastoral dialogue for either one or two voices (it is not clear), accompanied by two flutes and continuo. References to this work usually say that the author of the poem is unknown, or avoid the question altogether. But the *Unterhaltungen* reviewer clearly stated that "die Poesie ist von dem seel. Schlegel," which would mean Johann Elias Schlegel, who died at the age of 30 in 1749, and the poem may be found, just as Bach set it, in the Copenhagen edition of J. E. Schlegel's works, edited by his brother Johann Heinrich—who is not to be confused with his other brother, Johann Adolph, father of the two Romantic Schlegels, August Wilhelm and

Friedrich.¹ Finally, there is "Selma," to a poem by Voss, which was, like "Der Frühling," given both a setting for voice and keyboard, which appeared in Voss's *Musen-Almanach* for 1776, and an orchestral one, in this case for two flutes, strings, and continuo, which still exists only in manuscript. As in the case of "Der Frühling," here too the instrumental setting has a more elaborate introduction (and also a concluding violin flourish).

The point about these pieces is that they are all "number" cantatas, in which there is a neat separation between the section of music that sets one section of the poem and those that set others, and in which each section is itself a more or less self-contained form. The reason that mention of these earlier cantatas becomes relevant at this point is that during the period we are here concerned with, probably in about 1774, Bach wrote a quite different cantata. None of the others had been published in one of his song collections, but this one was. In fact, the full title of his 1789 posthumous collection, which I have been referring to as *Neue Lieder-Melodien*, ran as follows: *Neue Lieder-Melodien nebst eine Kantate zum Singen beym Klavier componirt von Karl Philipp Emanuel Bach.* That is, Bach not only published this new cantata along with his songs; he also took pains to inform the public that this collection contained a cantata as well as songs. And to top it off, he placed it last, after 21 songs, and in the collection's table of contents he denominated it as "Die Grazien. Eine Kantate."

One quick glance at this remarkable work suffices to make clear why Bach should have gone to such trouble to set it off sharply to the attention of his public. In one of the letters that Voss sent from Hamburg to J. M. Miller "und den Bund" back in Göttingen, written April 4, 1774, he tells of a conversation he and Bach had "von der musikalischen Poesie": "He is not at all satisfied with cantatas of the usual sort, because the emotions do not flow into one another sufficiently" (Suchalla, *Briefe und Dokumente*, p. 382). This seems to me a clear expression of Bach's dissatisfaction with the sort of "number" cantatas he and others had been writing, and also of his desire to try something different. Also, this was probably just shortly before he composed "Die Grazien." We have seen how completely he made "the emotions . . . flow into one another" in his second setting of the Haller poem. Indeed, his desire to accomplish this aim is the only reasonable justification for his returning to a poem he had already set. Though the second Haller setting was probably written a little after "Die Grazien," in 1775 or 1776, he may well have had the ideas for the two pieces in his mind at the same time. Besides, the chronology for these compositions is not perfectly definite. At any rate, the music of "Die Grazien," a piece about 50 bars longer than "An Doris," follows the suggestions of the verse even more closely and flexibly than that of "An Doris."

Moreover, "Die Grazien" is an even more complex poem. Its author is Heinrich Wilhelm von Gerstenberg, whom we encountered in Chapter Eleven, in connection with the puzzling circumstances under which Bach's Cramer settings came to be composed. Gerstenberg had burst upon the literary scene in 1759, with his first collection of poems, *Tändeleyen*. It was Lessing who introduced him, *Tändeleyen*, and specifically "Die Grazien" to the public, in the thirty-second of his *Literaturbriefe*, which appeared on April 12. Herculaneum had recently been excavated, and Lessing prefaced his printing of the whole of "Die Grazien" with the false claim that it was a German translation of a Greek poem discovered in the ruins, one of the lost Ἐρωτοπαίγνια (i.e., *Love Games*) of the 2nd century A.D. Athenian poet Alciphron. After citing the poem, Lessing of course confessed the ruse, and twitted his readers on their supposed snobbish preference for anything and everything Greek:

> Well, what do you have to say to that? Oh yes, you're simply enchanted: "What a delightful little fantasy! Never has a poet more prettily exalted his maiden! Nothing could be finer! O the Greeks! the Greeks!" Return from your enchanted state—I have been deceiving you. The scholar in Naples has made no discovery; Alciphron has written no Ἐρωτοπαίγνια; what you have read is not translated from the Greek; "Die Grazien" is an original work by a German.²

Gerstenberg was born in 1737 at Tondern (now Tønder, in Denmark), the son of an officer serving under the Danes. He attended school at Husum, in Schleswig-Holstein, and at 14 moved on to the Gymnasium at Altona, just outside of Hamburg. In May 1757, he entered the University of Jena to study law, but he seems to have devoted most of his time and attention to literature and the other arts. He joined a "Deutsche Gesellschaft," modeled on the one founded by Gottsched at Leipzig, and there he made the acquaintance of Jakob Friedrich Schmidt, a theologian teaching at Jena. Schmidt encouraged Gerstenberg in his literary ambitions, and persuaded him to send some of his poems to Gellert. He also sent the manuscript of *Tändeleyen* to Gleim, who was so pleased with the work that he helped to get it published. Then came Lessing's boost, and Gerstenberg was on his way.

It is not clear exactly how he and Bach got acquainted. In his 1931 book on Bach's chamber music, Ernst Fritz Schmid writes: "Gerstenberg had been friendly with Bach since the latter's Berlin days, and he renewed the friendship in Hamburg."[3] But Schmid gives no details and cites no evidence. From the letters collected in Suchalla's *Briefe und Dokumente*, however, it is clear that while Bach and Gerstenberg did not meet before the early 1770s, they had indeed been in some sort of contact before Bach left Berlin for Hamburg—perhaps through Friedrich Nicolai, of whom more later.

Bach enters the surviving correspondence of Gerstenberg and his friends in late 1766, less than two years before the publication of his tragedy *Ugolino* would make Gerstenberg famous. He had long since left the law for a military career, and had taken part in the Russian campaign of 1762. In 1766 he was a cavalry officer—Bach's letters address him as "Hochwohlgeborener, höchstgeehrtester Herr Rittmeister"—stationed at Copenhagen. Copenhagen was of course the seat of an active musical and poetic community with close ties to Hamburg. J. A. Scheibe, whom we have met as the editor of *Der critische Musikus* and who had known Bach since he was a boy, was Kapellmeister to the Danish court; and, as we know, both Klopstock and Cramer were also still attached to the court—though Klopstock would leave for Hamburg in 1770 and Cramer for Lübeck the following year. It may well have been from them or from other Copenhagen friends that Bach first got wind of Gerstenberg.

In any case, on September 22, 1766, the poet Matthias Claudius wrote his (and Gerstenberg's) friend Gottfried Friedrich Ernst Schönborn and asked about Bach's progress with a promised setting of a Gerstenberg poem based on Samuel Richardson's novel *Clarissa*, just then very popular in Germany (*Briefe und Dokumente*, pp. 88-89). Like Gerstenberg and Claudius, Schönborn, a man of letters who had opted for a career in the diplomatic service, was about a decade older than the founding members of the "Göttinger Hainbund." But he too would become closely involved with Voss and the other members, and would eventually contribute to the volumes of the *Musen-Almanach*.

We do not know how long the project involving the *Clarissa* poem had been under discussion between Bach and Gerstenberg. This is the first we hear of it, and the earliest surviving letters between Bach and Gerstenberg date from 1772. But in the letters that pass amongst Gerstenberg, Claudius, and Schönborn in the years 1767-1772 we hear quite a bit more about it. On November 4, 1768, after Bach has got settled in Hamburg, Claudius, who is now also in Hamburg and has been to see Bach, reports to Gerstenberg that the composer sends regards but has simply not had time to get down to work on the *Clarissa* poem (pp. 166-167). A couple of months later, in January or February, Claudius writes, with an irritation that will steadily grow more intense, that Bach is never at home to him or else keeps him waiting, and he has thus not been able to find out anything about the *Clarissa* setting: "Give me 10 commissions—but nothing involving Bach!" (pp. 174-175). But a year later, sometime in February 1770, Claudius was able to tell his friend: "Bach will compose the *Clarissa* and have it printed himself" (pp. 196-197). It appears, however, that Bach never did get around to setting Gerstenberg's *Clarissa* poem—though a reference to an unidentified aria in a letter Claudius wrote to Schönborn on July 27, 1770, leads Suchalla to leave open the possibility "that Bach actually did set Gerstenberg's *Clarissa* to music, but that the composition has simply disappeared" (p. 203).

In fact, we do not even know which Gerstenberg poem on *Clarissa* Bach was considering setting to music. Volume II of Gerstenberg's *Vermischte Schriften*, in the edition published at Altona in 1815-1816, contains a 64-line lyric poem, in unrhymed trimeter quatrains, entitled simply "Clarissa" (pp. 255-258). That Suchalla thinks this is the poem referred to in the letters is clear not only from the fact that he gives it that title but also from the fact that he cites its first line-and-a-half ("Die Sonne, hinter Nebeln, / Der Nacht") in an explanatory note to Claudius's letter to Schönborn of September 22, 1766 (*Briefe und Dokumente*, p. 89).

But Gerstenberg also wrote what his biographer, Albert Malte Wagner, calls a tragic cantata entitled "Clarissa im Sarge" or "Clarissa Harlowe im Sarge." Since "Clarissa im Sarge" is the title used by both Heinrich Miesner in *Philipp Emanuel Bach in Hamburg* (p. 40) and by Schmid in *Carl Philipp Emanuel Bach und seine Kammermusik* (p. 73), it is clear that they thought this was the work Bach was considering.

Which of these poems Bach had in mind is now, perhaps, undecidable. Both are elaborated versions of Richardson's endlessly protracted account of Clarissa's death. The lyric imagines her ascending to heaven in the company of her "Schutzgeist," her every step illumined by the glow of the morning sun. On the other hand, the cantata, which is apparently unfinished and which Gerstenberg never allowed to be published, is dismissed by Wagner as "an extremely tasteless half-dialogue, half-monologue versification of Richardson's *Clarissa*." There is a long conversation about the heroine, following her death, between Lovelace and Belford. The tone is heavily moralistic, and (as Wagner nicely puts it) "of the magic that surrounds the person of the seducer in the original, not a trace remains in Gerstenberg."[4] It is not difficult to imagine how a man of Bach's religious sensibility might have found neither of these works to his taste.

A more interesting bond between Bach and Gerstenberg than that created by the abortive *Clarissa* project was their shared interest in the relations between *Ton* and *Wort*. It was this interest that led Gerstenberg, probably sometime in 1767, to create the fusion of Bach's C-minor Fantasy and Hamlet's "To be or not to be" soliloquy that was mentioned in passing in Chapter Eleven.

The setting of the *Hamlet* soliloquy to Bach's fantasy is first mentioned in a letter that Gerstenberg wrote on December 5, 1767, to his friend Friedrich Nicolai, the Berlin writer, editor, and bookseller best known as the editor of the influential *Allgemeine deutsche Bibliothek*. After referring to himself as "a dedicated lover of music" who is, nonetheless, "not very knowledgeable about it," and praising Bach as a composer of songs, Gerstenberg writes:

> Because I'm chattering on so about music with you today, I must tell you that I've been making some musical experiments, of which I'd like to know your opinion. I assume, first of all, that music without words communicates only general [*allgemeine*] ideas, which receive their full definition [*Bestimmung*] through added words; second I make an experiment with instrumental solos in which the expression is clear and vivid. On these principles I have taken some Bach keyboard pieces, which were not at all made to be sung, and have underlaid them with text. Klopstock and everyone tells me that these would be the most expressive songs that one could hear. Under the Fantasy in the sixth sonata that he composed for application of his *Versuch*, for example, I put Hamlet's soliloquy in which he fantasizes about life and death, and which determines a kind of middle position for his agitated soul.
>
> [P. 127]

Gerstenberg's reason for setting Hamlet's soliloquy to Bach's fantasy was thus that he wanted to demonstrate the truth of his conviction that purely instrumental music necessarily has a less precise emotional or expressive or cognitive content than texted music—"that music without words communicates only general ideas"—but that this content can be made more precise, can in effect be fully realized, if the appropriate text is combined with the music. It is most important to note that Gerstenberg does not think he is in any way changing the content of the music or imposing a new content upon it by adding words: he is merely bringing to full clarity what was there in the music all the time, though vaguely and generally so. As we saw in Chapter One, this curious notion was memorably expressed by Krause in *Von der musikalischen Poesie*, was held by many 19th-century music historians, and still continues to play a part in musical aesthetics.

In another letter to Nicolai, written April 27, 1768, Gerstenberg responded to his friend's request to see the *Hamlet* fantasy by sending it to him—with, however, the caveat that Nicolai was not to share it with potentially unfriendly critics:

> You ask that I send you my text for the Bach Fantasy? I'll risk it. But I warn you in advance that I am sharing this text only with friends who treat my amusements with indulgence, not with strict critics. Here it is.
>
> [P. 144]

A few months later, probably at the end of July or beginning of August 1768, Claudius tells Gerstenberg that he was been to see Bach, "who calls your Fantasy a very nice piece, but says that because of the church music with which he is now occupied, he has still not had time to compose it" (p. 160). Suchalla, in his note to this passage, takes the "Fantasy" in question to be the C-minor Keyboard Fantasy with the *Hamlet* text. But why should Bach have felt it necessary to apologize for not having had time "to compose it"? That piece he had, after all, already composed! I think, rather, that Claudius is referring to whichever *Clarissa* poem of Gerstenberg's Bach had contracted to set to music. As the account given above of the two poems makes clear, either one could justly be spoken of as a "Fantasy."

In fact we do not have any clear evidence as to what Bach thought of Gerstenberg's tinkering with his C-minor Fantasy. As Eugene Helm has pointed out, "We do know that Bach made no special objection" to what Gerstenberg had done, and that "there is no record . . . of his having objected to the experiment's publication in 1787," in C. F. Cramer's magazine *Flora*.[5] It is, however, interesting to examine Bach's reactions to the general theoretical position on which Gerstenberg based his experiment, his conviction that the content of instrumental music is necessarily imprecise, yet can be made precise by the addition of a verbal text.

Gerstenberg expressed his ideas at far greater length in a letter he probably sent to Bach in September 1773. The letter itself is lost, but a very long, much corrected draft survives, as does Bach's reply, dated October 21.

After an account of a Copenhagen performance of some "Passions-Musik" by Bach—probably the *Passions-Cantate* (H. 776)—Gerstenberg tells of a recent evening on which he had heard some concertos based on biblical passages by Johann Nikolaus Tischer (1706/7-1774), a minor composer and the town organist of Schmalkalden, in Thuringia. The sophisticated Copenhagen audience laughed at the old-fashioned literal-mindedness that led poor Tischer to attach a biblical phrase to each concerto—like a tag around a dog's neck, as Stravinsky once unkindly said of Wagner's *Leitmotive*. But Gerstenberg did not laugh:

> I believed, however, that there was still something to be said in his defense. That he had performed that which he set out to perform without any particular genius—that I understood. On the other hand, any attempt to give the clavier expression and meaning, even if it fails, seems to me honorable.
>
> [P. 322]

Obviously, we can see here the same interest in clarifying (and thus heightening) the expressiveness of instrumental music that lay behind the *Hamlet* experiment. But Gerstenberg had another reason for not joining in the laughter: he liked the idea of instrumental pieces being concerned with the emotions embodied in the biblical passages because he felt strongly "that feelings of this sort are precisely those, of all feelings, to which music is most appropriate" (p. 322).

Gerstenberg knew, he tells Bach, that he had not persuaded anybody of the value of Tischer's efforts. "But I also believe," he continued, "that arguments of this kind only have value when they can be supported by brilliantly chosen examples" (p. 323). He then picks as examples some psalms, and shows how a composer—if he were a genius—could make very effective sonatas out of them:

> What a beautiful *Adagio mesto* could be made of that place in the sixth Psalm: "all the night I make my bed to swim; I water my couch with my tears. Mine eye is consumed because of grief; it waxeth old because of all mine enemies." And what an expressive *Andante patetico* would follow: "Depart from me, all ye workers of iniquity; for the Lord hath heard the voice of my weeping," etc. And how well would the sonata close with this *Allegro:* "Let all mine enemies be ashamed and sore vexed; let them return and be ashamed suddenly."
>
> [P. 323]

Gerstenberg continues this hypothetical fitting of music to biblical text through several more psalms. If indeed he was instrumental in getting Bach to set the Cramer psalms, this may have been part of the effort. More likely, he knew that Bach was already working on the settings, and would have the psalms very much in mind. Or of course it may have been pure coincidence. The point is that Gerstenberg is here imagining the creation of the same moment-to-moment, point-by-point correspondence between *Ton* and *Wort* (or *Ton* and *Empfindung*) that we saw Bach creating in the through-composed "An Doris" and will see him creating, on a larger scale, in his setting of Gerstenberg's "Die Grazien."

What Gerstenberg is doing here is also, quite obviously, related to what he was doing in setting Hamlet's soliloquy to Bach's C-minor Fantasy. Yet in that case he was bringing an already composed verbal utterance into combination with an already composed piece of music in order to render the expressive content of the music clearer, more precise. Here he is suggesting that an already composed verbal utterance can help to create—can, as it were, function as the skeleton or framework for—a piece of instrumental music without itself being part of the resulting work. It would seem as though Gerstenberg's thinking on these matters had shifted somewhat.

That this is indeed the case becomes clear as we read further. He finally sums up his paean of praise for the sort of music that might be created from biblical materials after this fashion by exclaiming: "The very idea of such music! And what precision of expression, which is otherwise so difficult to achieve" (p. 324)! Precision of expression, of course, is exactly what Gerstenberg had earlier denied could be attained by instrumental music: "music without words communicates only general ideas." Now, however, he seems almost possessed by the need to believe that this is not the case:

> Of course it is just this precision, this fully determined significance of a musical piece, whose possibility is always most doubted. But why impossible? So far as I, a layman who collects mere *facta* [things that have been done] and from them concludes *facienda* [things that can or ought to be done] understand these difficulties, it must be entirely possible to carry over the clearly defined [*marquirten*] feelings contained in the text into the composition in an equally clearly defined form. Indeed, the feelings that a certain admirable man so often evokes in me with his clavier sonatas are already such clearly defined feelings, even without the help of a text.
>
> [P. 324]

The fevered questions, the short breathless clauses, the skimpy punctuation—all testify to Gerstenberg's state of high excitement. This is a man who has discovered something of the first importance for himself—is, perhaps, discovering it even as he writes to the composer he so much admires.

What he has discovered is that his earlier, rather austere and legalistic theory about untexted music necessarily being imprecise and general in its content simply will not stand up to his own experience of the best music he knows—namely the keyboard music of that "certain admirable man," who is, of course, C.P.E. Bach himself. One almost wants to applaud from the wings. For Gerstenberg has done what all too few aestheticians, and perhaps musical aestheticians especially, have done: he has faced, head-on, the conflict between his theory and his aesthetic experience. While it may seem, when one is at some distance from the experience of great music, that because instrumental music is non-referential it must therefore be less precise in its content than verbal discourse, no sensitive listener can keep hold of that conviction when he is actually experiencing great music.

That this passage, and the discovery it embodies, were of great importance to Gerstenberg is shown by the fact that later in his draft he rewrites it, more soberly and decisively:

> So far as I, a layman who collects *facta* and from them concludes *facienda*, understand the matter, it must not be impossible to express these clearly defined feelings in clavier compositions because what I find expressed in the compositions of a certain admirable man, whom I will not name, really evokes in me very clearly defined feelings.
>
> [P. 325]

The change from the ardent "it must be entirely possible" to the cautious double negative "it must not be impossible" says it all.

Bach's reply is the second of his surviving letters to Gerstenberg. The first, dated May 15, 1772, is brief and formal yet extremely cordial. Most of it is taken up with Bach's apology for not having written earlier owing to illness. The one written in response to the fair copy that resulted from Gerstenberg's draft is downright affectionate. After a chatty opening paragraph in which he again apologizes for not having replied sooner—"letter-writing is not my strongest side"—Bach wittily gets down to business with a pun on "Tischer" and "Tischler" (carpenter or cabinetmaker): "Now to old Tischer! I mean the composer of that name—otherwise it might seem as though I wanted to order my coffin" (p. 336).

Bach agrees that Tischer has little genius, but genially adds that the poor man cannot help that. He then directly addresses the substance of Gerstenberg's letter:

> Your Honor is completely correct when you say that feelings of devotion are those that are most suitable to music, and I, as a keyboard player, venture to maintain that on our instrument one can indeed say a great deal in a good performance. I am not speaking here of mere ear tickling, but demand that the heart must be set in motion. Such a keyboard player, especially if he has a genius rich in emotion, can do a great deal. However, words always remain words, and the human voice always has an advantage over us. As long as we can have what is nearer [*das Nähere*], we need not search pointlessly for what is farther away [*das Weitere*].
>
> [Pp. 336-337]

Intending to duplicate the course of Gerstenberg's argument, Bach first agrees with one of the two reasons that Gerstenberg did not join in the laughter at Tischer's expense: the feelings associated with religious devotion are indeed exactly those best suited to music. But of course this was the less important of Gerstenberg's two reasons. He was more interested in Tischer's pieces because he saw them as attempts to give (as he put it) expression and significance to keyboard music. As we know from his own experiment with Bach's C-minor Fantasy, Gerstenberg had doubts about the expressivity and the actual content of instrumental music, and he here seems to be welcoming Tischer's similar experiments as offering proof that one can justify—if that is not too strong a word—the existence and usefulness of music that lacks the clear referential meaning given by an accompanying text or even by an epigraph or motto of the sort apparently provided by Tischer. As we saw, Gerstenberg (more or less) manages to convince himself, by the end of his draft, that untexted music can indeed communicate feelings as "marquirt," as sharply particularized, as those communicated by texted music.

Bach, however, has no such doubts. He has found and perfected his voice as a composer of songs by working with religious texts—first Gellert, and just now Cramer. Moreover, his job is to oversee the musical life of Hamburg's five great churches. Therefore the superiority of religious feelings to any other sort of feelings as the subject matter for music is naturally very much in his mind. And thus he adds, almost casually and in far less technical language than that used by Gerstenberg, that yes, a keyboard player giving a good performance can indeed say a good deal.

This leads him on to a favorite theme: he feels impelled, quite unnecessarily it would seem, to make it clear to Gerstenberg that he is not speaking of mere ear-tickling but rather of music that moves the heart—as, indeed, he demands all music must do. Gerstenberg would doubtless agree. But what interests Gerstenberg is the degree of emotional precision or definiteness instrumental music can attain, whereas Bach seems rather to be interested in emotional intensity. The two are certainly not opposed, but they are different. Such a keyboard player, Bach adds, if he has a richly emotional talent, can do a great deal—again the pointed casualness of language.

The last two sentences of this passage are undoubtedly the most difficult: "As long as we can have what is nearer, we need not search pointlessly for what is farther away." To follow his statement about the keyboard player who can do a great deal without benefit of words, providing that he has the emotional gifts, with the remark that words, meanwhile or nevertheless, always remain (merely?) words seems to be dismissing language, viewed in abstraction, as a means of emotional communication. But what is the relation of this dismissal to the second half of the sentence? Is the "and" that joins the sentence's two halves really closer in feeling to "but"? The human voice remains always preferable to us—compared, apparently, with mere words viewed in abstraction from the act of singing or speech, words as seen on the page. But how strong a contrast is intended between the words and the voice? They are obviously being to some degree contrasted since the latter is said to be preferable to the former, but how strong is the contrast? Are both nonetheless being viewed together over against the wordless performance of the keyboard player, who speaks directly to the heart? Or are words, when embodied in song, just as effective a means of emotional communication? Only after all these questions are answered can we determine exactly what "das Nähere" and "das Weitere" refer to.

Perhaps it will help to read on a bit further and then come back to these troubling sentences. In his draft, Gerstenberg objected to the mockery with which Tischer's music had been received, pointing out that if affixing biblical mottos to the pieces helped to make clear their expressive content for the listener, this was all to the good: "Whoever would rather have fixed than vacillating ideas is grateful to the musician for any aid whose employment itself constitutes an enlargement of his pleasure" (p. 324). Gerstenberg then used the illustrative analogy of a painter who writes captions below his pictures:

> So far as I am concerned, the painter might even place a motto under a praying David if he really believed himself capable of accurately expressing the content of the motto through his painting. To me it would always be preferable to perceive in the painting *what* David prays, not *that* he prays.
>
> [P. 324]

Yet, as Gerstenberg has already affirmed, music—even music without words—can in fact make clear its precise meaning without such captions: "Good for Music, if she has so great an advantage over her sister, Painting" (p. 324).

To return to Bach's reply. Immediately after the two puzzling sentences examined above, Bach writes as follows, once again echoing the words of Gerstenberg's draft:

> One should of course not join in the hollow mockery of the honest painter who wrote under his painted bird: "This is a bird"—especially if one says nothing about a sickness that might have provided the opportunity for certain experiments. Indeed, I remember many years ago, when I had my *Sanguineus and Cholericus* printed, that I was not wholly unaffected when a good friend said about me in jest certain things that he did not mean maliciously but that did not please me. How weak we are!
>
> [P. 337]

In agreeing with Gerstenberg that one should not join in mocking poor Tischer, Bach picks up the analogy of the painter who captions his painting, and adds that one should especially not make fun of such explicit labeling if one has engaged in it oneself. Humorously referring to the state of mind that led him to do so as a sickness, Bach then disarmingly tells of making his own early "experiment," a trio sonata composed in 1749 and published two years later.

This work was Bach's only piece that had a written program. It depicted a conversation between a sanguine man and a melancholy one—not a choleric one, as he misremembered when he wrote about it to Gerstenberg, over 20 years later. It was published as the first of a pair of trio sonatas, and Bach thus began his preface to it:

> In the first Trio one has attempted, so far as is possible, to express through instruments something for which one otherwise might more conveniently use a singing voice and words. It presents a conversation between a *Sanguineus* and a *Melancholicus,* who, in the whole first and almost until the end of the second movement, quarrel with each other and each try to win the other over to his side. Until at the end of the second movement they reach an agreement: the *Melancholicus* gives up, and accepts the other's predominance.[6]

The preface concludes with an extraordinarily detailed list of the various stages of the conversation, cued by letters to the music that follows.

So Bach is letting Gerstenberg know that he has been all through this business of attempting to give a piece of music the conceptual precision of verbal discourse. And what is more, he has been criticized for it. In his essay on Gerstenberg's experiment with the C-minor Fantasy, Eugene Helm suggests that the friend who hurt Bach's feelings by making fun of his experiment was Dr. Charles Burney, and Helm cites the following passage from Burney's 1789 *General History of Music*:

> That truly great musician, Emanuel Bach, some years ago, attempted, in a duet [i.e., for two violins and continuo], to carry on a disputation between two persons of different principles; but with all his powers of invention, melody, and modulation, the opinions of the disputants remained as obscure and unintelligible, as the warbling of larks and linnets.[7]

This seems a perfectly convincing solution.

Helm and others have discussed this dialogue between Bach and Gerstenberg in relation to a justly famous report of a conversation with Bach that Claudius gave to Gerstenberg in a letter written around July 5, 1768. That morning, a Tuesday, Claudius had gone to Bach's house and had found him "in negligé"—in his nightgown. He asked Bach's pardon, but was not to be put off (one sees, quite clearly, why Bach would soon not be at home to Claudius!). He said he had just come from Copenhagen, and Bach politely inquired about the state of music there. Claudius replied that it was only so-so ("sehr mässig"), the composers most in favor being Johann Schobert and Bach's brother Johann Christian, whom C. P. E. Bach disapproved of for many reasons. Schobert, Bach replied, "is a sensible man, but behind his and my brother's recent music there is nothing." "Yet it falls nicely into the ear," offered Claudius, to which Bach responded: "It falls in and fills it, but leaves the heart empty. That is my judgment of the new music, the new comic music, which, as Galuppi has told me, is also fashionable in Italy." The opposition of heart and ear reminds us directly of the opposition, in his reply to Gerstenberg, of moving the heart and merely tickling the ear. And a moment later, after Claudius had remarked that this sort of superficial, fashionable music might be compared to real music "as wit to pathos," Bach reinforced the opposition: "Not a bad comparison. Music has higher aims: it should not just fill the ear, but should set the heart in motion" (p. 149).

At this point something very interesting happens. Having got this far in eliciting Bach's views on the nature of musical communication, Claudius determines to press harder. "Here I looked him directly in the face," he proudly tells Gerstenberg. Either because Gerstenberg had asked him to do so, or simply because his interests were running along the same lines as Gerstenberg's, Claudius inquires about the works of Bach's that, leaving aside the trio sonata mentioned earlier, come closest to being program music, 24 short "character pieces" that he had composed for solo keyboard between the years of 1754 and 1757. Like those composed in the 1930s and 1940s by Virgil Thomson, each of these pieces attempted to sum up one of Bach's friends. When Claudius asks if Bach has done anything more in this line, the composer dismisses them as merely occasional and now forgotten. When Claudius presses on, insisting that such pieces represent a new departure or approach ("ein neuer Weg"), Bach replies: "But only a small one; you can get nearer to it if you add words" (p. 149). Bach's use of the word "näher," and the metaphor of nearness and distance that it brings into play, also reminds us of his reply to Gerstenberg's draft, and puts us in a position to return to those two troublesome sentences.

Bach, we recall, has just affirmed that a keyboard player, providing he has sufficient emotional gifts, can "do a great deal" so far as the communication of feelings goes. The intensification in emphasis from Bach's earlier expression, "say a great deal," seems to me significant: he is now insisting a little more firmly that words are not necessary for the precision and/or intensity of emotional content that both he and Gerstenberg have in mind. And the fact that Bach then goes on to mention words explicitly suggests that he has shifted somewhat, from thinking mainly in terms of emotional intensity to thinking more in terms of what Gerstenberg means by precision.

The first half of the first of our two problem sentences—"However, words always remain words"—does, then, seem to be dismissive of language in the abstract, as perhaps in Tischer's mottos or in the carefully laid-out stages of the argument between the sanguine and the melancholy man in Bach's preface to his trio sonata. Words thus artificially affixed to music—from the outside, as it were—remain simply words, as the words of Bach's preface did for Dr. Burney. But words sung by a human voice are something else again. It is, however, most interesting that in the second half of that sentence Bach does not quite put it that way since he does not explicitly mention words again: "and the human voice always has an advantage over us." This would seem to imply that even though that voice will in fact be singing words, it is the living humanity of the voice and of its present and visible owner, rather than the sense of the words it is singing, that makes song an effective medium of emotional communication. Is it more effective than the playing of the keyboard player? I do not think we can say; intentionally or unintentionally, Bach leaves it open.

What then do "das Nähere" and "das Weitere" refer to? Bach tells Claudius that providing words for his character pieces—turning them into songs, in effect—would have been a nearer, more natural, and therefore more sensible, perhaps also less foolishly pretentious, way of embodying the very particularized sort of meaning that he meant to embody. The pieces would then have been clearer, more effective portraits of his friends. So Bach does not intend to say that words are simply to be dismissed. It all depends on the sort of piece you are composing. Just so, when speaking more generally, of more types of music, in the reply to Gerstenberg, Bach says that the nearer way would be to write either an instrumental piece or a vocal piece, depending (one assumes) on your particular aim. The farther way—the unnecessary, awkward, less effective long way around—would be to bring music and words together not in the natural and customary ways but unnaturally, as Gerstenberg has done by underlaying Bach's fantasy with Hamlet's soliloquy and as he proposes doing by writing purely instrumental sonatas based on the psalms—rather than the songs that Bach is even then composing to Cramer's psalms.

That Gerstenberg came to see the artificiality of his *Hamlet* experiment is suggested by the fact that when it was published in C. F. Cramer's magazine, the fantasy had two texts: Hamlet's soliloquy and a grotesquely melodramatic version, probably also by Gerstenberg, of the death of Socrates. This Socrates, in marked contrast to Plato's humble and elegant wise man, is a ranting heaven-stormer. Unlike the Socrates of *Phaedo* 118a, he does not die reminding Crito that they owe a cock to Asclepius but rather in mid-rant:

> "O Rufer durch die Nacht!
> O Todesrufer!
> Sey mir gesegnet,
> Ich folge dir. . . ."

It seems highly unlikely that Gerstenberg would have printed two such different texts with the same piece of music had he still retained his old faith that the one right text would bring out, clarify, make explicit the meaning only imperfectly expressed by the music itself. The experiment seems to have become something closer to a parlor game.

It is important to see that the relation between Gerstenberg and Bach in this discussion is not that of high-powered aesthetic theorist to plainspoken untheoretical man of sense. What I earlier called the pointed casualness of Bach's language is, I think, just that: pointed, studied, intentional. In speaking of these matters more informally and less technically than Gerstenberg does, Bach is not showing his lack of experience and sophistication as a thinker about aesthetic questions; he is, rather, implicitly insisting on the primacy of aesthetic experience—of a commonsense realization that when "das Nähere" is within one's reach there is no need to go questing after "das Weitere"–which was, as we saw, what led Gerstenberg to change his mind, in mid-draft, about the degree of emotional precision attainable in untexted music. Bach, after all, had made his own aesthetic experiments, and had learned from them.

In view of their shared theoretical interests, it is, then, scarcely surprising that Gerstenberg too, like Bach, should have considered how the "strophic problem" might be solved. In his letter to Nicolai of December 5, 1767, the same letter in which he told about his experiment with Bach's C-minor Fantasy, Gerstenberg, almost as an afterthought, makes the following interesting request of Nicolai in a postscript:

> Could you not persuade Herr Bach to compose some songs with variations, so that the simple melody would always be sung, with the variations adjusted to suit the contents of the various strophes? . . . It goes without saying that this could be done only with charming or happy songs; the character of dignity, simplicity, etc. would exclude the possibility of such alterations.

[P. 128]

The suggestion here is plainly that the voice will continue to sing the same melody throughout while the keyboard player plays the successive variations as accompaniment. Thus the song would change—in accordance, presumably, with the changes in the verbal text—while yet remaining the same; the result would be the desired variety within unity.

These shared interests are also reflected in a comment that Gerstenberg makes, in another of his letters to Nicolai, in reference to the experiment with the Bach fantasy and Hamlet's soliloquy. This is the letter of April 27, 1768, with which Gerstenberg enclosed his setting of the *Hamlet* soliloquy. Immediately after agreeing to send it, Gerstenberg writes out the opening bar of the vocal part and then lists, in order, the principal phrases of the text, marking each one with a Roman numeral to indicate in what system of the musical score it appears. Plainly, he is attempting to give Nicolai an idea of the precise pace at which the emotions of the text change in the musical setting. "How shall I make comprehensible to you without notes the underlaying of my text?" he asks; this schematic listing is his answer.

Unfortunately, Suchalla omits this portion of the letter from *Briefe und Dokumente*.[8] If he had included it, the point of the remarks that Gerstenberg makes directly afterward would have been clearer. Gerstenberg writes:

> Incidentally, I cannot help observing that this Fantasy of Bach's rather clearly refutes Herr Lessing's opinion in No. 27 of *Hamburgische Dramaturgie,* that the composer cannot change, in the same piece, from one passion to its opposite, e.g., from peace to violence, or from tenderness to terror. Herr Lessing seems not to have taken into account the transitions, of which we have many remarkable examples in this Fantasy and, I believe, in many other sonatas by Bach.
>
> [P. 145]

This concern with music's ability to make seamless transitions from one emotion to another quite different one reminds us of Bach's dissatisfaction, expressed six years later in his conversation with Voss, with cantatas in which the various emotions did not flow into one another, in which (that is) the transitions from one to another were not sufficiently smooth and seamless: "He is not at all satisfied with cantatas of the usual sort, because the emotions do not flow into one another sufficiently" (p. 382). Interestingly enough, the letter in which Voss told Miller (and the "Bund") of this conversation was written on April 4, 1774, just shortly before Bach began putting his ideas into practice by making a cantata out of Gerstenberg's "Die Grazien."

The passage usually cited from No. 27 of Lessing's *Hamburgische Dramaturgie* to explain Gerstenberg's remark is the assertion that "in a symphony just one passion must predominate, and each separate movement must sound forth and seek to awaken in us that same passion, though with various modifications, according to the degree of its strength and vivacity or its varied intermixtures with other, related passions."[9] This comes near the end of a detailed examination of the incidental music provided by Johann Friedrich Agricola—at Lessing's instigation, as it happens—for Voltaire's very popular tragedy *Sémiramis,* which was just then (August 1767) playing in Hamburg.[10]

Lessing, understandably, praises Agricola's music highly, not only for its immediate effect in the theater but also for what its success demonstrates about the possibilities of combining music with spoken drama. Like Gerstenberg, Lessing questions music's ability to communicate ideas and feelings as specific and determinate as those communicated by language. Most difficult of all for untexted music to communicate would be those quicksilver shifts from one emotion to its virtual opposite—as Gerstenberg puts it—which are so common in drama, especially tragic drama:

> Now we melt with sadness and then suddenly we are to rage. How? Why? Against whom? Against him for whom our soul had only pity? Or against someone else? Music is unable to determine any of this; it leaves us in uncertainty and confusion; we

feel, without perceiving the correct consequence of our feelings; we feel as though in a dream; and all these confused feelings are more wearying than delightful.

[V, 127]

Poetry, however, can supply all these lacks, and so music combined with poetry has great advantages over absolute or untexted music:

Poetry, on the other hand, never allows us to lose the thread of our feelings; we know not only what we are to feel but also why we are to feel it; and this "why" alone is enough to make the sudden transitions not only tolerable but even pleasant. Indeed this explanation of the sudden transitions is one of the greatest advantages that music gains from its union with poetry; perhaps it is the greatest.

[V, 127]

Yet since Lessing is speaking of incidental music for the theater, he is not speaking of a true union of music and poetry, such as we get in opera, oratorio, cantata, and song. He is, rather, trying to determine the proper construction and appropriate emotional content of what he terms a symphony and what we should call an overture or entr'acte. Like Gerstenberg, he has not finally settled for himself his questions about the relative efficacy of music and poetry as conveyors of emotional or cognitive meaning, and so his essay contains statements that do not exactly square with one another.

As we saw, immediately after declaring that "in a symphony just one passion must predominate," Lessing can back down a little and allow certain "modifications"—so long as the basic "passion" retains its identity. And while he can sternly announce that "a symphony that expresses different, mutually contradictory passions in its different movements is a musical monstrosity," he can praise Agricola's "Anfangssymphonie" (or overture) in the following terms: "the violence of the first movement flows [*zerfliesst*] into the grief of the second, which in the third rises to a kind of solemn dignity" (V, 128). The word "zerfliesst" not only suggests that Lessing did have some conception of music's ability to make emotional transitions, but literally recalls Bach's word "zerfliessen," used in his complaint to Voss about contemporary cantatas.

Therefore Gerstenberg is somewhat oversimplifying Lessing's essay when he says Lessing has given no thought to transitions and offers his own *Hamlet* experiment, along with various Bach sonatas, as flat refutations of Lessing's point of view. But the important point is that the whole matter of transitions, and music's ability to make them effectively, was very much on Gerstenberg's mind and also on Bach's when they came to collaborate in producing the cantata "Die Grazien." In his excellent essay "Gerstenberg und die Musik seiner Zeit," Bernhard Engelke speculated that Bach's setting "Die Grazien" was "a compensation for the rejected 'Clarissa.'"[11] Whatever the truth of the matter, we do know that on April 21, 1774, only a little over two weeks after Bach's remark to Voss, Bach wrote to Gerstenberg, thanking him for subscribing to the Cramer Psalms and enclosing two copies of the work. Immediately following his opening salutation, Bach wrote:

From time to time you obligate a man who has never yet been able to free himself, even a little, from so great a debt, and who has no other merit than that he has the luck to please you with his middling musical talent. As much as I realize this, just so much do I wish, and think myself soon to be in a position, Your Honor, to show myself a grateful votary of your generous assistance. *Basta! Tempus docturus!* [Enough! Time will teach us!]

[Pp. 394–395]

Suchalla suggests (p. 397) that Bach is here suggesting that he would like to set one of Gerstenberg's poetic texts.

I would venture a step further. The mixture of courtliness and playfulness—"Basta! Tempus docturus"—in Bach's tone suggests that he is already at work on a Gerstenberg setting and will soon be able to show his full indebtedness to the poet by producing it as a finished piece. At any rate, on July 13 Reichardt wrote Carl Gottlieb Bock that he had heard "Die Grazien" performed "a few days earlier," and that he found it "an excellent composition" (p. 416). The following day Bach sent a copy of the work to Gerstenberg, modestly remarking:

> Your beautiful Graces have fallen into bad hands. They appear herewith. They will probably bring suit against me before their worthy author. Take my side and do not judge too strictly. At least my intentions were good.
>
> [P. 422]

III

It is, at long last, time to have a look at Gerstenberg's poem. Like many of the *Tändeleyen*, it is a mélange of poetry and prose. As we shall see, the text found in the three printed editions of *Tändeleyen* is somewhat different from the one that appears in Bach's *Neue Lieder-Melodien*; it is the latter that I give here:

> Als an einem Frühlingsabende sich die drey Grazien neben einem Walde in acidalischen Quellen belustigten, verlohr sich plötzlich Aglaja, die schönste der Grazien. Wie erschracken die Töchter der Anmuth, als sie Aglajen vermissten! wie liefen sie durch die Bäume und suchten und riefen!
>
> > So ängstlich bebt auf Cremonesersaiten
> > Der zärtste Silberton.
> > Aglaja!—rief der Silberton.
> > Aglaja!—half der Nachhall sanft verbreiten.
> > Umsonst, Aglaja war entflohn.
> > "Ach, Pan schlich längst ihr nach! der Frevler hat sie schon!
> > "Ach, Acidalia! blick her von deinem Thron!
> > "Soll sie nach langen Ewigkeiten
> > "Nur itzt nicht länger uns begleiten?
> > "Zwo Grazien sind aller Welt zum Hohn,
> > "Und ach! die Dritte hat er schon!"—
> > So klagten sie. Umsonst! Aglaja war entflohn.
>
> Nun schlichen sie an den Büschen herum, und schlugen leise an die Blätter, und flohen nach jedem Schlage furchstam zurück.
>
> > Denn stellten sie sich gleich, den Räuber auszuspähen,
> > So zitterten sie doch für Furcht, ihn nur zu sehen.
>
> Endlich kamen sie an ein Rosengebüsche, das meine Chloe versteckte—und mich. Chloe sass vor mir, ich hinter Chloen.
>
> Itzt bog ich schlau an ihrem Hals mich langsam über,
>   Und stahl ihr schnell ein Küsschen ab;

> Itzt bog sie sie unvermerkt den Hals zu mir herüber,
> Und jedes nahm den Kuss auf halben Weg sich ab,
> Den jedes nahm und jedes gab.
>
> In diesem Spiele überraschten uns die Grazien, und sie lachten laut, da sie uns küssen sahen, und hüpften fröhlich zu uns herbey. Da ist Aglaja!—riefen sie. Die Schleicherin!—Du küssest, da man unruhig herumirrt, und dich nicht finden kann?—Und itzt liefen sie mit meiner Chloe davon.
>
> Was! rief ich, lose Räuberinnen!
> Wie sollte sie Aglaja seyn?
> Ihr irrt euch sehr, ihr Huldgöttinnen!
> Für Grazien ist das nicht fein!
> Gebt Chloen mir zurück! Betrogne, sie ist mein!
>
> Doch die Grazien hörten mich nicht, und liefen mit meiner Chloe davon. Zornig wollte ich ihnen nacheilen, als plötzlich Aglaja hinter einer Buche hervortrat, und mir winkte, und freundlich lächelnd also zu mir sprach:
>
> Warum willst du zu Chloen eilen?
> Beglückter Sterblicher, Aglaja liebet dich.
> Küss itzt einmal statt Chloen mich;
> Wünsch nicht dein Mädchen zu ereilen:
> Ich, eine Göttinn, liebe dich.
>
> Schüchtern sah ich die Huldgöttinn an.
>
> Auf ihren Wangen sprach Entzücken,
> Und Jugend und Gefühl aus den verschämten Blicken.
>
> Gefährliche Reizungen!—Aber mit dreister Hand ergriff ich die Huldgöttinn, führte sie zu ihren Schwestern, und sprach: Hier ist Aglaja, ihr Grazien.—
>
> O Chloe, meine Lust, mein Glück! —
> Gebt meine Chloe mir zurück!
> Ist dies Aglajens Mund und Blick?
> Da! nehmt die Huldgöttinn zurück.

In the chapter of the second volume of his critical biography of Gerstenberg that is devoted to Gerstenberg's early lyric poetry, Albert Malte Wagner has some very interesting things to say about *Tändeleyen*. The so-called Anacreontic mode, Wagner argues, has been wrongly dismissed, by most literary historians, as an alien excrescence, of French or English or classical origin, that therefore has little or nothing to do with the development of German literature. "Literary history," he writes, "has dealt with the German Anacreontic poets as with their French counterparts: it has thrown them all in the same pot" (II, 206). Wagner, on the other hand, wants to show that there are important distinctions to be made amongst the Anacreontic poets, and that they played a most significant role in the formation of classic German lyric poetry: "The road to Goethe was still a long one, but it led through the Anacreontics, not through Klopstock" (II, 216). While the Anacreontic poets of the 18th century have usually been pictured as turning away from real life to create imagined worlds, Wagner sees Gerstenberg's Anacreontic poetry, as we find it in *Tändeleyen*, quite differently:

> Gerstenberg's lyrics are not just more "social" poetry, but are poetry of the individual, behind which stands not some poeticized Phyllis but rather a living, beloved being.

That he is still not capable of expressing all the oscillations of his soul through the oscillation of his verse is the fate of a transitional artist.

[II, 207]

The subtitle of Wagner's second volume, it is worth noting, is *Gerstenberg als Typus der Übergangszeit*. That Gerstenberg is a transitional figure writing in a time of transition is responsible both for the necessity of the elegant surface characteristic of Anacreontic poetry and also for Gerstenberg's need to disrupt that surface by mixing poetry and prose:

It is perfectly clear: in this transitional period, the man who feels more strongly must stand back, behind the surface imprinted on the form, because he must fight for the expression of his stronger feeling. But the resulting "formlessness" is more productive, because more indicative of the future, than the slick polish of universally beloved poets, which depends merely upon clever imitation.

[II, 212]

All of this seems to me very well said and very relevant to "Die Grazien." We can perhaps agree with Alfred Anger's objection that Wagner lays too much stress on the "experiential character" of *Tändeleyen*, the intrusions into the pastoral fantasy world of what we must consider as Gerstenberg's own literal life experience.[12] Yet we must nonetheless agree that, in "Die Grazien" at least, Gerstenberg is doing something quite novel and individual with pastoral convention—something that may remind readers of English poetry of the intricacies of Marvell.

The scene is set in even, unremarkable prose—the joke of course being that it is not just anyone taking an outing this particular spring evening, but the three Graces. Moreover, as they were disporting themselves in the Acidalian spring, Aglaia, the most beautiful of them, has suddenly and mysteriously vanished. Gerstenberg probably got the Acidalian spring from Virgil. Near the end of the first book of the *Aeneid*, after Venus has instructed Cupid to impersonate Ascanius and sit on Dido's lap, filling her with thoughts of love for Aeneas, Venus is referred to as Cupid's Acidalian mother (I, 720). The fourth- or fifth-century commentator Servius tells us that the reference is to a spring in Boeotia where Venus and the Graces, who attended her, used to bathe.[13]

Aglaia might also have come from Virgil, for she is mentioned in passing in the *Catalepton* (IX, 60). But Gerstenberg probably had also met her in Hesiod's *Theogony*, where she is mentioned, along with Euphrosyne and Thalia, as one of the three Graces (907-909) and also as the wife of Hephaestus (945-946). Aglaia seems to have been one of the many minor Greek divinities who began life as an abstract noun, for the Greek word ἀγλαίη, spelled just like the Grace's name, is used by Homer to mean beauty or radiance—that of Penelope, for example (*Odyssey*, XVIII, 180). The fact that Hesiod makes Aglaia the wife of Hephaestus enforces the Graces' connection to Venus/Aphrodite. For usually, as in the *Odyssey* (VIII, 266-269), Hephaestus's wife is Aphrodite, while in the *Iliad* (XVIII, 382-383) he is married to Charis, another minor deity allegorized from a common noun, in this case χάρις, the word for grace in both classical and New Testament Greek. It is sometimes suggested that Aglaia was not only the most beautiful but also the first and only Grace, as their story and cult gradually evolved out of their close association with Aphrodite.[14]

We are thus dealing with beings of no mean status, and further comedy is added by having these "Töchter der Anmuth" recoiling in horror, running about, and shouting for the lost Aglaia. In the poetic section that follows, these Graces turn out to be rather modern young ladies after all: their anxiety is given voice in the "zärtste Silberton" of "Cremonesersaiten." It was not until the early sixteenth century, when the Amati family established the tradition, that Cremona became known for the production of fine violins. (When he cited "Die Grazien" in *Literaturbrief* No. 32, Lessing disguised the poem's modernity by changing "Cremonesersaiten" to "Manethuser Saiten," an allusion I have been unable to trace.) The silvery tone with which the Graces' anxiety is expressed, together with the gentleness of its echo, gives the whole scene a delicacy that reconciles the seeming contradiction of the Graces behaving in this apparently ungraceful manner.

There is more gentle comedy in the fact that they seem perturbed not only by Aglaia's abduction but also by the unseemly appearance that will be created by there being, for the moment at least, only two Graces rather than the three the world is accustomed to and has come to expect: "Zwo Grazien sind aller Welt zum Hohn." So they continue to search, beating the bushes (quite literally) and keeping their eyes peeled for Pan while scaring themselves in the process.

Then the poem suddenly changes direction as the speaker tells us that they have come upon the spot where he and his Chloe have hidden themselves. We are amused by his naive overexplicitness: "Chloe sass vor mir, ich hinter Chloen." And we are charmed, as he breaks into verse, by the almost childlike quality of the kissing game. But this idyll is immediately cut short by the loud laughter and dancing about of the Graces. And the poem changes direction once again as they address Chloe as Aglaia, chide her for getting involved in a kissing game when they are searching for her, and—much to the speaker's amazement and distress—spirit her away.

This is, obviously, the turning point of "Die Grazien." The meaning of the poem as a whole will depend on how we interpret the fact that Aglaia and Chloe have, to our surprise as well as the narrator's, turned out to be the same person, while the narrator himself, formerly detached and objective, has suddenly become intimately involved in the action.

In his startled helplessness, he calls out to them, insisting that this is not their Aglaia but his Chloe that they have taken away, and (in his earlier naive mode) that such behavior is "nicht fein" for Graces. But of course they pay no attention. He is about to rush angrily after them when suddenly Aglaia—and it is significant that he now calls her Aglaia, not Chloe—steps out from behind a beech tree and, smiling invitingly, addresses him. Why should he hurry after Chloe when Aglaia loves him? Kiss me instead of her, she entreats him; don't rush off after your "Mädchen"—and the mildly contemptuous tone of the word is enforced by the majesty of the next line: "Ich, eine Göttinn, liebe dich."

Awestruck, he gazes at her shyly—who, after all, would not want to be loved by a goddess? But after taking due note of her charms (in poetry), he suddenly (in prose) turns on them: "Gefährliche Reizungen!" And with that he firmly leads her back to her sisters and orders them to take her with them.

But do they do so? The concluding quatrain leaves us, I think, in doubt:

> O Chloe, meine Lust, mein Glück!—
> Gebt meine Chloe mir zurück!
> Ist dies Aglajens Mund und Blick?
> Da! nehmt die Huldgöttinn zurück.

The first two lines are clear enough, yet another plea to the Graces to return his Chloe to him. But what about the third line? What does "dies" refer to? It seems that Aglaia is still present to him, her mouth and her look close enough for him to refer to them collectively as "dies." And the final line, which repeats his earlier demand that her sisters reclaim her, makes it clear that, somehow or other, they have not yet done so. Finally, why does he ask, in a tone of wonderment, if this mouth and this look belong to Aglaia?

Plainly, this is a poem about the joys, frustrations, and dangers of idealizing one's lover into a goddess. The opening portions give us a speaker who describes, with a certain degree of wit and detachment, a scene that seems to have nothing whatever to do with him: the loss of Aglaia by her sisters. And yet, as we noticed, he has brought these mythic beings of ancient Greece into the modern present: it is "Cremonersaiten" that produce the "zärtste Silberton" of their lament. This seems merely a pleasing and idle fantasy, only half-conscious and thus vague in its outlines, that the girl beside him, his Chloe, is a goddess—one of the three Graces, say.

But then suddenly the fantasy becomes reality. The two other Graces materialize by the rosebush where he is snuggling with Chloe, and, without anger or surprise—as though this has happened before—they chide Chloe/Aglaia for having run away, and take her with them. In fact, they seem relieved that it is only a mortal, and not Pan, who has got her this time.

He of course bewails the loss of his loved one. But just as he is about to run after her and the others, she suddenly appears nearby and—this is the point—he too now sees her not as Chloe but as Aglaia, thus acknowledging, albeit unwillingly and probably unconsciously, that the fantasy that turned her into Aglaia was of his own making. Yet he also sees the dangers of idealizing a beloved human being into a goddess—"Gefährliche Reizungen!"—and sternly rejects her advances, handing her back to her sisters while continuing to lament the loss of Chloe and ask that the goddesses return her to him.

But of course this is impossible, for Chloe and Aglaia really are, so far as he is concerned, the same person: to have one is to have the other; to lose one is to lose the other. And so the two are fused in the poem's concluding quatrain, leaving him in complete confusion. What—to return to the final question asked above—is the tone of "Ist dies Aglajens Mund und Blick?" Is he pleased or repelled by the idea that the girl beside him is (or may be) the goddess? No clear answer is possible, I think. The closest one can come is the term I used above: wonderment. He is, quite understandably, amazed at how all this has worked out, at the way in which his fantasy has taken over the real scene. But he does not know either how to feel about it or what to do about it.

This seems to me a masterly achievement. From its graceful beginning, "Die Grazien" gradually gathers a rather eerie power and compulsive attraction for the reader. The important, though often unacknowledged, role that myths, whether Grecian or of some other variety, play in the ways in which we construct our inner and outer lives is clearly and tellingly dramatized—though, certainly, no clear "solution" or "answers" emerge at the end. For better or worse, idealization and mythmaking seem an undeniable and inalienable part of human lovemaking. We are left with a problem rather than a solution.

What sort of setting did C. P. E. Bach contrive for this remarkably complex and interesting poem? And how successful was he? In his essay "Gerstenberg und die Musik seiner Zeit," Bernhard Engelke referred to it as "in part, a very successful composition" (p. 434), and made a few perceptive remarks about its beginning and end, but he said nothing about the remainder of the work. I know of no other critic who has ventured even that much commentary on "Die Grazien." This is, as we shall see, a pity.

Just as Gerstenberg alternates prose and poetry, so Bach moves between recitative and song—but with other stages in between, half-recitative and half-song. This is, after all, Bach's greatest experiment in creating a cantata in which emotional states would not simply be juxtaposed, in set pieces, but in which smooth, gradual transitions between them would be created in more perfect accordance with the text. One mark of his success, I think, is the extreme difficulty one experiences in breaking up "Die Grazien" into manageable sections for analysis. One cannot, however, simply print out a piece of music 206 bars long; so here, for a start, is Bach's setting of Gerstenberg's poem down to the narrator's description of the Graces' search for Aglaia and their discovery of him and Chloe:

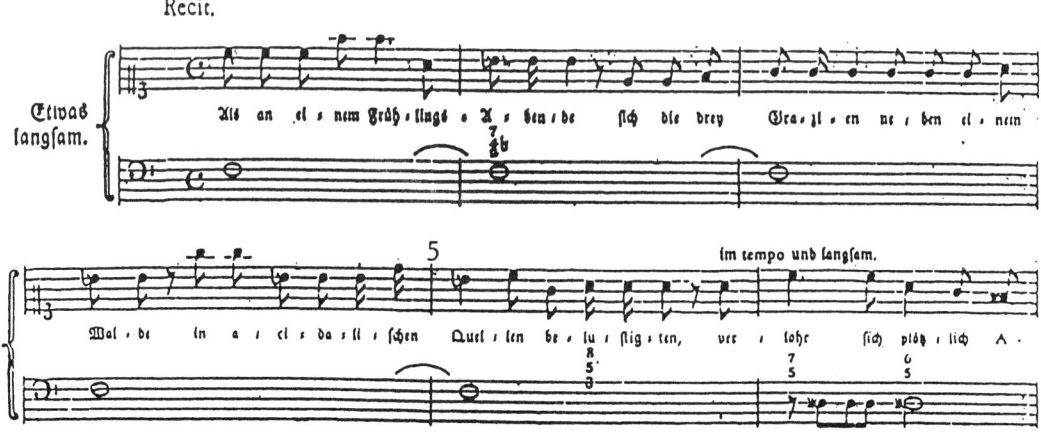

A Cantata for Gerstenberg 367

The tone of the opening, with its sustained chords in the keyboard instrument, is just as calm and peaceful as we should expect. The fact that the bass remains on F when the harmony changes in m. 2 adds to the sense of continuity and even stasis. But then, at the word "verlohr," as the harmony changes to a diminished seventh, the rhythm of the accompaniment takes on a little urgency (m. 6). And a couple of bars later, the pounding of the accompanying eighth notes becomes steady as the bass line descends. Notice the repeated 7-6 changes in the harmony (mm. 8-9): as Bach's notation of the two small notes at the beginning of m. 8 makes clear, the intent is to produce a series of yearning sighs in the accompaniment's upper voice, perfectly capturing the two remaining Graces' gradually dawning sadness at Aglaia's absence, which they have just noticed. The formality and decisiveness of the cadence to B minor in m. 10, which contrasts nicely with the tentativeness of the preceding bars, signals their full awareness of their sister's disappearance—and of what it might mean. The melodic line in the next few bars, moving mostly by step, is finely pathetic, and the harmony, especially the change from the B-minor chord in m. 10 to the bleak C-minor of m. 11—a change admired by Engelke—shows the Graces' increasing uneasiness.

In m. 14 it sounds as though we are about to embark on an F-major cadence, rather like the one we will have a bit later, at mm. 25-26. But instead of beginning to move through the familiar cadential pattern, the harmony slips into a dark F minor as the bass line moves down a whole step. At this point the Graces' lament for their lost sister ceases to be a recitative and takes on something of the character of song. The accompaniment picks up the eighth-note urgency heard earlier and produces a series of rather graceful, harmonically shifting figures that enter into a sort of duet with the vocal line (mm. 17-20). Notice the delicacy with which the echo of their lament is captured, *pianissimo*, in m. 19.

The G-minor cadence in m. 21 pulls us back into recitative, as the sisters are forced to admit the futility of their efforts. But these efforts are renewed at m. 26—with an increased urgency that is mirrored in the increased complexity of the accompaniment and its relation to the vocal line. Finally, at m. 31, the two voices, vocal line and accompaniment, merge, and in mm. 34-35 the keyboard, in octaves, joins the vocal line in a series of assertively striding upward-moving figures that dramatize their (slightly comic) embarrassment at suddenly being only two Graces, rather than the three the world expects. A reprise (m. 37) of the restlessly moving figures heard earlier takes us back into recitative and the desperate, rather melodramatic declarations of the following three bars.

Here is how Bach sets the narrator's description of the search, the discovery, and the little kissing game that he and Chloe were playing when the Graces came upon them:

As we noted above, the Graces' discovery of Chloe and the narrator marks the first big turning point in Gerstenberg's poem. We should therefore expect it to be vividly registered by a change in the music. Yet no such change occurs. The straight, rather impersonal and wholly conventional narration of the recitative continues just as it began, through the words "Endlich kamen sie an ein Rosengebüsche, das meine Chloe versteckte—und mich," and even beyond. In fact, far from registering shock or surprise, the music turns to a warm E-flat major on the word "Rosengebüsche," before moving back through B minor to the A minor of the recitative's opening bars. The only real change—and it is a small one—comes at bar 47, with the sudden off-beat diminished chord, and it registers not the surprise of Chloe and the narrator at being caught but the rising fear of the Graces as they pursue their search.

The change in the music comes rather at the point where the narrator begins describing the kissing game—and it is quite different from the change we expected. Just as Gerstenberg breaks into verse at this point, so Bach breaks into song. The little C-major melody looks at first glance sprightly and cheerful enough, and the accompaniment, by remaining silent on the first eighth note of each measure, and then furnishing a series of off-beats, suggests the rhythm of a dance. But the tempo marking is "Etwas langsam," giving the song an air of sweet recollection and throwing the unheard strong beat of each measure into sharp relief. The effect reminds one of those recollected marches and dance tunes that float through Ives's *Three Places in New England*. There are other finely imagined details: the neat contrary motion of upper and lower voices in bars 59-60 catches the playful reciprocity of the game, and the turn toward F major that begins at bar 65 heightens the tenderness of the memory.

But the song comes to an abrupt end with the suspension and resolution, on a fermata, at bars 74-75, as the vocal line reiterates "jedes nahm und jedes gab." The same words are reiterated yet again, after the fermata, *forte* and in the earlier triumphant F major: it is as though the narrator, even after having broken off his song of remembrance, wants, still more firmly, to insist on the reality of the experience that inspired it. The section closes with a delightful eight-bar keyboard postlude, in which the two hands, alternately soft and loud, imitate each other and then finally join together, in one final dramatization of the kissing game. A downward rush of thirty-second notes takes us, at last, into the shocked reaction to the Graces' intrusion that we expected so much earlier.

Here then is what Bach makes of that reaction:

We have, once again, what looks like rather conventional recitative. But we note the inexorable stepwise descent of the bass line as the narrator tells of the Graces' closing in on him and Chloe. Their search ends, in bar 89, with a whispered reprise, in octaves, of the little motif that represented that search earlier (m. 39), bringing us back to A minor and the Graces' triumphant cry: "Da ist Aglaja!" As they chide her for amusing herself in this way while they were searching for her, the bass line (mm. 92-93) marches back up with the same purposiveness with which it had earlier marched down. There is a fermata, and then the narrator breaks out with his anguished plaint: "und itzt liefen sie mit meiner Chloe davon."

As he turns to address the Graces directly, Gerstenberg once again shifts into verse and Bach follows him by shifting into song—or rather into three quite different songs, or fragments of song, that follow one another with bewildering speed. The meter changes abruptly to $\frac{3}{8}$ and the key to D major as the narrator begins a brisk little ballad of heroic self-assertion—ending, however, in the despairing "Was! Wie!," followed by another fermata. These words, we notice, do not appear at this point in the text. Bach has extracted them from the preceding two lines to form an anguished distillation of the narrator's plaint. Though this section of the poem reads continuously, Bach has broken it up to heighten the dramatic effect.

After the fermata, we shift tempo and meter once again, this time to a moderato $\frac{3}{4}$, a sort of slow mazurka. Plainly, the narrator is trying a new tack with the Graces. Rather than being briskly aggressive, as before, he is now decorous, formal, almost courtly—he is, after all, addressing them as "ihr Huldgöttinen." This is a tenderly persuasive lament. Each of the first two phrases is made up of a higher and a lower two-note stepwise descent, while the two latter phrases rise, as if to ask a question, with the bass in contrary motion, but then also end in a two-note stepwise descent, the familiar *empfindsam* "sigh" so common in Bach's work.

But once again the tempo and mood change, this time to a briskly urgent $\frac{2}{4}$, and this time without benefit of fermata. The narrator is now distraught, even desperate. The left-hand accompaniment is similar to that in the little song about the kissing game, but the quicker tempo and the character of the melodic line make all the difference. In phrases that mainly move stepwise, the melodic line gradually ascends, finally reaching high G as the narrator cries "Betrogne, sie ist mein!" Then, after a fermata and a slowing of the tempo, Bach once again repeats the words of the text: "gebt Chloen mir zurück, sie ist mein." But the slower tempo, the gradual descent of the melodic line, and another reprise of the "search" motive (m. 123) make it clear that the narrator has realized the futility of his plea and has utterly given up. The Graces' search for Aglaia may be ended, but so also is his for Chloe. Once again we return from song to recitative.

We have reached the next great turning point in the poem, Aglaia's surprising reappearance and her address to the narrator:

As we noted earlier in our examination of the poem, the narrator is just about to dash off angrily ("zornig") after Aglaia/Chloe and the others when she suddenly steps out from behind the beech tree. But just as Bach has, in the preceding bars, made it clear that the narrator has given up, so in this little recitative he does not make it sound in the least as though the narrator is still angry. At bar 126 we expect a cadence on G minor, but the deflection into C major, for the words "Zornig eilt ich ihnen nach," is perfectly conventional, and communicates nothing of the anger spoken of in the text. In view of this fact, it is interesting that both the three published editions of Gerstenberg's poem and the text as printed in Bach's *Neue Lieder-Melodien* read "Zornig wollte ich ihnen nacheilen." Thus, while in effect writing the narrator's anger out of his musical setting of the poem, Bach has, paradoxically, altered Gerstenberg's text to make the statement about the narrator's anger simpler and more straightforward: not only did he wish to hurry angrily after the Graces; in Bach's altered version, he actually did so! Perhaps Bach shortened the line in order to slip over it as quickly as possible. But why not simply omit mention of the anger?

At any rate, it soon becomes clear what Bach, in directing our attention away from the narrator's supposed anger, is directing it toward: as Aglaia is described waving or beckoning to the narrator ("winkte," m. 129), the vocal line recalls the beginning of the song about the kissing game (cf. m. 54). The point is that even though the narrator has just referred to her, for the first time, as Aglaia, he still sees her as Chloe. It is not, as before, that the Graces have made a mistake in thinking that Chloe was Aglaia; the two are, the narrator now unconsciously admits, one and the same—in his mind and, hence, in the world of the poem. Aglaia is his idealization of Chloe; Chloe is his Aglaia.

Yet Aglaia, in her little song, continues to treat Chloe as a being quite separate from herself: why, she asks, would he want to be with a mere "Mädchen" when "Ich, eine Göttinn, liebe dich"? The song is sung tenderly (Zärtlich"), and probably at a medium tempo. The gently descending melodic line is full of those 7-6 "sighs" that we have noticed so often before. "Aglaja liebet dich," she declares triumphantly, with an upward leap of a seventh. But then the same line is repeated, *piano*, in the minor and with dark low notes in the keyboard's left hand. Suddenly we are in C major, *forte*, as she urges the narrator to kiss her instead of Chloe, the phrase ending with a jaunty upward arpeggio in the bass. Similarly, she once again rises to a triumphant climax, ascending to high A, as she declares, with a suitably dramatic eighth-rest pause, "ich eine Göttinn liebe dich"—only to repeat "ich liebe dich" immediately, *piano* and in an intimate little turning phrase.

There thus seems something open and yet hidden, out in the daylight yet darkly mysterious, about this Aglaia and her declaration of love. And as she ends her song, we have a little keyboard postlude, graceful and seductive, filled with sinuous sixteenth-note phrases, that captures the narrator's wonderment at what he has just experienced. But in its final bars the postlude seems to spin off into space, to wander almost aimlessly into the keyboard's highest register. The clear suggestion is that the identity of Chloe and Aglaia is, after all, just a fantasy on the part of the narrator.

He therefore boldly takes matters into his own hands—though, as we saw in examining the poem, with very problematical and puzzling results. Here is Bach's setting of the poem's troubling conclusion:

Like all the preceding sections into which we have divided "Die Grazien" for purposes of analysis, this final one begins as a recitative. But unlike them, this section shifts into something closer to song after two measures. The narrator begins, neutrally and objectively, to tell us that he shyly approached Aglaia, in seeming obedience to her invitation. But the force of her beauty almost immediately pushes him into song. The first two bars (mm. 167-168) are in a slow, serene, pastoral-sounding $\frac{4}{4}$. Then we move, predictably enough, to the dominant—and suddenly the bass line begins to descend chromatically as the harmony becomes dense and tortured, capturing his inner struggle as he battles against her attraction for him. "Gefährliche Reizungen!" he exclaims, the music veering back into recitative as he regains control of himself. At first, however, the harmony is still somewhat wrenching (m. 171), but it gradually smooths out. By the approach of the F-major cadence (mm. 175-176), he seems to have mastered his feelings: we notice the firm rhythm of the vocal line, as it descends in an orderly fashion, and the decisive punctuation of the two concluding chords. "Hier ist Aglaja, ihr Grazien," he says, handing her over to her sisters, and the matter would seem to be closed. But he immediately breaks into a D-minor lament—"Etwas langsam und nachdrücklich"—for his lost Chloe. "O Chloe, meine Lust, mein Glück!" he sings, and the gracious music that immediately follows (mm. 181-183) recalls, for us as for him, that remembered happiness. But once again he pulls himself together, and sternly demands that the Graces return Chloe to him. Bach then has him repeat the words "meine Lust, Mein Glück" (mm. 185-187), but now they too sound stern and almost harsh, rather than plaintive and gently reminiscent, as they did only a few bars earlier.

We then arrive at the line we puzzled over so long in our examination of Gerstenberg's poem: "Ist dies Aglajas Mund und Blick?" The courtly, dancelike music to which Bach sets the line—not just once, we notice, but twice: the second time a whole step higher than the first—recalls the music of the narrator's first address to the Graces: "für Grazien ist das nicht fein" (mm. 110-113). The rhythm is similar, and there too we had a line that was repeated, the repetition pitched a whole step higher than the initial statement. The surprising, dramatic shift in tone suggests that the narrator, for all his firm resolution, has once again fallen under Aglaia's spell—her sisters, as we speculated earlier, having not taken her away after all.

But the tone immediately shifts once again, for the last time. "Da! Da!" shouts the narrator, his voice rising in pitch and intensity, "nehmt die Huldgöttinn zurück, nehmt die Göttinn zurück." The repetition of the final phrase, and the shortening of "Huldgöttinn" to "Göttinn," give the ending a sharper focus than it had in Gerstenberg's poem: the issue is not just this particular "Huldgöttinn"; it is the idea of having a goddess—any goddess—as a lover. The final phrase is sung in unison with keyboard octaves, to a darkly sinister phrase. The eight bars of keyboard postlude that follow, with the chromatically descending bass line, thunderous repeated chords, and far-flung right-hand arpeggios to a dotted rhythm, give the conclusion an air of high drama, an almost tragic sweep, that Bernard

Engelke saw as "a typical example of C.P.E. Bach's daemonic nature" (p. 434), and that could not have been predicted from the carefully ambiguous, rather enigmatic ending of Gerstenberg's poem.

Like the poem, this setting seems to me a very fine achievement. The consistently sharp and alert musical imagination with which Bach followed (and sometimes elaborated upon) the twists and turns of Gerstenberg's mélange of poetry and prose has created a work of considerable psychological depth and complexity. If some of Gerstenberg's playfulness is lacking—one of the few textual changes Bach requested was the substitution of the more proper "Küsschen" for the slightly vulgar "Mäulchen" in the account of the kissing game—the gain in intensity and high seriousness dictated by Bach's "daemonic nature" more than compensates. With "Die Grazien," we may say, Bach has fully realized his object of creating a cantata in which the emotions flow into one another sufficiently. It seems most fitting that this was the composition to stand last, in the place of honor, in Bach's final collection of songs.

Chapter Fourteen

The Sturm Songs

C. P. E. Bach's third and last large songwriting project was to set some of the poems of Christoph Christian Sturm, *Hauptpastor* of St. Peter's Church, Hamburg, from 1778 until his death eight years later. Bach chose 60 of Sturm's poems, most of them taken from *Lieder und Kirchengesänge*, published at Hamburg in 1780. Bach's settings appeared in two collections of 30 songs each, also published at Hamburg, in 1780 and 1781. It is worth noting that these two volumes were not published by Bach himself, as the Cramer psalms and various other works of this period had been. The publisher was Johann Henrich Herold, a friend of both Bach and Sturm who ran a book and music shop in Hamburg and who had also been the publisher of Sturm's *Lieder und Kirchengesänge*. In the preface to that volume Sturm writes:

> Lovers of melodies that are simple and yet lift the heart will perhaps be pleased to learn that Herr Kapellmeister Bach has provided a selection of these poems with melodies, which will soon appear in print.

Gudrun Busch, who cites this passage from Sturm's preface, comments: "We do not know whether Sturm himself asked Bach to set his poems to music or the idea came from Herold."[1]

What does seem clear, however, is that the three men were working closely with one another. Sturm's preface to *Lieder und Kirchengesänge* is dated March 20, 1780; the preface to the first of Bach's two collections, which (interestingly enough) is by Herold rather than by either Sturm or Bach himself, is dated the following July 4. The title pages of Bach's two collections are almost identical. At the top is the title, which reads in full: *Herrn Christoph Christian Sturms, Hauptpastors an der Hauptkirche St. Petri und Scholarchen in Hamburg, geistliche Gesänge mit Melodien zum Singen bey dem Claviere von Herrn Kapellmeister Carl Philipp Emanuel Bach, Musikdirektor in Hamburg*. Beneath the title is an elaborate engraving that shows a cloud floating over Hamburg, its five great churches clearly visible in the skyline to the lower right. The cloud, which is huge and which dominates the picture, is floating toward the right. To its right side sits the main figure, a muselike representation of the spirit of music. Crowned with a laurel wreath, she plays a small organ, surrounded by handmaidens and seraphim who sing to her playing. At the cloud's lower left, three cherubs hold a medallion, on which are inscribed, in profile, the faces of Bach and Sturm. The only difference between the two title pages is that on the earlier one the profiles are idealized while on the later they are realistically depicted. "Too bad," one reviewer of the 1780 volume had complained, "that the two heads intended to represent the poet and the composer are not better likenesses!"[2] One gets the sense that these two collections, the joint productions of Sturm, Bach, and Herold, are intended as a sort of civic celebration of or tribute to Hamburg.

Unlike his two predecessors as the subjects of major Bach song projects, Gellert and Cramer, Sturm was a close, perhaps even an intimate, friend of Bach's. Also unlike them, he was scarcely even thought of as a poet by most people. Gellert, as we saw, was a formidable poet, one of the more important figures of mid-18th-century German lyric verse. But, as we have also seen, he achieved fame late in life as a model Christian, a kind of Pietist saint, and this fact was not irrelevant to the decisive role he played in Bach's career as a composer of songs. Cramer, a close associate of Gellert and his first biographer, was certainly a lesser poet though a general all-round man of letters and, like Gellert, an admirable man. In Cramer's case, it may have been the man at least as much as the poet who attracted Bach's attention. Though often compared with Gellert in histories of German poetry, Cramer always suffers by the comparison. For example, Rudolf Haller, in *Geschichte der deutschen Lyrik vom Ausgang der Mittelalter bis zu Goethes Tod*, writes: "Even in his own special domain, that of the religious poem, Johann Andreas Cramer is surpassed by Gellert."[3] Sturm, so far as I can gather, is never even mentioned in ordinary histories of German poetry. To find him, one must go to a more specialized work, such as Eduard Emil Koch's *Geschichte des Kirchenlieds und Kirchengesangs der christlichen, insbesondere der deutschen evangelischen Kirche* (1869). And even Koch does not venture a judgment of Sturm's poetry, but merely cites the praise of another writer, J. P. Lange, for Sturm's "excellent talent for expression, his gift for freshly flowing utterance."[4]

At the highest estimate, Bach wrote between 290 and 300 compositions that we may class as songs. Taken together, the 55 Gellert songs, the 42 Cramer psalms, and the 60 Sturm songs make up a total of 157. That is, over half of his total song production was based on the work of these three poets. Yet there were better poets to be had, and Bach was a man sensitive to literature and personally in close touch with some of those better poets—Klopstock and Lessing, to cite only the most obvious examples. (He seems not to have known Hagedorn, or to have known him only slightly.) And of these better poets, Bach set precious little—though he did use a Klopstock text for one of his large choral works, *Klopstocks Morgengesang am Schöpfungsfeste*. As we have seen, Bach really found himself as a composer of songs with the Gellert collection. And though he was rather nervously conscious of not having employed the sort of musical idiom that Gellert plainly thought appropriate to his poems, Bach went out of his way, in his preface to the collection, to say that his aim was the same as Gellert's: namely, "Erbauung." In the Cramer preface, as we also saw, he went out of his way to avoid praising Cramer as a poet, praising instead the "divine content" of his versions of the psalms and noting his importance as a "theological scholar." For the two Sturm collections Bach wrote no preface at all.

The point is not merely that Bach saw his principal mission as a composer of songs, as embodied in his three large songwriting projects, to be the increasing of religious and spiritual "Erbauung"— though this is, I think, certainly true. The point is also that the three poets he chose decline in stature, from Gellert to Cramer to Sturm, and that in the former two cases, as we have seen, his choice of a poet seems to have been partially based on his admiration for the man's life and work. In this chapter we shall see that this was probably also true in the case of Sturm, who was not only the least important of the three poets but also the only one whom Bach knew really well.

I

Christoph Christian Sturm, who was born at Augsburg on January 25, 1740, came from a distinguished family. His father, Johann Jakob, was a well-known jurist, and his grandfather, Johann Christoph, was a famous mathematician and scientist whose picture graced the walls of the Royal Society, London. But Sturm's most illustrious ancestor was the educator Johannes Sturm (1507–1589), head of a school at Strasbourg and author of educational treatises, whose learning and eloquence had won him the appellation "the German Cicero."[5]

After study at the local academy, Sturm left Augsburg in 1760 to study philosophy at the University of Jena. The following year he was awarded the degree of *Magister* for a thesis that offered illustrations from medieval German history of Hobbes's views concerning natural law. At the end of 1761 Sturm moved on to study theology at the University of Halle, which ever since its founding in 1694 had been a center of Pietist and Enlightenment thought, the university of Francke, Thomasius, and Wolff. At the time of Sturm's matriculation, the theology faculty included Johann Salomo Semler and Sigmund Jakob Baumgarten. After a few months Sturm was offered a teaching position at the Paedagogium, a secondary school in Halle. He remained in Halle, teaching at the Paedagogium, until 1765, when he was offered the job of associate rector at a Gymnasium at Sorau (now Zary, in Poland). But early in 1767 he was called back to Halle, to serve as one of the preachers at the Marktkirche. The following year he married Johanne Christiane Bunning, and a year later, in 1769, he accepted a post as one of the preachers at the Church of the Holy Spirit in Magdeburg. Here he was to remain for almost nine years, a period he often later referred to as the happiest and quietest of his life. On April 26, 1778, he was appointed *Hauptpastor* of St. Peter's in Hamburg, succeeding the recently deceased Dr. Johann Christoph Friderici (or Friederici). Sturm's inauguration took place the following September 1, to music by C. P. E. Bach, who had also provided the music for Friderici's inauguration, less than three years earlier.

The reasons why Sturm's time in Hamburg, where he remained until his death, on August 26, 1786, was neither so happy nor so quiet as his time in Magdeburg are essential to an understanding of why the highly cultivated Bach chose this virtually unknown lesser poet for his last big song project. These reasons center on a fascinating character named Johan Melchior Goeze, who served as *Hauptpastor* of St. Catherine's in Hamburg from 1755 until his death, just three months before Sturm's, in 1786. More important, Goeze occupied, from 1760 until his resignation in 1770, the very powerful post of *Senior*: he was, that is, the city's representative in religious matters, in charge of Hamburg's *Ministerium*, which consisted of the *Hauptpastoren* of the five great churches, their junior clergy, and the preachers at the various minor churches and chapels of the city and its suburbs.

Goeze's name is known today principally because of a famous controversy he had with Lessing. Though Lessing lived in Hamburg for only three years, from Easter 1767 to Easter 1770, he naturally played an important role in the social and intellectual life of the city. Not only were he and Bach friends, they also moved in the same circles. The friends they had in common included Johann Georg Büsch, economist and Professor of Mathematics at the Gymnasium (Hamburg had no university); the translator and writer on music Dr. Christoph Daniel Ebeling; the poet Barthold Heinrich Brockes, who was known for his translations of Pope's *An Essay on Man* and Thomson's *Seasons*, and was also a member of the Hamburg Senate; the composer, oboist, and publisher Johann Joachim Christoph Bode; and the philosopher Herman Samuel Reimarus and his son Johann Albert, a doctor and scientist.

Taken together, these names represent what we might call the liberal or progressive element of Hamburg intellectual society. These men, and others like them, were the ones who in 1765 formed the second Patriot Society, which did much to improve the lot of the poor in Hamburg, and who exerted steady pressure for religious toleration on the conservative Lutheran orthodoxy, pressure that finally resulted in the toleration mandate of 1785.

That orthodoxy, on the other hand, was chiefly represented by Goeze. His career, which included the writing and publication of over 100 books and pamphlets, was one long battle against anyone and everyone whom he suspected of attempting to sully the purity of Lutheran dogma or of challenging Lutheranism's position as the only religion whose adherents were entitled to free exercise of public worship in Hamburg. In turn, he was widely satirized and caricatured in pamphlets and broadsides. "Der Inquisitor," "Der Papst Hammoniens" ("Hammonia" being the old Latin name for Hamburg), and "Melchior Cromwell" were only a few of the names Goeze got called.

Hermann Samuel Reimarus (1694–1768), at whose house the discussions that led to the founding of the second Patriot Society were held, was best known for two books, *Abhandlungen von den vornehmsten Wahrheiten der natürlichen Religion* (1754) and *Allgemeine Betrachtungen über die Triebe der Tiere, hauptsächlich über ihren Kunsttrieb* (1760). In both he sought for evidence in the natural world of the wisdom and goodness of God. To an ultra-orthodox theologian like Goeze, who not only saw no need for such a search but also viewed it as a dangerous temptation to stray from the true path, as laid out in the Bible and in Luther's writings, such books—and indeed the very phrase "natürliche Religion"—were as a red rag to a bull. Thus Reimarus joined the swelling ranks of Goeze's enemies.

At some point during his later years, Reimarus responded to the denunciations directed against him by Goeze and others of Hamburg's orthodox clergy. But this was not known during his lifetime. After his death, in 1768, his daughter Elise found among his effects a manuscript of some two thousand pages entitled *Apologie oder Schützschrift für die vernünftigen Verehrer Gottes*. This she passed on to Lessing, who was a close friend of hers.

Lessing left Hamburg in 1770 to become librarian of the Duke of Brunswick's library at Wolfenbüttel. He had been seeking this sort of post, which would give him a steady income and time to pursue his scholarly and theological interests in congenial circumstances, in Berlin, just before he came to Hamburg. Once ensconced at Wolfenbüttel, he began issuing books, mainly concerned with theological issues, based on the library's resources. The Reimarus manuscript fitted in perfectly with this project.

In 1774 he issued the first of the Reimarus fragments, together with an introduction stating that he had discovered it in the library and had no idea who the author might have been. This fragment, urging the toleration of deists, attracted little notice. Three years later, in 1777, Lessing published five more fragments that had a quite different effect. These pointed out inconsistencies in the Bible, discounted revelation in favor of "natural religion," and proposed calling off the missionary movement and leaving believers in non-Christian faiths to themselves.[6]

The first responses, directed against Reimarus himself, were polite enough. But Goeze soon attacked Lessing directly. Lessing was not slow to reply. The intensity and bitterness of his responses were at least partly due to personal tragedy. On December 24, 1777, his wife Eva, to whom he had been married only a little over a year, gave birth to a child that died almost immediately. Then on the following January 10, she too died. Fired by the controversy, Lessing published yet another fragment, the longest and most controversial one, in 1778. Once again Goeze responded, with three papers that bore the collective title *Lessings Schwächen*.[7] Lessing's replies specifically to Goeze, grouped under the title *Anti-Goeze*, can be found in even very selective compilations of his works—in German. We in the English-speaking world tend to think of Lessing as a dramatist (*Minna von Barnhelm*, *Nathan der Weise*), drama critic (*Hamburg Dramaturgy*), aesthetician (*Laocoon*), and, perhaps, lyric poet. But his father was an orthodox Lutheran pastor who sent him to the University of Leipzig to study theology. In time he gained his father's permission to abandon theology in favor of the theater, which had become his main interest, but theology remained a lifelong concern. It was rekindled by the controversy over the *Wolfenbütteler Fragmente* or *Fragmente eines Ungenannten*, as the portions of Reimarus's manuscript published by Lessing came to be known.

There is no need here to go into the intricacies of the *Fragmentenstreit*. Suffice it to say that it was not at all a simple, black-and-white battle between *Aufklärung* rationalism and stodgy Lutheran orthodoxy. Sir Herbert Butterfield, best known for his book *The Whig Interpretation of History*, has pointed out in a penetrating article that we must not view the modern struggle for religious toleration in "whiggish" terms, as a steady, step-by-step march forward, out of the darkness of medieval bigotry and superstition and into the bright dawn of the Enlightenment. "One must not infer," writes Butterfield tartly, "that persecution is always doomed to failure." The growth of toleration in modern Europe is yet another "historical transition to which we are tempted to attach a too simple linear cause," but which "ought rather to be seen as a gradual change of texture taking place in a complicated piece of material."[8] In earlier years Lessing and Goeze had in fact been friends. Lessing had sought out Goeze in Hamburg, and had even taken Goeze's side in the argument over which Goeze resigned the *Seniorat* in 1770, an argument over the proper form for the Penance-Day (*Busstag*) prayer. But when Goeze had objected, in 1775, and perhaps with some reason, that Goethe's *Die Leiden des jungen Werthers* glorified and encouraged adultery and suicide, Lessing had been on the other side. Moreover, in his notes to the Reimarus fragments and in *Anti-Goeze*, Lessing takes issue with Reimarus almost as often as he does with Goeze. For Lessing was just as devoted to polemics as was Goeze, and his whole position toward Lutheran orthodoxy was tortuously complex.

This was the world into which Christoph Christian Sturm innocently stepped when he accepted the post of *Hauptpastor* at St. Peter's in 1778, the very year in which the *Fragmentenstreit* reached its apex. As we might suspect from his choice of Halle as a place to study theology, Sturm was of a far more liberal persuasion than Goeze. J. S. Semler, of the Halle theology faculty, stood high on Goeze's enemies' list. Goeze's extremely sympathetic 19th-century biographer, Pastor Georg Reinhard Röpe, writes of Goeze: "Thus he . . . polemicized his whole life against Semler and his rationalist theology; in countless books and essays he pointed out to him his superficiality and untruths, and drew the consequences of his assertions."[9]

Although Sturm was not known as a poet, by the time he came to Hamburg, in 1778, he had already become a popular writer. Two of what were to remain, in German and in many translated versions, his most popular works were already in print: *Unterhaltungen mit Gott in den Morgenstunden, auf jeden Tag des Jahrs* was published at Halle in 1768; *Betrachtungen über die Werke Gottes im Reiche der Natur und der Vorsehung, auf alle Tage des Jahrs* appeared five years later, also published at Halle. Both books were collections of gently pious, easygoing prose ruminations on every imaginable corner of the human and natural worlds, suited to the changing of the seasons and, of course, redounding ultimately to the glory of God. Their popularity in England and America (and Sturm's low standing as a poet, even in his native country) is demonstrated by the fact that most large American university libraries contain several copies of each book in English translation, while a copy of Sturm's *Lieder und Kirchengesänge* in its original Hamburg edition of 1780 is apparently not to be found in this country and is rare in Germany. An English-speaking public reared on Wordsworth quite naturally took Sturm—the Sturm of the prose works, that is—to its heart. The preface to the seventh (1858) Bohn's Library edition of *Morning Communings with God* opens with the observation that "the name of Sturm has become so naturalized amongst us, that we scarcely remember that the honour of his birth appertains not to our country."

From all accounts, Sturm the man lived up to the persona of his books. He seems really to have been a perfect storybook old-time pastor: wise, warmhearted, generous, always there to help anyone in need, universally beloved. The only biography of him was written by his friend Jacob Friedrich Feddersen, and appeared soon after his death, in 1786—published, incidentally, by Johann Henrich Herold. It is uniformly praising of Sturm's life and character, and if one reads it without knowing the Hamburg background, and particularly without knowing of Goeze's character and power, it seems rather monotonous, unrelieved pious pap. In fact, it is a masterly little production.

Only a hundred pages long, Feddersen's *Christoph Christian Sturms . . . Leben und Charakter* is divided almost precisely in two: the first half is devoted to Sturm's life and character, the second to his writings. After giving Sturm's family history, more or less as I have summarized it above, and the story of his career up to his appointment in Hamburg, Feddersen jumps to an account of Sturm's death. He then launches into just the sort of stereotyped praise we should expect of an 18th-century pastor: "The goodness of his heart and the piety of his life were sincere and unmistakable, for they were the fruit of the religion of Jesus. . . . To the end he remained true to the solemn resolution and vow he took when he assumed office at Hamburg" (pp. 12, 18).

But only a few pages later we begin to notice, if we are aware of Goeze's character and polemical activities, that Feddersen's praise of Sturm is unobtrusively taking on greater particularity:

> He was utterly incapable of flattery or of speaking against his convictions. He candidly told everyone his opinion, without regard to the person or his position, without thinking of his own advantage or disadvantage. Many people therefore judged him to be unfit, and soon came to suspect him of an inclination toward innovation and argumentativeness.
>
> [P. 21]

This too could perhaps be taken as stereotyped praise of an honest man of God, determined to speak the truth no matter what it cost him. But the word "innovation" is, I think, a tip-off to the reader who knows something of Goeze. For of course it was precisely innovations in church doctrine, or what Goeze took to be innovations, that he came down on hardest. And his style of argument was relentlessly logical: one after another of his pamphlets bears a title beginning with the word "Proof" or the phrase "Proof that." And, as we have seen, the books that Sturm published, to great acclaim, even before arriving in Hamburg were of the sort that would open him to charges, from a man of Goeze's views, of an "inclination toward innovation," and also, from a man of Goeze's polemical style, of an "inclination toward argumentativeness." Add to these considerations the fact that Goeze was, preeminently, a "person of position" in contemporary Hamburg, and those two words in Feddersen's description also take on a sharper significance.

A few pages later, Feddersen quotes Sturm as having said, privately, in his own defense after something he had written had come in for some criticism: "You know how much I honor the religion of reason, but it must not be taught and praised at cost to or to the disparagement of the religion of Christ, for that alone is the source of all its genuine illumination" (p. 25). Feddersen is clearly making the point—or letting Sturm make it for himself—that, *pace* Goeze, it was possible to reconcile the religion of reason with the religion of Christ, so long as one remembered that it was from the latter that the former derived all its power.

This brings Feddersen to an account of Sturm's various good works—which Goeze, with his exclusive emphasis on faith over works, would also have found, at the very least, suspicious. He cites a writer whom he identifies only as "a learned and active patriot in Hamburg"—that is, a member of the second Patriot Society—who bore the initials L. G., as having praised the recently deceased Sturm, "who so willingly worked, at the right place and in the right way, for the advancement of civic contentment, unpretentiously and unobtrusively but with warmth and vigor" (p. 26). Feddersen himself then adds, in a significant phrase, that Sturm worked "for the enlightenment and improvement" of his fellow citizens—the former term, of course, being another that was anathema to Goeze. As examples Feddersen cites Sturm's work on the new *Hamburger Gesangbuch*, a project against which Goeze fulminated in print, and Sturm's founding, with Professor Büsch, of the *Hamburgische Krankeninstitut*.

A slightly different sort of example of Sturm's involvement with his fellow citizens is given a few pages later by Feddersen:

> In the last days of his life he cared, in a fatherly manner, for an able, upright young man who had converted from Judaism to the Christian religion. Through his goodness and learning he won the love of the young man, gave him free access to his house, and was in all things his advocate, having persuaded several of his friends to underwrite a yearly stipend for the continuation of the young man's studies. He himself contributed first, and, as was customary with him, very generously. Dying, he charged his friends with seeing to the young man's academic success.
>
> [P. 32]

The young man, whose name evidently was Christiani, is now studying at Kiel, to whose "generous scholars" Feddersen commends him.

It is hard to say what the reaction of a man like Goeze to such a good deed would have been. As a convert, the young man was certainly entitled to all the privileges of an ordinary Lutheran dwelling in Hamburg. Yet it is difficult, if one knows Goeze's driving concerns, to imagine that he himself would have taken in such a person, or even that he would be much interested in the project. At any rate, Feddersen skillfully uses this anecdote to lead up to one of the main differences between Goeze and Sturm: their position on the whole issue of religious toleration.

Two pages later he very pointedly writes of Sturm: "Christian reasonableness, peacefulness, and religious tolerance of the differences in theological ideas. These highly prized virtues and sacred duties of a Christian religious teacher he practiced continually" (p. 34). Sturm agreed wholeheartedly, Feddersen tells us, with Johann Christoph Döderlein (1746-1792), a well-known spokesman for religious toleration, "regarding the eternal bliss of the heathens":

> The inescapable consequences of honest and active benevolence toward everyone—modesty, humility, and justice toward the merit of other people—these are the qualities that the friends and companions of a noble person recognize in him most often and as most worthy of love. You students of human nature who knew Sturm intimately and associated with him, shall you not bear witness that he was wholly free of everything that betrays pride and envy?
>
> [Pp. 34-35]

The point could scarcely be clearer. The inevitable damnation of all those born outside the orbit of Christianity was one of Goeze's favorite themes; the virtues here attributed to Sturm, as the inevitable result of his generously tolerant attitude, are those which Goeze signally lacked, while the vices from which Sturm is said to be free are those evidenced by Goeze—alongside, it must be said, other, far finer qualities—throughout his long and combative life.

Yet to make the point still clearer, Feddersen now tells an anecdote about his own early acquaintance with Sturm. He and Sturm had frequent "literary quarrels" so intense that they went out of their way to avoid each other, even though they lived not far apart—Sturm in Halle, Feddersen in Bernburg. But then Providence stepped in:

> Providence led us both to Magdeburg at the same time and furnished a remarkable opportunity, since we were able to explain our principles and convictions to each other calmly in conversation. From that day forward we became fond of each other, our hearts grew ever closer, and soon we were the most intimate friends—so we remained until his death, without a moment of coldness or lessening of our tender affection. We often joked, thereafter, about our youthful feud [*Fehde*].
>
> [Pp. 37-38]

To a contemporary Hamburger, the very word *Fehde,* so often applied to Goeze, would bring him instantly to mind, underlining the contrast between his life, which was in effect one long *Fehde*, and that of Sturm, who put such squabbling behind him early in life and made his sometime opponent his lifelong friend.

Such a reader, thinking back over the preceding few pages of Feddersen's biography, would doubtless also recall that the particular *Fehde* that forced Goeze to submit his resignation as *Senior*, in 1770, concerned the Lutheran Church's attitude toward non-Christians. The prayer said annually on Penance-Day or *Busstag* included verse 6 of Psalm 79, which in the King James Version reads as follows: "Pour out thy wrath upon the heathen that have not known thee, and upon the kingdoms that have not called upon thy name." Julius Gustav Alberti, who had been a *Pastor* at St. Catherine's since April 1755, a few months before Goeze became *Hauptpastor*, wanted this verse dropped from the prayer because he found its vivid depiction of an angry God inconsistent with the message of the Gospels. Goeze objected strenuously, but was overruled by the municipal authorities, and so felt he had to resign. When Alberti died suddenly in 1772, Goeze was popularly held responsible—a situation, as we shall see, that was to arise at least twice more.

Feddersen concludes the purely biographical section of his book by noting Sturm's "gracious and goodnatured attitude toward his enemies": "In his sermons and writings he never repaid bitterness with bitterness" (p. 44). Once, when Sturm had become embroiled in controversy, Feddersen offered to defend him—but Sturm rejected the offer:

> He embraced me. "Thanks, my friend! But do not do it. My enemies will just become more embittered, and they will receive discontent as a reward for their good intentions."
>
> [P. 45]

Feddersen neither names the enemy in question nor tells us what the controversy was about, but Koch clears up both questions. Sturm's rejection of his friend's offer occurred "in 1782, when he [Sturm], because of the teaching regarding the redemption of the heathens, which he had expounded in his writings, was strongly attacked for his rationalism and thereby entangled in a long-lasting battle by the watchman standing guard on the Lutheran church tower, Senior Götze [*sic*]" (p. 359). Koch then adds that this protracted quarrel with Goeze undermined Sturm's health, and led directly to his death, four years later.

Feddersen, who says he was reluctant even to mention Sturm's quarrel and has done so only for the light that it casts on his friend's character, says nothing of the rumor that it caused Sturm's death—which indeed seems unlikely. But by this time Goeze's chronic pugnaciousness had isolated him, even from Hamburg's clerical community, and most people were ready to believe the worst of him. Moreover, there was not only the earlier rumor about his having been responsible for Alberti's death to contend with but also a similar one about Sturm's predecessor at St. Peter's, Friderici. Shortly after his arrival in Hamburg in 1775, it was noted that Friderici's sermons dealt almost solely with moral, rather than theological, matters, and that he carefully dodged the question of whether or not he believed in the divinity of Christ. This of course provoked Goeze, who instantly went on the attack, and when Friderici died two years later the rumors were heard again.

Finally, Feddersen tells us not only that Sturm spoke well of his (still unnamed) opponent in the controversy—"He is one of the most learned preachers that I know"—but also that he delivered a moving speech about him after his death—Goeze, we recall, died three months before Sturm:

> At the memorial service after the learned man's death, he spoke with good sense and honesty, praising him as he deserved. Thousands heard this, and I have read a copy of it.
>
> [P. 45]

One is amused to note the care that Feddersen, afraid that the reader will suspect him of gilding the lily, takes to reassure us that he is not inventing this final testimony to Sturm's generous and forgiving nature, that the speech actually exists in print.

Despite Feddersen's reluctance to name names, then, his biography of Sturm gives us a vivid picture of the degree to which Goeze's reactionary brand of Lutheran orthodoxy influenced religious, social, and political life in Hamburg during the third quarter of the 18th century, and suggests how important a role Sturm played as a member of the more liberal, tolerant counterforce. A few more details of this picture—but only a few—are filled in by the contemporary biography of Goeze, also published in 1786, immediately after his death.

The first odd thing about this book, entitled *Wahrhafte Nachricht von dem Leben des weiland Hochwürdigen Herrn Johan Melchior Goeze, Hauptpastors an der St. Catherinen Kirche in Hamburg*, is that the author chose not to divulge his name. On its title page he stands identified only as "J. C. M. St***." His name, evidently, was Steineck, but I have been unable to discover who he was, and, unlike Feddersen, he does not tell us what relation, if any, he bore to the subject of his book.

The second odd thing is the tone of his *Vorrede*, which begins with the following arresting sentence:

> I have dared to write the life history of a man who made a great stir in the learned, and especially in the theological, world; who, because he constantly and firmly defended the ancient principles of the evangelical-Lutheran church against all attacks, was subjected to much, and often groundless, opposition; and whose inquisitorial vigilance and unflagging zeal were called willful stubbornness.
>
> [Pp. V-VI]

"I have dared"?—as though merely writing the biography of this man were an act of daring, a risky undertaking? That, plainly, is the suggestion, which is intensified by the sentence's uneasy prolixity—as though poor Steineck felt he had to go on and on, justifying both Goeze and himself.

The third odd thing is that Goeze's name does not even get mentioned until page 18! The preceding pages are all cast in an elaborately impersonal mode that reminds one of the language lawyers refer to scornfully as "boilerplate." Tortuous rhetorical questions of virtually Faulknerian length force us to grapple with general issues, rather in the mode of a defense attorney who knows that he has a losing case on his hands and that his only chance of victory lies in keeping his argument as abstract (and as confusing) as possible, and thus keeping the jurors from recalling how disreputable a client he is representing. Could anyone raised in the traditional Lutheran faith remain silent in the face of the exclusively moral emphasis of the newer pastors and theologians? Doesn't any collection of writings that claims divine origin inevitably lead to argument and conflict? Aren't our religious leaders, after all, men, and therefore prone to conflict with one another? And so it goes—all without so much as a whisper of Goeze's dread name.

And even once his name has been mentioned, the impersonality of the language continues. Instead of generalizations about humankind as a whole, we are treated to generalizations about society and family life in the era of Goeze's birth and youth. The one hint that Goeze had, apart from theological conflict, an emotional life comes when Steineck recounts his marriage, to one Johanna Rosina Derlingen, who "had made the tenderest impression upon his heart" (p. 33). The poor woman suffered from emotional instability, which "der selige Goeze" (as Steineck always calls him) "not only bore with quiet patience, which often can also be the consequence of a cold indifference, but also exercised the tenderest concern in order to lessen the sufferings of his wife" (p. 34).

This strikes me as a very curious sentence. Was or was not the quiet patience with which Goeze bore his wife's infirmity the result of a coldly indifferent nature? If it was not, why raise the possibility that it might have been? It sounds very much as though Steineck, perhaps unconsciously, is attempting to have it both ways: his mention of Goeze's tender concern makes it seem as though he is defending his subject, but he has also given himself what, in political circles, has come to be called "deniability" in the face of the charge that Goeze was, as everyone knows, a coldly indifferent man.

At one point (p. 46) Steineck asserts, in language too verbose to be worth citing here, that discussing a man's quarrels only leads one into the investigation of humanity's lowest passions. Yet there is very little besides Goeze's quarrels, and the many publications that both caused and resulted from them, that poor Steineck can find to discuss. That he is nervously aware of the shortcomings of his book is shown by his admission, in the *Vorrede*, that he had only two months to prepare it and that many of the salient documents were not available to him. Perhaps he tried to make up for them by his endless recital of who said (or wrote) what when on which theological point of dispute. Now and then he remembers to praise Goeze, yet again, as a noble, misunderstood defender of the faith, but the whole tone and method of his book make his praise ring hollow.

For Goeze was, as Steineck is forced to admit, a man of violent temperament who could not bear to leave a piece of writing with which he differed, on no matter how small a point, unanswered. Yet with all that was undeniably hateful about the man, there are a few points where one sympathizes with his conservative stand against Pietism and the Enlightenment. A Pietist named Bardt published a translation of the New Testament in the early 1770s. Shocked by its sugary elaboration of what Steineck nicely calls "the powerful and true-hearted language of Luther" (p. 121), Goeze fired back a pamphlet, *Beweis, dass die Bardtische Verdeutschung des neuen Testaments keine Uebersetzung, sondern eine vorsetzliche Verfälschung und frevelhafte Schändung des lebendigen Gottes sey*. The one example of Bardt's "translation" that Steineck gives puts one immediately and wholeheartedly on Goeze's side. For the first half of Matthew 5:4 Bardt has "Wohl denen, welche die süssen Melancholien der Tugend, den rauschenden Freuden des Lasters vorziehen." After which the bare, noble words of Luther strike one like a thunderbolt: "Selig sind, die da Leid tragen." By comparison, even the King James Version's "Blessed are they that mourn" seems namby-pamby.

So Steineck's biography of Goeze is an interesting and revealing book—not in spite of but because of its many oddities. But the reader who comes to it looking for illumination of the relation between Goeze and Sturm is sorely disappointed—until, that is, the last three of its 228 pages. Only then do we encounter Sturm's name.

In 1784, Steineck relates, Goeze had the unpleasant task of replying to an anonymous pamphlet on the seemingly obscure theological question of whether or not criminals should be accompanied to their place of execution by a pastor. The pamphlet, though published anonymously, is duly listed in the catalogue of Sturm's writings at the end of Feddersen's biography: *Ueber die Gewohnheit, Missethäter durch Prediger zur Hinrichtung begleiten zu lassen*. When Goeze wrote his reply, *Gewissenhafte Erinnerungen zu der Schrift: Ueber die Gewohnheit, Missethäter durch Prediger zur Hinrichtung begleiten zu lassen*, he did not know (or at least claimed not to know) that Sturm was the author. Surprisingly, since one thinks of Sturm as a progressive and humane man, he opposed the custom, apparently on the grounds that it was based on Roman Catholic superstition. Stung by Goeze's response, Sturm published a counter-response, this time acknowledging authorship: *Meine erste und letzte Erklärung in Absicht auf die gewissenhaften Erinnerungen des Hrn. Past. Goeze gegen meine Schrift*. In it he not only answered Goeze's criticisms but also went on to accuse Goeze of having, for the preceding five years, in both sermons and writings, attacked him—not by name but in a way that would make it clear to any reader exactly who the target was. Certainly the fact that Sturm called his pamphlet his first and last explanation does suggest that his patience—and we know that he, unlike Goeze, was a patient man—has finally run out. Goeze replied with protestations of what Steineck calls "collegial love and friendship" (p. 227).

The fact that Steineck mentions Sturm in only his last few pages might suggest a certain reluctance to take on this beloved Hamburg figure, recently deceased or just possibly still alive when Steineck's biography appeared. In his biography of Goeze, frankly titled *Johan Melchior Goeze: Eine Rettung*, even Röpe calls Sturm "the much-loved Sturm" (p. 272), and his references to him are extremely scanty, even a bit reluctant. Interestingly, the conflict between Goeze and Sturm that Röpe mentions is neither the one over the status of heathens that Feddersen was apparently alluding to nor the one about criminals' being accompanied by a preacher that we learn of from Steineck. It was, rather, a controversy in which Goeze's main opponent was one Johann Heinrich Daniel Moldenhawer. It began about 1782 but persisted until 1784, the time of the criminals controversy. Moldenhawer was interested in the ways in which foreign trade and travel could help to spread the gospel, while Goeze insisted that this should only be done through established missions. According to Röpe, Sturm gave sermons in support of Moldenhawer's position. One interesting fact: Moldenhawer's pamphlets were published by Herold, publisher of Sturm's poems and also of Bach's settings.

The fact that different authorities come up with different controversies in which Sturm and Goeze opposed each other suggests that this may have happened even more than three times. Certainly Feddersen's tone concerning the unnamed Goeze implies that he was a steady irritant to Sturm, as to so many others. His reputation went speedily downhill in the early years of the 19th century, and it was only in 1860 that Röpe saw fit to publish his *Rettung*, his attempt to salvage something of Goeze's earlier power and fame. Perhaps the death-blow to his reputation was given by Lessing, though not in the *Fragmentenstreit*. In 1779 Lessing's boss, the Duke of Brunswick, ruled that Lessing could publish no more polemical theological writings. Therefore Lessing gave Goeze an undesirable immortality by portraying him as the bigoted Patriarch of Jerusalem in his dramatic plea for religious toleration, *Nathan der Weise*.

Thus we can see that in the third quarter of the 18th century, Hamburg was torn by religious and social controversy, and that Sturm took an active part as one of the liberal group associated with the second Patriot Society, a group to which Bach seems also to have been sympathetic. So much for Sturm the man: now what about Sturm the poet?

II

One of the few books that mentions Sturm as a poet is Feodor Wehl's 1856 *Hamburgs Literaturleben im achtzehnten Jahrhundert*—though he gets only about two pages of a summary chapter devoted to Hamburg poets of the time.[10] The poem that Wehl quotes as a fair specimen of Sturm's work is, as it happens, one that Bach set, "Gottes Grösse in der Natur":

> Gross ist der Herr! Von seiner Macht
> Erzählen Himmel, Erd' und Meere.
> Ihn preist die sternenvolle Nacht,
> Die Sonn' und aller Sonnen Heere.

> Ihn rühmt die blühende Natur,
> Ihr Schmuck und ihres Segens Menge;
> Die Frucht der garbenschweren Flur
> Sind seiner Allmacht Lobgesänge.

> Ihn preist in seiner Felsenkluft
> Des Löwen furchtbares Gebrülle;
> Der Rabe, der um Speise ruft,
> Der Wurm in seines Staubes Hülle.

> Der Rebenberg, das Waizenthal,
> Der Schmerlenbach, der Auen Blüthe,
> Die Luft und jeder Sonnenstrahl
> Verkündigt des Allmächt'gen Güte.

> Des Westes Kühlung sendet Er,
> Den Donnersturm in Ungwittern.
> Er spricht! Und still ist Erd' und Meer!
> Er spricht! Und Meer und Erde zittern!

> Vom Aufgang bis zum Niedergang,
> Von hier bis zu den fernsten Sphären,
> Schallt der Geschöpfe Lobgesang
> Zu unsers Weltenschöpfers Ehren.

> Gross ist der Herr! Zu ihm empor
> Soll meine frohe Seele dringen.
> In aller Creaturen Chor
> Soll meines Liedes Jubel singen.

It is natural at this point, I think, to recall Gellert's poem "Die Ehre Gottes aus der Natur," which we looked at briefly in Chapter Nine. One of the most frequently set of Gellert's poems, it called forth from Bach the most splendid of the Gellert volume's "outward-turning" songs: robust, dignified, exuberant. Yet the poem itself, a rather repetitious recital of the earthly evidences of God's power, did not seem one of Gellert's best. It looks considerably better when we place it alongside the poem of Sturm's just cited. Despite its repetitiousness, Gellert's poem has a certain metrical variety, gained by the introduction of two three-syllable feet into the first and third lines of each quatrain:

> Die Himmel rühmen des Ewigen Ehre
>   Ihr Schall pflanzt seinen Namen fort.
> Ihn rühmt der Erdkreis, ihn preisen die Meere;
>   Vernimm, o Mensch, ihr göttlich Wort!

This gives the effect of repeated bursts of energy and enthusiasm repeatedly steadied by sober declarations of faith. Gellert makes this effect work especially well at the poem's turning point, when in reply to the speaker's increasingly excited questionings, God himself steps in as speaker:

> Kannst du der Wesen unzählbare Heere,
>   Den kleinsten Staub fühllos beschaun?
> Durch wen ist alles? O gieb ihm die Ehre!
>   Mir, ruft der Herr, sollst du vertraun.

Gellert's poem thus has both variety of movement and a certain drama to it, whereas Sturm's is both static and rhythmically dead, more like a list than a poem.

    The reason the comparison is a natural one to make is that in 1774 Sturm had published a collection of poems by himself and, among others, Gellert and Cramer, *Sammlung geistlicher Gesänge über die Werke Gottes in der Natur*. This was, Feddersen tells us (p. 85), the first such collection of poems devoted entirely to *Naturreligion*. That Sturm clearly saw himself in the line of poets inaugurated by Gellert and extended by Cramer makes it quite reasonable to see his "Gottes Grösse in der Natur" as a conscious descendant of Gellert's "Die Ehre Gottes aus der Natur"—and it also helps us to see why Sturm, despite his limitations as a poet, should have been chosen by Bach to follow Gellert and Cramer as the source of texts for his third and last big songwriting project.

    Bach's setting of Sturm's "Gottes Grösse in der Natur," while a good song, lacks the ebullience and majesty of his setting of Gellert's "Die Ehre Gottes aus der Natur":

The key to the song lies, I think, in the seemingly paradoxical tempo direction, "Lebhaft und prächtig." For the song itself is a playful, lighthearted duel between the *prächtig* (or would-be *prächtig*) melody, with its firm quarter notes and wide skips (at least at the beginnings of phrases) and the *lebhaft* little bass-figure (two sixteenth notes followed by two eighths) that drives the rhythm and finally takes over, winning the duel hands down.

The first phrase is very regular, with its opening octave leap, and we expect the little train of eighth notes in bar 3 to continue right on down to the tonic, rounding off the phrase in bar 4. But no—instead the melodic line turns around and heads back up, without a break, moving in rhythm with the bass line. Precisely because the first phrase has been a regular four-bar one, we expect the same of the second—at least until the melodic line's turnabout jars us slightly. We are jarred further by what seems the rushed ending to the second phrase and the uncertainty about phrase boundaries that sets in at this point.

The second phrase seems to end in bar 6, but then the bass administers the *coup de grâce* in bar 7. And exactly what is bar 7, anyway? After the rather rushed and flustered ending to the preceding phrase, the slight pause before the melodic line's leisurely little fanfare in bar 8 is a witty surprise. And is bar 8 to be heard as the beginning of the third phrase or as a drawn-out pickup to it? The bass line's imitative rise in bar 9 presages its takeover of the rhythm two bars later, with its little motivic phrase recalled from the song's opening.

The fourth phrase, like the first, begins with the melodic line setting a pattern of staid quarter notes and wide skips, this time moving up a step each time, more or less in parallel. Meanwhile, underneath the bass drives the rhythm forward with its repeated figure—until, in bar 15, the melody responds with its little grace-noted flourish. The sudden high chord, in voice and keyboard, in the next bar is another fine surprise: for just a second, owing to the absence of an E-flat from the chord, the drama of the moment suggests a diminished seventh. But then the bass comes in with a solid E-flat upward arpeggio, a tonic version of the dominant arpeggio in bar 9 but this time done to the rhythm of the bass line's characteristic motif. The melody rises to the tonic over two playful skips in the bass, followed by a downward arpeggio in the bass, answering the upward one two bars earlier. The song ends with a repetition of the last phrase.

The reviewer for the *Gesammelte Beyträge zu der Hamburger Neuen Zeitung* also saw the song as combining a melody and a bass line of quite different characters: "how simple and powerful the melody," he exclaimed, "how sublime the fiery bass!" And, calling attention to Bach's little appended refrain, he added: "and how happy the repetition of 'Gross ist der Herr' at the end" (*Spiegel*, p. 103). This is a good song, but it lacks the majesty and depth of feeling of the setting of Gellert's "Die Ehre Gottes aus der Natur," and of similar outward-turning songs in the Gellert collection. This may be partly owing to the lower quality of Sturm's poetry—indeed, the *Allgemeine deutsche Bibliothek*'s reviewer, judging the melodies of the 1780 Sturm volume to be inferior to those of the Cramer psalms, perceptively observed: "the cause is probably the poetry of these songs" (*Spiegel*, p. 192). But I think that by the time he came to set Sturm's songs, Bach was, for whatever reason, less interested in the outward-turning poems celebrating evidence of God's goodness in the natural world than he had been almost a quarter-century earlier. For the triumphs of the Sturm collections are almost exclusively the darker songs, specifically the ones concerned with Christ's passion. Despite Sturm's fame, because of his prose works, as a champion of *Naturreligion*, it seems to have been the *Christusreligion* in his poetry that most strongly appealed to Bach.

III

In Bach's two collections of Sturm settings, there are three songs entitled *Passionslied*. Here is the first of the three:

For many reasons, this immediately invites comparison with the "Passionslied" in Bach's Gellert collection that we examined back in Chapter Nine:

The tempo directions, "Traurig" and "Langsam," are more or less equivalent, and each song begins with a seven-bar phrase that ends in a half-cadence and then is repeated. In each case, too, the seven-bar phrase is composed of a four-bar segment dominated by a dragging short-long-short melodic rhythm, and a three-bar segment whose truncation, and rather rushed ending, add to the effect of weariness created by the dragging rhythm of the melody. In both songs the contrasting second part begins with insistently repeated quarter notes on the same pitch—signifying, apparently, a new resolve. But in both songs the rather weary and resigned mood of the opening gradually returns.

Of course there are differences too. In the Gellert song the cadence in bars 3 and 4 is on the tonic, G minor, while in the Sturm song it is on the relative major, giving the music a momentary hopeful turn. But notice how, in bar 4, Bach has the keyboard's left hand ceremoniously round off the cadence with its descent to low D, and then immediately reassert B, the relative minor, as we sweep into the opening phrase's second segment. Something like this occurs, we recall, in bar 4 of the Gellert song, where the E-flat triad just following the cadence has the same, momentarily hopeful effect. This device of raising the listener's hope for just a moment before returning, through the truncated three-bar segment that completes the phrase, to the initial sadness and weariness creates the same emotional movement on the phrase level that we saw to be created, in both songs, by the whole piece.

The contrasting second part of the Sturm song is also quite differently constructed from that of the Gellert song, which is a full ten bars longer. In the Sturm song, the insistent repeated notes occur again, in bars 18 and 19, a step lower than before. The first segment of the song's second part is three bars long, and the second one, which begins with the second set of repeated notes, is four bars long, lengthened out by the little melisma on "verlassen." I think the ear expects symmetry here, something like this:

The rather beseeching nature of the phrase to which the words "Gott verlassen" are sung makes us feel it precisely as a lengthened, intensified version of its predecessor. The fact that the song is rounded off with yet another three-bar phrase compounds this impression.

What of the poem to which this song is written? It has nothing of the precision and intricacy of Gellert's, and the relation between Christ's sacrifice and man's innate sinfulness is treated baldly, without any of Gellert's subtlety. In the opening stanza Christ is depicted, rather vaguely, as encompassed by the curse of (man's) sins, the familiar mixture of blood and sweat pouring from his face:

> Einst, als dich im Gerichte
> Der Sünden Fluch umgab,
> Da floss vom Angesichte
> Dir Schweiss, wie Blut, herab:

In the second stanza he is said to battle as a mediator—"Wie Mittler kämpftest du!"—while his whole soul prays "Um Linderung, um Ruh." And as if this weren't confusing enough, there are the badly mixed metaphors of the stanza's final lines:

> Doch ach! da war kein Tröster nicht;
> Du dürstetest vergebens
> Nach Freudigkeit und Licht.

In the next stanza the disciples are taken to task:

> Auch sie, die so entschlossen,
> So männlich dich bekannt,
> Sind muthlos, sind verdrossen,
> Vom Schlummer übermannt.

>   Sie schauen deiner Seele Schmerz:
>   Und keiner deiner Brüder
>   Spricht Labsal dir ins Herz.

Do the disciples, though mysteriously overcome by sleep, nonetheless literally see the pain of Christ's soul? Or is one (or perhaps both) of these words being used metaphorically? Since the poem seems merely a string of clichéd attitudes about Gethsemane, one suspects that the period after "übermannt" gave Sturm the sense that what he said next did not have to bear any relation to what had just preceded. In the fourth stanza Christ responds to the disciples' contemptible weakness "Mit göttlicher Geduld" (a phrase found also in Gellert's poem), and commands them to wake up: "O wacht mit mir und betet! / Nah ist des Feindes Macht."

Finally, in the concluding two stanzas the speaker asks Christ to protect him since he suddenly feels in dire need: "Wie leicht sink ich darnieder, / Verführt durch stolzen Wahn!" He too, he tells us, has slumbered in complacency, "ruhig bey Gefahren, / Die meiner Seele dräun." We have, of course, seen nothing of these attitudes in the speaker heretofore: they have found their way into Sturm's poem merely because they tend to turn up in moralizings about Christ's passion. In Gellert's "Passionslied," on the other hand, the speaker's connection with Judas the betrayer, and the whole matter of original sin, was beautifully worked out. Finally, Sturm's poem concludes with more unmotivated self-condemnation and a plea to Christ for assurance of eventual salvation:

>   Herr, rette du mich Schwachen,
>   Wenn Stolz und Sicherheit
>   Den Geist verdrossen machen:
>   Gieb Muth und Kraft im Streit.
>   Flöss meiner Seele Tröstung ein:
>   Sprich zu ihr: Wach und bete!
>   Bald ist die Krone dein.

What we have here, then, is an expressive and effective song, in a mode we are by now very familiar with, that has only a loose and general connection with the poem it sets. The general mood of weariness rising temporarily to hope and again sinking back upon itself suits a good deal of the poem—though not its ending, perhaps. And the drawn-out phrase in bars 19-21 comes at what is the climactic point of at least most of Sturm's stanzas. But this song does not mark an advance over Bach's previous song composition like the one marked, say, by the experiments considered in the preceding chapter. And in this it is typical of Bach's Sturm songs. The reviewer for the *Gesammelte Beyträge zu der Hamburger Neuen Zeitung* only said the obvious when he remarked, near the end of his review: "Herr B. has now given us a companion-piece to his Gellert songs" (*Spiegel*, p. 103). Though the great majority of the Sturm settings are not formally experimental, however, there are some that extend Bach's expressive range as a composer of songs.

One of these is the third "Passionslied." Here is the poem that it sets:

>   In Todesängsten hängst du da,
>   O Gottessohn auf Golgotha!
>   Wer kann dein Leiden fassen?
>   Laut seufzest du: mein Gott! mein Gott!
>   Wie hast du mich verlassen!
>
>   Die Zunge klebt am dürren Gaum:
>   Du athmest vor Verschmachten kaum.
>   Doch ach! mit bitterm Spotte

Lacht deine letzten heissen Dursts
Der Missethäther Rotte.

    Du, dessen Wort den Müden Kraft,
Erquickung Dürstenden verschafft,
Ach du, du willst verschmachten?
Mich dürstet! rufst du. Niemand will
Auf deine Klagen achten.

    Dir, der des Weinstocks Früchte schuf,
Dir, Mächtiger, auf dessen Ruf
Sich Quell und Ström' ergiessen,
Dir kann des heissen Durstes Pein
Kein Labetrunk versüssen.

    Doch Gott hat dich im Tod erquickt,
Dich ewig alle Quaal entrückt,
Und dein Gebet erhöret.
Durch dich wird in des Todes Angst
Erquickung mir gewähret.

The first stanza is perfectly conventional crucifixion material: Christ hanging on the cross, his suffering, his crying out to God. But in the second stanza the poem is more or less taken over by the metaphor of physical thirst, and of the refreshment offered by a drink, for physical and spiritual suffering and its opposite, the ultimate refreshment or renewal offered by the prospect of eternal life.

In fact, this metaphor is so thoroughly worked out—worked over, one might almost say—that from the second stanza on, the poem takes on a rather dreary, mechanical air. In the second stanza the suffering Christ—expiring of a burning thirst, his tongue cleaving to the roof of his mouth—is bitterly mocked by the crowd. The third baldly sets before us the irony of Christ, the supplier of spiritual refreshment to those who thirsted for it, now being the one who cries out "I thirst!"—while no one listens. The fourth further extends (and labors) the same irony: Christ, who as God created the fruit of the vine and caused the waters of the earth to flow, has now no drink to soothe the pain of his thirst. Finally, in the last stanza the sharp juxtaposition of opposites we have all been waiting for arrives: "Gott hat dich im Tod erquickt." Paradoxically, it is in Christ's death (or "death"?) that he is renewed and refreshed—and, it must follow as the night the day, the speaker (symbolizing all of us) is also promised "Erquickung."

Nothing, it seems to me, in the rather pat and trite phrasing of the poem could prepare us for the intricacy and power of Bach's setting:

The melody begins by moving soberly forward in straight quarter notes, but almost immediately the harmony surprises us. Moreover, we notice that this song is not completely strophic: Bach has provided different music for the final stanza of Sturm's poem.

The melodic line, starting out unaccompanied, makes its first move downward, and because by that time the three lower voices have joined in, and are moving upward, the ear, I believe, expects the melody to continue downward. Not only does it move up, however, it moves to a surprising B-flat major chord at the beginning of bar 2. Then it moves up once more, and once more drops a semitone. So the sequence of rising melodic notes (D-flat, E-flat, F), each of which drops a semitone, is completed, and we arrive where we more or less expected to arrive, at a half-cadence (bar 2). But the route we traveled has not been one we expected. The B-flat-major chord, interposed between the F-minor tonic and C-major dominant, taken together with the rise in the melodic line, has given the music a sense of opening outward mysteriously, even miraculously, instantly giving the notion of Christ's suffering on the cross greater drama than we expect to encounter this early in the song.

The next two-bar phrase, falling to a gently concessive rhythm over a repeated middle C in the bass, is a languishing lament that ends, once again, on the dominant and thus carries us no further harmonically. But in the third two-bar phrase the resolute, even quarter notes return for a bar—only to be supplanted in bar 6 by the gently falling syncopated rhythm heard earlier. As the falling phrases continue, in bar 7, the bass line, almost ceaselessly active until this point, seems to lose impulse, entering only on the weak beats. The music seems temporarily stalled, static—rather as in the setting of the Gellert "Passionslied" alluded to earlier. Yet we reach the expected cadence on the dominant (our third) in bar 8, and the last line of the poem's stanza is given added poignancy by the little two-bar extension, in which the melodic line is harmonized a sixth lower and reinforced by the bass line's sudden, dark descent to low E. The cadence, we notice, occurs to the same rhythm (with an added grace note) as that in bar 4.

The special music written for the poem's last stanza is one of Bach's finest surprises. The text of the poem, as we observed, stresses continuity: after the scene-setting opening stanza, Sturm focuses his attention on developing the irony of Christ, even as he is bringing refreshment to the world, thirsting for it himself. The conclusion, which logically extends this irony to the familiar Christian paradox of life in death, seems all too predictable. But there is nothing predictable about Bach's setting of Sturm's final stanza. We might have expected something like the ebullient "Triumph! Triumph!" choruses from Bach's oratorio, *Auferstehung und Himmelfahrt Jesu;* what we get is very different indeed.

The change in dynamics, from the steadily maintained *piano* of the other strophes to *fortissimo,* is in itself not surprising, given the text. But we are surprised to find ourselves still in the minor mode—though now in G minor—and to note the reminiscences of the earlier strophes: the resolute quarter notes of the accompaniment have now become the insistently hammered-out D-seventh chords of the first bar-and-a-half, and the first phrase of the melody reminds us of the phrases in bars 2-3 and 5-8. Yet the text of this first phrase is "Doch Gott hat dich im Tod erquickt," the final glorious reassurance toward which we have been heading all along. Instead of sounding reassuring and triumphant, however, it sounds tough, harsh, almost grim. There is, for Bach as opposed to Sturm, nothing easy about this resolution: the paradox remains a paradox, both sides of it kept firmly in view. Christ's suffering—the "Tod" side of the paradox—is in fact felt far more powerfully and directly than earlier in the song. This is not, as earlier, pathos: this is pain. The death by which Christ gains (and gains for us) eternal life is really death—not just "death." Anyone who has had a Christian upbringing can, I am sure, recall many Easter sermons in which the horror of Good Friday was effortlessly swept aside amidst flowers, smiles, and general good cheer. Bach does not let us off so easily.

In the next phrase (bars 13-14) the music turns toward the major, and the harshness softens slightly—but only slightly: note that Bach reduces the dynamic level only to *forte*. The phrases are again reminiscent of the song's earlier section as we cadence first on E-flat and then, the music softening still further, on A-flat. Moreover, both cadences are rhythmically similar to the one in bars 3-4. So Bach too retains continuity with what has preceded—even as he stresses the sharp and enigmatic nature of the paradox far more effectively than Sturm does. And the softening continues in bars 17-18, with the melodic line's sixteenth notes (on the second "durch") and the bass's rhythmic suspension over the bar-line. The dynamics, however, do not change.

Bach has one more surprise in store for us. At the beginning of the penultimate bar, the bass suddenly springs upward an octave, on the word "Erquickung," and the melodic line responds with a quite uncharacteristic little turning figure in thirty seconds. Then, as the all-important word is repeated, the bass jumps another octave and, harmonized a third above, it is joined by another little turning figure in the melody—after which the song concludes with an F-minor cadence almost exactly like that which ended its earlier strophes. The effect is quite astonishing. There is something driven, almost desperate, about this leap into eternal life, and yet we end where we ended before. There is no turn to the major, no triumphant blaring of trumpets: the pain and suffering of before—and rendered more loudly than in earlier strophes—are still with us, even in the midst of the promise of eternal life. This ending is surely the song's most brilliant fusion of continuity and change.

Many of the other songs in the two Sturm volumes deal with particular stages of the crucifixion or with particular aspects of Christ's sacrifice and its implications for man. Two of the finest (and most famous) of these songs are "Jesus in Gethsemane" and "Über die Finsterniss kurz vor dem Tode Jesu." Moreover, these two songs set two of Sturm's most interesting and ambitious poems. Take first "Jesus in Gethsemane":

> Schau hin! Dort in Gethsemane
> Klagt, trauret, bebt der Heiligste
> Und ringt mit Todesquaal.
> O sieh ihn weinen, beten, knien:
> Herb ist der Kelch: doch trinkt er ihn.
>
> Schau hin, dort geht er ins Gericht;
> Sein bluthbeflossnes Angesicht
> Liegt vor dem Herrn im Staub.
> Doch fleht der peinlich Leidende:
> Nicht mein, dein Wille, Gott, gescheh!
>
> Schau hin zum Oelberg, wenn die Lust
> Der Eitelkeit in deiner Brust
> Sich gegen Gott empört.
> Ach sieh, die Arbeit jener Nacht
> Hat deine Sünde ihm gemacht.
>
> Schau hin, wenn bey des Leidens Schmerz
> Dein mattes, jammervolles Herz
> In Thränen sich ergiesst.

> Auch in der Nächte dunkelm Graun,
> Christ, lerne deinem Gott vertraun.
>
>   Schau hin! Nach Labung dürstest du,
> Du wünschest Heiterkeit und Ruh.
> Er, Er errang sie dir,
> Nun lässt der Richter auf dein Flehn
> Vor dir den Kelch vorüber gehn.
>
>   Schau hin, wenn einst das Grab dich schreckt
> Und kalter Schweiss die Stirn bedeckt:
> Sein Trauren, seine Quaal,
> Sein Flehn, sein Ringen mit dem Tod
> Versüsst dir deine letzte Noth.

Though each of the poem's six stanzas begins with the urgent injunction "Schau hin," the force of that injunction changes subtly as we move through the poem. In the first stanza we are told precisely where to direct our gaze: "Dort in Gethsemane," the location of Christ's so-called agony in the garden, an episode found, in closely matching versions, in all three synoptic gospels. The two series of grieving, self-abasing actions—"Klagt, trauret, bebt" and "weinen, beten, knien"—and the desperate "Todesquaal" are sharply juxtaposed against the ringing phrase "der Heiligste." Finally, we are told, "Herb ist der Kelch: doch trinkt er ihn"—which of course answers to the phrase we know, in the King James Version, as "let this cup pass from me" (Matthew 26:39). (In Luther's translation, his word for cup in all three versions of this passage is *Kelch*.) But of course Christ does not drink from that cup— as he does from the cup that precedes it, at the Last Supper, and from the cup of vinegar or sour wine that follows it, just after the crucifixion. For that cup, the one that he asks God to let pass from him, is not there at all but is only a metaphorical cup. So Sturm is extending his perspective somewhat in this first stanza's final line: Christ did indeed drink from the bitter cup, but later, not at Gethsemane.

A similar compression of time takes place in the second stanza. Its final line, "Nicht mein, dein Wille, Gott gescheh," indicates that our basic focus is still Gethsemane. For this thought appears, in all three synoptic gospels, directly after the line about the cup. As we find it in Matthew: "nevertheless not as I will, but as thou wilt." Yet the first line of the stanza has Christ already before his judges, and the second speaks of his face as "blutbeflossnes." In the versions found in Matthew and Mark, Christ's face is not yet bloodied, but at Luke 22:44 we find "his sweat was as it were great drops of blood falling down to the ground"—or, in Luther, "Es ward aber sein Schweiss wie Blutstropfen, die fielen auf die Erde." Yet this verse and the preceding one fail to appear in many early manuscripts of Luke, and so seem to have been added precisely to compress time, to give an inkling of Christ's physical suffering on the cross proleptically, as it were, while he is suffering spiritually in the garden. Anyway, it is as clear from the Greek—"ὡσεὶ θρόμβοι αἵματος"—as from the translations just cited that an analogy is being made: these are not literal drops of blood—not yet. Yet the third and fourth lines of the stanza, like the final one, bring us back to the literal scene in the garden. This sort of compression or telescoping of time is, of course, perfectly appropriate when one is dealing with a divine being, and is one of the pervasive rhetorical techniques that separate the Gospel According to St. John from the synoptics.

In the third stanza our focus changes somewhat, from Gethsemane, which is in the Kidron Valley just east of Jerusalem, at the foot of the Mount of Olives, to the mount itself. This scene, we recall, directly precedes the agony in the garden, and so we are now moving slightly backward in time. Since this is the scene in which Christ predicts that Peter will deny him three times, the speaker of the poem moves from merely asking us to look at an external scene to asking us to look within. As we gaze at the Mount of Olives, we are to recall what went on there, to banish from our hearts the vanity that sometimes turns us against God, and to realize the meaning, for us, of Christ's coming sacrifice: "Ach sieh, die Arbeit jener Nacht / Hat deine Sünde ihm gemacht." In the fourth stanza, no particular place is mentioned, but the advice of the third stanza is generalized: "lerne deinem Gott vertraun."

In the two concluding stanzas, we, the addressees of the poem, are not only told to see—in the nonphysical sense of understand—what Christ has done for us; we are also analogically associated with Christ. Like him, we thirst, we long for rest and good cheer rather than life's manifold sufferings. But, as it happens, we already possess these gifts since Christ has won them for us: "Er, Er errang sie dir." The words "Richter," "Flehn," and "Kelch" in the last two lines of the fifth stanza vividly recall Christ's situation in Gethsemane as depicted earlier; yet now Christ is the judge who allows the bitter cup of suffering to pass from us. Similarly, in the last stanza it is we who, like Christ in Gethsemane, fear the grave and have the sweat of suffering on our foreheads; yet it is precisely his grief, his torture, his pleas to God, his struggles with death that have made sweet, with the promise of eternal life, our final agony. The insistence that we are both like and unlike Christ—which of course is the meaning of the incarnation—is, I think, very skillfully managed in these stanzas.

Here is Bach's setting:

Set against the background of the regularly pulsing eighth-note accompaniment, the unexpected upward leap of a tritone on the words "Schau hin!" causes them to pierce the listener's heart. And this of course happens with each stanza of the poem, even though it is only the first and fifth stanzas in which those two words are set apart from their context by an exclamation point. The noble curve of the melody soon brings us, at the beginning of bar 3, to the expected half-cadence. But melody and harmony are immediately, restlessly off again, this time leading us, rather surprisingly, into C minor. This turns out, of course, merely to be the subdominant, and we move right to a cadence on the tonic, G minor. But once again the music refuses to rest, even for a moment. A diminished passing chord carries us still further to the flat side of the spectrum, first to F minor and then, astonishingly, to D-flat, the richness and mellowness of which seem quite out of key with the text ("Todesquaal" in the opening stanza!). Thus ends the first half of the song.

The second half is restless in a quite different way. Leaving behind the constantly changing harmony and broken, irregular phrases of the opening, we arrive at a very orderly-seeming sequence of three long descending phrases, each a step higher than the one preceding. Taken together, these three phrases form a lament of steadily increasing intensity. In bar 10 the tension breaks as the melodic line is silent for a dramatic moment and then enters on a repeated high E-flat—the highest note in the song—with a declamatory phrase that harks back to those in bars 2 and 5. A gradual stepwise descent to the cadence on the tonic closes the song. It is most interesting, I think, to note the way in which Bach uses the long melisma that links the first and second of the three long descending phrases—something quite unusual in his songs—to break up what might otherwise have been the rather pat parallelism of the three phrases to one another.

The general movement of the song is thus from tension and comparative disorder—the opening outburst on "Schau hin!"—through the restless and uneven phrases that follow to a sort of order, stability, and resolution. But even though the three long descending phrases are, in themselves and in their relation to one another, orderly and regular, their almost desperately grieving air keeps alive the disturbing quality of the song's first section—as does that dramatic, repeated E-flat in the vocal line at the beginning of bar 10. So the move toward order and resolution is clouded by reminders of disorder and tension. This, it seems to me, is Bach's way of solving the strophic problem in dealing with this particular poem, which moves from the appalling vision of Christ in Gethsemane to a reassurance that is, nonetheless, marked by so many of the same words—"Trauren," "Quaal," "Flehn," "Ringen"—found, in slightly different forms, at the beginning. The poem's final word is "Noth," though it has, we are assured, been "Versüsst" by Christ's sacrifice, just as the restlessness of the song's first section is "Versüsst" by that sudden D-flat sonority that leads into its second section.

"Über die Finsterniss kurz vor dem Tode Jesu" is, perhaps, a still more interesting poem:

>Nacht und Schatten decken
>Des Mittlers Angesicht:
>Und des Richters Schrecken
>Erträgt die Seele nicht!
>Ach, wie ist ihm bange
>Um Freudigkeit und Licht!
>Vater, ach wie lange
>Verzeucht dein Angesicht!
>Herr, Herr, erbarme dich!
>Herr, Herr, erbarme dich!
>Gott, erbarme dich!

>Nacht und Schatten decken
>Das Mördervolle Land:
>Und bewehrt mit Schrecken
>Ist, Rächer, deine Hand.
>Selbst die Frevler zagen:
>Nun ruht ihr frecher Spott:
>Wehgeschrey und Klagen
>Ertönen auf zu Gott.
>Herr, Herr, erbarme dich!
>Herr, Herr, erbarme dich!
>Gott, erbarme dich!

>Ach nun fühlt der Spötter,
>Der Gottes Sohn entehrt,
>Dass der Gott der Götter
>Ihn vor der Welt verklärt.

An des Abgrunds Stufen,
Dem er sich frech genaht,
Möcht er itzt noch rufen
Zu ihm, der für ihn bat.
Herr, Herr, erbarme dich!
Herr, Herr, erbarme dich!
Gott, erbarme dich!

The descent of darkness over the land during the first three of Christ's six hours on the cross is described in all three of the synoptic gospels. In Mark 15:33-39 Christ cries out, asking why God has forsaken him; he is given sour wine to drink; he breathes his last; the curtain of the temple is torn from top to bottom; and the centurion who has been watching him remarks: "Truly this man was the Son of God." In Matthew 27:45-54 several other portents follow upon the tearing of the temple curtain: the earth shakes, rocks split, and the saints are released from their tombs. Moreover, it is not only the centurion who recognizes Christ as the son of God but also those who are standing with him; and they are all said to be terrified by this recognition. The account given in Luke 23:44-49 is somewhat more upbeat. Christ does not ask why God has forsaken him but instead declares: "Father, into thy hands I commend my spirit." And the centurion first praises God and then pronounces Jesus to have been a just or righteous (δίκαιος) man. (The New Revised Standard Version's "innocent" seems to beg the legal question.) The bystanders then smite their breasts, presumably out of a mix of compassion and guilt, and return home. But Christ's "acquaintance," presumably including the disciples, who in Luke's account are still with Christ, stand off at a distance, "beholding these things." There is no account of the falling of darkness in John, who concentrates instead on insisting that every saying and act of Christ and of the others fulfilled some bit of scripture. This is of course implicit in the synoptic gospels: Christ's lament, the sour wine, and the darkness itself all have Old Testament precedents, and the tearing of the temple curtain is thought to symbolize the destruction of the old covenant by which only Jews had direct access to God. But John is concerned with making the continuity between Old and New Testaments explicit at every point, and so he tells a simpler, more stripped-down version of the crucifixion story.

But what sort of poem has Sturm made of all this? The opening two lines are clear enough: night and shadow cover—and of course from the title we expect that the land will be the direct object. But no. Sturm saves that until later. For the moment he is interested in the face of Christ, the "Mittler," the mediator. This too, he tells us, is darkened. But the next two lines are quite troubling: "Und des Richters Schrecken / Erträgt die Seele nicht." But who is the judge? It would seem to be Pilate, but "Richter" is a word commonly applied both to God the father and to Christ, who shall come to judge both the quick and the dead at the latter day. And is "des Richters Schrecken" objective or subjective genitive? There is even a potential confusion in the phrase "die Seele": does this soul belong to the judge (whoever he may be) or to the one being judged?

There is no point in spelling out, and laboriously investigating, all the possible interpretations. The point is that Sturm seems intentionally to be confusing the two roles of judge and judged, making us see double (as it were). At the moment Pilate is in the position of judge, but eventually the judge of Pilate and all the rest of us will be Christ. This technique of telescoping or compressing time, we said earlier, is particularly common in St. John's gospel. And it may in fact have been a line in John that gave Sturm the idea of playing with the word "Richter" as he does in this poem.

In Chapter 19 of St. John's gospel, the Jews are urging a fearful and reluctant Pilate to crucify Jesus because he has been representing himself as King of the Jews. Finally they threaten Pilate: "If thou let this man go, thou art not Caesar's friend: whosoever maketh himself a king speaketh against Caesar" (19:12). Pilate then (19:13) brings Jesus out, and (as the passage is usually translated) sits in the judgment seat, preparatory to handing Jesus over to the Jews. In Luther's translation that verse reads as follows: "Da Pilatus das Wort hörete, führete er Jesum heraus und setzte sich auf den Richterstuhl an der Stätte, die da heisst Hochpflaster, auf ebräisch aber Gabbatha." But in the Greek the verb is ἐκάθισεν, first aorist third singular of the verb καθίζω, which can mean either to sit down oneself or to seat someone else. There is no direct object in the same clause with ἐκάθισεν, but Ἰησοῦν, from the preceding clause, can be understood as carrying over into this one. Noting the ambiguity in his commentary on St. John, R. H. Lightfoot remarks that "it would be in accordance with St. John's method" to exploit the verb's ambiguity in order to "remind readers who at this moment is truly Judge . . . and who the judged." Lightfoot adds that the reading according to which Pilate places Jesus upon the judgment seat gains credence from "a tradition in the second century that (not Pilate, but) the Jews placed the Lord in this position."[11]

But how does this ambiguity, and the telescoping of time that it involves, work in the remainder of Sturm's poem? The rest of the opening stanza is easy enough. It seems pretty clearly (or at least primarily) the suffering Christ, whether we consider him as judge or judged or as both, who, at this moment anyway, yearns for cheerfulness and light, and wishes that God would show his face—which, by implication, embodies those qualities, quite unlike the darkened and shadowed face of Christ himself. It is interesting that as the stanza proceeds, the speaker of the poem identifies himself with Christ: with the lines "Vater, ach wie lange / Verzeuchst dein Angesicht!" he stops referring to Christ in the third person. A plea for mercy closes the stanza.

The second stanza gives us, as it were, the other side of the coin, the crucifixion scene as it relates not to Christ but to his tormentors. The land too is darkened—and not just literally but also figuratively. What is being done to Christ disfigures the whole place, making it not just the land where a murder happens to be occurring but "das Mördervolle Land." The hand of the avenger who strikes down Christ is, ironically, armed with terror—the word "Schrecken," like the stanza's opening line, answering to its counterpart in the first stanza. Even the criminals who torment Christ, presumably both those in the crowd and those who are crucified with him, are afraid, and cease mocking him. The "Wehgeschrey und Klagen" that arise in place of their mockery are borrowed from Luke's account. Again the stanza closes with a plea for mercy, but this time it presumably comes from the now terrified tormentors rather than from Christ.

Though this stanza is considerably less difficult than the first one, it has much in common with it. As we saw, the possible multiple meanings of "Und des Richters Schrecken / Erträgt die Seele nicht" prevent the first stanza from having a straightforward, linear dramatic development. As is so often true in the Bible, the future seems already contained in the present, the terror that Christ the judge will cause to his tormentors already contained in the terror that they cause in him by inflicting their judgment upon him. Similarly, in the second stanza the corresponding lines, "Und bewehrt mit Schrecken / Ist, Rächer, deine Hand," can point ahead to the terror that the hand of Christ the avenger will arouse in the hearts of his tormentors at the last judgment. Moreover, the darkness over the land, the terror (whomever it belongs to), the cessation of the tormentors' mockery, and their bursting forth into tears and lamentation seem all to be happening simultaneously, not following one another in a clear causal sequence.

The third and final stanza is more clearly focused temporally, by "nun" in the first line and "itzt" in the seventh. Also, the sense is clearer and more straightforward than in the preceding stanzas. The mocker who dishonored God's son now feels that God has revealed him to all the world. Brought to the very edge of the abyss by his impudence, he now cries out to him who has already interceded on his behalf. Yet *verklären*, though it can mean to reveal or make clear, usually means to transfigure. And since "Gottes Sohn" is the noun phrase standing closest to "Ihn" at the beginning of line four, we feel for a moment that the him referred to is Christ—though this cannot of course be sustained through the stanza. Still, "transfigured" would make better sense with Christ than with the mocker—though it might also apply there. The poem has moved from its concentration on Christ in the first stanza to the large body of Christ's tormentors in the second to a single, now penitent mocker in the third. As the focus changes and narrows, the repeated refrain at the end of each stanza ties the poem neatly together and enforces the sense of community that unites Christ and the sinning, suffering humanity redeemed by his sacrifice.

Here is the quite remarkable song that Bach wrote to this poem:

One is surprised at how soft a song this is. The poem, after all, was filled with terror, anguish, mockery, more terror, lamentation, and talk of the abyss. Yet aside from the two brief *forte* outbursts at bars 6 and 14, the song is to be delivered *piano* or *pianissimo*. Also, this is a song that, almost to its end, seems clearly to be in G—and yet it ends in D. Why should this be so? Finally, we notice that the last three lines of Sturm's eleven-line stanza, the little refrain, take up almost half the song, fourteen of its thirty bars. This too seems rather strange.

Looking more closely, we realize that the opening of the song is not merely soft but ineffably quiet. The vocal line that enters alone and *pianissimo*, its unhurried rise and fall, the even, gently pulsating quarter notes of the accompaniment, the drift toward the subdominant—all these create, by the beginning of bar 4, a feeling of infinite peace that is not seriously disturbed by the somewhat more rhythmically active few bars that follow, taking us to the cadence on D. Yet in the poem these lines tell us of the darkness that covers the savior's face and the murderous land, and of the mocker who dishonors the son of God! The music seems appropriate to a welcoming, even romantic darkness rather than to one that brings an earthquake and the opening of tombs. Also, the tonality, right up through the cadence at the beginning of bar 6, is uncertain. We have heard an unadorned G triad only fleetingly, on the second beat of the first bar. This blurring of boundaries also helps to make the darkness invoked by the text seem friendly rather than ominous or threatening.

It is interesting that the first *forte* outburst comes on the lines that, in each stanza, we found to be perhaps ambiguous or otherwise problematical. It is also interesting that it is these bars, differentiated from the preceding ones not only by their sudden loudness but also by their decisive dotted-eighth-and-sixteenth rhythms and the firmly sustained half notes in the lower voices, that take us to our first cadence (though a rather thin one) on what will seem, until the end, to be the tonic.

The very thinness of that cadence in bar 8 makes one hear a decrescendo as we move into the next section, which is marked *piano*. At the end of the *forte* outburst the music seems suddenly to withdraw into itself. The next couple of bars give us a taste of the sort of music that will later come to dominate the song: a steady quarter-note movement, with ever-changing harmony, maintained by voices filled with suspensions and overlappings. The effect just here is to mute the defiance of the preceding outburst to a rather wispy poignancy.

At the end of bar 10, however, a new note is struck. As the bass rises, majestically and in half notes, by fourths, the vocal line, reinforced a third below, quietly takes us back into D with a graceful little turning phrase that moves stepwise. This of course perfectly suits the first stanza's text, "um Freudigkeit und Licht." And a singer could make it suit that of the second stanza by giving a bit of stress to the word "ruht" in the line "Nun ruht ihr frecher Spott." The third stanza's phrase, "Dem er sich frech genaht," referring as it does to the yawning abyss to which the mocker's impudence has brought him, requires some stretching, but might be said to work proleptically since it is in the next line that the reformed mocker calls out to Christ. This phrase becomes of increasing importance the better one knows the song. For it very firmly establishes, and gives a distinctive tone to, the key of D major, which is, as we shall see, the key in which the song will conclude.

The general sunniness of D major is, however, somewhat shadowed in the phrase that follows (bars 12-14) as the dynamic level sinks still further, to *pianissimo*, and the repeated C-sharp in the bass clashes with the grace note C-natural and the appoggiatura B-flat, pulling the D chord back to dominant status. In the brief second *forte* outburst (bars 14-16), an E-flat is added to the offending chord, making it an Italian sixth and confirming the dominant function of D. As with the earlier outburst, this one too seems almost to shrivel up, to withdraw into itself as it reaches its cadence. Thus ends the first of the song's two sections.

It is at this point that the texture we noted in bars 8-10 takes over. As opposed to the rapid changes in texture and volume to which we have become accustomed, the next ten bars are smoothly flowing, uniform in texture, and all at the same dynamic level, *piano*. They are also extraordinarily, heartbreakingly beautiful, one of the great passages in C.P.E. Bach's song output. The melody is resolutely diatonic, rising and then falling in even half notes. But the quarter-note harmony below is ravishingly chromatic. Note especially the gentle clash of F (in the bass) and E (in the alto) on the third beat of bar 21.

The first two phrases of this section are each four bars long (17-20, 21-24). At the end of each phrase the melody rests for half a bar while the inner voices continue, leading into the next phrase. But the third phrase, we notice, is only two bars long. Moreover, it seems to break off in the middle. The preceding phrases have conditioned us to expect that the melodic line in bar 25 will rise to B in bar 26. But instead the dynamic level drops to *pianissimo*, the bass drops out, and we have what sounds very much like the beginning of the preparation, complete with dominant pedal-point, for the final cadence in G major. Something like this, perhaps:

But Bach lingers just a little too long on the alternation between D major and its dominant, causing us to lose our sense of G major as our destined home base. The remarkable thing is that when one plays the passage over at the piano, the song does not sound incomplete or unsatisfying. It simply seems to have traveled into another, quite compatible world, a world associated in our minds with the "Freudigkeit und Licht" spoken of earlier, a world in which the forgiveness begged in the concluding lines of each stanza has already been granted. The softening of the dynamics in the penultimate bar also contributes to this effect, as do our memories of the mysterious calm of the song's opening. All in all, "Ueber die Finsterniss kurz vor dem Tode Jesu" seems to me one of Bach's finest achievements.

Finally, we might look at a song that does not directly concern the crucifixion, but that has strong connections to those that do, "Der Tag des Weltgerichts." Here is Sturm's poem:

> Wann der Erde Gründe beben,
> Und in Todtengrüften Leben
> Und im Staube Jugendstärke wallt:
> Wann des Auferweckers Stimme schallt:
> Gott! erbarm dich unser!
>
> Wann mit donnerndem Getümmel,
> O Allmächtger, deine Himmel
> Und des Erdballs Reiche schnell vergehn,
> Und wir wankend auf den Trümmern stehn:
> Gott! erbarm dich unser!
>
> Wann auf deinem Wolkenwagen,
> Von zehntausenden getragen,
> Weltenrichter, du herniederfährst
> Und den Uebelthätern Rache schwörst:
> Gott! erbarm dich unser!
>
> Wann mit Zittern und Entzücken
> Alle Völker nach dir blicken,
> Und dein flammend Richterangesicht
> Fluch und Lohn in ihre Seele spricht:
> Gott! erbarm dich unser!
>
> Wann auch ich dann vor dir stehe,
> Und mein Aug zu deiner Höhe
> Bebend nur empor zu schauen wagt:
> Wann in mir die ganze Menschheit zagt:
> Gott! erbarm dich meiner!

There is of course every reason why a poem on the last judgment should have a good deal in common with poems on the crucifixion. Even in Mark it is stressed that Christ's mission has three phases: his teaching on earth, his passion and death, and his coming again as judge at the end of the world. And as we read through the four gospels, in order of their probable composition and increasing intellectual complexity–from Mark to Matthew to Luke to John–the second and third phases of that mission draw ever closer to each other, almost becoming, in effect, two sides of the same coin.

Not only are the two scenes in some ways similar—the earth trembles in this poem just as it did in "Ueber die Finsterniss kurz vor dem Tode Jesu." Some of the promises seemingly latent in the ambiguities of terms used in that and the other poems are fulfilled in this one. We noted that when Pilate (apparently) is called "Richter," the word resonates with the fact that the tables will be turned at the last judgment when the "Richter" will be Christ; and that the reference to Christ's tormentors collectively as "Rächer" inevitably brings to mind the thought that Christ will one day have his own revenge on those who failed to believe in him. In "Der Tag des Weltgerichts" he is addressed as the "Weltenrichter" who has sworn "Rache" to all evildoers. Similarly, in the crucifixion poems we heard a good bit about Christ's "Angesicht," covered with sweat and/or blood, and about his yearning to see the face of God. In this poem what we see is Christ's own "flammend Richterangesicht." And just as the speaker in those poems sometimes presented himself as a representative of all redeemed (or at least redeemable) humanity, so this poem ends with his presenting himself as the representative of all those who come at the latter day to be judged.

The rather curious treatment of time and action in this poem is also reminiscent of that in the crucifixion poems. Each stanza, we notice, begins with the word "Wann." In the first stanza the earth trembles and the "Auferwecker," presumably a stand-in for Gabriel and his trumpet, announces the judgment. In the second, the heavens and the kingdoms of the earth instantly vanish, leaving only ruins. In the third, Christ, accompanied by the angels, descends in his "Wolkenwagen." In the fourth, the assembled multitudes confront him. And in the fifth the focus narrows to the speaker alone. Yet are the various happenings occurring one after the other, in a clear temporal (and perhaps causal) sequence? It would seem not.

On the contrary, the repeated "Wann" at the beginning of each stanza sounds not like a storyteller's patient placing of events in sequence but rather like the excited exclamation of a child who is beholding something so stunningly complex and many-faceted that he is unable to sum it up, but must simply take it one aspect at a time. This sense of simultaneity is also, of course, created by the refrain at the end of each stanza—slightly altered in the last one. Moreover, the refrain itself is interesting in its relation to the rest of the poem. Grammatically, of course, it is simply the apodosis to the protasis formed, in each stanza, by the "Wann" clause. But in all five stanzas it is preceded by a colon, which suggests a different, and more intimate, relation to the stanza's earlier lines. Moreover, in three of the first four stanzas, the colon is immediately preceded by a verb that suggests speech: "schallt," "schwörst," and "spricht." There is thus the suggestion that "Gott! erbarm dich unser!" are not just words spoken by the speaker to complete the grammar of the stanza but are the words actually intoned by the voice of the "Auferwecker," the words that echo, in the souls of the damned, Christ's oath of vengeance, the words of "Fluch und Lohn" that he speaks (or causes to be spoken) in the souls of "alle Völker." This, I think, is why the alteration of the refrain in the final stanza seems so satisfying and right: this time "Gott! erbarm dich meiner!" is both what the speaker says to complete the stanza grammatically and also—since the subject of this stanza is the speaker himself—the words that embody the fear of all humanity as it manifests itself in the speaker.

So this poem shares some of the characteristics of the poems that deal with the crucifixion. But what has Bach made of it? Here is his setting:

The first thing we notice is how radically the music changes at just the point where the refrain enters. The ruggedly insistent bass octaves cease, the dynamics (hitherto unspecified) soften to *piano*, and the rhythm alters in a way that makes it sound as though the tempo has been halved. This does not, on the face of it, sort very well with what I have just been saying about the way in which Sturm makes the refrain seem closely related to the earlier portion of the stanza. The naked power of the first ten bars seems sharply, even absolutely, contrasted with the poignant pleading—reminiscent of "Ueber die Finsterniss kurz vor dem Tode Jesu"—of the last five.

Yet this is not quite true. After the little three-beat introduction, the first phrase of the melody (bars 1-3) is boldly declarative, characterized by leaps of fairly wide intervals before it comes to rest. Its general course, however, is clearly downward, emphasized by the stepwise descent of the lowest right-hand voice in the keyboard part. In the phrases that follow, the pattern of stepwise descent more or less takes control of the melody, first making itself strongly felt in the melodic appoggiaturas of bars 4 and 5, and in the appoggiatura in the alto voice at the beginning of bar 6. Despite the aggressive force of the drumming left-hand octaves, these appoggiaturas, and the clashes they produce in the harmony, introduce a certain poignancy into the music, a poignancy intensified by the two sudden high D's in the melody in bar 8. Thus, although we are surprised by the breaking off of the melody, by the harmony's turn to E-flat on the words "Gott! Gott!," and by the slow, quiet music that completes the song, we have been subtly prepared for these changes.

The poignancy that Bach allows to accumulate, even in the face of the persistently powerful and aggressive octaves in the keyboard's left hand, seems intended to betray a steadily increasing anxiety in the speaker-singer that is not present, or anyway not so clearly present, in Sturm's poem. And of course the song makes far more of the concluding plea for mercy than does the poem. Having ended on the relative major of the tonic, E-flat, the music of Bach's song, freed from the rhythmic constraints that had been so prominent earlier, floats languorously upward, through a series of rather indecisive harmonies, to close, wistfully and by no means triumphantly, in C minor, where it began.

These seem to me some of the very best songs in Bach's two Sturm collections. Even more decisively than in the Gellert volume, the best songs are concerned with poems that turn inward, especially those that contemplate aspects of Christ's mission as teacher, savior, and judge. Yet it would be unfair to leave the Sturm songs without sampling at least one of the best outer-directed songs. Also, it is interesting to see the best of what Bach furnished when confronted by Sturm's characteristic celebration of external nature as evidence of God's goodness and power.

IV

One of the most famous of these songs, praised by contemporary reviewers and twice reprinted in modern editions, is "Empfindungen in der Sommernacht," from the second collection. The poem, which is brief and undistinguished, goes as follows:

Der Mond ist aufgegangen:
Die güldnen Sterne prangen
Am blauen Himmelszelt.
Gebüsch und Haine schallen
Vom Lied der Nachtigallen:
O Gott, wie schön ist deine Welt!

Schön, wenn vom Abendthaue
Beperlet Wald und Aue
In deinem Segen stehn;
Und wenn in Ungewittern
Die Donner sie erschüttern,
Ist deine Welt, o Vater, schön.

Aus deiner Allmacht Fülle
Strömt in der Nächte Stille
Erquickung auf die Flur:
Und durch die kühlen Lüfte
Bringt ihre Balsamdüfte
Zum Abendopfer die Natur.

Mit ihrem Opfer walle
Mein Dank empor! Ich falle
Vor dir anbetend hin.
Du schufst in hoher Ferne
Den Mond: du schufst die Sterne:
Du schufst der Haine Sängerin.

There is, it seems to me, little to be said here in the way of analysis. The first two stanzas are really little more than mood music. The moon rises, the stars shine in the sky, the groves echo with the song of the nightingale, forest and meadow are besprent with dew, the storm's thunder manifests God's power and control over this beautiful world. The third stanza imagines a ceremonious exchange of gifts: renewing life flows forth, in the stillness of the night, from God to the fields; and they, in return, send up their sweet odors to God, as an offering of thanks. In the last stanza, the speaker of the poem joins this ceremony of thanksgiving, falling on his knees in prayer and glorifying God for having created the moon, the stars, and "der Haine Sängerin."

Here, however, is what Bach makes of Sturm's poem:

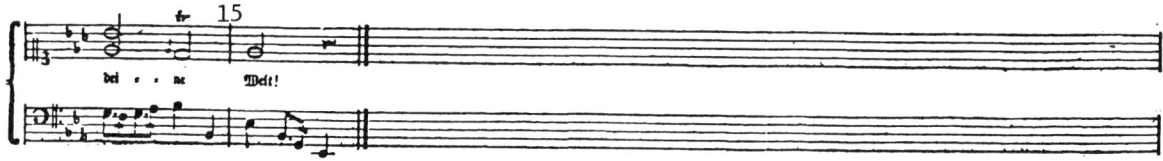

Bach's 19th-century biographer, C. H. Bitter, was especially fond of this song, which he called "a song that bears within itself a mood utterly foreign to the time of its composer, the Romantic mood."[12] And one can certainly see the sense in this judgment. The gentle lift of an octave in the bass, and the descent of the upper two voices, in thirds, instantly set a tone of languishing ease. Yet no sooner have we arrived at the expected subdominant than we note that each chord is marked with a vertical dash or wedge (*Keil*).

This is a mark not often employed by Bach in his songs. It occurs in only four of the remaining 59 Sturm songs, and these are all in the 1781 collection: numbers 1, 8, 13, and 14. It is found somewhat more frequently in the Gellert collection, in 11 of the 55 songs: numbers 12, 15, 16, 18, 20, 22, 27, 34, 39, 42, and 43. Moreover, even in the songs in which it occurs, it is used sparingly, for special emphasis. In *A Performer's Guide to Baroque Music*, Robert Donington writes: "Dots, dashes and wedges are staccato signs not distinct from one another until very late in the baroque period, when the dot tended (no more) to imply a lighter staccato."[13] But Bach himself, in the *Versuch*, makes no distinction between vertical dashes (or wedges) and dots, and employs dots simply because of the danger of confusing dashes with fingering numerals.[14] Here and elsewhere in his songs, however, it does seem as though Bach means something more by the vertical dash than simply what we mean by the familiar staccato dot. He usually places it over the notes in both staves (when there are notes in both staves), and he frequently places it over half notes. Sometimes he seems to mean little more by it than we mean by the staccato dot—for example, in the left hand's opening bar of the Gellert song, "Die Ehre Gottes aus der Natur" (where he also means it to apply to more than just the first three notes):

But usually, as in the song under consideration, he seems to want a sudden, strong accent where we should otherwise not expect one. As we learnt long ago, C.P.E. Bach is preeminently a composer of surprises; this marking is one of his means of getting them.

Its effect in the first phrase (and elsewhere) in "Empfindungen in der Sommernacht" is precisely to prevent us from sinking immediately into the romantic languor that seems promised by the song's opening phrase—and that Bitter, writing in the midst of the Romantic age, evidently finds characteristic of the song as a whole. Instead, the four notes bearing the marking, occurring (appropriately) on the words "ist aufgegangen," summon us back to business, redirecting our attention from the rather vague "Romantic" associations with the moon—and it had plenty of them by 1781—to our view of the actual physical moon rising (or already risen) in the night sky. Thus in the first bar-and-a-half we have a juxtaposition of idioms.

Bach continues to build on this juxtaposition throughout the course of the song. The motion initiated by the four notes marked with the vertical dash suddenly halts on the bass half note C in bar 2 (which, we notice, does not have a dash). The melodic phrase that enters is a version, a fourth higher, of the song's opening phrase, but this time it really does descend languishingly, as the bass line rises beneath it. At the end of bar 3, where the bass goes into close intervals, the texture darkens somewhat, the song's center of gravity seeming to lower. The cadence on F minor is approached thoughtfully and lingeringly—but then we notice the neat descent in the bass, complete with its brisk dotted-eighth-and-sixteenth rhythm: once more, back to business!

Each of the next two phrases (bars 6–8 and 8–10) begins with a descent, over a sustained bass, that seems once again to promise some sort of Romantic ease—but each time Bach once again pulls us up short, combining the use of the vertical dash with a briskly rhythmic bass arpeggio. Finally, however, the song's long concluding phrase (bars 10–15), spun out with syncopations and grace notes, seems to give us the rather sentimental repose Bach has been offering and then withdrawing all along. And the phrase really is quite beautiful—just as the song's first-stanza text declares God's world to be. But then in the penultimate bar we notice the left hand's busy little turning figure and, in the final bar, one last descending bass arpeggio.

Bitter's idea that "Empfindungen in der Sommernacht" is a proto-Romantic song born too early to achieve its full realization is thus completely mistaken. It was part of the Romantics' teleological view of art to see the eighteenth century as dominated by order, prose, and reason—except for those rare moments when the first rays of the Romantic dawn began to break through. It was too easily forgotten that the very sentimental novels of Samuel Richardson, which had perhaps even more influence in Germany than in England, appeared in the 1740s, along with Young's equally influential *Night Thoughts*. Several decades of Romantic languor had already passed before Bach composed "Empfindungen in der Sommernacht." He was not dimly glimpsing a world of Romantic sentiment still unborn; he was, rather, wittily playing off allusions to that world against a bracing and exuberant sense of God's power actively at work in his creation. In so doing, he was giving us a good deal more than Sturm gave us in his poem.

The reviewer for the *Gesammelte Beyträge zu der Hamburger Neuen Zeitung* said of Bach's first Sturm collection: "Since everyone knows his Gellert songs, we need say little more than that Bach remains always the same" (*Spiegel*, p. 102). And, as we have seen, it is in many ways true that in his two Sturm collections Bach returned to the idiom he had discovered and explored in his Gellert collection of almost a quarter century earlier. The songs are almost entirely strophic, and there is almost none of the experimentation that we have seen in so many of the songs intervening between the Gellert and Sturm collections. Bach no longer seems interested either in modest or extended through-composition, of the sort we saw in Chapters Ten and Thirteen, or in creating the sort of larger dramatic organization amongst songs or groups of songs that we saw in the Cramer Psalms.

Yet the religious feeling evidenced in many of the Sturm songs seems both stronger and darker than that found in the Gellert collection. The concentration on the crucifixion and on various other facets of Christ's mission and sacrifice attests to that. As we have seen from the beginning, Bach, like many of his contemporaries, was vexed, all through his career as a composer of songs, by the strophic problem. Perhaps one of the many reasons he felt so drawn, as he neared the end of his songwriting career, to poems dealing with Christ's sacrifice was precisely that they are so naturally fitted to the form of the strophic song. As the Gospels, and particularly St. John's gospel, repeatedly emphasize, almost everything that Christ does is a repetition of an earlier act, a fulfillment of a promise made earlier, in the Old Testament. As he himself often says, he comes not to destroy but to fulfill the law and the prophets. Thus Sturm's poems that deal with Christ's mission tend not to be straightforwardly dramatic but to be filled with correspondences, glances forward and back at later and earlier words and phrases. Moreover, since Christ on the cross represents all mankind, and since the speaker of Sturm's poems often puts himself forward as the representative of all mankind thus represented by Christ, the lines between characters become blurred. Thus the repetition of the same strophe of music for each stanza of poetry makes a kind of *prima facie* sense that it does not ordinarily make with a straightforwardly dramatic poem. The strophic problem is thus given at least a partial solution by the poetic text.

Chapter Fifteen

The Last Songs

During the last seven years of his life, from the publication of the second Sturm collection in 1781 to his death in 1788, C.P.E. Bach wrote relatively few songs. What mainly occupied him were his six volumes of solo keyboard pieces "für Kenner und Liebhaber." These were published in 1779, 1780, 1781, 1783, 1785, and 1787. Though some of the pieces had been composed earlier, the great majority date from 1778-1786. The only major choral work composed during that time is the 1783 *Klopstocks Morgengesang am Schöpfungsfeste*, though of course there were also many occasional passions. In the last two years of his life, Bach, freed from the burden of the *Kenner und Liebhaber* collections, had a final burst of creative energy in which he composed the F-sharp minor keyboard fantasy known as "C.P.E. Bachs Empfindungen"; the three Quartets for Keyboard, Flute, Viola, and Bass; and the fine Double Concerto for Harpsichord, Forte-Piano, and Orchestra.

The songs that he managed to compose along the way may be divided into three groups. First, there are two that were written, probably in 1781, for the 1782 edition of Voss's *Musen-Almanach*. Second, there are six songs that were added to others composed earlier, including the long cantata to Gerstenberg's poem "Die Grazien," to form the collection *Neue Lieder-Melodien*, which was posthumously published in 1789 but had probably been prepared for the press by Bach just before his death. Of these six songs, all but one were composed in 1782 or a bit earlier, and that one was composed in 1785. Third, there are 12 Masonic songs, probably composed about 1787, that Bach contributed to a volume entitled *Freimäurer-Lieder* that was published at Copenhagen and Leipzig in 1788 and that also contained songs by J. A. P. Schulz and the Dresden Kapellmeister Johann Gottlieb Naumann (1741-1801). We also know of a few songs from this period that have been lost, and it should further be noted that Bach contributed two litanies for double chorus to the *Vollständige Sammlung der Melodien zu den Gesängen des neuen allgemeinen Schleswigen-Holsteinschen Gesangbuchs* (Leipzig, 1785) and composed 14 chorales that appeared in *Neue Melodien zu einigen Liedern des neuen Hamburgischen Gesangbuchs* (Hamburg, 1787). These, like his earlier compositions of this sort, do not fall within our area of investigation; yet it is most significant that Bach composed them at this time.[1]

I

In Chapter Twelve we traced Bach's relations with Voss and the *Musen-Almanach*. In October 1780, as we saw at the end of that chapter, Voss expressed his dissatisfaction with Bach's setting of his poem "Tischlied" to his close collaborator J. A. P. Schulz. And on March 4, 1782, Voss told Schulz how much better he liked Schulz's simpler, more "volkstümlich" setting of the poem. Even before the former letter, on September 4, 1780, Voss had written the poet Leopold Friedrich Günther Goeckingk that he was "completely dissatisfied with the melody of 'Tischlied,'" and Voss had added: "But brother Schulz is a splendid fellow! If I can shake myself loose of Bach, Schulz alone will take care of the future compositions." Yet in the same letter in which he told Schulz of his preference for Schulz's setting of "Tischlied," Voss had also included some backhanded praise of Bach's recent work: "Wherever you seem to be making concessions to fashion, you, like Bach with his Rondos, always turn out to be the leader, not the slave, of fashion." The point of the compliment is that with his second *Kenner und Liebhaber* collection, published in 1780, Bach had begun including Rondos, then regarded as a *Modegattung*, a fashionable or popular form, along with the Sonatas—a practice that continued through the later collections, to which Fantasias were also added. And two months later, on May 13, 1782, again writing to Schulz, Voss praised Bach's setting of his poem "Die Schlummernde," which had appeared in the 1775 *Musen-Almanach*, as "very well composed."[2]

It is clear, then, that during the early 1780s Voss's attitude toward Bach, especially in relation to the *Volkslied* movement that he and Schulz were vigorously promoting, was ambivalent. Despite his intense dislike of the "Tischlied" setting—which he reiterated in a letter written to Schulz on April 10, 1787 (*Briefwechsel*, p. 61)—Voss still welcomed contributions from Bach to the 1782 *Musen-Almanach*. As we shall see over the course of this chapter, the poems that Bach chose to set in his last years strongly suggest that he too was deeply preoccupied with the *Volkslied* movement and, specifically, with what his own relation to it ought to be.

One of the two songs Bach contributed is in fact to a rather odd and witty poem by Voss himself, "Das Milchmädchen":

>Mädchen, nehmt die Eimer schnell,
>>Habt ihr ausgemolken!
>
>Seht, die Sterne blinken hell,
>Und der Vollmond guckt so grell
>>Aus den krausen Wolken!
>
>Lieg' und wiederkäu' in Ruh'
>>Dein gesundes Futter!
>
>Alles, gute fromme Kuh,
>Milch und Käse schenkest du,
>>Rahm und süsse Butter!
>
>Ruhig läuten durch das Feld
>>Dumpfe Rinderglocken;
>
>Und der Hund im Dorfe bellt,
>Und der Schlag der Wachtel gellt
>>Im betauten Roggen!
>
>Mädchen, singt mit frohem Schall;
>>Wer nicht singt, den grauet!
>
>Hört den schönen Widerhall
>Dort im Wald' und Erlental,
>>Wo der Hase brauet!
>
>"Töchterlein, nimm dich in acht,
>>Komm mir bald zu Hause!"
>
>Sagt die Mutter: "in der Nacht

Schwärmt des Teufels wilde Jagd
    Mit des' Sturms Gesause!

Ein gehörnter schwarzer Mann
    Kommt oft hulter pulter!
Guckt mit glühndem Aug' dich an,
Kneipt dich mit der Krall', und dann
    Hockt er auf die Schulter!"

Mädchen, wandelt früh und spät,
    Trotz den klugen Müttern!
Wer auf guten Wegen geht,
Und auf Kreuze sich versteht,
    Darf vor Spuk nicht zittern!

Zwar mich fasst ein Bösewicht
    Manchmal um den Nacken;
Aber rot ist sein Gesicht,
Und mit Krallen kneipt er nicht
    Freundlich meine Backen!

Dieser heisst, das Ohr gespitzt!
    Wilhelm und so ferner:
Zwar sein blaues Auge blitzt;
Aber, wenigstens bis itzt,
    Trägt er keine Hörner!

 From the title, and from what we know of Voss, we expect this poem to be some sort of pastoral—a sketch of idyllic village life, showing the milkmaid going cheerfully about her work in an immaculately idealized setting. The first word, "Mädchen," suggests that the poet is going to address her fondly—but then the imperative verbs that follow all turn out to be plural, not singular. Moreover, the speaker is telling the milkmaids to hurry: they seem to be quite late with their evening chores. The stars are already out, and so is the full moon—though, we notice, it is scarcely the full moon of song and story: it glares harshly from amongst wispy clouds. The cow, addressed affectionately in the second stanza, is the only one in this poem who inhabits an ideal world. The cowbells have none of the expected charm but ring heavily and dully; a dog barks; the call of the quail is shrill. Moreover, the injunction to the maidens to sing a happy song carries with it a threat: sing so that you won't be afraid of the storm brewing in the valley.[3] As if this were not bad enough, an unspecified, generic mother tells a dark tale of the devil, who rides out on stormy nights, fixes his evil eye on likely young girls, snatches them up in his claws, and spirits them away.

 At this point the poem changes direction. Never mind all that, says the speaker—whose identity we still do not know. Wander around all you like, early and late; no good Christian need worry about spooks. And then finally the speaker is revealed to be the milkmaid of the title, a kind of leader of the group, bolder and cheekier than the others. Having taunted and scared them sufficiently, she confesses that she is indeed often seized by a "Bösewicht"—but not by the one in the old wives' tale. This one's face is red, not black, and when he nips at her cheeks he does it in a friendly way, and not with his claws—but, the reader supplies, with his lips. His blue eyes may indeed blaze, but he does not have horns—or not yet, at least! The possibility that he may, one of these days, push his advances to the point where he would become, at least in a mother's watchful eyes, something of a devil is raised by the speaker but is not contemplated with fear or distaste. Indeed, she may rather be hoping for it. Moreover, the fact that he does not yet "wear horns" can also mean that she has not yet cheated on him—though she may do so. Perfectly poised in its irony, the poem leaves all these possibilities open.

Let us now see what Bach made of this admirable poem. Here is his song, as it appears, somewhat modernized, in Otto Vrieslander's 1922 collection, *Lieder und Gesänge*:

One's first impression is of concerted energy and bustling good humor. Melody and bass line move together rhythmically but in contrary motion through the first phrase. The second phrase, by comparison, seems rather graceful, its curving melody and concluding turn contrasting sharply with the stepwise motion of the opening phrase. Again the pause at the end of the phrase is filled by a bass arpeggio—but this time by one that descends rather than ascending, the neatness of the symmetry heightening the wit of the song.

At the beginning of bar 5, however, we have a surprise: as expected, the bass descends through an octave, but its low G unexpectedly forms the seventh of a V^7/ii, taking us into D minor. The darkening of the harmony, and the bass line's imitation, in bar 6, of the preceding bar's melodic line, momentarily give the music greater drama and density than we were prepared for. But after dwelling for one more bar in D minor—where the ear expects a turn to the dominant and thence to the concluding tonic—the music brightens once more. Of course the song cannot end, as the various earlier symmetries have led the ear to expect, in bar 8, for Voss's poem has a five-line stanza. Bach turns this fact to advantage by staying on the dominant through bar 8, as the melody once again moves upward, and then, with mock-pomposity, extending the cadence under the melody's dancing sixteenth notes, and ending with a trill.

This setting seems to suit Voss's poem very well indeed. Without in the least making it more serious and important than it is, Bach has managed, by the little movement into D minor, to catch the poem's moments of slight harshness and disturbance. But, just as in the poem, everything turns out for the best, and the music has about it a witty knowingness that seems appropriate to Voss's speaker. It would be very interesting to know what Voss thought of it, but so far as I know, he never expressed himself on the matter.

There was, however, another setting of "Das Milchmädchen," of which we do know Voss's opinion. On May 13, 1782, Voss sent his friend Schulz three poems to set for the 1783 *Musen-Almanach*, along with a number of other poems of his own, in hopes that Schulz might use them in the forthcoming first volume of his *Lieder im Volkston* series. But on July 7 Schulz wrote him to say that he had already sent off his manuscript, and was expecting copies any day. Schulz did, however, mention that "Das Milchmädchen" was among the poems that he had set for the volume. On May 22, 1783, Voss, whose wife had been ill and whose oldest son had died recently, finally got around, with many apologies, to thanking Schulz for *Lieder im Volkston*. He mentioned "the playful [*muthwillige*] song of my *Milchmädchen*" only in passing, as one of a group of songs of which he exclaimed: "All, all are excellent" (*Briefwechsel*, pp. 20-22, 28-32).

Here is Schulz's setting:

Mutwillig, surely, is not the first word one would think of applying to this song. It has none of the mischievous playfulness of Voss's poem—or of Bach's setting. Lacking the hymnic solemnity of Schulz's setting of Voss's "Tischlied," it is perhaps even worse: not simple, but merely arid and banal, the musical equivalent of those dreadful pastorals by Ambrose ("Namby-Pamby") Philips over which Pope and Gay had so much sport earlier in the century. Trapped in its own relentless diatonicism—not an accidental in sight!—it goes nowhere and says nothing. The final proof of Schulz's utter lack of invention is his failure to turn the somewhat unusual five-line stanza to musical advantage—as we saw Bach doing. Indeed, Schulz has not really written a ten-bar song at all: this setting of Voss's poem is really an eight-bar setting of which bars 5 and 6 had to be repeated in order to make the music stretch to the end of the stanza.

Bach's other song to appear in the 1782 *Musen-Almanach* is a setting of a poem by another member of the "Göttinger Hainbund," Count Friedrich Leopold Stolberg. The poem is titled, simply, "Lied":

> Ich ging unter Erlen am kühligen Bach,
> Und dachte wohl manchem und manchem wohl nach;
> Es war mir im Herzen so leicht und so wohl,
> Doch wurden von Thränen die Augen mir voll.
>
> Es entschwebte den säuselden Wellen das Bild
> Von meiner Geliebten, holdselig und mild;

Da sank ich an's Ufer in's schwellende Moos,
Mir stürtzten die Thränen hinab in den Schoos.

   Nun lag ich im Schatten am kühligen Bach,
Und dachte wohl manchem und manchem wohl nach;
Die Nachtigall sang, und es rauschte der Bach;
Da dacht' ich dem Einen und Einen nur nach.

   Schon flammten die Wolken im röthenden Strahl,
Schon senkten sich bräunere Schatten in's Thal,
Schon bebte durch Erlen der Mond auf dem Bach;
Ich dachte dem Einen und Einen nur nach.

   Nun wankt' ich von dannen mit weinendem Blick,
Und sah nach dem Bach und den Erlen zurück;
Sie schwanden. Es schwand nicht das liebliche Bild,
Das immer und immer die Seele mir füllt.

The remarkable thing about this fine poem is the enormous disparity between the power of the emotional experience it recounts and the quiet, hypnotically lulling tone in which it is recounted. Aside from his constant thinking, the only acts the speaker commits are simple physical acts: he walks to the side of the brook, sinks down on the bank, lies in the shadows, walks unsteadily away, and finally looks back at the scene as he departs. Everything else—everything that constitutes the powerful experience he undergoes—is something that happens to him, not something he does: tears fill his eyes (though his heart is light), his beloved's image appears in the waves of the brook, the tears pour down into his lap, and the image of his lost love refuses to go away, continuing, "immer und immer," to fill his soul. Moreover, his thinking, the most important act he performs, seems curiously undirected and lacking in conscious purpose—almost as if someone else were pulling the strings. The object of his reflections is at first the vague, unspecified "manchem und manchem" (presumably an undifferentiated mass of past experience), but gradually—as his sadness increases and the sun sets—it becomes directed to "dem Einen und Einen" (presumably that image of his beloved that stubbornly refuses to leave his consciousness). The one point at which the lulling, constantly flowing movement of the verse is broken is in the penultimate line: though the details of the landscape disappear as he walks away from the place, the painful yet cherished image remains. The contrast is thus deftly enforced.

The air of dissociation from his own experience that so clearly marks the speaker of the poem is all the more effective for being presented in such a muted, underplayed manner. The poem is much sadder (and more frightening) than many far more dramatic poems about lost love. Here is what Bach made of it:

Though neither so sad nor so frightening as Stolberg's poem, this setting is admirable for its reticence and its air of delicate melancholy.

The tempo direction, we note, is only *Etwas langsam*: slow yet not so slow as to deaden the dance-like movement created in the accompaniment by the delayed entrance in bar 1 and kept alive, at the end of the first phrase, by the bass line's descent to low E on the second beat of bar 4. While the first phrase is openly lyrical, with the bass moving freely beneath, the second phrase, over a chromatically descending bass line, seems to shrink in upon itself, to become constricted and even a little contorted as it probes the fourth between B and F-sharp—just a fifth above the interval through which the bass is steadily descending. Suddenly, at the end of bar 8, the melody bursts out alone—a somewhat restrained cry in the wilderness that is repeated, in more decorated form, a step higher. The final phrase, a stepwise descent beginning on C that leads into the cadence, echoes bars 2–3—with the splendid change of the original F-sharp to an F-natural: the quasi-modal poignancy of the ♭II⁶ chord turns the conclusion into a kind of relapse, a final withdrawal into the self that is most appropriate to the speaker of Stolberg's poem.

Once again we have no idea what Voss thought of this setting, or how he saw it in relation to the folksong movement. What we do know, however, is that when Bach turned to composing songs for his own *Neue Lieder-Melodien*, he kept experimenting with folk poems, themes, and musical idioms. Plainly, the new movement made an impression upon him that extended far beyond what he may have considered his obligations to Voss. It will perhaps be most useful to consider the songs that wound up in *Neue Lieder-Melodien* in order of increasing musical complexity.

II

The simplest is the setting of a faux-naïf little poem by Gleim called "Mittel, freundlich zu werden":

> Mein Vater küsst die Mutter,
> Die Mutter küsst den Vater,
> Und wenn sie beyde küssen,
> So sind sie beyde freundlich.
> Wie oft sagt meine Mutter:

418 ∾ Chapter Fifteen

> Mein Wilhelm werde freundlich!
> Nun will ich es schon werden;
> Denn unsers Nachbars Tochter
> Lässt sich recht gerne küssen.

There is not much that needs saying about this. The joke of course is that when Wilhelm's mother tells him to be friendly, she is trying to turn him from a moody adolescent into a sociable adult—not into the seducer of their neighbor's daughter. And yet his justification of his behavior—whether genuinely naive or simply tongue-in-cheek—is perfectly logical: when his parents kiss, they act friendly to each other; therefore this must be what his mother has in mind.

Bach's setting is not inappropriately pretentious, and yet it manages to make the poem rather more interesting than it seems when it stands alone:

Though there is nothing particularly complex about this song, it is plainly in a different world from the two settings by Schulz that we have examined.

Nothing could be simpler than the first phrase—or than the way it is slightly varied in the phrase that immediately follows (bars 1–4). But the slight irregularities in the bass line's playful little octave jumps throw us off balance just enough to keep things interesting. When the melody launches out on its own in bar 5, and the harmony turns toward F minor, it sounds as though things may be getting a bit more serious—but the octave jump at the beginning of bar 6 keeps the tone playful, as does the one in bar 8, at the cadence. With the citation of mother's injunction to be friendly, we begin the rise to a climax (though still with the octave jumps beneath), which is reached in bar 13, having been ushered in by the rather grand little rising arpeggio in the bass. But in the following bar the bass again turns playful. Yet again, in bar 17, the solidly repeated quarter notes in the bass seem to promise an increase in seriousness—and yet again the promise is not kept: as the melodic phrase is repeated in bars 19-20, the bass turns to dancing eighth notes. The move to the final cadence sustains the playful tone.

It is interesting to notice how Bach has apportioned the 24 bars of his song to Gleim's nine lines of poetry. To each of the first six lines—through "Mein Wilhelm werde freundlich!"—Bach gives two bars. But the seventh line, "Nun will ich es schon werden," comes at bar 13, the climax of the song, and is stretched out to cover four bars. Line eight again gets two bars, as does line nine, but it is then repeated, stretched out over four bars. By letting the music expand at the climax, and also by taking pains to retain a playful tone throughout, Bach gives the speaker of Gleim's poem a triumphant exit, and makes it seem, as Gleim did not in his poem, that Wilhelm is very conscious of the sophistry that leads him to justify kissing the neighbor's daughter by referring back to his mother's advice. All in all, an excellent song.

Next come two pastoral vignettes. The first of these, "Lied der Schnitterinnen," is also by Gleim. It appears thus in Bach's *Neue Lieder-Melodien*:

> Singend gehn wir, fröhlich singend
> Unser bestes Hirten-Lied!
> Zu der Arbeit gehn wir springend,
> Dass uns hört, wer uns nicht sieht.
> Singend gehn wir zum Getümmel,
> Zu den Heerden gehen wir;
> Singend gehn wir; unterm Himmel
> Ist kein Volk so froh wie wir.

There is, if anything, even less to be said about this poem than there was about "Mittel, freundlich zu werden." Indeed, it seems almost too straightforward. The only question is why these female mowers are going "Zu den Heerden": surely they are not intending to shear the sheep with their sickles? One is amused to notice that in the standard (1811) edition of Gleim's *Sämmtliche Werke*, the sixth line of "Die Schnitterinnen" reads thus: "In die Ernte, alle wir!" This of course makes far better sense. But one is still left wondering why the poem should ever have been printed as it is in Bach's collection.

Here is Bach's setting:

There are many more of the *Volkslied* trademarks in this setting than in "Mittel, freundlich zu werden": The quasi-drone bass, for example, and the predominant melodic rhythm—in this case eighth-quarter-eighth. But the further we go into the song, the more differences we see between it and, say, Schulz's setting of "Das Milchmädchen."

The eighth-quarter-eighth syncopated rhythm really does dominate at least the early portions of the song. It appears in six of the first eight bars! Moreover, the harmonic rhythm of those bars moves very slowly: four of tonic, then four of dominant—all outlined clearly by the unvarying quarter-note drone bass. Or almost unvarying: we notice that it drops out for a beat in bars 3 and 7. In the next eight bars, however, the eighth-quarter-eighth melodic rhythm appears in only three bars, being supplanted in bars 10 and 14 by the elegant little turning figures and in bar 15 by straight eighth notes. We also note the way in which the bass delays for half a beat at the end of bar 14, coming in with an eighth note to pick up the end of the melodic turning figure and move into the cadence. At the beginning of the third eight bars, the harmony thickens—rather as in bars 17-18 of "Mittel, freundlich zu werden"—and the melodic rhythm is again somewhat loosened, the passage ending with a rather expansive bass arpeggio. Finally, in the fourth and last eight-bar section the rhythm breaks free. On the words "Singend gehn wir," the two upper voices move lyrically in thirds while the bass sustains—and then, in the next bar, imitates the upper voice. Only at this point, as the song begins to pull together, does Bach allude to the eighth-quarter-eighth rhythm. Bars 29-30, sung to the words "ist kein Volk so froh," have a fine air of decision and finality about them, and the fast-moving eighth-note cadential phrase, complete with concluding bass arpeggio, ends the song forcefully.

This seems to me a charming piece, just as stylized and monotonous as it needs to be to suit Gleim's poem, yet skillfully (and very gradually) freeing itself from its initial mannerisms as it goes along. Bach's other pastoral sets a quite different poem, written by another "Göttinger Hainbund" member, Johann Martin Miller, and called (as it originally appeared in the 1775 *Göttinger Musen-Almanach* and as printed in Bach's collection) "Das mitleidige Mädchen":

> Der fromme Damon dauert mich
> Von ganzen Herzen;
> Voll innern Harms verzehrt er sich
> In Liebes-Schmerzen:
> Wie Sommer-Rosen welkt er hin.
> Doch weinen kann ich nur um ihn.
>
> Er schwankt des Tages zehenmal
> Mein Haus vorüber;

Und immer wird bey seiner Qual
Mein Auge trüber.
Ich blicke traurig nach ihm hin:
Doch weinen kann ich nur um ihn.

    Ach dir, Amyntas, schlägt allein
Diess Herz im Stillen;
Du nur kannst seine süsse Pein
Durch Liebe stillen!
O Liebe! lenke du sein Herz,
Und lindr', o lindre Damons Schmerz.

The speaker of the poem, it seems, is the compassionate maiden herself. She sees Damon suffering the pangs of disappointed love, and sympathizes with his plight. Ten times a day, she tells us, he staggers by her house, and each time she sees him she grows sadder. But why does he pass her house so often? Is she the lover who has rejected him? It would seem not, since she repeatedly says that all she can do for him is to cry about the pain he is undergoing. With the third and final stanza a new character suddenly enters the poem. She turns from addressing us and speaks to Amyntas: it is for you that his heart secretly beats (she says); only you can ease his pain through your love. But who is Amyntas?

Amyntas is a shepherd first encountered in Theocritus's *Idyll* VII but better known for his several appearances in Virgil's *Eclogues*.[4] So we are suddenly, and somewhat to our surprise, thrust back into the homoerotic world of the Alexandrian and Roman pastoral. In the final lines of Miller's poem, the maiden asks love to guide or direct Damon's heart and soothe his distress. But what, exactly, does this mean? Miller evidently did not think he had made himself clear on this point, for his final version of the poem, as it appears in his collected works, substitutes the words "lenke mir sein Herz" for the troublingly ambiguous "lenke du sein Herz" of the version used by Bach. She is asking that love incline Damon's heart away from Amyntas and toward her.

Once puzzled out, this poem seems more like a tour de force than a poem. The poetry of Horace, Virgil, and Ovid of course had a powerful and fructifying influence on the German lyric poetry of the mid- and late eighteenth century. But the casual bisexuality of the classical pastoral does not fit naturally into the rather lavishly sentimental and comradely world of the German "Anacreontic" poets. That Miller retitled the poem "Das Mitleiden" may well indicate that he came to see it more as an exercise, an attempt to depict a certain very special emotional state, than as the anguished monologue of an actual *Mädchen*.

In any case, here is Bach's setting:

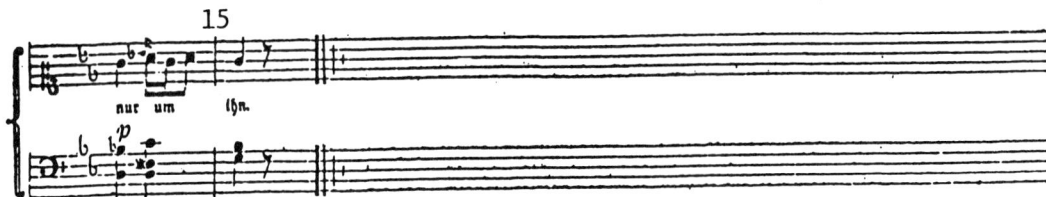

Clearly, we have moved far from the qualified folksong idiom of the preceding two songs.

The song begins as a rather conventional lament, the melody, in even eighths with frequent repeated notes, slowly working its way downward to a thinly voiced accompaniment in even quarters. But at the beginning of bar 4 there is a mild disruption: the phrase-ending seems sudden, abrupt. The melody of the second phrase begins in a manner similar to that of the first, but the accompaniment is now only on the off-beats. Moreover, while we seem to be heading into F, the diminished seventh at the end of bar 6 pushes us toward B-flat. Both melodic and bass lines become more active in bar 7, and the phrase-ending again seems a bit abrupt. The bass line's high B-flat at the end of bar 8 leads without a break into the next phrase, which begins with a wistfully lyrical little passage in thirds. As the harmony moves, at the end of bar 10, to a D chord, we expect the phrase to end back in the tonic, G minor. But again, just as in the preceding phrase, we are deflected further to the flat side of the spectrum—this time, by a twisting, contorted melodic detour (bars 11–12) into C minor. The expected four-bar phrase is thus extended to five bars. The song ends, once again abruptly, with the simplest of two-bar cadences. After all the various deflections—harmonic, melodic, and rhythmic—the simplicity of this little phrase seems to speak not so much of conclusion as of submission, of giving up because there is no way to go on. Though it does not seem very intimately connected to Miller's poem, this is nonetheless an interesting and touching piece.

The first of the two non-strophic songs intended for *Neue Lieder-Melodien* is the only religious one of the group. It sets an untitled poem by Countess Elise von der Recke (1756–1833):

> Ich hoff auf Gott mit festem Muth,
> Er wird mir Hülfe geben.
> Wie Gott mich führt, so ist es gut,
> Sein ist mein ganzes Leben.
> Schickt er mir Leidensstunden zu,
> So schaft er mir auch Trost und Ruh,
> Und hilft mir überwinden.
>
> Zwar wird es meiner Seele schwer,
> Wenn Leiden mich ergreifen.
> Oft ist mein Herz am Troste leer,
> Wenn sie zu stark sich häufen.
> Doch seufz' ich Gott zu dir hinauf,
> Dann richtest du mich wieder auf,
> Du Tröster meiner Seele!
>
> Verlassen hab' ich mich auf dich
> Seit frühsten Jugend-Tagen;
> Du treuster Gott, wirst ferner mich
> Auf Vater-Armen tragen.
> Ich hoff auf Gott, auf Gott allein!
> Diess soll mein Trost und Labsal seyn
> Im Leiden und im Sterben.

This poem certainly seems trite enough, both in style and in content. Yet the noble young poetess, commonly referred to simply as "Elise," was apparently well regarded. She and a friend had visited Bach at the end of October 1785, and his song is dated November 1. That he set her poem, and did it so promptly, perhaps demonstrates his respect for her work, as Ernst Suchalla hypothesizes. On the other hand, she was young, of noble birth, probably charming, and certainly lavish in her admiration for the aging Bach.

Here is his quite interesting setting:

Though the poem's second stanza deals at slightly greater length with the speaker's occasional sufferings than do its other two stanzas, we should certainly have expected Bach to compose a strophic setting for it. But he has not done that. Instead he has employed a three-part form, a sort of modified ABA, in which the first and third parts differ in expressive detail but not in general layout.

Though this is a religious song, it is by no means somber. The tempo marking suggests not only liveliness but also firm resolve—and we encounter both qualities immediately, in the very first phrase. The vocal line launches out boldly on its own, its two emphatic quarter notes and playful little descending phrase being answered, as if in wholehearted agreement, by a cadential phrase in octaves. The little downward bass flourish at the end—a gesture made frequently, in both directions, in this A section—decisively caps the matter. The next few bars (3-5) are somewhat more lyrical, with cheerful, dancelike activity in the bass line, leading to the emphatic declaration "so ist es gut" (bars 5-6), given in quarter notes that recall the very opening. Again the music grows a little lyrical, even tender, and then darkens momentarily (bars 9-10) as we move into D minor for mention of the speaker's "Leidens-Stunden." But then three descending melodic phrases, each initiated by a pair of sixteenth notes, immediately lighten the tone (bars 11-12). The section closes with a little turning figure in the melody answered, as at the beginning, by a descent in octaves to the cadence.

As we move into the poem's second stanza, the key changes to C minor and the volume drops to *piano*—but without the tempo slowing. The bass off-beats (bar 15) add to the drama and tension. But the music keeps veering toward the major, and some of the phrases strongly suggest those of the A section. Therefore we cannot take the "Leiden" spoken of in bar 17 quite seriously—we have too often seen the sort of music C.P.E. Bach can provide when he really wants to communicate suffering. The rather breathless drama of bars 23-24, in which the highly placed, off-beat left-hand chords nicely catch the speaker's sighing, is almost operatic in effect, and so are the sudden climax in bar 25, the equally sudden slowing of the tempo in bar 27, and the rush to the close of the section. Is Bach perhaps having a little fun with the countess's poem? It does not seem impossible.

The first five bars of the second A section are exactly the same as those of the first one—with one small but significant difference: the opening phrase of the vocal line is made slightly more assertive by the addition of a third C before the little descending figure, which this time comes off the beat, where we should expect it, rather than on the beat as before. It is only in bar 35 that the changes set in. Instead of repeating the solidly insistent quarter notes of bar 6, the vocal line exuberantly cuts loose and we travel a somewhat different harmonic route to reach the dominant in bar 37. The dynamics are increased to *forte*, and instead of the diminished seventh moving to D minor that we had back in bar 9, at the mention of "Leidens-Stunden," we have the joyous proclamation "Ich hoff auf Gott," set to a melodic line reminiscent of that in bars 5-6 ("so ist es gut") over a leaping A-major arpeggio in the bass. Therefore when we do touch momentarily on D minor in bar 39, it is felt merely as a transitional chord leading us to the three lighthearted descending phrases in bars 39-41 (which parallel those in bars 10-12) rather than as a dark sonority associated with suffering. As so often, Bach has one concluding surprise: at the end of bar 41 the dynamics soften to *piano*, and instead of the triumphant end we expected, the music turns inward, moving through the subdominant to a quiet, almost prayerful close.

The finest, and most formally complex, of the last songs written for *Neue Lieder-Melodien* is, interestingly, to an anonymous folk poem in Swiss dialect described only by the phrase "Aus dem Canton Schweiz." The six-stanza poem, entitled "Nonnelied," is the unhappy monologue of a girl who deeply regrets her decision to enter a convent. In the version presented in Bach's *Neue Lieder-Melodien* it runs as follows:

> 'S ist kein verdriesslicher Lebe,
> Als in das Klösterli gehe.
> Man muss darinne verbliebe,
> Muss alle Schäzli miede.
> O Liebe, was hab ich gethan!
> O Liebe, was hab ich gethan!
>
> Dort kömmet mie Vater und Muter,
> In Klösterli finde sie mich;
> Hab'n alle hübsche Kleidli an;
> Weder ich muss in dem Kütli stahn.
> O Liebe, was hab ich gethan!
> O Liebe, was hab ich gethan!
>
> Wenn ich in die Kirche gehe,
> Sing ich die Vesper alleine;
> Wenn ich das Gloriabäteli sing,
> Liegt mir mie Schäzli nur im Sinn.
> O Liebe, was hab ich gethan!
> O Liebe, was hab ich gethan!
>
> Wenn ich dann zu Tischli gehe,
> Steht mir das Tischli alleine;
> Ich esse das Fleisch, und trinke den Wie,
> Und denke, o Schäzli, wärst du dabie!
> O Liebe, was hab ich gethan!
> O Liebe, was hab ich gethan!

Wenn ich denn auch schlafe gehe,
Steht mir das Bettli alleine;
Ich liege darin, dass Gott erbarm!
Und denke Dich, Schäzli, in mine Arm.
O Liebe, was hab ich gethan!
O Liebe, was hab ich gethan!

In der Nacht, wenn ich erwach,
Da greif ich hin und her.
Da mag ich greife, wo ich will,
Wo ich greife, ist alles still.
O Liebe, was hab ich gethan!
O Liebe, was hab ich gethan!

One is not sure just how a reader in Lutheran Hamburg of the 1780s would be most likely to respond to this poem about a young nun in Catholic Switzerland. Bach had undoubtedly come across it in the 1777 edition of Voss's *Musen-Almanach*. Such *Nonnelieder* were, Gudrun Busch tells us, quite popular at the time, and she shrewdly observes: "The reader can choose either to shed sentimental tears of compassion or, as an Enlightened person, to protest against such a suppression of personal freedom."[5] Perhaps the reason such poems were popular was precisely that they offered poets the opportunity to satisfy (and their readers the opportunity to indulge) so many favorite literary cravings: for *Empfindsamkeit* pathos, perfectly exemplified in the life of a young girl forever denied a normal life in the world; for the carefree praise of wine, women, and song, common to Horatian or "Anacreontic" verses; and for gothic spookiness, easily associated with the mysterious life led behind the walls of a venerable cloister. Johann Martin Miller, a member of the "Göttinger Hainbund" who was born at Ulm, in Catholic south Germany, and who eventually returned there to serve as a pastor and a professor of theology, wrote many such poems, which explore the relations amongst these various emotional states from several different angles. Of Miller's boyhood, spent in Leipheim on the Danube, August Sauer wrote: "Here, in the company of Capuchins and Piarists, the Protestant developed that predilection for the monastic life that later so clearly left its mark on *Siegwart*."[6]

This particular *Nonnelied* shows up in most of the major collections of such poems. As printed in Ludwig Tobler's late 19th-century *Schweizerische Volkslieder*, it is different in two ways from the text used by Bach. First, the refrain repeated after each stanza reads: "O Himmel, was hab i getan! / die Liebi ist Schuld daran." Second, the second stanza of Bach's version is moved to the end of the poem.[7] Thus the final emphasis is not on the girl's loneliness for her sweetheart as she awakens in the middle of the night but rather on the shame and alienation she feels when her parents visit her, in their fine clothes, as she stands before them in her coarse woolen habit. Though this is perhaps a psychologically more penetrating ending, one can well understand why the more obviously "romantic" one would have had a stronger appeal in the late 18th century. In either version, the poem makes its effect through the sadly reiterated "alleine": though the speaker has joined what is supposed to be a religious community, she feels more alone than ever.

For this poem too Bach devised a non-strophic setting, which Gudrun Busch justly calls "the most mature representative of the modified strophic song" in his entire output (Busch, p. 360):

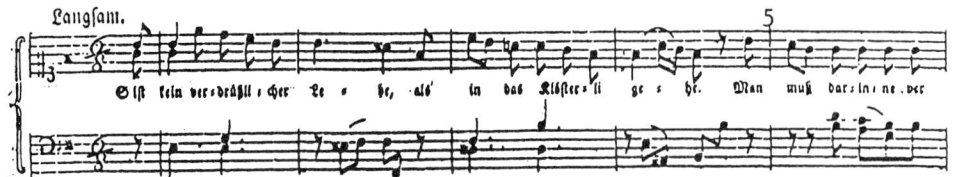

Though the tempo marking is "Langsam," the amount of eighth-note movement in the melody, supported and urged forward by bass figures that begin on the off-beat, suggests that this song should not be taken too slowly. Each strophe, except for the climactic final one, is fifteen bars long. The first eight bars, in which we move from the initial E minor to a cadence on G major, take us through the body of each stanza. The last seven bars, in which we move back to E minor, embody the refrain.

The impression given by the first four bars of the opening strophe is one of simple, lyrical pathos. The melody has an easy swing to it, and there is a pleasing symmetry between melody and bass line:

when the melody moves, the bass is stable, and vice versa. But in bar 5 the melody starts alone, and is imitated by the bass. We are not sure where we are tonally until the end of bar 6, when the ascending bass line and the F in the melody make it clear that we have embarked on a I-IV-V-I cadence on G (bar 8). During bars 9 and 10 we are again momentarily uncertain: are we still in G or have we returned to E minor? The little appoggiatura in bar 10, over the gently lulling bass arpeggios, is especially seductive. But then, with bar 11 and its powerfully dramatic assertion of the V of E minor, everything is suddenly clear. After this outburst, bar 13 (and its pickup)—the only bar to be repeated unchanged until the song's final strophe—represents a quiet, introspective withdrawal. But then we have another sudden outburst: the wonderfully dark F#-minor chord, delivered *forte*, in bar 14. The E-minor cadence that closes the strophe is a rhythmic copy, in both melody and bass, of the G-major one seven bars earlier. The two outbursts, it is worth noting, occur on the "was" of the speaker's anguished question: "Was hab ich gethan!"

The rhythm of the melody at the beginning of the second strophe (bar 16) is slightly different, but only because of the layout of the poetic line. The only changes of consequence come in bars 21 and 22, with the sixteenth notes on "weder" and "muss in." Again, one might say that this change too is merely forced on Bach by the poem's verbal layout. But he was not forced to make each pair of sixteenths change pitch, nor to omit the melodic F at the end of bar 21 that smooths the passage to the IV chord in the bar following. The drop of a fourth and rise of a sixth that he chose to make—rather, say, than having each pair of sixteenths on a repeated pitch—give the vocal line a slight air of decisiveness or force, dramatizing the speaker's feelings of shame and isolation.

The third strophe begins (bar 31) with the same, slightly altered rhythm as the second, but there are more changes this time. Bars 35 and 36, in which the girl mentions the "Gloria-Bäteli," are quite different from the corresponding bars in either of the two preceding strophes. The bass is steady on low B throughout bar 35, and the melody describes a descending G-major triad in its latter half. The sixteenth notes that rise a sixth at the beginning of bar 36, though differently placed within the bar, give the same feeling of assertiveness as did those in bar 22 of the second strophe. A further change, small yet significant, is that the bass line in the last bar of the strophe (bar 45) is extended to the end of the bar by the addition of a D#.

This slight alteration links the end of the third strophe to the beginning of the fourth, which is dramatically different from those of the preceding ones. For the first two bars (46 and 47) the vocal line stays high rather than descending, as before, while the bass performs a pair of off-beat downward octave leaps, and then drops out for a half-bar. The result is greatly to increase the urgency of the young nun's lament, an effect heightened by the chromatic descent of the melodic line into bar 48. Bars 50–55 are also quite different from the corresponding bars in any preceding stanza. Already in bar 50 the harmony moves to IV, and in bar 51 the bass momentarily drops out and then continues the melody's downward line. In bar 52 the hurried sixteenths capture the intensity with which the girl yearns for her sweetheart, and the new, passionate line to which the words "O Liebe, O Liebe" are sung (bars 53–55) heightens the effect still further. (We note that the lulling, repetitive bass line has been replaced, in bar 55, by a more active and irregular one.) Again the strophe ends with a bass line that leads into the next one.

At the beginning of strophe five (bar 61) the bass line just keeps right on moving up, continuing the motion begun at the end of the preceding strophe as the melody traces an extended version of its earlier line at this point, ending in bar 62 on an A# that intensifies the clash produced by the B chord in the following bar. And this time the rather soothing, temporarily reassuring effect that the cadence on G major had in the preceding strophes is marred by the suggestion of a diminished seventh created in bar 66 by the collision of Eb and F#. Again, at the end of bar 67, a rush of sixteenth notes captures the nun's urgency as she speaks of her loved one. The curious, confused overlapping keyboard and vocal lines also dramatize the girl's increasing agitation. On the repetition of the word "Liebe" (bar 70), we come to a dramatic dead stop, *fortissimo*. The rest of the strophe is precisely like the first and other earlier ones, thus stabilizing and controlling the song's musical form even as the differences between the earlier portion of this strophe and the preceding ones reflect the poem's dramatic progression.

The sixth and final strophe, on the other hand, is almost the same as earlier ones through its first half but altogether different at its end. Only the sixteenth-note pickups and the restless off-beat accompaniment (bars 75–76) point up this final stanza's greater urgency. The very sameness of melodic line and accompaniment through the next five bars, as the poor girl describes her desperate reaching out in the dark for her beloved, helps to emphasize her helplessness in the confinement of the convent. Only at the end of the phrase—"wo ich greife, ist alles still"—does the melodic line alter slightly, closing *piano* as the accompaniment momentarily drops out (bar 83), making us sense acutely her loneliness. She then suddenly bursts out, *forte*, with a real *cri de coeur*, repeating (as in no earlier stanza) the phrase "o Liebe." In these two bars (84–85) the keyboard's left hand stands comparatively still, focusing our attention on the melody. And the harmony is simplified: we do not move from the gently lulling V^7/V in the G major where we have apparently settled to the stark V^7 of the E minor to which we are returning. Instead (bars 85–86) we pass quickly to the apparent V chord and thence to a stark diminished seventh, with D-sharp, the former melody note, now in the bass, commencing a chromatic upward movement that is continued in the following bar as we resolve in E minor, just as in the earlier strophes. We then reach the climax of the entire song: the Neapolitan sixth on which the girl repeats, with horror, the single word "was," *fortissimo*. After a moment of dead silence, the carefully nuanced dynamics descend once again to *piano* as we begin the slow, painful movement to the final E-minor cadence. The utter bleakness of this ending seemingly negates whatever light or semihumorous overtones the song may have had up until this point. "Nonnelied" is surely one of C. P. E. Bach's triumphs as a composer of songs.

It was in fact recognized as such by the first reviewers of *Neue Lieder-Melodien*. All but one of those five reviewers were very enthusiastic about the collection, and particularly enthusiastic about the non-strophic songs it contained. "It should be unnecessary to say that these melodies are all stamped by the musical genius of their great composer," began the review in the *Hamburgischer Correspondent*, which soon zeroed in on the four non-strophic songs:

> The Swiss nun's song: *'S ist kein verdrüssliches Lebe, als in das Klöterli gehe* etc. receives in each strophe a melody that is uncommonly characteristic. The same honor is accorded Herr von Haller's poem: *Das Tageslicht hat sich verdunkelt*, etc. One will sing this song, with its new melody, with new enjoyment, since it is so well suited to and so expressive of the words. The ending of the last strophe is especially beautifully expressed. All the strophes of Elise's poem: *Ich hoff' auf Gott*, etc. are also excellently composed. . . . Ebeling's song on the birthday of a friend is full of emotion.

Especially noteworthy here is the reviewer's clear assumption that non-strophic, or modified strophic, songs would yield greater delight because they fit their texts more closely and thus were more fully expressive. It is no surprise that this reviewer closes by praising the Gerstenberg cantata: "*Finis coronat opus*: and so here Gerstenberg's cantata *Die Grazien* crowns this collection."[8]

The reviewer for the *Hamburger Neue Zeitung* was also led by his praise of the songs' expressiveness and richness of content—"expressive of every emotion, full of charm and attractive because of the novelty and beauty of the thoughts"—into singling out the non-strophic songs for special attention:

> Some songs have melodies for each strophe. Thus the purposely naive Swiss nun's song, and the verses on p. 32 ["Auf den Geburtstag eines Freundes"], to which Bach's spirited music gives life and power; moreover, the emotional religious song on p. 35 ["Ich hoffe auf Gott"] is a masterpiece of expressive melodic twistings and turnings.

Just as incomparably set are the first 8 stanzas of Haller's Doris, and declamation filled with feeling reigns from beginning to end.

This reviewer too goes on to praise "Die Grazien": "The recitatives, the arioso, the ariettas with all their changes of tempo, interludes, minute scene-painting, above all with the most charming melodies, perfectly suited to the excellent poem" (*Spiegel*, p. 175)!

The other two positive reviews were considerably shorter, and although they did not specifically mention "Nonnelied," they also both expressed an implicit preference for the non-strophic songs of the collection by concentrating their attention on "Die Grazien." The reviewer for the *Neuester Altonaischer gelehrter Mercurius* concluded thus: "At the end comes a cantata, for which Herr B. has chosen von Gerstenerg's charming *Tändelei*, 'die Grazien.' Through Bach's composition it has become one of the most beautiful vocal works that was ever assembled out of recitatives and arias" (*Spiegel*, p. 195). *Allgemeine Literatur Zeitung*'s reviewer concurred: "Connoisseurs will rediscover their old friend at many points, and especially in the cantata will wonder at the richness of the harmony and the inexhaustible fullness of thought that are his alone—and are so inimitable" (*Spiegel*, p. 179).

From these four reviews it would seem clear that the first reviewers of Bach's *Neue Lieder-Melodien* were not part of the *Volkslied* movement, as conceived and carried on by Voss, Schulz, and others. Rather, these reviewers retained—or, perhaps, had newly attained, for themselves—the feeling common during the *liederlose Zeit*, that the expressive potential of vocal music is most fully realized in non-strophic settings of poems with a consistent stanzaic form. Moreover, these reviewers welcomed Bach precisely because of his ability to compose this sort of song well, and probably assumed that he wholeheartedly shared their preference. The fifth reviewer, who is far less impressed with *Neue Lieder-Melodien* yet nonetheless considers Bach a great composer, considerably complicates the picture.

This review, which appeared in Friedrich Nicolai's *Allgemeine deutsche Bibliothek* in 1792, several years later than the others, begins with the firm assertion that although Bach is a great composer, he is not well served by the volume under consideration: "The already immortal C.P.E. Bach is indisputably one of the greatest composers of the 18th century, even if these songs, published (as we recall) shortly after his death, are distinguished neither by the usual Bachian originality nor by novelty and melodic charm." The problem is that in these songs, as opposed (by implication) to his other works, Bach "has apparently tried to write in a light, easy style, and in this he has been successful." Yet the cost of this success has been that Bach, in order to attain it, has been forced to go against his own nature as a composer: "Yet perhaps because of this very effort, and constraints to which Bach's genius was unaccustomed, the songs are for the most part rather insignificant" (*Spiegel*, 193).

The reviewer then condemns, as "dull and dry," a couple of the strophic songs, "Todtengräberlied" and "An den Schlaf," both of which we examined in earlier chapters; the non-strophic songs, on the other hand, "at least exhausted this reviewer" (*Spiegel*, p. 193). Of "Nonnelied" he tells us, rather vaguely: "It seems to us that Bach, if he had really wanted to compose this song, would have done it in a different tone" (*Spiegel*, p. 194). The reviewer then makes some fussy, pedantic objections to "word-painting" in the new setting of "An Doris" and to the "scansion, declamation, and punctuation" of "Auf den Geburtstag eines Freundes"—namely, to Bach's rather playful placing of unimportant words on strong beats of the bar, and important words on weak beats.

But the reviewer's strongest objections, as we by now expect, are reserved for "Die Grazien"— though his criticisms are, again, annoyingly vague:

> Similar, and still greater, inaccuracies can be found on almost every page, especially in the cantata by Gerstenberg, entitled "Die Grazien." We should have to enter into a detailed examination of the composition of this cantata if we were to take note of everything that cannot withstand criticism. But whoever is free of an exclusive preference for the works of this composer already knows that Bach is far from being a classic song

composer, and accordingly should in no sense be classed with Handel, Hasse, Graun, Schulz, Naumann, G. Benda, Reichardt, Hiller, Homilius, Rolle, et. al.

[*Spiegel*, p. 194]

This list is, as we shall see, a most interesting and revealing one.

The reviewer then declares, quite defensively, that anyone who disagrees with this judgment is simply not facing facts: "And yet Bach's enthusiastic admirers seem either to be deaf and blind to his undeniably hard and stiff style, as well as to his errors of purpose and artistic execution, or zealously to wish to be so. And woe to him who does not in every case join with them, vigorously and without restraint, in their praise of Bach!" (*Spiegel*, pp. 194-195). His tone suggests that he has already been burned once or twice by these enthusiastic—and here we must recall the 18th-century religious overtones of the word—admirers of Bach! Yet the review closes with a return to the high praise of its opening: "We merely cannot acknowledge that the otherwise so deserving composer is one of the best song composers of the present century, though with full conviction we consider him, especially during his middle years, the greatest keyboard composer of his time" (*Spiegel*, p. 195).

The author of this review was the well-known composer, conductor, and musical pedagogue Daniel Gottlob Türk (1750-1813).[9] He received his primary musical education at the Dresden Kreuzschule under Gottfried August Homilius (1714-1785), whose name appears on Türk's list of "classical" song composers. Homilius had, in turn, been a pupil of J. S. Bach, and was also the teacher of Hiller and Reichardt, whose names also appear on Türk's list. In 1772 Türk moved on to Leipzig University, to continue his studies under Hiller, to whom Homilius had recommended him, and two years later, on Hiller's recommendation, he became Kantor of the Ulrichskirche, Halle, and a teacher at the Gymnasium there. In 1779 Türk was appointed director of music at Halle University, lecturing on theory and composition, and in 1787 he also became organist and musical director of the Marktkirche, the principal church in Halle. These were the posts he held when he wrote his review of Bach's *Neue Lieder-Melodien*. Finally, in 1808, five years before his death, he was promoted to a professorship at Halle University.

The critical position that emerges from Türk's review is both interesting and complex, and can, I believe, be traced to his musical education and related to the character of his music (what we know of it) and of his writings. The training he received at both Dresden and Leipzig was very much in the tradition of J. S. Bach, and we know that he was also introduced to C.P.E. Bach's *Versuch* and keyboard compositions. Most of his own early compositions have been lost, but while at Halle he wrote a number of sonatas, cantatas, lieder, and other vocal works that have survived. Most of these are evidently of a strongly pedagogical nature, as are his books of this period. His first book, *Von den wichtigsten Pflichten eines Organisten* (1787), bore the subtitle *ein Beytrag zur Verbesserung der musikalischen Liturgie*, and was concerned with reforming church music, which had fallen into neglect during the Enlightenment. His *Kurze Anweisung zum Generalbassspielen* (1791, 1800) similarly attempted to reform the figured bass tradition, which was also in a state of disrepair. In addition, Türk produced a scholarly and widely respected *Clavierschule* (1789, 1802) and an *Anleitung zu Temperaturberechnungen* (1808), which treated problems of equal and unequal temperament from a comprehensive scientific point of view.

In a sense, then, Türk may fairly be labeled a musical conservative—in a wholly non-derogatory sense of that much abused term. He knew music theory and the musical practices of the High Baroque thoroughly, and he strove in his writings and his teaching to preserve traditions that he thought worth preserving. On the other hand, the concerts that he gave at Halle often featured the symphonies of Haydn and Mozart, and he gave concert performances of a number of Mozart operas. During the years just before his death, Türk undertook the musical education of Carl Loewe, who had joined his choir in 1810 and who would soon become a famous composer of Romantic ballads. It would, then, be quite wrong to conclude that Türk's conservatism implied a rejection of everything new and important that was happening in music at the turn of the 19th century. Türk did, however, have his troubles with early Beethoven; of an 1810 concert performance of the First Symphony, Loewe reports: "Türk excised the 'comic' violin introduction to the finale of the now old-fashioned master's C-Major Symphony because he thought the audience would laugh so loudly that the orchestra would be embarrassed."[10]

We can thus begin to understand the case that Türk was—rather inadequately, to be sure—making in his review of Bach's *Neue Lieder-Melodien*. For him C.P.E. Bach was J. S. Bach's son, the author of the *Versuch*, the creator of a remarkably original and adventurous keyboard literature. Songs, on the other hand, and especially secular songs like most of those in *Neue Lieder-Melodien*, were for Türk a very different genre of composition, demanding gifts very different from those Bach customarily manifested in his work. In accordance with standard 18th-century doctrine, secular songs were to be natural, easy, flowing, and thus demanded a light touch—of which the composer of C.P.E. Bach's keyboard works would, by definition as it were, be incapable. So when Bach adopted the light touch, the striving necessary to achieve it showed through, spoiling the effect. Yet Türk liked Bach's Gellert songs, to which, he insisted, the songs of *Neue Lieder-Melodien* were not at all to be compared. For the Gellert songs, being deeply religious, were a special case: they did not require the light touch, and so were within Bach's range of competence.

But precisely what is so interesting about Bach's work as a song composer is of course that it demonstrates, perhaps more clearly than any other area of his output, how able he was to adapt his great gifts to any type of music he attempted, and usually to do so in a highly individual and surprising way. So the cherished canons of 18th-century genre criticism simply do not hold for him. One wonders how Türk would have reacted to Bach's other major song project of these last years, the twelve songs he contributed to the 1788 volume of *Freimäurer-Lieder*, which, as we have seen, also contained songs by two more of the "classical" song composers on Türk's list, J. A. P. Schulz and Johann Gottlieb Naumann.

III

The first question that comes to mind is why Bach should have had any interest in contributing to a volume of Masonic songs. He was himself not a Mason, so far as we know.[11] Yet we know that he conducted several concerts in the hall of the house, on Grosse Bäckerstrasse in Hamburg, that was used for meetings by the Absalom, St. Georg, and Emanuel Masonic Lodges. In the chronology of Bach's concerts that appears in the program book for the celebration of his 200th birthday held in Hamburg in 1988, he is said to have conducted Handel's *Messiah* in that hall on February 23, 1777, and April 12, 1778.[12] Moreover, in a talk given at a C.P.E. Bach conference also held at Hamburg in 1988, Gudrun Busch adduces evidence to show that Bach also conducted Handel's *Judas Maccabaeus* and *Alexander's Feast* in the same hall, the former in the autumn of 1774 and the latter in the winter of 1776-1777.[13] The secrecy with which Masonic affairs have traditionally been conducted has perhaps concealed from scholarly view other concerts that Bach conducted at the Masonic hall. So the question of what connections, if any, he had with the Masons remains. To answer it, albeit tentatively, we must delve briefly into the history of Freemasonry.

Most books on the Enlightenment and its history make either scant mention or no mention at all of the Masonic movement (as we may call it). Yet Freemasonry was, in many ways, the Enlightenment movement *par excellence*. It started in England, with the founding of the Modern London Grand Lodge in 1717. In ways that are still obscure, the movement grew out of the group practices of actual stonemasons. Or, as it is now customary to put it, Speculative Masonry (what we ordinarily call Freemasonry) grew out of Operative Masonry (the group practices of English stonemasons). However it may have come about, the tools of the mason's craft—the compass, the T-square, and so on—took on symbolic value in the rituals of Freemasonry. God was viewed as the master mason or architect who created the world, and Masons busily invented myths that traced the origins of their organization to the builders of the great pyramids and the designer of the temple of Solomon.[14]

Freemasonry was, in the words of one Viennese Mason, "an institution dedicated to teaching its members the tenets of a universal moral system and to improving society."[15] While it did not itself constitute a specific religion, it sought to instill in its members the ethical tenets recognized by all major religions. A cosmopolitan institution, it minimized differences amongst nations and creeds, seeking to recommend (and to practice) the universal constructive principles conducive to peace, harmony, virtue, and the advancement of human knowledge.

After the founding of the Modern London Grand Lodge, Freemasonry swiftly spread to the European continent and also to America. Montesquieu visited England in the 1720s, and was persuaded by J. T. Desaguliers, holder of a chair in Experimental Philosophy at Oxford and a member of the Royal Society, to join the movement and to carry it back to France. In time the Nine Sisters Lodge of Paris numbered amongst its members Benjamin Franklin, who had joined a Philadelphia lodge in 1731, and Voltaire, who was inducted only a few days before his death, in 1778. French Masons were suspected of attempting to subvert the government of Louis XV and the state religion—a decree against the Masons was issued by Louis in 1737, and a papal bull followed a year later—but the members of the Nine Sisters Lodge, like other Masons elsewhere, were more interested in the cultivation of sociability and brotherhood than in revolution, though many of them sided with America in her revolution.

Another prominent early Masonic outpost was the True Harmony Lodge at Vienna. It sponsored a scientific journal, the *Journal für Freimäurer*, in which Joseph II was favorably compared to Solomon and all manner of recent scientific investigations were described and debated. Haydn and Mozart were members, and so was Kapellmeister Naumann, whose Masonic opera *Osiris* (1781) influenced Mozart's *Die Zauberflöte* of a decade later.

Meanwhile the original London Lodge established and maintained close ties with the Royal Society through Desaguliers and other prominent members. The thought of English Masons was, generally, Newtonian, whiggish, and deistic. Yet although the members of course had political interests and the Lodge itself mounted projects with political implications, the concern was less with partisan politics than with philanthropy and the general well-being of society. A General Charity Committee was founded, largely by members, in 1729, and remained active for several decades, distributing funds to the poor, sponsoring London hospitals and schools, and giving financial aid to those emigrating to America.

Such activities recall those carried on by the members of the second Patriot Society in Hamburg during Bach's time of residence, and in which several of his friends took an active part. From what we know of the comparatively tolerant and progressive intellectual climate of 18th-century Hamburg, it is no surprise that when Freemasonry came to Germany, it came first to Hamburg. The Absalom Lodge was officially founded on December 6, 1737. Not only were the goals of English and Continental Masons—charity, religious toleration, the dissemination of scientific knowledge—markedly similar to those of the first and second Patriot Societies of Hamburg; there was actually a direct personal connection between the Hamburg groups and the Masons.

In the early 1730s Count Albrecht Wolfgang von Schaumburg-Lippe, a colorful character who had become a Mason in England and would later play a major role in the secret induction of Frederick the Great into the order, visited Hamburg. He there established a circle of friends who, a few years later, founded the Absalom Lodge.[16] His closest Hamburg associate, with whom he corresponded after his visit, seems to have been the poet, and then senator, Barthold Heinrich Brockes, who had been instrumental in founding the first Patriot Society in 1724. Brockes himself apparently never became a Mason. In 1735 he had left town to take a position as magistrate in nearby Ritzebüttel, and there is no mention in his biographies of his having joined the Absalom or any other Lodge between the time of his return to Hamburg, in 1741, and his death six years later.[17] But in addition to helping the first Patriot Society, Brockes had led a group called the *Deutschegesinnten Gesellschaft*, which was also known as the *Brüderschaft der drei Rosen*, and which in 1770 became the Masonic Lodge *Zu den drei Rosen*. Moreover, one of the founding members of the Absalom Lodge, Peter Carpser, was Brockes's doctor.

The ties between the Hamburg Masons and the faction of Hamburg intellectual society with which C. P. E. Bach was known to be sympathetic were, then, very close indeed. It therefore does not seem at all unlikely that his conducting performances in the hall of the house at which several Masonic Lodges held their meetings was what we should nowadays call a gesture of solidarity. And we may perhaps conclude the same of his contributing to an anthology of Masonic songs. For if Bach himself was not a Mason, two of his most illustrious friends, Lessing and Klopstock, were. Also, of course, the Masonic project gave Bach another, doubtless welcome, opportunity to write songs in a simple, *volkstümlich* style.

Music has always played an important role in Masonic rituals and social gatherings, and this has perhaps been truer in Germany and Austria than elsewhere. The first Masonic song published in Germany appeared in 1745, in the third and last *Fortsetzung* to "Sperontes'" *Singende Muse an der Pleisse*. As the last of the 50 songs in the volume, it occupied a prominent position. Also, the Masonic symbols of plummet and compasses were printed beneath it.[18] Therefore Spitta, in his famous 1885 essay that identified "Sperontes" as Johann Sigismund Scholze, hypothesized that Scholze must have been a Mason. But a search of the Lodge records for the cities where Scholze was known to have spent time—Leipzig, Halle, and Altenburg—turned up no member of that name. Therefore Spitta offered the suggestion that since the university student clubs of that time frequently aped the customs and rituals of the Masons, Scholze might possibly have belonged to one of these clubs rather than to the Masons.[19] The text of the song, however, makes this seem unlikely.

Like most of the songs collected in the *Singende Muse an der Pleisse* volumes, this one is of negligible worth musically. But the text, which extends for a full nine stanzas, is very interesting indeed. Therefore I give music and text in full, as they stand in the volume of *Denkmäler deutscher Tonkunst* devoted to Scholze's collections:[20]

```
4.  Unser Zweck bei jeder Tat,
      Nach den strengsten Liebes-Pflichten,
    Lauter Gutes zu verrichten,
      Hat Vernunft zum Oberrat,
    Mit andern, inzwischen, die Pflichten gemein:
    Bescheiden, gelassen, gefällig zu sein.

5.  Auf der vorgesetzten Bahn
      Denen Lastern zu entstehen,
    Und den Tugendweg zu gehen,
      Ehren wir soviel man kann,
    Den Herren des Himmels, die Fürsten der Welt,
    Und tun, was Gesetz und Verordnung enthält.

6.  Bei dem allen, was ergötzt,
      Jeder vor sich selbst empfindet,
    Uns zusammen fest verbindet,
      Bleibt der Wohlstand unverletzt.
    Als Bürger und Freie, als Bruder und Freund,
    Hält uns das traulichste Bündnis vereint.

7.  Unsre Logen sind allzeit
      Der Vergnügung reine Tempel,
    Und ein richtiges Exempel
      Unverbotner Lustbarkeit:
    Was ehrbar, was mäßig, was löblich nur ist,
    Wird nirgends in unsrer Gesellschaft vermißt.

8.  Also seht ihr überführt,
      Daß wir immer darnach streben,
    Nützlich und vergnügt zu leben:
      Daß dem Orden, der uns ziert,
    Auch weder Verspottung, Verleumdung, noch Bann
    In Zukunft mehr Eintrag und Schaden tun kann.

9.  Wer nun aber überhaupt,
      Von dem allen, was wir treiben,
    Und was viele davon schreiben,
      Weder richtig denkt, noch glaubt;
    Dem wird das Geheimnis der Freimäurerei
    Zum ewigen Rätsel. Es bleibet dabei!
```

Scholze himself may or may not have been a Mason; but the text of the poem makes it virtually certain that its author, whoever he may have been, was a Mason. For what we have here is a version of the Masonic creed, as I have outlined it briefly above, presented in a way that stamps it as coming from the early years of German Freemasonry, when the order was still widely suspected of attempting to foment revolution.

The poem is addressed to all "Vernünftler," which seems to have been the German 18th-century equivalent of the contemporary English phrase "men of sense." The assumption is that such men harbor dark suspicions concerning the Masons and their activities. So the speaker of the poem boldly asks these men to declare precisely what they know (or think) of the Masons and their secrets. In the third stanza he asserts that the men he is addressing would have to be "voll Unvernunft" to believe that such worthy men as make up the Masonic order could possibly be plotting the downfall of either virtue or the state. The order is, in fact, organized along reasonable principles—"Hat Vernunft zum Oberrat"—and seeks only to do good, honoring the lord of heaven and the princes of this world, performing only what is demanded by law and the social order. Their fellowship is devoted to innocent pleasure, enjoyed in an atmosphere free of ridicule and slander. Their goal is "Nützlich und vergnügt zu leben"—"Vergnügung," as we have seen, being (along with "Zufriedenheit") one of the dominant terms in the poetry of this time (and especially in the poetry of the *Singende Muse an der Pleisse*). To anyone who does not believe all this, the poem concludes, the secret of Freemasonry will indeed always remain a riddle—and so be it!

One could scarcely ask for a clearer statement of Masonic goals and belief. And when one considers how new Freemasonry was to Germany, and indeed to the rest of Continental Europe, in the 1740s, one can understand the tone of somewhat combative defensiveness. But this was to change rapidly, as Freemasonry spread and entered the cultural mainstream.

Indeed it is just a year after the publication of this third and last Spérontes *Fortsetzung*, in 1746, that the first volume of *Freimäurer-Lieder* proper—songs not written in defense of the order but songs written to be sung at Lodge meetings—appeared in Germany. It contains only nine songs, and the title page lists no place of publication; the poet is one Ludwig Friedrich Lenz (1717-1780) and the composer is unknown, the music evidently undistinguished. But it was the first in a stream of collections that was to quicken as the century went on. It was followed in 1749 by *Neue Freimäurer-Lieder, mit bequemen Melodien*, with both words and music provided by J. A. Scheibe, whom we have encountered before as the editor of *Der critische Musikus*. Since 1744 Scheibe had been in charge of the orchestra at the Danish court, and he had evidently become active in Masonic affairs. His volume of songs was dedicated to the "Zorobabel" Lodge in Copenhagen, of which he was a member.

In 1776, the year of his death, Scheibe brought out another book of Masonic songs, *Vollständiges Liederbuch für Freimaurer mit Melodien, in zwey Büchern*. It bore the subtitle *Herausgegeben von einem alten Mitgliede der Loge Zorobabel*. The phrase *in zwey Büchern* seems to have meant that a companion volume was planned and would soon follow. The reason it did not do so was, presumably, Scheibe's death. But it did appear in 1785, published by Christian Gottlieb Proft, a Leipzig printer and publisher who had moved to Copenhagen in 1782. The volume is evidently quite obscure, for the author of the *MGG* entry under "Freimaurermusik" notes that it is mentioned by neither Friedlaender nor Eitner. The volume to which Bach, Naumann, and Schulz contributed was the third and final one in the collection. Its full title is *Freymäurer-Lieder mit ganz neuen Melodien von den Herrn Capellmeistern Bach, Naumann und Schulz*, and it too was published by Proft, who was now operating out of both Copenhagen and Leipzig. In his brief preface, Proft makes it clear that the collection is for general consumption: "The well-deserved reputation of these three famous German composers insures that many lovers of song, even outside of our Order, will want to have this collection." And he gives us a hint of how the volume came into being when he mentions Bach's friend and sometime student, Niels Schiörring, "who has the good fortune to be prized by these three excellent men, whose friendship for him we have to thank for this collection."

IV

The layout of the volume is both interesting and important. Unfortunately, it has been misrepresented in both catalogues of C.P.E. Bach's works, Wotquenne's of 1905 and E. Eugene Helm's of 1989.

There are 38 songs in all, 12 of which were composed by Bach, 16 by Naumann, and 10 by Schulz. They appear in the order in which a selection from them would be likely to be sung during the course of a Masonic meeting or ritual. The first 13 songs set the stage for the meeting. After two settings of the same opening prayer, we encounter two that officially open the Lodge and greet the assembled members, three that celebrate "das Fest des heiligen Johannes," one in which the Master of the Lodge engages in dialogue with the members and another—for special occasions?—to celebrate the Master's wedding, and four that evoke the darkness, stillness, and solemnity of the Lodge at meeting time, including one that welcomes new members. Then come 16 songs in which particular Masonic duties or states of mind appropriate to the Masonic life are celebrated and explored: loyalty, patriotism (again perhaps with the accusation of subversion in mind!), zeal, renewal of friendship, continuity of past and present, the power of divine law, contentment, secrecy, compassion, joyfulness, and the appreciation of nature. There are then five songs declaring the power and fame of the order and yet delicately making clear the position of women, excluded yet essential. Finally, there are three songs of consolation for death and assurance of eternal life, and one that officially closes the meeting.

Bach's 12 contributions are most interestingly placed within the volume. Eight of them occur in the opening group of 13, while the other four come in the penultimate group of five. Within the whole collection, Bach's songs are numbers 3, 4, 6, 7, 8, 9, 10, 12, 30, 31, 32, and 34. What does this signify? Perhaps that Bach, who apparently was not a Mason, was allowed to deal only with the more general introductory and concluding songs, and not with any that explored in detail the duties and goals of Masonic life. Those songs were all given to Naumann and Schulz. Though one cannot be sure of the reason behind it, the distribution is nonetheless striking, and scarcely seems coincidental.

Wotquenne and Helm misrepresent the distribution of Bach's songs within the volume by listing their incipits in an incorrect order: 1, 2, 3, 5, 4, 9, 6, 7, 11, 10, 12, 8. That Helm repeats Wotquenne's error is all the more remarkable in light of the fact that Helm prefaces his entry on the Masonic songs by telling us that the Bach songs appear "in the order shown here, not that shown in the incipits in Wotquenne"—and then giving the incipits precisely in Wotquenne's order.[21] This would give Bach's songs the following locations within the collection: 3, 4, 6, 8, 7, 30, 9, 10, 32, 31, 34, 12. Thus Bach's ninth song, in praise of the everlasting power of the Masonic order, is boosted from thirtieth place up to sixth, among the songs about St. John; and his eighth, one of the solemn opening songs, is pushed down to thirty-fourth place, with the songs in praise of women. Granted, this mistake of Wotquenne's and Helm's is not terribly serious; yet it does seem to mar what is apparently the intended ritualistic order of the songs.

There is certainly no need to examine all 12 of Bach's songs. The very fact that he was writing songs to be sung by a group rather than by an individual singer naturally limited the expressive and technical means at his disposal. Yet, as always, he brought to this unusual project his own highly individual gifts. We can better appreciate how he made use of these gifts if we compare two of his settings with ones on similar themes by Naumann and Schulz.

It will be easiest to dispose first of Schulz. As I suggested above, the last few songs in the introductory group of 13 evoke the atmosphere of stillness and solemnity appropriate to the meeting that is just getting under way. Of these songs, the second-to-last was written by Bach (his eighth, number twelve in the volume), and the last by Schulz; though the poems they set are rather similar, the songs themselves are worlds apart.

Here, first, is "Das stille Glück der Maurerey," the poem set by Bach:

>   Lasst andre stolz nach Ehre dürsten,
>   Der grösste Rang ist Sklaverey.
>   Der nächste Liebling grosser Fürsten
>   Ist nur ihr Sklave—niemals frey.

>   Lasst andre Krösus Schätze häufen,
>   Geniessen sie dann wohl ihr Geld?
>   Wenn sie in Goldgeiz sich ersäufen,
>   Was nutzen sie sich und der Welt?

>   Lasst andre sich in Wollust wiegen,
>   Ganz ihrer Lüste Sklaven seyn.
>   Nie fühlen sie ein rein Vergnügen
>   Und ihrer Wollust folgt nur Pein.

>   Der Maurer, stets mit sich zufrieden,
>   Baut sein und andrer Menschen Glück,
>   Fühlt seinen Himmel schon hienieden,
>   Und segnet dankbar sein Geschick.

>   Der Himmel trübt sich;—doch die Dicke
>   Des Pfades schreckt den Maurer nie.

Er duldet;—und giebt's Sonnenblicke,
So sammlet und geniesst er sie.

   Theilt mit den Brüdern seine Leiden,
Die er getheilt nur halb noch fühlt,
Und schmecket doppelt jede Freuden,
Weil sie der Bruder mit ihm fühlt.

   O Brüder! was sind Thron und Reiche,
Was Moguls Schätze, Pomp und Pracht,
Wenn ich sie mit dem Bund' vergleiche
Der uns im Schurzfell glücklich macht?

   Lasst Thoren sich bey Erdeschätzen
Im Ungenuss, bloss scheinbar freun,
Uns sey der Orden nur Ergötzen;
Uns soll er Dreymal heilig seyn.

After the first three stanzas have pictured various sorts of slavery—to ambition, to greed, to lust—the central fourth stanza presents a contrasting view of the Mason, gaining lasting spiritual satisfaction from his ability to contribute to his own happiness and that of his fellow man. The concluding four stanzas fill out this idealized picture in more detail.

   Here is Bach's setting:

The poem might well have called forth a triumphant, exultant, even rather boastful song, a sort of public declaration delivered, as it were, from a public platform. Clearly, Bach has taken an entirely different tack.

Taking the $\frac{3}{4}$ time signature together with the tempo direction, "Sanft und etwas langsam," we see that what Bach has written is, in effect, a gently graceful slow minuet. From first note to last, the tone is one of quiet assurance—the music, we notice, never stops: the pauses at phrase-endings are all filled by entries of lower voices. The first phrase is completely diatonic, and it looks, from the little bass lead-in, as if the second phrase will be too. But then at the beginning of bar 7 we are struck by the unexpected Bb-minor triad caused by the middle voice's ascent from C to D-flat. It would of course have been perfectly easy to have the middle voice hold on to its C for a beat and then move up, but Bach plainly wanted to break up the uniformly diatonic feel of the song at just this point. The text at this point, in the first stanza, says "Sklaverey"—and so the dissonance has a certain local appropriateness. As it does in the following two stanzas, when it falls on the ironic juxtaposition "wohl ihr Geld" and on the word "Sklaven." But what about the other five, more "positive" stanzas? How is the just slightly disturbing clash related to their content?

If we look ahead to the end of the song, we notice that from this point onward there are a great many upward moves of a half-step, particularly in the inner voices but also in the melody. To a certain extent, this is of course generic: every dominant-tonic shift involves a movement upward of a half-step. But not all of the ones in this song occur on dominant-to-tonic shifts, and anyway, such shifts also necessarily involve a corresponding downward half-step movement—and Bach has not arranged his voice-leading so as to call attention to this fact.

If we combine the constant upward (and inward) pressure created by these half-step movements with the consistent downward motion of all four of the song's phrases, and also perhaps with the fact that the music never stops flowing, I think we see why the song so strongly gives an impression of comforting self-enclosure. The melody falls as the other voices rise to meet it, creating an aural image of the safe and secure Masonic community praised in the text. As for the recurring dissonance at the beginning of bar 7, I think it acts as a continuing reminder of difficulties to be overcome, work to be done, opponents to be kept at a distance.

It is, I think, instructive to compare what Bach made of his poem with what Schulz made of the one he was given to set for the song just following. Here is the poem, which is untitled:

> Aus dämmernder, westlicher Ferne,
> Blickt schimmernd der Führer der Sterne,
> Der Herold der kommenden Nacht:
> Jetzt geht er als Hesperus nieder,
> Einst kehrt er als Phosphorus wieder,
> Ein Herold des Tags, der erwacht.
>
> Sey freundlich, o Nacht! uns willkommen,
> Du gütige Freundin der Frommen,
> Die liebreich dein Schleyer verbirgt;

Damit sie nicht Arglist bespähe,
Damit sie Verläumdung nicht schmähe,
Nicht Bosheit ergreife, die würgt.

    Zwar öfters, doch ungern, bedeckest
Du Laster, indem du sie schreckest:
Wir aber bedürfen es nicht,
Dass deine gefälligen Schatten,
Hier Lastern die Zuflucht verstatten;
Wir wandeln auch finster im Licht.

    Verschwiegene Freundin, umhülle
Uns jetzo mit Dunkel und Stille!
Deck unsre Geheimnisse zu!
Die Sorgen, die Sterbliche quälen,
Lass schlummern, und geuss in die Seelen
Der Gnügsamkeit selige Ruh.

    Das aber verbirg nicht dem Neide,
Dass uns hier in Unschuld und Freude,
Die nächtlichen Stunden verfliehn:
Und dass in verschlossnen Gemächern,
Bey nüchternen, fröhlichen Bechern,
Wir Menschen zur Weisheit erziehn.

Night, though she often (albeit unwillingly) conceals crimes and shelters those who commit them, is being summoned to envelop the Masons "mit Dunkel und Stille," to conceal their secrets from the wicked world so that they may get on with their good works. The poem hinges on the paradox that the Masons, who do only good, need the darkness and stillness of night just as much as do those who do only evil. For it is only through being literally in the dark that they can move figuratively toward the light of knowledge and wisdom: "Wir wandeln auch finster im Licht."

    Certainly one would expect a setting that was, in one way or another, brooding and complex, though with some hint of final triumph and security. Here, however, is what the hapless Schulz provided:

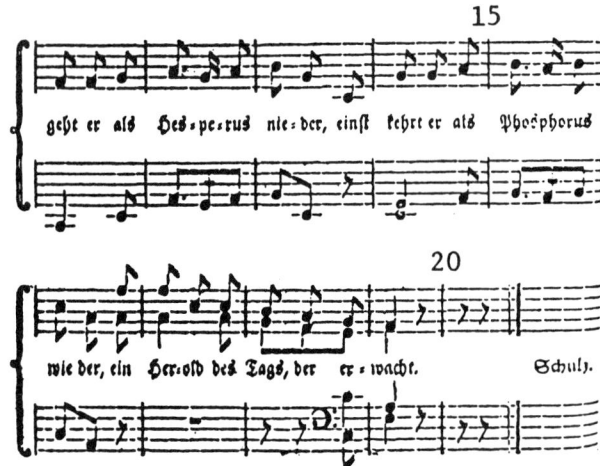

The jaunty triple rhythm, the "horn fifths" in the harmony, the short choppy phrases—everything suggests a cheerful hunting song. Only the tempo direction "Gemässigt" (where the music cries out for "Lebhaft"!) gives the slightest indication that Schulz had any notion of what the poem was about. One can scarcely imagine anything more inappropriate. Perhaps the last words of the first stanza, where Venus as the morning star is called "ein Herold des Tags, der erwacht," were all of the poem that Schulz bothered to read.

Naumann is far more accomplished. To see how his contributions compare with those of Bach, it will perhaps be best to look at the three songs devoted to St. John, numbers five through seven. The first of these was composed by Naumann, the latter two, his third and fourth, by Bach. First, however, it is necessary to say a word about the special importance of St. John to the history of the Freemasons.

At least since the 16th century, the patron saint of the mason's craft in Scotland and England was St. John. There was, however, a good deal of confusion about whether this meant St. John the Baptist or St. John the Evangelist. Eventually the Masons, and after them the Freemasons, seem to have settled for both. "In every country where Freemasonry is encouraged," writes Albert G. Mackey, "its festival days are celebrated with great ceremony. These are the festival of St. John the Baptist, on the 24th of June, and that of St. John the Evangelist, on the 27th of December."[22] The two saints, the announcer of Christ's coming and the apostle traditionally thought to have been the poet of the apocalypse, stand in a pleasingly symmetrical relation to each other. So also do their feast days, occurring within a few days of the summer and winter solstices. St. John the Baptist's case may also have been strengthened by the fact that Hermes Trismegistus, supposed author of the Hermetic corpus, composed during the early centuries A.D. by Greeks residing in Egypt, figured importantly in the early Masonic mythology. And since Hermes was, like John the Baptist, a messenger, it seemed natural enough to conflate the two figures.[23] (For that matter, since the Hermetic corpus was an apocalyptic body of writing, it might also have seemed natural to conflate Hermes Trismegistus with the other St. John—once you start this sort of thing, where does it stop?)

The poem that Naumann set for song five does not need to be cited in its entirety. As the first stanza, printed below with the music, makes clear, it is a traditional call to celebrate the saint's feast day—the roses and garlands suggest June rather than December, and hence the Baptist rather than the Evangelist, but it is not made clear which saint is being honored. The only slightly unexpected (though characteristically Masonic) touch is the admonition, in later stanzas, not to forget the poor in the midst of all this gaiety: "Doch bey allen diesen Freuden, / Brüder, übt die schönste Pflicht, / Denkt an fremde Menschenleiden / Und vergesst der Armen nicht."

Here then is Naumann's setting:

Not an outstanding song, to be sure, but miles ahead of Schulz. Not only is the music generally appropriate to the poem; there is also a good deal of tasteful variation and surface polish in the writing. Notice the way the accompaniment shifts octaves: low and compact for the solo singer, high and spread out for the group. Or the way in which the bass figuration gradually gets more elaborate as we move through the song. Or—a nice final touch—the way the dominant chord on the last beat of bar 24 is a simple triad while the one in the following bar has its seventh added.

The poem that Bach set in the following song, "Auf das Fest des heiligen Johannis," does not need to be cited in its entirety either. It is simply a call, uttered in St. John's name, for unity and brotherhood. From a couplet in the fourth of the poem's six stanzas it seems clear that for these Masons, at any rate, one or the other St. John, or perhaps both, represented simply the spirit of joy resulting from good fellowship: "Auch an dem schwächern Freudenton / Kennt man doch Johannis Sohn." The only interesting formal feature of the poem is that in the last stanza the two-line refrain is sung three times.

Bach therefore provided a modified strophic setting:

The spirit of this song, like that of the preceding one by Naumann, is generally jubilant, but it also has a somewhat martial air because of the insistent dotted rhythms. There is, however, a good deal more going on here than in Naumann's song.

Like the first phrase (bars 1-8) of the Naumann song, Bach's first phrase has a sort of call-and-response feel to it, and we rather expect the second phrase to be similar. So it seems at first: bars 5-6, which carry us into the dominant, are rhythmically identical to the opening two bars of the song. But the two bars that follow, which we expect to bring us neatly back to the tonic, instead take us in the other direction, to V/V. Moreover, the phrase-lengths seem to be expanding as the next few bars firmly establish C major. Then comes the pleasant surprise of the little unison fanfare, a whole step lower, in B flat, and a cadence that brings us back to the tonic. With the repetition of these four bars, the strophe ends. For the poem's final stanza, however, Bach replaces the B-flat fanfare and its repetition with three fanfares that ascend in pitch from B flat to C to D, each one followed by the formulaic cadence, which is somewhat emphasized and strengthened the last time. The wit of the song lies in the juxtaposition of the firm military rhythms and the leisurely expansiveness that is capped, finally, by the splendid "dreimal hoch!" of the threefold rising fanfare.

In the next song, also to a poem titled "Auf das Fest des heiligen Johannis," Bach again demonstrates, though this time in a quite different style, his ability to infuse a determinedly simple song with just enough ingenuity and inventiveness to make it a little special. This time the poem is rather earnestly folkish, delivered by a naive speaker who tells us he has just been with Johannis, and then describes the man and the experience. We all, he tells us, have within us the spirit of love that Johannis personifies, a spirit that enables us to heal the pain of our brothers here on earth and to continue to love one another in the life to come—a spirit, it should be added, firmly distinguished (as "Liebe") from the quite different "Amor" and "Leidenschaft."

Here is Bach's setting:

On its surface, the song is certainly simple enough: two rhythmically identical four-bar phrases with bass lines that are virtually identical rhythmically. And yet there seems something a little odd about it. Initially, we hear the opening bars as asserting the tonic, G major. But then suddenly a cadence carries us to C major. Because this seems a little early for a move to the subdominant, we reinterpret: the song is, after all, in C major, and the opening bars were on the dominant, leading into the cadence. But then, almost before we know it, the second phrase whisks us back to G major and the end of the strophe! Perhaps the rather genially skipping melodic line makes us expect a more expansive song, and makes it difficult to hear the overly condensed move to IV and then back to I as a complete unit. I am not sure. But it seems to me that Bach is here having a quiet, affectionate joke at the expense of the earnestly maintained "simplicity" of *Volkslied* composers like Schulz.

Actually, the song's two phrases make more musical sense if you reverse them (making the necessary adjustments in the bass line), and hear them not as a complete unit but rather as the opening of a longer song. Thus:

Whatever we say about this song, it seems to me that its mix of village-maiden naiveté (to borrow a favorite phrase of Tovey's) and tongue-in-cheek musical sophistication is enough to distinguish it not only from the products of Schulz's labor but also from the more accomplished songs of Naumann.

The rest of Bach's contributions are similarly distinguished. Take, for example, song number 10, which sets yet another poem glorifying the Masonic brotherhood and its solemn quest for wisdom within the confines of the Lodge or "temple":

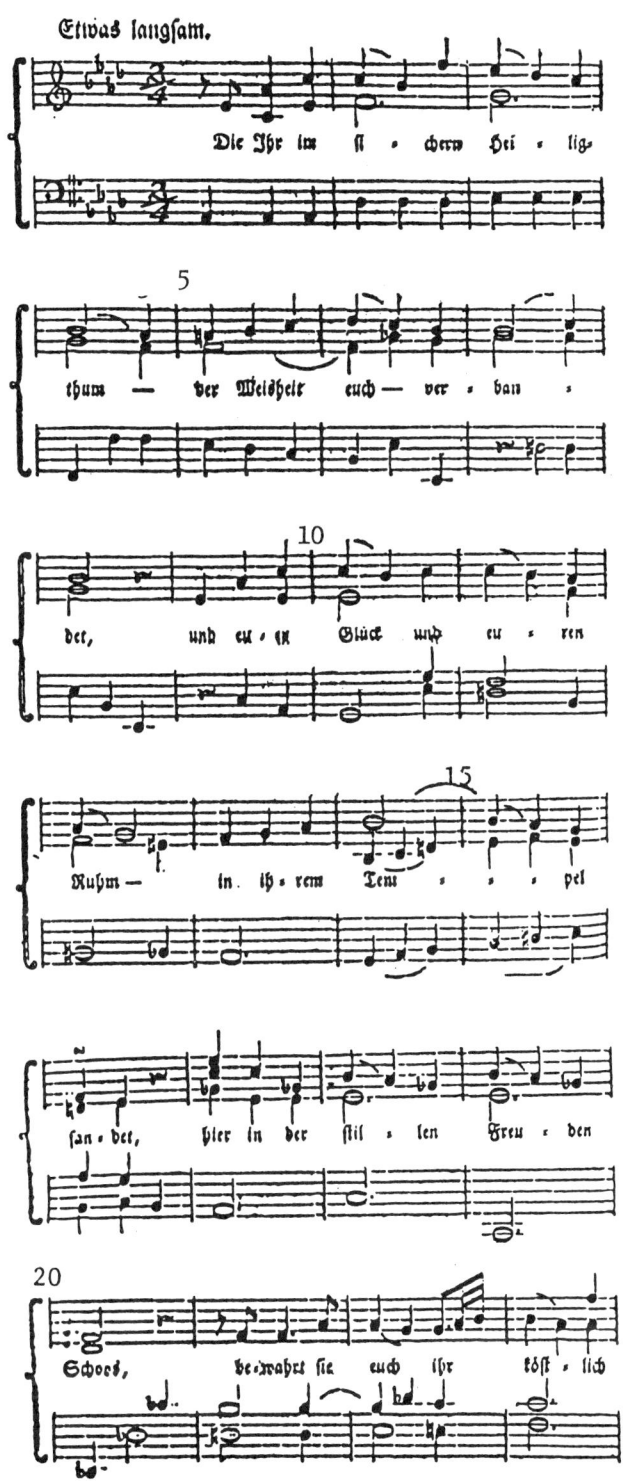

It is immediately obvious that this is a beautiful and solemn song; but the art by which Bach keeps it from becoming monotonous requires comment.

The first impression is of evenness, steadiness, order. The repeated melodic rises followed by a drop of a step create a sense of quiet security and fulfillment. But notice how the texture lightens just a little at the end of the first eight-bar phrase, with the first-beat rest in the bass and the two upper voices only a step apart in bar 7. The half-cadence sounds somewhat tentative, almost more like a question than the straightforward proclamations we have been hearing. The repeat of the opening bar that begins the second eight-bar phrase is similarly lightened, and this time we head not to IV, but to V and then V/V. The voice-leading becomes chromatic (bars 12–13) and the inner parts come to the fore (bars 14–15) as the second eight-bar phrase approaches its end.

But it does not end. Instead of the cadence on the dominant that we expect, we get a deceptive cadence that sweeps us right on to an unexpected V^7/IV that is prolonged for three bars before its resolution in bar 20. Then, as the bass line begins to climb chromatically, the melodic line forsakes its even quarter notes and becomes forcefully rhetorical and, in the final four bars, even more straightforward and emphatic. It is quite easy, I think, to imagine these final eight bars, sung by a male chorus, achieving a splendid climax to the gradual growth and deepening of feeling presented in the song.

Another fine, though much simpler, solemn song is number 30, Bach's ninth, set to a poem that praises the everlastingness of the temple, its columns, and the work that goes on within its walls:

As in the song just examined, so here too the first impression is one of steadiness—brought about in this case by the even quarter notes in the bass and the alternation, in the melody, of bars with even quarter notes and ones with eighth-quarter-eighth syncopation. The predominantly stepwise motion of the melody also contributes. But then suddenly, at the beginning of the second of the two eight-bar segments, the harmony unexpectedly moves to V/vi and the melody, starting high, makes a dramatic downward jump of a fifth. After the resolution to vi, the harmony moves to V/ii and the melody leaps still higher, this time to drop a sixth. After the resolution to ii, the melody returns to its earlier patterns and the song closes quietly.

Thus the song seems at first to break into halves. But then we look back and notice that the melody did, after all, begin, in the opening bar, with a drop of a fourth. So the two later, increasingly larger, drops of a fifth and a sixth, which in context seem a new departure—so accustomed have we become to the melody's stepwise movement—were really foreshadowed from the start. There is something pleasing about this blend of difference and similarity within a song of such limited scope.

Finally, we should look at song number 31, Bach's tenth, which is untitled. Its poem is a little more ambitious and interesting than most of the others:

> Hoch wie des Adlers kühnster Flug
> Und voll wie Davids Ton,
> Stark wie der Griechen Pindar schlug
> Und klug wie Salomon.
>
> So sollte stets dein Loblied seyn,
> Sonst ist der Rauch umsonst,
> Sonst ist das Opfer dir zu klein,
> Du königliche Kunst!
>
> Du hast der Wiege von der Welt
> Dein Kleinod anvertraut,
> Und Hanochs Stadt und Jabals Zelt
> Und Noahs Schiff gebaut.
>
> Du hast den Thurm in Sinear
> Zum Wunder ausgedacht,

In deinen Pyramiden war
Am Nilus Witz und Pracht.

Izt rauscht Europa deinen Ruhm
Von Tagus bis zum Belt,
Und dennoch bleibt dein Heiligthum
Ein Räzel für die Welt.

The poem is addressed to the art of masonry in the broadest sense: the art of building and design, metaphorically extended from its literal significance to include as well intellectual creativity and spiritual imagination. This art, we are told, merits a song of praise higher than the eagle's flight, as richly laden with meaning as the psalms of David, as strong as the odes of Pindar, as wise as Solomon. Anything less would be unsuitable for the art that has, over the ages, created Hanoch's city (Midian, presumably); the tent of Jabal, "the father of such as dwell in tents, and such as have cattle" (Genesis 4:20); Noah's ark; the Tower of Babel at Shinar; and the Pyramids—an art, it might be added, that has now won fame throughout Europe, from the Tagus (or Tajo or Tejo) River in Portugal, the longest river on the Iberian peninsula, to the great Belt, the forty-mile passage that separates the Danish islands of Fyn and Sjaelland. Much of the poem's attractiveness derives from the sweepingly allusive nature of its language, which is utterly uncharacteristic of the poems set in this volume of songs.

So this is yet another song of triumphant praise. Here is Bach's setting:

The first thing that strikes us is the direction "Pathetisch," which certainly seems surprising for a song of praise—and especially for a song of praise that makes the claims that this one does.

But other surprises are in store. The vocal line is downright plaintive, as it moves through the B-minor cadence in bars 2-3. Moreover, the three-bar phrase, followed by its perfunctory little two-bar addendum, seems off balance, denying the positive thrust of the A-major cadence, topped off with an upward flourish in bar 5. The first chord of the next phrase, with its added seventh jumping an octave in the bass, is also a little offputting. Once again the length of the whole phrase is an irregular five bars, though this time the ending in the major is more elaborately turned out, complete with trill, and somewhat more convincing. The third phrase, which also begins with a high, light texture, again consists of three bars plus a two-bar addendum. But this time the addendum presses on, with the firmly descending bass line at the end of bar 15 and the octave leap to high A in the melody. The concluding phrase, we note, is not only more convincing than the preceding ones in its positive assertion of the major but is also a regular four-bar phrase.

Thus it seems as though the song, far from being a straightforward *Loblied*, had needed to begin rather tentatively—"Pathetisch," in fact—and then had gathered assurance as it moved along through its curiously irregular phrases, finally achieving the appropriate degree of assertiveness. The song, we note further, is not strictly strophic. Bach has indicated that the first four strophes are to be sung "gerade durch," or straight through the music. Thus the first time through the music sets stanzas one and two of the poem. But then with stanza three we must return to the music's rather tentative beginning and work through the whole process again. The fifth stanza, however, will begin with the pickup to bar 11, thus repeating and reaffirming the assurance gained in the fourth.

It is worth remarking on the song's carefully devised form because it has been misrepresented. In *Emanuel und Friedemann Bach und deren Brüder*, C. H. Bitter prints the song thus:[24]

Plainly, Bitter either ignored or misunderstood Bach's direction "Vier Strophen gerade durch," and focused his attention on the later direction "Die 5te strophe fängt hier an." He therefore took it that only the fifth and last stanza of the poem was to be sung to the last nine bars of music. This led him to label the stanzas of the text incorrectly. The second stanza, beginning "So sollte stets dein Loblied seyn," became the fifth since it was the one printed under the last nine bars of music, while stanzas 3 through 5 became 2 through 4. Yet the full text of the poem, with the stanzas in their proper order, was printed directly below the music of the song in the volume of *Freimäurer-Lieder*. How could Bitter have made this mistake? He tells us that he found the song in Speyer's *Musikalische Real-Zeitung* for 1788; one can only assume that the poem was incorrectly printed there.

What difference does Bitter's error make? A good deal, so far as the song's effect is concerned. Sung Bitter's way, with each of the first four stanzas set to the first 10 bars of music, there is no rise in assurance as we move from stanza 1 to stanza 2, or from 3 to 4. The second, third, and fourth stanzas all revert to the "Pathetisch" opening of the music. What Bach seems rather to have wanted was for the first two stanzas to build gradually to the triumphant assertiveness of the song's final bars. The third stanza would then return to the song's opening bars, which nicely suit the intimate lines about the holy art of masonry entrusting its treasure to the cradle of the world. Then, as the geographical references begin to add power and grandeur to the poem, they would be complemented by the growing assurance of the music in the song's second half. This effect would be reinforced by having the song's second half repeated for the equally grand fifth stanza of the poem.

V

And so we come to the end of our traversal of the songs of C. P. E. Bach. At the conclusion of his career as a composer of songs we find him as he has been ever since he found his true voice and vocation in the Gellert volume: restlessly experimenting with various forms, from simple *volkstümlich* strophic songs to a complex through-composed song like "Nonnelied" to songs with mixed forms—like the one just considered. There remain, however, two lost songs, apparently composed very near the end of Bach's life, that deserve mention.

Both of them, interestingly, were to texts by Friedrich von Hagedorn. As we have seen, though Hagedorn was one of the most frequently set poets of the time, there are only two surviving Bach songs to Hagedorn poems: "Morgen" and "An die Liebe." Apparently, Hagedorn's generally "Horatian" themes did not appeal to Bach as did those of more thoughtful, speculative poets. Yet at the end of his life, "in der letzten Zeit des Lebens," as his widow put it in an August 1791 letter to

Johann Jakob Heinrich Westphal, Bach turned to Hagedorn.[25] Lacking further documentation, as well as the songs themselves, we of course do not know why. But one is tempted to say that Bach chose these two poems, "Die Alster" and "Harvstehude," because both of them pay affectionate tribute to Hamburg.

The Alster is a small, pretty river that runs through Hamburg, widening into a large, man-made lake. Hagedorn begins his poem by contrasting the Alster with the Elbe, the large river that handles Hamburg's commercial traffic:

> Beförderer vieler Lustbarkeiten,
> Du angenehmer Alsterfluss!
> Du mehrest Hamburgs Seltenheiten
> Und ihren fröhlichen Genuss.
> Dir schallen zur Ehre,
> Du spielende Fluth!
> Die singenden Chöre,
> Der jauchzende Muth.
>
> Der Elbe Schifffahrt macht uns reicher;
> Die Alster lehrt gesellig seyn!
> Durch jene füllen sich die Speicher;
> Auf dieser schmeckt der fremde Wein.
> In treibenden Nachen
> Schifft Eintracht und Lust,
> Und Freyheit und Lachen
> Erleichtern die Brust.

While the Elbe has made Hamburg the commercial capital of Germany, it is the Alster that has made it possible for Hamburg's citizenry to enjoy the good life that riches bring. The remaining four stanzas of the poem elaborate upon the pleasures of this life—with the classical allusions that we should expect from Hagedorn. The pretty girls that line the Alster's banks on a summer night compare favorably with the nymphs that accompanied Diana on the hunt; Flora herself has taken care of the decorations. Hagedorn closes by evoking the celebratory, music-filled nights along the river:

> Hier lärmt, in Nächten voll Vergnügen,
> Der Pauken Schlag, des Waldhorns Schall;
> Hier wirkt, bey Wein und süssen Zügen,
> Die rege Freyheit überall.
> Nichts lebet gebunden,
> Was Freundschaft hier paart.
> O glückliche Stunden!
> O liebliche Fahrt!

It is interesting that Hagedorn's delightful vision includes not only "Vergnügen" but also "rege Freyheit": worldly success brings political as well as sensuous benefits, Hamburg's heritage of moderation and toleration as well as festivity.

Harvstehude (now known as Harvestehude) is an idyllic district near the Alster that had an interesting and important history. During the 1520s Hamburg made the transition to Lutheranism gradually and bloodlessly. The only incident that marred the peaceful acceptance of Lutheran teachings was the violent destruction, in 1530, of a monastery in Harvstehude. Hagedorn begins his poem with a generous expression of tolerance that alludes to the monastery:

> Ich bin ein Freund der Klosterländer,
> Und gönn und wünsch insonderheit
> Den rechten Kern der Segenspfänder
> Der jüngferlichen Geistlichkeit.
> Was Heilige für sich verwalten,
> Das kann, das wird, das muss gedeyn,
> Und frommer Schwestern Wohlverhalten
> Sollt immer reich an Pfründen seyn.
>
> Ihr edlen Johanniterinnen,
> Euch strömen Gut und Ehre zu;
> Ihr seyd ein Muster keuscher Sinnen
> In Harvstehudens sichrer Ruh.
> Wie selten höret ihr die Klagen
> Der buhlerischen Schmeicheley!
> Euch drücken keine Landesplagen,
> Kein Alp und keine Ketzerei.

After more praise of the place's beauty, the poem becomes somewhat obscure. Hagedorn alludes to a man named Stoppe, who built a small inn called "Der Parnass," in honor of the Greek mountain sacred to Apollo and the Muses, on the hill overlooking the lake. If we go there, he assures us, we shall be welcomed as graciously as Phoenix, Ajax, and Odysseus were welcomed by Achilles at his tent when they came, in Book IX of the *Iliad*, to try and persuade him to rejoin the war:

> Wo findet man so gute Wirthe,
> Als an den Helden jener Zeit?
> Wann sich ein Wandersmann verirrte,
> So stand für ihn ihr Haus bereit.
> Hier folgt man täglich dem Exempel
> Und tränkt und speiset jeden Gast,
> Und uns macht diesen Comustempel
> Auch ein Cornaro nicht verhasst.

Comus is of course the god of sensual pleasure, child of Bacchus and Circe, whom Hagedorn would have encountered in Milton's masque. Cornaro is Luigi or Lodovico Cornaro (1467?-1566), a Venetian nobleman who, in his eighty-third year, wrote *Discorsi della Vita Sobria* (1558), a book extolling the virtues of temperance. Hagedorn would probably have known of it from *Spectator* No. 195, where Addison recommends a recent English translation, *Sure and certain Methods of attaining a long and healthful Life: With Means for correcting a bad Constitution*.

As we have seen in the last few chapters, C.P.E. Bach came, in his later years, to play a prominent part in the intellectual and general cultural life of Hamburg. There is something very pleasing in the quite unverifiable supposition that he closed his long and productive career as a composer of songs by setting two poems in praise of the city he loved and served so well for 20 years.

Appendix One

Near the end of Chapter One, I promised that one of the main contentions of this book would be that the strophic song, despite the difficulties it presents to both composers and singers, is not just a compromise form, a necessary second best to the musically and aesthetically superior through-composed song, but is a special sort of work of art with special advantages of its own. Certainly the musical aesthetics of the mid-18th century, with its Horatian advocacy of unity in variety, and the practice of the song composers, the vast majority of whose songs were cast in strophic form, suggest that they saw strophic songs as possessing such unique advantages.

More convincing and specific evidence is offered by the songwriting career of C.P.E. Bach. As we saw, his songs were, from the beginning, rather different from those of his contemporaries. His main aim was constant, moment-to-moment expression of the text, while they paid less attention to expressing the text than they did to following a loose set of abstract rules: make the harmony move fast, use contrary motion whenever possible, keep it brisk and cheery unless the text is downright funereal. Since the very nature of the strophic song, with its one strophe of music applied to all the stanzas of the poem, no matter how varied they may be, would seem to work dead against Bach's goal of continuous expressivity, one would have expected him to have written through-composed rather than strophic songs.

And so he did—but only very seldom. Those three early "arias" (Wq. 211; H. 669), of which we know only that they were "written in his early years,"[1] were through-composed, but they probably came before the 1730s and the revival of the strophic song. Once he had launched himself on his songwriting career, Bach was extremely faithful to the strophic song. Yet it may well be significant that one of his very earliest songs—the fourth one he wrote, in fact—was the through-composed "Die Küsse." He may well have wanted to show others (and perhaps to prove to himself) that he could also handle a through-composed song. In fact, his through-composed solo vocal works, though few, are spotted throughout his career: "Die Küsse" (1750-1753), "Auf den Geburtstag eines Freundes" (1767 or later), "Phyllis" (1768 or earlier), the more "experimental" Cramer Psalms (1773-1774), "Die Grazien" (1774), "An Doris" (1775 or 1776), "Nonnelied" (1782 or earlier?), and "Ich hoff auf Gott" (1785). It is also significant, I think, that his two longest and most ambitious through-composed solo vocal pieces, "An Doris" and "Die Grazien," were written at about the same time he was composing short, folksong-like pieces for Voss—at the other end of the musical spectrum, so to speak—as well as worrying about the problem of transition in music and the failure of most cantatas to flow smoothly from one emotion to the next.

As we have seen, Bach—and he was not alone in this—grumbled in the prefaces to his vocal collections about the constraints of the strophic song. Yet the through-composed pieces just listed all fared well with contemporary critics. One gets the impression that despite the popularity of the newly reborn strophic song, Bach's reputation, even quite early in his career, was powerful enough to have sold plenty of collections of long, through-composed songs. If he wrote well over 90 percent of his songs strophically, he must have wanted to—despite his grumbling about how strophic form limited the opportunities for expression. Therefore there must have been compensating benefits of the strophic form over and above those discussed by the theorists. But what were they?

Perhaps the best answer to this question was provided by Goethe. In July 1800 he had begun translating Voltaire's play *Tancrède* into German. During the next several months, he worked on and off at the translation, in an old palace at Jena. By December, when he was rushing to complete the work before Christmas, the palace had grown cold and drafty, and poor Goethe was very ill with erysipelas. He didn't finish and arrive home in Weimar until the day after Christmas, and within a week, his condition, which had steadily worsened, had brought him near death. For several days he was delirious, and his life hung in the balance. By January 19 he was out of danger, 10 days later he and Schiller were holding rehearsals of the new play *Tankred*, and he wrote the following in his diary about one of the actors, whose name was Ehlers:

> Ehlers was useful and pleasing in many roles as actor and singer—especially welcome in the latter capacity for sociable entertainment when he performed ballads and songs of that sort with the guitar, rendering the words of the text with the greatest precision, absolutely incomparably. He was tireless in his quest for the proper expression, which consists in this: the singer must know how to bring out the varying significance of the different stanzas by just *one* melody, and thus must perform simultaneously the duties of both the lyric and the epic poet. Thus inspired, he was happy to accede to my request that he repeat the same song, with all its shadings exactly as before, for several more hours—indeed, until deep into the night. For his successful demonstration showed convincingly how objectionable is all the so-called "through-composition" of songs, by which all the lyrical character is lost, and a false sympathy is demanded and excited by each separate strophe.[2]

This seems to me a wonderfully clear and eloquent testimony to the special artistic potential of the strophic song. Whereas the strophic song is usually considered rather rough and imprecise when compared to the closeness with which a through-composed song can follow the progress of the poem, it is Ehlers's precision in suiting the song's music to the words of each stanza that intrigues Goethe. When he says that the singer of a strophic song must be at once both a lyric and an epic poet, what he means is that he must both repeat his tune and yet tell a continuously changing story, thus combining unity and variety. And what he finds wrong with through-composed songs is that they are too full of novelty and short on the artistic unity given the strophic song by the music's pervasive dramatization of the *herrschendes Affekt*.

Appendix Two

I have mentioned several times, in passing, the three arias for tenor, strings, and continuo (Wq. 211; H. 669) that C.P.E. Bach evidently composed in his youth. These have never been published, and I publish them now by the kind permission of Mr. Johan Eeckeloo, librarian of the Koninklijk Conservatorium/Conservatoire Royal of Brussels, which owns the manuscript. Here first are the three poems, which are of unknown authorship:

1. Edle Freiheit, Götterglück,
   Ohne dich ist Glanz und Würde
   Nur ein schimmernd Missgeschick,
   Eine Sklavenbürde.
   Für den Liebling ihrer Brust
   Hat die Gottheit dich erkoren,
   Und der Mann, der dich verloren,
   Lechzt unsonst nach andrer Lust.

2. Himmelstochter, Ruh der Seelen,
   Ewig wirst du Fürsten fehlen,
   Denn dich schreckt des Purpurs Glanz.
   Ungewinkt, mit leisem Schritte,
   Eilst du zu des Schäfers Hütte,
   Windest mit an seinem Veilchenkranz.
   Seine Tage fliessen heiter,
   Wie ein Frühlingsbach dahin.
   Stille Tugend, sein Begleiter,
   Lässt auf seinem Pfade Rosen buh'n.

3. Reiche bis zum Wolkensitze,
   Noch ist Demuth deine Pflicht.
   Dich beschirmt von nahem Blitze
   Ruhm und Gold und Hoheit nicht.
   Gestern Herr von sieben Reichen,
   Heut ist kaum ein Hügel dein.
   Flüchtiger als Weste weichen,
   Kann dein Glück entwichen sein.

I have given the text with modern German spelling and capitalization, as one finds it in Bitter (I, 192), and also with some corrections: Bitter's text is at odds with the manuscript at a couple of points. On the six pages that follow are the three arias, as they appear in the manuscript.

1st Aria (beg.)

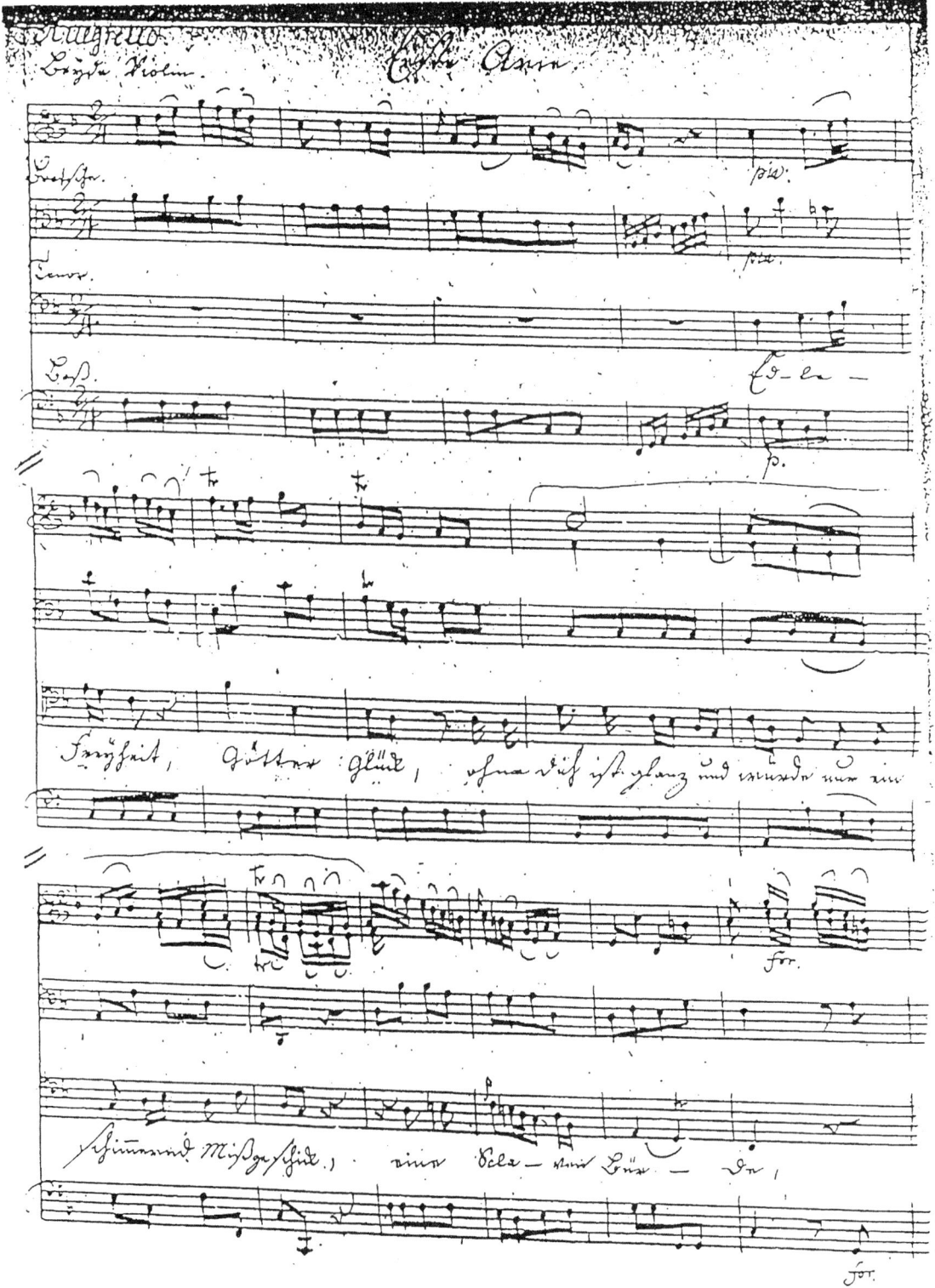

1st Aria (concl.)

2nd Aria (beg.)

2nd Aria (concl.)

3rd Aria (beg.)

3rd Aria (concl.)

Certainly there is no hint, in these three little well-turned pieces, of C. P. E. Bach the harmonist—as he would soon be known. Yet there are some small surprises, of the sort Bach would later delight in. He has given no notice that flutes are to be in the ensemble until bar 19, the antepenultimate bar, of the 3rd Aria. At that point he asks that the little G-major arpeggio (an imitation of that played by the violins in the bar preceding) be played by the flutes, and just below this bar he has a brief note: "From this measure on the two flutes should play in unison, and should end with the first note of the last bar." It is surely no coincidence that the flutes enter just after the west wind is mentioned. Also, the tempo change—"Ein wenig hurtiger" (a little faster)—comes at just the point in the 2nd Aria at which the speaker of the poem begins to discuss in detail the shepherd's way of life. Therefore the intimacy and warmth added by the change in tempo and change in time signature are most appropriate.

Bitter notes, in his review of Bach's compositions, that "in his earliest youth Bach had certainly composed some arias" (I, 138). But Bitter evidently does not know that the (flawed) text he produces fifty-five pages later belongs to the three arias. Bach's job at Hamburg was not only to direct the music at the five great churches but also to be cantor of the Johanneum, the city Gymnasium. It is in the course of explaining Bach's duties at the Johanneum that Bitter introduces what turns out to be the text of the three early arias. He is explaining that Bach not only had to lecture on music theory but also had to give individual lessons and even provide music for school dramatic productions. On March 12-15, 1776, the school players presented a five-act dramatization of Julius Caesar's life, ending in his murder. Bach's arias and various of his symphonic movements were used as entr'actes. While the program identified the arias as being by Bach, it evidently said nothing about their being very early works.

Notes

CHAPTER ONE

[1] See Hans Aarsleff, *From Locke to Saussure: Essays on the Study of Language and Intellectual History* (Minneapolis: University of Minnesota Press, 1982).

[2] Christian Friedrich Daniel Schubart, *Ideen zu einer Ästhetik der Tonkunst* (Vienna, 1806). There is a reprint edition of this work, published in 1969 by Georg Olms, Hildesheim, and edited by Fritz and Margrit Kaiser.

[3] Johann Friedrich Reichardt, *Über die Deutsche comische Oper* (Hamburg, 1774). There is a reprint edition of this work, published in 1974 by Musikverlag Emil Katzbichler, Munich.

[4] Johann Friedrich Reichardt, *Briefe eines aufmerksamen Reisenden die Musik betreffend,* 2 vols. (Frankfurt and Leipzig, 1774; Frankfurt and Breslau, 1776). The *New Grove Dictionary of Music and Musicians* says that there has been a modern reprint edition of this important and entertaining work, but gives no date of publication. The Harvard Music Library has been unable to trace such an edition. Substantial passages dealing with Reichardt's opinion of C.P.E. Bach are, however, reprinted in Ernst Suchalla's two-volume *Carl Philipp Emanuel Bach: Briefe und Dokumente* (Göttingen: Vanderhoeck and Ruprecht, 1994).

[5] See Manfred Schenker, *Charles Batteux und seine Nachahmungstheorie in Deutschland* (Leipzig: H. Haessel Verlag, 1909).

[6] Quoted by Gudrun Busch, *C. Ph. E. Bach und seine Lieder* (Regensburg: Gustav Bosse Verlag, 1957), p. 248.

[7] Samuel Johnson, *Lives of the English Poets,* ed. George Birkbeck Hill, 3 vols. (Oxford: Clarendon Press, 1905), III, 233.

[8] Samuel Taylor Coleridge, *Biographia Literaria,* ed. J. Shawcross, 2 vols. (Oxford: Oxford University Press, 1907), II, 12.

[9] Ernst Otto Lindner, *Geschichte des deutschen Liedes im XVIII. Jahrhundert* (Leipzig: Breitkopf und Härtel, 1871).

[10] See A. Peter Brown, "Joseph Haydn and C.P.E. Bach: The Question of Influence," in *Joseph Haydn's Keyboard Music: Sources and Style* (Bloomington: Indiana University Press, 1986), pp. 203-229.

[11] Donald Francis Tovey, *Essays in Musical Analysis,* Volume I, *Symphonies* (London: Oxford University Press, 1935), p. 192.

[12] See my essay, "The Operas of Haydn," *The Atlantic Monthly,* September 1983, pp. 110-115.

[13] Quoted by Reinhard G. Pauly, *Music in the Classical Period,* 3rd ed. (Englewood Cliffs, N.J.: Prentice-Hall, 1988), p. 196.

[14] Quoted by Otto Erich Deutsch, *Mozart: A Documentary Biography,* trans. Eric Blom, Peter Branscombe, and Jeremy Noble (Stanford, Calif.: Stanford University Press, 1965), p. 305.

[15] Karl Christian Friedrich Krause, *Darstellungen aus der Geschichte der Musik,* ed. Aug. Wünsche (Leipzig: Dieterische Verlagsbuchhandlung, 1911).

[16] I have used the English translation: R. G. Kiesewetter, *History of the Modern Music of Western Europe,* trans. Robert Müller (London: T. C. Newby, 1848).

[17] Gustav Schilling (ed.), *Encyclopädie der gesammten musikalischen Wissenschaften, oder Universal-Lexicon der Tonkunst,* 7 vols., 2nd ed. (Stuttgart: Franz Heinrich Köhler, 1840).

[18] Franz Brendel, *Geschichte der Musik in Italien, Deutschland und Frankreich* (Leipzig: Bruno Hinze, 1852).

[19] August Reissmann, *Allgemeine Geschichte der Musik,* Vol. III (Leipzig: Fues's Verlag, 1864). All my citations of Reissmann are from this volume.

[20] See William S. Newman, *The Sonata since Beethoven,* 2nd ed. (New York: W. W. Norton, 1972), Chapter II.

[21] Arrey von Dommer, *Handbuch der Musikgeschichte,* 2nd ed. (Leipzig: Wilhelm Grunow, 1878).

[22] While it is true that mid-19th-century academic music historians found the formal and theoretical problems presented by untexted instrumental music quite puzzling, it should be mentioned here that there were other writers on music, mainly poets, who did not. As early as the last years of the 18th century, such men as Wilhelm Heinrich Wackenroder, Ludwig Tieck, and E. T. A. Hoffmann welcomed the new instrumental music as a richer and more precise medium of communication than verbal language, much as Wagner and others would do half a century later. The relevant writings of Wackenroder (and of Tieck, who collaborated with him to a degree still undetermined) are most conveniently found in Heinrich Wackenroder, *Werke und Briefe* (Heidelberg: Schneider, 1967); those of Hoffmann, in his *Schriften zur Musik,* ed. Friedrich Schnapp (Munich: Winkler, 1977). For English versions, see Wackenroder's *Confessions and Fantasies,* trans. and ed. Mary Hurst Schubert (University Park, Pennsylvania State University Press, 1971), and Hoffmann's *Musical Writings,* ed. David Charlton and trans. Martyn Clarke (Cambridge: Cambridge University Press, 1989). See also Carl Dahlhaus, *The Idea of Absolute Music,* trans. Roger Lustig (Chicago: University of Chicago Press, 1989), and John Neubauer, *The Emancipation of Music from Language* (New Haven: Yale University Press, 1986), Chapter XIV.

[23] C. H. Bitter, *Carl Philipp Emanuel und Wilhelm Friedemann Bach und deren Brüder,* 2 vols. (Berlin: Wilhelm Müller, 1868).

[24] C.P.E.. Bach, *Essay on the True Art of Playing Keyboard Instruments,* trans. and ed. William J. Mitchell (New York: W. W. Norton, 1949).

[25] I have used the English translation: Emil Naumann, *The History of Music,* trans. F. Praeger, Vol. IV (London: Cassell & Co., [1886]).

[26] Wilhelm Langhans, *Die Geschichte der Musik des 17. 18. und 19. Jahrhunderts,* vol. II (Leipzig: F. E. C. Leuckart, 1887).

[27] George Grove (ed.), *A Dictionary of Music and Musicians,* 4 vols. (London: Macmillan and Co., 1879-1889).

[28] C. Hubert H. Parry, *The Art of Music,* 2nd ed. (London: Kegan Paul, Trench, Trübner, & Co., 1894).

[29] Charles Darwin, *The Origin of Species,* ed. Gillian Beer (Oxford: Oxford University Press, 1996). This is a reprint of the work's 2nd edition, which originally appeared January 7, 1860, about six weeks after the 1st edition.

[30] W. H. Hadow, *The Viennese Period,* The Oxford History of Music, Vol. V (Oxford: Clarendon Press, 1905).

[31] I have used the English translation: Hugo Riemann, *Catechism of Musical History,* Part II (New York: G. Schirmer, 1892).

[32] Hugo Riemann, "Die Söhne Bachs," in *Präludien und Studien,* vol. III (Leipzig: H. Seemann, 1901), pp. 173-184.

[33] Ernst Fritz Schmid, *C.P.E. Bach und seine Kammermusik* (Kassel: Bärenreiter, 1931).

[34] *Denkmäler der Tonkunst in Bayern,* Jahrgang III/1, Volume IV (1902).

[35] *Denkmäler der Tonkunst in Österreich,* Jahrgang XV/2, Volume XXXI (1908).

[36] Hugo Riemann, *Handbuch der Musikgeschichte,* vol. 2, part 3, *Die Musik des 18. und 19. Jahrhunderts: Die grossen deutschen Meister* (Leipzig: Breitkopf und Härtel, 1913).

[37] Guido Adler (ed.), *Handbuch der Musikgeschichte,* Part 2, 2nd rev. ed. (Berlin: Max Hesses Verlag, 1930).

[38] Guido Adler, "Haydn and the Viennese Classical School," trans. W. Oliver Strunk, *The Musical Quarterly,* XVIII (1932), 191-207.

[39] Gerald Abraham, "18th-Century Music and the Problems of Its History," *Current Musicology,* IX (1969), 49-51.

[40] Donald Francis Tovey, *Essays in Musical Analysis,* 6 vols. (London: Oxford University Press, 1935-1939).

[41] Donald Francis Tovey, *A Musician Talks: 1. The Integrity of Music* (London: Oxford University Press, 1941).

[42] *The Encyclopaedia Britannica,* 29 vols., 11th ed. (New York: The Encyclopaedia Britannica Company, 1911).

[43] Donald Francis Tovey, *Musical Articles from the "Encyclopaedia Britannica"* (London: Oxford University Press, 1944).

⁴⁴Donald Francis Tovey, *Essays and Lectures on Music* (London: Oxford University Press, 1949).

⁴⁵*The Age of Enlightenment: 1745-1790,* ed. Egon Wellesz and Frederick Sternfeld, New Oxford History of Music, Vol. VII (London: Oxford University Press, 1973).

⁴⁶*Perspectives in Musicology,* ed. Barry S. Brook, Edward O. D. Downes, and Sherman Van Solkema (New York: W. W. Norton, 1972), p. 145.

⁴⁷Charles Rosen, *The Classical Style: Haydn, Mozart, Beethoven* (New York: Viking Press, 1971) and *Sonata Forms* (New York: W. W. Norton, 1980).

⁴⁸Giorgio Pestelli, *The Age of Mozart and Beethoven,* trans. Eric Cross (Cambridge: Cambridge University Press, 1984).

⁴⁹Max Friedlaender, *Das deutsche Lied im 18. Jahrhundert* (Stuttgart and Berlin: J. G. Cotta'sche Buchhandlung, 1902).

⁵⁰W. K. von Jolizza, *Das Lied und seine Geschichte* (Vienna and Leipzig: A. Hartleben's Verlag, 1910).

⁵¹Hermann Kretzschmar, *Geschichte des neuen deutschen Liedes* (Leipzig: Druckerei Lokay, 1911).

⁵²Otto Vrieslander, *Carl Philipp Emanuel Bach* (Munich: R. Piper, 1923).

⁵³Hertha Wien-Claudi, *Zum Liedschaffen Carl Philipp Emanuel Bachs* (Reichenberg: Gebrüder Stiepel, 1928).

⁵⁴Gudrun Busch, *C. Ph. E. Bach und seine Lieder* (Regensburg: Gustav Bosse Verlag, 1957).

⁵⁵Reinhard G. Pauly, *Music in the Classical Period,* 3rd ed. (Englewood Cliffs, N.J.: Prentice-Hall, 1988).

⁵⁶*A History of Song,* ed. Denis Stevens, rev. ed. (London: Hutchinson & Co., 1960).

CHAPTER TWO

¹Quoted in E. Eugene Helm, *Thematic Catalogue of the Works of Carl Philipp Emanuel Bach* (New Haven and London: Yale University Press, 1989), p. 147, from *Verzeichniss des musikalischen Nachlasses des verstorbenen Capellmeisters Carl Philipp Emanuel Bach...* (Hamburg, 1790), p. 64. See Appendix Two, pp. 457-464.

²Hans Joachim Moser, *The German Solo Song and the Ballad* (Cologne: Arno Volk Verlag, 1958), p. 5.

³August Reissmann, *Das deutsche Lied in seiner historischen Entwicklung* (Cassel: Verlag von Oswald Bertram, 1861), quoted p. 74.

⁴K. E. Schneider, *Das Musikalische Lied in geschichtlicher Entwickelung* (Leipzig: Breitkopf und Härtel, 1865), III, iv.

[5] Ernst Otto Lindner, *Geschichte des deutschen Liedes im XVIII. Jahrhundert* (Leipzig: Breitkopf und Härtel, 1871), p. 1.

[6] Johann Mattheson, *Critica musica,* I, 100; II, 309; cited Lindner, p. 2. *Critica musica* was reprinted, in two individually paginated volumes, in 1964 by Frits A. M. Knuf, Amsterdam.

[7] Johann Gottfried Walther, *Musikalisches Lexicon oder musikalische Bibliothek* (Leipzig, 1732), p. 584. There is a reprint edition of this work, published in 1953 by Bärenreiter-Verlag, Kassel.

[8] Johann Adolph Scheibe, *Critischer Musikus,* p. 583; partially cited Lindner, p. 28. The 1745 Leipzig "vermehrte und verbesserte" edition of *Critischer Musikus* was reprinted by Georg Olms Verlag, Hildesheim, in 1970. Since the whole work is contained in one continuously paginated volume, only page references need be given.

[9] The word "Oden" (songs) is in Scheibe's text but is omitted by Lindner.

[10] The word "fast" (almost) is in Scheibe's text but is omitted by Lindner. The ellipsis in this quotation is my own.

[11] August Reissmann, *Geschichte des deutschen Liedes* (Berlin: Verlag von J. Gutentag, 1874), p. v.

[12] For an account of the rise of positivist historiography, see R. G. Collingwood, *The Idea of History* (Oxford: Clarendon Press, 1946), Part III.

[13] Leopold von Ranke, *Fürsten und Völker,* ed. Willy Andreas (Wiesbaden: Emil Vollmer Verlag, 1957), p. 4.

[14] Max Friedlaender, *Das deutsche Lied im 18. Jahrhundert* (Stuttgart and Berlin: J. G. Cotta'sche Buchhandlung, 1902), I/i, xi.

[15] W. K. von Jolizza, *Das Lied und seine Geschichte* (Vienna and Leipzig: A. Hartleben's Verlag, 1910), p. 145.

[16] Hermann Kretzschmar, *Geschichte des neuen deutschen Liedes* (Leipzig: Druckerei Lokay, 1911), p. 1.

[17] Lewis White Beck, *Early German Philosophy: Kant and His Predecessors* (Cambridge, Mass.: Harvard University Press, 1969), p. 245. Chapters XI-XIV of Beck's book give an excellent account of German thought during C.P.E. Bach's lifetime.

[18] The best account of the changes undergone by German literature during this period may be found in Eric A. Blackall's splendid book, *The Emergence of German as a Literary Language,* 2nd ed. (Ithaca: Cornell University Press, 1978).

[19] Herbert Butterfield, *The Whig Interpretation of History* (London: G. Bell and Sons, 1931), pp. 5-6.

[20] Günther Müller, *Geschichte des deutschen Liedes vom Zeitalter des Barock bis zur Gegenwart* (Munich: Drei Masken Verlag, 1925), p. 108.

[21] Walther Vetter, *Das frühdeutsche Lied,* 2 vols. (Münster: Helios-Verlag, 1928), I, xi. All citations will be to the first of Vetter's two volumes.

[22] See Harold Bloom, *The Anxiety of Influence: A Theory of Poetry* (Oxford: Oxford University Press, 1973). Bloom elaborates into a general theory Walter Jackson Bate's view of the relation of English poets to their predecessors during a particular historical period, 1660-1830, in *The Burden of the Past and the English Poet* (Cambridge, Mass.: Harvard University Press, 1970).

[23] Ernst Bücken, *Das deutsche Lied: Probleme und Gestalten* (Hamburg: Hanseatische Verlagsanstalt, 1939), p. 9.

[24] Siegfried Kross, *Geschichte des deutschen Liedes* (Darmstadt: Wissenschaftliche Buchgesellschaft, 1989), p. 54.

CHAPTER THREE

[1] See Hermann Kretzschmar, *Geschichte des neuen deutschen Liedes* (Leipzig: Druckerei Lokay, 1911), pp. 2-7.

[2] Jan Racek, *Stilprobleme der italienischen Monodie,* Opera Universitatis Purkynianae Brunensis Facultas Philosophica, No. 103 (Prague: Státní pedagogické nakladetelství), p. 156.

[3] John Herschel Baron, "Foreign Influences on the German Secular Continuo Lied of the Mid-Seventeenth Century" (Ph.D. diss., Brandeis University, 1967), p. 112.

[4] See particularly the two essays "Entstehung und Wurzeln des begleiteten deutschen Sololiedes" (1926) and "Wort und Ton in der Musik des 18. Jahrhunderts" (1923), in *Gesammelte Schriften und Vorträge,* ed. F. Blume (Tutzing: Schneider, 1929), pp. 156-172 and 173-231, respectively.

[5] Heinrich Albert's *Arien* were published in 1907 as Volumes XII and XIII of *Denkmäler deutscher Tonkunst,* edited by Eduard Bernoulli. There is now a revised edition of these volumes edited by Hans Joachim Moser (Wiesbaden: Breitkopf und Härtel, 1958).

[6] Andreas Hammerschmidt's *Weltliche Oden oder Liebesgesänge* have been published as Volume XLIII of *Das Erbe deutscher Musik,* edited by Hans Joachim Moser (Mainz: B. Schott's Söhne, 1962).

[7] Adam Krieger's *Arien* were published in 1905 as Volume XIX of *Denkmäler deutscher Tonkunst,* edited by Alfred Heuss. There is now a revised edition of this volume edited by Hans Joachim Moser (Wiesbaden: Breitkopf und Härtel, 1958).

[8] Heinrich Elmenhorst's *Geistliche Lieder* were published in 1911 as Volume XLV of *Denkmäler deutscher Tonkunst,* edited by Joseph Kromolicki and Wilhelm Krabbe. There is now a revised edition of this volume edited by Hans Joachim Moser (Wiesbaden: Breitkopf und Härtel, 1961).

[9] Philipp Heinrich Erlebach's *Harmonische Freude musikalischer Freunde* was published in 1914 as Volumes XLVI and XLVII of *Denkmäler deutscher Tonkunst,* edited by Otto

Kinkeldey. There is now a revised edition of these volumes, edited by Hans Joachim Moser (Wiesbaden: Breitkopf und Härtel, 1959)

[10] The four volumes of Valentin Rathgeber's *Ohren-vergnügendes und Gemüths-ergözendes Tafel-Confect* have been published as Volume XIX of *Das Erbe deutscher Musik,* edited by Hans Joachim Moser (Mainz: B. Schott's Söhne, 1942).

[11] The four volumes of *Singende Muse an der Pleisse* were published in 1909 as Volumes XXXV and XXXVI of *Denkmäler deutscher Tonkunst,* edited by Edward Buhle. There is now a revised edition of these volumes, edited by Hans Joachim Moser (Wiesbaden: Breitkopf und Härtel, 1958).

[12] Spitta's essay on "Sperontes" was reprinted in his *Musikgeschichtliche Aufsätze* (Berlin: Verlag von Gebrüder Paetel, 1894), pp. 177-295. This volume was in turn reprinted in 1976 by Georg Olms Verlag of Hildesheim. In making references to Spitta's essay, I have given the page numbers of the Olms reprint.

[13] Marpurg's *Kritische Briefe über die Tonkunst* was published at Berlin in 1759-1764, in four parts ("Theile") that made up two separately paginated volumes. This edition was reprinted in 1964 by Georg Olms Verlag, Hildesheim.

[14] Mizler, *Neu eröffnete musikalische Bibliothek,* I, iii, 76-77. The original four-volume Leipzig edition of Mizler's periodical, which appeared in 1739-1754, was reprinted in the Netherlands in 1966. Not only each volume but also each part ("Theil") of the periodical is paginated individually. Hence I give references to volume, part, and page—as above.

[15] Scheibe, *Critischer Musikus,* p. 588. For an explanation of the edition and its organization, see Note 8 to Chapter Two.

[16] See Imanuel Willheim's 1964 University of Illinois doctoral dissertation, "Johann Adolph Scheibe: German Musical Thought in Transition," pp. 35-36.

[17] Johann Mattheson, *Critica musica,* I, 16, 319; Johann Christoph Gottsched, *Versuch einer critischen Dichtkunst,* 4th ed. (Leipzig, 1751), p. 723. For an explanation of the edition of *Critica musica* and its organization, see Note 6 to Chapter Two. The 1751 edition of Gottsched's *Versuch einer critischen Dichtkunst* was reprinted by the Wissenschaftliche Buchgesellschaft, Darmstadt, in 1962.

[18] See Rainer Kahleyss, *Conrad Friedrich Hurlebusch (1691-1765): Sein Leben und Wirken* (Frankfurt am Main: Haag und Herchen Verlag, 1984), pp. 99ff.

[19] Manfred F. Bukofzer, *Music in the Baroque Era* (New York: W. W. Norton, 1947), p. 261.

[20] Hermann Kretzschmar, *Geschichte des neuen deutschen Liedes* (Leipzig: Druckerei Lokay, 1911), p. 215.

[21] Max Friedlaender, *Das deutsche Lied im 18. Jahrhundert* (Stuttgart and Berlin: J. G. Cotta'sche Buchhandlung, 1902).

[22] Telemann's *Vier und zwanzig, theils ernsthafte, theils scherzende Oden* and Görner's three-part *Sammlung neuer Oden und Lieder* were published together in 1917 as Volume LVII of *Denkmäler deutscher Tonkunst,* edited by Wilhelm Krabbe and Joseph Kromolicki. There is

now a revised edition of this volume, edited by Hans Joachim Moser (Wiesbaden: Breitkopf und Härtel, 1959). The passages cited from Krabbe may be found on pp. x, xi, xv, and xvii. Cf. Friedlaender, I/i, 82.

[23] Lothar Hoffmann-Erbrecht, "Der 'galante Stil' in der Musik des 18. Jahrhunderts," *Studien zur Musikwissenschaft* XXV (1962), 259.

[24] Lukas Richter, "Telemanns Lieder nach Hagedorn," *Telemann und seine Dichter* (Magdeburg, 1977), pp. 91, 94.

[25] J. W. Smeed, *German Song and Its Poetry, 1740-1900* (London: Croom Helm, 1987), pp. 35, 15.

[26] Herbert Butterfield, *The Whig Interpretation of History* (London: G. Bell and Sons, 1931), p. v.

[27] Henry Knight Miller, "The 'Whig Interpretation' of Literary History," *Eighteenth-Century Studies,* VI (1972-1973), 62, 63.

[28] George Saintsbury, *A History of Criticism and Literary Taste in Europe,* 3 vols., 4th ed. (Edinburgh and London: William Blackwood and Sons, 1922-23), III, 184.

[29] Hugo Leichtentritt, *Music, History, and Ideas* (Cambridge, Mass.: Harvard University Press, 1938), p. 176.

[30] Karin Zauft, *Telemanns Liedschaffen und seine Bedeutung für die Entwicklung des deutschen Liedes in der ersten Hälfte des 18. Jahrhunderts* (Magdeburg, 1967), pp. 14–15.

[31] Friedlaender, *Das deutsche Lied im 18. Jahrhundert,* I/i, 97ff.

CHAPTER FOUR

[1] Henry Knight Miller, "The 'Whig Interpretation' of Literary History," *Eighteenth-Century Studies,* VI (1972-1973), 60-84.

[2] Hugo Goldschmidt, *Die Musikästhetik des 18. Jahrhunderts und ihre Beziehungen zu seinem Kunstschaffen* (Zürich and Leipzig: Verlag von Rascher & Co., 1915); Walter Serauky, *Die musikalische Nachahmungsästhetik im Zeitraum von 1700 bis 1850* (Münster: Helios-Verlag, 1929).

[3] A good introduction to Gottsched is provided by P. M. Mitchell in *Johann Christoph Gottsched (1700-1766): Harbinger of German Classicism* (Columbia, S.C.: Camden House, 1995). For a more general view of the period, see Stephen D. Martinson, *On Imitation, Imagination and Beauty: A Critical Reassessment of the Concept of the Literary Artist during the Early German "Aufklärung"* (Bonn: Bouvier Verlag Herbert Grundmann, 1977).

[4] Imanuel Willheim, "Johann Adolph Scheibe: German Musical Thought in Transition" (Ph.D. diss., University of Illinois, 1963).

[5] John Richard Edwards, "Christian Gottfried Krause: Mentor of the First Berlin Song School" (Ph.D. diss., University of Iowa, 1973).

⁶Howard Jay Serwer, "Friedrich Wilhelm Marpurg (1718-1795): Music Critic in a *Galant* Age" (Ph.D. diss., Yale, 1969).

⁷Ludwig Wittgenstein, *Philosophical Investigations,* trans. G. E. M. Anscombe, 2nd rev. ed. (Oxford: Basil Blackwell, 1958), I, paras. 66-67, pp. 31^e-32^e.

⁸William E. Kennick, "Does Traditional Aesthetics Rest on a Mistake?," *Mind,* N.S. LXVII (1958), 317-334.

⁹I have borrowed this example from John Hospers, "What Is Explanation?," which may be most conveniently found in Anthony Flew, ed., *Essays in Conceptual Analysis* (London: Macmillan & Co., 1956), pp. 94-119, but which was originally published in *The Journal of Philosophy,* 1946.

¹⁰G. E. Moore, "Wittgenstein's Lectures in 1930-33," *Philosophical Papers* (New York: Collier Books, 1962), p. 308. Moore's account of Wittgenstein's lectures first appeared, in three installments, in *Mind,* 1954-1955.

¹¹Paul Oskar Kristeller, "The Modern System of the Arts: A Study in the History of Aesthetics," *Journal of the History of Ideas,* XII (1951), 496-527; and XIII (1952), 17-46.

¹²Samuel Johnson, *Lives of the English Poets,* ed. George Birkbeck Hill, 3 vols. (Oxford: Clarendon Press, 1905), I, 410, 412.

¹³Sir Robert Howard, "Preface to *The Great Favourite, or The Duke of Lerma,*" J. E. Spingarn, ed., *Critical Essays of the Seventeenth Century,* 3 vols. (Oxford: Clarendon Press, 1908-1909), II, 106, 109, 106-107.

¹⁴*Essays of John Dryden,* ed. W. P. Ker, 2 vols. (Oxford: Clarendon Press, 1900), I, 23-108. All later references to Dryden's critical essays will be to the first volume of this edition.

¹⁵Frank Sibley, "Aesthetic Concepts," *Philosophical Review,* LXVIII (1959), 421-450. See also Sibley's later essay, "Aesthetic and Nonaesthetic," *Philosophical Review,* LXXIV (1965), 135-159.

¹⁶*The New Yorker,* May 6, 1967, p. 170.

¹⁷Friedrich Waismann, "Verifiability," most conveniently available in A. G. N. Flew, ed., *Logic and Language* (First Series) (Oxford: Basil Blackwell, 1951), pp. 117-144.

CHAPTER FIVE

¹ The relevant sections of Bouhours's book are conveniently available, in English translation, in Scott Elledge and Donald Schier, ed., *The Continental Model: Selected French Critical Essays of the Seventeenth Century,* rev. ed. (Ithaca: Cornell University Press, 1970), pp. 160-192.

² Henry More, *Enchiridion Ethicum,* trans. Robert Southwell (1690). Reproduced from the 1st ed. (New York: The Facsimile Text Society, 1930), pp. 6-7.

³ It is much to be regretted that there is no good modern edition of Cudworth's major works. The best introduction to his thought is J. A. Passmore, *Ralph Cudworth: An Interpretation* (Cambridge: Cambridge University Press, 1951). See also A. N. Prior, *Logic and the Basis of Ethics* (Oxford: Clarendon Press, 1949); W. D. Hudson, *Ethical Intuitionism* (New York: St. Martin's Press, 1967); and my own "Founding English Ethics: Locke, Mathematics, and the Innateness Question," *Eighteenth Century Life,* XVI (1992), 12–45.

⁴ Dubos's work was translated into English, as *Critical Reflections on Poetry, Painting and Music,* by Thomas Nugent, and first appeared in 1719. The 5th ed., 3 vols. (London, 1748) was reprinted by AMS Press, New York, in 1978.

⁵ The first (1725) edition of Hutcheson's *Inquiry into the Original of our Ideas of Beauty and Virtue* was reprinted by Georg Olms, Hildesheim, in 1971 as Volume I in their seven-volume *Collected Works of Francis Hutcheson.* The best introduction to Hutcheson's thought is Peter Kivy, *The Seventh Sense: A Study of Francis Hutcheson's Aesthetics and Its Influence in Eighteenth-Century Britain* (New York: Burt Franklin & Co., 1976).

⁶ All references to Gottsched's *Versuch einer critischen Dichtkunst* are to the first edition of 1730, which has, to my knowledge, never been reprinted.

⁷ This passage is taken from Chapter II of Miscellany III of Shaftesbury's *Miscellaneous Reflections,* a work that first appeared in 1711 and became the third and final volume of Shaftesbury's *Characteristicks of Men, Manners, Opinions, Times* (1711). It may be found in John L. Robertson's edition of *Characteristics,* 2 vols. (London: Grant Richards, 1900) at II, 257. Gottsched refers to it as appearing on p. 164, which was its location in Volume III of the early 18th-century editions of 1711 *et seq.* Later in the *Versuch* (pp. 185–186), Gottsched translates the two-and-a-half paragraphs that follow the passage from Shaftesbury quoted earlier, and gives the English in a footnote.

⁸ Batteux's *Les Beaux-Arts réduits à un même principe* and the essays he added to it to make up the *Cours de belles-lettres* (1750) were translated into English by John Miller, as *A Course of the Belles Lettres or the Principles of Literature,* 4 vols. (London, 1761). Later references to this edition will appear in parentheses or brackets in the body of the text. The German translation of *Les Beaux-Arts réduit à un même principe,* incidentally, was made by Johann Adolph Schlegel, and was published in 1751, as *Einschränkung der Schönen Künste auf einen einzigen Grundsatz.* For Batteux's influence in Germany, see Manfred Schenker, *Charles Batteux und seine Nachahmungstheorie in Deutschland* (Leipzig: H. Haessel Verlag, 1909).

⁹ Marshall R. Schwartz, "L'Abbé Batteux: A 'Philosophe' Defender of Aristotle" (Ph.D. diss., University of Chicago, 1966), p. 46.

¹⁰ See Anthony Kenny, "Cartesian Privacy," in *Wittgenstein: The Philosophical Investigations,* ed. George Pitcher (Garden City, N.Y.: Doubleday Anchor, 1966), pp. 352–370.

CHAPTER SIX

¹ The original text of Baumgarten's *Meditationes philosophicae,* together with an English translation, *Reflections on Poetry,* by Karl Aschenbrenner and William B. Holther, is avail-

able (Berkeley and Los Angeles: University of California Press, 1954). The Latin text of Baumgarten's *Aesthetica,* as it appeared in 1750 and 1758, was republished, in one volume, by Georg Olms, Hildesheim, in 1970. Apparently, though incredibly, this seminal work has never been translated into a modern language. Even before Baumgarten's work was published, his thought was popularized in Germany by his admirer Georg Friedrich Meier, whose three-volume *Anfangsgründe aller schönen Wissenschaften,* which appeared in 1748, was also republished, in 1970, by Olms. See also Ernst Bergmann, *Die Begründung der deutschen Ästhetik durch Alex. Gottlieb Baumgarten und Georg Friedrich Meier* (Leipzig: Röder & Schunke, 1911); Hans Rudolf Schweizer, *Ästhetik als Philosophie der sinnlichen Erkenntnis* (Basel and Stuttgart: Schwab & Co., 1973), which contains lengthy excerpts from Baumgarten's *Aesthetica,* in Latin and German on facing pages; and Friedhelm Solms, *Disciplina aethetica: Zur Frühgeschichte der ästhetischen Theorie bei Baumgarten und Herder* (Stuttgart: Klett-Cotta, 1990).

[2] R. R. Bolgar, *The Classical Heritage and Its Beneficiaries* (Cambridge: Cambridge University Press, 1954), pp. 115-116.

[3] A good modern edition of Vida's poem, with translation and commentary, is Ralph G. Williams, *The "De Arte Poetica" of Marco Girolamo Vida* (New York: Columbia University Press, 1976).

[4] Webbe's "Cannons or general cautions of Poetry" and Fabricius's Latin original may both be found in G. Gregory Smith, ed., *Elizabethan Critical Essays,* 2 vols. (Oxford: Oxford University Press, 1904), I, 290-301, 417-421.

[5] F. R. Leavis, *Revaluation* (London: Chatto & Windus, 1936), p. 19.

[6] Scheibe, *Critischer Musikus,* p. 62. For an explanation of the edition and its organization, see Note 8 to Chapter Two.

[7] Boileau's *L'Art poétique* and the Soames-Dryden translation appear on facing pages in the Elledge and Schier anthology, *The Continental Model,* pp. 208-269. See Note 1 to Chapter Five. All references to Boileau will be to this book.

[8] C. O. Brink, *Horace on Poetry: The "Ars Poetica"* (Cambridge: Cambridge University Press, 1971), p. 86. Later references to this work appear in parentheses or brackets, in the body of the text.

[9] Batteux, *A Course of the Belles Lettres,* trans. Miller (London, 1761), III, 254-255. See Note 8 to Chapter Five.

[10] Jean-Pierre de Crousaz, *Traité du Beau* (Amsterdam, 1715), p. 16. This volume was reprinted in 1970 by Slatkine Reprints, of Geneva. I have been unable to discover a contemporary English translation of Crousaz's book. Portions of it appeared in German translation in Johann Nikolaus Forkel's *Musikalisch-critische Bibliothek* in 1778-1779.

[11] Ernst Cassirer, *The Philosophy of the Enlightenment,* trans. Fritz C. A. Koelln and James P. Pettegrove (Boston: Beacon Press, 1955), p. 289n.

[12] See *The Making of Homeric Verse: The Collected Papers of Milman Parry,* ed. Adam Parry (Oxford: Oxford University Press, 1971). See also Albert Bates Lord, *The Singer of Tales* (Cambridge Mass.: Harvard University Press, 1960).

CHAPTER SEVEN

[1] Mattheson, *Critica musica,* I, 100; II, 309. For an explanation of the edition and its organization, see Note 6 to Chapter Two.

[2] For an explanation of the edition of Mizler's journal that I cite, and its organization, see Note 14 to Chapter Three.

[3] See Note 8 to Chapter Two.

[4] Cited James H. Mallard, "A Translation of Christian Gottfried Krause's *Von der musikalischen Poesie,* with a Critical Essay on His Sources and the Aesthetic Views of His Time" (Ph.D. diss., University of Texas at Austin, 1978), p. 19n.

[5] J. E. Spingarn (ed.), *Critical Essays of the Seventeenth Century,* 3 vols. (Oxford: Clarendon Press, 1908-1909), II, 298.

[6] Cited James H. Mallard, "A Translation of Christian Gottfried Krause's *Von der musikalischen Poesie,*" p. 16n. See Note 4, above.

[7] Krause's book has not, so far as I know, received a modern reprinting. The copy I used was the second edition, dated 1753, which is, reportedly, virtually identical to the first edition of 1752.

[8] Peter Kivy, *The Corded Shell: Reflections on Musical Expression* (Princeton, N.J.: Princeton University Press, 1980), pp. 105, 109-110.

[9] Johann Jacob Breitinger, *Critische Dichtkunst,* 2 vols. (Zürich, 1740), I, 18. This edition has been reprinted by the J. B. Meltzerische Verlagsbuchhandlung, Stuttgart, 1966.

[10] For an excellent account of this process, see John Neubauer, *The Emancipation of Music from Language* (New Haven: Yale University Press, 1986).

[11] Marpurg's *Historisch-Kritische Beyträge* was reprinted by Georg Olms, Hildesheim, in 1970, in five large, individually paginated volumes. Later references to this periodical will be given by volume and page number.

[12] Marpurg's *Kritische Briefe über die Tonkunst* was reprinted by Georg Olms, Hildesheim, in 1974, in two individually paginated volumes. Later references to this periodical will be given by volume and page number.

[13] *The Spectator,* ed. Donald F. Bond, 5 vols. (Oxford: Clarendon Press, 1965), I, 506. In a note, Bond points out that Dryden uses the same figure to describe the difference between tragedies and epics in the Dedication to *Aeneis* (*Essays,* ed. W. P. Ker, II, 158).

[14] Donald Francis Tovey, *Essays in Musical Analysis,* Volume I, *Symphonies* (London: Oxford University Press, 1935), p. 165.

[15] Max Friedlaender, *Das deutsche Lied im 18. Jahrhundert,* I/i, 105-106.

CHAPTER EIGHT

[1] This passage comes in the fifth paragraph of the Preface that Wordsworth contributed to the second edition of his and Coleridge's *Lyrical Ballads* in 1800. It may be found in most anthologies of English criticism or in Wordsworth's *Poetical Works,* ed. E. de Selincourt, 5 vols. (Oxford: Clarendon Press, 1944–1949), II, 386. For a full critical and textual examination of Wordsworth's Preface, see W. J. B. Owen, *Wordsworth's Preface to "Lyrical Ballads,"* Anglistica, Vol. IX (Copenhagen: Rosenkilde and Bagger, 1957).

[2] In her superb recording of Haydn's version, Elly Ameling sings the final strophe of the song with increasing bathos, descending into outright parody for the last three lines—and then dismisses it all with a laugh in the final phrase. Ameling's recordings of Haydn songs, once available as a 3-LP set (Philips 6769064), have to my knowledge never appeared on compact disc.

[3] Charles Rosen, *The Classical Style* (New York: Viking Press, 1971), p. 147.

[4] A. Peter Brown, "Joseph Haydn and Leopold Hoffman's 'Street Songs,'" *Journal of the American Musicological Society,* XXXIII (1980), 356-383. Later references to this essay appear in parentheses or brackets, in the body of the text.

[5] Rosen, *The Classical Style,* p. 163.

[6] George Puttenham, *The Arte of English Poesie,* ed. Gladys Doidge Willcock and Alice Walker (Cambridge: Cambridge University Press, 1936), pp. 38-39.

[7] Carl Philipp Emanuel Bach, *Quartette für Klavier, Flöte, Bratsche und Violoncello,* ed. Ernst Fritz Schmid (Kassel: Bärenreiter, 1952). Schmid's remark may be found on the first of the four unnumbered pages of his "Vorlagenbericht," which comes at the end of the volume.

[8] Hermann Kretzschmar, *Geschichte des neuen deutschen Liedes* (Leipzig: Druckerei Lokay, 1911), p. 218.

[9] W. K. von Jolizza, *Das Lied und seine Geschichte* (Vienna and Leipzig: A. Hartleben, 1910), pp. 241-242.

[10] Marpurg, *Kritische Briefe über die Tonkunst,* I, 170. For an explanation of the edition and its organization, see Note 12 to Chapter Seven.

[11] See *The Complete Works of Horace,* trans. Charles E. Passage (New York: Frederick Ungar, 1983), p. 161.

[12] Christoph Nichelmann, *Die Melodie nach ihrem Wesen sowohl, als nach ihren Eignschaften* (Dantzig, 1755), p. 2. So far as I knew, Nichelmann's book has never been reprinted. I am grateful to Thomas Christensen for calling it to my attention, in his essay "Nichelmann contra C. Ph. E. Bach: Harmonic Theory and Musical Politics at the Court of Frederick the Great," in Hans Joachim Marx, ed., *Carl Philipp Emanuel Bach und die europäische Musikkultur des mittleren 18. Jahrhunderts* (Göttingen: Vandenhoeck & Ruprecht, 1990), pp. 189-220.

¹³ Marpurg, *Historisch-Kritische Beyträge,* I, 431-439. For an explanation of this edition and its organization, see Note 11 to Chapter Seven.

¹⁴ Pope, *An Essay on Criticism,* lines 297-300.

CHAPTER NINE

¹ Gudrun Busch, *C. Ph. E. Bach und seine Lieder* (Regensburg: Gustav Bosse Verlag, 1957), p. 61.

² *Christian Fürchtegott Gellerts sämmelte Schriften,* 10 vols. (Leipzig, 1839), X, 243. Later references will appear in parentheses or brackets, in the body of the text.

³ Busch, pp. 58-67; *Gellerts sämmelte Schriften,* VIII, 63.

⁴ Carsten Schlingmann, *Gellert: Eine literarhistorische Revision* (Berlin: Verlag Gehlen, 1967), p. 147.

⁵ Samuel Johnson, *Lives of the English Poets,* ed. George Birkbeck Hill, 3 vols. (Oxford: Clarendon Press, 1905), I, 19; III, 233.

⁶ Christian Friedrich Daniel Schubart, *Deutsche Chronik auf das Jahr 1774* (Augsburg and Ulm, 1775), p. 280.

⁷ Max Friedlaender, *Das deutsche Lied im 18. Jahrhundert* (Stuttgart and Berlin: J. G. Cotta'sche Buchhandlung Nachfolger, 1902), I/i, 138.

⁸ Helmut Banning, *Johann Friedrich Doles: Leben und Werke* (Leipzig: Fr. Kistner and C. F. W. Siegel, 1939), pp. 56-64, 96-97.

⁹ Carsten Schlingmann, *Gellert: Eine Literarhistorische Revision.* Later references appear in parentheses or brackets, in the body of the text.

¹⁰ Emil Werth, *Untersuchungen zu Chr. F. Gellerts geistlichen Oden und Liedern* (Breslaue: Paul Plischke, 1936). The list of biblical passages alluded to in "Busslied" that directly follows is adapted from Werth, pp. 79-80.

¹¹ The only fact I have been able to discover about the mysterious Rackemann is his birth date.

¹² Adapted from Werth, pp. 43-44.

¹³ *The New Jerome Biblical Commentary,* ed. Raymond E. Brown, Joseph A. Fitzmeyer, and Roland E. Murphy (Englewood Cliffs, N.J.: Prentice Hall, 1990), p. 531.

¹⁴ Ernst Suchalla (ed.), *Carl Philipp Emanuel Bach im Spiegel seiner Zeit: Die Dokumentensammlung Johann Jakob Heinrich Westphals* (Hildesheim: Georg Olms Verlag, 1990), p. 120.

¹⁵ Marpurg, *Historisch-Kritische Beyträge,* III, 558. For an explanation of this edition and its organization, see Note 11 to Chapter Seven.

¹⁶ Marpurg, *Kritische Briefe über die Tonkunst,* I, 250. See Note 12 to Chapter Seven.

¹⁷ *Carl Philipp Emanuel Bach im Spiegel seiner Zeit,* p. 102.

CHAPTER TEN

[1] Gudrun Busch, *C. Ph. E. Bach und seine Lieder* (Regensburg: Gustav Bosse, 1957), pp. 54-58.

[2] Deryck Cooke, "Wagner's Musical Language," in *The Wagner Companion*, ed. Peter Burbidge and Richard Sutton (London: Faber and Faber, 1979), pp. 227-228.

[3] Ernst Otto Lindner, *Geschichte des deutschen Liedes im XVIII. Jahrhundert* (Leipzig: Breitkopf und Härtel, 1871), p. 59.

[4] Hans-Günter Ottenberg, *C.P.E. Bach*, trans. Philip J. Whitmore (Oxford: Oxford University Press, 1987), p. 93.

[5] Max Friedlaender, *Das deutsche Lied im 18. Jahrhundert* (Stuttgart and Berlin: G. A. Cotta'sche Buchhandlung Nachfolger, 1902), II, 11-13. Later writers have followed Friedlaender in giving the number of stanzas in Haller's poem incorrectly, as 22 rather than 24.

[6] Matthias Lexer, *Mittelhochdeutsches Handwörterbuch*, 3 vols. (Leipzig: S. Hirzel, 1872-1878), s.v. "prîvilêgje."

[7] H. F. Jolowicz, *Historical Introduction to the Study of Roman Law* (Cambridge: Cambridge University Press, 1952), p. 25.

[8] Jaroslav Pelikan, *Christian Doctrine and Modern Culture (since 1700)* (Chicago: University of Chicago Press, 1989), p. 135. The whole of Pelikan's third chapter, "The Theology of the Heart" (pp. 118-173), is very much worth reading in connection with these issues.

[9] C. H. Bitter, *Carl Philipp Emanuel und Wilhelm Friedemann Bach und deren Brüder*, 2 vols. (Berlin: Wilhelm Müller, 1868), I, 162.

[10] For details, see Gudrun Busch, *C. Ph. E. Bach und seine Lieder*, pp. 78-85, and Ada Kadelbach, "Die Kirchenliedkompositionen C. Ph. E. Bachs in Choralbüchern seiner Zeit," in *Carl Philipp Emanuel Bach und die europäische Musikkultur des mittleren 18. Jahrhunderts*, ed. Hans Joachim Marx (Göttingen: Vandenhoeck and Ruprecht, 1990), pp. 389-402.

[11] Eduard Emil Koch, *Geschichte des Kirchenlieds und Kirchengesangs der christlichen*, vol. VI (Stuttgart: Verlag der Chr. Belser'schen Verlagshandlung, 1869), p. 354.

CHAPTER ELEVEN

[1] Baumgarten's most accessible work is the 1735 *Meditationes philosophicae*. Both the original text and an English translation, by Karl Aschenbrenner and William B. Holther, are available in *Reflections on Poetry* (Berkeley and Los Angeles: University of California Press, 1954).

[2] See Elizabeth M. Wilkinson, *Johann Elias Schlegel: A German Pioneer in Aesthetics* (Oxford: Basil Blackwell, 1945).

[3] See Joyce S. Rutledge, *Johann Adolph Schlegel* (Bern and Frankfurt am Main: Herbert Lang, 1974), especially Chapters IV and VII.

[4] See Christel Matthias Schröder, *Die "Bremer Beiträge": Vorgeschichte und Geschichte einer deutschen Zeitschrift des achtzehnten Jahrhunderts* (Bremen: Carl Schumann Verlag, 1956).

[5] Eduard Emil Koch, *Geschichte des Kirchenlieds und Kirchengesangs der christlichen, insbesondere der deutschen evangelischen Kirche*, 7 vols. (Stuttgart, 1866-1872), VI, 336.

[6] Adolf Blümcke, *Beitraege zur Kenntnis der Lyrik Johann Andreas Cramer's (1742-1761)* (Greifswald: Buchdruckerei Hans Adler, 1910), p. 48.

[7] Hermann von Hase, "Carl Philipp Emanuel Bach und Joh. Gottl. Im. Breitkopf," Bach-Jahrbuch VIII (1911), 93-94.

[8] Gudrun Busch, *C. Ph. E. Bach und seine Lieder* (Regensburg: Gustav Bosse Verlag, 1957), p. 105.

[9] See Eugene Helm, "The *Hamlet* Fantasy and the Literary Element in C.P.E. Bach's Music," *The Musical Quarterly*, LVIII (1972), 277-296; Friedrich Chrysander, "Eine Klavier-Phantasie von Karl Philipp Emanuel Bach mit nachträglich von Gerstenberg eingefügten Gesangsmelodien zu zwei verschiedenen Texten," *Vierteljahrsschrift für Musikwissenschaft*, VIII (1891), 1-25.

[10] Ernst Fritz Schmid, *Carl Philipp Emanuel Bach und seine Kammermusik* (Kassel: Bärenreiter, 1931), pp. 51-52.

[11] Busch, *C. Ph. E. Bach und seine Lieder*, p. 106.

[12] *Carl Philipp Emanuel Bach im Spiegel seiner Zeit*, ed. Ernst Suchalla (Hildesheim: Georg Olms Verlag, 1993), p. 69.

[13] *Carl Philipp Emanuel Bach: Briefe und Dokumente*, ed. Ernst Suchalla, 2 consecutively paginated vols. (Göttingen: Vandenhoeck & Ruprecht, 1994), p. 164.

[14] The Gerstenberg and Claudius passages are both cited by Gudrun Busch, *Carl Ph. E. Bach und seine Lieder*, p. 107.

[15] Suchalla, *Briefe und Dokumente*, p. 306.

[16] Busch, *C. Ph. E. Bach und seine Lieder*, pp. 109-110n.

[17] Suchalla, *Briefe und Dokumente*, I, 306.

[18] Ernst Boll, *Geschichte Mecklenburgs*, 4 vols. (Berlin: Evangelische Verlagsanstalt, 1952), II, 431.

[19] Karl Schmaltz, *Kirchengeschichte Mecklenburgs*, 4 vols. (Berlin: Evangelische Verlagsanstalt, 1952), III, 167.

[20] C. H. Bitter, *Carl Philipp Emanuel und Wilhelm Friedemann Bach und deren Brüder,* 2 vols. (Berlin, 1868), II, 60-61.

[21] Cited by Bitter, *Carl Philipp Emanuel und Wilhelm Friedemann Bach und deren Brüder,* II, 165.

[22] Busch, *C. Ph. E. Bach und seine Lieder,* pp. 112-114; Suchalla, *Briefe und Dokumente,* pp. 405-406.

[23] Bitter *Carl Philipp Emanuel und Wilhelm Friedemann Bach und deren Brüder,* II, 66.

[24] Suchalla, *Spiegel,* pp. 110-111.

[25] Suchalla, *Spiegel,* pp. 114-115.

[26] Sigmund Mowinckel, *The Psalms in Israel's Worship,* trans. D. R. Ap-Thomas, 2 vols. in one (Sheffield: JSOT Press, 1992), especially Chapters I-III.

[27] Mowinckel, *The Psalms in Israel's Worship,* II, 6-8.

[28] Martin Luther, *Works,* ed. Jaroslav Pelikan (St. Louis: Concordia Publishing House, 1955-), XII, 98.

[29] Howard E. Smither, *A History of the Oratorio,* 3 vols. (Chapel Hill: University of North Carolina Press, 1977-1987), III, 331-340.

CHAPTER TWELVE

[1] Wilhelm Herbst, *Johann Heinrich Voss,* 3 vols. (Leipzig: Teubner, 1872-1876), I, 27. The account of Voss's life that follows is largely taken from Herbst's biography.

[2] *Der Göttinger Dichterbund,* ed. August Sauer, 3 pts. (Berlin and Stuttgart, 1885-1887), I, xiii-xiv.

[3] Cited by Rudolf Haller, *Geschichte der deutschen Lyrik vom Ausgang des Mittelalters bis zu Goethes Tod* (Bern and Munich: Francke Verlag, 1967), p. 314.

[4] Most of the letters of Voss cited in this chapter are taken from *Carl Philipp Emanuel Bach: Briefe und Dokumente,* ed. Ernst Suchalla, 2 vols. (Göttingen: Vandenhoeck & Ruprecht, 1994). This is true as well of the correspondence, cited later in this chapter, between Bach and Gerstenberg. References will appear in brackets or parentheses, in the body of the text.

[5] Cited by Hans Grantzkow, *Geschichte des Göttinger und des Vossischen Musenalmanachs* (Berlin: Emil Eberling, 1909), p. 96.

[6] Karl Kindt, *Klopstock,* 2nd ed. (Berlin-Spandau: Wichern-Verlag Herbert Renner, 1948), p. 229.

[7] Ernst Otto Lindner, *Geschichte des deutschen Liedes im XVIII. Jahrhundert* (Leipzig: Breitkopf und Härtel, 1871), p. 104n.

[8] Grantzkow, *Geschichte des Göttinger und des Vossischen Musenalmanachs,* p. 97.

⁹It was Vrieslander who first called attention to, and reprinted in facsimile, Bach's correction of "Lyda." See his *Carl Philipp Emanuel Bach* (Munich: R. Piper & Co., 1923), pp. 121-123.

¹⁰Cited by Gudrun Busch, *C. Ph. E. Bach und seine Lieder*, p. 248.

¹¹*Briefwechsel zwischen Johann Abraham Peter Schulz und Johann Heinrich Voss*, ed. Heinz Gottwaldt and Gerhard Hahne (Kassel: Bärenreiter, 1960), p. 16. Later references to this work will appear in parentheses or brackets, in the body of the text.

¹²See Heinrich W. Schwab, "Carl Philipp Emanuel Bach und das geistliche 'Lied im Volkston,'" in Hans Joachim Marx, ed., *Carl Philipp Emanuel Bach und die europäische Musikkultur des mittleren 18. Jahrhunderts* (Göttingen: Vandenhoeck & Ruprecht, 1990), p. 369. See also Schwab's excellent book, *Sangbarkeit, Popularität und Kunstlied* (Regensburg: Gustav Bosse Verlag, 1965).

CHAPTER THIRTEEN

¹Johann Adolph and Johann Elias Schlegel are often confused with each other. Though Johann Elias was the one more deeply concerned with aesthetic theory, it was Johann Adolph who produced the first German translation of Batteux's *Les Beaux-Arts réduits à un même principe*. See Notes 2 and 3 to Chapter Eleven.

²Gotthold Ephraim Lessing, *Werke*, ed. Julius Petersen and Waldemar von Olshaufen, 25 vols. (Berlin and Vienna: Deutsches Verlagshaus Bong & Co., 1925-1935), IV, 84-85.

³Ernst Fritz Schmid, *Carl Philipp Emanuel Bach und seine Kammermusik* (Kassel: Bärenreiter, 1931), p. 49.

⁴Albert Malte Wagner, *Heinrich Wilhelm von Gerstenberg und der Sturm und Drang*, 2 vols. (Heidelberg: Carl Winter, 1920-1924), II, 277.

⁵Eugene Helm, "The *Hamlet* Fantasy and the Literary Element in C.P.E. Bach's Music," *The Musical Quarterly*, LVIII (1972), 288.

⁶Cited by Hans Mersmann, "Ein Programmtrio Karl Philipp Emanuel Bachs." *Bach-Jahrbuch*, XIV (1917), 139.

⁷Cited by Helm, "The *Hamlet* Fantasy and the Literary Element in C.P.E. Bach's Music," p. 292.

⁸The entire letter may be found in Richard Maria Werner, "Gerstenbergs Briefe an Nicolai nebst einer Antwort Nicolais," *Zeitschrift für deutsche Philologie*, XXIII (1891), 60-63.

⁹Lessing, *Werke*, V, 128.

¹⁰*Die Musik in Geschichte und Gegenwart*, I, column 161.

¹¹Bernhard Engelke, "Gerstenberg und die Musik seiner Zeit," *Zeitschrift der Gesellschaft für Schleswig-Holsteinische Geschichte*, LVI (1927), 433.

¹²Heinrich Wilhelm von Gerstenberg, *Tändeleyen*, facsimile reprint of the 3rd ed., 1765, with afterword by Alfred Anger (Stuttgart: J. B. Metzlersche Verlagsbuchhandlung, 1966), pp. 17*-18*.

¹³See, for example, *The Aeneid of Virgil,* ed. R. D. Williams, 2 vols. (London: Macmillan, 1972), I, 212.

¹⁴The fullest and most helpful account of the graces is the entry under *Charites* in Pauly-Wissowa, *Real-Encyclopädie der classischen Altertumswissenschaft.*

CHAPTER FOURTEEN

¹Gudrun Busch, *C. Ph. Bach und seine Lieder* (Regensburg: Gustav Bosse Verlag, 1957), pp. 141-142.

²*Carl Philipp Emanuel Bach im Spiegel seiner Zeit,* ed. Ernst Suchalla (Hildesheim: Georg Olms Verlag, 1993), p. 112. Later references to this work will appear in parentheses or brackets, in the body of the text.

³Rudolf Haller, *Geschichte der deutschen Lyrik vom Ausgang des Mittelalters bis zu Goethes Tod* (Bern and Munich: A. Francke Verlag, 1967), p. 245.

⁴Eduard Emil Koch, *Geschichte des Kirchenlieds und Kirchengesangs der christlichen, insbesondere der deutschen evangelischen Kirche,* 7 vols. (Stuttgart, 1866-1872), VI, 362.

⁵Jacob Friederich Feddersen, *Christoph Christian Sturms . . . Leben und Charakter* (Hamburg: Johann Henrich Herold, 1786), p. 5. The account given here of Sturm's life is largely taken from Feddersen and Koch.

⁶See Henry Chadwick, ed., *Lessing's Theological Writings* (Stanford, Calif.: Stanford University Press, 1956).

⁷See Hans Höhne, "Johann Melchior Goeze im Urteil seiner Zeitgenossen und der Literatur über ihn bis heute," in *Verspätete Orthodoxie: Über D. Johann Melchior Goeze (1717-1786),* ed. Heimo Reinitzer and Walter Sparn (Wiesbaden: Otto Harrassowitz, 1989), pp. 27-62.

⁸Herbert Butterfield, "Toleration in Early Modern Times," *Journal of the History of Ideas,* XXXVIII (1977), 579, 582.

⁹Georg Reinhard Röpe, *Johan Melchior Goeze: Eine Rettung* (Hamburg, 1860), p. 85. Also of interest is August Boden's response to Röpe, *Lessing und Goeze: Ein Beitrag zur Literarur- und Kirchengeschichte des achtzehnten Jahrhunderts. Zugleich als Widerlegung der Röpe'schen Schrift: "Johan Melchior Goeze, eine Rettung"* (Leipzig and Heidelberg, 1862).

¹⁰Feodor Wehl, *Hamburgs Literaturleben im achtzehnten Jahrhundert* (Hamburg, 1856), pp. 240-241.

¹¹R. H. Lightfoot, *St. John's Gospel: A Commentary,* ed. C. F. Evans (Oxford: Clarendon Press, 1956), pp. 325-326.

¹²C. H. Bitter, *Carl Philipp Emanuel und Wilhelm Friedemann Bach und deren Brüder,* 2 vols. (Berlin, 1868), II, 73.

¹³Robert Donington, *A Performer's Guide to Baroque Music* (New York: Charles Scribner's Sons, 1973), p. 285.

¹⁴C. P. E. Bach, *Essay on the True Art of Playing Keyboard Instruments,* trans. and ed. William J. Mitchell (New York: W. W. Norton, 1949), p. 154.

CHAPTER FIFTEEN

¹In *C. Ph. E. Bach und seine Lieder,* Gudrun Busch discusses these "non-lied" compositions. See also Heinrich W. Schwab, "Carl Philipp Emanuel Bach und das geistliche 'Lied im Volkston,'" and Ada Kadelbach, "Die Kirchenliedkompositionen C. Ph. E. Bachs in Choralbüchern seiner Zeit," both of which may be found in *Carl Philipp Emanuel Bach und die europäische Musikkultur des mittleren 18. Jahrhunderts,* ed. Hans Joachim Marx (Göttingen: Vandenhoeck & Ruprecht, 1990), pp. 369-388 and 389-402, respectively. Schwab's book, *Sangbarkeit, Popularität und Kunstlied* (Regensburg: Gustav Bosse Verlag, 1965), is also of interest.

²*Briefwechsel zwischen Johann Abraham Peter Schulz und Johann Heinrich Voss,* ed. Heinz Gottwaldt and Gerhard Hahne (Kassel: Bärenreiter, 1960), pp. 16, 19; *Carl Philipp Emanuel Bach: Briefe und Dokumente,* ed. Ernst Suchalla (Göttingen: Vandenhoeck & Ruprecht, 1994), pp. 855-866; *Briefwechsel,* p. 20.

³In the first part of his three-part *Der Göttinger Dichterbund* (Berlin and Stuttgart, 1885-1887), August Sauer has the following note on line 20 of "Das Milchmädchen": "*Der Hase brauet* [i.e., the hare is brewing] is what one says when the clouds hang low over the meadows" (p. 250).

⁴In a note on *Eclogues* III 66, Wendell Clausen explains that while both Amyntas and Antigenes were, in Theocritus, the names of real people, Virgil treats both as fictitious pastoral names. Antigenes, however, is mentioned only once by Virgil whereas Amyntas appears eleven times and thus became an established pastoral figure. In addition to Tasso's well-known *Aminta,* Clausen cites as examples a pastoral fragment published in Gow's *Bucoli Graeci* and eclogues by the first-century A.D. Roman poet Calpurnius Siculus and the third-century Carthaginian Nemesianus. See Wendell Clausen, *A Commentary on Virgil, Eclogues* (Oxford: Clarendon Press, 1994), p. 108.

⁵Gudrun Busch, *C. Ph. E. Bach und seine Lieder,* pp. 191-192.

⁶Sauer, *Der Göttinger Dichterbund,* II, 121.

⁷*Schweizerische Volkslieder,* ed. Ludwig Tobler, 2 vols. (Frauenfeld: Verlag von J. Huber, 1882, 1884), II, 202-203. In his general introduction to the two-volume collection (I, cxxiv), Tobler mentions several analogues and other versions of this poem, and the collections in which they may be found.

⁸*Carl Philipp Emanuel Bach im Spiegel seiner Zeit,* ed. Ernst Suchalla (Hildesheim: Georg Olms Verlag, 1993), pp. 174-175. Later references to this work appear in parentheses or brackets, in the body of the text.

⁹Türk is identified as the author of the review by Gustav C. F. Parthey, *Die Mitarbeiter an Friedrich Nicolai's Allgemeiner Deutscher Bibliothek nach ihren Namen und Zeichen in zwei Registern geordnet* (Berlin, 1842), p. 43.

[10] *Dr. Carl Loewe's Selbstbiographie,* ed. C. H. Bitter (Berlin: Verlag von Wilhelm Müller, 1870), p. 28.

[11] On the question of whether or not Bach was a Mason, Heinrich Miesner reports: "To confirm from documents that he was a Mason has until now not been possible." To which he adds the following explanatory footnote: "Herr Staatsrat Dr. Hagedorn-Hamburg has, at my urging, taken the trouble to search through the Hamburg lodge archives, for which I extend to him my sincere thanks." See Miesner's *Philipp Emanuel Bach in Hamburg* (Leipzig: Breitkopf und Härtel, 1929), p. 20.

[12] Waltraut Schardig and Stefan Erdmann, "'Zur Ehre Gottes, zum Besten der Jugend, zum Nutzen des Publici.' Bachs Konzerttätigkeit in Hamburg," in *Programmbuch: Der Hamburger Bach und die neue Musik des 18. Jahrhunderts,* ed. Hans Joachim Marx (Hamburg: Grömmer-Druck, 1988), pp. 180-181.

[13] Gudrun Busch, "Wirkung in die Nähe: Carl Philipp Emanuel Bachs Braunschweiger und Wolfenbütteler Freunde," in *Carl Philipp Emanuel Bach und die europäischer Musikkultur des mittleren 18. Jahrhunderts,* ed. Hans Joachim Marx (Göttingen: Vandenhoeck & Ruprecht, 1990), pp. 149-150.

[14] I am indebted, for this account of Freemasonry, to R. William Weisberger's *Speculative Freemasonry and the Enlightenment* (Boulder: Eastern European Monographs, 1993), an excellent introduction to the subject. A more penetrating, though controversial, examination of the contemporary significance of early Freemasonry is Margaret C. Jacob's *Living the Enlightenment* (New York: Oxford University Press, 1991).

[15] This passage is cited, in English, by Weisberger, *Speculative Freemasonry and the Enlightenment,* p. 139. It is taken from an article by one Karl Reinhold that appeared in 1785 in the *Journal für Freymaurer,* which was published by the True Harmony Lodge of Vienna.

[16] Manfred Steffens, *Freimaurer in Deutschland* (Flensburg: Christian Wolff Verlag, 1964), pp. 122-127. For more on the colorful Schaumburg-Lippe, see Ferdinand Runkel, *Geschichte der Freimaurerei in Deutschland,* 3 vols. (Berlin: Reimar Hobbing, 1932), I, 113-143.

[17] See Alois Brandl, *Barthold Heinrich Brockes* (Innsbruck: Verlag der Wagner'schen Universitäts-Buchhandlung, 1878), and *Barthold Heinrich Brockes: Dichter und Amtmann in Ritzebüttel von 1735 bis 1741* (Curhaven: Deichverlag, 1935), a collection of essays anonymously edited.

[18] Philipp Spitta, "Sperontes' 'Singende Muse an der Pleisse,'" in *Musikgeschichtliche Aufsätze* (Berlin: Verlag von Gebrüder Paetel, 1894; reprint ed., Hildesheim: Georg Olms Verlag, 1976), p. 204.

[19] Spitta, "Sperontes' 'Singende Muse an der Pleisse,'" p. 206.

[20] This song may be found in *Denkmäler deutscher Tonkunst,* XXXV-XXXVI, 238.

[21] E. Eugene Helm, *Thematic Catalogue of the Works of Carl Philipp Emanuel Bach* (New Haven: Yale University Press, 1989), p. 173. Cf. Alfred Wotquenne, *Thematisches Verzeichnis der Werke von Carl Philipp Emanuel Bach (1714–1788)* (Leipzig: Breitkopf und Härtel, 1905), pp. 93-94.

[22] Cited from Albert G. Mackey, *Mackey's Masonic Ritualist,* 3rd ed. (New York: Maynard, Merrill & Co., 1871), p. 199, by Arthur Preuss, *A Study in American Freemasonry,* 2nd ed. (St. Louis: B. Herder, 1908), p. 82.

[23] Arthur Preuss, *A Study in American Freemasonry,* p. 244. See also David Stevenson, *The Origins of Freemasonry: Scotland's Century, 1590-1710* (Cambridge: Cambridge University Press, 1988), pp. 20-25, 82-87.

[24] C. H. Bitter, *Carl Philipp Emanuel und Wilhelm Friedemann Bach und deren Brüder* (Berlin: Wilhelm Müller, 1868), II, 75-76.

[25] E. Eugene Helm, *Thematic Catalogue of the Works of Carl Philipp Emanuel Bach* (New Haven: Yale University Press, 1989), p. 173.

APPENDIX ONE

[1] See Appendix 2.

[2] This delightful passage may be found in the fifth paragraph of the 1801 entries in Goethe's *Tag- und Jahres-Hefte*. In the edition of *Goethes Werke* published in 1892 by Hermann Bohlau of Weimar, the passage occurs at XXXV, 90-91. In the 1926 "Festausgabe" published by the Bibliographisches Institut, Leipzig, to mark its centenary, and edited by Robert Petsch, the passage is at XVII, 293-294.

Bibliography

Aarsleff, Hans. *From Locke to Saussure: Essays on the Study of Language and Intellectual History.* Minneapolis: University of Minnesota Press, 1982.

Abert, Hermann. *Gesammelte Schriften und Vorträge.* Edited by F. Blume. Tutzing: Schneider, 1929.

Abraham, Gerald. "18th-Century Music and the Problems of its History." *Current Musicology,* IX (1969), 49-51.

Adler, Guido. "Haydn and the Viennese Classical School." Translated by W. Oliver Strunk. *The Musical Quarterly,* XVIII (1932), 191-207.

Adler, Guido. *Denkmäler der Tonkunst in Österreich,* Jahrgang XV/2, Volume XXXI.

Adler, Guido, ed. *Handbuch der Musikgeschichte.* Part 2, 2nd rev. ed. Berlin: Max Hesses Verlag, 1930.

Albert, Heinrich. *Arien.* Denkmäler deutscher Tonkunst, vols. XII and XIII, ed. Eduard Bernoulli, 1907. Reprint, ed. Hans Joachim Moser. Wiesbaden: Breitkopf und Härtel, 1958.

Allen, William Dwight. *Philosophies of Music History.* New York: Dover, 1962.

Bach, Carl Philipp Emanuel. *Essay on the True Art of Playing Keyboard Instruments.* Edited and translated by Willam J. Mitchell. New York: W. W. Norton, 1949.

Bach, Carl Philipp Emanuel. *Quartette für Klavier, Flöte, Bratsche und Violoncello.* Edited by Ernst Fritz Schmid. Kassel: Bärenreiter, 1952.

Banning, Helmut. *Johann Friedrich Doles: Leben und Werke.* Leipzig: Fr. Kistner and C.F.W. Siegel, 1939.

Baron, John Herschel. "Foreign Influences on the German Secular Continuo Lied of the Mid-Seventeenth Century." Ph.D. dissertation, Brandeis University, 1967.

Batteux, Charles. *A Course of the Belles Lettres.* Translated by John Miller. 4 vols. London, 1761.

Baumgarten, Alexander Gottlieb. *Aesthetica.* Frankfurt an der Oder, 1750, 1758. Reprint. Hildesheim: Georg Olms Verlag, 1970.

Baumgarten, Alexander Gottlieb. *Reflections on Poetry.* Translated, with the Original Text, and Introduction and Notes, by Karl Aschenbrenner and William B. Holthier. Berkeley: University of California Press, 1954.

Beck, Lewis White. *Early German Philosophy: Kant and His Predecessors.* Cambridge, Mass.: Harvard University Press, 1969.

Bergmann, Ernst. *Die Begründung des deutschen Ästhetik durch Alex. Gottlieb Baumgarten und Georg Friedrich Meier.* Leipzig: Verlag von Röder und Schunke, 1911.

Bitter, C. H. *Carl Philipp Emanuel und Wilhelm Friedemann Bach und deren Brüder.* 2 vols. Berlin: Wilhelm Müller, 1868.

Blackall, Eric A. *The Emergence of German as a Literary Language, 1700-1775.* 2nd ed. Ithaca, N.Y.: Cornell University Press, 1978.

Blümcke, Adolf. *Beitraege zur Kenntnis der Lyrik Johann Andreas Cramer's (1742-1761).* Greifswald: Buchdruckerei Hans Adler, 1910.

Bolgar, R. R. *The Classical Heritage and Its Beneficiaries.* Cambridge: Cambridge University Press, 1954.

Boll, Ernst. *Geschichte Mecklenburgs mit besonderer Berücksichtigung zur Culturgeschichte.* 2 pts. Neubrandenburg, 1856.

Bond, Donald F., ed. *The Spectator.* 5 vols. Oxford: Clarendon Press, 1965.

Brandl, Alois. *Barthold Heinrich Brockes.* Innsbruck: Verlag der Wagner'schen Universitäts-Buchhandlung, 1878.

Breitinger, Johann Jacob. *Critische Dichtkunst.* 2 vols. Zürich, 1740. Reprint. Stuttgart: J. G. Metzlersche Verlagsbuchhandlung, 1966.

Brendel, Franz. *Geschichte der Musik in Italien, Deutschland und Frankreich.* Leipzig: Bruno Hinze, 1852.

Brink, C. O. *Horace on Poetry: The "Ars Poetica."* Cambridge: Cambridge University Press, 1971.

Brook, Barry S.; Downes, Edward O. D.; and Solkema, Sherman Van, eds. *Perspectives in Musicology.* New York: W. W. Norton, 1972.

Brown, A. Peter. "Joseph Haydn and Leopold Hoffman's Street Songs." *Journal of the American Musicological Society,* XXXIII (1980), 356-383.

Brown, Raymond E.; Fitzmeyer, Joseph A.; and Murphy, Roland E., eds. *The New Jerome Biblical Commentary.* Englewood Cliffs, N.J.: Prentice-Hall, 1990.

Bücken, Ernst. *Das deutsche Lied: Probleme und Gestalten.* Hamburg: Hanseatische Verlagsanstalt, 1939.

Bücken, Ernst. *Musik der Deutschen: Kulturgeschichte der deutschen Musik.* Cologne: Staufen Verlag, 1941.

Bukofzer, Manfred F. *Music in the Baroque Era.* New York: W. W. Norton, 1947.

Busch, Gudrun. "Wirkung in der Nähe: Carl Philipp Emanuel Bachs Braunschweiger und Wolfenbütteler Freunde." In *Carl Philipp Emanuel Bach und die europäischer Musikkultur des mittleren 18. Jahrhunderts,* edited by Hans Joachim Marx, pp. 133-158. Göttingen: Vandenhoeck & Ruprecht, 1990.

Busch, Gudrun. *C. Ph. E. Bach und seine Lieder.* Regensburg: Gustav Bosse Verlag, 1957.

Butterfield, Herbert. "Toleration in Early Modern Times." *Journal of the History of Ideas,* XXXVIII (1977), 573-584.

Butterfield, Herbert. *The Whig Interpretation of History.* London: G. Bell & Sons, 1931.

Caccini, Giulio. *Le Nuove musiche.* Edited by H. Wiley Hitchcock. Madison, Wis.: A-R Editions, 1970.

Chadwick, Henry, ed. *Lessing's Theological Writings.* Stanford, Calif.: Stanford University Press, 1956.

Chrysander, Friedrich. "Eine Klavier-Phantasie von Karl Philipp Emanuel Bach mit nachträglich von Gerstenberg eingefügten Gesangsmelodien zu zwei verschiedenen Texten." *Vierteljahrsschrift für Musikwissenschaft,* VII (1891), 1-25.

Clark, Stephen L. "The Occasional Choral Works of C. P. E. Bach." Ph.D. dissertation, Princeton University, 1984.

Clark, Stephen L., ed. *C. P. E. Bach Studies.* Oxford: Clarendon Press, 1988.

Clark, Stephen L., trans. and ed. *The Letters of C. P. E. Bach.* Oxford: Clarendon Press, 1997.

Clausen, Wendell. *A Commentary on Virgil, Eclogues.* Oxford: Clarendon Press, 1994.

Coleridge, Samuel Taylor. *Biographia Literaria.* 2 vols. Edited by J. Shawcross. Oxford: Oxford University Press, 1907.

Collingwood, R. G. *An Essay on Metaphysics.* Oxford: Clarendon Press, 1940.

Cooke, Deryck. "Wagner's Musical Language." In *The Wagner Companion,* edited by Peter Burbidge and Richard Sutton, pp. 225-268. London: Faber & Faber, 1979.

Crousaz, Jean-Pierre de. *Traité du Beau.* Amsterdam, 1715. Reprint. Geneva: Slatkine Reprints, 1970.

Dahlhaus, Carl. *The Idea of Absolute Music.* Translated by Roger Lustig. Chicago: University of Chicago Press, 1989.

Darwin, Charles. *The Origin of Species.* 2nd ed., 1860. Reprint, ed. Gillian Beer. Oxford: Oxford University Press, 1996.

Deutsch, Otto Erich. *Mozart: A Documentary Biography*. Translated by Eric Blom, Peter Branscombe, and Jeremy Noble. Stanford, Calif.: Stanford University Press, 1965.

Dommer, Arrey von. *Handbuch der Musikgeschichte*. 2nd ed. Leipzig: Wilhelm Grunow, 1878.

Dryden, John. *Essays of John Dryden*. Edited by W. P. Ker. 2 vols. Oxford: Clarendon Press, 1900.

Dubos, Jean Baptiste. *Critical Reflections on Poetry, Painting and Music*. 3 vols. Translated by Thomas Nugent. 5th ed. London, 1748. Reprint. New York: AMS Press, 1978.

Edwards, John Richard. "Christian Gottfried Krause: Mentor of the First Berlin Song School." Ph.D. dissertation, University of Iowa, 1973.

Eliot, T. S. *Selected Essays*. New enl. ed. New York: Harcourt Brace, 1950.

Elledge, Scott, and Schier, Donald, eds. *The Continental Model: Selected French Critical Essays of the Seventeenth Century*. Ithaca: Cornell University Press, 1970.

Elmenhorst, Heinrich. *Geistliche Lieder*. Denkmäler deutscher Tonkunst, vol. XLV, ed. Joseph Kromolicki and Wilhelm Krabbe, 1911. Reprint, ed. Hans Joachim Moser. Wiesbaden: Breitkopf und Härtel, 1961.

Engelke, Bernhard. "Gerstenberg und die Musik seiner Zeit." *Zeitschrift der Gesellschaft für Schleswig-Holsteinische Geschichte*, LVI (1927), 417-448.

Erlebach, Philipp Heinrich. *Harmonische freude musikalischer Freunde*. Denkmäler deutscher Tonkunst, vols. XLVI and XLVII, ed. Otto Kinkeldy, 1914. Reprint, ed. Hans Joachim Moser. Wiesbaden: Breitkopf und Härtel, 1959.

Feddersen, Jacob Friederich. *Christoph Christian Sturms . . . Leben und Charakter*. Hamburg: Johann Henrich Herold, 1786.

Friedlaender, Max. *Das deutsche Lied im 18. Jahrhundert*. 2 vols. Stuttgart and Berlin: J. G. Cotta'sche Buchhandlung Nachfolger, 1902.

Frotscher, Gotthold. "Die Aesthetik des Berliner Liedes im XVIII. Jahrhundert." Doctoral dissertation, University of Leipzig, 1922.

Frotscher, Gotthold. "Die Ästhetik des Berliner Liedes in ihren Hauptproblemen." *Zeitschrift für Musikwissenschaft*, VI (1923-1924), 431-448.

Gellert, Christian Fürchtegott. *C. F. Gellerts sämmtliche Schriften*. 10 vols. Leipzig, 1839.

Gellinek, Janis Little. *Die weltliche Lyrik des Martin Opitz*. Bern and Munich: Francke Verlag, 1973.

Gerstenberg, Heinrich Wilhelm von. *Tändeleyen*. 3rd ed., 1765. Facsimile reprint, with afterword by Alfred Anger. Stuttgart: J. B. Metzlersche Verlagsbuchhandlung, 1966.

Goldschmidt, Hugo. *Die Musikästhetik des 18. Jahrhunderts und ihre Beziehungen zu seinem Kunstschaffen*. Zurich and Leipzig: Verlag von Rascher & Co., 1915.

Gottsched, Johann Christoph. *Versuch einer critischen Dichtkunst vor die Deutschen*. Leipzig, 1730.

Gottsched, Johann Christoph. *Versuch einer critischen Dichtkunst*. 4th enl. ed. Leipzig, 1951. Reprint. Darmstadt: Wissenschaftliche Buchgesellschaft, 1962.

Gottwaldt, Heinz, and Hahne, Gerhard, eds. *Briefwechsel zwischen Johann Abraham Peter Schulz und Johann Heinrich Voss*. Kassel: Bärenreiter, 1960.

Grantzkow, Hans. *Geschichte des Göttinger und des Vossischen Musenalmanachs*. Berlin: Emil Eberling, 1909.

Grove, George, ed. *A Dictionary of Music and Musicians*. 4 vols. London: Macmillan & Co., 1879-1889.

Hadow, W. H. *The Viennese Period*. The Oxford History of Music, vol. 5. Oxford: Clarendon Press, 1905.

Haller, Rudolf. *Geschichte der deutschen Lyrik vom Ausgang des Mittelalters bis zu Goethes Tod*. Bern and Munich: Francke Verlag, 1967.

Hammerschmidt, Andreas. *Weltliche Oden oder Liebesgesänge*. Das Erbe deutscher Musik, vol. XLIII, ed. Hans Joachim Moser. Mainz: B. Schott's Söhne, 1962.

Hase, Hermann von. "Carl Philipp Emanuel Bach und Joh. Gottl. Im. Breitkopf." *Bach-Jahrbuch*, VIII (1911), 86-104.

Hay, Gerhard. *Die Beiträger des Voss'schen Musenalmanachs.* Hildesheim: Georg Olms Verlag, 1975.

Helm, E. Eugene. "The *Hamlet* Fantasy and the Literary Element in C. P. E. Bach's Music." *The Musical Quarterly,* LVIII (1972), 277-296.

Helm, E. Eugene. *Thematic Catalogue of the Works of Carl Philipp Emanuel Bach.* New Haven and London: Yale University Press, 1989.

Herbst, Wilhelm. *Johann Heinrich Voss.* 3 vols. Leipzig: Teubner, 1872-1876.

Hoffmann-Erbrecht, Lothar. "Der 'galante Stil' in der Musik des 18. Jahrhunderts." *Studien zur Musikwissenschaft,* XXV (1962), 257-274.

Höhne, Hans. "Johan Melchior Goeze im Urteil seiner Zeitgenossen und der Literatur über ihn bis heute." In *Verspätete Orthodoxie,* ed. Heimo Reinitzer and Walter Sparn. Wiesbaden: Otto Harrasowitz, 1989, pp. 27-62.

Hospers, John. "What Is Explanation?" In *Essays in Conceptual Analysis,* edited by Anthony Flew, pp. 94-119. London: Macmillan & Co., 1956.

Hutcheson, Francis. *An Inquiry into the Origin of Our Ideas of Beauty and Virtue.* London, 1725. Reprint. Vol. I of *Collected Works of Francis Hutcheson.* 7 vols. Hildesheim: Georg Olms Verlag, 1971.

Jacob, Margaret C. *Living the Enlightenment.* New York: Oxford University Press, 1991.

Johnson, Samuel. *Lives of the English Poets.* 3 vols. Edited by George Birkbeck Hill. Oxford: Clarendon Press, 1905.

Jolizza, W. K. von. *Das Lied und seine Geschichte.* Vienna and Leipzig: A. Hartleben, 1910.

Kadelbach, Ada. "Die Kirchenliedkompositionen C. Ph. E. Bachs in Choralbüchern seiner Zeit." In *Carl Philipp Emanuel Bach und die europäische Musikkultur des mittleren 18. Jahrhunderts.* Edited by Hans Joachim Marx. Göttingen: Vandenhoeck & Ruprecht, 1990, pp. 389-402.

Kahleyss, Rainer. *Conrad Friedrich Hurlebusch (1691-1765): Sein Leben and Wirken.* Frankfurt am Main: Haag und Herchen Verlag, 1984.

Kennick, William E. "Does Traditional Aesthetics Rest on a Mistake?" *Mind,* N.S. LXVII (1958), 317-334.

Kenny, Anthony. "Cartesian Privacy." In *Wittgenstein: The Philosophical Investigations,* edited by George Pitcher, pp. 286-323. Garden City, N.Y.: Doubleday Anchor, 1966.

Kiesewetter, R. G. *History of the Modern Music of Western Europe.* Translated by Robert Miller. London: T. C. Newby, 1848.

Kindt, Karl. *Klopstock.* 2nd ed. Berlin-Spandau: Wichern-Verlag Herbert Renner, 1948.

Kivy, Peter. *The Corded Shell: Reflections on Musical Expression.* Princeton, N.J.: Princeton University Press, 1980.

Kivy, Peter. *The Seventh Sense: A Study of Francis Hutcheson's Aesthetics and Its Influence in Eighteenth-Century Britain.* New York: Burt Franklin & Co., 1976.

Koch, Eduard Emil. *Geschichte des Kirchlieds und Kirchengesangs der christlichen, insbesondere der deutschen evangelischen Kirche.* 7 vols. Stuttgart, 1866-1872.

Kohlschmidt, Werner. *A History of German Literature, 1760-1805.* Translated by Ian Hilton. New York: Holmes and Meier, 1975.

Krause, Karl Christian Friedrich. *Darstellungen aus der Geschichte der Musik.* Edited by August Wünsche. Leipzig: Dieterische Verlagsbuchhandlung, 1911.

Kretzschmar, Hermann. *Geschichte des neuen deutschen Liedes.* Leipzig: Druckerei Lokay, 1911.

Krieger, Adam. *Arien.* Denkmäler deutscher Tonkunst, vol. XIX, ed. Alfred Heuss, 1905. Reprint, ed. Hans Joachim Moser. Wiesbaden: Breitkopf und Härtel, 1958.

Kristeller, Paul Oskar. "The Modern System of the Arts: A Study in the History of Aesthetics." *Journal of the History of Ideas,* XII (1951), 496-527; and XIII (1952), 17-46.

Kross, Siegfried. *Geschichte des deutschen Liedes*. Darmstadt: Wissenschaftliche Buchgesellschaft, 1989.
Langhans, Wilhelm. *Die Geschichte der Musik des 17, 18, und 19, Jahrhunderts*. Vol. 2. Leipzig: F. E. C. Leukart, 1887.
Leavis, F. R. *Revaluation*. London: Chatto & Windus, 1936.
Leichtentritt, Hugo. *Music, History, and Ideas*. Cambridge, Mass.: Harvard University Press, 1938.
Lessing, Gotthold Ephraim. *Werke*. Edited by Julius Petersen and Waldemar von Olshaufen. 25 vols. Berlin and Vienna: Deutsches Verlagshaus Bong & Co., 1925-1935.
Lightfoot, R. H. *St. John's Gospel: A Commentary*. Edited by C. F. Evans. Oxford: Clarendon Press, 1956.
Lindner, Ernst Otto. *Geschichte des deutschen Liedes im XVIII. Jahrhundert*. Leipzig: Breitkopf und Härtel, 1871.
Loewe, Carl. *Selbstbiographie*. Edited by C. H. Bitter. Berlin: Verlag von Wilhelm Müller, 1870.
Lohmeier, Dieter, ed. *Carl Philipp Emanuel Bach: Musik und Literatur in Norddeutschland*. Heide in Holstein: Westholsteinische Verlagsdruckerei Boyens & Co., 1988.
Luther, Martin, *Works*. Edited by Jaroslav Pelikan. St. Louis: Concordia Publishing House, 1955- .
Mackinnon, Flora Isabel, ed. *Philosophical Writings of Henry More*. New York: Oxford University Press, 1925.
Mallard, James H. "A Translation of Christian Gottfried Krause's *Von der musikalischen Poesie*, with a Critical Essay on his Sources and the Aesthetic Views of his Time." 2 pts. Ph.D. dissertation, University of Texas at Austin, 1978.
Marpurg, Friedrich Wilhelm. *Der critische Musikus an der Spree*. Berlin, 1749-1750. Reprint. Hildesheim: Georg Olms Verlag, 1970.
Marpurg, Friedrich Wilhelm. *Historisch-Kritische Beyträge zur Aufnahme der Musik*. Berlin, 1754-1778. Reprint, 5 vols. Hildesheim: Georg Olms Verlag, 1970.
Marpurg, Friedrich Wilhelm. *Kritische Briefe über die Tonkunst*. 2 vols. Berlin, 1759-1764. Reprint. Hildesheim: Georg Olms Verlag, 1974.
Martinson, Steven D. *On Imitation, Imagination and Beauty: A Critical Reassessment of the Concept of the Literary Artist During the Early German "Aufklärung."* Bonn: Bouvier Verlag Herbert Grundmann, 1977.
Marx, Hans Joachim, ed. *Carl Philipp Emanuel Bach und die europäische Musikkultur des mittleren 18. Jahrhunderts*. Göttingen: Vandenhoeck & Ruprecht, 1990.
Mattheson, Johann. *Critica musica*. Hamburg, 1722-1725. Reprint (2 vols.). Amsterdam: Frits A. M. Knuf, 1964.
May, Kurt. *Das Weltbild in Gellerts Dichtung*. Frankfurt am Main: Verlag Moritz Diesterweg, 1928.
Meier, Georg Friedrich. *Anfangsgründe aller schönen Wissenschaften*. 2nd ed. 3 vols. Halle, 1754. Reprint. Hildesheim: Georg Olms Verlag, 1976.
Menke, Werner. *Das Vokalwerk Georg Philipp Telemann's: Überlieferung und Zeitfolge*. Kassel: Bärenreiter, 1942.
Mersmann, Hans. "Ein Programmtrio Karl Philipp Emanuel Bachs." *Bach-Jahrbuch*, XIV (1917), 137-170.
Miesner, Heinrich. *Philipp Emanuel Bach in Hamburg*. Leipzig: Breitkopf und Härtel, 1929.
Miller, Henry Knight. "The 'Whig Interpretation' of Literary History." *Eighteenth-Century Studies*, VI (1972-1973), 60-84.
Mitchell, P. M. *Johann Christoph Gottsched (1700-1766): Harbinger of German Classicism*. Columbia, S.C.: Camden House, 1995.
Mizler, Lorenz. *Neu eröffnete musikalische Bibliothek*. Leipzig, 1739-1754. Reprint (4 vols.). The Netherlands, 1966.

Moore, G. E. "Wittgenstein's Lectures in 1930-33." In *Philosophical Papers*, pp. 247-318. New York: Collier Books, 1962.

More, Henry. *Enchiridion Ethicum*. Translated by Robert Southwell. London, 1690. Reprint. New York: The Facsimile Text Society, 1930.

Moser, Hans Joachim. *Corydon: Geschichte des mehrstimmigen Generalbassliedes und des Quodlibets im deutschen Barock*. 2 vols. 2nd rev. ed. Hildesheim: Georg Olms Verlag, 1966.

Moser, Hans Joachim. *The German Solo Song and the Ballad*. Cologne: Arno Volk Verlag, 1958.

Mowinckel, Sigmund. *The Psalms in Israel's Worship*. Translated by D. R. Ap-Thomas. 2 vols. in one. Sheffield: JSOT Press, 1992.

Müller, Günther. *Geschichte des deutschen Liedes vom Zeitalter des Barock bis zur Gegenwart*. Munich: Drei Masken Verlag, 1925.

Naumann, Emil. *The History of Music*. Vol. 4. Translated by F. Praeger. London: Cassell & Co., 1886.

Neubauer, John. *The Emancipation of Music from Language: Departure from Mimesis in Eighteenth-Century Aesthetics*. New Haven: Yale University Press, 1986.

Newman, William S. *The Sonata Since Beethoven*. 2nd ed. New York: W. W. Norton, 1972.

Nichelmann, Christoph. *Die Melodie nach ihrem Wesen sowohl, als nach ihren Eigenschaften*. Danzig, 1755.

Ottenberg, Hans-Günter. *Carl Philipp Emanuel*. Translated by Philip J. Whitmore. New York: Oxford University Press, 1987.

Ottenberg, Hans-Günter. *Die Entwicklung des theoretisch-ästhetischen Denkens innerhalb der Berliner Musikkultur von den Anfängen bis Reichardt*. Leipzig: VEB Deutscher Verlag für Musik, 1976.

Ottenberg, Hans-Günter, ed. *Der Critische Musikus an der Spree: Berliner Musikschrifttum von 1748 bis 1799*. Leipzig: Reclam, 1984.

Owen, W. J. B. *Wordsworth's Preface to "Lyrical Ballads."* Anglistica, Volume IX. Copenhagen: Rosenkilde and Bagger, 1957.

Parry, C. Hubert H. *The Art of Music*. 2nd ed. London: Kegan Paul, Trench, Trübner, & Co., 1894.

Parry, C. Hubert H. *The Evolution of the Art of Music*. London: Kegan Paul, 1905.

Parry, Milman. *The Making of Homeric Verse: The Collected Papers of Milman Parry*. Edited by Adam Parry. Oxford: Oxford University Press, 1971.

Parthey, Gustav C. F. *Die Mitarbeiter an Friedrich Nicolai's Allgemeiner Deutscher Bibliothek nach ihren Namen und Zeichen in zwei Registern geordnet*. Berlin, 1842.

Passmore, J. A. *Ralph Cudworth: An Interpretation*. Cambridge: Cambridge University Press, 1951.

Pauly, Reinhard G. *Music in the Classical Period*. 3rd ed. Englewood Cliffs, N.J.: Prentice-Hall, 1988.

Pelikan, Jaroslav. *Christian Doctrine and Modern Culture (since 1700)*. Vol. 5, *The Christian Tradition: A History of the Development of Doctrine*. Chicago: University of Chicago Press, 1989.

Pelikan, Jaroslav. *Reformation of Church and Dogma (1300-1700)*. Vol. 4, *The Christian Tradition: A History of the Development of Doctrine*. Chicago: University of Chicago Press, 1983.

Pestelli, Giorgio. *The Age of Mozart and Beethoven*. Translated by Eric Cross. Cambridge: Cambridge University Press, 1984.

Petzoldt, Richard. *Georg Philipp Telemann*. Translated by Horace Fitzpatrick. New York: Oxford University Press, 1974.

Pfeiffer, Johannes. *Dichtkunst und Kirchenlied: Über das geistliche Lied im Zeitalter der Säkularisation*. Hamburg: Friedrich Wittig Verlag, 1961.

Potter, Pamela M. *Most German of the Arts: Musicology and Society from the Weimar Republic to the End of Hitler's Reich*. New Haven: Yale University Press, 1998.

Preuss, Arthur. *A Study in American Freemasonry*. 2nd ed. St. Louis: B. Herder, 1908.

Puttenham, George. *The Arte of English Poesie*. Edited by Gladys Doidge Willcock and Alice Walker. Cambridge: Cambridge University Press, 1936.

Racek, Jan. *Stilprobleme der italienischen Monodie*. Prague: Statní Pedagogicke Nakladatelstvı, 1965.

Radandt, Friedhelm. *From Baroque to Storm and Stress.* London: Croom Helm, 1977.

Rathgeber, Valentin. *Ohren-vergnügendes und Gemuths-ergözendes Tafel-Confect.* Das Erbe deutscher Musik, vol. XIX, ed. Hans Joachim Moser. Mainz: B. Schott's Söhne, 1942.

Reichardt, J. F. *Musikalisches Kunstmagazin.* Berlin, 1782-1791.

Reichardt, Johann Friedrich. *Briefe eines aufmerksamen Reisenden die Musik betreffend.* 2 vols. Frankfurt and Leipzig, 1774; Frankfurt and Breslau, 1776.

Reichardt, Johann Friedrich. *Über die Deutsche comische Oper.* Hamburg, 1774. Reprint. Munich: Musikverlag Emil Katzbichler, 1974.

Reissmann, August. *Allgemeine Geschichte der Musik.* Vol. 3. Leipzig: Fues's Verlag, 1864.

Reissmann, August. *Das deutsche Lied in seiner historischen Entwicklung.* Kassel, 1861.

Reissmann, August. *Geschichte des deutschen Liedes.* Berlin: Verlag von J. Gutentag, 1874.

Richter, Lukas. "Telemanns Lieder nach Hagedorn." In *Telemann und seine Dichter,* pp. 87-97. Magdeburg, 1977.

Riemann, Hugo. "Die Musik des 18. und 19. Jahrhunderts: Die grossen deutschen Meister." Vol. 2, part 3 of *Handbuch der Musikgeschichte.* Leipzig: Breitkopf und Härtel, 1913.

Riemann, Hugo. "Die Söhne Bachs." *Präludien und Studien,* vol. 3, pp. 173-184. Leipzig: H. Seemann, 1901.

Riemann, Hugo. *Catechism of Musical History.* Part 2. Anonymous translation. New York: G. Schirmer, 1892.

Riemann, Hugo. *Denkmäler der Tonkunst in Bayern,* Jahrgang III/1, Volume IV (1902).

Rogers, Robert W. "Critiques of the *Essay on Man* in France and Germany, 1736-1755." *ELH: A Journal of English Literary History,* XV (1948), 176-193.

Röpe, Dr. Georg Reinhard. *Johan Melchior Goeze: Eine Rettung.* Hamburg: Gustav Eduard Nolte, 1860.

Rosen, Charles. *The Classical Style.* New York: Viking Press, 1971.

Rosen, Charles. *Sonata Forms.* New York: W. W. Norton, 1980.

Rosenkaimer, Eugen. *Johann Adolph Scheibe als Verfasser seines "Critischen Musikus."* Bonn: L. Neuendorff, 1929.

Runkel, Ferdinand. *Geschichte der Freimaurerei in Deutschland.* 3 vols. Berlin: Reimar Hobbing, 1932.

Rutledge, Joyce S. *Johann Adolph Schlegel.* Bern and Frankfurt am Main: Herbert Lang, 1974.

Sauer, August, ed. *Der Göttinger Dichterbund.* 3 pts. Berlin and Stuttgart, 1885-1887.

Schardig, Waltraut, and Erdmann, Stefan. "'Zur Ehre Gottes, zum Besten der Jugend, zum Nutzen des Publici.' Bachs Konzerttätigkeit in Hamburg." In *Programmbuch: Der Hamburger Bach und die neue Musik des 18. Jahrhunderts,* edited by Hans Joachim Marx, pp. 169-190. Hamburg: Grommer-Druck, 1988.

Scheibe, Johann Adolph. *Critischer Musikus.* Leipzig, 1745. Reprint. Hildesheim: Georg Olms Verlag, 1970.

Schenker, Manfred. *Charles Batteux und seine Nachahmungstheorie in Deutschland.* Leipzig: H. Haessel Verlag, 1909.

Schilling, Gustav, ed. *Encyclopädie der gesammten musikalischen Wissenschaften, oder Universal-Lexicon der Tonkunst.* 2nd ed. 7 vols. Stuttgart: Franz Heinrich Köhler, 1840.

Schlingmann, Carsten. *Gellert: Eine literarhistorische Revision.* Berlin: Verlag Gehlen, 1967.

Schmaltz, Karl. *Kirchengeschichte Mecklenburgs.* 4 vols. Berlin: Evangelische Verlagsanstalt, 1952.

Schmid, Ernst Fritz. *Carl Philipp Emanuel Bach und seine Kammermusik.* Kassel: Bärenreiter, 1931.

Schmidt, Erich, ed. *Goezes Streitschriften gegen Lessing.* Stuttgart, 1893.

Schmitz, Eugen. *Geschichte der weltlichen Solokantate.* 2nd rev. ed. Leipzig: Breitkopf und Härtel, 1955.

Schneider, K. E. *Das Musikalische Lied in geschichtlicher Entwickelung.* 3 vols. Leipzig: Breitkopf und Härtel, 1863-1865.
Schröder, Christel Matthias. *Die "Bremer Beiträge": Vorgeschichte und Geschichte einer deutschen Zeitschrift des achtzehnten Jahrhunderts.* Bremen: Carl Schumann Verlag, 1956.
Schubart, Christian Friedrich Daniel. *Deutsche Chronik auf das Jahr 1774.* Augsburg and Ulm, 1775.
Schubart, Christian Friedrich Daniel. *Ideen zu einer Ästhetik der Tonkunst.* Vienna, 1806. Reprint, ed. Fritz and Margrit Kaiser. Hildesheim: Georg Olms, 1969.
Schwab, Heinrich W. *Sangbarkeit, Popularität und Kunstlied.* Regensburg: Gustav Bosse Verlag, 1965.
Schwartz, Marshall R. "L'Abbé Batteux: A 'Philosophe' Defender of Aristotle." Ph.D. dissertation, University of Chicago, 1966.
Schweizer, Hans Rudolf. *Ästhetik als Philosophie der sinnlichen Erkenntnis.* Basel: Schwabe & Co., 1973.
Serauky, Walter. *Die musikalische Nachahmungsästhetik im Zeitraum von 1700 bis 1850.* Münster: Helios-Verlag, 1929.
Serwer, Howard Jay. "Friedrich Wilhelm Marpurg: Music Critic in a *Galant* Age." Ph.D. dissertation, Yale University, 1969.
Shaftesbury, Anthony Ashley Cooper, 3rd Earl of. *Characteristics of Men, Manners, Opinions, Times.* Edited by John M. Robertson. 2 vols. London: Grant Richards, 1900.
Sibley, Frank. "Aesthetic and Nonaesthetic." *Philosophical Review,* LXXIV (1965), 135-159.
Sibley, Frank. "Aesthetic Concepts." *Philosophical Review,* LXVIII (1959), 421-450.
Smeed, J. W. *German Song and its Poetry, 1740-1900.* London: Croom Helm, 1987.
Smith, G. Gregory, ed. *Elizabethan Critical Essays.* 2 vols. Oxford: Clarendon Press, 1904.
Smither, Howard E. *A History of the Oratorio.* 3 vols. Chapel Hill: University of North Carolina Press, 1977-1987.
Solms, Friedheim. *Disciplina aesthetica: Zur Frühgeschichte der ästhetischen Theorie bei Baumgarten und Herder.* Stuttgart: Klett-Cotta, 1990.
"Sperontes." *Singende Muse an der Pleisse.* Edited by Edward Buhle. Denkmäler deutscher Tonkunst, Volumes XXXV and XXXVI, 1909. Reprint, ed. Hans Joachim Moser. Wiesbaden: Breitkopf und Härtel, 1958.
Spingarn, J. E. *Critical Essays of the Seventeenth Century.* 3 vols. Oxford: Clarendon Press, 1908-1909.
Spitta, Philipp. "Sperontes' 'Singende Muse an der Pleisse.'" In *Musikgeschichtliche Aufsätze.* Berlin: Verlag von Gebrüder Paetel, 1894. Reprint. Hildesheim: Georg Olms Verlag, 1976.
St*** [Steineck], J. C. M. *Wahrhafter Nachricht von dem Leben des weiland Hochwürdigen Herrn Johan Melchior Goeze.* Hamburg, 1786.
Steffens, Manfred. *Freimaurer in Deutschland.* Flensburg: Christian Wolff Verlag, 1964.
Stevenson, David. *The Origins of Freemasonry: Scotland's Century, 1590-1710.* Cambridge: Cambridge University Press, 1988.
Stoljar, Margaret Mahony. *Poetry and Song in Late Eighteenth Century Germany: A Study in the Musical "Sturm und Drang."* London: Croom Helm, 1985.
Suchalla, Ernst, ed. *Carl Philipp Emanuel Bach: Briefe und Dokumente, kritische Gesamtausgabe.* 2 vols. Göttingen: Vandenhoeck & Ruprecht, 1994.
Suchalla, Ernst, ed. *Carl Philipp Emanuel Bach im Spiegel seiner Zeit.* Hildesheim: Georg Olms Verlag, 1993.
Telemann, Georg Philipp. *Vierundzwanzig Oden.* Görner, Johann Valentin. *Sammlung neuer Oden und Lieder.* Denkmäler deutscher Tonkunst, vol. LVII, ed. Wilhelm Krabbe and Joseph Kromolicki, 1917. Reprint, ed. Hans Joachim Moser. Wiesbaden: Breitkopf und Härtel, 1959.
The Encyclopaedia Britannica. 11th ed. 29 vols. New York: The Encyclopaedia Company, 1911.
Thomas, R. Hinton. *Poetry and Song in the German Baroque.* Oxford: Clarendon Press, 1963.

Tovey, D. F. *Essays in Musical Analysis.* 7 vols. London: Oxford University Press, 1935-1944.

Tovey, Donald Francis. *A Musician Talks: 1. The Integrity of Music.* London: Oxford University Press, 1941.

Tovey, Donald Francis. *Essays and Lectures on Music.* London: Oxford University Press, 1949.

Tovey, Donald Francis. *Musical Articles from the "Encyclopaedia Britannica."* London: Oxford University Press, 1944.

Vetter, Walther. *Das frühdeutsche Lied.* 2 vols. Münster: Helios-Verlag, 1928.

Vida, Marco Girolamo. *The "De Arte Poetica" of Marco Girolamo Vida.* With translation and commentary by Ralph G. Williams. New York: Columbia University Press, 1976.

Vrieslander, Otto. *Carl Philipp Emanuel Bach.* Munich: R. Piper & Co., 1923.

Wagner, Albert Malte. *Heinrich Wilhelm von Gerstenberg und der Sturm und Drang.* 2 vols. Heidelberg: Carl Winters Universitätsbuchhandlung, 1920-1924.

Waismann, Friedrich. "Verifiability." In *Logic and Language (First Series),* edited by A. G. N. Flew, pp. 117-144. Oxford: Basil Blackwell, 1951.

Wehl, Feodor. *Hamburgs Literaturleben im achtzehnten Jahrhundert.* Hamburg, 1856.

Weisberger, R. William. *Speculative Freemasonry and the Enlightenment.* Boulder: Eastern European Monographs, 1993.

Weiser, Artur. *The Psalms: A Commentary.* Translated by Herbert Hartwell. London: SCM Press, 1962.

Wellesz, Egon, and Sternfield, Frederick, eds. *The Age of Enlightenment.* The New Oxford History of Music, vol. 7. London: Oxford University Press, 1973.

Werth, Emil. *Untersuchungen zu Chr. F. Gellerts Geistlichen Oden und Liedern.* Breslau: Paul Plischke, 1936.

Whaley, Joachim. *Religious Toleration and Social Change in Hamburg, 1529-1819.* Cambridge: Cambridge University Press, 1985.

Whitehead, Alfred North. *Science and the Modern World.* New York: Macmillan, 1925.

Wien-Claudi, Hertha. *Zum Liedschaffen Carl Philipp Emanuel Bach.* Reichenberg: Gebrüder Stiepel, 1928.

Willheim, Imanuel. "Johann Adolph Scheibe: German Musical Thought in Transition." Ph.D. dissertation, University of Illinois, 1963.

Wilkinson, Elizabeth M. *Johann Elias Schlegel: A German Pioneer in Aesthetics.* Oxford: Basil Blackwell, 1945.

Wittgenstein, Ludwig. *Philosophical Investigations.* Translated by G. E. M. Anscombe. 2nd rev. ed. Oxford: Basil Blackwell, 1958.

Youngren, William H. "The Operas of Haydn." *The Atlantic Monthly,* September 1983, pp. 110-115.

Zauft, Karin. *Telemanns Liedschaffen und seine Bedeutung für die Entwicklung des deutschen Liedes in der ersten Hälfte des 18. Jahrhunderts.* Magdeburg, 1967.

Index

"Abendlied" (Gellert), 239
Abert, Hermann, 49, 59
Abraham, Gerald, 24
Addison and Steele (*Tatler* and *Spectator*), 5, 47, 84, 90, 125, 156, 157
Adler, Guido
    on Mannheim *vs.* Viennese schools, 24, 29
aesthetic judgment
    See also taste
    nature of, 96-106, 116, 120-122
    and rules in art, 96-97, 99-105, 106
Affektenlehre (theory of emotions)
    See also strophic problem; *Ton* and *Wort*
    and musical expression, 90
    and neo-classic creed, 92
    and rationalist aesthetics, 92, 93, 94
    and reinstatement of strophic song, 52
    and strophic song, 40, 52, 149, 150, 156, 158-159, 163
    as unifying idea, 142, 149, 150-151, 163
Agricola, Johann Friedrich, 191, 258, 273
    music of, 360, 361
Albert, Heinrich
    Arien und Melodeyn, 43, 59
    and German lied, 43, 49, 59
    and Italian monody, 43, 49-50
    and Schütz, 46
    and strophic form, 59
Allgemeinheit (generality), in music, 12, 14-15, 148, 152, 352-353
    See also Bestimmtheit
"Die Alster" (Hagedorn), 224, 266, 452-453
"Am Communion-Tage" (unnamed poet), 268
"Am neueren Jahr" (Gellert), 239
Ambros, August Wilhelm, music history of, 18
"Amint" ("Amynt") (Kleist), 184-191
Amthor, Christoph H., 135

"An den Schlaf" (Röding), 258-261, 431
"An den Schlaf" (Hagedorn), 71-83, 88
"An die Liebe" (Hagedorn), 224, 266-268, 452
"An Doris" (Haller), 32, 243, 341, 342, 343-349, 350, 354, 431, 455
"An Gott" (Karsch), 250-254
"An Phyllis" (Günter), 66-69
"An Thyrsis" ("Schäferlied," "Chloe an Thyrsis") (Ziegler), 165, 167-171, 172, 186-187
Anacreontic style, and German lyric poetry, 363-364, 421, 426
Anhang songs. *See* C. P. E. Bach, songs
Arien und Melodeyn (Albert), 43, 59
Aristotle, 90, 94, 105, 123, 132, 145
Ars poetica. See Horace
art
    and aesthetic judgment. *See* aesthetic judgment
    as imitation, 5, 90, 91, 189
    nature of, 5, 90, 92, 97, 99, 100
    in neo-classical and Romantic thought, 5, 91, 92
    and rationalist aesthetics, 90, 91, 92, 96, 97
L'Art poétique (Boileau), 92, 93, 125, 130, 145
"Auf das Fest des heiligen Johannis" (Masonic), 444-447
"Auf den Geburtstag eines Freundes" (Ebeling), 261-263, 265, 349, 430, 431, 455
"Auf die Auferstehung des Erlösers" (unnamed poet), 268
Auferstehung und Himmelfahrt Jesu.
    See C. P. E. Bach, oratorios
Aufklärung. See reform, of German letters
Aufschwung (reinstatement of strophic lied)
    beginning and end of, 35, 44, 48, 83, 84
    and Berlin song school, 84, 88
    causes of, 40, 44, 48, 64, 139

Aufschwung (continued)
   and reform of German letters, 57
   and strophic form, 40, 57-58, 88, 89
   transitional nature of, 82

Bach, Carl Philipp Emanuel (C. P. E.)
   catalogues, of works of, 1, 30, 31, 32, 437
   critics' views of, 3-6, 8-33
   as Haydn forerunner, 7, 9, 11, 12, 15, 17, 21, 23, 26, 28, 29, 33
   influence of, 21, 22, 23, 29, 30, 33
   as link between eras, 7, 8, 15, 23-26, 29, 178
   musical output of, 1, 30, 35, 203, 224, 311, 411
Bach, C. P. E., cantatas
   Neue Lieder-Melodien nebst eine Kantate zum Singen beym Klavier componirt, 6, 258, 261, 311, 330, 340, 350, 362, 374, 411
   Phillis und Thirsis (Schlegel), 258, 349
   Der Wirth und die Gäste, 258
   "Der Frühling" (Wieland), 258, 349, 350
   "Die Grazien" (Gerstenberg), 258, 350, 354, 360, 361, 362, 366-377, 411, 430, 431, 455
   "Selma" (Voss), 32, 258, 350
   cantata output, 1, 258, 269, 308, 311, 349
   critics' views of, 3, 9, 240
   emotional transitions in, 350, 360, 361, 366, 377, 455
   keyboard introductions in, 170
   lost cantatas, 35
   number cantatas, 349-350
Bach, C. P. E., choral works
   Heilig, 5, 311, 325
   Klopstocks Morgengesang am Schöpfungsfeste, 380, 411
   Magnificat, 2, 22
   passions, 411
Bach, C. P. E., chorale form
   chorale output, 1, 256, 263, 269, 278, 279, 308, 411
   critics' views of, 3, 240, 280
Bach, C. P. E., instrumental music
   Kenner und Liebhaber collections, 311, 411, 412
   Sechs Sonaten fürs Clavier mit veränderten Reprisen, 155
   Versuch über die wahre Art das Clavier zu spielen, 16, 52, 224, 409
   C-minor Fantasy (Hamlet soliloquy), 352-354, 356, 357, 359-360
   character pieces, 358, 359
   expressive power of, 224, 352, 355-358, 359

   importance of, 11, 12, 16, 21, 23, 29, 33
   instrumental output, 1, 35, 203, 311, 411
   keyboard works, 1, 7, 12, 21, 31
   sonata form, 4, 10, 12, 15, 16, 17, 20, 21, 22, 26-29
   symphonies, 1, 7, 17, 20, 23, 24, 26, 29, 311
   vis-à-vis vocal music, 16, 31
Bach, C. P. E., oratorios, 309-310
   Auferstehung und Himmelfahrt Jesu, 22, 294, 309, 310, 311
   Die Israeliten in der Wüste, 4, 5, 22, 263, 294, 309
   Passions-Cantate (Die letzten Leiden des Erlösers), 22, 309, 310
   critics' views of, 4, 9, 21, 22, 25
Bach, C. P. E., as song composer, 1-2
   See also C. P. E. Bach, songs
   attributes of, 31, 174, 175, 181, 262, 377, 409, 433
   and Berlin song school, 30-31, 52, 165, 184, 201, 203, 248
   vis-à-vis contemporaries, 177, 178, 240
   critics' views of, 29-33, 430-433. *See also under* Bach, songs—Cramer settings; Bach, songs—Gellert settings
   and German lied, 17, 22, 30, 31, 35
   formal experimentation by, 250, 258, 263, 269, 308, 310, 340, 349, 452
   Freemasonry and, 433, 435. *See also under* Bach, songs: Masonic songs
   song output of, 1, 31, 35, 203, 311, 379, 380, 411
   songs, earliest, 35, 165-201, 203
   popularity and reputation of, 2, 3, 6, 29, 33, 340
Bach, C. P. E., songs
   See also C. P. E. Bach, cantatas
   Anhang songs, 239, 250, 254, 256, 263, 278
   Clavierstücke verschiedener Art von Carl Philipp Emanuel Bach, 246, 248, 250
   Neue Lieder-Melodien, 6, 30, 258, 261, 311, 340, 350, 362, 374, 411, 417, 419, 422, 425, 430, 431, 433
   Oden mit Melodien, 6, 53, 165, 172, 179, 186, 193, 241, 242, 243
   "Abendlied" (Gellert). See C. P. E. Bach, songs—Gellert settings
   "Die Alster" (Hagedorn), 224, 266, 452-453
   "Am Communion-Tage" (unnamed poet), 268
   "Am neueren Jahr" (Gellert). See C. P. E. Bach, songs—Gellert settings
   "Amint" (Kleist), 184, 186-191
   "An den Schlaf" (Röding), 258, 260-261, 431

"An die Liebe" (Hagedorn), 224, 266, 267-268, 452
"An Doris" (Haller). *See* C. P. E. Bach, through-composed songs
"An Gott" (Karsch poems), 250, 251-252, 253-254
"Auf das Fest des heiligen Johannis" (Masonic), 444-447
"Auf den Geburtstag eines Freundes" (Ebeling). *See* C. P. E. Bach, through-composed songs
"Auf die Auferstehung des Erlösers" (unnamed poet), 268
"Der Bauer" (Miller), 330
"Bitten" (Gellert). *See* C. P. E. Bach, songs—Gellert settings
"Busslied" (Gellert). *See* C. P. E. Bach, songs—Gellert settings
"Communionlied" (Münter), 268-269
"Doris" (Haller), 32, 243, 246
"Die Ehre Gottes aus der Natur" (Gellert). *See* C. P. E. Bach, songs—Gellert settings
"Empfindungen in der Sommernacht" (Sturm). *See* C. P. E. Bach, songs—Sturm settings
"Freude, du Lust der Götter und Menschen" (unnamed poet). *See* C. P. E. Bach, through-composed songs
"Der Frühling" (Miller), 330, 331
"Das Gebet" (Gellert). *See* C. P. E. Bach, songs—Gellert settings
"Gottes Grösse in der Natur" (Sturm). *See* C. P. E. Bach, songs—Sturm settings
"Harvstehude" (Hagedorn), 224, 266, 452-453
"Herausforderungslied vor der Schlacht bey Rossbach" (Gleim), 241-243, 265
"Ich hoff auf Gott" (Recke, von der). *See* C. P. E. Bach, through-composed songs
"Jesus in Gethsemane" (Sturm). *See* C. P. E. Bach, songs—Sturm settings
"Klagen einer Schäferinn" (unnamed poet), 268
"Die Küsse" (Giseke). *See* C. P. E. Bach, through-composed songs
"Lied" (Stolberg), 415, 416-417
"Lied der Schnitterinnen" (Gleim), 419-420
"Lyda" ("Edone") (Klopstock), 315, 320, 321-324, 325
"Das Milchmädchen" (Voss), 412, 414-415
"Das mitleidige Mädchen" (Miller), 420, 421-422

"Mittel, freundlich zu werden" (Gleim), 417, 418-419, 420
"Der Morgen," (Hagedorn), 178-179, 181-183, 266, 452
"Morgengesang" (Gellert). *See* C. P. E. Bach, songs—Gellert settings
"Nonnelied" (anonymous), *See* C. P. E. Bach, through-composed songs
"Osterlied" (Gellert). *See* C. P. E. Bach, songs—Gellert settings
"Passionslied" (Gellert). *See* C. P. E. Bach, songs—Gellert settings
"Passionslied" (Sturm). *See* C. P. E. Bach, songs—Sturm settings
"Phyllis" (Kleist). *See* C. P. E. Bach, through-composed songs
"Das Privilegium" (Giseke), 246, 248, 249-250
Psalm 88 (anonymous), 254, 255, 256-258, 300-301
"Schäferlied" (Ziegler), 165, 167-168, 186-187
"Die Schlummernde" (Voss), 315, 325, 327, 329-330, 412
"Selma" (Voss), 32, 258
"Das stille Glück der Maurerey" (Masonic), 438, 439-440
"Der Tag des Weltgerichts" (Sturm). *See* C. P. E. Bach, songs—Sturm settings
"Tischlied" (Voss), 337-338, 339, 340
"Todtengräberlied" (Hölty), 331, 335-336, 431
"Der Traum" (poet unknown), 243
"Die Tugend" (Haller), 243
"Über die Finsterniss kurz vor dem Tode Jesu" (Sturm). *See* C. P. E. Bach, songs—Sturm settings
"Der Unbeständige" (unnamed poet), 268
untitled poem (Countess von Recke), 423-425
"Vaterlandslied" (Klopstock), 314-315, 317-319, 320
"Weihnachtslied" (Gellert). *See* C. P. E. Bach, songs—Gellert settings
"Wider den Übermut" (Gellert). *See* C. P. E. Bach, songs—Gellert settings
"Der Zufriedene" (Stahl), 172, 173-175, 345
in Gräfe collections, 30, 35, 39, 64
and *Hausmusik*, 1, 2, 170
lost songs (Hagedorn), 411, 452, 453
Masonic songs, 411, 433, 435, 437-438, 442, 444-452
Nichelmann's revisions of. *See* Nichelmann

Bach, C. P. E., songs (*continued*)
    and non-strophic forms, 154, 349, 422, 424, 426, 430. *See also* C. P. E. Bach, through-composed songs
    and pastoral genre, 167, 168, 177-178, 419, 420
    psalms. *See* C. P. E. Bach, songs—Cramer settings
    in Ramler-Krause collections, 35, 154, 193
    and strophic form, 1, 33, 53, 201, 269, 280, 300, 308, 335, 336, 349, 410, 455-456
    and strophic problem, 222, 225, 252, 254, 269, 275, 277, 318, 324, 331, 359, 400, 410
    unpublished arias, 457-464
    and Volkslied, 6, 32, 339, 340, 411, 412, 417, 420, 435, 446, 455

Bach, C. P. E., songs—Cramer settings
    See also Cramer
    Herrn Doctor Cramers übersetzte Psalmen mit Melodien, 53, 310
    Psalm 1, 283, 284-286, 296
    Psalm 4, 284, 286-288, 296
    Psalm 6, 278, 279, 283, 284, 289, 291-292, 296
    Psalm 8, 280, 281, 283, 284, 292-298, 310
    Psalm 33, 280, 281, 283
    Psalm 65, 281, 283
    Psalm 67, 280, 281, 283, 298-299
    Psalm 86, 278, 283, 298, 299-300
    Psalm 88, 298, 300-302
    Psalm 90, 298, 302-303
    Psalm 91, 278-279, 283, 298, 303-306
    Psalm 93, 280, 281, 283, 298, 306-308
    Psalm 103, 278, 279, 283
    Psalm 110, 283
    Psalm 130, 278, 279-280, 283
    Psalm 145, 283
    Psalm 150, 283
    Psalm mentions, 278, 279, 282, 283
    and Book of Psalms, 279, 281, 282-283
    cantata form in, 280, 281, 296
    chorale form in, 278-280, 281, 283, 301-302, 303-304, 305, 310
    critics' views of, 3, 31, 240, 279-281, 283
    demand for, 274-278
    oratorio form in, 308-310
    ordering of musical forms in, 281, 283, 298, 308, 310, 349
    poems, appeal of, for Bach, 278, 284, 380
    psalm table, 282
    selection criteria for, 277, 280, 281
    and strophic form, 277, 280, 281, 295, 296, 349

    and through-composed form, 280, 281, 292, 294, 295

Bach, C. P. E., songs—Gellert settings
    See also Gellert
    Anhang. See under C. P. E. Bach, songs
    Geistliche Oden und Lieder, 30, 161, 201, 203, 212, 224, 236, 239, 282
    "Abendlied," 239
    "Am neueren Jahr," 239
    "Bitten," 227, 228-229, 230
    "Busslied," 220-222, 225
    "Die Ehre Gottes aus der Natur," 237, 238-239, 390, 391
    "Das Gebet," 230-231, 234
    "Morgengesang," 239
    "Osterlied," 239
    "Passionslied," 224, 231, 234-236
    "Weihnachtslied," 239
    "Wider den Übermut," 31
    and chorale form, 211, 212, 256
    critics' views of, 22, 30-31, 32, 161, 239-240, 433
    distinctive voice in, 30-31, 161, 201, 212, 248, 308, 452
    and Gellert's aims, 223-224, 239
    Gellert's views of, 211
    order of musical forms in, 281
    poems, appeal of, for Bach, 204, 224-225, 236
    and song output, 203, 380
    and strophic form, 222-223, 308

Bach, C. P. E., songs—Sturm settings
    See also Sturm
    "Empfindungen in der Sommernacht," 407, 408-410
    "Gottes Grösse in der Natur," 389, 390-391
    "Jesus in Gethsemane," 397, 399-400
    "Passionslied" poems, 391-397
    "Der Tag des Weltgerichts," 405, 406-407
    "Über die Finsterniss kurz vor dem Tode Jesu," 397, 403-405
    collections of, 311, 379, 407
    poems, appeal of, for Bach, 391, 410
    strophic form in, 396, 410
    and Sturm friendship, 380

Bach, C. P. E., through-composed songs
    See also C. P. E. Bach, cantatas
    Clarissa (Gerstenberg), 351-352, 353, 361
    "An Doris" (Haller), 32, 243, 341, 342, 343-349, 350, 354, 431, 455
    "Auf den Geburtstag eines Freundes" (Ebeling), 261-263, 265, 349, 430, 431, 455

"Freude, du Lust der Götter und Menschen" (unnamed poet), 258
"Ich hoff auf Gott" (Recke, von der), 422-425, 455
"Die Küsse" (Giseke), 52-53, 191, 193-201, 261, 265, 349, 455
"Nonnelied" (anonymous), 425, 426-431, 452, 455
"Phyllis" (Kleist), 263, 264-265, 349, 455
and contemporary views, 22, 32-33
Bach, Johann Christoph Friedrich, 268
Bach, Johann Sebastian, 1, 94, 125, 211
    and Baroque era (era of Bach and Handel), 7, 54
    chorales of, 278, 279
    and German lied, 40, 54
    music of, 7, 8, 13-14
    Scheibe's attack on, 57
    Ziegler settings of, 165
Bach und seine Lieder, C. Ph. E. (Busch), 31, 242
Bach, "Lieder und Gesänge," Carl Philipp Emanuel (Vrieslander), 318, 414
Bacon, 47
Baron, John
    on strophic variation, 58-59
Baroque era
    and transition to Classical, 7, 8, 15-16, 25
Barr, Raymond A., on Krause, 146
Batteux, Charles
    Ars poetica translation of, 123, 131-132
    Cours de belles lettres, 5, 90, 123, 131
    Les Beaux-Arts réduits à un même principe, 5, 90, 91, 100, 133, 155, 271
    on art as imitation, 5, 90, 91
    influence of, 5, 90, 271
    and rationalist thought, 90-92
    on taste and rules in art, 119-121
    on variety within unity, 132, 133
"Der Bauer" (Miller), 315, 330
Baumgarten, Alexander Gottlieb
    and influence of Horace, 123-124, 132
    philosophical aesthetics of, 93-94, 113, 123, 147, 271
Les Beaux-Arts réduits à un même principe (Batteux), 5, 90, 91, 100, 133, 155, 271
Beck, Lewis White, 47
Beckmann, Gustav, 319
Beethoven, Ludwig van
    and Classical era, 7
    Gellert settings of, 204, 214, 225
    and instrumental music, 20, 433
    and sonata form, 13
    songs of, 2

Benda, Georg, 268
Berlin song school (first)
    See also under C. P. E. Bach, songs
    characteristics of, 31, 52, 69-70, 80, 88, 183-184, 190, 191, 201, 210, 219, 220, 228, 249
    and influence of Horace, 146
    "manifesto" of, 83, 146
    and Marpurg, 161
    and Ramler-Krause, 52, 83, 84, 93, 146
    and reform of German letters, 212
    and strophic song, 2, 33, 52
Berlin song school (second). *See* Volkslied movement
Berlinische Oden und Lieder (Marpurg), 185
Bestimmtheit (definiteness), in music, 12-15, 19-20, 148, 352-353, 356, 360
    See also Allgemeinheit
Birnstiel, F. W., 278
"Bitten" (Gellert), 225-229, 230
Bitter, Carl Hermann
    Emanuel und Friedemann Bach und deren Brüder, 16, 451
    on Bach, 16-17, 22, 258
    on Bach's Cramer settings, 279-281, 283
    on Bach's "Empfindungen in der Sommernacht," 409, 410
    on Bach's Gellert settings, 278
    on Bach's lost arias, 457, 464
    on Bach's Masonic songs, 451-452
    on strophic form, 280
Blümcke, Adolf
    on Cramer, 271, 273
Bodmer, Johann Jakob
    and *Aufschwung*, 44
    and Longinian sublime, 271
    and reform of German letters, 90, 93
Böhm, Georg, 59
Boie, Ernestine, 314, 325
Boie, Heinrich Christian
    and Hainbund, 313
    and *Musen-Almanach*, 312, 314-315. *See also Musen-Almanach*
    and Voss, 311, 312, 313-314
Boileau
    L'Art poétique, 92, 93, 125, 130, 145
    and influence of Horace, 125, 130, 145, 179
    and Longinian sublime, 130
    and rationalist thought, 5, 91, 92
    on rules in art, 91, 125, 130-131
    and taste, ideas of, 107
Bokemeyer, Heinrich, 38
Bollioud-Mermot, Louis, 153

Borchward, Ernst Samuel Jacob, 204, 210
Bouhours, Father Dominique
    and ideas of taste in art, 107
Brahms, Johannes, and strophic form, 32
Breitinger, Johann Jakob
    critical writings of, 148, 271
    and reform of German letters, 90, 93
Breitkopf, publisher, 311, 319
    Cramer psalms and settings, 272, 273, 274, 275, 276
Bremer Beiträge, 204, 272
Bremner, publisher, 311
Brendel, Franz
    on Bach, 11, 12
    on Gluck, 11
    and Wagner, 10-11
Brink, C. O., on *Ars poetica*, 126, 128, 129, 132
Brockes, Barthold Heinrich
    and Bach, 381
    and Freemasons, 434-435
    and reform of German letters, 47, 57
Buch von der Deutschen Poeterey (Opitz), 59, 93, 124
Bücken, Ernst
    on aria and German lied, 50-51
Bukofzer, 69
Bürger, Gottfried August, 3, 313
Burney, Charles, 6, 23, 263
    on Bach, 21
    on Bach's C-minor Fantasy, 357, 358
Busch, Gudrun
    C. Ph. E. Bach und seine Lieder, 31, 242
    Bach chronology of, 31-32
    on Bach's Cramer settings, 274
    on Bach and Gellert, 203, 204, 211
    on Bach and Sturm, 379
    on other Bach settings, 31, 242, 248, 258, 265, 315, 336, 426
    on *Nonnelieder*, 426
"Busslied" (Gellert), 212-222, 225, 226
Butterfield, Sir Herbert
    See also progressivist thought
    The Whig Interpretation of History, 46-48, 78
    on tolerance, 382

C-minor Fantasy (Bach), 274, 352-354, 356, 357, 359-360, 361
Caccini, Francesca
    See also monody, Italian
    Le nuove musiche, 43, 45, 58
    and German lied, 43, 45, 46
    and strophic form, 58
Calzabigi, Raniero de, 156
Canitz, Friedrich Rudolf Ludwig von, 124-125, 134
    and influence of Horace, 64, 133
cantata form
    See also under C. P. E. Bach, cantatas
    epic vs. dramatic, 144
    German lied and, 36, 44, 45, 46, 57-58, 60, 150
    "number" cantatas, 350
    vs. ode form, 149-150, 151
    and strophic form, 49, 54, 58, 60, 136-138, 143-145, 152
Carissimi, 8
Cassirer, Ernst, 132
"Chloe an Thyrsis" ("Schäferlied," "An Thyrsis") (Ziegler), 165, 167-171, 172, 186-187
Chrysander, 16, 17
Cicero, 47
Clarissa (Gerstenberg), 351-352, 353, 361
Classical era, Classical style
    Bach and, 7, 10, 15, 17, 21, 23, 25, 27, 28, 29, 33, 178, 201, 249
    characteristics of, 7, 8, 23, 24, 171
    and German lied, 78
    instrumental music and, 6, 13, 15, 27, 29
    pastoral genre and, 171, 172, 177, 178
    sonata form and, 25
    symphonic output of, 27
    and transition from Baroque, 7, 8, 14, 15, 25
    Viennese composers and, 2, 24, 165
Claudius, Mattias, 358, 359
    and Bach's Cramer settings, 274-275
    and Bach's Gerstenberg settings, 351, 353
    and Hainbund, 313
    and *Volkslied* movement, 3, 314
Cleveland, John, 124, 125
Clodius (Klöde, Christian), song collection of, 48
Coleridge, 5, 121
Colles, H. C., 18
"Communionlied" (Münter), 268-269
Condillac, Etienne Bonnot de, 2
Cooke, Deryck, 242
Corelli, 19, 29
Corneille, 94
Cours de belles lettres (Batteux), 5, 90, 123, 131
Cowley, Abraham, 124, 125
Cramer, Carl Friedrich, 278, 313, 353, 359
Cramer, Johann Andreas, 271-273, 278, 351
    See also C. P. E. Bach, songs—Cramer settings
    Psalm 1, 285-286
    Psalm 4, 287-288
    Psalm 6, 289-292

Psalm 8, 294-297
Psalm 67, 298-299
Psalm 86, 299-300
Psalm 88, 301
Psalm 90, 302-303
Psalm 91, 304-305
Psalm 93, 307
and Luther's Bible, 284-286, 288-292, 297-307
Gellert biography of, 203-204, 278
stature of, 380
Critica musica (Mattheson), 38, 52, 66, 139
criticism. *See* aesthetic judgment
Der critische Musikus (Scheibe), 39, 40, 64, 93, 125, 139, 141, 143, 150, 183
Der critische Musikus an der Spree (Marpurg), 40, 153
Crousaz, Jean-Pierre de
on variety and unity, 132
Cudworth, Ralph, 108
Czerny, Carl, 13

Dach, Simon, 124, 125
and influence of Horace, 133
Dacier, André, on Horace, 145
Darwin, Charles
See also progressivist thought
Origin of Species, 7, 16, 19
influence of, on music historians, 7, 16, 18, 19-21, 38, 78
D'Aubignac, 93
de Giovannini, 64, 265
"An den Schlaf" (Hagedorn), 71, 73-74, 75, 81, 82, 83, 88
"Sinne" (poet called "K"), 69-71
Denkmäler early music editions, 22, 23, 24, 77, 435
Descartes, René, 47, 123
introspective philosophy of, 93, 121, 122
and rationalist thought, 91, 92, 115
Das deutsche Lied im 18. Jahrhundert (Friedlaender), 29, 35, 41, 160, 167
Das deutsche Lied in seiner historischen Entwicklung (Reissmann), 36
Doles, Johann Friedrich
Neue Lieder nebst ihren Melodien, 162
"Busslied" (Gellert), 216-217, 218
other Gellert settings of, 155, 162, 211-212, 237
Dommer, Arrey von
on Bach, 15, 18
on *Bestimmtheit* and *Allgemeinheit* in music, 13-15

Donington, Robert, 409
"Doris" (Haller), 32, 243, 246, 341-349, 350, 431
Drant, Thomas, 124
Drijvers, Pius. *See* psalms
Dryden, John, 124, 125
See also rationalist thought
critical works of, 100-105
and rationalist thought, 5
on rules in art, 101-105, 106, 108
Dubos, Jean Baptiste
Réflexions critiques sur la Poésie et sur la Peinture, 92, 94, 108
and rationalist aesthetics, 92, 94
on sixth sense (taste), 94, 108-110, 117, 118, 119, 120, 121
Durchkomponierung. *See* through-composed song

Ebeling, Christoff Daniel, 381
See also under C. P. E. Bach, songs
"Auf den Geburtstag eines Freundes," 261-263, 430
"Edone" ("Lyda") (Klopstock), 315, 320-324, 325-327
Edwards, John Richard
on Krause and German letters, 93-94, 95
"Die Ehre Gottes aus der Natur" (Gellert), 224, 236-239, 390, 391, 409
Einstein, Alfred, 49
Eitner, Robert, 41
Elmenhorst, Heinrich, 59
"Empfindungen in der Sommernacht" (Sturm), 407-410
Engelke, Bernhard
on Bach's "Die Grazien," 361, 366, 368, 377
Enlightenment, 177
See also progressivist thought; rationalist thought
in England and France, 47, 84, 177
and Freemasonry, 433-434
in Germany, 47, 52, 57, 84, 133, 141, 381, 432
Erk, Ludwig, folksong collections of, 42
Erlebach, Philipp Heinrich
Harmonische Freude musikalischer Freunde collections, 52, 59
and *liederlose Zeit*, 60-61
and opera, influence of, 51, 52, 59-61
song settings of, 60
Ernst, Counts Christian and Heinrich. *See* Wernigerode songbook
Erste Sammlung auserlesener moralischer Oden (Mizler), 80, 143, 160

Fabricius, Georg, 124
Fasch, Carl F., 191
    Cramer settings of, 274
Feddersen, Jacob Friedrich, on Sturm, 383-386, 388, 390
Fétis, François-Joseph
    music history of, 18, 41
Fleischer, Friedrich Gottlob, 162-163
Fleming, Paul
    and Horace, influence of, 133
    and reform of German letters, 124
folksong movement. *See* Volkslied movement
Fontenelle
    and ideas about art, 92
Forkel, E. N., 6
Forkel, Johann Nikolaus, 94
form, in music, 11, 12, 13, 14-16, 18, 19, 25
    See also *Allgemeinheit*; *Bestimmtheit*.
    See also specific musical form
Franck, Johann Wolfgang, 51, 59
Franz, 6
Freemasonry, 433-437, 442
    See also Masonic songs
"Freude, du Lust der Götter und Menschen" (unnamed poet), 258
Friedlaender, Max
    Das deutsche Lied im 18. Jahrhundert, 29, 35, 41, 160, 167
    on Bach, 29-30, 32, 211
    on German song, 42, 43
    on *liederlose Zeit*, 42, 48
    song compendium of, 29, 32, 35, 41, 42
    on Telemann and Görner settings, 77, 81
"Der Frühling" (Miller), 330-331
"Der Frühling" (Wieland), 349-350
Fünfzig Psalmen, geistliche Oden und Lieder (Gräfe), 217-218, 273-274

Gabrieli, Giovanni, 43
Gärtner, Karl Christian
    and *Bremer Beiträge*, 204, 272
Gay, John
    and *Aufschwung*, 44
"Das Gebet" (Gellert), 229-231, 234
Geistliche, moralische und weltliche Oden, von verschiedenen Dichtern und Componisten. See Marpurg
Geistliche Oden, in Melodien gesetzt von einigen Tonkünstlern in Berlin. See Marpurg
Geistliche Oden und Lieder. See C. P. E. Bach—Gellert settings; Gellert

Gellert, Christian Fürchtegott
    See also C. P. E. Bach, songs—Gellert settings
    Geistliche Oden und Lieder, 30, 155, 161, 203, 204-205, 210, 211, 212, 213, 217, 239, 241
    other writings of, 203-204
    "Bitten," 225-229
    "Busslied," 212-222, 225, 226
    "Die Ehre Gottes aus der Natur," 224, 236-239, 390, 391, 409
    "Das Gebet," 229-231
    "Passionslied," 224, 231-236, 394
    other poem mentions, 224, 239
    aims of, 206, 209, 210, 211, 212, 222-224
    and *Aufschwung*, 44
    biblical language, in songs of, 208, 213-215, 217, 224, 226, 230, 232, 236-237
    and Bach, 203, 204, 222
    on Bach settings, 211, 276
    and Cramer, 203, 217, 272
    and Gottsched, 203, 207
    and Gräfe volumes, 64
    and influence of Horace, 203, 206, 208
    reputation and popularity of, 203, 204, 212, 241, 268, 380
    on sacred poetry and song, 205-211
    on taste and rules, 206-207
German lied
    See also *Aufschwung*; Berlin song school; *Hausmusik*; *Liederlose Zeit*; song collections; Volkslied
    and Bach, 17, 22, 30, 35
    and foreign influences, 36, 37, 38, 42, 43, 45, 46, 47, 49, 59, 61
    histories of, 6, 29-32, 36-55
    musical literacy and, 89
    popularity and stature of, 2, 3, 57, 89, 141
    as Romantic genre, 2, 6, 22, 78-79
    and strophic form, 2, 36, 37, 38, 44, 57-58
Gerstenberg, Heinrich Wilhelm von
    Clarissa (Clarissa im Sarge, Clarissa Harlowe im Sarge), 351-352
    Tändeleyen collection, 350, 351, 362, 363, 364
    Ugolino, 351
    "Die Grazien," 350, 354, 361, 362-377, 411
    as Anacreontic poet, 363-364
    and Bach, 351, 352, 359
    and Bach's C-minor Fantasy (*Hamlet* soliloquy), 274, 352-354, 356, 357, 359-360, 361
    and Bach's Cramer settings, 274-275, 350, 354, 361

on expressive power of instrumental music, 352-357, 359, 361
Geschichte des deutschen Liedes (Reissmann), 6, 41
Geschichte des deutschen Liedes im XVIII. Jahrhundert (Lindner), 6, 38, 42
Geschichte des neuen deutschen Liedes (Kretzschmar), 30, 44-45
Giseke, Nicolaus Dietrich
    See also under C. P. E. Bach, songs
    "Die Küsse," 191-201
    "Das Privilegium," 246-250
Gleim, Johann Wilhelm Ludwig, 145
    See also under C. P. E. Bach, songs
    "Herausforderungslied vor der Schlacht bey Rossbach," 241-243
    "Lied der Schnitterinnen," 419-420
    "Mittel, freundlich zu werden," 417-419
    and Gerstenberg, 351
    and Karsch, 250
    and *Musen-Almanach*, 314
    song collections of, 241, 419
Gluck, Christoph Willibald
    "Vaterlandslied" (Klopstock), 314-315, 319-320
    and *Aufschwung*, 44
    critics' views of, 7-13, 18, 26-27, 28, 29
    as link between eras, 7-9, 25, 27
    and reform of opera, 7, 9-10, 11, 13, 27
Goethe, Johann Wolfgang von, 44, 314, 337, 382
    on influence of Mozart, 7-8
    and Ossian "translations," 3
Goeze, Johan Melchior
    and Lessing, 381-383, 389
    and Moldenhawer, 388
    religious orthodoxy of, 381-382, 384-386
    and Semler, 383
    Steineck biography of, 386-388
    and Sturm, 381, 383-386, 388
Goldschmidt, Hugo
    Die Musikästhetik des 18. Jahrhunderts, 90
    on rationalist thought, 90-92, 96
    on taste and rules in art, 104, 122
    as whig historian, 90
Görner, Johann Valentin
    Sammlung neuer Oden und Lieder volumes, 76, 80, 161, 183, 266
    "An den Schlaf" (Hagedorn), 76-79, 80, 82
    "An die Liebe" ("Die Liebe") (Hagedorn), 266-267
    "Der Lauf der Welt" (Hagedorn), 84, 86-87
    "Der Morgen" (Hagedorn), 183-184

    and Berlin song school, 183-184, 191
    and German lied, 52
"Gottes Grösse in der Natur" (Sturm), 389-391
Göttinger Hainbund. *See* Hainbund
Göttinger Musen-Almanach. *See* Musen-Almanach
Gottsched, Johann Christoph
    Versuch einer critischen Dichtkunst vor die Deutschen, 39, 53, 90, 91, 112-113, 123, 125, 133, 134, 137, 139, 271
    other writings of, 47, 90, 92
    on ancient song, 134-135
    Ars poetica translation of, 123
    on cantatas, 136-138, 140
    and Cramer, 271-272
    and Gellert, 203, 206
    in Gräfe collections, 64
    and Horace, influence of, 123, 133, 137, 138, 141, 142, 145
    influence of, 62-63, 90, 91, 207, 271, 351
    opposition to, 93, 271-272
    and rationalist thought, 5, 51, 90-91, 92, 94
    and reform of German letters, 39-40, 47, 57, 90, 93, 133, 207, 212
    and reinstatement of strophic song, 44, 134, 139, 145
    on strophic song, 39, 135-137, 138
    on taste and aesthetic judgment, 91, 92, 93, 112-119, 120, 121
    on variety within unity, 137-138, 142, 145
    on Wechseloden, 40, 135, 138
Gräfe, Johann Friedrich
    Fünfzig Psalmen, geistliche Oden und Lieder, 217-218, 273-274
    Sammlung verschiedener und auserlesener Oden volumes, 30, 35, 39, 63-65, 69, 70, 73, 141, 160, 165, 172
    "Bitten" (Gellert), 227, 228, 230
    "Busslied" (Gellert), 218-219, 222
    "Die Ehre Gottes aus der Nature" (Gellert), 237, 238
    "Das Gebet" (Gellert), 230-231
    other setting mentions, 65-66
    and *Aufschwung*, 35
    and Bach, 30, 35, 39, 165, 172
    Cramer settings, 217-218, 273-274
    Gellert settings, 217-218, 273
    on German lied, state of, 63
    and rationalist thought, 51
    song collections of, 39, 63-66, 141, 143, 160
    as song composer, 83, 218
    and Sperontes volumes, 63, 160-161
    on strophic problem, 219
Grandval, Nicolas Rogot de, 153

Graun, Carl Heinrich, 191, 258
    operas of, 5, 146, 155
    songs of, 4, 64
"Die Grazien" (Gerstenberg), 258, 350, 354, 360, 361, 362-377, 411, 430, 431, 455
Grove, Sir George, 18
Grove's Dictionary of Music and Musicians, 18, 21, 41
    See also New Grove Dictionary
Gryphius, 125
Gunkel, Hermann, and psalm scholarship, 283
Günther, Johann Christian
    "An Phyllis," 66-69
    and Gräfe collections, 64, 65
    and influence of Horace, 133
    and reform of German letters, 47, 57, 133
    and reinstatement of strophic song, 48, 57, 125

Hadow, W. H.
    on Bach, 21-22
    on sonata form and Classical style, 25
Hagedorn, Friedrich von
    See also under C. P. E. Bach, songs
    Oden und Lieder, 52, 57, 73, 80
    Sämmelte poetische Werke, 71, 84
    "Die Alster," 224, 266, 453
    "An den Schlaf," 71-83
    "An die Liebe," 224, 266-268, 452
    "Harvstehude," 224, 266, 453-454
    "Der Lauf der Welt," 84-88
    "Der Morgen," 179-184, 266, 452
    and Gräfe volumes, 64
    and influence of Horace, 77-78, 133, 179, 266
    popularity of, 224, 266, 452
    and reform of German letters, 47, 52, 57
    and reinstatement of strophic song, 52, 57, 125
Hainbund (Göttinger Hainbund), 313-314
    and Bach, 330, 331, 415, 420
    members of, 278, 313, 351, 415, 426
    and *Musen-Almanach*, 314
Haller, Albrecht von
    See also under C. P. E. Bach, songs
    "Doris," 32, 243, 246, 341-349, 350, 431
    "Die Tugend," 243
Haller, Rudolf, on Cramer and Gellert, 380
Hamman, Johann George, 136-137
Hammerschmidt, Andreas
    and Schütz, 46
    and strophic form, 59
Handel, Georg Friedrich
    Neun deutsche Arien, 51, 54
    and Baroque era, 7
    and German lied, 51, 54
    and modern music, 8, 11
Harmonische Freude musikalischer Freunde collections (Erlebach), 52, 59
"Harvstehude" (Hagedorn), 224, 266, 452-453
Hase, Hermann von, 273
Hasse
    operas of, 5, 8, 146, 155
Hassler, polyphonic songs of, 46
Hausmusik
    Bach and, 1, 2, 170
    Berlin song school and, 83
    foreign influences and, 42
    Italian monody and, 43
    popularity of, 89
    strophic song and, 89
Haydn, Franz Josef
    "Schäferlied" ("An Thyrsis") (Ziegler), 168, 169-171, 172
    "Der Zufriedene" ("Die Landlust") (Stahl), 172, 175-177
    and Bach, 7, 9, 10, 11, 12, 16, 26, 28
    as Bach forerunner, 23, 24
    and Classical era, 7, 171
    and Freemasons, 434
    music of, 2, 28, 148, 159, 189
    and opera, 170
    and pastoral genre, 171, 177-178, 327
    and sonata form, 12, 13, 16, 27
    songs of, 2, 170
    and Viennese Classical school, 24
Hegel, 38, 90
Heilig. See C. P. E. Bach, choral works
Helm, E. Eugene
    Thematic Catalogue of the Works of Carl Philipp Emanuel Bach, 1, 31, 437
    on Bach's C-minor Fantasy, 353, 357
    on Bach's Masonic songs, 437, 438
"Herausforderungslied vor der Schlacht bey Rossbach" (Gleim), 241-243, 265
Herbst, Wilhelm
    on Voss, 312, 313
Herder, Johann Gottfried von
    Auszug aus einem Briefwechsel über Ossian und die Lieder alter Völker, 3
    Volkslieder, 3
    other writings of, 2, 3
    on ancient song, 2, 3, 33
    and Ossian "translations," 3
    and reputation of Bach, 3

and Volkslied movement, 3, 146, 314, 340
Herold, Johann Heinrich, publisher
    Bach's Sturm settings, 379
    Sturm poems and biography, 383, 388
Hesse, Johann Heinrich, 163
    Lieder zum unschuldigen Vergnügen, 163
Hiller, Johann Adam, 160, 162, 268
    Lieder mit Melodien fürs Clavier, 162
histories, of music. *See* music histories
Historisch-Kritische Beyträge zur Aufnahme der Musik. See Marpurg
Hobbes, 47
    and contemporary philosophy, 108, 121, 205
Hoffmann, A. H. von Fallersleben
    song history of, 6
Hoffmann-Erbrecht, Lothar
    on Hagedorn settings, 78
Hofmannswaldau, Christian Hofmann von
    and reform of German letters, 57, 64, 124, 125, 133
Hölty, Ludwig Christoph Heinrich
    See also under C. P. E. Bach, songs
    "Todtengräberlied," 331-336
    and Hainbund, 313
    and Volkslied movement, 3
Horace
    Ars poetica, 123-138, 140-141, 144, 145, 146-147, 149, 152
    and German poetry, 421, 426
    influence of, 122, 123-126, 133, 141, 142, 203, 208
    and reform of German letters, 124, 125, 145
    and rules in art, 105, 130, 142, 206
    and variety within unity, 128, 131-132, 144, 145, 152
Howard, Sir Robert
    on rules and taste in art, 100-104, 109
Hughes, Rosemary
    on 18th-century song, 32
Hume
    An Enquiry concerning Human Understanding, 205
    A Treatise of Human Nature, 121, 205
    and contemporary philosophy, 47, 121, 123, 205
Hurd, Richard, 208
Hurlebusch, Conrad Friedrich
    "An Phyllis" (Günther), 66, 68-69
    and Gräfe collection, 63-64, 66
    stature of, 65, 66, 69
Hutcheson, Francis
    writings of, 110, 112, 132
    on pleasure and taste in art, 110, 111-112, 114, 117, 120, 121, 147
    on variety within unity, 111-112, 132

"Ich hoff auf Gott" (Recke, von der), 422-425, 455
instrumental form, in music
    See also Allgemeinheit; *Bestimmtheit*
    and Bach, 11, 12, 23
    and Classical era, 2, 6, 13-15, 29
    expressivity in, 15, 353, 354, 355, 356
    as independent form, 11, 12, 19-20, 152
    in music historical writing, 6, 8, 11-17, 19, 27, 29, 55
    vs. texted music, 12, 13, 148, 352-355
    vocal music, relation to, 2, 16, 45, 356, 358
Isaac, polyphonic songs of, 46
Iskra, Augustinus, 124
Die Israeliten in der Wüste. See C. P. E. Bach, oratorios

"Jesus in Gethsemane" (Sturm), 397-400
Joachim, Joseph, 10
Johnson, Dr., 5, 79, 131, 209
    on Dryden, 100
Jolizza, W. K. von
    Das Lied und seine Geschichte, 30, 42
    on Bach, 30
    on Caccini, 43
    on German lied, 42-44, 45
    on Görner's Hagedorn settings, 183
    on *Liederlose Zeit*, 44
    on *Tafel-Confect* and Sperontes volumes, 44, 63
Jolowicz, H. F., 248
Jonson, Ben
    Horace translation of, 124, 125

Kant, 11
    and rationalist thought, 92
    and reform of German letters, 40
Karsch, Anna Louisa, 250, 263
    See also under C. P. E. Bach, songs
    "An Gott" poems, 250-254
Keiser, Reinhard
    on German lied, 36, 41
    songs and operas of, 38, 50, 53
Kennick, William E.
    on aesthetic judgment, 97, 99, 100, 105, 106
Kiesewetter, Raphael Georg
    on Bach, 9
    on Western music and song, 8-9, 11
Kindt, Karl, 316, 320

Kirnberger, Johann Philipp, 94, 339
 "Doris" (Haller), 243
 "Das Privilegium" (Giseke), 248-249
Kittel, Caspar, songs of, 50, 58-59
Kivy, Peter, on texted music, 148
"Klagen einer Schäferinn" (unnamed poet), 268
Kleist, Ewald Christian von
 See also under C. P. E. Bach, songs
 "Amint," 184-191
 "Phyllis," 263-265
Klopstock, 263, 268, 351
 See also under C. P. E. Bach, songs
 "Lyda" ("Edone"), 315, 320-324, 325-327
 "Vaterlandslied," 314-320
 and *Aufschwung*, 44
 and Bach, 224, 277, 380, 435
 and Cramer, 272, 278
 on "Doris" (Haller), 243
 and Hainbund, 313, 317
 and *Musen-Almanach*, 314
 on "Vaterlandslied," Gluck vs. Bach settings of, 314-315, 320
 and *Volkston*, 316, 320
 and Voss, 312, 314
Klopstocks Morgengesang am Schöpfungsfeste. See C. P. E. Bach, choral works
Kluge, 75
Koch, Eduard Emil
 on Cramer, 273
 on Münter, 268
 on Sturm, 380, 386
Koloraturlied, 45, 46
König, Johann Ulrich von, 125
Krabbe, Wilhelm
 on Görner and Telemann, 77
Krause, Christian Friedrich, music history of, 8-9, 11
Krause, Christian Gottfried
 See also Ramler; Ramler-Krause song collections
 Von der musikalischen Poesie, 64, 93, 123, 145-146, 153, 155, 353
 "Der Lauf der Welt" (Hagedorn), 84, 87-88
 on *Affektenlehre* (theory of emotions), 150, 151, 153, 158-159
 and Berlin song school, 93, 146
 Cramer settings of, 273
 Gleim settings of, 241
 and Gräfe volumes, 64
 and influence of Horace, 123, 145-146, 152, 155
 on *liederlose Zeit*, 150
 and Marpurg, on song composition, 156-160

 musical output of, 145
 on non-strophic forms, 151
 and reinstatement of strophic song, 64, 92, 152
 on strophic form, 150-152, 158-159
 on texts and musical settings, 94, 146-153, 353
 on variety within unity, 146, 152-153
Krebs, Johann Ludwig, 78
Kretzschmar, Hermann
 Geschichte des neuen deutschen Liedes, 30, 44-45
 on "An den Schlaf" (Hagedorn) settings, 75, 77, 80
 on Bach, 30-31
 on Caccini and Albert, 45, 49-50, 58
 on German lied, 44-46, 59
 on *liederlose Zeit*, 46, 47-49
 and *Volkslied*, 62
Krieger, Adam
 and German lied, 49
 and Schütz, 46
 and strophic form, 59
Kristeller, Paul Oskar
 on notion of fine art, 100
Kritische Briefe über die Tonkunst. See Marpurg
Kross, Siegfried
 Dokumentation zur Geschichte des deutschen Liedes (editor), 53
 Geschichte des deutschen Liedes, 53
 on *Liederlose Zeit*, 53-54
"Die Küsse" (Giseke), 52-53, 191-201, 261, 265, 349, 455
Kusser, operas of, 50, 53

"Die Landlust" ("Der Zufriedene") (Stahl), 172-177, 178, 345
Landon, H. C. Robbins
 on 18th-century symphonic output, 27
Lang, Paul Henry, 94
Lange, J. P., on Sturm, 380
Langhans, Wilhelm, 18
"Der Lauf der Welt" (Hagedorn), 84-88
Leavis, F. R., 124
Le Bossu, 93
Leibniz, 132, 243
Lessing
 and *Aufschwung*, 44
 and Bach, 277, 380, 381, 435
 on expressive power of music, 360-361
 and Gerstenberg, 350, 351, 360, 364
 and Goeze controversy, 381-383, 389
Lexer, 75

"Die Liebe" ("An die Liebe") (Hagedorn), 224, 266-268, 452
lied. *See* German lied
"Lied" (Stolberg), 415-417
"Lied der Schnitterinnen" (Gleim), 419-420
Das Lied und seine Geschichte (Jolizza), 30, 42
Lieder der Deutschen mit Melodien volumes (Ramler-Krause), 80
Lieder im Volkston collections (Schulz), 3, 338, 340, 415
Lieder und Kirchengesänge (Sturm), 379
liederlose Zeit (songless time)
    See also strophic problem
    and Bach, 35
    causes of, 37, 40, 44, 46, 48, 49, 54, 150
    end of, 35, 37, 44, 48, 52, 53
    Erlebach and, 60, 61
    and foreign influences, 36, 37, 38, 42, 44, 46, 49, 50-51, 55, 60, 150
    and German poetry, 42, 44, 46, 49, 55
    historians' views of, 36-55, 78
    and Italian monody, 54
    and Kretzschmar, 48
    and music historical writing, 36
    and Ramler-Krause, 44
    and song collections, 35, 89
    and song quality, 141
    and strophic form, 37, 40, 49, 53, 54, 58, 89, 431
    and Telemann, 53
Lightfoot, R. H., 402
Lindner, Ernst Otto
    Geschichte des deutschen Liedes im XVIII. Jahrhundert, 6, 38, 42
    on Bach songs, 6, 242, 319
    on contemporary criticism, 38-40, 55
    on contemporary song collections, 39, 40
    on *liederlose* Zeit, 40, 55
    on opera, influence of, 38
    on reinstatement of strophic song, 139
    on *Wechseloden*, 40
Liszt, 10, 11, 31
Locke, John
    and intuitionism, 108, 121, 205
    on pleasure in understanding, 110-111
Loewe, 6, 432
Lohenstein, Daniel Casper von, 124, 125, 133
Longinian sublime, 130, 271
Losius, J. C., 53
Luther, Martin, Bible translation of
    Bach and, 224
    Cramer's psalm translations and, 284-307
    Gellert and, 208-209, 213, 224, 232

    and Psalm 88 (poet unknown), 254-255
"Lyda" ("Edone") (Klopstock), 315, 320-324, 325-327

Macaulay, 47
Mackey, Albert G., on Freemasonry, 442
Macpherson, James, Ossian "translations" of, 3
Magnificat. *See* C. P. E. Bach, choral works
Mannheim school
    influence of, 15, 23, 24-25
Marini, Giambattista, influence of, 124-125
Marpurg, Friedrich Wilhelm
    Anleitung zur Singcomposition, 159
    Berlinische Oden und Lieder, 185
    Der critische Musikus an der Spree, 40, 153
    Geistliche, moralische und weltliche Oden, von verschiedenen Dichtern und Componisten, 219, 227, 239, 248, 273
    Geistliche Oden, in Melodien gesetzt von einigen Tonkünstlern in Berlin, 155, 219, 239, 273
    Historisch-Kritische Beyträge zur Aufnahme der Musik, 40, 153, 154, 155-156, 187, 191, 239
    Kritische Briefe über die Tonkunst, 40, 155-156, 159, 184, 240
    Musikalisches Allerley, 274
    Neue Lieder zum Singen beym Claviere, 179
    "Amint" ("Amynt") (Kleist), 184, 185-186, 187
    "Bitten" (Gellert), 227-228, 229
    "Busslied" (Gellert), 219-220, 222
    "Doris" (Haller), 243
    "Die Ehre Gottes aus der Natur" (Gellert), 237, 238
    on Bach, 155, 161, 239-240, 274
    and Berlin song school, 153, 161
    and contemporary aesthetic ideas, 94-96
    and Cramer psalm settings, 273, 274
    Gellert collections of, 239
    on German music, state of, 154
    on Görner, 184
    on Gräfe volumes, 65, 160
    musical output of, 153
    and Nichelmann, 187, 191
    progressivist leanings of, 94-95
    and Rameau, influence of, 94, 187
    on Ramler-Krause, 155, 161
    and reform of German letters, 39-40
    and reinstatement of strophic song, 92, 163
    on song collections, 65, 155, 158, 159-163, 184
    on song composition, 156-157

Marpurg, Friedrich Wilhelm (*continued*)
    on Sperontes volumes, 63, 65, 160
    on strophic song, 155, 157-158, 162
    on Telemann, 65
Marvell, 177, 245
Marx, Adolf Bernhard
    on Bach, 10
    on Gluck, 9-10, 11
    on sonata form, 13
Mascov, 113
Masonic songs, 433, 435-452
    See also under C. P. E. Bach, songs
    Freimäurer-Lieder volumes, 436-452
Mattheson, Johann, 38-41
    Critica musica, 38, 52, 66, 139
    and *Affektenlehre*, 93, 94
    and *liederlose Zeit*, 54
    and reform of German letters, 39-40, 47, 57
    on strophic form, 38, 39, 49, 52, 139
Meier, Georg Friedrich
    and Horace, influence of, 123-124, 132
    and ideas of taste, 113
melismatic style, 38, 39, 59, 79, 139, 393, 400
Mencke, Johann Burkhard, 112
Mendelssohn, Felix, 17, 41
Mendelssohn, Moses, 250
"metaphysical" poets, 124, 134
Meusel, J. G., 324
"Das Milchmädchen" ("Das Mitleiden") (Voss), 412-415, 420
Miller, Henry Knight
    See also progressivist thought
    on "whig" history, 78, 89-90
Miller, Johann Martin, 315
    See also under C. P. E. Bach, songs
    "Der Bauer," 315, 330
    "Der Frühling," 330-331
    "Das mitleidige Mädchen" ("Das Mitleiden"), 420-422
    and Hainbund, 313
    and *Nonnelieder*, 426
Milton, 208
    vis-à-vis rationalist thought, 92, 93
Minnesingers, 36
"Das mitleidige Mädchen" ("Das Mitleiden") (Miller), 420-422
"Mittel, freundlich zu werden" (Gleim), 417-419, 420
Mizler von Kolof, Lorenz Christoph
    Erste Sammlung auserlesener moralischer Oden, 80, 143, 160
    Neu eröffnete musikalische Bibliothek, 39, 139, 140

    on *Ars poetica*, 140-141
    and Gottsched, 39, 57, 139, 140, 141
    on Gräfe collections, 64, 66
    influence of, 139
    and reform of German letters, 57
    and reinstatement of strophic song, 139
    on strophic form, 39, 40, 140
    on texts and musical settings, 140
Moldenhawer, Johann Heinrich Daniel
    and Goeze, 388
Monn, Matthias Georg, 24
monody, Italian
    See also Caccini
    and German lied, 43, 45, 51, 54, 59, 83, 89
    and strophic variation, 45, 58, 89
    Ton and *Wort* in, 43, 44, 48, 58, 83
Montaigne, 47
Montesquieu, 47
Monteverdi
    and German lied, evolution of, 8, 31, 43
    and strophic variation, 58
Moore, G. E., 99
More, Henry, and ideas of taste, 107
"Der Morgen" (Hagedorn), 178-184, 266, 452
"Morgengesang" (Gellert), 239
Moscheles, Ignaz, 10
Mowinckel, Sigmund, 283, 302
    See also psalm scholarship
Mozart, Wolfgang Amadeus
    on Bach, 7
    and Classical era, 7, 23
    and Freemasons, 434
    and Gluck, 9, 11
    and sonata form, 13, 27
    songs of, 2
Müller, Günther
    Geschichte des deutschen Liedes, 49
    on *liederlose Zeit*, 49
Münter, Balthasar
    See also under C. P. E. Bach, songs
    "Communionlied," 268-269
Musen-Almanach
    See also Boie
    and Bach settings, 311, 315, 318, 320, 338, 350, 411-412, 415
    and Gluck settings, 319
    and Klopstock, influence of, 314
    and Voss, 311, 312, 313, 314, 336, 338
music histories, 2-33
    See also under historian name
    song histories, 2, 6, 29-32, 36-55

Das musikalische Lied in geschichtlicher Entwickelung (Schneider), 6, 36, 41, 42
Musikalisches Allerley (Marpurg), 274

Naumann, Emil
    music history of, 17
    on Bach, 17-18
Naumann, Johann Gottlieb
    Masonic music of, 411, 433, 434, 437, 438, 442-444
Nauwach, Johann
    and Schütz, 46
    and strophic variation, 58
Neefe, C. G., 3
neoclassicism
    See also rationalist thought
    characteristics of, 5, 8, 28, 91, 189, 209
    and rules in art, 94, 206-207
Neu eröffnete musikalische Bibliothek (Mizler), 39, 139, 140
Neue Lieder-Melodien. *See* C. P. E. Bach, songs
Neue Lieder zum Singen beym Claviere (Marpurg), 179
Neue Sammlung verschiedener und auserlesener Oden (editor unknown), 160
Neukirch, 142
Neumeister, Erdmann, 63
New Grove Dictionary of Music and Musicians, 54, 146, 171, 224
Nichelmann, Christoph
    See also under C. P. E. Bach, songs
    "Amint" (Patzke), 185
    on Bach's "Amint," 188-191
    on Bach's "Die Küsse," 196-201
    and Berlin song school, 191, 219
    on harmony and melody, 187-191, 196-201
    and influence of Horace, 201
    and influence of Rameau, 187, 188
Nicolai, Friedrich
    Allgemeine deutsche Bibliothek, 352, 431
    and Bach's C-minor Fantasy, 274, 352, 353, 359, 360
    on Gluck, 7
    and progressivist thought, 94
    Volkslied satire of, 340
"Nonnelied" (anonymous), 425, 426-431, 452, 455
Nonnelieder, popularity of, 426
North German composers. *See* Berlin song school
Nottebohm, Gustav, 18
Le nuove musiche (Caccini), 43, 45, 58

ode
    vs. "lied," 39, 157
    and song settings, 135, 149-151, 157-158
    and strophic form, 39, 135, 151
Oden mit Melodien (Bach). *See* C. P. E. Bach, songs
Oden mit Melodien (Ramler-Krause). *See* Ramler-Krause song collections
Oden und Lieder (Hagedorn), 52, 57, 73, 80
Olms, Georg, 53
opera
    and Classical style, 7
    and German lied, 32, 36, 37, 42, 43, 44, 51, 52, 60, 61, 84, 154, 160
    and *liederlose Zeit*, 46, 49, 54, 57, 60
    reform of. *See* Gluck
    and reinstatement of German lied, 145
    and strophic form, 37, 49, 58
    and strophic variation, 58
    and Western music, 8-9
Opitz, Martin
    Buch von der Deutschen Poeterey, 59, 93, 124
    on expressiveness in art, 148
    and Gräfe volumes, 64
    and Horace, influence of, 124, 125, 133, 145
    influence of, 93, 118, 124-125
    and reform of German letters, 57, 59, 124, 125, 133
oratorio
    See also C. P. E. Bach, oratorios
    dramatic vs. lyric, 308-309, 310
    and German lied, 36, 45, 49, 54, 57-58, 60
Ossian, and ancient poetry, 3
"Osterlied" (Gellert), 239
Ottenberg, Hans-Günter, 242
Ovid, influence of, on German poetry, 421
Oxford History of Music, 21, 41
    New Oxford History of Music, 27, 32

"parody" settings, 62, 141, 150
    See also Ton and Wort
Parry, Hubert
    The Evolution of the Art of Music, 18
    on Bach, 20-21
    on evolution of musical forms, 19-20, 25
Passions-Cantate (Die letzten Leiden des Erlösers). *See* C. P. E. Bach, oratorios
"Passionslied" (Gellert), 224, 231-236, 394
"Passionslied" poems (Sturm), 391-397
pastoral genre
    See also under C. P. E. Bach, songs

pastoral genre (*continued*)
    characteristics of, 72, 167-168, 173, 176, 177-178, 421
    classical style and, 171, 172, 177
Patriot Society, 434-435
Patzke, Johann Samuel, 185
Pauly, Reinhard G., on German lied, 32
Pelikan, Jaroslav, 256
Pestelli, Giorgio, 29
Petri, Georg Gottfried, 163
Philips, Ambrose, 80
Phillis und Thirsis (Schlegel), 258, 349
"Phyllis" (Kleist), 263-265, 349, 455
Pindar, 83, 135, 206, 208, 313, 450
Pope, Alexander
    An Essay on Criticism, 4, 125, 130, 142, 145, 207, 209-210
    and Horace, influence of, 125, 130, 142, 145, 179
    on nature and art, 4
    and rationalist thought, 5, 189, 209
    on rules and freedom in art, 131, 142, 207
    and variety within unity, ideas of, 132-133
Printz, Wolfgang Caspar, 187
"Das Privilegium" (Giseke), 246-250
Proft, Christian Gottlieb, 437
progressivist thought
    See also Darwin; Enlightenment
    and music historical writing, 6-7, 8, 18-21, 25, 36, 41, 46, 78
    and "whig" history, 46-47, 78, 89-90, 92, 95
Psalm 88 setting (anonymous), 254, 255, 256-258, 300-301
psalm settings. See C. P. E. Bach, songs—Cramer settings
psalms
    See also Luther
    Cramer translations of. See Cramer
    Drijvers' psalm table, 282-283
    and Gellert poems. See Gellert, biblical language
    psalm scholarship, 283, 302
Pufendorf, on demonstrative science of law and morals, 115
Puttenham, on pastoral mode, 178

Quantz, Johann Joachim
    Neue Kirchenmelodien (Gellert songs), 161, 237
    Gellert settings of, 161, 237

Racek, Jan, 58
Racine, 91

Rackemann, Friedrich Christian
    "Busslied" (Gellert), 219, 220
Radcliffe, Philip
    on Bach, 32
Raguenet, Abbé François, 38
Rameau
    as Gluck forerunner, 11
    on harmony, 94, 187, 188
Ramler, Karl Wilhelm
    See also Krause; Ramler-Krause song collections
    Auferstehung und Himmelfahrt Jesu, 311
    Batteux translations of, 5, 155
    and Berlin song school, 93
    and *Musen-Almanach*, 314
    on poems and musical settings, 83-84, 153-154, 206
    and reform of German letters, 84
    on song in Germany, 153-154
    textual changes by, 81, 82, 83, 87-88, 153
Ramler-Krause song collections
    See also Krause; Ramler
    Lieder der Deutschen mit Melodien volumes, 80
    Oden mit Melodien, 35, 44, 52, 83, 84, 93, 153, 155, 161, 186, 193, 206, 210
    and *Aufschwung*, 35, 44, 64, 83, 84
    and Berlin song school, 52, 80, 83, 84, 93
    and reinstatement of strophic song, 64
    and strophic song, 154, 162
Ranke, Leopold von, and positivist thought, 41
Rapin, on rules in art, 105
Rathgeber, Johann Valentin. See *Tafel-Confect* volumes
rationalist thought
    See also Descartes; Dryden; Horace; progressivist thought
    and aesthetic judgment, 97-106. See also aesthetic judgment
    and anti-rational bias, 122, 146
    and Berlin song school, 52
    characteristics of, 51, 91, 92, 96, 105, 112, 189, 313
    and influence of Gottsched, 90-92
    and intuitionism, 92-93
    and reconciliation of opposites, 5, 92, 104, 106, 189
    and reform of German letters, 91
    and rules in art, 91, 92, 94, 96-106
    and taste, ideas of. See taste
    and variety within unity, 105, 112, 132
rebirth (reinstatement), of strophic song. See *Aufschwung*

Recke, Countess Elise von der
    See also under C. P. E. Bach, songs
    "Ich hoff auf Gott," 422-425, 455
reform, of German letters *(Aufklärung)*
    and Berlin song school, 212
    and German lied, 84
    and Gottsched, 39-40, 47, 57, 90, 91, 93, 133
    and influence of Horace, 124, 125
    and Opitz, 59, 124
    and taste in poetry, 207
    and variety within unity, 133
Reicha, Anton, 13
Reichardt, Johann Friedrich
    writings of, 3, 4, 5, 324
    "Lyda" (Klopstock), 324, 325-327
    on Bach, 3-6, 240, 324-325, 362
    on Bach's "Die Grazien," 362
    on goals of art, 5
    and Volkslied movement, 3, 325
Reimarus, Hermann Samuel
    and Goeze controversy, 381-383
reinstatement, of strophic song. *See Aufschwung*
Reissmann, August
    Das deutsche Lied in seiner historischen
        Entwicklung, 36
    Geschichte des deutschen Liedes, 6, 41
    other writings of, 11, 41
    on Bach, 6, 12, 22
    on *Bestimmtheit* (definiteness), in music, 11-13
    on German lied, 6, 36, 38
    on Gluck, 11
Richardson, Samuel, 203, 351, 352, 410
Richter, Lukas
    and folksong revival, 78, 79
    on Telemann and Görner, 78, 79, 80
Riemann, Hugo, 49
    writings of, 22, 23
    on Bach, 22-24
    and *Denkmäler* volumes, 23
    on Haydn as Bach forerunner, 23, 24
    on Mannheim vs. Viennese schools, 23-24,
        25, 29
Rist, Johann, 43
Röding, J. H.
    See also under C. P. E. Bach, songs
    "An den Schlaf," 258-261
Romantic genre
    and Bach, 11
    characteristics of, 5, 15, 29, 32, 168, 188,
        215, 312, 410
    German lied as, 2, 6, 22, 51, 78-79
    and progressivist ideas, 78
    vs. rationalism, 92

Röpe, Georg Reinhard
    on Goeze, 383, 388-389
    on Sturm, 388
Roscommon, Earl of (Wentworth Dillon), 145
Rosen, Charles
    on Bach and Gluck, 28
    on Haydn and pastoral genre, 170, 177-178
Rousseau, Jean-Jacques
    on early language and song, 2
    and Rameau, 187
rules, in art. *See* rationalist thought, and rules
    in art

Sack, Heinrich Wilhelm, 204
Saintsbury, 78, 92
Sammartini
    and modern symphony, 29
    and sonata form, 15, 27
Sammlung neuer Oden und Lieder volumes
    (Görner), 76, 80, 161, 183, 266
Sammlung verschiedener und auserlesener Oden
    volumes. *See* Gräfe
Sauer, August, 426
Scaliger, Julius Caesar, 124, 206
Scarlatti, Domenico, and sonata form, 12
"Schäferlied" ("An Thyrsis," "Chloe an Thyrsis")
    (Ziegler), 165-172, 178,
    186-187
Schale, Cramer setting of, 273
Scheibe, Johann Adolph
    Der critische Musikus, 39, 40, 64, 93, 125,
        139, 141, 143, 150, 183
    and *Affektenlehre*, 93, 142, 150
    and Bach, 351
    on J. S. Bach, 125
    on German lied, 40, 141
    and Gottsched, 39, 53, 57, 93
    and influence of Horace, 142, 145
    and *liederlose Zeit*, 54, 141
    Masonic songs of, 437
    Münter settings of, 268
    on non-strophic forms, 40, 141, 142, 143-144
    and rationalist thought, 51, 92-93
    and reform of German letters, 39-40, 57
    and reinstatement of strophic song,
        92, 139
    on rules in art, 40
    on song, attributes of, 79, 80, 143, 183
    on strophic form, 40, 49, 141-144
    on Telemannm, 53, 64-65, 79, 143,
        161, 183
    on *Ton* and *Wort*, in Gräfe collections, 64-65,
        143

Scheibe, Johann Adolph (*continued*)
    as transitional figure, 92-93, 95, 96
    on variety within unity, 143-145
Schein
    and Schütz, 46
Schering, Arnold, 13
Schiebeler, Daniel
    Die Israeliten in der Wüste librettist, 263
Schilling, Gustav
    music encyclopedia of, 9
Schlegel, Johann Adolph
    Batteux translation of, 271-272
    and Cramer, 272
    and Gottsched, opposition to, 272
    and Gräfe collections, 64
Schlegel, Johann Elias
    Phyllis und Thirsis, 349
    and Gottsched, opposition to, 271
Schlingmann, Carsten, on Gellert, 213, 230
"Die Schlummernde" (Voss), 315, 325, 327-330, 412
Schmid, Ernst Fritz
    on Bach, 23, 178, 274, 351, 352
    on Gerstenberg, 351
Schmidt, Jakob Friedrich, and Gerstenberg, 351
Schmitz, Eugen, 17
Schneider, K. E.
    Das musikalische Lied in geschichtlicher Entwickelung, 6, 36, 41, 42
    on Bach songs, 6
    on foreign influences, 37, 44, 47-48
    on German lied, 36-38
    on *liederlose Zeit*, causes of, 37, 48
    progressivist views of, 36-37, 43, 46-47
Schoenberg, 51
Scholze, Johann Sigismund
    See also Singende Muse an der Pleisse volumes
    "Sinne" (poet called "K"), 69-71
    "parody" settings of, 62, 63, 65, 70, 150, 160
    as Sperontes, 62, 160, 435
Schönborn, Gottfried Friedrich Ernst, 351, 352
    and Hainbund, 351
Schubart, Christian Friedrich Daniel
    "Die Forelle," 3
    on Bach, 3, 211, 240
    on early song, 2
Schubert, Franz
    "Die Forelle" (Schubart), 3
    "Todtengräberlied" (Hölty), 331, 333-335, 336
    and Bach, 6, 22, 31
    and German lied, 2, 6, 22, 32, 44, 51

Schulz, Johann Abraham Peter
    Lieder im Volkston collections, 3, 338, 340, 415
    "Das Milchmädchen" (Voss), 415, 420
    "Tischlied" (Voss), 338, 339-340, 411, 412, 415
    on Bach, 339
    Masonic songs of, 411, 433, 437, 438, 440, 441-442
    and *Volkslied* movement, 3, 325, 339-340, 412
Schumann, Robert, 10, 22, 41, 280
    and German lied, 6
Schütz, 43
    and German lied, 45-46
Schwab, Heinrich W.
    on Bach songs, 340
Schwabe, Johann Joachim, 271
Schwartz, Marshall R.
    on Batteux and taste, 119-120
"Selma" (Voss), 32, 258, 350
Senfl, polyphonic songs of, 46
Serauky, Walter
    Die musikalische Nachahmungsästhetik im Zeitraum von 1700 bis 1850, 90
    on *Affektenlehre*, 94
    on Batteux and Gottsched, 90-92
    on rationalist thought, 91, 92, 96, 117
    on rules and taste in art, 104, 122
    as whig historian, 90
Serwer, Howard Jay
    on Marpurg, 94-95
Shaftesbury, 3rd Earl of (Anthony Ashley Cooper)
    and ideas of taste, 107, 110, 112, 113
Shakespeare, 208
    rationalist thought and, 92, 93, 104-105
Sibley, Frank
    on critical discussion, 105-106
Silesian School, Second, 124
Simon, Johann Caspar, 160
Singende Muse an der Pleisse volumes
    See also Scholze; Sperontes
    and *Aufschwung*, 48, 54, 83
    Masonic songs in, 435
    "parody" settings in, 62, 65, 141, 160
    popularity of, 54, 62, 63
    quality of, 39, 54, 63
    and resurgence of song collections, 35, 44, 138
    Ton and *Wort* (text and melody) in, 44, 48, 63, 65
Singspiel
    and *Aufschwung*, 44

"Sinne" (poet called "K"), 69-71
Smeed, J. W.
    German Song and its Poetry, 52
    on *Aufschwung*, 52
    on Bach, 52-53
    on strophic form, 52-53
    on Telemann and Görner, 78
Smither, Howard E.
    on oratorio, 308-309, 310
Soames, Sir William, 125
sonata form
    See also C. P. E. Bach, instrumental music
    and *Bestimmtheit* (definiteness),
        12-13, 15
    evolution of, and Bach, 15-29
song, songs
    See also German lied
    origins and evolution of, 2-3, 36-37, 134-135
    and Western music, 8-9
song collections
    See also under specific collection, collector or
        composer
    and Albert, influence of, 43, 46, 59
    Arien und Melodeyn. See Albert
    and *Aufschwung*, 35, 44, 83, 141
    Bach, "Lieder und Gesänge." See Vrieslaender
    Das deutsche Lied im 18. Jahrhundert. See
        Friedlaender
    Geistliche Oden und Lieder. See C. P. E. Bach,
        songs; Gellert
    Geistliche, moralische und weltliche Oden.
        See Marpurg
    Lieder im Volkston collections. See Schulz
    and *Liederlose Zeit*, 37, 39, 48, 53, 61, 89
    Marpurg's reviews of, 65, 163
    See Masonic songs
    See *Musen-Almanach*
    Neue Lieder-Melodien. See C. P. E. Bach, songs
    Oden mit Melodien. See C. P. E. Bach, songs;
        Ramler-Krause song collections
    *Sammlung geistlicher Gesänge über die Werke
        Gottes in der Natur*. See Sturm
    Sammlung neuer Oden und Lieder volumes.
        See Görner
    Sperontes. See *Singende Muse an der Pleisse*
        volumes
    See *Tafel-Confect* volumes
    *Vier und zwanzig, theils ernsthafte, theils
        scherzende, Oden*. See Telemann
    Volkslieder. See Herder
    See Wernigerode songbooks
song histories, 2, 6, 29-32, 36-55
    See also under historian name

songless time. See *liederlose Zeit*
Spenser, 177, 208
Sperontes
    See also Scholze; *Singende Muse an der Pleisse*
        volumes
    identity of, 62, 160
Spitta, Philipp, 16, 17, 280
    on Scholze, 435
    on Sperontes and "parody" settings,
        62, 150, 160
Stahl
    See also under C. P. E. Bach, songs
    "Der Zufriedene" ("Die Landlust"),
        172-176, 178
Stamitz, Johann
    and Bach, 24
    as Haydn forerunner, 24
    and Mannheim school, 23
    and modern symphony, 29
Steele. See Addison and Steele
Steffan, Josef Anton
    "Schäferlied" ("Chloe an Thyrsis") (Ziegler),
        171-172, 178
Steineck, J. C. M., on Goeze, 386-388
Sternfeld, F. W., 27
    "Das stille Glück der Maurerey" (Masonic), 438,
        439-440
Stolberg, Christian von, 313
Stolberg, Count Friedrich Leopold von
    See also under C. P. E. Bach, songs
    "Lied," 415-417
    and Hainbund, 313
Stoljar, Margaret Mahony
    on Bach, 52
strophic problem
    and *Affektenlehre*, 40, 140, 156, 159
    and *Liederlose Zeit*, 40, 49, 54, 60
    nature of, 39, 139
    and non-strophic forms, 58, 61,
        136-137, 143
strophic song
    See also German lied; strophic problem
    characteristics of, 32-33, 58, 89, 136,
        158-159
    expressive power of, 32, 38, 336,
        455-456
    origins of, 134-135
    prevalence of, 2, 6, 58, 61, 89, 139
    reinstatement of. See *Aufschwung*
strophic variation
    See also through-composed form;
        Wechseloden
    and German lied, 45, 58, 59, 61, 89

strophic variation (*continued*)
    and Italian monody, 58, 89
    Ton and *Wort* in, 58
Sturm, Christoph Christian
    See also Bach, songs—Sturm settings
    Lieder und Kirchengesänge, 379
    Sammlung geistlicher Gesänge über die Werke Gottes in der Natur, 390
    other writings of, 383, 388
    "Empfindungen in der Sommernacht," 407-410
    "Gottes Grösse in der Natur," 389-391
    "Jesus in Gethsemane," 397-400
    "Passionslied" poems, 391-397
    "Der Tag des Weltgerichts," 405-407
    "Über die Finsterniss kurz vor dem Tode Jesu," 397, 400-405
    Bach settings of, 32, 311, 379, 380, 410
    and Bach, 311, 380, 390
    and Goeze controversies, 381, 383-386, 388, 389
    stature of, as poet, 383, 389, 391
Suchalla, Ernst, 315
    on Bach's Gerstenberg settings, 351, 352, 353, 360, 362
    on other Bach settings, 423
Sulzer, Johann Georg, 204, 250
symphonic form
    vast 18th c. symphony output, 27
    evolution of, 19, 27, 29
    Mannheim school and, 23, 24-25

Tafel-Confect volumes
    and *Aufschwung*, 35, 39, 44, 48, 141
    popularity of, 54, 62
    quality of, 39, 44, 61-62
"Der Tag des Weltgerichts" (Sturm), 405-407
Tändeleyen collection (Gerstenberg), 350, 351, 362, 363, 364
taste
    See also aesthetic judgment
    emerging ideas of, 107-122
    and rationalist thought, 92, 117
    role of, 89, 91, 93, 101, 102, 104
    and rules, 104, 106, 119
    and sixth sense, 108-110, 117
Telemann
    Der getreue Music-Meister, 53, 183
    Singe-, Spiel- und Generalbass-Übungen, 53, 183
    Vier und zwanzig, theils ernsthafte, theils scherzende, Oden, 53, 64, 73, 79, 143, 160, 183

    "An den Schlaf" (Hagedorn), 73, 74-79, 80, 82
    and *Aufschwung*, 54, 82
    and Berlin song school, 191
    and German lied, 52, 53, 183
    and Görner, 183
    and *liederlose Zeit*, 53
    songs of, 79-80, 143, 160-161
    Ton and *Wort* in, 64-65, 80, 143
Thematic Catalogue of the Works of Carl Philipp Emanuel Bach (Helm), 1, 31, 437
Theodor, Carl, 23
Thomas, R. Hinton
    on German lied, 51-52
through-composed form
    See also strophic variation; Wechseloden
    and Caccini, influence of, 43, 58, 83
    expressive power of, 143, 149, 152
    German lied and, 32-33, 89
    Koloraturlied, 45, 46
    recitative and, 43
    vs. strophic form, 40, 144, 149
    and strophic problem, 40, 54
    and strophic variation, 45, 58
    Ton and *Wort* in, 58, 83
    and variety within unity, 143, 144
Tischer, Johann Nikolaus, 353, 355, 356
"Tischlied" (Voss), 336-340, 411, 412, 415
Tobler, Ludwig, 426
"Todtengräberlied" (Hölty), 331-336, 431
Ton and *Wort* (melody and text), in song settings
    See also Affektenlehre; monody, Italian
    and German lied, 37, 43, 44
    and Gräfe settings, 65
    and poems for musical settings, 146
    and Sperontes volumes, 44, 48, 63
    and strophic form, 38, 83-84, 163
    and strophic variation, 58
    in Telemann and Görner, 78-80
Tovey, Donald Francis, 7, 78, 447
    Essays in Musical Analysis, 25
    other writings of, 25-27, 28
    on Bach, 25-27, 28
    on Gluck, 26-27, 29
    on Haydn, 159, 189
"Der Traum" (poet unknown), 243
Trevelyan, 47
"Die Tugend" (Haller), 243
Türk, Daniel Gottlob, 223
    on Bach, 432-433

"Über die Finsterniss kurz vor dem **Tode Jesu**" (Sturm), 397, 400-405

"Der Unbeständige" (unnamed poet), 268
unity and variety, in art. See under Horace; rationalist thought
Unterhaltungen, 263, 266, 268, 349

"Vaterlandslied" (Klopstock), 314-320
Versuch einer critischen Dichtkunst vor die Deutschen. See Gottsched
Vetter, Walther
  Das frühdeutsche Lied, 49
  on German lied, 49-50, 51
Vida, Marco Girolamo
  and influence of Horace, 124
Viennese Classical school. See under Classical era, Classical style
Vier und zwanzig, theils ernsthafte, theils scherzende, Oden (Telemann), 53, 64, 73, 79, 143, 160, 183
Virgil, 313
  influence of, on German poetry, 177, 184, 192, 364, 421
Vivaldi, 29, 69
vocal music
  instrumental music, relation to, 11-12, 14, 16
  in music historical writing, 6, 11, 16, 55
  and role of text, 12, 13, 15, 16
  in Western music, 2, 9
Volkslied (*Volkston*)
  German lied and, 37, 45, 47, 50, 314
  and Herder, 3
  and *Liederlose Zeit*, 42
  and Ossian "translations," 3
  popularity of, 62, 316, 340
  strophic song and, 145
Volkslied movement (second Berlin song school)
  See also Schulz; Voss
  and *Aufschwung*, 44
  characteristics of, 3, 146, 316, 325, 339, 340, 420
  goals of, 339, 340
  and Herder, 146, 340
  origins of, 3
  and strophic form, 145
Volkslieder (Herder), 3
Von der musikalischen Poesie. See Krause
Voss, Johann Friedrich, 145
Voss, Johann Heinrich
  See also under C. P. E. Bach, songs
  Musen-Almanach, editor, 311, 312, 313, 314, 336, 338
  "Das Milchmädchen," 412-415
  "Die Schlummernde," 315, 327-330, 412
  "Selma," 32, 350
  "Tischlied," 336-340
  and Bach, 314, 315, 317, 338, 350, 412
  and Bach's "Lyda," 322-323, 325, 338, 339
  on Bach's "Tischlied," 338, 339, 340, 411-412
  and Boie, 312-314
  and Hainbund, 313
  and Hölty, 313
  influence of, 311
  and Klopstock, 312
  and Schulz, 338-339, 415
  and *Volkslied* movement, 316, 325, 339, 340, 412
Vrieslander, Otto
  Carl Philipp Emanuel Bach, 31
  Carl Philipp Emanuel Bach, "Lieder und Gesänge," 318, 414
  on Bach songs, 31
  and Bach's "Lyda," 322-323
  and Bach's "Die Schlummernde," 329, 330
  and Bach's "Vaterlandslied," 318-319

Wagenseil, Georg Christoph, 24, 171
Wagner, 10-11, 18, 176, 332
Wagner, Albert Malte, 352
  on Gerstenberg and Anacreontic poets, 363-364
Waismann, Friedrich, 106
Walther, Johann Gottfried
  on melismatic style, 39
Waniek, Gustav, 91
Warton, Joseph, 208
Warton, Thomas, 208
Webbe, William
  on Horace, 124, 125
Wechseloden form, 40, 58, 135, 138, 143
  See also strophic variation
Wehl, Feodor, on Sturm, 389
"Weihnachtslied" (Gellert), 239
Wellesz, Egon, 27
Wernigerode songbooks, 263, 269, 278
Werth, Emil
  on biblical texts in Gellert, 213, 226, 230, 232, 236
"whig" history. See Butterfield; Miller, Henry Knight; progressivist thought
"Wider den Übermut" (Gellert), 31
Wieland, Christoph Martin, 314
  "Der Frühling," 349-350
Wien-Claudi, Hertha
  on Bach, 31

Willheim, Imanuel
    on Scheibe, 92-93, 95
Winckelmann, J. J., 8
Der Wirth und die Gäste. See C. P. E. Bach, cantatas
Wittgenstein
    See also rationalist thought
    on critical argument, 97, 99
Wockenfuss, Peter Laurentius, 59
Wolff, Christian, 139, 381
    and reform of German letters, 47, 57, 91
Wordsworth, 98-99
    and pastoral genre, 167, 340
Wotquenne, Alfred
    Bach catalogue of, 30, 32, 437, 438

Zauft, Karen
    on Telemann, 79
Zedler
    on Sperontes, 62
Ziegler, Christina Mariana von
    See also under C. P. E. Bach, songs
    "Schäferlied," 165-172, 178
"Der Zufriedene" ("Die Landlust") (Stahl),
    172-177, 178, 345

About the Author

William H. Youngren was born in Evanston, Illinois, and attended Amherst College. He then studied English literature at Harvard, which awarded him a Ph.D. in 1961. He has taught at M.I.T., Smith College, and (since 1971) Boston College. He is married, has three children, and lives in West Newton, Massachusetts.

Dr. Youngren is the author of *Semantics, Linguistics, and Criticism* (1972) and several articles on eighteenth-century aesthetics and criticism. In recent years, however, he has written mainly about music and records for *Partisan Review, Hudson Review, Commentary, Yale Review, The Atlantic, Fanfare,* and other magazines. In 1983 he entered the doctoral program in musicology at Brandeis, which awarded him a Ph.D. in 1999.

NOV 10 2004

HEWLETT-WOODMERE PUBLIC LIBRARY

3 1327 00429 5671

28 Day Loan

Hewlett-Woodmere Public Library
Hewlett, New York 11557-0903

Business Phone 516-374-1967
Recorded Announcements 516-374-1667